Data-Driven Science and Engineering

Data-driven discovery is revolutionizing the modeling, prediction, and control of complex systems. This textbook brings together machine learning, engineering mathematics, and mathematical physics to integrate modeling and control of dynamical systems with modern methods in data science. It highlights many of the recent advances in scientific computing that enable data-driven methods to be applied to a diverse range of complex systems such as turbulence, the brain, climate, epidemiology, finance, robotics, and autonomy.

Aimed at advanced undergraduate and beginning graduate students in the engineering and physical sciences, the text presents a range of topics and methods from introductory to state of the art.

Steven L. Brunton is Associate Professor of Mechanical Engineering at the University of Washington. He is also Adjunct Associate Professor of Applied Mathematics and a Data-Science Fellow at the eScience Institute. His research applies data science and machine learning for dynamical systems and control to fluid dynamics, biolocomotion, optics, energy systems, and manufacturing. He is an author of two textbooks, received the Army and Air Force Young Investigator Program awards, and was awarded the University of Washington College of Engineering teaching and Junior Faculty awards.

J. Nathan Kutz is the Robert Bolles and Yasuko Endo Professor of Applied Mathematics at the University of Washington, and served as department chair until 2015. He is also Adjunct Professor of Electrical Engineering and Physics and a Senior Data-Science Fellow at the eScience institute. His research interests are in complex systems and data analysis where machine learning can be integrated with dynamical systems and control for a diverse set of applications. He is an author of two textbooks and has received the Applied Mathematics Boeing Award of Excellence in Teaching and an NSF CAREER award.

Data-Driven Science and Engineering

Machine Learning, Dynamical Systems, and Control

STEVEN L. BRUNTON

University of Washington

J. NATHAN KUTZ

University of Washington

CAMBRIDGE
UNIVERSITY PRESS

University Printing House, Cambridge CB2 8BS, United Kingdom

One Liberty Plaza, 20th Floor, New York, NY 10006, USA

477 Williamstown Road, Port Melbourne, VIC 3207, Australia

314–321, 3rd Floor, Plot 3, Splendor Forum, Jasola District Centre, New Delhi – 110025, India

79 Anson Road, #06–04/06, Singapore 079906

Cambridge University Press is part of the University of Cambridge.

It furthers the University's mission by disseminating knowledge in the pursuit of education, learning, and research at the highest international levels of excellence.

www.cambridge.org
Information on this title: www.cambridge.org/9781108422093
DOI: 10.1017/9781108380690

First published 2019

A catalogue record for this publication is available from the British Library.

Library of Congress Cataloging-in-Publication Data
Names: Brunton, Steven L. (Steven Lee), 1984– author. | Kutz, Jose Nathan, author.
Title: Data-driven science and engineering : machine learning, dynamical systems, and control / Steven L. Brunton,
University of Washington, J. Nathan Kutz, University of Washington.
Description: Cambridge : Cambridge University Press, 2019. |
Includes bibliographical references and index.
Identifiers: LCCN 2018029888 | ISBN 9781108422093 (hardback : alk. paper)
Subjects: LCSH: Engineering–Data processing. | Science–Data processing. |
    Mathematical analysis.
Classification: LCC TA330 .B78 2019 | DDC 620.00285/631–dc23
LC record available at https://lccn.loc.gov/2018029888

ISBN 978-1-108-42209-3 Hardback

Contents

Preface

This book is about the growing intersection of data-driven methods, applied optimization, and the classical fields of engineering mathematics and mathematical physics. We have been developing this material over a number of years, primarily to educate our advanced undergrad and beginning graduate students from engineering and physical science departments. Typically, such students have backgrounds in linear algebra, differential equations, and scientific computing, with engineers often having some exposure to control theory and/or partial differential equations. However, most undergraduate curricula in engineering and science fields have little or no exposure to data methods and/or optimization. Likewise, computer scientists and statisticians have little exposure to dynamical systems and control. Our goal is to provide a broad entry point to applied data science for both of these groups of students. We have chosen the methods discussed in this book for their (1) relevance, (2) simplicity, and (3) generality, and we have attempted to present a range of topics, from basic introductory material up to research-level techniques.

Data-driven discovery is currently revolutionizing how we model, predict, and control complex systems. The most pressing scientific and engineering problems of the modern era are not amenable to empirical models or derivations based on first-principles. Increasingly, researchers are turning to data-driven approaches for a diverse range of complex systems, such as turbulence, the brain, climate, epidemiology, finance, robotics, and autonomy. These systems are typically nonlinear, dynamic, multi-scale in space and time, high-dimensional, with dominant underlying patterns that should be characterized and modeled for the eventual goal of sensing, prediction, estimation, and control. With modern mathematical methods, enabled by unprecedented availability of data and computational resources, we are now able to tackle previously unattainable challenge problems. A small handful of these new techniques include robust image reconstruction from sparse and noisy random pixel measurements, turbulence control with machine learning, optimal sensor and actuator placement, discovering interpretable nonlinear dynamical systems purely from data, and reduced order models to accelerate the study and optimization of systems with complex multi-scale physics.

Driving modern data science is the availability of vast and increasing quantities of data, enabled by remarkable innovations in low-cost sensors, orders-of-magnitudes increases in computational power, and virtually unlimited data storage and transfer capabilities. Such vast quantities of data are affording engineers and scientists across all disciplines new opportunities for data-driven discovery, which has been referred to as the fourth paradigm of scientific discovery [245]. This fourth paradigm is the natural culmination of the first three paradigms: empirical experimentation, analytical derivation, and computational investigation. The integration of these techniques provides a transformative framework for data-driven discovery efforts. This process of scientific discovery is not new, and indeed mimics the efforts of leading figures of the scientific revolution: Johannes Kepler (1571–1630) and Sir Isaac Newton (1642–1727). Each played a critical role in developing the theoretical underpinnings of celestial mechanics, based on a combination of empirical data-driven and analytical approaches. Data science is not replacing mathematical physics and engineering, but is instead augmenting it for the twenty-first century, resulting in more of a renaissance than a revolution.

Data science itself is not new, having been proposed more than 50 years ago by John Tukey who envisioned the existence of a scientific effort focused on learning from data, or *data analysis* [152]. Since that time, data science has been largely dominated by two distinct cultural outlooks on data [78]. The *machine learning* community, which is predominantly comprised of computer scientists, is typically centered on prediction quality and scalable, fast algorithms. Although not necessarily in contrast, the *statistical learning* community, often centered in statistics departments, focuses on the inference of interpretable models. Both methodologies have achieved significant success and have provided the mathematical and computational foundations for data-science methods. For engineers and scientists, the goal is to leverage these broad techniques to infer and compute models (typically nonlinear) from observations that correctly identify the underlying dynamics *and* generalize qualitatively and quantitatively to unmeasured parts of phase, parameter, or application space. Our goal in this book is to leverage the power of both statistical and machine learning to solve engineering problems.

Themes of This Book

There are a number of key themes that have emerged throughout this book. First, many complex systems exhibit *dominant low-dimensional patterns* in the data, despite the rapidly increasing resolution of measurements and computations. This underlying structure enables efficient sensing, and compact representations for modeling and control. Pattern extraction is related to the second theme of finding *coordinate transforms* that simplify the system. Indeed, the rich history of mathematical physics is centered around coordinate transformations (e.g., spectral decompositions, the Fourier transform, generalized functions, etc.), although these techniques have largely been limited to simple idealized geometries and linear dynamics. The ability to derive *data-driven* transformations opens up opportunities to generalize these techniques to new research problems with more complex geometries and boundary conditions. We also take the perspective of *dynamical systems and control* throughout the book, applying data-driven techniques to model and control systems that evolve in time. Perhaps the most pervasive theme is that of *data-driven applied optimization*, as nearly every topic discussed is related to optimization (e.g., finding *optimal* low-dimensional patterns, *optimal* sensor placement, machine learning *optimization*, *optimal* control, etc.). Even more fundamentally, most data is organized into arrays for analysis, where the extensive development of numerical linear algebra tools from the early 1960s onward provides many of the foundational mathematical underpinnings for matrix decompositions and solution strategies used throughout this text.

Acknowledgments

We are indebted to many wonderful students, collaborators, and colleagues for valuable feedback, suggestions, and support. We are especially grateful to Joshua Proctor, who was instrumental in the origination of this book and who helped guide much of the framing and organization. We have also benefited from extensive interactions and conversations with Bing Brunton, Igor Mezić, Bernd Noack, and Sam Taira. This work would also not be possible without our many great colleagues and collaborators, with whom we have worked and whose research is featured throughout this book.

Throughout the writing of this book and teaching of related courses, we have received great feedback and comments from our excellent students and postdocs: Travis Askham, Michael Au-Yeung, Zhe Bai, Ido Bright, Kathleen Champion, Emily Clark, Charles Delahunt, Daniel Dylewski, Ben Erichson, Charlie Fiesler, Xing Fu, Chen Gong, Taren Gorman, Jacob Grosek, Seth Hirsh, Mikala Johnson, Eurika Kaiser, Mason Kamb, James Kunert, Bethany Lusch, Pedro Maia, Krithika Manohar, Niall Mangan, Ariana Mendible, Thomas Mohren, Megan Morrison, Markus Quade, Sam Rudy, Susanna Sargsyan, Isabel Scherl, Eli Shlizerman, George Stepaniants, Ben Strom, Chang Sun, Roy Taylor, Meghana Velagar, Jake Weholt, and Matt Williams. Our students are our inspiration for this book, and they make it fun and exciting to come to work every day.

We would also like to thank our publisher Lauren Cowles at Cambridge University Press for being a reliable supporter throughout this process.

Online Material

We have designed this book to make extensive use of online supplementary material, including codes, data, videos, homeworks, and suggested course syllabi. All of this material can be found at the following website:

databookuw.com

In addition to course resources, all of the code and data used in the book are available. The codes online are more extensive than those presented in the book, including code used to generate publication quality figures. Data visualization was ranked as the top used data-science method in the Kaggle 2017 *The State of Data Science and Machine Learning* study, and so we highly encourage readers to download the online codes and make full use of these plotting commands.

We have also recorded and posted video lectures on YouTube for most of the topics in this book. We include supplementary videos for students to fill in gaps in their background on scientific computing and foundational applied mathematics. We have designed this text both to be a reference as well as the material for several courses at various levels of student preparation. Most chapters are also modular, and may be converted into stand-alone *boot camps*, containing roughly 10 hours of materials each.

How to Use This Book

Our intended audience includes beginning graduate students, or advanced undergraduates, in engineering and science. As such, the machine learning methods are introduced at a beginning level, whereas we assume students know how to model physical systems with differential equations and simulate them with solvers such as **ode45**. The diversity of topics covered thus range from introductory to state-of-the-art research methods. Our aim is to provide an integrated viewpoint and mathematical toolset for solving engineering and science problems. Alternatively, the book can also be useful for computer science and statistics students who often have limited knowledge of dynamical systems and control. Various courses can be designed from this material, and several example syllabi may be found on the book website; this includes homework, data sets, and code.

First and foremost, we want this book to be fun, inspiring, eye-opening, and empowering for young scientists and engineers. We have attempted to make everything as simple as possible, while still providing the depth and breadth required to be useful in research. Many of the chapter topics in this text could be entire books in their own right, and many of them are. However, we also wanted to be as comprehensive as may be reasonably expected for a field that is so big and moving so fast. We hope that you enjoy this book, master these methods, and change the world with applied data science!

Common Optimization Techniques, Equations, Symbols, and Acronyms

Most Common Optimization Strategies

Least-Squares (discussed in Chapters 1 and 4) minimizes the sum of the squares of the residuals between a given fitting model and data. Linear least-squares, where the residuals are linear in the unknowns, has a closed form solution which can be computed by taking the derivative of the residual with respect to each unknown and setting it to zero. It is commonly used in the engineering and applied sciences for fitting polynomial functions. Nonlinear least-squares typically requires iterative refinement based upon approximating the nonlinear least-squares with a linear least-squares at each iteration.

Gradient Descent (discussed in Chapters 4 and 6) is the industry leading, convex optimization method for high-dimensional systems. It minimizes residuals by computing the gradient of a given fitting function. The iterative procedure updates the solution by *moving downhill* in the residual space. The Newton–Raphson method is a one-dimensional version of gradient descent. Since it is often applied in high-dimensional settings, it is prone to find only local minima. Critical innovations for big data applications include stochastic gradient descent and the backpropagation algorithm which makes the optimization amenable to computing the gradient itself.

Alternating Descent Method (ADM) (discussed in Chapter 4) avoids computations of the gradient by optimizing in one unknown at a time. Thus all unknowns are held constant while a line search (non-convex optimization) can be performed in a single variable. This variable is then updated and held constant while another of the unknowns is updated. The iterative procedure continues through all unknowns and the iteration procedure is repeated until a desired level of accuracy is achieved.

Augmented Lagrange Method (ALM) (discussed in Chapters 3 and 8) is a class of algorithms for solving constrained optimization problems. They are similar to penalty methods in that they replace a constrained optimization problem by a series of unconstrained problems and add a penalty term to the objective which helps enforce the desired constraint. ALM adds another term designed to mimic a Lagrange multiplier. The augmented Lagrangian is not the same as the method of Lagrange multipliers.

Linear Program and Simplex Method are the workhorse algorithms for convex optimization. A linear program has an objective function which is linear in the unknown and the constraints consist of linear inequalities and equalities. By computing its feasible region, which is a convex polytope, the linear programming algorithm finds a point in the polyhedron where this function has the smallest (or largest) value if such a point exists. The simplex method is a specific iterative technique for linear programs which aims to take a given basic feasible solution to another basic feasible solution for which the objective function is smaller, thus producing an iterative procedure for optimizing.

Most Common Equations and Symbols
Linear Algebra
Linear System of Equations

$$\mathbf{Ax} = \mathbf{b}. \tag{0.1}$$

The matrix $\mathbf{A} \in \mathbb{R}^{p \times n}$ and vector $\mathbf{b} \in \mathbb{R}^p$ are generally known, and the vector $\mathbf{x} \in \mathbb{R}^n$ is unknown.

Eigenvalue Equation

$$\mathbf{AT} = \mathbf{T\Lambda}. \tag{0.2}$$

The columns $\boldsymbol{\xi}_k$ of the matrix $\mathbf{T}$ are the eigenvectors of $\mathbf{A} \in \mathbb{C}^{n \times n}$ corresponding to the eigenvalue λ_k: $\mathbf{A}\boldsymbol{\xi}_k = \lambda_k \boldsymbol{\xi}_k$. The matrix $\mathbf{\Lambda}$ is a diagonal matrix containing these eigenvalues, in the simple case with n distinct eigenvalues.

Change of Coordinates

$$\mathbf{x} = \mathbf{\Psi a}. \tag{0.3}$$

The vector $\mathbf{x} \in \mathbb{R}^n$ may be written as $\mathbf{a} \in \mathbb{R}^n$ in the coordinate system given by the columns of $\mathbf{\Psi} \in \mathbb{R}^{n \times n}$.

Measurement Equation

$$\mathbf{y} = \mathbf{Cx}. \tag{0.4}$$

The vector $\mathbf{y} \in \mathbb{R}^p$ is a measurement of the state $\mathbf{x} \in \mathbb{R}^n$ by the measurement matrix $\mathbf{C} \in \mathbb{R}^{p \times n}$.

Singular Value Decomposition

$$\mathbf{X} = \mathbf{U\Sigma V}^* \approx \tilde{\mathbf{U}}\tilde{\mathbf{\Sigma}}\tilde{\mathbf{V}}^*. \tag{0.5}$$

The matrix $\mathbf{X} \in \mathbb{C}^{n \times m}$ may be decomposed into the product of three matrices $\mathbf{U} \in \mathbb{C}^{n \times n}$, $\mathbf{\Sigma} \in \mathbb{C}^{n \times m}$, and $\mathbf{V} \in \mathbb{C}^{m \times m}$. The matrices $\mathbf{U}$ and $\mathbf{V}$ are *unitary*, so that $\mathbf{UU}^* = \mathbf{U}^*\mathbf{U} = \mathbf{I}_{n \times n}$ and $\mathbf{VV}^* = \mathbf{V}^*\mathbf{V} = \mathbf{I}_{m \times m}$, where * denotes complex conjugate transpose. The columns of $\mathbf{U}$ (resp. $\mathbf{V}$) are orthogonal, called left (resp. right) *singular vectors*. The matrix $\mathbf{\Sigma}$ contains decreasing, nonnegative diagonal entries called *singular values*.

Often, $\mathbf{X}$ is approximated with a low-rank matrix $\tilde{\mathbf{X}} = \tilde{\mathbf{U}}\tilde{\mathbf{\Sigma}}\tilde{\mathbf{V}}^*$, where $\tilde{\mathbf{U}}$ and $\tilde{\mathbf{V}}$ contain the first $r \ll n$ columns of $\mathbf{U}$ and $\mathbf{V}$, respectively, and $\tilde{\mathbf{\Sigma}}$ contains the first $r \times r$ block of $\mathbf{\Sigma}$. The matrix $\tilde{\mathbf{U}}$ is often denoted $\mathbf{\Psi}$ in the context of spatial modes, reduced order models, and sensor placement.

Regression and Optimization

Overdetermined and Underdetermined Optimization for Linear Systems

$$\underset{\mathbf{x}}{\mathrm{argmin}} \left(\|\mathbf{A}\mathbf{x} - \mathbf{b}\|_2 + \lambda g(\mathbf{x}) \right) \qquad \text{or} \qquad (0.6a)$$

$$\underset{\mathbf{x}}{\mathrm{argmin}}\, g(\mathbf{x}) \text{ subject to } \|\mathbf{A}\mathbf{x} - \mathbf{b}\|_2 \leq \epsilon, \qquad (0.6b)$$

Here $g(\mathbf{x})$ is a regression penalty (with penalty parameter λ for overdetermined systems). For over- and underdetermined linear systems of equations, which result in either no solutions or an infinite number of solutions of $\mathbf{A}\mathbf{x} = \mathbf{b}$, a choice of constraint or penalty, which is also known as *regularization*, must be made in order to produce a solution.

Overdetermined and Underdetermined Optimization for Nonlinear Systems

$$\underset{\mathbf{x}}{\mathrm{argmin}} \left(f(\mathbf{A}, \mathbf{x}, \mathbf{b}) + \lambda g(\mathbf{x}) \right) \qquad \text{or} \qquad (0.7a)$$

$$\underset{\mathbf{x}}{\mathrm{argmin}}\, g(\mathbf{x}) \text{ subject to } f(\mathbf{A}, \mathbf{x}, \mathbf{b}) \leq \epsilon \qquad (0.7b)$$

This generalizes the linear system to a nonlinear system $f(\cdot)$ with regularization $g(\cdot)$. These over- and underdetermined systems are often solved using gradient descent algorithms.

Compositional Optimization for Neural Networks

$$\underset{\mathbf{A}_j}{\mathrm{argmin}} \left(f_M(\mathbf{A}_M, \cdots f_2(\mathbf{A}_2, (f_1(\mathbf{A}_1, \mathbf{x})) \cdots) + \lambda g(\mathbf{A}_j) \right) \qquad (0.8)$$

Each $\mathbf{A}_k$ denotes the weights connecting the neural network from the kth to $(k + 1)$th layer. It is typically a massively underdetermined system which is regularized by $g(\mathbf{A}_j)$. Composition and regularization are critical for generating expressive representations of the data as well as preventing overfitting.

Dynamical Systems and Reduced Order Models

Nonlinear Ordinary Differential Equation (Dynamical System)

$$\frac{d}{dt}\mathbf{x}(t) = \mathbf{f}(\mathbf{x}(t), t; \boldsymbol{\beta}). \qquad (0.9)$$

The vector $\mathbf{x}(t) \in \mathbb{R}^n$ is the state of the system evolving in time t, $\boldsymbol{\beta}$ are parameters, and $\mathbf{f}$ is the vector field. Generally, $\mathbf{f}$ is Lipschitz continuous to guarantee existence and uniqueness of solutions.

Linear Input–Output System

$$\frac{d}{dt}\mathbf{x} = \mathbf{A}\mathbf{x} + \mathbf{B}\mathbf{u} \qquad (0.10a)$$

$$\mathbf{y} = \mathbf{C}\mathbf{x} + \mathbf{D}\mathbf{u}. \qquad (0.10b)$$

The state of the system is $\mathbf{x} \in \mathbb{R}^n$, the inputs (actuators) are $\mathbf{u} \in \mathbb{R}^q$, and the outputs (sensors) are $\mathbf{y} \in \mathbb{R}^p$. The matrices $\mathbf{A}, \mathbf{B}, \mathbf{C}, \mathbf{D}$ define the dynamics, the effect of actuation, the sensing strategy, and the effect of actuation feed-through, respectively.

Nonlinear Map (Discrete-Time Dynamical System)

$$\mathbf{x}_{k+1} = \mathbf{F}(\mathbf{x}_k). \tag{0.11}$$

The state of the system at the kth iteration is $\mathbf{x}_k \in \mathbb{R}^n$, and $\mathbf{F}$ is a possibly nonlinear mapping. Often, this map defines an iteration forward in time, so that $\mathbf{x}_k = \mathbf{x}(k\Delta t)$; in this case the flow map is denoted $\mathbf{F}_{\Delta t}$.

Koopman Operator Equation (Discrete-Time)

$$\mathcal{K}_t g = g \circ \mathbf{F}_t \quad \Longrightarrow \quad \mathcal{K}_t \varphi = \lambda \varphi. \tag{0.12}$$

The linear Koopman operator $\mathcal{K}_t$ advances measurement functions of the state $g(\mathbf{x})$ with the flow $\mathbf{F}_t$. Eigenvalues and eigenvectors of $\mathcal{K}_t$ are λ and $\varphi(\mathbf{x})$, respectively. The operator $\mathcal{K}_t$ operates on a Hilbert space of measurements.

Nonlinear Partial Differential Equation

$$\mathbf{u}_t = \mathbf{N}(\mathbf{u}, \mathbf{u}_x, \mathbf{u}_{xx}, \cdots, x, t; \boldsymbol{\beta}). \tag{0.13}$$

The state of the PDE is $\mathbf{u}$, the nonlinear evolution operator is $\mathbf{N}$, subscripts denote partial differentiation, and x and t are the spatial and temporal variables, respectively. The PDE is parameterized by values in $\boldsymbol{\beta}$. The state $\mathbf{u}$ of the PDE may be a continuous function $u(x, t)$, or it may be discretized at several spatial locations, $\mathbf{u}(t) = \begin{bmatrix} u(x_1, t) & u(x_2, t) & \cdots & u(x_n, t) \end{bmatrix}^T \in \mathbb{R}^n$.

Galerkin Expansion
The continuous Galerkin expansion is:

$$u(x, t) \approx \sum_{k=1}^{r} a_k(t) \psi_k(x). \tag{0.14}$$

The functions $a_k(t)$ are temporal coefficients that capture the time dynamics, and $\psi_k(x)$ are spatial modes. For a high-dimensional discretized state, the Galerkin expansion becomes: $\mathbf{u}(t) \approx \sum_{k=1}^{r} a_k(t)\boldsymbol{\psi}_k$. The spatial modes $\boldsymbol{\psi}_k \in \mathbb{R}^n$ may be the columns of $\boldsymbol{\Psi} = \tilde{\mathbf{U}}$.

Complete Symbols

Dimensions

K Number of nonzero entries in a K-sparse vector $\mathbf{s}$

m Number of data snapshots (i.e., columns of $\mathbf{X}$)

n Dimension of the state, $\mathbf{x} \in \mathbb{R}^n$

p Dimension of the measurement or output variable, $\mathbf{y} \in \mathbb{R}^p$

q Dimension of the input variable, $\mathbf{u} \in \mathbb{R}^q$

r Rank of truncated SVD, or other low-rank approximation

Scalars

s Frequency in Laplace domain

t Time

δ learning rate in gradient descent

Δt Time step

x Spatial variable

Δx Spatial step

σ Singular value

λ Eigenvalue

λ Sparsity parameter for sparse optimization (Section 7.3)

λ Lagrange multiplier (Sections. 3.7, 8.4, and 11.4)

τ Threshold

Vectors

$\mathbf{a}$ Vector of mode amplitudes of $\mathbf{x}$ in basis $\mathbf{\Psi}$, $\mathbf{a} \in \mathbb{R}^r$

$\mathbf{b}$ Vector of measurements in linear system $\mathbf{Ax} = \mathbf{b}$

$\mathbf{b}$ Vector of DMD mode amplitudes (Section 7.2)

$\mathbf{Q}$ Vector containing potential function for PDE-FIND

$\mathbf{r}$ Residual error vector

$\mathbf{s}$ Sparse vector, $\mathbf{s} \in \mathbb{R}^n$

$\mathbf{u}$ Control variable (Chapters 8, 9, and 10)

$\mathbf{u}$ PDE state vector (Chapters 11 and 12)

$\mathbf{w}$ Exogenous inputs

$\mathbf{w}_d$ Disturbances to system

$\mathbf{w}_n$ Measurement noise

$\mathbf{w}_r$ Reference to track

$\mathbf{x}$ State of a system, $\mathbf{x} \in \mathbb{R}^n$

$\mathbf{x}_k$ Snapshot of data at time t_k

$\mathbf{x}_j$ Data sample $j \in Z := \{1, 2, \cdots, m\}$ (Chapters 5 and 6)

$\tilde{\mathbf{x}}$ Reduced state, $\tilde{\mathbf{x}} \in \mathbb{R}^r$, so that $\mathbf{x} \approx \tilde{\mathbf{U}}\tilde{\mathbf{x}}$

$\hat{\mathbf{x}}$ Estimated state of a system

$\mathbf{y}$ Vector of measurements, $\mathbf{y} \in \mathbb{R}^p$

$\mathbf{y}_j$ Data label $j \in Z := \{1, 2, \cdots, m\}$ (Chapters 5 and 6)

$\hat{\mathbf{y}}$ Estimated output measurement

$\mathbf{z}$ Transformed state, $\mathbf{x} = \mathbf{Tz}$ (Chapters 8 and 9)

$\boldsymbol{\epsilon}$ Error vector

Vectors, continued

$\boldsymbol{\beta}$ Bifurcation parameters

$\boldsymbol{\xi}$ Eigenvector of Koopman operator (Sections 7.4 and 7.5)

$\boldsymbol{\xi}$ Sparse vector of coefficients (Section 7.3)

$\boldsymbol{\phi}$ DMD mode

$\boldsymbol{\psi}$ POD mode

$\boldsymbol{\Upsilon}$ Vector of PDE measurements for PDE-FIND

Matrices

$\mathbf{A}$ Matrix for system of equations or dynamics

$\tilde{\mathbf{A}}$ Reduced dynamics on r-dimensional POD subspace

$\mathbf{A_X}$ Matrix representation of linear dynamics on the state $\mathbf{x}$

$\mathbf{A_Y}$ Matrix representation of linear dynamics on the observables $\mathbf{y}$

$(\mathbf{A}, \mathbf{B}, \mathbf{C}, \mathbf{B})$ Matrices for continuous-time state-space system

$(\mathbf{A}_d, \mathbf{B}_d, \mathbf{C}_d, \mathbf{B}_d)$ Matrices for discrete-time state-space system

$(\hat{\mathbf{A}}, \hat{\mathbf{B}}, \hat{\mathbf{C}}, \hat{\mathbf{B}})$ Matrices for state-space system in new coordinates $\mathbf{z} = \mathbf{T}^{-1}\mathbf{x}$

$(\tilde{\mathbf{A}}, \tilde{\mathbf{B}}, \tilde{\mathbf{C}}, \tilde{\mathbf{B}})$ Matrices for reduced state-space system with rank r

$\mathbf{B}$ Actuation input matrix

$\mathbf{C}$ Linear measurement matrix from state to measurements

$\mathcal{C}$ Controllability matrix

$\mathcal{F}$ Discrete Fourier transform

$\mathbf{G}$ Matrix representation of linear dynamics on the states and inputs $[\mathbf{x}^T \mathbf{u}^T]^T$

$\mathbf{H}$ Hankel matrix

$\mathbf{H}'$ Time-shifted Hankel matrix

$\mathbf{I}$ Identity matrix

$\mathbf{K}$ Matrix form of Koopman operator (Chapter 7)

$\mathbf{K}$ Closed-loop control gain (Chapter 8)

$\mathbf{K}_f$ Kalman filter estimator gain

$\mathbf{K}_r$ LQR control gain

$\mathbf{L}$ Low-rank portion of matrix $\mathbf{X}$ (Chapter 3)

$\mathcal{O}$ Observability matrix

$\mathbf{P}$ Unitary matrix that acts on columns of $\mathbf{X}$

$\mathbf{Q}$ Weight matrix for state penalty in LQR (Sec. 8.4)

$\mathbf{Q}$ Orthogonal matrix from QR factorization

$\mathbf{R}$ Weight matrix for actuation penalty in LQR (Sec. 8.4)

$\mathbf{R}$ Upper triangular matrix from QR factorization

$\mathbf{S}$ Sparse portion of matrix $\mathbf{X}$ (Chapter 3)

$\mathbf{T}$ Matrix of eigenvectors (Chapter 8)

$\mathbf{T}$ Change of coordinates (Chapters 8 and 9)

$\mathbf{U}$ Left singular vectors of $\mathbf{X}$, $\mathbf{U} \in \mathbb{R}^{n \times n}$

$\hat{\mathbf{U}}$ Left singular vectors of economy SVD of $\mathbf{X}$, $\mathbf{U} \in \mathbb{R}^{n \times m}$

$\tilde{\mathbf{U}}$ Left singular vectors (POD modes) of truncated SVD of $\mathbf{X}$, $\mathbf{U} \in \mathbb{R}^{n \times r}$

$\mathbf{V}$ Right singular vectors of $\mathbf{X}$, $\mathbf{V} \in \mathbb{R}^{m \times m}$

$\tilde{\mathbf{V}}$ Right singular vectors of truncated SVD of $\mathbf{X}$, $\mathbf{V} \in \mathbb{R}^{m \times r}$

Matrices, continued

$\boldsymbol{\Sigma}$ Matrix of singular values of $\mathbf{X}$, $\boldsymbol{\Sigma} \in \mathbb{R}^{n \times m}$

$\hat{\boldsymbol{\Sigma}}$ Matrix of singular values of economy SVD of $\mathbf{X}$, $\boldsymbol{\Sigma} \in \mathbb{R}^{m \times m}$

$\tilde{\boldsymbol{\Sigma}}$ Matrix of singular values of truncated SVD of $\mathbf{X}$, $\boldsymbol{\Sigma} \in \mathbb{R}^{r \times r}$

$\mathbf{W}$ Eigenvectors of $\tilde{\mathbf{A}}$

$\mathbf{W}_c$ Controllability Gramian

$\mathbf{W}_o$ Observability Gramian

$\mathbf{X}$ Data matrix, $\mathbf{X} \in \mathbb{R}^{n \times m}$

$\mathbf{X}'$ Time-shifted data matrix, $\mathbf{X}' \in \mathbb{R}^{n \times m}$

$\mathbf{Y}$ Projection of $\mathbf{X}$ matrix onto orthogonal basis in randomized SVD (Sec. 1.8)

$\mathbf{Y}$ Data matrix of observables, $\mathbf{Y} = \mathbf{g}(\mathbf{X})$, $\mathbf{Y} \in \mathbb{R}^{p \times m}$ (Chapter 7)

$\mathbf{Y}'$ Shifted data matrix of observables, $\mathbf{Y}' = \mathbf{g}(\mathbf{X}')$, $\mathbf{Y}' \in \mathbb{R}^{p \times m}$ (Chapter 7)

$\mathbf{Z}$ Sketch matrix for randomized SVD, $\mathbf{Z} \in \mathbb{R}^{n \times r}$ (Sec. 1.8)

$\boldsymbol{\Theta}$ Measurement matrix times sparsifying basis, $\boldsymbol{\Theta} = \mathbf{C}\boldsymbol{\Psi}$ (Chapter 3)

$\boldsymbol{\Theta}$ Matrix of candidate functions for SINDy (Sec. 7.3)

$\boldsymbol{\Gamma}$ Matrix of derivatives of candidate functions for SINDy (Sec. 7.3)

$\boldsymbol{\Xi}$ Matrix of coefficients of candidate functions for SINDy (Sec. 7.3)

$\boldsymbol{\Xi}$ Matrix of nonlinear snapshots for DEIM (Sec. 12.5)

$\boldsymbol{\Lambda}$ Diagonal matrix of eigenvalues

$\boldsymbol{\Upsilon}$ Input snapshot matrix, $\boldsymbol{\Upsilon} \in \mathbb{R}^{q \times m}$

$\boldsymbol{\Phi}$ Matrix of DMD modes, $\boldsymbol{\Phi} \triangleq \mathbf{X}'\mathbf{V}\boldsymbol{\Sigma}^{-1}\mathbf{W}$

$\boldsymbol{\Psi}$ Orthonormal basis (e.g., Fourier or POD modes)

Tensors

$(\mathcal{A}, \mathcal{B}, \mathcal{M})$ N-way array tensors of size $I_1 \times I_2 \times \cdots \times I_N$

Norms

$\| \cdot \|_0$ ℓ_0 pseudo-norm of a vector $\mathbf{x}$ the number of nonzero elements in $\mathbf{x}$

$\| \cdot \|_1$ ℓ_1 norm of a vector $\mathbf{x}$ given by $\|\mathbf{x}\|_1 = \sum_{i=1}^{n} |x_i|$

$\| \cdot \|_2$ ℓ_2 norm of a vector $\mathbf{x}$ given by $\|\mathbf{x}\|_2 = \sqrt{\sum_{i=1}^{n}(x_i^2)}$

$\| \cdot \|_2$ 2-norm of a matrix $\mathbf{X}$ given by $\|\mathbf{X}\|_2 = \max_{\mathbf{x}} \frac{\|\mathbf{X}\mathbf{x}\|_2}{\|\mathbf{x}\|_2}$

$\| \cdot \|_F$ Frobenius norm of a matrix $\mathbf{X}$ given by $\|\mathbf{X}\|_F = \sqrt{\sum_{i=1}^{n} \sum_{j=1}^{m} |X_{ij}|^2}$

$\| \cdot \|_*$ Nuclear norm of a matrix $\mathbf{X}$ given by $\|\mathbf{X}\|_* = \text{trace}\left(\sqrt{\mathbf{X}^*\mathbf{X}}\right) = \sum_{i=1}^{m} \sigma_i$ (for $m \leq n$)

$\langle \cdot, \cdot \rangle$ Inner product. For functions, $\langle f(x), g(x) \rangle = \int_{-\infty}^{\infty} f(x)g^*(x)dx$.

$\langle \cdot, \cdot \rangle$ Inner product. For vectors, $\langle \mathbf{u}, \mathbf{v} \rangle = \mathbf{u}^*\mathbf{v}$.

Operators, Functions, and Maps

$\mathcal{F}$ Fourier transform

$\mathbf{F}$ Discrete-time dynamical system map

$\mathbf{F}_t$ Discrete-time flow map of dynamical system through time t

$\mathbf{f}$ Continuous-time dynamical system

$\mathcal{G}$ Gabor transform

Operators, Functions, and Maps, continued

G	Transfer function from inputs to outputs (Chapter 8)
g	Scalar measurement function on $\mathbf{x}$
$\mathbf{g}$	Vector-valued measurement functions on $\mathbf{x}$
J	Cost function for control
ℓ	Loss function for support vector machines (Chapter 5)
$\mathcal{K}$	Koopman operator (continuous time)
$\mathcal{K}_t$	Koopman operator associated with time t flow map
$\mathcal{L}$	Laplace transform
$\mathbf{L}$	Loop transfer function (Chapter 8)
$\mathbf{L}$	Linear partial differential equation (Chapters 11 and 12)
$\mathbf{N}$	Nonlinear partial differential equation
$\mathcal{O}$	Order of magnitude
$\mathbf{S}$	Sensitivity function (Chapter 8)
$\mathbf{T}$	Complementary sensitivity function (Chapter 8)
$\mathcal{W}$	Wavelet transform
μ	Incoherence between measurement matrix $\mathbf{C}$ and basis $\mathbf{\Psi}$
κ	Condition number
φ	Koopman eigenfunction
∇	Gradient operator
$*$	Convolution operator

Most Common Acronyms

CNN	Convolutional neural network
DL	Deep learning
DMD	Dynamic mode decomposition
FFT	Fast Fourier transform
ODE	Ordinary differential equation
PCA	Principal components analysis
PDE	Partial differential equation
POD	Proper orthogonal decomposition
ROM	Reduced order model
SVD	Singular value decomposition

Other Acronyms

ADM	Alternating directions method
AIC	Akaike information criterion
ALM	Augmented Lagrange multiplier
ANN	Artificial neural network
ARMA	Autoregressive moving average
ARMAX	Autoregressive moving average with exogenous input
BIC	Bayesian information criterion
BPOD	Balanced proper orthogonal decomposition
DMDc	Dynamic mode decomposition with control
CCA	Canonical correlation analysis
CFD	Computational fluid dynamics
CoSaMP	Compressive sampling matching pursuit
CWT	Continuous wavelet transform
DEIM	Discrete empirical interpolation method
DCT	Discrete cosine transform
DFT	Discrete Fourier transform
DMDc	Dynamic mode decomposition with control
DNS	Direct numerical simulation
DWT	Discrete wavelet transform
ECOG	Electrocorticography
eDMD	Extended DMD
EIM	Empirical interpolation method
EM	Expectation maximization
EOF	Empirical orthogonal functions
ERA	Eigensystem realization algorithm
ESC	Extremum-seeking control
GMM	Gaussian mixture model
HAVOK	Hankel alternative view of Koopman
JL	Johnson–Lindenstrauss
KL	Kullback–Leibler
ICA	Independent component analysis

Other Acronyms, continued

KLT	Karhunen–Loève transform
LAD	Least absolute deviations
LASSO	Least absolute shrinkage and selection operator
LDA	Linear discriminant analysis
LQE	Linear quadratic estimator
LQG	Linear quadratic Gaussian controller
LQR	Linear quadratic regulator
LTI	Linear time invariant system
MIMO	Multiple input, multiple output
MLC	Machine learning control
MPE	Missing point estimation
mrDMD	Multi-resolution dynamic mode decomposition
NARMAX	Nonlinear autoregressive model with exogenous inputs
NLS	Nonlinear Schrödinger equation
OKID	Observer Kalman filter identification
PBH	Popov–Belevitch–Hautus test
PCP	Principal component pursuit
PDE-FIND	Partial differential equation functional identification of nonlinear dynamics
PDF	Probability distribution function
PID	Proportional-integral-derivative control
PIV	Particle image velocimetry
RIP	Restricted isometry property
rSVD	Randomized SVD
RKHS	Reproducing kernel Hilbert space
RNN	Recurrent neural network
RPCA	Robust principal components analysis
SGD	Stochastic gradient descent
SINDy	Sparse identification of nonlinear dynamics
SISO	Single input, single output
SRC	Sparse representation for classification
SSA	Singular spectrum analysis
STFT	Short time Fourier transform
STLS	Sequential thresholded least-squares
SVM	Support vector machine
TICA	Time-lagged independent component analysis
VAC	Variational approach of conformation dynamics

Part I

Dimensionality Reduction and Transforms

1 Singular Value Decomposition (SVD)

The singular value decomposition (SVD) is among the most important matrix factorizations of the computational era, providing a foundation for nearly all of the data methods in this book. The SVD provides a numerically stable matrix decomposition that can be used for a variety of purposes and is guaranteed to exist. We will use the SVD to obtain low-rank approximations to matrices and to perform pseudo-inverses of non-square matrices to find the solution of a system of equations $\mathbf{Ax} = \mathbf{b}$. Another important use of the SVD is as the underlying algorithm of principal component analysis (PCA), where high-dimensional data is decomposed into its most statistically descriptive factors. SVD/PCA has been applied to a wide variety of problems in science and engineering.

In a sense, the SVD generalizes the concept of the fast Fourier transform (FFT), which will be the subject of the next chapter. Many engineering texts begin with the FFT, as it is the basis of many classical analytical and numerical results. However, the FFT works in idealized settings, and the SVD is a more generic data-driven technique. Because this book is focused on data, we begin with the SVD, which may be thought of as providing a basis that is *tailored* to the specific data, as opposed to the FFT, which provides a *generic* basis.

In many domains, complex systems will generate data that is naturally arranged in large matrices, or more generally in arrays. For example, a time-series of data from an experiment or a simulation may be arranged in a matrix with each column containing all of the measurements at a given time. If the data at each instant in time is multi-dimensional, as in a high-resolution simulation of the weather in three spatial dimensions, it is possible to reshape or *flatten* this data into a high-dimensional column vector, forming the columns of a large matrix. Similarly, the pixel values in a grayscale image may be stored in a matrix, or these images may be reshaped into large column vectors in a matrix to represent the frames of a movie. Remarkably, the data generated by these systems are typically low rank, meaning that there are a few dominant patterns that explain the high-dimensional data. The SVD is a numerically robust and efficient method of extracting these patterns from data.

1.1 Overview

Here we introduce the SVD and develop an intuition for how to apply the SVD by demonstrating its use on a number of motivating examples. The SVD will provide a foundation for many other techniques developed in this book, including classification methods in Chapter 5, the dynamic mode decomposition (DMD) in Chapter 7, and the proper orthogonal decomposition (POD) in Chapter 11. Detailed mathematical properties are discussed in the following sections.

High dimensionality is a common challenge in processing data from complex systems. These systems may involve large measured data sets including audio, image, or video data. The data may also be generated from a physical system, such as neural recordings from a brain, or fluid velocity measurements from a simulation or experiment. In many naturally occurring systems, it is observed that data exhibit dominant patterns, which may be characterized by a low-dimensional attractor or manifold [252, 251].

As an example, consider images, which typically contain a large number of measurements (pixels), and are therefore elements of a high-dimensional vector space. However, most images are highly compressible, meaning that the relevant information may be represented in a much lower-dimensional subspace. The compressibility of images will be discussed in depth throughout this book. Complex fluid systems, such as the Earth's atmosphere or the turbulent wake behind a vehicle also provide compelling examples of the low-dimensional structure underlying a high-dimensional state-space. Although high-fidelity fluid simulations typically require at least millions or billions of degrees of freedom, there are often dominant coherent structures in the flow, such as periodic vortex shedding behind vehicles or hurricanes in the weather.

The SVD provides a systematic way to determine a low-dimensional approximation to high-dimensional data in terms of dominant patterns. This technique is *data-driven* in that patterns are discovered purely from data, without the addition of expert knowledge or intuition. The SVD is numerically stable and provides a hierarchical representation of the data in terms of a new coordinate system defined by dominant correlations within the data. Moreover, the SVD is guaranteed to exist for any matrix, unlike the eigendecomposition.

The SVD has many powerful applications beyond dimensionality reduction of high-dimensional data. It is used to compute the pseudo-inverse of non-square matrices, providing solutions to underdetermined or overdetermined matrix equations, $\mathbf{Ax} = \mathbf{b}$. We will also use the SVD to de-noise data sets. The SVD is likewise important to characterize the input and output geometry of a linear map between vector spaces. These applications will all be explored in this chapter, providing an intuition for matrices and high-dimensional data.

Definition of the SVD

Generally, we are interested in analyzing a large data set $\mathbf{X} \in \mathbb{C}^{n \times m}$:

$$
\mathbf{X} = \begin{bmatrix} | & | & & | \\ \mathbf{x}_1 & \mathbf{x}_2 & \cdots & \mathbf{x}_m \\ | & | & & | \end{bmatrix}.
\tag{1.1}
$$

The columns $\mathbf{x}_k \in \mathbb{C}^n$ may be measurements from simulations or experiments. For example, columns may represent images that have been reshaped into column vectors with as many elements as pixels in the image. The column vectors may also represent the state of a physical system that is evolving in time, such as the fluid velocity at a set of discrete points, a set of neural measurements, or the state of a weather simulation with one square kilometer resolution.

The index k is a label indicating the kth distinct set of measurements. For many of the examples in this book, $\mathbf{X}$ will consist of a *time-series* of data, and $\mathbf{x}_k = \mathbf{x}(k \Delta t)$. Often the *state-dimension n* is very large, on the order of millions or billions of degrees of freedom.

The columns are often called *snapshots*, and m is the number of snapshots in $\mathbf{X}$. For many systems $n \gg m$, resulting in a *tall-skinny* matrix, as opposed to a *short-fat* matrix when $n \ll m$.

The SVD is a unique matrix decomposition that exists for every complex-valued matrix $\mathbf{X} \in \mathbb{C}^{n \times m}$:

$$\mathbf{X} = \mathbf{U}\mathbf{\Sigma}\mathbf{V}^* \tag{1.2}$$

where $\mathbf{U} \in \mathbb{C}^{n \times n}$ and $\mathbf{V} \in \mathbb{C}^{m \times m}$ are *unitary* matrices[1] with orthonormal columns, and $\mathbf{\Sigma} \in \mathbb{R}^{n \times m}$ is a matrix with real, nonnegative entries on the diagonal and zeros off the diagonal. Here $*$ denotes the complex conjugate transpose[2]. As we will discover throughout this chapter, the condition that $\mathbf{U}$ and $\mathbf{V}$ are unitary is used extensively.

When $n \geq m$, the matrix $\mathbf{\Sigma}$ has at most m nonzero elements on the diagonal, and may be written as $\mathbf{\Sigma} = \begin{bmatrix} \hat{\mathbf{\Sigma}} \\ \mathbf{0} \end{bmatrix}$. Therefore, it is possible to *exactly* represent $\mathbf{X}$ using the *economy* SVD:

$$\mathbf{X} = \mathbf{U}\mathbf{\Sigma}\mathbf{V}^* = \begin{bmatrix} \hat{\mathbf{U}} & \hat{\mathbf{U}}^\perp \end{bmatrix} \begin{bmatrix} \hat{\mathbf{\Sigma}} \\ \mathbf{0} \end{bmatrix} \mathbf{V}^* = \hat{\mathbf{U}}\hat{\mathbf{\Sigma}}\mathbf{V}^*. \tag{1.3}$$

The full SVD and economy SVD are shown in Fig. 1.1. The columns of $\hat{\mathbf{U}}^\perp$ span a vector space that is complementary and orthogonal to that spanned by $\hat{\mathbf{U}}$. The columns of $\mathbf{U}$ are called *left singular vectors* of $\mathbf{X}$ and the columns of $\mathbf{V}$ are *right singular vectors*. The diagonal elements of $\hat{\mathbf{\Sigma}} \in \mathbb{C}^{m \times m}$ are called *singular values* and they are ordered from largest to smallest. The rank of $\mathbf{X}$ is equal to the number of nonzero singular values.

Computing the SVD

The SVD is a cornerstone of computational science and engineering, and the numerical implementation of the SVD is both important and mathematically enlightening. That said, most standard numerical implementations are mature and a simple interface exists in many modern computer languages, allowing us to abstract away the details underlying the SVD computation. For most purposes, we simply use the SVD as a part of a larger effort, and we take for granted the existence of efficient and stable numerical algorithms. In the sections that follow we demonstrate how to use the SVD in various computational languages, and we also discuss the most common computational strategies and limitations. There are numerous important results on the computation of the SVD [212, 106, 211, 292, 238]. A more thorough discussion of computational issues can be found in [214]. Randomized numerical algorithms are increasingly used to compute the SVD of very large matrices as discussed in Section 1.8.

Matlab. In Matlab, computing the SVD is straightforward:

```
>>X = randn(5,3);     % Create a 5x3 random data matrix
>>[U,S,V] = svd(X);   % Singular Value Decomposition
```

---

[1] A square matrix $\mathbf{U}$ is unitary if $\mathbf{U}\mathbf{U}^* = \mathbf{U}^*\mathbf{U} = \mathbf{I}$.
[2] For real-valued matrices, this is the same as the regular transpose $\mathbf{X}^* = \mathbf{X}^T$.

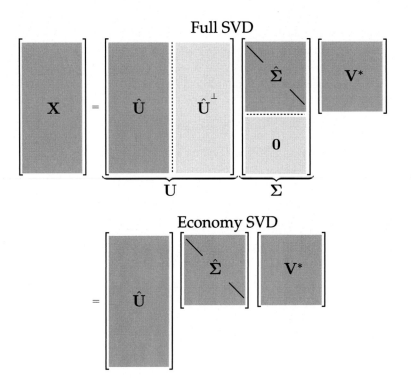

Figure 1.1 Schematic of matrices in the full and economy SVD.

For non-square matrices $\mathbf{X}$, the economy SVD is more efficient:

```
>> [Uhat,Shat,V] = svd(X,'econ');   % economy sized SVD
```

Python

```
>>> import numpy as np
>>> X = np.random.rand(5, 3)   % create random data matrix
>>> U, S, V = np.linalg.svd(X,full_matrices=True) % full SVD
>>> Uhat, Shat, Vhat = np.linalg.svd(X, full_matrices=False)
    % economy SVD
```

R

```
> X <- replicate(3, rnorm(5))
> s <- svd(X)
> U <- s$u
> S <- diag(s$d)
> V <- s$v
```

Mathematica

```
In:= X=RandomReal[{0,1},{5,3}]
In:= {U,S,V} = SingularValueDecomposition[X]
```

Other Languages

The SVD is also available in other languages, such as Fortran and C++. In fact, most SVD implementations are based on the LAPACK (Linear Algebra Package) [13] in Fortran. The

SVD routine is designated **DGESVD** in LAPACK, and this is wrapped in the C++ libraries **Armadillo** and **Eigen**.

Historical Perspective

The SVD has a long and rich history, ranging from early work developing the theoretical foundations to modern work on computational stability and efficiency. There is an excellent historical review by Stewart [502], which provides context and many important details. The review focuses on the early theoretical work of Beltrami and Jordan (1873), Sylvester (1889), Schmidt (1907), and Weyl (1912). It also discusses more recent work, including the seminal computational work of Golub and collaborators [212, 211]. In addition, there are many excellent chapters on the SVD in modern texts [524, 17, 316].

Uses in This Book and Assumptions of the Reader

The SVD is the basis for many related techniques in dimensionality reduction. These methods include principal component analysis (PCA) in statistics [418, 256, 257], the Karhunen–Loève transform (KLT) [280, 340], empirical orthogonal functions (EOFs) in climate [344], the proper orthogonal decomposition (POD) in fluid dynamics [251], and canonical correlation analysis (CCA) [131]. Although developed independently in a range of diverse fields, many of these methods only differ in how the data is collected and pre-processed. There is an excellent discussion about the relationship between the SVD, the KLT and PCA by Gerbrands [204].

The SVD is also widely used in system identification and control theory to obtain reduced order models that are balanced in the sense that states are hierarchically ordered in terms of their ability to be observed by measurements and controlled by actuation [388].

For this chapter, we assume that the reader is familiar with linear algebra with some experience in computation and numerics. For review, there are a number of excellent books on numerical linear algebra, with discussions on the SVD [524, 17, 316].

1.2   Matrix Approximation

Perhaps the most useful and defining property of the SVD is that it provides an *optimal* low-rank approximation to a matrix $\mathbf{X}$. In fact, the SVD provides a *hierarchy* of low-rank approximations, since a rank-r approximation is obtained by keeping the leading r singular values and vectors, and discarding the rest.

Schmidt (of Gram-Schmidt) generalized the SVD to function spaces and developed an approximation theorem, establishing truncated SVD as the optimal low-rank approximation of the underlying matrix $\mathbf{X}$ [476]. Schmidt's approximation theorem was rediscovered by Eckart and Young [170], and is sometimes referred to as the Eckart-Young theorem.

Theorem 1 (Eckart-Young [170]) *The optimal rank-r approximation to* $\mathbf{X}$, *in a least-squares sense, is given by the rank-r SVD truncation* $\tilde{\mathbf{X}}$:

$$\underset{\tilde{\mathbf{X}}, \; s.t. \; \mathrm{rank}(\tilde{\mathbf{X}})=r}{\mathrm{argmin}} \quad \|\mathbf{X} - \tilde{\mathbf{X}}\|_F = \tilde{\mathbf{U}}\tilde{\mathbf{\Sigma}}\tilde{\mathbf{V}}^*. \tag{1.4}$$

Here, $\tilde{\mathbf{U}}$ and $\tilde{\mathbf{V}}$ denote the first r leading columns of $\mathbf{U}$ and $\mathbf{V}$, and $\tilde{\mathbf{\Sigma}}$ contains the leading $r \times r$ sub-block of $\mathbf{\Sigma}$. $\| \cdot \|_F$ is the Frobenius norm.

Here, we establish the notation that a truncated SVD basis (and the resulting approximated matrix $\tilde{\mathbf{X}}$) will be denoted by $\tilde{\mathbf{X}} = \tilde{\mathbf{U}}\tilde{\mathbf{\Sigma}}\tilde{\mathbf{V}}^*$. Because $\mathbf{\Sigma}$ is diagonal, the rank-r SVD approximation is given by the sum of r distinct rank-1 matrices:

$$\tilde{\mathbf{X}} = \sum_{k=1}^{r} \sigma_k \mathbf{u}_k \mathbf{v}_k^* = \sigma_1 \mathbf{u}_1 \mathbf{v}_1^* + \sigma_2 \mathbf{u}_2 \mathbf{v}_2^* + \cdots + \sigma_r \mathbf{u}_r \mathbf{v}_r^*. \tag{1.5}$$

This is the so-called *dyadic* summation. For a given rank r, there is no better approximation for $\mathbf{X}$, in the ℓ_2 sense, than the truncated SVD approximation $\tilde{\mathbf{X}}$. Thus, high-dimensional data may be well described by a few dominant patterns given by the columns of $\tilde{\mathbf{U}}$ and $\tilde{\mathbf{V}}$.

This is an important property of the SVD, and we will return to it many times. There are numerous examples of data sets that contain high-dimensional measurements, resulting in a large data matrix $\mathbf{X}$. However, there are often dominant low-dimensional patterns in the data, and the truncated SVD basis $\tilde{\mathbf{U}}$ provides a coordinate transformation from the high-dimensional measurement space into a low-dimensional pattern space. This has the benefit of *reducing* the size and dimension of large data sets, yielding a tractable basis for visualization and analysis. Finally, many systems considered in this text are *dynamic* (see Chapter 7), and the SVD basis provides a hierarchy of modes that characterize the observed attractor, on which we may project a low-dimensional dynamical system to obtain reduced order models (see Chapter 12).

Truncation

The truncated SVD is illustrated in Fig. 1.2, with $\tilde{\mathbf{U}}, \tilde{\mathbf{\Sigma}}$ and $\tilde{\mathbf{V}}$ denoting the truncated matrices. If $\mathbf{X}$ does not have full rank, then some of the singular values in $\hat{\mathbf{\Sigma}}$ may be zero, and the truncated SVD may still be exact. However, for truncation values r that are smaller than the number of nonzero singular values (i.e., the rank of $\mathbf{X}$), the truncated SVD only approximates $\mathbf{X}$:

$$\mathbf{X} \approx \tilde{\mathbf{U}}\tilde{\mathbf{\Sigma}}\tilde{\mathbf{V}}^*. \tag{1.6}$$

There are numerous choices for the truncation rank r, and they are discussed in Sec. 1.7. If we choose the truncation value to keep all non-zero singular values, then $\mathbf{X} = \tilde{\mathbf{U}}\tilde{\mathbf{\Sigma}}\tilde{\mathbf{V}}^*$ is exact.

Example: Image Compression

We demonstrate the idea of matrix approximation with a simple example: image compression. A recurring theme throughout this book is that large data sets often contain underlying patterns that facilitate low-rank representations. Natural images present a simple and intuitive example of this inherent *compressibility*. A grayscale image may be thought of as a real-valued matrix $\mathbf{X} \in \mathbb{R}^{n \times m}$, where n and m are the number of pixels in the vertical and horizontal directions, respectively[3]. Depending on the basis of representation (pixel-space, Fourier frequency domain, SVD transform coordinates), images may have very compact approximations.

---

[3] It is not uncommon for image size to be specified as horizontal by vertical, i.e. $\mathbf{X}^T \in \mathbb{R}^{m \times n}$, although we stick with vertical by horizontal to be consistent with generic matrix notation.

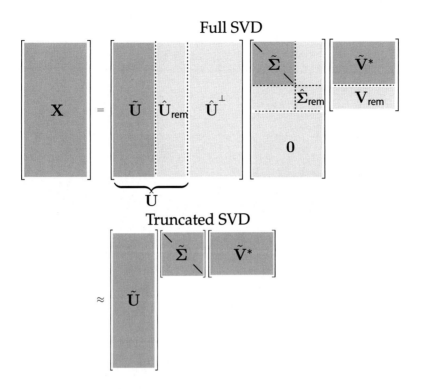

Figure 1.2 Schematic of truncated SVD. The subscript 'rem' denotes the remainder of $\hat{U}$, $\hat{\Sigma}$ or V after truncation.

Consider the image of Mordecai the snow dog in Fig. 1.3. This image has 2000×1500 pixels. It is possible to take the SVD of this image and plot the diagonal singular values, as in Fig. 1.4. Figure 1.3 shows the approximate matrix $\tilde{X}$ for various truncation values r. By $r = 100$, the reconstructed image is quite accurate, and the singular values account for almost 80% of the image variance. The SVD truncation results in a compression of the original image, since only the first 100 columns of U and V, along with the first 100 diagonal elements of Σ, must be stored in $\tilde{U}$, $\tilde{\Sigma}$ and $\tilde{V}$.

First, we load the image:

```
A=imread('../DATA/dog.jpg');
X=double(rgb2gray(A)); % Convert RBG->gray, 256 bit->double.
nx = size(X,1); ny = size(X,2);
imagesc(X), axis off, colormap gray
```

and take the SVD:

```
[U,S,V] = svd(X);
```

Next, we compute the approximate matrix using the truncated SVD for various ranks ($r = 5, 20,$ and 100):

```
for r=[5 20 100]; % Truncation value
    Xapprox = U(:,1:r)*S(1:r,1:r)*V(:,1:r)'; % Approx. image
    figure, imagesc(Xapprox), axis off
    title(['r=',num2str(r,'%d'),']);
end
```

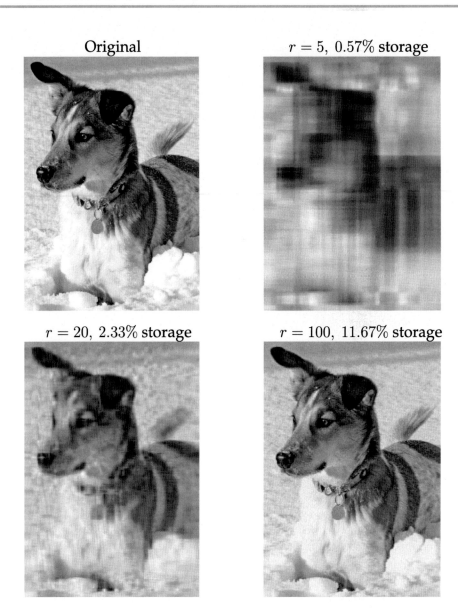

Original

$r = 5, \ 0.57\%$ storage

$r = 20, \ 2.33\%$ storage

$r = 100, \ 11.67\%$ storage

Figure 1.3 Image compression of Mordecai the snow dog, truncating the SVD at various ranks r. Original image resolution is 2000×1500.

Finally, we plot the singular values and cumulative energy in Fig. 1.4:

```
subplot(1,2,1), semilogy(diag(S),'k')
subplot(1,2,2), plot(cumsum(diag(S))/sum(diag(S)),'k')
```

1.3   Mathematical Properties and Manipulations

Here we describe important mathematical properties of the SVD including geometric interpretations of the unitary matrices $\mathbf{U}$ and $\mathbf{V}$ as well as a discussion of the SVD in terms of

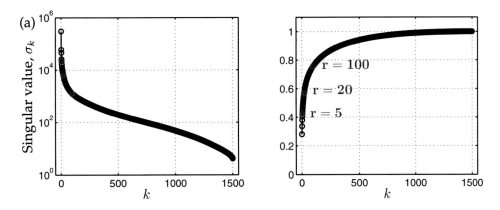

Figure 1.4 (a) Singular values σ_k. (b) Cumulative energy in the first k modes.

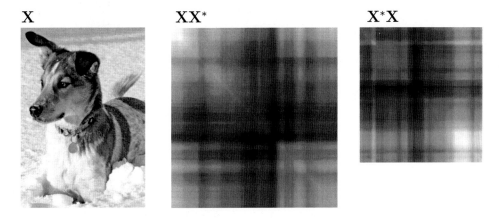

Figure 1.5 Correlation matrices $\mathbf{XX}^*$ and $\mathbf{X}^*\mathbf{X}$ for a matrix $\mathbf{X}$ obtained from an image of a dog. Note that both correlation matrices are symmetric.

dominant correlations in the data $\mathbf{X}$. The relationship between the SVD and correlations in the data will be explored more in Section 1.5 on principal components analysis.

Interpretation as Dominant Correlations

The SVD is closely related to an eigenvalue problem involving the correlation matrices $\mathbf{XX}^*$ and $\mathbf{X}^*\mathbf{X}$, shown in Fig. 1.5 for a specific image, and in Figs. 1.6 and 1.7 for generic matrices. If we plug (1.3) into the row-wise correlation matrix $\mathbf{XX}^*$ and the column-wise correlation matrix $\mathbf{X}^*\mathbf{X}$, we find:

$$\mathbf{XX}^* = \mathbf{U}\begin{bmatrix}\hat{\boldsymbol{\Sigma}}\\\mathbf{0}\end{bmatrix}\mathbf{V}^*\mathbf{V}\begin{bmatrix}\hat{\boldsymbol{\Sigma}} & \mathbf{0}\end{bmatrix}\mathbf{U}^* = \mathbf{U}\begin{bmatrix}\hat{\boldsymbol{\Sigma}}^2 & \mathbf{0}\\\mathbf{0} & \mathbf{0}\end{bmatrix}\mathbf{U}^* \tag{1.7a}$$

$$\mathbf{X}^*\mathbf{X} = \mathbf{V}\begin{bmatrix}\hat{\boldsymbol{\Sigma}} & \mathbf{0}\end{bmatrix}\mathbf{U}^*\mathbf{U}\begin{bmatrix}\hat{\boldsymbol{\Sigma}}\\\mathbf{0}\end{bmatrix}\mathbf{V}^* = \mathbf{V}\hat{\boldsymbol{\Sigma}}^2\mathbf{V}^*. \tag{1.7b}$$

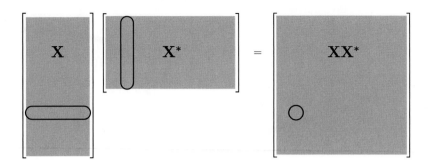

Figure 1.6 Correlation matrix $\mathbf{X}\mathbf{X}^*$ is formed by taking the inner product of rows of $\mathbf{X}$.

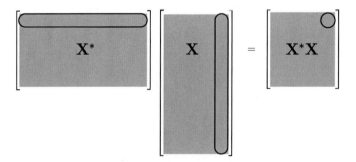

Figure 1.7 Correlation matrix $\mathbf{X}^*\mathbf{X}$ is formed by taking the inner product of columns of $\mathbf{X}$.

Recalling that $\mathbf{U}$ and $\mathbf{V}$ are unitary, $\mathbf{U}$, $\boldsymbol{\Sigma}$, and $\mathbf{V}$ are solutions to the following eigenvalue problems:

$$\mathbf{X}\mathbf{X}^*\mathbf{U} = \mathbf{U}\begin{bmatrix} \hat{\boldsymbol{\Sigma}}^2 & \mathbf{0} \\ \mathbf{0} & \mathbf{0} \end{bmatrix}, \tag{1.8a}$$

$$\mathbf{X}^*\mathbf{X}\mathbf{V} = \mathbf{V}\hat{\boldsymbol{\Sigma}}^2. \tag{1.8b}$$

In other words, each nonzero singular value of $\mathbf{X}$ is a positive square root of an eigenvalue of $\mathbf{X}^*\mathbf{X}$ and of $\mathbf{X}\mathbf{X}^*$, which have the same nonzero eigenvalues. It follows that if $\mathbf{X}$ is self-adjoint (i.e. $\mathbf{X} = \mathbf{X}^*$), then the singular values of $\mathbf{X}$ are equal to the absolute value of the eigenvalues of $\mathbf{X}$.

This provides an intuitive interpretation of the SVD, where the columns of $\mathbf{U}$ are eigenvectors of the correlation matrix $\mathbf{X}\mathbf{X}^*$ and columns of $\mathbf{V}$ are eigenvectors of $\mathbf{X}^*\mathbf{X}$. We choose to arrange the singular values in descending order by magnitude, and thus the columns of $\mathbf{U}$ are hierarchically ordered by how much correlation they capture in the columns of $\mathbf{X}$; $\mathbf{V}$ similarly captures correlation in the rows of $\mathbf{X}$.

Method of Snapshots
It is often impractical to construct the matrix $\mathbf{X}\mathbf{X}^*$ because of the large size of the state-dimension n, let alone solve the eigenvalue problem; if $\mathbf{x}$ has a million elements, then $\mathbf{X}\mathbf{X}^*$

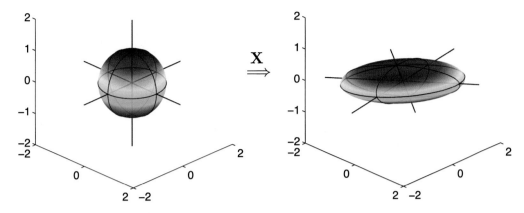

Figure 1.8 Geometric illustration of the SVD as a mapping from a sphere in $\mathbb{R}^n$ to an ellipsoid in $\mathbb{R}^m$.

has a trillion elements. In 1987, Sirovich observed that it is possible to bypass this large matrix and compute the first m columns of $\mathbf{U}$ using what is now known as the method of snapshots [490].

Instead of computing the eigen-decomposition of $\mathbf{X}\mathbf{X}^*$ to obtain the left singular vectors $\mathbf{U}$, we only compute the eigen-decomposition of $\mathbf{X}^*\mathbf{X}$, which is much smaller and more manageable. From (1.8b), we then obtain $\mathbf{V}$ and $\hat{\mathbf{\Sigma}}$. If there are zero singular values in $\hat{\mathbf{\Sigma}}$, then we only keep the r non-zero part, $\tilde{\mathbf{\Sigma}}$, and the corresponding columns $\tilde{\mathbf{V}}$ of $\mathbf{V}$. From these matrices, it is then possible to approximate $\tilde{\mathbf{U}}$, the first r columns of $\mathbf{U}$, as follows:

$$\tilde{\mathbf{U}} = \mathbf{X}\tilde{\mathbf{V}}\tilde{\mathbf{\Sigma}}^{-1}. \tag{1.9}$$

Geometric Interpretation

The columns of the matrix $\mathbf{U}$ provide an orthonormal basis for the column space of $\mathbf{X}$. Similarly, the columns of $\mathbf{V}$ provide an orthonormal basis for the row space of $\mathbf{X}$. If the columns of $\mathbf{X}$ are spatial measurements in time, then $\mathbf{U}$ encode spatial patterns, and $\mathbf{V}$ encode temporal patterns.

One property that makes the SVD particularly useful is the fact that both $\mathbf{U}$ and $\mathbf{V}$ are *unitary* matrices, so that $\mathbf{U}\mathbf{U}^* = \mathbf{U}^*\mathbf{U} = \mathbf{I}_{n\times n}$ and $\mathbf{V}\mathbf{V}^* = \mathbf{V}^*\mathbf{V} = \mathbf{I}_{m\times m}$. This means that solving a system of equations involving $\mathbf{U}$ or $\mathbf{V}$ is as simple as multiplication by the transpose, which scales as $\mathcal{O}(n^2)$, as opposed to traditional methods for the generic inverse, which scale as $\mathcal{O}(n^3)$. As noted in the previous section and in [57], the SVD is intimately connected to the spectral properties of the compact self-adjoint operators $\mathbf{X}\mathbf{X}^*$ and $\mathbf{X}^*\mathbf{X}$.

The SVD of $\mathbf{X}$ may be interpreted geometrically based on how a hypersphere, given by $S^{n-1} \triangleq \{\mathbf{x} \mid \|\mathbf{x}\|_2 = 1\} \subset \mathbb{R}^n$ maps into an ellipsoid, $\{\mathbf{y} \mid \mathbf{y} = \mathbf{X}\mathbf{x} \text{ for } \mathbf{x} \in S^{n-1}\} \subset \mathbb{R}^m$, through $\mathbf{X}$. This is shown graphically in Fig. 1.8 for a sphere in $\mathbb{R}^3$ and a mapping $\mathbf{X}$ with three non-zero singular values. Because the mapping through $\mathbf{X}$ (i.e., matrix multiplication) is linear, knowing how it maps the unit sphere determines how all other vectors will map.

For the specific case shown in Fig. 1.8, we construct the matrix $\mathbf{X}$ out of three rotation matrices, $\mathbf{R}_x$, $\mathbf{R}_y$, and $\mathbf{R}_z$, and a fourth matrix to stretch out and scale the principal axes:

$$\mathbf{X} = \underbrace{\begin{bmatrix} \cos(\theta_3) & -\sin(\theta_3) & 0 \\ \sin(\theta_3) & \cos(\theta_3) & 0 \\ 0 & 0 & 1 \end{bmatrix}}_{\mathbf{R}_z} \underbrace{\begin{bmatrix} \cos(\theta_2) & 0 & \sin(\theta_2) \\ 0 & 1 & 0 \\ -\sin(\theta_2) & 0 & \cos(\theta_2) \end{bmatrix}}_{\mathbf{R}_y}$$

$$\times \underbrace{\begin{bmatrix} 1 & 0 & 0 \\ 0 & \cos(\theta_1) & -\sin(\theta_1) \\ 0 & \sin(\theta_1) & \cos(\theta_1) \end{bmatrix}}_{\mathbf{R}_x} \begin{bmatrix} \sigma_1 & 0 & 0 \\ 0 & \sigma_2 & 0 \\ 0 & 0 & \sigma_3 \end{bmatrix}.$$

In this case, $\theta_1 = \pi/15$, $\theta_2 = -\pi/9$, and $\theta_3 = -\pi/20$, and $\sigma_1 = 3$, $\sigma_2 = 1$, and $\sigma_3 = 0.5$. These rotation matrices do not commute, and so the order of rotation matters. If one of the singular values is zero, then a dimension is removed and the ellipsoid collapses onto a lower-dimensional subspace. The product $\mathbf{R}_x\mathbf{R}_y\mathbf{R}_z$ is the unitary matrix $\mathbf{U}$ in the SVD of $\mathbf{X}$. The matrix $\mathbf{V}$ is the identity.

Code 1.1 Construct rotation matrices.

```
theta = [pi/15; -pi/9; -pi/20];
Sigma = diag([3; 1; 0.5]);            % scale x, y, and z

Rx = [1 0 0;                          % rotate about x-axis
      0 cos(theta(1)) -sin(theta(1));
      0 sin(theta(1)) cos(theta(1))];

Ry = [cos(theta(2)) 0 sin(theta(2));  % rotate about y-axis
      0 1 0;
      -sin(theta(2)) 0 cos(theta(2))];

Rz = [cos(theta(3)) -sin(theta(3)) 0; % rotate about z-axis
      sin(theta(3)) cos(theta(3)) 0;
      0 0 1];

X = Rz*Ry*Rx*Sigma;                   % rotate and scale
```

Code 1.2 Plot sphere.

```
[x,y,z] = sphere(25);
h1=surf(x,y,z);
```

Code 1.3 Map sphere through $\mathbf{X}$ and plot resulting ellipsoid.

```
xR = 0*x;   yR = 0*y;   zR = 0*z;
for i=1:size(x,1)
    for j=1:size(x,2)
        vecR = X*[x(i,j); y(i,j); z(i,j)];
        xR(i,j) = vecR(1);
        yR(i,j) = vecR(2);
        zR(i,j) = vecR(3);
    end
end
h2=surf(xR,yR,zR,z);   % using sphere z-coord for color
```

Invariance of the SVD to Unitary Transformations

A useful property of the SVD is that if we left or right-multiply our data matrix $\mathbf{X}$ by a unitary transformation, it preserves the terms in the SVD, except for the corresponding left or right unitary matrix $\mathbf{U}$ or $\mathbf{V}$, respectively. This has important implications, since the discrete Fourier transform (DFT; see Chapter 2) $\mathcal{F}$ is a unitary transform, meaning that the SVD of data $\hat{\mathbf{X}} = \mathcal{F}\mathbf{X}$ will be exactly the same as the SVD of $\mathbf{X}$, except that the modes $\hat{\mathbf{U}}$ will be be the DFT of modes $\mathbf{U}$: $\hat{\mathbf{U}} = \mathcal{F}\mathbf{U}$. In addition, the invariance of the SVD to unitary transformations enable the use of compressed measurements to reconstruct SVD modes that are sparse in some transform basis (see Chapter 3).

The invariance of SVD to unitary transformations is geometrically intuitive, as unitary transformations rotate vectors in space, but do not change their inner products or correlation structures. We denote a left unitary transformation by $\mathbf{C}$, so that $\mathbf{Y} = \mathbf{CX}$, and a right unitary transformation by $\mathbf{P}^*$, so that $\mathbf{Y} = \mathbf{XP}^*$. The SVD of $\mathbf{X}$ will be denoted $\mathbf{U_X}\mathbf{\Sigma_X}\mathbf{V_X^*}$ and the SVD of $\mathbf{Y}$ will be $\mathbf{U_Y}\mathbf{\Sigma_Y}\mathbf{V_Y^*}$.

Left Unitary Transformations

First, consider a left unitary transformation of $\mathbf{X}$: $\mathbf{Y} = \mathbf{CX}$. Computing the correlation matrix $\mathbf{Y}^*\mathbf{Y}$, we find

$$\mathbf{Y}^*\mathbf{Y} = \mathbf{X}^*\mathbf{C}^*\mathbf{CX} = \mathbf{X}^*\mathbf{X}. \tag{1.10}$$

The projected data has the same eigendecomposition, resulting in the same $\mathbf{V_X}$ and $\mathbf{\Sigma_X}$. Using the method of snapshots to reconstruct $\mathbf{U_Y}$, we find

$$\mathbf{U_Y} = \mathbf{Y}\mathbf{V_X}\mathbf{\Sigma_X^{-1}} = \mathbf{CX}\mathbf{V_X}\mathbf{\Sigma_X^{-1}} = \mathbf{CU_X}. \tag{1.11}$$

Thus, $\mathbf{U_Y} = \mathbf{CU_X}$, $\mathbf{\Sigma_Y} = \mathbf{\Sigma_X}$, and $\mathbf{V_Y} = \mathbf{V_X}$. The SVD of $\mathbf{Y}$ is then:

$$\mathbf{Y} = \mathbf{CX} = \mathbf{CU_X}\mathbf{\Sigma_X}\mathbf{V_X^*}. \tag{1.12}$$

Right Unitary Transformations

For a right unitary transformation $\mathbf{Y} = \mathbf{XP}^*$, the correlation matrix $\mathbf{Y}^*\mathbf{Y}$ is:

$$\mathbf{Y}^*\mathbf{Y} = \mathbf{PX}^*\mathbf{XP}^* = \mathbf{PV_X}\mathbf{\Sigma_X^2}\mathbf{V_X^*}\mathbf{P}^*, \tag{1.13}$$

with the following eigendecomposition

$$\mathbf{Y}^*\mathbf{Y}\mathbf{PV_X} = \mathbf{PV_X}\mathbf{\Sigma_X^2}. \tag{1.14}$$

Thus, $\mathbf{V_Y} = \mathbf{PV_X}$ and $\mathbf{\Sigma_Y} = \mathbf{\Sigma_X}$. We may use the method of snapshots to reconstruct $\mathbf{U_Y}$:

$$\mathbf{U_Y} = \mathbf{Y}\mathbf{PV_X}\mathbf{\Sigma_X^{-1}} = \mathbf{XV_X}\mathbf{\Sigma_X^{-1}} = \mathbf{U_X}. \tag{1.15}$$

Thus, $\mathbf{U_Y} = \mathbf{U_X}$, and we may write the SVD of $\mathbf{Y}$ as:

$$\mathbf{Y} = \mathbf{XP}^* = \mathbf{U_X}\mathbf{\Sigma_X}\mathbf{V_X^*}\mathbf{P}^*. \tag{1.16}$$

1.4 Pseudo-Inverse, Least-Squares, and Regression

Many physical systems may be represented as a linear system of equations:

$$\mathbf{Ax} = \mathbf{b}, \tag{1.17}$$

where the constraint matrix **A** and vector **b** are known, and the vector **x** is unknown. If **A** is a square, invertible matrix (i.e., **A** has nonzero determinant), then there exists a unique solution **x** for every **b**. However, when **A** is either singular or rectangular, there may be one, none, or infinitely many solutions, depending on the specific **b** and the column and row spaces of **A**.

First, consider the *underdetermined system*, where $\mathbf{A} \in \mathbb{C}^{n \times m}$ and $n \ll m$ (i.e., **A** is a short-fat matrix), so that there are fewer equations than unknowns. This type of system is likely to have full column rank, since it has many more columns than are required for a linearly independent basis[4]. Generically, if a short-fat **A** has full column rank, then there are infinitely many solutions **x** for every **b**. The system is called *underdetermined* because there are not enough values in **b** to uniquely determine the higher-dimensional **x**.

Similarly, consider the *overdetermined system*, where $n \gg m$ (i.e., a tall-skinny matrix), so that there are more equations than unknowns. This matrix cannot have a full column rank, and so it is guaranteed that there are vectors **b** that have no solution **x**. In fact, there will only be a solution **x** if **b** is in the column space of **A**, i.e. $\mathbf{b} \in \mathrm{col}(\mathbf{A})$.

Technically, there may be some choices of **b** that admit infinitely many solutions **x** for a tall-skinny matrix **A** and other choices of **b** that admit zero solutions even for a short-fat matrix. The solution space to the system in (1.17) is determined by the four fundamental subspaces of $\mathbf{A} = \tilde{\mathbf{U}}\tilde{\mathbf{\Sigma}}\tilde{\mathbf{V}}^*$, where the rank r is chosen to include all nonzero singular values:

- The column space, $\mathrm{col}(\mathbf{A})$, is the span of the columns of **A**, also known as the *range*. The column space of **A** is the same as the column space of $\tilde{\mathbf{U}}$;
- The orthogonal complement to $\mathrm{col}(\mathbf{A})$ is $\mathrm{ker}(\mathbf{A}^*)$, given by the column space of $\hat{\mathbf{U}}^{\perp}$ from Fig. 1.1;
- The row space, $\mathrm{row}(\mathbf{A})$, is the span of the rows of **A**, which is spanned by the columns of $\tilde{\mathbf{V}}$. The row space of **A** is equal to $\mathrm{row}(\mathbf{A}) = \mathrm{col}(\mathbf{A}^*)$;
- The kernel space, $\mathrm{ker}(\mathbf{A})$, is the orthogonal complement to $\mathrm{row}(\mathbf{A})$, and is also known as the *null space*. The null space is the subspace of vectors that map through **A** to zero, i.e., $\mathbf{A}\mathbf{x} = \mathbf{0}$, given by $\mathrm{col}(\hat{\mathbf{V}}^{\perp})$.

More precisely, if $\mathbf{b} \in \mathrm{col}(\mathbf{A})$ and if $\dim(\mathrm{ker}(\mathbf{A})) \neq 0$, then there are infinitely many solutions **x**. Note that the condition $\dim(\mathrm{ker}(\mathbf{A})) \neq 0$ is guaranteed for a short-fat matrix. Similarly, if $\mathbf{b} \notin \mathrm{col}(\mathbf{A})$, then there are no solutions, and the system of equations in (1.17) are called *inconsistent*.

The fundamental subspaces above satisfy the following properties:

$$\mathrm{col}(\mathbf{A}) \oplus \mathrm{ker}(\mathbf{A}^*) = \mathbb{R}^n \tag{1.18a}$$

$$\mathrm{col}(\mathbf{A}^*) \oplus \mathrm{ker}(\mathbf{A}) = \mathbb{R}^n. \tag{1.18b}$$

Remark 1 *There is an extensive literature on random matrix theory, where the above stereotypes are almost certainly true, meaning that they are true with high probability. For example, a system $\mathbf{A}\mathbf{x} = \mathbf{b}$ is extremely unlikely to have a solution for a random matrix $\mathbf{A} \in \mathbb{R}^{n \times m}$ and random vector $\mathbf{b} \in \mathbb{R}^n$ with $n \gg m$, since there is little chance that **b** is in*

---

[4] It is easy to construct degenerate examples where a short-fat matrix does not have full column rank, such as
$$\mathbf{A} = \begin{bmatrix} 1 & 1 & 1 & 1 \\ 1 & 1 & 1 & 1 \end{bmatrix}.$$

the column space of **A**. *These properties of random matrices will play a prominent role in compressed sensing (see Chapter 3).*

In the overdetermined case when no solution exists, we would often like to find the solution **x** that minimizes the sum-squared error $\|\mathbf{Ax} - \mathbf{b}\|_2^2$, the so-called *least-squares* solution. Note that the least-squares solution also minimizes $\|\mathbf{Ax} - \mathbf{b}\|_2$. In the underdetermined case when infinitely many solutions exist, we may like to find the solution **x** with minimum norm $\|\mathbf{x}\|_2$ so that $\mathbf{Ax} = \mathbf{b}$, the so-called *minimum-norm* solution.

The SVD is the technique of choice for these important optimization problems. First, if we substitute an exact truncated SVD $\mathbf{A} = \tilde{\mathbf{U}}\tilde{\boldsymbol{\Sigma}}\tilde{\mathbf{V}}^*$ in for **A**, we can "invert" each of the matrices $\tilde{\mathbf{U}}$, $\tilde{\boldsymbol{\Sigma}}$, and $\tilde{\mathbf{V}}^*$ in turn, resulting in the Moore-Penrose *left pseudo-inverse* [425, 426, 453, 572] $\mathbf{A}^\dagger$ of **A**:

$$\mathbf{A}^\dagger \triangleq \tilde{\mathbf{V}}\tilde{\boldsymbol{\Sigma}}^{-1}\tilde{\mathbf{U}}^* \implies \mathbf{A}^\dagger\mathbf{A} = \mathbf{I}_{m \times m}. \tag{1.19}$$

This may be used to find both the minimum norm and least-squares solutions to (1.17):

$$\mathbf{A}^\dagger\mathbf{A}\tilde{\mathbf{x}} = \mathbf{A}^\dagger\mathbf{b} \implies \tilde{\mathbf{x}} = \tilde{\mathbf{V}}\tilde{\boldsymbol{\Sigma}}^{-1}\tilde{\mathbf{U}}^*\mathbf{b}. \tag{1.20}$$

Plugging the solution $\tilde{\mathbf{x}}$ back in to (1.17) results in:

$$\mathbf{A}\tilde{\mathbf{x}} = \tilde{\mathbf{U}}\tilde{\boldsymbol{\Sigma}}\tilde{\mathbf{V}}^*\tilde{\mathbf{V}}\tilde{\boldsymbol{\Sigma}}^{-1}\tilde{\mathbf{U}}^*\mathbf{b} \tag{1.21a}$$

$$= \tilde{\mathbf{U}}\tilde{\mathbf{U}}^*\mathbf{b}. \tag{1.21b}$$

Note that $\tilde{\mathbf{U}}\tilde{\mathbf{U}}^*$ is not necessarily the identity matrix, but is rather a projection onto the column space of $\tilde{\mathbf{U}}$. Therefore, $\tilde{\mathbf{x}}$ will only be an exact solution to (1.17) when **b** is in the column space of $\tilde{\mathbf{U}}$, and therefore in the column space of **A**.

Computing the pseudo-inverse $\mathbf{A}^\dagger$ is computationally efficient, after the expensive upfront cost of computing the SVD. Inverting the unitary matrices $\tilde{\mathbf{U}}$ and $\tilde{\mathbf{V}}$ involves matrix multiplication by the transpose matrices, which are $\mathcal{O}(n^2)$ operations. Inverting $\tilde{\boldsymbol{\Sigma}}$ is even more efficient since it is a diagonal matrix, requiring $\mathcal{O}(n)$ operations. In contrast, inverting a dense square matrix would require an $\mathcal{O}(n^3)$ operation.

One-Dimensional Linear Regression

Regression is an important statistical tool to relate variables to one another based on data [360]. Consider the collection of data in Fig. 1.9. The red ×'s are obtained by adding Gaussian white noise to the black line, as shown in Code 1.4. We assume that the data is linearly related, as in (1.17), and we use the pseudo-inverse to find the least-squares solution for the slope x below (blue dashed line), shown in Code 1.5:

$$\begin{bmatrix} | \\ \mathbf{b} \\ | \end{bmatrix} = \begin{bmatrix} | \\ \mathbf{a} \\ | \end{bmatrix} x = \tilde{\mathbf{U}}\tilde{\boldsymbol{\Sigma}}\tilde{\mathbf{V}}^* x. \tag{1.22a}$$

$$\implies x = \tilde{\mathbf{V}}\tilde{\boldsymbol{\Sigma}}^{-1}\tilde{\mathbf{U}}^*\mathbf{b}. \tag{1.22b}$$

In (1.22b), $\tilde{\boldsymbol{\Sigma}} = \|\mathbf{a}\|_2$, $\tilde{\mathbf{V}} = 1$, and $\tilde{\mathbf{U}} = \mathbf{a}/\|\mathbf{a}\|_2$. Taking the left pseudo-inverse:

$$x = \frac{\mathbf{a}^*\mathbf{b}}{\|\mathbf{a}\|_2^2}. \tag{1.23}$$

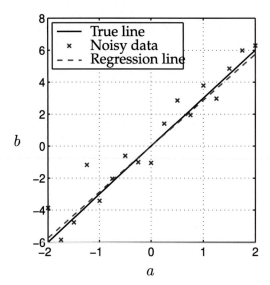

Figure 1.9 Illustration of linear regression using noisy data.

This makes physical sense, if we think of x as the value that best maps our vector **a** to the vector **b**. Then, the best single value x is obtained by taking the dot product of **b** with the normalized **a** direction. We then add a second normalization factor $\|\mathbf{a}\|_2$ because the **a** in (1.22a) is not normalized.

Note that strange things happen if you use row vectors instead of column vectors in (1.22). Also, if the noise magnitude becomes large relative to the slope x, the pseudo-inverse will undergo a phase-change in accuracy, related to the hard-thresholding results in subsequent sections.

Code 1.4 Generate noisy data for Fig. 1.9.

```
x = 3;                              % True slope
a = [-2:.25:2]';
b = a*x + 1*randn(size(a));         % Add noise
plot(a,x*a,'k')                     % True relationship
hold on, plot(a,b,'rx')             % Noisy measurements
```

Code 1.5 Compute least-squares approximation for Fig. 1.9.

```
[U,S,V] = svd(a,'econ');
xtilde = V*inv(S)*U'*b;             % Least-square fit
plot(a,xtilde*a,'b--')              % Plot fit
```

The procedure above is called *linear regression* in statistics. There is a **regress** command in Matlab, as well as a **pinv** command that may also be used.

Code 1.6 Alternative formulations of least-squares in Matlab.

```
xtilde1 = V*inv(S)*U'*b
xtilde2 = pinv(a)*b
xtilde3 = regress(b,a)
```

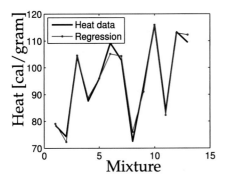

Figure 1.10 Heat data for cement mixtures containing four basic ingredients.

Multilinear regression
Example 1: Cement heat generation data
First, we begin with a simple built-in Matlab dataset that describes the heat generation for various cement mixtures comprised of four basic ingredients. In this problem, we are solving (1.17) where $\mathbf{A} \in \mathbb{R}^{13 \times 4}$, since there are four ingredients and heat measurements for 13 unique mixtures. The goal is to determine the weighting $\mathbf{x}$ that relates the proportions of the four ingredients to the heat generation. It is possible to find the minimum error solution using the SVD, as shown in Code 1.7. Alternatives, using **regress** and **pinv**, are also explored.

Code 1.7 Multilinear regression for cement heat data.

```
load hald;    % Load Portlant Cement dataset
A = ingredients;
b = heat;

[U,S,V] = svd(A,'econ');
x = V*inv(S)*U'*b;           % Solve Ax=b using the SVD

plot(b,'k');   hold on       % Plot data
plot(A*x,'r-o',);            % Plot fit

x = regress(b,A);            % Alternative 1  (regress)
x = pinv(A)*b;               % Alternative 2  (pinv)
```

Example 2: Boston Housing Data
In this example, we explore a larger data set to determine which factors best predict prices in the Boston housing market [234]. This data is available from the UCI Machine Learning Repository [24].

There are 13 attributes that are correlated with house price, such as per capita crime rate and property-tax rate. These features are regressed onto the price data, and the best fit price prediction is plotted against the true house value in Fig. 1.11, and the regression coefficients are shown in Fig. 1.12. Although the house value is not perfectly predicted, the trend agrees quite well. It is often the case that the highest value outliers are not well-captured by simple linear fits, as in this example.

This data contains prices and attributes for 506 homes, so the attribute matrix is of size 506×13. It is important to pad this matrix with an additional column of ones, to take

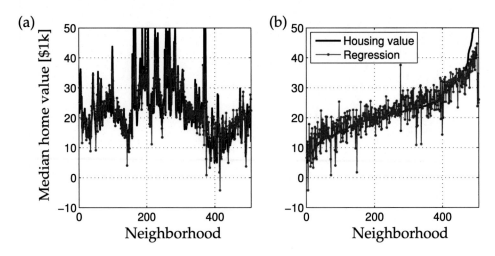

Figure 1.11 Multilinear regression of home prices using various factors. (a) Unsorted data, and (b) Data sorted by home value.

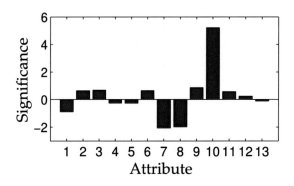

Figure 1.12 Significance of various attributes in the regression.

into account the possibility of a nonzero constant offset in the regression formula. This corresponds to the "y-intercept" in a simple one-dimensional linear regression.

Code 1.8 Multilinear regression for Boston housing data.

```
load housing.data

b = housing(:,14);       % housing values in $1000s
A = housing(:,1:13);     % other factors,
A = [A ones(size(A,1),1)];  % Pad with ones y-intercept

x = regress(b,A);
plot(b,'k-o');
hold on, plot(A*x,'r-o');

[b sortind] = sort(housing(:,14)); % sorted values
plot(b,'k-o')
hold on, plot(A(sortind,:)*x,'r-o')
```

Caution

In general, the matrix $\mathbf{U}$, whose columns are left-singular vectors of $\mathbf{X}$, is a unitary square matrix. Therefore, $\mathbf{U}^*\mathbf{U} = \mathbf{U}\mathbf{U}^* = \mathbf{I}_{n\times n}$. However, to compute the pseudo-inverse of $\mathbf{X}$, we must compute $\mathbf{X}^\dagger = \tilde{\mathbf{V}}\tilde{\mathbf{\Sigma}}^{-1}\tilde{\mathbf{U}}^*$ since only $\tilde{\mathbf{\Sigma}}$ is invertible (if all singular values are nonzero), although $\mathbf{\Sigma}$ is not invertible in general (in fact, it is generally not even square).

Until now, we have assumed that $\mathbf{X} = \tilde{\mathbf{U}}\tilde{\mathbf{\Sigma}}\tilde{\mathbf{V}}^*$ is an exact SVD, so that the rank r includes all nonzero singular values. This guarantees that the matrix $\tilde{\mathbf{\Sigma}}$ is invertible.

A complication arises when working with a truncated basis of left singular vectors $\tilde{\mathbf{U}}$. It is still true that $\tilde{\mathbf{U}}^*\tilde{\mathbf{U}} = \mathbf{I}_{r\times r}$, where r is the rank of $\mathbf{X}$. However, $\tilde{\mathbf{U}}\tilde{\mathbf{U}}^* \neq \mathbf{I}_{n\times n}$, which is easy to verify numerically on a simple example. Assuming that $\tilde{\mathbf{U}}\tilde{\mathbf{U}}^*$ is equal to the identity is one of the most common accidental misuses of the SVD[5].

```
>> tol = 1.e-16;
>> [U,S,V] = svd(X,'econ')
>> r = max(find(diag(S)>max(S(:))*tol));
>> invX = V(:,1:r)*S(1:r,1:r)*U(:,1:r)';   % only approximate
```

1.5 Principal Component Analysis (PCA)

Principal components analysis (PCA) is one of the central uses of the SVD, providing a data-driven, hierarchical coordinate system to represent high-dimensional correlated data. This coordinate system involves the correlation matrices described in Sec. 1.3. Importantly, PCA pre-processes the data by mean subtraction and setting the variance to unity before performing the SVD. The geometry of the resulting coordinate system is determined by principal components (PCs) that are uncorrelated (orthogonal) to each other, but have maximal correlation with the measurements. This theory was developed in 1901 by Pearson [418], and independently by Hotelling in the 1930s [256, 257]. Jolliffe [268] provides a good reference text.

Typically, a number of measurements are collected in a single experiment, and these measurements are arranged into a row vector. The measurements may be features of an observable, such as demographic features of a specific human individual. A number of experiments are conducted, and each measurement vector is arranged as a row in a large matrix $\mathbf{X}$. In the example of demography, the collection of experiments may be gathered via polling. Note that this convention for $\mathbf{X}$, consisting of rows of features, is different than the convention throughout the remainder of this chapter, where individual feature "snapshots" are arranged as columns. However, we choose to be consistent with PCA literature in this section. The matrix will still be size $n \times m$, although it may have more rows than columns, or vice versa.

Computation

We now compute the row-wise mean $\bar{\mathbf{x}}$ (i.e., the mean of all rows), and subtract it from $\mathbf{X}$. The mean $\bar{\mathbf{x}}$ is given by

$$\bar{\mathbf{x}}_j = \frac{1}{n}\sum_{i=1}^{n}\mathbf{X}_{ij}, \tag{1.24}$$

---

[5] The authors are not immune to this, having mistakenly used this fictional identity in an early version of [96].

and the mean matrix is

$$\bar{\mathbf{X}} = \begin{bmatrix} 1 \\ \vdots \\ 1 \end{bmatrix} \bar{\mathbf{x}}. \tag{1.25}$$

Subtracting $\bar{\mathbf{X}}$ from $\mathbf{X}$ results in the mean-subtracted data $\mathbf{B}$:

$$\mathbf{B} = \mathbf{X} - \bar{\mathbf{B}}. \tag{1.26}$$

The covariance matrix of the rows of $\mathbf{B}$ is given by

$$\mathbf{C} = \frac{1}{n-1} \mathbf{B}^* \mathbf{B}. \tag{1.27}$$

The first principal component $\mathbf{u}_1$ is given as

$$\mathbf{u}_1 = \underset{\|\mathbf{u}_1\|=1}{\operatorname{argmax}} \ \mathbf{u}_1^* \mathbf{B}^* \mathbf{B} \mathbf{u}_1, \tag{1.28}$$

which is the eigenvector of $\mathbf{B}^*\mathbf{B}$ corresponding to the largest eigenvalue. Now it is clear that $\mathbf{u}_1$ is the left singular vector of $\mathbf{B}$ corresponding to the largest singular value.

It is possible to obtain the principal components by computing the eigen-decomposition of $\mathbf{C}$:

$$\mathbf{CV} = \mathbf{VD}, \tag{1.29}$$

which is guaranteed to exist, since $\mathbf{C}$ is Hermitian.

pca *Command*

In Matlab, there the additional commands **pca** and **princomp** (based on **pca**) for the principal components analysis:

```
>> [V,score,s2] = pca(X);
```

The matrix $\mathbf{V}$ is equivalent to the $\mathbf{V}$ matrix from the SVD of $\mathbf{X}$, up to sign changes of the columns. The vector **s2** contains eigenvalues of the covariance of $\mathbf{X}$, also known as principal component variances; these values are the squares of the singular values. The variable **score** simply contains the coordinates of each row of $\mathbf{B}$ (the mean-subtracted data) in the principal component directions. In general, we often prefer to use the **svd** command with the various pre-processing steps described earlier in the section.

Example: Noisy Gaussian Data

Consider the noisy cloud of data in Fig. 1.13 (a), generated using Code 1.9. The data is generated by selecting $10,000$ vectors from a two-dimensional normal distribution with zero mean and unit variance. These vectors are then scaled in the x and y directions by the values in Table 1.1 and rotated by $\pi/3$. Finally, the entire cloud of data is translated so that it has a nonzero center $\mathbf{x}_C = \begin{bmatrix} 2 & 1 \end{bmatrix}^T$.

Using Code 1.10, the PCA is performed and used to plot confidence intervals using multiple standard deviations, shown in Fig. 1.13 (b). The singular values, shown in Table 1.1, match the data scaling. The matrix $\mathbf{U}$ from the SVD also closely matches the rotation matrix, up to a sign on the columns:

Table 1.1 Standard deviation of data and normalized singular values.

	σ_1	σ_2
Data	2	0.5
SVD	1.974	0.503

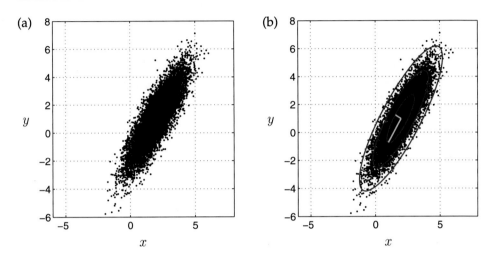

Figure 1.13 Principal components capture the variance of mean-subtracted Gaussian data (a). The first three standard deviation ellipsoids (red), and the two left singular vectors, scaled by singular values ($\sigma_1 u_1 + x_C$ and $\sigma_2 u_2 + x_C$, cyan), are shown in (b).

$$\mathbf{R}_{\pi/3} = \begin{bmatrix} 0.5 & -0.8660 \\ 0.8660 & 0.5 \end{bmatrix}, \qquad \mathbf{U} = \begin{bmatrix} -0.4998 & -0.8662 \\ -0.8662 & 0.4998 \end{bmatrix}.$$

Code 1.9 Generation of noisy cloud of data to illustrate PCA.

```
xC = [2; 1;];                        % Center of data (mean)
sig = [2; .5;];                      % Principal axes

theta = pi/3;                        % Rotate cloud by pi/3
R = [cos(theta) -sin(theta);         % Rotation matrix
    sin(theta) cos(theta)];

nPoints = 10000;                     % Create 10,000 points
X = R*diag(sig)*randn(2,nPoints) + diag(xC)*ones(2,nPoints);
scatter(X(1,:),X(2,:),'k.','LineWidth',2)
```

Code 1.10 Compute PCA and plot confidence intervals.

```
Xavg = mean(X,2);                    % Compute mean
B = X - Xavg*ones(1,nPoints);        % Mean-subtracted Data
[U,S,V] = svd(B/sqrt(nPoints),'econ'); % PCA via SVD
scatter(X(1,:),X(2,:),'k.','LineWidth',2) % Plot data

theta = (0:.01:1)*2*pi;
Xstd = U*S*[cos(theta); sin(theta)]; % 1-std conf. interval
```

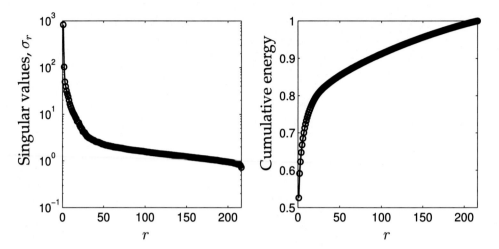

Figure 1.14 Singular values for the Ovarian cancer data.

```
plot(Xavg(1)+Xstd(1,:),Xavg(2) + Xstd(2,:),'r-')
plot(Xavg(1)+2*Xstd(1,:),Xavg(2) + 2*Xstd(2,:),'r-')
plot(Xavg(1)+3*Xstd(1,:),Xavg(2) + 3*Xstd(2,:),'r-')
```

Finally, it is also possible to compute using the **pca** command:

```
>> [V,score,s2] = pca(X);
>> norm(V*score' - B)

ans =
   2.2878e-13
```

Example: Ovarian Cancer Data

The ovarian cancer data set, which is built into Matlab, provides a more realistic example to illustrate the benefits of PCA. This example consists of gene data for 216 patients, 121 of whom have ovarian cancer, and 95 of whom do not. For each patient, there is a vector of data containing the expression of 4000 genes. There are multiple challenges with this type of data, namely the high dimension of the data features. However, we see from Fig. 1.14 that there is significant variance captured in the first few PCA modes. Said another way, the gene data is highly correlated, so that many patients have significant overlap in their gene expression. The ability to visualize patterns and correlations in high-dimensional data is an important reason to use PCA, and PCA has been widely used to find patterns in high-dimensional biological and genetic data [448].

More importantly, patients with ovarian cancer appear to cluster separately from patients without cancer when plotted in the space spanned by the first three PCA modes. This is shown in Fig. 1.15, which is generated by Code 1.11. This inherent clustering in PCA space of data by category is a foundational element of machine learning and pattern recognition. For example, we will see in Sec. 1.6 that images of different human faces will form clusters in PCA space. The use of these clusters will be explored in greater detail in Chapter 5.

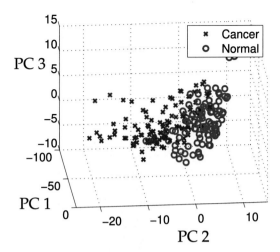

Figure 1.15 Clustering of samples that are normal and those that have cancer in the first three principal component coordinates.

Code 1.11 Compute PCA for ovarian cancer data.

```
load ovariancancer;    % Load ovarian cancer data
[U,S,V] = svd(obs,'econ');
for i=1:size(obs,1)
    x = V(:,1)'*obs(i,:)';
    y = V(:,2)'*obs(i,:)';
    z = V(:,3)'*obs(i,:)';
    if(grp{i}=='Cancer')
        plot3(x,y,z,'rx','LineWidth',2);
    else
        plot3(x,y,z,'bo','LineWidth',2);
    end
end
```

1.6 Eigenfaces Example

One of the most striking demonstrations of SVD/PCA is the so-called eigenfaces example. In this problem, PCA (i.e. SVD on mean-subtracted data) is applied to a large library of facial images to extract the most dominant correlations between images. The result of this decomposition is a set of *eigenfaces* that define a new coordinate system. Images may be represented in these coordinates by taking the dot product with each of the principal components. It will be shown in Chapter 5 that images of the same person tend to cluster in the eigenface space, making this a useful transformation for facial recognition and classification [510, 48]. The eigenface problem was first studied by Sirovich and Kirby in 1987 [491] and expanded on in [291]. Its application to automated facial recognition was presented by Turk and Pentland in 1991 [537].

Here, we demonstrate this algorithm using the Extended Yale Face Database B [203], consisting of cropped and aligned images [327] of 38 individuals (28 from the extended database, and 10 from the original database) under 9 poses and 64 lighting conditions[6].

---

[6] The database can be downloaded at http://vision.ucsd.edu/~iskwak/ExtYaleDatabase/ExtYaleB.html.

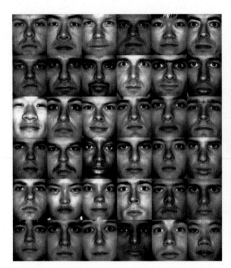

Figure 1.16 (left) A single image for each person in the Yale database, and (right) all images for a specific person. Left panel generated by Code (1.12).

Each image is 192 pixels tall and 168 pixels wide. Unlike the previous image example in Section 1.2, each of the facial images in our library have been reshaped into a large column vector with $192 \times 168 = 32,256$ elements. We use the first 36 people in the database (left panel of Fig. 1.16) as our training data for the eigenfaces example, and we hold back two people as a test set. An example of all 64 images of one specific person are shown in the right panel. These images are loaded and plotted using Code 1.12.

Code 1.12 Plot an image for each person in the Yale database (Fig. 1.16 (a))

```
load ../DATA/allFaces.mat

allPersons = zeros(n*6,m*6);        % Make an array to fit all
    faces
count = 1;
for i=1:6            % 6 x 6 grid of faces
    for j=1:6
        allPersons(1+(i-1)*n:i*n,1+(j-1)*m:j*m) ...
            =reshape(faces(:,1+sum(nfaces(1:count-1))),n,m);
        count = count + 1;
    end
end
imagesc(allPersons), colormap gray
```

As mentioned before, each image is reshaped into a large column vector, and the average face is computed and subtracted from each column vector. The mean-subtracted image vectors are then stacked horizontally as columns in the data matrix $\mathbf{X}$, as shown in Fig. 1.17. Thus, taking the SVD of the mean-subtracted matrix $\mathbf{X}$ results in the PCA. The columns of $\mathbf{U}$ are the eigenfaces, and they may be reshaped back into 192×168 images. This is illustrated in Code 1.13.

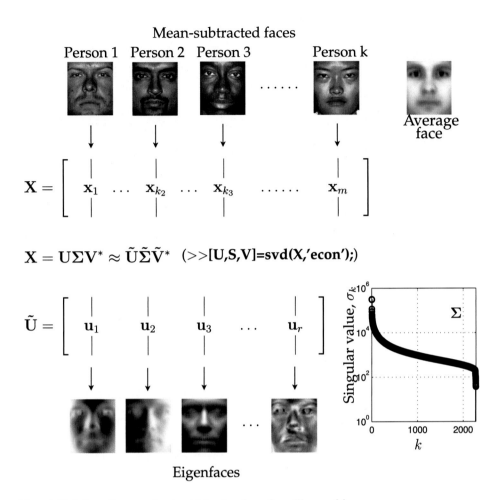

Figure 1.17 Schematic procedure to obtain eigenfaces from library of faces.

Code 1.13 Compute eigenfaces on mean-subtracted data.

```
% We use the first 36 people for training data
trainingFaces = faces(:,1:sum(nfaces(1:36)));
avgFace = mean(trainingFaces,2);  % size n*m by 1;

% Compute eigenfaces on mean-subtracted training data
X = trainingFaces-avgFace*ones(1,size(trainingFaces,2));
[U,S,V] = svd(X,'econ');

imagesc(reshape(avgFace,n,m))  % Plot avg face
imagesc(reshape(U(:,1),n,m))   % Plot first eigenface
```

Using the eigenface library, $\tilde{\mathbf{U}}$, obtained by this code, we now attempt to approximately represent an image that was not in the training data. At the beginning, we held back two individuals (the 37th and 38th people), and we now use one of their images as a test image, $\mathbf{x}_{\text{test}}$. We will see how well a rank-r SVD basis will approximate this image using the following projection:

$$\tilde{\mathbf{x}}_{\text{test}} = \tilde{\mathbf{U}}\tilde{\mathbf{U}}^*\mathbf{x}_{\text{test}}.$$

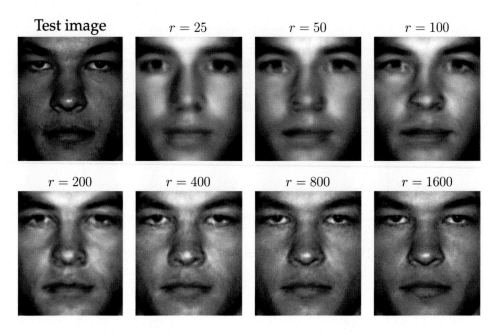

Figure 1.18 Approximate representation of test image using eigenfaces basis of various order r. Test image is not in training set.

The eigenface approximation for various values of r is shown in Fig. 1.18, as computed using Code 1.14. The approximation is relatively poor for $r \leq 200$, although for $r > 400$ it converges to a passable representation of the test image.

It is interesting to note that the eigenface space is not only useful for representing human faces, but may also be used to approximate a dog (Fig. 1.19) or a cappuccino (Fig. 1.20). This is possible because the 1600 eigenfaces span a large subspace of the 32256 dimensional image space corresponding to broad, smooth, nonlocalized spatial features, such as cheeks, forehead, mouths, etc.

Code 1.14 Approximate test-image that was omitted from training data.

```
testFaceMS = testFace - avgFace;
for r=[25 50 100 200 400 800 1600]
    reconFace = avgFace + (U(:,1:r)*(U(:,1:r)'*testFaceMS));
    imagesc(reshape(reconFace,n,m))
end
```

We further investigate the use of the eigenfaces as a coordinate system, defining an eigenface space. By projecting an image $\mathbf{x}$ onto the first r PCA modes, we obtain a set of coordinates in this space: $\tilde{\mathbf{x}} = \tilde{\mathbf{U}}^* \mathbf{x}$. Some principal components may capture the most common features shared among all human faces, while other principal components will be more useful for distinguishing between individuals. Additional principal components may capture differences in lighting angles. Figure 1.21 shows the coordinates of all 64 images of two individuals projected onto the 5th and 6th principal components, generated by Code 1.15. Images of the two individuals appear to be well-separated in these coordinates. This is the basis for image recognition and classification in Chapter 5.

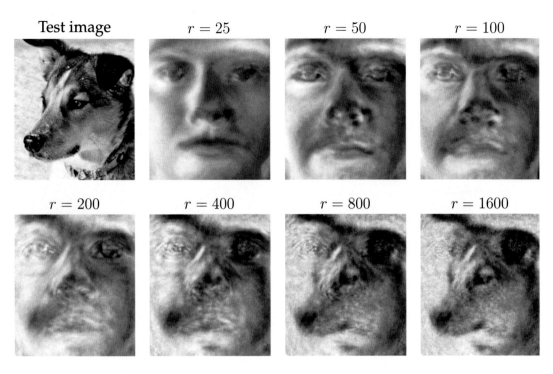

Figure 1.19 Approximate representation of an image of a dog using eigenfaces.

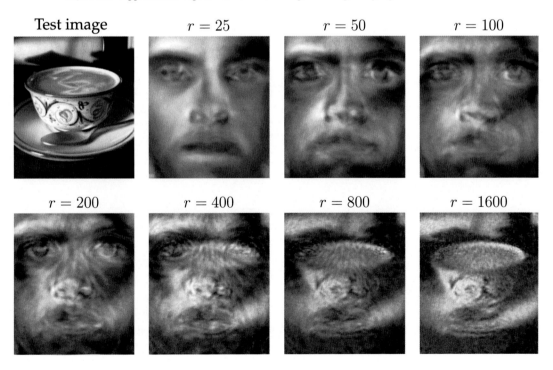

Figure 1.20 Approximate representation of a cappuccino using eigenfaces.

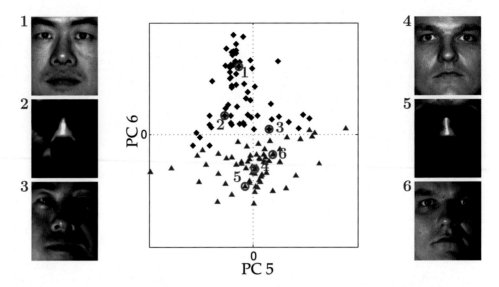

Figure 1.21 Projection of all images from two individuals onto the 5th and 6th PCA modes. Projected images of the first individual are indicated with black diamonds, and projected images of the second individual are indicated with red triangles. Three examples from each individual are circled in blue, and the corresponding image is shown.

Code 1.15 Project images for two specific people onto the 5th and 6th eigenfaces to illustrate the potential for automated classification.

```
P1num = 2;   % Person number 2
P2num = 7;   % Person number 7

P1 = faces(:,1+sum(nfaces(1:P1num-1)):sum(nfaces(1:P1num)));
P2 = faces(:,1+sum(nfaces(1:P2num-1)):sum(nfaces(1:P2num)));

P1 = P1 - avgFace*ones(1,size(P1,2));
P2 = P2 - avgFace*ones(1,size(P2,2));

PCAmodes = [5 6];    % Project onto PCA modes 5 and 6
PCACoordsP1 = U(:,PCAmodes)'*P1;
PCACoordsP2 = U(:,PCAmodes)'*P2;

plot(PCACoordsP1(1,:),PCACoordsP1(2,:),'kd')
plot(PCACoordsP2(1,:),PCACoordsP2(2,:),'r^')
```

1.7   Truncation and Alignment

Deciding how many singular values to keep, i.e. where to truncate, is one of the most important and contentious decisions when using the SVD. There are many factors, including specifications on the desired rank of the system, the magnitude of noise, and the distribution of the singular values. Often, one truncates the SVD at a rank r that captures a pre-determined amount of the variance or energy in the original data, such as 90% or 99% truncation. Although crude, this technique is commonly used. Other techniques involve identifying "elbows" or "knees" in the singular value distribution, which may denote the transition from singular values that represent important patterns from those that represent noise. Truncation may be viewed as a hard threshold on singular values, where values larger than a threshold τ are kept, while remaining singular values are truncated. Recent work by Gavish and Donoho [200] provides an optimal truncation value, or hard threshold, under certain conditions, providing a principled approach to obtaining low-rank matrix approximations using the SVD.

In addition, the alignment of data significantly impacts the rank of the SVD approximation. The SVD essentially relies on a separation of variables between the columns and rows of a data matrix. In many situations, such as when analyzing traveling waves or misaligned data, this assumption breaks down, resulting in an artificial rank inflation.

Optimal Hard Threshold

A recent theoretical breakthrough determines the *optimal* hard threshold τ for singular value truncation under the assumption that a matrix has a low-rank structure contaminated with Gaussian white noise [200]. This work builds on a significant literature surrounding various techniques for hard and soft thresholding of singular values. In this section, we summarize the main results and demonstrate the thresholding on various examples. For more details, see [200].

First, we assume that the data matrix $\mathbf{X}$ is the sum of an underlying low-rank, or approximately low-rank, matrix $\mathbf{X}_{\text{true}}$ and a noise matrix $\mathbf{X}_{\text{noise}}$:

$$\mathbf{X} = \mathbf{X}_{\text{true}} + \gamma \mathbf{X}_{\text{noise}}. \tag{1.30}$$

The entries of $\mathbf{X}_{\text{noise}}$ are assumed to be independent, identically distributed (i.i.d.) Gaussian random variables with zero mean and unit variance. The magnitude of the noise is characterized by γ, which deviates from the notation in [200][7].

When the noise magnitude γ is known, there are closed-form solutions for the optimal hard threshold τ:

1. If $\mathbf{X} \in \mathbb{R}^{n \times n}$ is square, then

    $$\tau = (4/\sqrt{3})\sqrt{n}\gamma. \tag{1.31}$$

2. If $\mathbf{X} \in \mathbb{R}^{n \times m}$ is rectangular and $m \ll n$, then the constant $4/\sqrt{3}$ is replaced by a function of the aspect ratio $\beta = m/n$:

    $$\tau = \lambda(\beta)\sqrt{n}\gamma, \tag{1.32}$$

    $$\lambda(\beta) = \left(2(\beta + 1) + \frac{8\beta}{(\beta + 1) + \left(\beta^2 + 14\beta + 1\right)^{1/2}} \right)^{1/2}. \tag{1.33}$$

    Note that this expression reduces to (1.31) when $\beta = 1$. If $n \ll m$, then $\beta = n/m$.

When the noise magnitude γ is unknown, which is more typical in real-world applications, then it is possible to estimate the noise magnitude and scale the distribution of singular values by using σ_{med}, the *median* singular value. In this case, there is no closed-form solution for τ, and it must be approximated numerically.

---

[7] In [200], σ is used to denote standard deviation and y_k denotes the kth singular value.

3.   For unknown noise γ, and a rectangular matrix $\mathbf{X} \in \mathbb{R}^{n \times m}$, the optimal hard threshold is given by

$$\tau = \omega(\beta)\sigma_{\text{med}}. \tag{1.34}$$

Here, $\omega(\beta) = \lambda(\beta)/\mu_\beta$, where μ_β is the solution to the following problem:

$$\int_{(1-\beta)^2}^{\mu_\beta} \frac{\left[\left((1+\sqrt{\beta})^2 - t\right)\left(t - (1 - \sqrt{\beta})^2\right)\right]^{1/2}}{2\pi t} dt = \frac{1}{2}.$$

Solutions to the expression above must be approximated numerically. Fortunately [200] has a Matlab code supplement[8] [151] to approximate μ_β.

The new method of optimal hard thresholding works remarkably well, as demonstrated on the examples below.

Example 1: Toy Problem

In the first example, shown in Fig. 1.22, we artificially construct a rank-2 matrix (Code 1.16) and we contaminate the signal with Gaussian white noise (Code 1.17). A de-noised and dimensionally reduced matrix is then obtained using the threshold from (1.31) (Code 1.18), as well as using a 90% energy truncation (Code 1.19). It is clear that the hard threshold is able to filter the noise more effectively. Plotting the singular values (Code 1.20) in Fig. 1.23, it is clear that there are two values that are above threshold.

Code 1.16 Compute the underlying low-rank signal. (Fig. 1.22 (a))

```
clear all, close all, clc

t = (-3:.01:3)';

Utrue = [cos(17*t).*exp(-t.^2) sin(11*t)];
Strue = [2 0; 0 .5];
Vtrue = [sin(5*t).*exp(-t.^2) cos(13*t)];

X = Utrue*Strue*Vtrue';
figure, imshow(X);
```

Code 1.17 Contaminate the signal with noise. (Fig. 1.22 (b))

```
sigma = 1;
Xnoisy = X+sigma*randn(size(X));
figure, imshow(Xnoisy);
```

Code 1.18 Truncate using optimal hard threshold. (Fig. 1.22 (c))

```
[U,S,V] = svd(Xnoisy);

N = size(Xnoisy,1);
cutoff = (4/sqrt(3))*sqrt(N)*sigma; % Hard threshold
r = max(find(diag(S)>cutoff)); % Keep modes w/ sig > cutoff
Xclean = U(:,1:r)*S(1:r,1:r)*V(:,1:r)';
figure, imshow(Xclean)
```

---

[8] http://purl.stanford.edu/vg705qn9070

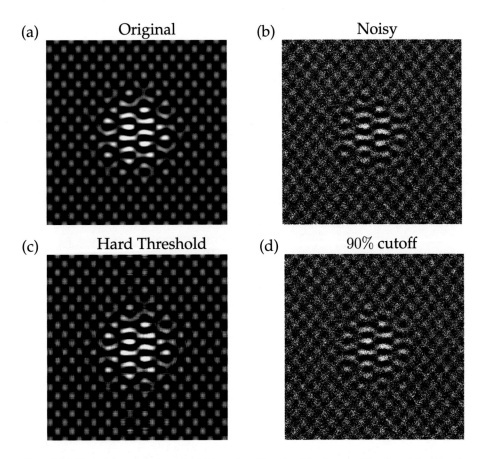

Figure 1.22 Underlying rank 2 matrix (a), matrix with noise (b), clean matrix after optimal hard threshold $(4/\sqrt{3})\sqrt{n}\sigma$ (c), and truncation based on 90% energy (d).

Code 1.19 Truncate using 90% energy criterion. (Fig. 1.22 (d))

```
cdS = cumsum(diag(S))./sum(diag(S));   % Cumulative energy
r90 = min(find(cdS>0.90));   % Find r to capture 90% energy

X90 = U(:,1:r90)*S(1:r90,1:r90)*V(:,1:r90)';
figure, imshow(X90)
```

Code 1.20 Plot singular values for hard threshold example. (Fig. 1.23)

```
semilogy(diag(S),'-ok','LineWidth',1.5), hold on, grid on
semilogy(diag(S(1:r,1:r)),'or','LineWidth',1.5)
```

Example 2: Eigenfaces

In the second example, we revisit the eigenfaces problem from Section 1.6. This provides a more typical example, since the data matrix $\mathbf{X}$ is rectangular, with aspect ratio $\beta = 3/4$, and the noise magnitude is unknown. It is also not clear that the data is contaminated with white noise. Nonetheless, the method determines a threshold τ, above which columns of $\mathbf{U}$ appear to have strong facial features, and below which columns of $\mathbf{U}$ consist mostly of noise, shown in Fig. 1.24.

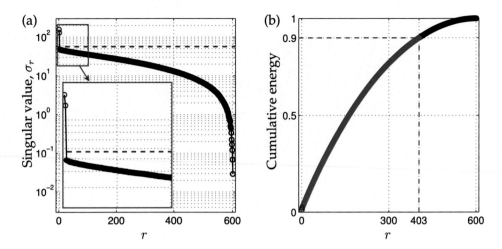

Figure 1.23 Singular values σ_r (a) and cumulative energy in first r modes (b). The optimal hard threshold $\tau = (4/\sqrt{3})\sqrt{n}\sigma$ is shown as a red dashed line (- -), and the 90% cutoff is shown as a blue dashed line (- -). For this case, $n = 600$ and $\sigma = 1$ so that the optimal cutoff is approximately $\tau = 56.6$.

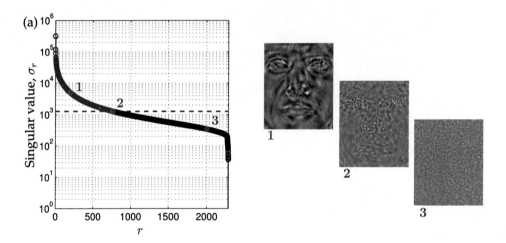

Figure 1.24 Hard thresholding for eigenfaces example.

Importance of Data Alignment

Here, we discuss common pitfalls of the SVD associated with misaligned data. The following example is designed to illustrate one of the central weaknesses of the SVD for dimensionality reduction and coherent feature extraction in data. Consider a matrix of zeros with a rectangular sub-block consisting of ones. As an image, this would look like a white rectangle placed on a black background (see Fig. 1.25 (a)). If the rectangle is perfectly aligned with the x- and y- axes of the figure, then the SVD is simple, having only one nonzero singular value σ_1 (see Fig. 1.25 (c)) and corresponding singular vectors $\mathbf{u}_1$ and $\mathbf{v}_1$ that define the width and height of the white rectangle.

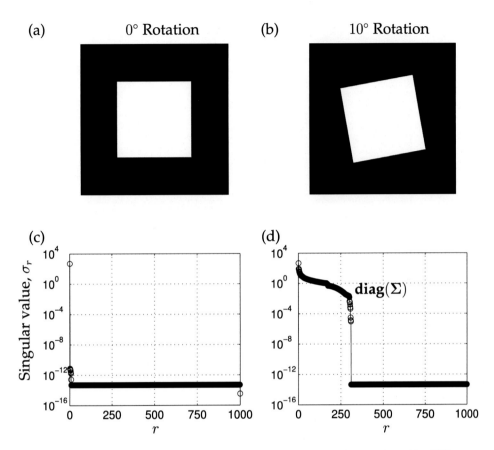

Figure 1.25 A data matrix consisting of ones with a square sub-block of zeros (a), and its SVD spectrum (c). If we rotate the image by $10°$, as in (b), the SVD spectrum becomes significantly more complex (d).

When we begin to rotate the inner rectangle so that it is no longer aligned with the image axes, additional non-zero singular values begin to appear in the spectrum (see Figs. 1.25 (b,d) and 1.26).

Code 1.21 Compute the SVD for a well-aligned and rotated square (Fig. 1.25).

```
n = 1000;     % 1000 x 1000 square
X = zeros(n,n);
X(n/4:3*n/4,n/4:3*n/4) = 1;
imshow(X);

Y = imrotate(X,10,'bicubic');   % rotate 10 degrees
Y = Y - Y(1,1);
nY = size(Y,1);
startind = floor((nY-n)/2);
Xrot = Y(startind:startind+n-1, startind:startind+n-1);
imshow(Xrot);
[U,S,V] = svd(X);       % SVD well-aligned square
[U,S,V] = svd(Xrot);    % SVD rotated square
semilogy(diag(S),'-ko')
semilogy(diag(S),'-ko')
```

(a) (b)

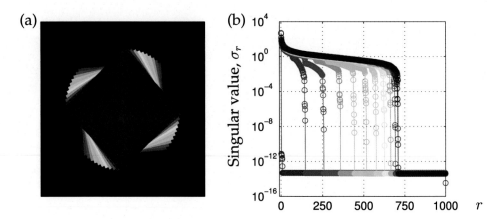

Figure 1.26 A data matrix consisting of zeros with a square sub-block of ones at various rotations (a), and the corresponding SVD spectrum, **diag(S)**, (b).

The reason that this example breaks down is that the SVD is fundamentally *geometric*, meaning that it depends on the coordinate system in which the data is represented. As we have seen earlier, the SVD is only generically invariant to unitary transformations, meaning that the transformation preserves the inner product. This fact may be viewed as both a strength and a weakness of the method. First, the dependence of SVD on the inner product is essential for the various useful geometric interpretations. Moreover, the SVD has meaningful units and dimensions. However, this makes the SVD sensitive to the alignment of the data. In fact, the SVD rank explodes when objects in the columns translate, rotate, or scale, which severely limits its use for data that has not been heavily pre-processed.

For instance, the eigenfaces example was built on a library of images that had been meticulously cropped, centered, and aligned according to a stencil. Without taking these important pre-processing steps, the features and clustering performance would be underwhelming.

The inability of the SVD to capture translations and rotations of the data is a major limitation. For example, the SVD is still the method of choice for the low-rank decomposition of data from partial differential equations (PDEs), as will be explored in Chapters 11 and 12. However, the SVD is fundamentally a data-driven separation of variables, which we know will not work for many types of PDE, for example those that exhibit traveling waves. Generalized decompositions that retain the favorable properties and are applicable to data with symmetries is a significant open challenge in the field.

Code 1.22 SVD for a square rotated through various angles (Fig. 1.26).

```
nAngles = 12;   % sweep through 12 angles, from 0:4:44
Xrot = X;
for j=2:nAngles
    Y = imrotate(X,(j-1)*4,'bicubic'); % rotate (j-1)*4
    startind = floor((size(Y,1)-n)/2);
    Xrot1 = Y(startind:startind+n-1, startind:startind+n-1);
    Xrot2 = Xrot1 - Xrot1(1,1);
    Xrot2 = Xrot2/max(Xrot2(:));
    Xrot(Xrot2>.5) = j;

    [U,S,V] = svd(Xrot1);
```

```
      subplot(1,2,1), imagesc(Xrot), colormap([0 0 0; cm])
      subplot(1,2,2), semilogy(diag(S),'-o','color',cm(j,:))
end
```

1.8   Randomized Singular Value Decomposition

The accurate and efficient decomposition of large data matrices is one of the cornerstones of modern computational mathematics and data science. In many cases, matrix decompositions are explicitly focused on extracting dominant low-rank structure in the matrix, as illustrated throughout the examples in this chapter. Recently, it has been shown that if a matrix $\mathbf{X}$ has low-rank structure, then there are extremely efficient matrix decomposition algorithms based on the theory of random sampling; this is closely related to the idea of sparsity and the high-dimensional geometry of sparse vectors, which will be explored in Chapter 3. These so-called *randomized* numerical methods have the potential to transform computational linear algebra, providing accurate matrix decompositions at a fraction of the cost of deterministic methods. Moreover, with increasingly vast measurements (e.g., from 4K and 8K video, internet of things, etc.), it is often the case that the *intrinsic* rank of the data does not increase appreciable, even though the dimension of the ambient measurement space grows. Thus, the computational savings of randomized methods will only become more important in the coming years and decades with the growing deluge of data.

Randomized Linear Algebra

Randomized linear algebra is a much more general concept than the treatment presented here for the SVD. In addition to the randomized SVD [464, 371], randomized algorithms have been developed for principal component analysis [454, 229], the pivoted LU decomposition [485], the pivoted QR decomposition [162], and the dynamic mode decomposition [175]. Most randomized matrix decompositions can be broken into a few common steps, as described here. There are also several excellent surveys on the topic [354, 228, 334, 177]. We assume that we are working with tall-skinny matrices, so that $n > m$, although the theory readily generalizes to short-fat matrices.

> **Step 0:**   Identify a target rank, $r < m$.
>
> **Step 1:**   Using random projections $\mathbf{P}$ to sample the column space, find a matrix $\mathbf{Q}$ whose columns approximate the column space of $\mathbf{X}$, i.e., so that $\mathbf{X} \approx \mathbf{Q}\mathbf{Q}^*\mathbf{X}$.
>
> **Step 2:**   Project $\mathbf{X}$ onto the $\mathbf{Q}$ subspace, $\mathbf{Y} = \mathbf{Q}^*\mathbf{X}$, and compute the matrix decomposition on $\mathbf{Y}$.
>
> **Step 3:**   Reconstruct high dimensional modes $\mathbf{U} = \mathbf{Q}\mathbf{U_Y}$ using $\mathbf{Q}$ and the modes computed from $\mathbf{Y}$.

Randomized SVD Algorithm

Over the past two decades, there have been several randomized algorithms proposed to compute a low-rank SVD, including the *Monte Carlo* SVD [190] and more robust approaches based on random projections [464, 335, 371]. These methods were improved by incorporating structured sampling matrices for faster matrix multiplications [559]. Here, we use the randomized SVD algorithm of Halko, Martinsson, and Tropp [228], which combined and expanded on these previous algorithms, providing favorable error bounds. Additional analysis and numerical implementation details are found in Voronin and Martinsson [544]. A schematic of the rSVD algorithm is shown in Fig. 1.27.

Step 1: We construct a random projection matrix $\mathbf{P} \in \mathbb{R}^{m \times r}$ to sample the column space of $\mathbf{X} \in \mathbb{R}^{n \times m}$:

$$\mathbf{Z} = \mathbf{XP}. \tag{1.35}$$

The matrix $\mathbf{Z}$ may be much smaller than $\mathbf{X}$, especially for low-rank matrices with $r \ll m$. It is highly unlikely that a random projection matrix $\mathbf{P}$ will project out important components of $\mathbf{X}$, and so $\mathbf{Z}$ approximates the column space of $\mathbf{X}$ with high probability. Thus, it is possible to compute the low-rank QR decomposition of $\mathbf{Z}$ to obtain an orthonormal basis for $\mathbf{X}$:

$$\mathbf{Z} = \mathbf{QR}. \tag{1.36}$$

Step 1

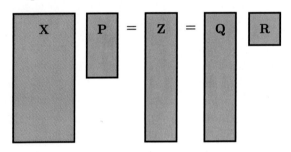

Step 2

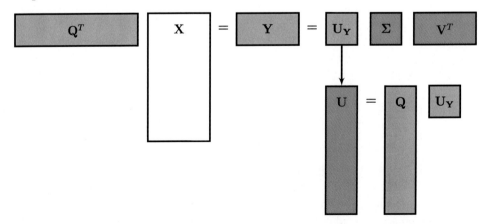

Figure 1.27 Schematic of randomized SVD algorithm. The high-dimensional data $\mathbf{X}$ is depicted in red, intermediate steps in gray, and the outputs in blue. This algorithm requires two passes over $\mathbf{X}$.

Step 2: With the low-rank basis $\mathbf{Q}$, we may project $\mathbf{X}$ into a smaller space:

$$\mathbf{Y} = \mathbf{Q}^*\mathbf{X}. \tag{1.37}$$

It also follows that $\mathbf{X} \approx \mathbf{Q}\mathbf{Y}$, with better agreement when the singular values σ_k decay rapidly for $k > r$.

It is now possible to compute the singular value decomposition on $\mathbf{Y}$:

$$\mathbf{Y} = \mathbf{U_Y}\mathbf{\Sigma}\mathbf{V}^*. \tag{1.38}$$

Because $\mathbf{Q}$ is a orthonormal and approximates the column space of $\mathbf{X}$, the matrices $\mathbf{\Sigma}$ and $\mathbf{V}$ are the same for $\mathbf{Y}$ and $\mathbf{X}$, as discussed in Section 1.3.

Step 3: Finally, it is possible to reconstruct the high-dimensional left singular vectors $\mathbf{U}$ using $\mathbf{U_Y}$ and $\mathbf{Q}$:

$$\mathbf{U} = \mathbf{Q}\mathbf{U_Y}. \tag{1.39}$$

Oversampling

Most matrices $\mathbf{X}$ do not have an exact low-rank structure, given by r modes. Instead, there are nonzero singular values σ_k for $k > r$, and the sketch $\mathbf{Z}$ will not exactly span the column space of $\mathbf{X}$. In general, increasing the number of columns in $\mathbf{P}$ from r to $r + p$, significantly improves results, even with p adding around 5 or 10 columns [370]. This is known as *oversampling*, and increasing p decreases the variance of the singular value spectrum of the sketched matrix.

Power Iterations

A second challenge in using randomized algorithms is when the singular value spectrum decays slowly, so that the remaining truncated singular values contain significant variance in the data $\mathbf{X}$. In this case, it is possible to preprocess $\mathbf{X}$ through q *power iterations* [454, 228, 224] to create a new matrix $\mathbf{X}^{(q)}$ with a more rapid singular value decay:

$$\mathbf{X}^{(q)} = \left(\mathbf{X}\mathbf{X}^*\right)^q \mathbf{X}. \tag{1.40}$$

Power iterations dramatically improve the quality of the randomized decomposition, as the singular value spectrum of $\mathbf{X}^{(q)}$ decays more rapidly:

$$\mathbf{X}^{(q)} = \mathbf{U}\mathbf{\Sigma}^{2q-1}\mathbf{V}^*. \tag{1.41}$$

However, power iterations are expensive, requiring q additional passes through the data $\mathbf{X}$. In some extreme examples, the data in $\mathbf{X}$ may be stored in a distributed architecture, so that every additional pass adds considerable expense.

Guaranteed Error Bounds

One of the most important properties of the randomized SVD is the existence of tunable error bounds, that are explicit functions of the singular value spectrum, the desired rank r, the oversampling parameter p and the number of power iterations q. The best attainable error bound for a deterministic algorithm is:

$$\|\mathbf{X} - \mathbf{Q}\mathbf{Y}\|_2 \geq \sigma_{r+1}(\mathbf{X}). \tag{1.42}$$

In other words, the approximation with the best possible rank-r subspace $\mathbf{Q}$ will have error greater than or equal to the next truncated singular value of $\mathbf{X}$. For randomized methods, it is possible to bound the *expectation* of the error:

$$\mathbb{E}\left(\|\mathbf{X} - \mathbf{QY}\|_2\right) \leq \left(1 + \sqrt{\frac{r}{p-1}} + \frac{e\sqrt{r+p}}{p}\sqrt{m-r}\right)^{\frac{1}{2q+1}} \sigma_{k+1}(\mathbf{X}), \qquad (1.43)$$

where e is Euler's number.

Choice of random matrix $\mathbf{P}$

There are several suitable choices of the random matrix $\mathbf{P}$. Gaussian random projections (e.g., the elements of $\mathbf{P}$ are i.i.d. Gaussian random variables) are frequently used because of favorable mathematical properties and the richness of information extracted in the sketch $\mathbf{Z}$. In particular, it is very unlikely that a Gaussian random matrix $\mathbf{P}$ will be chosen *badly* so as to project out important information in $\mathbf{X}$. However, Gaussian projections are expensive to generate, store, and compute. Uniform random matrices are also frequently used, and have similar limitations. There are several alternatives, such as Rademacher matrices, where the entries can be $+1$ or -1 with equal probability [532]. Structured random projection matrices may provide efficient sketches, reducing computational costs to $\mathcal{O}(nm\log(r))$ [559]. Yet another choice is a sparse projection matrix $\mathbf{P}$, which improves storage and computation, but at the cost of including less information in the sketch. In the extreme case, when even a single pass over the matrix $\mathbf{X}$ is prohibitively expensive, the matrix $\mathbf{P}$ may be chosen as random columns of the $m \times m$ identity matrix, so that it randomly selects columns of $\mathbf{X}$ for the sketch $\mathbf{Z}$. This is the fastest option, but should be used with caution, as information may be lost if the structure of $\mathbf{X}$ is highly localized in a subset of columns, which may be lost by column sampling.

Example of Randomized SVD

To demonstrate the randomized SVD algorithm, we will decompose a high-resolution image. This particular implementation is only for illustrative purposes, as it has not been optimized for speed, data transfer, or accuracy. In practical applications, care should be taken [228, 177].

Code 1.23 computes the randomized SVD of a matrix $\mathbf{X}$, and Code 1.24 uses this function to obtain a rank-400 approximation to a high-resolution image, shown in Fig. 1.28.

Code 1.23 Randomized SVD algorithm.

```
function [U,S,V] = rsvd(X,r,q,p);

% Step 1: Sample column space of X with P matrix
ny = size(X,2);
P = randn(ny,r+p);
Z = X*P;
for k=1:q
    Z = X*(X'*Z);
end
[Q,R] = qr(Z,0);

% Step 2: Compute SVD on projected Y=Q'*X;
Y = Q'*X;
```

Figure 1.28 Original high-resolution (left) and rank-400 approximations from the SVD (middle) and rSVD (right).

```
[UY,S,V] = svd(Y,'econ');
U = Q*UY;
```

Code 1.24 Compute the randomized SVD of high-resolution image.

```
clear all, close all, clc
A=imread('jupiter.jpg');
X=double(rgb2gray(A));
[U,S,V] = svd(X,'econ');        % Deterministic SVD

r = 400;  % Target rank
q = 1;    % Power iterations
p = 5;    % Oversampling parameter
[rU,rS,rV] = rsvd(X,r,q,p); % Randomized SVD

%% Reconstruction
XSVD = U(:,1:r)*S(1:r,1:r)*V(:,1:r)';        % SVD approx.
errSVD = norm(X-XSVD,2)/norm(X,2);
XrSVD = rU(:,1:r)*rS(1:r,1:r)*rV(:,1:r)'; % rSVD approx.
errrSVD = norm(X-XrSVD,2)/norm(X,2);
```

1.9   Tensor Decompositions and *N*-Way Data Arrays

Low-rank decompositions can be generalized beyond matrices. This is important as the SVD requires that disparate types of data be flattened into a single vector in order to evaluate correlated structures. For instance, different time snapshots (columns) of a matrix may include measurements as diverse as temperature, pressure, concentration of a substance, etc. Additionally, there may be categorical data. Vectorizing this data generally does not make sense. Ultimately, what is desired is to preserve the various data structures and types in their own, independent directions. Matrices can be generalized to *N*-way arrays, or

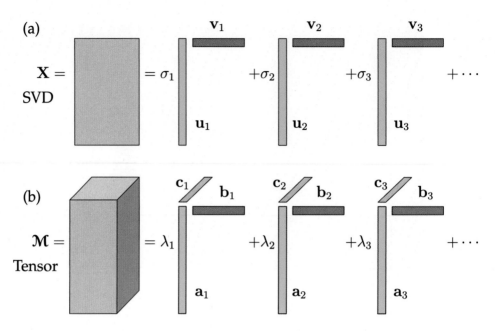

Figure 1.29 Comparison of the SVD and Tensor decomposition frameworks. Both methods produce an approximation to the original data matrix by sums of outer products. Specifically, the tensor decomposition generalizes the concept of the SVD to N-way arrays of data without having to flatten (vectorize) the data.

tensors, where the data is more appropriately arranged without forcing a data-flattening process.

The construction of data tensors requires that we revisit the notation associated with tensor addition, multiplication, and inner products [299]. We denote the rth column of a matrix $\mathbf{A}$ by $\mathbf{a}_r$. Given matrices $\mathbf{A} \in \mathbb{R}^{I \times K}$ and $\mathbf{B} \in \mathbb{R}^{J \times K}$, their Khatri-Rao product is denoted by $\mathbf{A} \odot \mathbf{B}$ and is defined to be the $IJ \times K$ matrix of column-wise Kronecker products, namely

$$\mathbf{A} \odot \mathbf{B} = \begin{pmatrix} \mathbf{a}_1 \otimes \mathbf{b}_1 & \cdots & \mathbf{a}_K \otimes \mathbf{b}_K \end{pmatrix}.$$

For an N-way tensor $\mathcal{A}$ of size $I_1 \times I_2 \times \cdots \times I_N$, we denote its $\mathbf{i} = (i_1, i_2, \ldots, i_N)$ entry by $a_{\mathbf{i}}$.

The inner product between two N-way tensors $\mathcal{A}$ and $\mathcal{B}$ of compatible dimensions is given by

$$\langle \mathcal{A}, \mathcal{B} \rangle = \sum_{\mathbf{i}} a_{\mathbf{i}} b_{\mathbf{i}}.$$

The Frobenius norm of a tensor $\mathcal{A}$, denoted by $\|\mathcal{A}\|_{\mathrm{F}}$, is the square root of the inner product of $\mathcal{A}$ with itself, namely $\|\mathcal{A}\|_{\mathrm{F}} = \sqrt{\langle \mathcal{A}, \mathcal{A} \rangle}$. Finally, the mode-$n$ matricization or unfolding of a tensor $\mathcal{A}$ is denoted by $\mathbf{mA}_{(n)}$.

Let $\mathcal{M}$ represent an N-way data tensor of size $I_1 \times I_2 \times \cdots \times I_N$. We are interested in an R-component CANDECOMP/PARAFAC (CP) [124, 235, 299] factor model

$$\mathcal{M} = \sum_{r=1}^{R} \lambda_r \, \mathbf{ma}_r^{(1)} \circ \cdots \circ \mathbf{ma}_r^{(N)}, \tag{1.44}$$

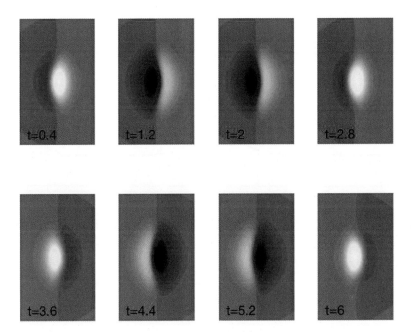

Figure 1.30 Example N-way array data set created from the function (1.45). The data matrix is $A \in \mathbb{R}^{121 \times 101 \times 315}$. A CP tensor decomposition can be used to extract the two underlying structures that produced the data.

where $\circ$ represents outer product and $\mathbf{ma}_r^{(n)}$ represents the rth column of the *factor matrix* $\mathbf{mA}^{(n)}$ of size $I_n \times R$. The CP decomposition refers to CANDECOMP/PARAFAC which stand for *parallel factors analysis* (PARAFAC) and *canonical decomposition* (CANDE-COMP) respectively. We refer to each summand as a *component*. Assuming each factor matrix has been column-normalized to have unit Euclidean length, we refer to the λ_r's as *weights*. We will use the shorthand notation where $\lambda = (\lambda_1, \ldots, \lambda_R)^{\mathsf{T}}$ [25]. A tensor that has a CP decomposition is sometimes referred to as a Kruskal tensor.

For the rest of this chapter, we consider a 3-way CP tensor decomposition (See Fig. 1.29) where two modes index state variation and the third mode indexes time variation:

$$\mathcal{M} = \sum_{r=1}^{R} \lambda_r \, \mathbf{A}_r \circ \mathbf{B}_r \circ \mathbf{C}_r.$$

Let $\mathbf{A} \in \mathbb{R}^{I_1 \times R}$ and $\mathbf{B} \in \mathbb{R}^{I_2 \times R}$ denote the factor matrices corresponding to the two state modes and $\mathbf{C} \in \mathbb{R}^{I_3 \times R}$ denote the factor matrix corresponding to the time mode. This 3-way decomposition is compared to the SVD in Fig. 1.29.

To illustrate the tensor decomposition, we use the MATLAB N-way toolbox developed by Rasmus Bro and coworkers [84, 15] which is available on the Mathworks file exchange. This simple to use package provides a variety of tools to extract tensor decompositions and evaluate the factor models generated. In the specific example considered here, we generate data from a spatio-temporal function (See Fig. 1.30)

$$F(x, y, t) = \exp(-x^2 - 0.5y^2) \cos(2t) + \operatorname{sech}(x) \tanh(x) \exp(-0.2y^2) \sin(t). \quad (1.45)$$

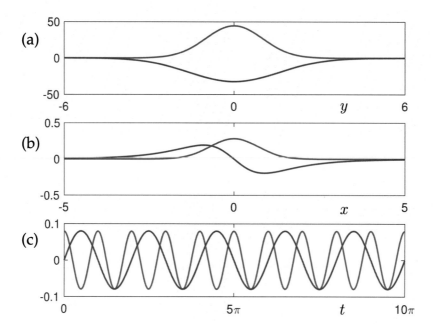

Figure 1.31 3-way tensor decomposition of the function (1.45) discretized so that the data matrix is $\mathbf{A} \in \mathbb{R}^{121 \times 101 \times 315}$. A CP tensor decomposition can be used to extract the two underlying structures that produced the data. The first factor is in blue, the second factor is in red. The three distinct directions of the data (parallel factors) are illustrated in (a) the y direction, (b) the x direction, and (c) the time t.

This model has two spatial modes with two distinct temporal frequencies, thus a two factor model should be sufficient to extract the underlying spatial and temporal modes. To construct this function in MATLAB, the following code is used.

Code 1.25 Creating tensor data.

```
x=-5:0.1:5; y=-6:0.1:6; t=0:0.1:10*pi;
[X,Y,T]=meshgrid(x,y,t);
A=exp(-(X.^2+0.5*Y.^2)).*(cos(2*T))+ ...
    (sech(X).*tanh(X).*exp(-0.2*Y.^2)).*sin(T);
```

Note that the **meshgrid** command is capable of generating N-way arrays. Indeed, MATLAB has no difficulties specifying higher-dimensional arrays and tensors. Specifically, one can easily generate N-way data matrices with arbitrary dimensions. The command $\mathbf{A} = \mathbf{randn}(10, 10, 10, 10, 10)$ generates a 5-way hypercube with random values in each of the five directions of the array.

Figure 1.30 shows eight snapshots of the function (1.45) discretized with the code above. The N-way array data generated from the MATLAB code produces $\mathbf{A} \in \mathbb{R}^{121 \times 101 \times 315}$, which is of total dimension 10^6. The CP tensor decomposition can be used to extract a two factor model for this 3-way array, thus producing two vectors in each direction of space x, space y, and time t.

The N-way toolbox provides a simple architecture for performing tensor decompositions. The PARAFAC command structure can easily take the input function (1.45) which is discretized in the code above and provide a two-factor model. The following code produces the output as **model**.

Code 1.26 Two factor tensor model.

```
model=parafac(A,2);
[A1,A2,A3]=fac2let(model);
subplot(3,1,1), plot(y,A1,'Linewidth',[2])
subplot(3,1,2), plot(x,A2,'Linewidth',[2])
subplot(3,1,3), plot(t,A3,'Linewidth',[2])
```

Note that in this code, the **fac2let** command turns the factors in the model into their component matrices. Further note that the **meshgrid** arrangement of the data is different from **parafac** since the x and y directions are switched.

Figure 1.31 shows the results of the N-way tensor decomposition for the prescribed two factor model. Specifically, the two vectors along each of the three directions of the array are illustrated. For this example, the exact answer is known since the data was constructed from the rank-2 model (1.45). The first set of two modes (along the original y direction) are Gaussian as prescribed. The second set of two modes (along the original x direction) include a Gaussian for the first function, and the anti-symmetric $\mathrm{sech}(x)\tanh(x)$ for the second function. The third set of two modes correspond to the time dynamics of the two functions: $\cos(2t)$ and $\sin(t)$, respectively. Thus, the two factor model produced by the CP tensor decomposition returns the expected, low-rank functions that produced the high-dimensional data matrix $\mathbf{A}$.

Recent theoretical and computational advances in N-way decompositions are opening up the potential for tensor decompositions in many fields. For N large, such decompositions can be computationally intractable due to the size of the data. Indeed, even in the simple example illustrated in Figs. 1.30 and 1.31, there are 10^6 data points. Ultimately, the CP tensor decomposition does not scale well with additional data dimensions. However, randomized techniques are helping yield tractable computations even for large data sets [158, 175]. As with the SVD, randomized methods exploit the underlying low-rank structure of the data in order to produce an accurate approximation through the sum of rank-one outer products. Additionally, tensor decompositions can be combined with constraints on the form of the parallel factors in order to produce more easily interpretable results [348]. This gives a framework for producing interpretable and scalable computations of N-way data arrays.

Suggested Reading
Texts
(1) **Matrix computations**, by G. H. Golub and C. F. Van Loan, 2012 [214].

Papers and reviews
(1) **Calculating the singular values and pseudo-inverse of a matrix**, by G. H. Golub and W. Kahan, *Journal of the Society for Industrial & Applied Mathematics, Series B: Numerical Analysis*, 1965 [212].

(2) **A low-dimensional procedure for the characterization of human faces**, by L. Sirovich and M. Kirby, *Journal of the Optical Society of America A*, 1987 [491].

(3)   **Finding structure with randomness: Probabilistic algorithms for constructing approximate matrix decompositions**, by N. Halko, P.-G. Martinsson, and J. A. Tropp, *SIAM Review*, 2011 [230].

(4)   **A randomized algorithm for the decomposition of matrices**, by P.-G. Martinsson, V. Rokhlin, and M. Tygert, *Applied and Computational Harmonic Analysis*, 2011 [371].

(5)   **The optimal hard threshold for singular values is** $4/\sqrt{3}$, by M. Gavish and D. L. Donoho, *IEEE Transactions on Information Theory*, 2014 [200].

2 Fourier and Wavelet Transforms

A central concern of mathematical physics and engineering mathematics involves the transformation of equations into a coordinate system where expressions simplify, decouple, and are amenable to computation and analysis. This is a common theme throughout this book, in a wide variety of domains, including data analysis (e.g., the SVD), dynamical systems (e.g., spectral decomposition into eigenvalues and eigenvectors), and control (e.g., defining coordinate systems by controllability and observability). Perhaps the most foundational and ubiquitous coordinate transformation was introduced by J.-B. Joseph Fourier in the early 1800s to investigate the theory of heat [185]. Fourier introduced the concept that sine and cosine functions of increasing frequency provide an orthogonal *basis* for the space of solution functions. Indeed, the Fourier transform basis of sines and cosines serve as eigenfunctions of the heat equation, with the specific frequencies serving as the eigenvalues, determined by the geometry, and amplitudes determined by the boundary conditions.

Fourier's seminal work provided the mathematical foundation for Hilbert spaces, operator theory, approximation theory, and the subsequent revolution in analytical and computational mathematics. Fast forward two hundred years, and the fast Fourier transform has become the cornerstone of computational mathematics, enabling real-time image and audio compression, global communication networks, modern devices and hardware, numerical physics and engineering at scale, and advanced data analysis. Simply put, the fast Fourier transform has had a more significant and profound role in shaping the modern world than any other algorithm to date.

With increasingly complex problems, data sets, and computational geometries, simple Fourier sine and cosine bases have given way to *tailored* bases, such as the data-driven SVD. In fact, the SVD basis can be used as a direct analogue of the Fourier basis for solving PDEs with complex geometries, as will be discussed later. In addition, related functions, called wavelets, have been developed for advanced signal processing and compression efforts. In this chapter, we will demonstrate a few of the many uses of Fourier and wavelet transforms.

2.1 Fourier Series and Fourier Transforms

Before describing the computational implementation of Fourier transforms on vectors of data, here we introduce the analytic Fourier series and Fourier transform, defined for continuous functions. Naturally, the discrete and continuous formulations should match in the limit of data with infinitely fine resolution. The Fourier series and transform are intimately related to the geometry of infinite-dimensional function spaces, or *Hilbert* spaces, which generalize the notion of vector spaces to include functions with infinitely many degrees of freedom. Thus, we begin with an introduction to function spaces.

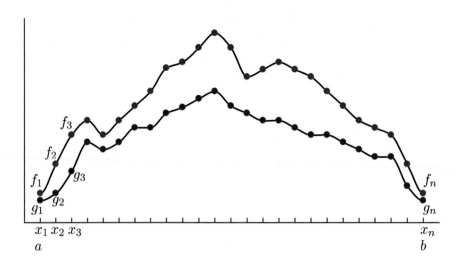

Figure 2.1 Discretized functions used to illustrate the inner product.

Inner Products of Functions and Vectors

In this section, we will make use of inner products and norms of functions. In particular, we will use the common Hermitian inner product for functions $f(x)$ and $g(x)$ defined for x on a domain $x \in [a, b]$:

$$\langle f(x), g(x) \rangle = \int_a^b f(x) \bar{g}(x) \, dx \tag{2.1}$$

where $\bar{g}$ denotes the complex conjugate.

The inner product of functions may seem strange or unmotivated at first, but this definition becomes clear when we consider the inner product of vectors of data. In particular, if we discretize the functions $f(x)$ and $g(x)$ into vectors of data, as in Fig. 2.1, we would like the vector inner product to converge to the function inner product as the sampling resolution is increased. The inner product of the data vectors $\mathbf{f} = \begin{bmatrix} f_1 & f_2 & \cdots & f_n \end{bmatrix}^T$ and $\mathbf{g} = \begin{bmatrix} g_1 & g_2 & \cdots & g_n \end{bmatrix}^T$ is defined by:

$$\langle \mathbf{f}, \mathbf{g} \rangle = \mathbf{g}^* \mathbf{f} = \sum_{k=1}^n f_k \bar{g}_k = \sum_{k=1}^n f(x_k) \bar{g}(x_k). \tag{2.2}$$

The magnitude of this inner product will grow as more data points are added; i.e., as n increases. Thus, we may normalize by $\Delta x = (b - a)/(n - 1)$:

$$\frac{b-a}{n-1} \langle \mathbf{f}, \mathbf{g} \rangle = \sum_{k=1}^n f(x_k) \bar{g}(x_k) \Delta x, \tag{2.3}$$

which is the Riemann approximation to the continuous function inner product. It is now clear that as we take the limit of $n \to \infty$ (i.e., infinite data resolution, with $\Delta x \to 0$), the vector inner product converges to the inner product of functions in (2.1).

This inner product also induces a norm on functions, given by

$$\|f\|_2 = (\langle f, f \rangle)^{1/2} = \sqrt{\langle f, f \rangle} = \left(\int_a^b f(x) \bar{f}(x) \, dx \right)^{1/2}. \tag{2.4}$$

The set of all functions with bounded norm define the set of square integrable functions, denoted by $L^2([a, b])$; this is also known as the set of Lebesgue integrable functions. The interval $[a, b]$ may also be chosen to be infinite (e.g., $(-\infty, \infty)$), semi-infinite (e.g., $[a, \infty)$), or periodic (e.g., $[-\pi, \pi)$). A fun example of a function in $L^2([1, \infty))$ is $f(x) = 1/x$. The square of f has finite integral from 1 to ∞, although the integral of the function itself diverges. The shape obtained by rotating this function about the x-axis is known as Gabriel's horn, as the volume is finite (related to the integral of f^2), while the surface area is infinite (related to the integral of f).

As in finite-dimensional vector spaces, the inner product may be used to *project* a function into an new coordinate system defined by a basis of orthogonal functions. A Fourier series representation of a function f is precisely a projection of this function onto the orthogonal set of sine and cosine functions with integer period on the domain $[a, b]$. This is the subject of the following sections.

Fourier Series

A fundamental result in Fourier analysis is that if $f(x)$ is periodic and piecewise smooth, then it can be written in terms of a Fourier series, which is an infinite sum of cosines and sines of increasing frequency. In particular, if $f(x)$ is 2π-periodic, it may be written as:

$$f(x) = \frac{a_0}{2} + \sum_{k=1}^{\infty} (a_k \cos(kx) + b_k \sin(kx)). \tag{2.5}$$

The coefficients a_k and b_k are given by

$$a_k = \frac{1}{\pi} \int_{-\pi}^{\pi} f(x) \cos(kx) dx \tag{2.6a}$$

$$b_k = \frac{1}{\pi} \int_{-\pi}^{\pi} f(x) \sin(kx) dx, \tag{2.6b}$$

which may be viewed as the coordinates obtained by projecting the function onto the orthogonal cosine and sine basis $\{\cos(kx), \sin(kx)\}_{k=0}^{\infty}$. In other words, the integrals in (2.6) may be re-written in terms of the inner product as:

$$a_k = \frac{1}{\|\cos(kx)\|^2} \langle f(x), \cos(kx) \rangle \tag{2.7a}$$

$$b_k = \frac{1}{\|\sin(kx)\|^2} \langle f(x), \sin(kx) \rangle, \tag{2.7b}$$

where $\|\cos(kx)\|^2 = \|\sin(kx)\|^2 = \pi$. This factor of $1/\pi$ is easy to verify by numerically integrating $\cos(x)^2$ and $\sin(x)^2$ from $-\pi$ to π.

The Fourier series for an L-periodic function on $[0, L)$ is similarly given by:

$$f(x) = \frac{a_0}{2} + \sum_{k=1}^{\infty} \left(a_k \cos\left(\frac{2\pi kx}{L}\right) + b_k \sin\left(\frac{2\pi kx}{L}\right) \right), \tag{2.8}$$

with coefficients a_k and b_k given by

$$a_k = \frac{2}{L} \int_0^L f(x) \cos\left(\frac{2\pi k x}{L}\right) dx \tag{2.9a}$$

$$b_k = \frac{2}{L} \int_0^L f(x) \sin\left(\frac{2\pi k x}{L}\right) dx. \tag{2.9b}$$

Because we are expanding functions in terms of sine and cosine functions, it is also natural to use Euler's formula $e^{ikx} = \cos(kx) + i\sin(kx)$ to write a Fourier series in complex form with complex coefficients $c_k = \alpha_k + i\beta_k$:

$$f(x) = \sum_{k=-\infty}^{\infty} c_k e^{ikx} = \sum_{k=-\infty}^{\infty} (\alpha_k + i\beta_k)(\cos(kx) + i\sin(kx))$$

$$= (\alpha_0 + i\beta_0) + \sum_{k=1}^{\infty} \left[(\alpha_{-k} + \alpha_k)\cos(kx) + (\beta_{-k} - \beta_k)\sin(kx) \right]$$

$$+ i\sum_{k=1}^{\infty} \left[(\beta_{-k} + \beta_k)\cos(kx) - (\alpha_{-k} - \alpha_k)\sin(kx) \right]. \tag{2.10}$$

If $f(x)$ is real-valued, then $\alpha_{-k} = \alpha_k$ and $\beta_{-k} = -\beta_k$, so that $c_{-k} = \bar{c}_k$.

Thus, the functions $\psi_k = e^{ikx}$ for $k \in \mathbb{Z}$ (i.e., for integer k) provide a basis for periodic, complex-valued functions on an interval $[0, 2\pi)$. It is simple to see that these functions are orthogonal:

$$\langle \psi_j, \psi_k \rangle = \int_{-\pi}^{\pi} e^{ijx} e^{-ikx} dx = \int_{-\pi}^{\pi} e^{i(j-k)x} dx = \left[\frac{e^{i(j-k)x}}{i(j-k)} \right]_{-\pi}^{\pi} = \begin{cases} 0 & \text{if } j \neq k \\ 2\pi & \text{if } j = k. \end{cases}$$

So $\langle \psi_j, \psi_k \rangle = 2\pi \delta_{jk}$, where δ is the Kronecker delta function. Similarly, the functions $e^{i2\pi kx/L}$ provide a basis for $L^2([0, L))$, the space of square integrable functions defined on $x \in [0, L)$.

In principle, a Fourier series is just a change of coordinates of a function $f(x)$ into an infinite-dimensional orthogonal function space spanned by sines and cosines (i.e., $\psi_k = e^{ikx} = \cos(kx) + i\sin(kx)$):

$$f(x) = \sum_{k=-\infty}^{\infty} c_k \psi_k(x) = \frac{1}{2\pi} \sum_{k=-\infty}^{\infty} \langle f(x), \psi_k(x) \rangle \psi_k(x). \tag{2.11}$$

The coefficients are given by $c_k = \frac{1}{2\pi} \langle f(x), \psi_k(x) \rangle$. The factor of $1/2\pi$ normalizes the projection by the square of the norm of ψ_k; i.e., $\|\psi_k\|^2 = 2\pi$. This is consistent with our standard finite-dimensional notion of change of basis, as in Fig. 2.2. A vector $\vec{f}$ may be written in the $(\vec{x}, \vec{y})$ or $(\vec{u}, \vec{v})$ coordinate systems, via projection onto these orthogonal bases:

$$\vec{f} = \langle \vec{f}, \vec{x} \rangle \frac{\vec{x}}{\|\vec{x}\|^2} + \langle \vec{f}, \vec{y} \rangle \frac{\vec{y}}{\|\vec{y}\|^2} \tag{2.12a}$$

$$= \langle \vec{f}, \vec{u} \rangle \frac{\vec{u}}{\|\vec{u}\|^2} + \langle \vec{f}, \vec{v} \rangle \frac{\vec{v}}{\|\vec{v}\|^2}. \tag{2.12b}$$

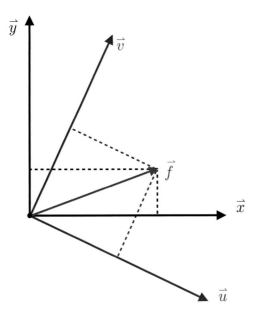

Figure 2.2 Change of coordinates of a vector in two dimensions.

Example: Fourier Series for a Continuous Hat Function

As a simple example, we demonstrate the use of Fourier series to approximate a continuous hat function, defined from $-\pi$ to π:

$$f(x) = \begin{cases} 0 & \text{for } x \in [-\pi, \pi/2) \\ 1 + 2x/\pi & \text{for } x \in [-\pi/2, 0) \\ 1 - 2x/\pi & \text{for } x \in [0, \pi/2) \\ 0 & \text{for } x \in [\pi/2, \pi). \end{cases} \tag{2.13}$$

Because this function is even, it may be approximated with cosines alone. The Fourier series for $f(x)$ is shown in Fig. 2.3 for an increasing number of cosines.

Figure 2.4 shows the coefficients a_k of the even cosine functions, along with the approximation error, for an increasing number of modes. The error decreases monotonically, as expected. The coefficients b_k corresponding to the odd sine functions are not shown, as they are identically zero since the hat function is even.

Code 2.1 Fourier series approximation to a hat function.

```
% Define domain
dx = 0.001;
L = pi;
x = (-1+dx:dx:1)*L;
n = length(x);   nquart = floor(n/4);

% Define hat function
f = 0*x;
f(nquart:2*nquart) = 4*(1:nquart+1)/n;
f(2*nquart+1:3*nquart) = 1-4*(0:nquart-1)/n;
plot(x,f,'-k','LineWidth',1.5), hold on

% Compute Fourier series
```

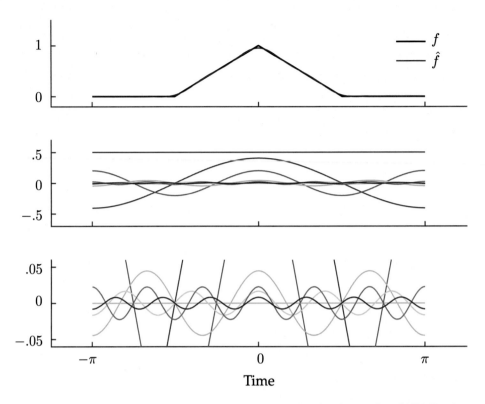

Figure 2.3 (top) Hat function and Fourier cosine series approximation for $n = 7$. (middle) Fourier cosines used to approximate the hat function, and (bottom) zoom in of modes with small amplitude and high frequency.

```
CC = jet(20);
A0 = sum(f.*ones(size(x)))*dx;
fFS = A0/2;
for k=1:20
    A(k) = sum(f.*cos(pi*k*x/L))*dx;  % Inner product
    B(k) = sum(f.*sin(pi*k*x/L))*dx;
    fFS = fFS + A(k)*cos(k*pi*x/L) + B(k)*sin(k*pi*x/L);
    plot(x,fFS,'-','Color',CC(k,:),'LineWidth',1.2)
end
```

Example: Fourier Series for a Discontinuous Hat Function

We now consider the discontinuous square hat function, defined on $[0, L)$, shown in Fig. 2.5. The function is given by:

$$f(x) = \begin{cases} 0 & \text{for } x \in [0, L/4) \\ 1 & \text{for } x \in [L/4, 3L/4) \\ 0 & \text{for } x \in [3L/4, L). \end{cases} \tag{2.14}$$

The truncated Fourier series is plagued by ringing oscillations, known as Gibbs phenomena, around the sharp corners of the step function. This example highlights the challenge of applying the Fourier series to discontinuous functions:

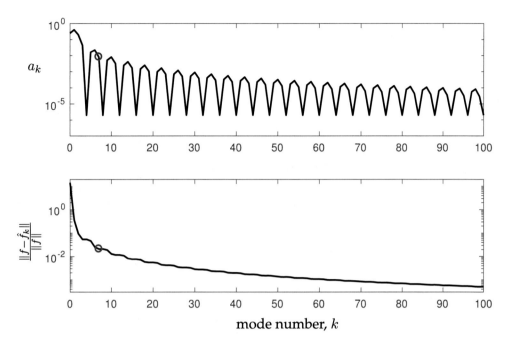

Figure 2.4 Fourier coefficients (top) and relative error of Fourier cosine approximation with true function (bottom) for hat function in Fig. 2.3. The $n = 7$ approximation is highlighted with a blue circle.

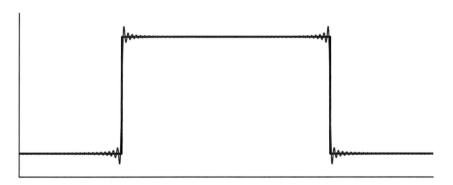

Figure 2.5 Gibbs phenomena is characterized by high-frequency oscillations near discontinuities. The black curve is discontinuous, and the red curve is the Fourier approximation.

```
dx = 0.01;  L = 10;
x = 0:dx:L;
n = length(x); nquart = floor(n/4);

f = zeros(size(x));
f(nquart:3*nquart) = 1;

A0 = sum(f.*ones(size(x)))*dx*2/L;
fFS = A0/2;
for k=1:100
    Ak = sum(f.*cos(2*pi*k*x/L))*dx*2/L;
    Bk = sum(f.*sin(2*pi*k*x/L))*dx*2/L;
```

```
        fFS = fFS + Ak*cos(2*k*pi*x/L) + Bk*sin(2*k*pi*x/L);
 end

 plot(x,f,'k','LineWidth',2), hold on
 plot(x,fFS,'r-','LineWidth',1.2)
```

Fourier Transform

The Fourier series is defined for periodic functions, so that outside the domain of definition, the function repeats itself forever. The Fourier transform integral is essentially the limit of a Fourier series as the length of the domain goes to infinity, which allows us to define a function defined on $(-\infty, \infty)$ without repeating, as shown in Fig. 2.6. We will consider the Fourier series on a domain $x \in [-L, L)$, and then let $L \to \infty$. On this domain, the Fourier series is:

$$f(x) = \frac{a_0}{2} + \sum_{k=1}^{\infty} \left[a_k \cos\left(\frac{k\pi x}{L}\right) + b_k \sin\left(\frac{k\pi x}{L}\right) \right] = \sum_{k=-\infty}^{\infty} c_k e^{ik\pi x/L} \qquad (2.15)$$

with the coefficients given by:

$$c_k = \frac{1}{2L} \langle f(x), \psi_k \rangle = \frac{1}{2L} \int_{-L}^{L} f(x) e^{-ik\pi x/L}\, dx. \qquad (2.16)$$

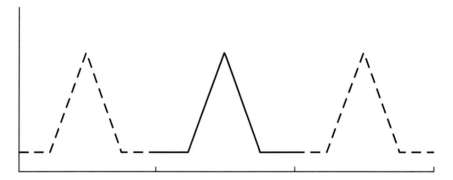

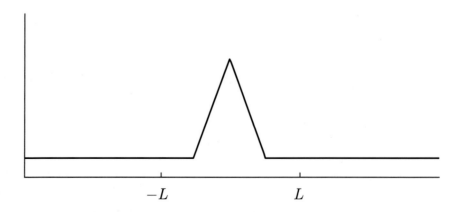

Figure 2.6 (top) Fourier series is only valid for a function that is periodic on the domain $[-L, L)$. (bottom) The Fourier transform is valid for generic nonperiodic functions.

Restating the previous results, $f(x)$ is now represented by a sum of sines and cosines with a discrete set of frequencies given by $\omega_k = k\pi/L$. Taking the limit as $L \to \infty$, these discrete frequencies become a continuous range of frequencies. Define $\omega = k\pi/L$, $\Delta\omega = \pi/L$, and take the limit $L \to \infty$, so that $\Delta\omega \to 0$:

$$f(x) = \lim_{\Delta\omega \to 0} \sum_{k=-\infty}^{\infty} \frac{\Delta\omega}{2\pi} \underbrace{\int_{-\pi/\Delta\omega}^{\pi/\Delta\omega} f(\xi)e^{-ik\Delta\omega\xi}\, d\xi}_{\langle f(x), \psi_k(x)\rangle} e^{ik\Delta\omega x}. \tag{2.17}$$

When we take the limit, the expression $\langle f(x), \psi_k(x)\rangle$ will become the Fourier transform of $f(x)$, denoted by $\hat{f}(\omega) \triangleq \mathcal{F}(f(x))$. In addition, the summation with weight $\Delta\omega$ becomes a Riemann integral, resulting in the following:

$$f(x) = \mathcal{F}^{-1}\left(\hat{f}(\omega)\right) = \frac{1}{2\pi}\int_{-\infty}^{\infty} \hat{f}(\omega)e^{i\omega x}\, d\omega \tag{2.18a}$$

$$\hat{f}(\omega) = \mathcal{F}(f(x)) = \int_{-\infty}^{\infty} f(x)e^{-i\omega x}\, dx. \tag{2.18b}$$

These two integrals are known as the *Fourier transform pair*. Both integrals converge as long as $\int_{-\infty}^{\infty} |f(x)|\, dx < \infty$ and $\int_{-\infty}^{\infty} |\hat{f}(\omega)|\, d\omega < \infty$; i.e., as long as both functions belong to the space of Lebesgue integrable functions, $f, \hat{f} \in L^1(-\infty, \infty)$.

The Fourier transform is particularly useful because of a number of properties, including linearity, and how derivatives of functions behave in the Fourier transform domain. These properties have been used extensively for data analysis and scientific computing (e.g., to solve PDEs accurately and efficiently), as will be explored throughout this chapter.

Derivatives of Functions The Fourier transform of the derivative of a function is given by:

$$\mathcal{F}\left(\frac{d}{dx}f(x)\right) = \int_{-\infty}^{\infty} \overset{dv}{\overbrace{f'(x)}}\, \overset{u}{\overbrace{e^{-i\omega x}}}\, dx \tag{2.19a}$$

$$= \left[\underbrace{f(x)e^{-i\omega x}}_{uv}\right]_{-\infty}^{\infty} - \int_{-\infty}^{\infty} \underbrace{f(x)}_{v}\underbrace{\left[-i\omega e^{-i\omega x}\right]}_{du}\, dx \tag{2.19b}$$

$$= i\omega \int_{-\infty}^{\infty} f(x)e^{-i\omega x}\, dx \tag{2.19c}$$

$$= i\omega \mathcal{F}(f(x)). \tag{2.19d}$$

This is an extremely important property of the Fourier transform, as it will allow us to turn PDEs into ODEs, closely related to the separation of variables:

$$u_{tt} = cu_{xx} \quad \overset{\mathcal{F}}{\Longrightarrow} \quad \hat{u}_{tt} = -c\omega^2\hat{u}. \tag{2.20}$$
$$\text{(PDE)} \qquad\qquad \text{(ODE)}$$

Linearity of Fourier Transforms The Fourier transform is a linear operator, so that:

$$\mathcal{F}(\alpha f(x) + \beta g(x)) = \alpha\mathcal{F}(f) + \beta\mathcal{F}(g). \tag{2.21}$$

$$\mathcal{F}^{-1}(\alpha \hat{f}(\omega) + \beta \hat{g}(\omega)) = \alpha \mathcal{F}^{-1}(\hat{f}) + \beta \mathcal{F}^{-1}(\hat{g}). \tag{2.22}$$

Parseval's Theorem

$$\int_{-\infty}^{\infty} |\hat{f}(\omega)|^2 \, d\omega = 2\pi \int_{-\infty}^{\infty} |f(x)|^2 \, dx. \tag{2.23}$$

In other words, the Fourier transform preserves the L_2 norm, up to a constant. This is closely related to unitarity, so that two functions will retain the same inner product before and after the Fourier transform. This property is useful for approximation and truncation, providing the ability to bound error at a given truncation.

Convolution The convolution of two functions is particularly well-behaved in the Fourier domain, being the product of the two Fourier transformed functions. Define the convolution of two functions $f(x)$ and $g(x)$ as $f * g$:

$$(f * g)(x) = \int_{-\infty}^{\infty} f(x - \xi)g(\xi) \, d\xi. \tag{2.24}$$

If we let $\hat{f} = \mathcal{F}(f)$ and $\hat{g} = \mathcal{F}(g)$, then:

$$\mathcal{F}^{-1}\left(\hat{f}\hat{g}\right)(x) = \frac{1}{2\pi} \int_{-\infty}^{\infty} \hat{f}(\omega)\hat{g}(\omega)e^{i\omega x} \, d\omega \tag{2.25a}$$

$$= \int_{-\infty}^{\infty} \hat{f}(\omega)e^{i\omega x} \left(\frac{1}{2\pi} \int_{-\infty}^{\infty} g(y)e^{-i\omega y} \, dy\right) d\omega \tag{2.25b}$$

$$= \frac{1}{2\pi} \int_{-\infty}^{\infty} \int_{-\infty}^{\infty} g(y)\hat{f}(\omega)e^{i\omega(x-y)} \, d\omega \, dy \tag{2.25c}$$

$$= \int_{-\infty}^{\infty} g(y)\underbrace{\left(\frac{1}{2\pi} \int_{-\infty}^{\infty} \hat{f}(\omega)e^{i\omega(x-y)} \, d\omega\right)}_{f(x-y)} dy \tag{2.25d}$$

$$= \int_{-\infty}^{\infty} g(y)f(x - y) \, dy = g * f = f * g. \tag{2.25e}$$

Thus, multiplying functions in the frequency domain is the same as convolving functions in the spatial domain. This will be particularly useful for control systems and transfer functions with the related Laplace transform.

2.2   Discrete Fourier Transform (DFT) and Fast Fourier Transform (FFT)

Until now, we have considered the Fourier series and Fourier transform for continuous functions $f(x)$. However, when computing or working with real-data, it is necessary to approximate the Fourier transform on discrete vectors of data. The resulting discrete Fourier transform (DFT) is essentially a discretized version of the Fourier series for vectors of data $\mathbf{f} = \begin{bmatrix} f_1 & f_2 & f_3 & \cdots & f_n \end{bmatrix}^T$ obtained by discretizing the function $f(x)$ at a regular spacing, Δx, as shown in Fig. 2.7.

The DFT is tremendously useful for numerical approximation and computation, but it does not scale well to very large $n \gg 1$, as the simple formulation involves multiplication by a dense $n \times n$ matrix, requiring $\mathcal{O}(n^2)$ operations. In 1965, James W. Cooley (IBM) and John W. Tukey (Princeton) developed the revolutionary *fast* Fourier transform (FFT)

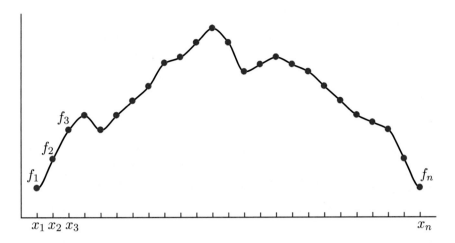

Figure 2.7 Discrete data sampled for the discrete Fourier transform.

algorithm [137, 136] that scales as $\mathcal{O}(n \log(n))$. As n becomes very large, the $\log(n)$ component grows slowly, and the algorithm approaches a linear scaling. Their algorithm was based on a fractal symmetry in the Fourier transform that allows an n dimensional DFT to be solved with a number of smaller dimensional DFT computations. Although the different computational scaling between the DFT and FFT implementations may seem like a small difference, the fast $\mathcal{O}(n \log(n))$ scaling is what enables the ubiquitous use of the FFT in real-time communication, based on audio and image compression [539].

It is important to note that Cooley and Tukey did not invent the idea of the FFT, as there were decades of prior work developing special cases, although they provided the general formulation that is currently used. Amazingly, the FFT algorithm was formulated by Gauss over 150 years earlier in 1805 to approximate the orbits of the asteroids Pallas and Juno from measurement data, as he required a highly accurate interpolation scheme [239]. As the computations were performed by Gauss in his head and on paper, he required a fast algorithm, and developed the FFT. However, Gauss did not view this as a major breakthrough and his formulation only appeared later in 1866 in his compiled notes [198]. It is interesting to note that Gauss's discovery even predates Fourier's announcement of the Fourier series expansion in 1807, which was later published in 1822 [186].

Discrete Fourier Transform

Although we will always use the FFT for computations, it is illustrative to begin with the simplest formulation of the DFT. The discrete Fourier transform is given by:

$$\hat{f}_k = \sum_{j=0}^{n-1} f_j e^{-i2\pi jk/n}, \tag{2.26}$$

and the inverse discrete Fourier transform (iDFT) is given by:

$$f_k = \frac{1}{n} \sum_{j=0}^{n-1} \hat{f}_j e^{i2\pi jk/n}. \tag{2.27}$$

Figure 2.8 Real part of DFT matrix for $n = 256$.

Thus, the DFT is a linear operator (i.e., a *matrix*) that maps the data points in $\mathbf{f}$ to the frequency domain $\hat{\mathbf{f}}$:

$$\{f_1, f_2, \cdots, f_n\} \quad \xrightarrow{\text{DFT}} \quad \{\hat{f}_1, \hat{f}_2, \cdots \hat{f}_n\}. \tag{2.28}$$

For a given number of points n, the DFT represents the data using sine and cosine functions with integer multiples of a fundamental frequency, $\omega_n = e^{-2\pi i/n}$. The DFT may be computed by matrix multiplication:

$$\begin{bmatrix} \hat{f}_1 \\ \hat{f}_2 \\ \hat{f}_3 \\ \vdots \\ \hat{f}_n \end{bmatrix} = \begin{bmatrix} 1 & 1 & 1 & \cdots & 1 \\ 1 & \omega_n & \omega_n^2 & \cdots & \omega_n^{n-1} \\ 1 & \omega_n^2 & \omega_n^4 & \cdots & \omega_n^{2(n-1)} \\ \vdots & \vdots & \vdots & \ddots & \vdots \\ 1 & \omega_n^{n-1} & \omega_n^{2(n-1)} & \cdots & \omega_n^{(n-1)^2} \end{bmatrix} \begin{bmatrix} f_1 \\ f_2 \\ f_3 \\ \vdots \\ f_n \end{bmatrix}. \tag{2.29}$$

The output vector $\hat{\mathbf{f}}$ contains the Fourier coefficients for the input vector $\mathbf{f}$, and the DFT matrix $\mathbf{F}$ is a unitary Vandermonde matrix. The matrix $\mathbf{F}$ is complex-valued, so the output $\hat{\mathbf{f}}$ has both a magnitude and a phase, which will both have useful physical interpretations.

The real part of the DFT matrix $\mathbf{F}$ is shown in Fig. 2.8 for $n = 256$. Code 2.2 generates and plots this matrix. It can be seen from this image that there is a hierarchical and highly symmetric multiscale structure to $\mathbf{F}$. Each row and column is a cosine function with increasing frequency.

Code 2.2 Generate discrete Fourier transform matrix.

```
clear all, close all, clc
n = 256;
w = exp(-i*2*pi/n);

% Slow
for i=1:n
    for j=1:n
        DFT(i,j) = w^((i-1)*(j-1));
    end
end

% Fast
[I,J] = meshgrid(1:n,1:n);
DFT = w.^((I-1).*(J-1));
imagesc(real(DFT))
```

Fast Fourier Transform

As mentioned earlier, multiplying by the DFT matrix $\mathbf{F}$ involves $\mathcal{O}(n^2)$ operations. The fast Fourier transform scales as $\mathcal{O}(n\log(n))$, enabling a tremendous range of applications, including audio and image compression in MP3 and JPG formats, streaming video, satellite communications, and the cellular network, to name only a few of the myriad applications. For example, audio is generally sampled at 44.1 kHz, or 44, 100 samples per second. For 10 seconds of audio, the vector $\mathbf{f}$ will have dimension $n = 4.41 \times 10^5$. Computing the DFT using matrix multiplication involves approximately 2×10^{11}, or 200 billion, multiplications. In contrast, the FFT requires approximately 6×10^6, which amounts to a speed-up factor of over 30, 000. Thus, the FFT has become synonymous with the DFT, and FFT libraries are built in to nearly every device and operating system that performs digital signal processing.

To see the tremendous benefit of the FFT, consider the transmission, storage, and decoding of an audio signal. We will see later that many signals are highly compressible in the Fourier transform domain, meaning that most of the coefficients of $\hat{\mathbf{f}}$ are small and can be discarded. This enables much more efficient storage and transmission of the compressed signal, as only the non-zero Fourier coefficients must be transmitted. However, it is then necessary to rapidly encode and decode the compressed Fourier signal by computing the FFT and inverse FFT (iFFT). This is accomplished with the one-line commands:

```
>>fhat = fft(f);    % Fast Fourier transform
>>f = ifft(fhat);   % Inverse fast Fourier transform
```

The basic idea behind the FFT is that the DFT may be implemented much more efficiently if the number of data points n is a power of 2. For example, consider $n = 1024 = 2^{10}$. In this case, the DFT matrix $\mathbf{F}_{1024}$ may be written as:

$$\hat{\mathbf{f}} = \mathbf{F}_{1024}\mathbf{f} = \begin{bmatrix} \mathbf{I}_{512} & -\mathbf{D}_{512} \\ \mathbf{I}_{512} & -\mathbf{D}_{512} \end{bmatrix} \begin{bmatrix} \mathbf{F}_{512} & \mathbf{0} \\ \mathbf{0} & \mathbf{F}_{512} \end{bmatrix} \begin{bmatrix} \mathbf{f}_{\text{even}} \\ \mathbf{f}_{\text{odd}} \end{bmatrix}, \qquad (2.30)$$

where $\mathbf{f}_{even}$ are the even index elements of $\mathbf{f}$, $\mathbf{f}_{odd}$ are the odd index elements of $\mathbf{f}$, $\mathbf{I}_{512}$ is the 512×512 identity matrix, and $\mathbf{D}_{512}$ is given by

$$\mathbf{D}_{512} = \begin{bmatrix} 1 & 0 & 0 & \cdots & 0 \\ 0 & \omega & 0 & \cdots & 0 \\ 0 & 0 & \omega^2 & \cdots & 0 \\ \vdots & \vdots & \vdots & \ddots & \vdots \\ 0 & 0 & 0 & \cdots & \omega^{511} \end{bmatrix}. \tag{2.31}$$

This expression can be derived from a careful accounting and reorganization of the terms in (2.26) and (2.29). If $n = 2^p$, this process can be repeated, and $\mathbf{F}_{512}$ can be represented by $\mathbf{F}_{256}$, which can then be represented by $\mathbf{F}_{128} \to \mathbf{F}_{64} \to \mathbf{F}_{32} \to \cdots$. If $n \neq 2^p$, the vector can be padded with zeros until it is a power of 2. The FFT then involves an efficient interleaving of even and odd indices of sub-vectors of $\mathbf{f}$, and the computation of several smaller 2×2 DFT computations.

FFT Example: Noise Filtering

To gain familiarity with how to use and interpret the FFT, we will begin with a simple example that uses the FFT to denoise a signal. We will consider a function of time $f(t)$:

$$f(t) = \sin(2\pi f_1 t) + \sin(2\pi f_2 t) \tag{2.32}$$

with frequencies $f_1 = 50$ and $f_2 = 120$. We then add a large amount of Gaussian white noise to this signal, as shown in the top panel of Fig. 2.9.

It is possible to compute the fast Fourier transform of this noisy signal using the **fft** command. The power spectral density (PSD) is the normalized squared magnitude of $\hat{\mathbf{f}}$, and indicates how much *power* the signal contains in each frequency. In Fig. 2.9 (middle), it is clear that the noisy signal contains two large peaks at 50 Hz and 120 Hz. It is possible to zero out components that have power below a threshold to remove noise from the signal. After inverse transforming the filtered signal, we find the clean and filtered time-series match quite well (Fig. 2.9, bottom). Code 2.3 performs each step and plots the results.

Code 2.3 Fast Fourier transform to denoise signal.

```
dt = .001;
t = 0:dt:1;
f = sin(2*pi*50*t) + sin(2*pi*120*t);  % Sum of 2 frequencies
f = f + 2.5*randn(size(t));  % Add some noise

%% Compute the Fast Fourier Transform FFT
n = length(t);
fhat = fft(f,n);            % Compute the fast Fourier transform
PSD = fhat.*conj(fhat)/n;  % Power spectrum (power per freq)
freq = 1/(dt*n)*(0:n);     % Create x-axis of frequencies in Hz
L = 1:floor(n/2);          % Only plot the first half of freqs

%% Use the PSD to filter out noise
indices = PSD>100;          % Find all freqs with large power
PSDclean = PSD.*indices;    % Zero out all others
fhat = indices.*fhat;       % Zero out small Fourier coeffs. in Y
ffilt = ifft(fhat);         % Inverse FFT for filtered time signal
```

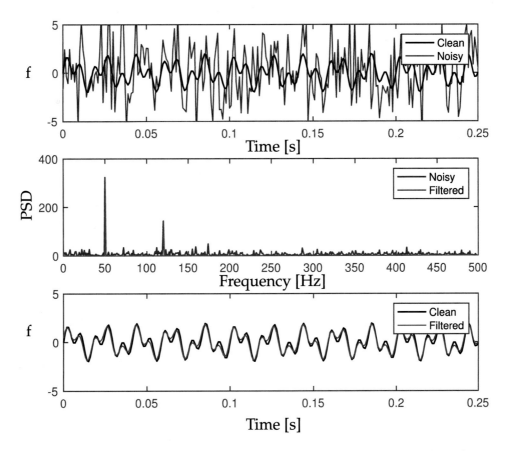

Figure 2.9 De-noising with FFT. (top) Noise is added to a simple signal given by a sum of two sine waves. (middle) In the Fourier domain, dominant peaks may be selected and the noise filtered. (bottom) The de-noised signal is obtained by inverse Fourier transforming the two dominant peaks.

```
%% PLOTS
subplot(3,1,1)
plot(t,f,'r','LineWidth',1.2), hold on
plot(t,f,'k','LineWidth',1.5)
legend('Noisy','Clean')

subplot(3,1,2)
plot(t,f,'k','LineWidth',1.5), hold on
plot(t,ffilt,'b','LineWidth',1.2)
legend('Clean','Filtered')

subplot(3,1,3)
plot(freq(L),PSD(L),'r','LineWidth',1.5), hold on
plot(freq(L),PSDclean(L),'-b','LineWidth',1.2)
legend('Noisy','Filtered')
```

FFT Example: Spectral Derivatives

For the next example, we will demonstrate the use of the FFT for the fast and accurate computation of derivatives. As we saw in (2.19), the continuous Fourier transform has

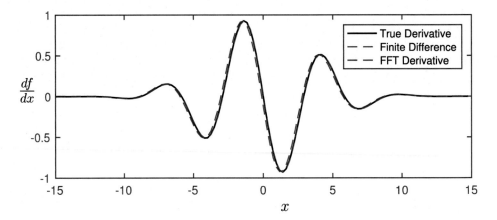

Figure 2.10 Comparison of the spectral derivative, computed using the FFT, with the finite-difference derivative.

the property that $\mathcal{F}(df/dx) = i\omega\mathcal{F}(f)$. Similarly, the numerical derivative of a vector of discretized data can be well approximated by multiplying each component of the discrete Fourier transform of the vector $\hat{\mathbf{f}}$ by $i\kappa$, where $\kappa = 2\pi k/n$ is the discrete wavenumber associated with that component. The accuracy and efficiency of the spectral derivative makes it particularly useful for solving partial differential equations, as explored in the next section.

To demonstrate this so-called *spectral* derivative, we will start with a function $f(x)$ where we can compute the analytic derivative for comparison:

$$f(x) = \cos(x)e^{-x^2/25} \implies \frac{df}{dx}(x) = -\sin(x)e^{-x^2/25} - \frac{2}{25}xf(x). \tag{2.33}$$

Fig. 2.10 compares the spectral derivative with the analytic derivative and the forward Euler finite-difference derivative using $n = 128$ discretization points:

$$\frac{df}{dx}(x_k) \approx \frac{f(x_{k+1}) - f(x_k)}{\Delta x}. \tag{2.34}$$

The error of both differentiation schemes may be reduced by increasing n, which is the same as decreasing Δx. However, the error of the spectral derivative improves more rapidly with increasing n than finite-difference schemes, as shown in Fig. 2.11. The forward Euler differentiation is notoriously inaccurate, with error proportional to $\mathcal{O}(\Delta x)$; however, even increasing the order of a finite-difference scheme will not yield the same accuracy trend as the spectral derivative, which is effectively using information on the whole domain. Code 2.4 computes and compares the two differentiation schemes.

Code 2.4 Fast Fourier transform to compute derivatives.

```
n = 128;
L = 30;
dx = L/(n);
x = -L/2:dx:L/2-dx;
f = cos(x).*exp(-x.^2/25);             % Function
df = -(sin(x).*exp(-x.^2/25) + (2/25)*x.*f);  % Derivative

%% Approximate derivative using finite Difference...
```

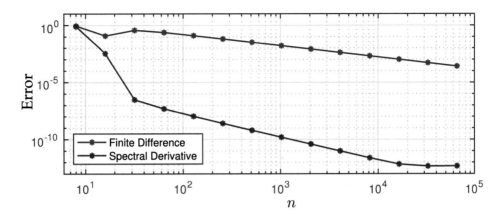

Figure 2.11 Benchmark of spectral derivative for varying data resolution.

```
for kappa=1:length(df)-1
    dfFD(kappa) = (f(kappa+1)-f(kappa))/dx;
end
dfFD(end+1) = dfFD(end);

%% Derivative using FFT (spectral derivative)
fhat = fft(f);
kappa = (2*pi/L)*[-n/2:n/2-1];
kappa = fftshift(kappa);   % Re-order fft frequencies
dfhat = i*kappa.*fhat;
dfFFT = real(ifft(dfhat));

%% Plotting commands
plot(x,df,'k','LineWidth',1.5), hold on
plot(x,dfFD,'b--','LineWidth',1.2)
plot(x,dfFFT,'r--','LineWidth',1.2)
legend('True Derivative','Finite Diff.','FFT Derivative')
```

If the derivative of a function is discontinuous, then the spectral derivative will exhibit Gibbs phenomena, as shown in Fig. 2.12.

2.3 Transforming Partial Differential Equations

The Fourier transform was originally formulated in the 1800s as a change of coordinates for the heat equation into an eigenfunction coordinate system where the dynamics decouple. More generally, the Fourier transform is useful for transforming partial differential equations (PDEs) into ordinary differential equations (ODEs), as in (2.20). Here, we will demonstrate the utility of the FFT to numerically solve a number of PDEs. For an excellent treatment of spectral methods for PDEs, see Trefethen [523]; extensions also exist for stiff PDEs [282].

Heat Equation

The Fourier transform basis is ideally suited to solve the heat equation. In one spatial dimension, the heat equation is given by

$$u_t = \alpha^2 u_{xx} \qquad (2.35)$$

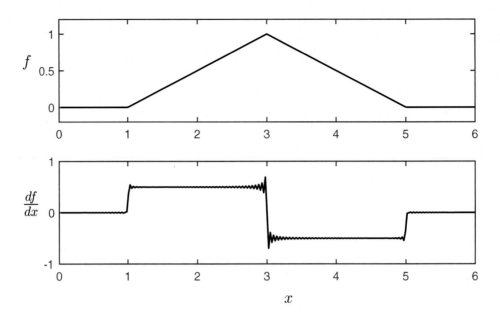

Figure 2.12 Gibbs phenomena for spectral derivative of function with discontinuous derivative.

where $u(t, x)$ is the temperature distribution in time and space. If we Fourier transform in space, then $\mathcal{F}(u(t, x)) = \hat{u}(t, \omega)$. The PDE in (2.35) becomes:

$$\hat{u}_t = -\alpha^2 \omega^2 \hat{u} \tag{2.36}$$

since the two spatial derivatives contribute $(i\omega)^2 = -\omega^2$ in the Fourier transform domain. Thus, by taking the Fourier transform, the PDE in (2.35) becomes an ODE for each fixed frequency ω. The solution is given by:

$$\hat{u}(t, \omega) = e^{-\alpha^2 \omega^2 t} \hat{u}(0, \omega). \tag{2.37}$$

The function $\hat{u}(0, \omega)$ is the Fourier transform of the initial temperature distribution $u(0, x)$. It is now clear that higher frequencies, corresponding to larger values of ω, decay more rapidly as time evolves, so that sharp corners in the temperature distribution rapidly smooth out. We may take the inverse Fourier transform using the convolution property in (2.24), yielding:

$$u(t, x) = \mathcal{F}^{-1}(\hat{u}(t, \omega)) = \mathcal{F}^{-1}\left(e^{-\alpha^2 \omega^2 t}\right) * u(0, x) = \frac{1}{2\alpha\sqrt{\pi t}} e^{-\frac{x^2}{4\alpha^2 t}} * u(0, x). \tag{2.38}$$

To simulate this PDE numerically, it is simpler and more accurate to first transform to the frequency domain using the FFT. In this case (2.36) becomes

$$\hat{u}_t = -\alpha^2 \kappa^2 \hat{u} \tag{2.39}$$

where κ is the discretized frequency. It is important to use the **fftshift** command to re-order the wavenumbers according to the Matlab convention.

Code 2.5 simulates the 1D heat equation using the FFT, as shown in Figs. 2.13 and 2.14. In this example, because the PDE is linear, it is possible to advance the system using **ode45**

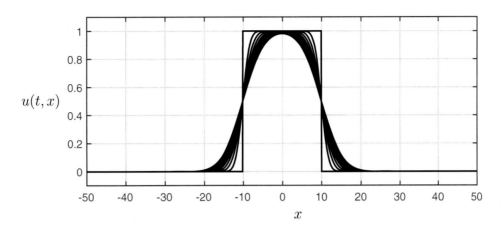

Figure 2.13 Solution of the 1D heat equation in time for an initial condition given by a square hat function. As time evolves, the sharp corners rapidly smooth and the solution approaches a Gaussian function.

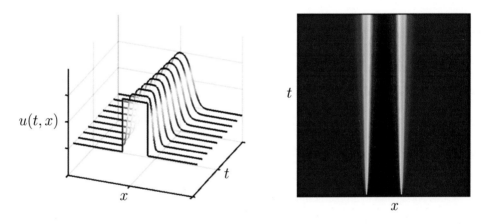

Figure 2.14 Evolution of the 1D heat equation in time, illustrated by a waterfall plot (left) and an x-t diagram (right).

directly in the frequency domain, using the vector field given in Code 2.6. Finally, the plotting commands are given in Code 2.7.

Figs. 2.13 and 2.14 show several different views of the temperature distribution $u(t, x)$ as it evolves in time. Fig. 2.13 shows the distribution at several times overlayed, and this same data is visualized in Fig. 2.14 in a waterfall plot (left) and in an x-t diagram (right). In all of the figures, it becomes clear that the sharp corners diffuse rapidly, as these correspond to the highest wavenumbers. Eventually, the lowest wavenumber variations will also decay, until the temperature reaches a constant steady state distribution, which is a solution of Laplace's equation $u_{xx} = 0$. When solving this PDE using the FFT, we are implicitly assuming that the solution domain is periodic, so that the right and left boundaries are identified and the domain forms a ring. However, if the domain is large enough, then the effect of the boundaries is small.

Code 2.5 Code to simulate the 1D heat equation using the Fourier transform.

```
a = 1;          % Thermal diffusivity constant
L = 100;        % Length of domain
N = 1000;       % Number of discretization points
dx = L/N;
x = -L/2:dx:L/2-dx; % Define x domain

% Define discrete wavenumbers
kappa = (2*pi/L)*[-N/2:N/2-1];
kappa = fftshift(kappa);     % Re-order fft wavenumbers

% Initial condition
u0 = 0*x;
u0((L/2 - L/10)/dx:(L/2 + L/10)/dx) = 1;

% Simulate in Fourier frequency domain
t = 0:0.1:10;
[t,uhat]=ode45(@(t,uhat)rhsHeat(t,uhat,kappa,a),t,fft(u0));

for k = 1:length(t) % iFFT to return to spatial domain
    u(k,:) = ifft(uhat(k,:));
end
```

Code 2.6 Right-hand side for 1D heat equation in Fourier domain, $d\hat{u}/dt$.

```
function duhatdt = rhsHeat(t,uhat,kappa,a)
duhatdt = -a^2*(kappa.^2)'.*uhat;   % Linear and diagonal
```

Code 2.7 Code to plot the solution of the 1D heat equation.

```
figure, waterfall((u(1:10:end,:)));
figure, imagesc(flipud(u));
```

One-Way Wave Equation

As second example is the simple linear PDE for the one-way equation:

$$u_t + cu_x = 0. \tag{2.40}$$

Any initial condition $u(0, x)$ will simply propagate to the right in time with speed c, as $u(t, x) = u(0, x - ct)$ is a solution. Code 2.8 simulates this PDE for an initial condition given by a Gaussian pulse. It is possible to integrate this equation in the Fourier transform domain, as before, using the vector field given by Code 2.9. However, it is also possible to integrate this equation in the spatial domain, simply using the FFT to compute derivatives and then transform back, as in Code 2.10. The solution $u(t, x)$ is plotted in Figs. 2.15 and 2.16, as before.

Code 2.8 Code to simulate the 1D wave equation using the Fourier transform.

```
c = 2;              % Wave speed
L = 20;             % Length of domain
N = 1000;           % Number of discretization points
dx = L/N;
x = -L/2:dx:L/2-dx; % Define x domain

% Define discrete wavenumbers
kappa = (2*pi/L)*[-N/2:N/2-1];
```

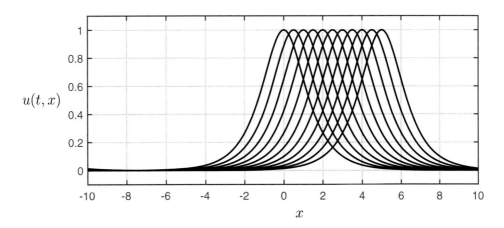

Figure 2.15 Solution of the 1D wave equation in time. As time evolves, the Gaussian initial condition moves from left to right at a constant wave speed.

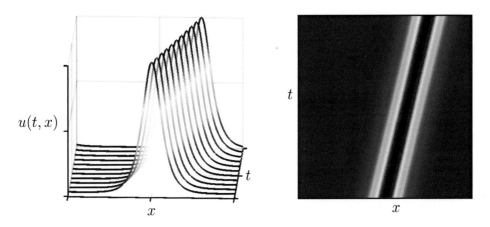

Figure 2.16 Evolution of the 1D wave equation in time, illustrated by a waterfall plot (left) and an x-t diagram (right).

```
kappa = fftshift(kappa');      % Re-order fft wavenumbers

% Initial condition
u0 = sech(x);
uhat0 = fft(u0);

% Simulate in Fourier frequency domain
dt = 0.025;
t = 0:dt:100*dt;
[t,uhat] = ode45(@(t,uhat)rhsWave(t,uhat,kappa,c),t,uhat0);

% Alternatively, simulate in spatial domain
[t,u] = ode45(@(t,u)rhsWaveSpatial(t,u,kappa,c),t,u0);
```

Code 2.9 Right hand side for 1D wave equation in Fourier transform domain.

```
function duhatdt = rhsWave(t,uhat,kappa,c)
duhatdt = -c*i*kappa.*uhat;
```

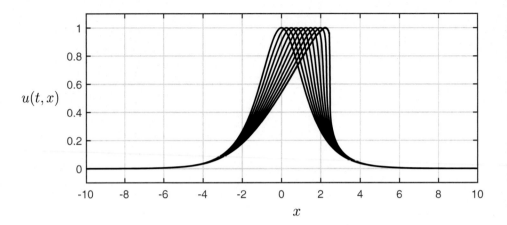

Figure 2.17 Solution of Burgers' equation in time. As time evolves, the leading edge of the Gaussian initial condition steepens, forming a shock front.

Code 2.10 Right hand side for 1D wave equation in spatial domain.

```
function dudt = rhsWaveSpatial(t,u,kappa,c)
uhat = fft(u);
duhat = i*kappa.*uhat;
du = ifft(duhat);
dudt = -c*du;
```

Burgers' Equation

For the final example, we consider the nonlinear Burgers' equation

$$u_t + uu_x = \nu u_{xx} \tag{2.41}$$

which is a simple 1D example for the nonlinear convection and diffusion that gives rise to shock waves in fluids [253]. The nonlinear convection uu_x essentially gives rise to the behavior of wave steepening, where portions of u with larger amplitude will convect more rapidly, causing a shock front to form.

Code 2.11 simulates the Burgers' equation, giving rise to Figs. 2.17 and 2.18. Burgers' equation is an interesting example to solve with the FFT, because the nonlinearity requires us to map into and out of the Fourier domain at each time step, as shown in the vector field in Code 2.12. In this example, we map into the Fourier transform domain to compute u_x and u_{xx}, and then map back to the spatial domain to compute the product uu_x. Figs. 2.17 and 2.18 clearly show the wave steepening effect that gives rise to a shock. Without the damping term u_{xx}, this shock would become infinitely steep, but with damping, it maintains a finite width.

Code 2.11 Code to simulate Burgers' equation using the Fourier transform.

```
clear all, close all, clc
nu=0.001;     % Diffusion constant

% Define spatial domain
L = 20;           % Length of domain
N = 1000;         % Number of discretization points
```

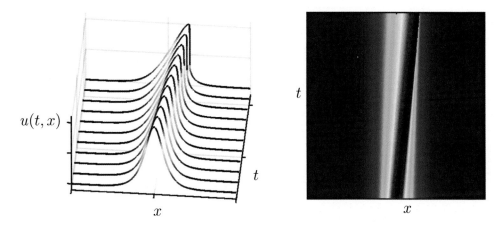

Figure 2.18 Evolution of Burgers' equation in time, illustrated by a waterfall plot (left) and an *x-t* diagram (right).

```
dx = L/N;
x = -L/2:dx:L/2-dx;  % Define x domain

% Define discrete wavenumbers
kappa = (2*pi/L)*[-N/2:N/2-1];
kappa = fftshift(kappa');     % Re-order fft wavenumbers

% Initial condition
u0 = sech(x);

% Simulate PDE in spatial domain
dt = 0.025;
t = 0:dt:100*dt;
[t,u] = ode45(@(t,u)rhsBurgers(t,u,kappa,nu),t,u0);
```

Code 2.12 Right hand side for Burgers' equation in Fourier transform domain.

```
function dudt = rhsBurgers(t,u,kappa,nu)
uhat = fft(u);
duhat = i*kappa.*uhat;
dduhat = -(kappa.^2).*uhat;
du = ifft(duhat);
ddu = ifft(dduhat);
dudt = -u.*du + nu*ddu;
```

2.4 Gabor Transform and the Spectrogram

Although the Fourier transform provides detailed information about the frequency content of a given signal, it does not give any information about when in time those frequencies occur. The Fourier transform is only able to characterize truly periodic and stationary signals, as time is stripped out via the integration in (2.18a). For a signal with nonstationary frequency content, such as a musical composition, it is important to simultaneously characterize the frequency content and its evolution in time.

The Gabor transform, also known as the short-time Fourier transform (STFT), computes a windowed FFT in a moving window [437, 262, 482], as shown in Fig. 2.19. This STFT

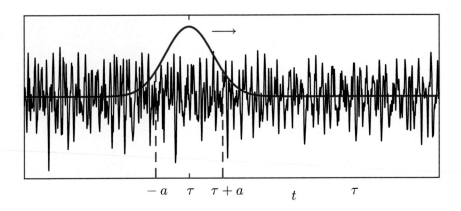

Figure 2.19 Illustration of the Gabor transform with a translating Gaussian window for the short-time Fourier transform.

enables the localization of frequency content in time, resulting in the *spectrogram*, which is a plot of frequency versus time, as demonstrated in Figs. 2.21 and 2.22. The STFT is given by:

$$\mathcal{G}(f)(t, \omega) = \hat{f}_g(t, \omega) = \int_{-\infty}^{\infty} f(\tau)e^{-i\omega\tau}\bar{g}(\tau - t)\, d\tau = \langle f, g_{t,\omega}\rangle \tag{2.42}$$

where $g_{t,\omega}(\tau)$ is defined as

$$g_{t,\omega}(\tau) = e^{i\omega\tau}g(\tau - t). \tag{2.43}$$

The function $g(t)$ is the kernel, and is often chosen to be a Gaussian:

$$g(t) = e^{-(t-\tau)^2/a^2}. \tag{2.44}$$

The parameter a determines the spread of the short-time window for the Fourier transform, and τ determines the center of the moving window.

The inverse STFT is given by:

$$f(t) = \mathcal{G}^{-1}\left(\hat{f}_g(t, \omega)\right) = \frac{1}{2\pi\|g\|^2}\int_{-\infty}^{\infty}\int_{-\infty}^{\infty}\hat{f}_g(\tau, \omega)g(t - \tau)e^{i\omega t}\, d\omega\, dt. \tag{2.45}$$

Discrete Gabor Transform
Generally, the Gabor transform will be performed on discrete signals, as with the FFT. In this case, it is necessary to discretize both time and frequency:

$$\nu = j\Delta\omega \tag{2.46}$$

$$\tau = k\Delta t. \tag{2.47}$$

The discretized kernel function becomes:

$$g_{j,k} = e^{i2\pi j\Delta\omega t}g(t - k\Delta t) \tag{2.48}$$

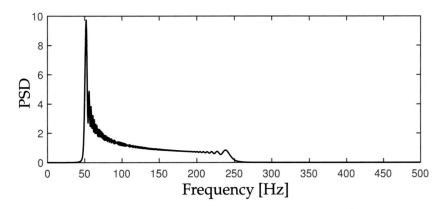

Figure 2.20 Power spectral density of quadratic chirp signal.

and the discrete Gabor transform is:

$$\hat{f}_{j,k} = \langle f, g_{j,k} \rangle = \int_{-\infty}^{\infty} f(\tau) \bar{g}_{j,k}(\tau) \, d\tau. \tag{2.49}$$

This integral can then be approximated using a finite Riemman sum on discretized functions f and $\bar{g}_{j,k}$.

Example: Quadratic Chirp

As a simple example, we construct an oscillating cosine function where the frequency of oscillation increases as a quadratic function of time:

$$f(t) = \cos(2\pi t \omega(t)) \quad \text{where} \quad \omega(t) = \omega_0 + (\omega_1 - \omega_0)t^2/3t_1^2. \tag{2.50}$$

The frequency shifts from ω_0 at $t = 0$ to ω_1 at $t = t_1$.

Fig. 2.20 shows the power spectral density obtained from the FFT of the quadratic chirp signal. Although there is a clear peak at 50 Hz, there is no information about the progression of the frequency in time. The code to generate the spectrogram is given in Code 2.13, and the resulting spectrogram is plotted in Fig. 2.21, where it can be seen that the frequency content shifts in time.

Code 2.13 Spectrogram of quadratic chirp, shown in Fig. 2.21.

```
t = 0:0.001:2;
f0 = 50;
f1 = 250;
t1 = 2;
x = chirp(t,f0,t1,f1,'quadratic');
x = cos(2*pi*t.*(f0 + (f1-f0)*t.^2/(3*t1^2)));
% There is a typo in Matlab documentation...
% ... divide by 3 so derivative amplitude matches frequency

spectrogram(x,128,120,128,1e3,'yaxis')
```

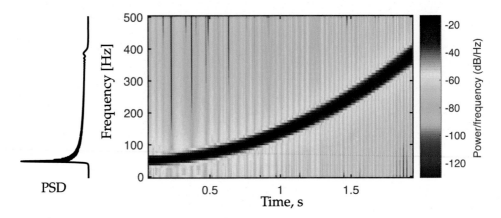

Figure 2.21 Spectrogram of quadratic chirp signal. The PSD is shown on the left, corresponding to the integrated power across rows of the spectrogram.

Example: Beethoven's Sonata Pathétique

It is possible to analyze richer signals with the spectrogram, such as Beethoven's Sonata Pathétique, shown in Fig. 2.22. The spectrogram is widely used to analyze music, and has recently been leveraged in the Shazam algorithm, which searches for key point markers in the spectrogram of songs to enable rapid classification from short clips of recorded music [545].

Fig. 2.22 shows the first two bars of Beethoven's Sonata Pathétique, along with the spectrogram. In the spectrogram, the various chords and harmonics can be seen clearly. A zoom-in of the frequency shows two octaves, and how cleanly the various notes are excited. Code 2.14 loads the data, computes the spectrogram, and plots the result.

Code 2.14 Compute spectrogram of Beethoven's Sonata Pathétique (Fig. 2.22).

```
% Download mp3read from http://www.mathworks.com/matlabcentral/
    fileexchange/13852-mp3read-and-mp3write
[Y,FS,NBITS,OPTS] = mp3read('beethoven.mp3');

%% Spectrogram using 'spectrogram' comand
T = 40;              % 40 seconds
y=Y(1:T*FS);         % First 40 seconds
spectrogram(y,5000,400,24000,24000,'yaxis');

%% Spectrogram using short-time Fourier transform 'stft'
wlen = 5000;    % Window length
h=400;          % Overlap is wlen - h
% Perform time-frequency analysis
[S,f,t_stft] = stft(y, wlen, h, FS/4, FS); % y axis 0-4000HZ

imagesc(log10(abs(S)));    % Plot spectrogram (log-scaled)
```

To invert the spectrogram and generate the original sound:

```
[x_istft, t_istft] = istft(S, h, FS/4, FS);
sound(x_istft,FS);
```

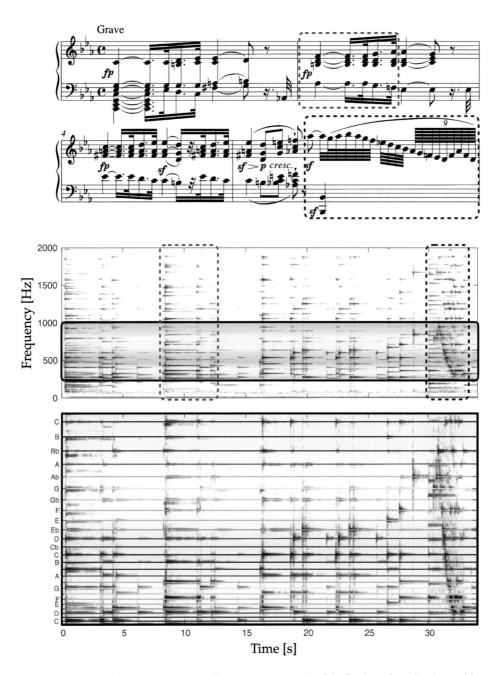

Figure 2.22 First two bars of Beethoven's Sonata Pathétique (No. 8 in C minor, Op. 13), along with annotated spectrogram.

Artists, such as Aphex Twin, have used the inverse spectrogram of images to generate music. The frequency of a given piano key is also easily computed. For example, the 40th key frequency is given by:

```
freq = @(n)(((2^(1/12))^(n-49))*440);
freq(40) % frequency of 40th key = C
```

Uncertainty Principles

In time-frequency analysis, there is a fundamental uncertainty principle that limits the ability to simultaneously attain high resolution in both the time and frequency domains. In the extreme limit, a time series is perfectly resolved in time, but provides no information about frequency content, and the Fourier transform perfectly resolves frequency content, but provides no information about when in time these frequencies occur. The spectrogram resolves both time and frequency information, but with lower resolution in each domain, as illustrated in Fig. 2.23. An alternative approach, based on a multi-resolution analysis, will be the subject of the next section.

Stated mathematically, the time-frequency uncertainty principle [429] may be written as:

$$\left(\int_{-\infty}^{\infty} x^2 |f(x)|^2 \, dx \right) \left(\int_{-\infty}^{\infty} \omega^2 |\hat{f}(\omega)|^2 \, d\omega \right) \geq \frac{1}{16\pi^2}. \tag{2.51}$$

This is true if $f(x)$ is absolutely continuous and both $xf(x)$ and $f'(x)$ are square integrable. The function $x^2 |f(x)|^2$ is the dispersion about $x = 0$. For real-valued functions, this is the second moment, which measures the variance if $f(x)$ is a Gaussian function. In other words, a function $f(x)$ and its Fourier transform cannot both be arbitrarily localized. If the

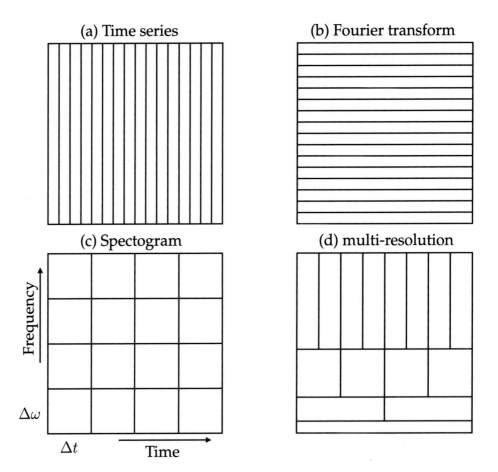

Figure 2.23 Illustration of resolution limitations and uncertainty in time-frequency analysis.

function f approaches a delta function, then the Fourier transform must become broadband, and vice versa. This has implications for the Heisenberg uncertainty principle [240], as the position and momentum wave functions are Fourier transform pairs.

In time-frequency analysis, the uncertainty principle has implication for the ability to localize the Fourier transform in time. These uncertainty principles are known as the Gabor limit. As the frequency content of a signal is resolved more finely, we lose information about when in time these events occur, and vice versa. Thus, there is a fundamental tradeoff between the simultaneously attainable resolutions in the time and frequency domains. Another implication is that a function f and its Fourier transform cannot both have finite support, meaning that they are localized, as stated in Benedick's theorem [8, 51].

2.5   Wavelets and Multi-Resolution Analysis

Wavelets [359, 145] extend the concepts in Fourier analysis to more general orthogonal bases, and partially overcome the uncertainty principle discussed above by exploiting a multi-resolution decomposition, as shown in Fig. 2.23 (d). This multi-resolution approach enables different time and frequency fidelities in different frequency bands, which is particularly useful for decomposing complex signals that arise from multi-scale processes such as are found in climatology, neuroscience, epidemiology, finance, and turbulence. Images and audio signals are also amenable to wavelet analysis, which is currently the leading method for image compression [16], as will be discussed in subsequent sections and chapters. Moreover, wavelet transforms may be computed using similar fast methods [58], making them scalable to high-dimensional data. There are a number of excellent books on wavelets [521, 401, 357], in addition to the primary references [359, 145].

The basic idea in wavelet analysis is to start with a function $\psi(t)$, known as the *mother* wavelet, and generate a family of scaled and translated versions of the function:

$$\psi_{a,b}(t) = \frac{1}{\sqrt{a}} \psi \left(\frac{t - b}{a} \right). \tag{2.52}$$

The parameters a and b are responsible for scaling and translating the function ψ, respectively. For example, one can imagine choosing a and b to scale and translate a function to fit in each of the segments in Fig. 2.23 (d). If these functions are orthogonal then the basis may be used for projection, as in the Fourier transform.

The simplest and earliest example of a wavelet is the *Haar* wavelet, developed in 1910 [227]:

$$\psi(t) = \begin{cases} 1 & 0 \le t < 1/2 \\ -1 & 1/2 \le t < 1 \\ 0 & \text{otherwise.} \end{cases} \tag{2.53}$$

The three Haar wavelets, $\psi_{1,0}$, $\psi_{1/2,0}$, and $\psi_{1/2,1/2}$, are shown in Fig. 2.24, representing the first two layers of the multi-resolution in Fig. 2.23 (d). Notice that by choosing each higher frequency layer as a bisection of the next layer down, the resulting Haar wavelets are orthogonal, providing a hierarchical basis for a signal.

The orthogonality property of wavelets described above is critical for the development of the discrete wavelet transform (DWT) below. However, we begin with the continuous

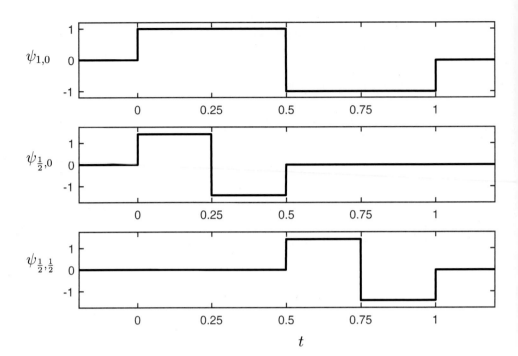

Figure 2.24 Three Haar wavelets for the first two levels of the multi-resolution in Fig. 2.23 (d).

wavelet transform (CWT), which is given by:

$$W_\psi(f)(a, b) = \langle f, \psi_{a,b} \rangle = \int_{-\infty}^{\infty} f(t) \bar{\psi}_{a,b}(t)\, dt, \tag{2.54}$$

where $\bar{\psi}_{a,b}$ denotes the complex conjugate of $\psi_{a,b}$. This is only valid for functions $\psi(t)$ that satisfy the boundedness property that

$$C_\psi = \int_{-\infty}^{\infty} \frac{|\hat{\psi}(\omega)|^2}{|\omega|}\, d\omega < \infty. \tag{2.55}$$

The inverse continuous wavelet transform (iCWT) is given by:

$$f(t) = \frac{1}{C_\psi} \int_{-\infty}^{\infty} \int_{-\infty}^{\infty} W_\psi(f)(a, b) \psi_{a,b}(t) \frac{1}{a^2}\, da\, db. \tag{2.56}$$

New wavelets may also be generated by the convolution $\psi * \phi$ if ψ is a wavelet and ϕ is a bounded and integrable function. There are many other popular mother wavelets ψ beyond the Haar wavelet, designed to have various properties. For example, the Mexican hat wavelet is given by:

$$\psi(t) = (1 - t^2)e^{-t^2/2} \tag{2.57a}$$

$$\hat{\psi}(\omega) = \sqrt{2\pi}\,\omega^2 e^{-\omega^2/2}. \tag{2.57b}$$

Discrete Wavelet Transform

As with the Fourier transform and Gabor transform, when computing the wavelet transform on data, it is necessary to introduce a discretized version. The discrete wavelet transform (DWT) is given by:

$$\mathcal{W}_\psi(f)(j,k) = \langle f, \psi_{j,k} \rangle = \int_{-\infty}^{\infty} f(t) \bar{\psi}_{j,k}(t) \, dt \qquad (2.58)$$

where $\psi_{j,k}(t)$ is a discrete family of wavelets:

$$\psi_{j,k}(t) = \frac{1}{a^j} \psi \left(\frac{t - kb}{a^j} \right). \qquad (2.59)$$

Again, if this family of wavelets is orthogonal, as in the case of the discrete Haar wavelets described earlier, it is possible to expand a function $f(t)$ uniquely in this basis:

$$f(t) = \sum_{j,k=-\infty}^{\infty} \langle f(t), \psi_{j,k}(t) \rangle \psi_{j,k}(t). \qquad (2.60)$$

The explicit computation of a DWT is somewhat involved, and is the subject of several excellent papers and texts [359, 145, 521, 401, 357]. However, the goal here is not to provide computational details, but rather to give a high-level idea of what the wavelet transform accomplishes. By scaling and translating a given shape across a signal, it is possible to efficiently extract multi-scale structures in an efficient hierarchy that provides an optimal tradeoff between time and frequency resolution. This general procedure is widely used in audio and image processing, compression, scientific computing, and machine learning, to name a few examples.

2.6 2D Transforms and Image Processing

Although we analyzed both the Fourier transform and the wavelet transform on one-dimensional signals, both methods readily generalize to higher spatial dimensions, such as two-dimensional and three-dimensional signals. Both the Fourier and wavelet transforms have had tremendous impact on image processing and compression, which provides a compelling example to investigate higher-dimensional transforms.

2D Fourier Transform for Images

The two-dimensional Fourier transform of a matrix of data $\mathbf{X} \in \mathbb{R}^{n \times m}$ is achieved by first applying the one-dimensional Fourier transform to every row of the matrix, and then applying the one-dimensional Fourier transform to every column of the intermediate matrix. This sequential row-wise and column-wise Fourier transform is shown in Fig. 2.25. Switching the order of taking the Fourier transform of rows and columns does not change the result.

Code 2.15 Two-dimensional Fourier transform via one-dimensional row-wise and column-wise FFTs.

```
A = imread('../../CH01_SVD/DATA/dog.jpg');
B = rgb2gray(A);        % Convert to grayscale image
subplot(1,3,1), imagesc(B);              % Plot image

for j=1:size(B,1);    % Compute row-wise FFT
```

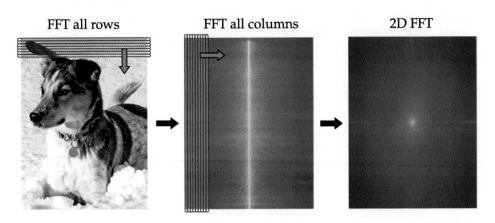

FFT all rows   FFT all columns   2D FFT

Figure 2.25 Schematic of 2D FFT. First, the FFT is taken of each row, and then the FFT is taken of each column of the resulting transformed matrix.

```
    Cshift(j,:) = fftshift(fft(B(j,:)));
    C(j,:) = (fft(B(j,:)));
end
subplot(1,3,2), imagesc(log(abs(Cshift)))

for j=1:size(C,2);  % Compute column-wise FFT
    D(:,j) = fft(C(:,j));
end
subplot(1,3,3), imagesc(fftshift(log(abs(D))))

D = fft2(B); % Much more efficient to use fft2
```

The two-dimensional FFT is effective for image compression, as many of the Fourier coefficients are small and may be neglected without loss in image quality. Thus, only a few large Fourier coefficients must be stored and transmitted.

Code 2.16 Image compression via the FFT.

```
Bt=fft2(B);     % B is grayscale image from above
Btsort = sort(abs(Bt(:)));  % Sort by magnitude

% Zero out all small coefficients and inverse transform
for keep=[.1 .05 .01 .002];
    thresh = Btsort(floor((1-keep)*length(Btsort)));
    ind = abs(Bt)>thresh;        % Find small indices
    Atlow = Bt.*ind;             % Threshold small indices
    Alow=uint8(ifft2(Atlow));    % Compressed image
    figure, imshow(Alow)         % Plot Reconstruction
end
```

Finally, the FFT is extensively used for denoising and filtering signals, as it is straightforward to isolate and manipulate particular frequency bands. Code 2.17 and Fig. 2.27 demonstrate the use of a FFT threshold filter to denoise an image with Gaussian noise added. In this example, it is observed that the noise is especially pronounced in high frequency modes, and we therefore zero out any Fourier coefficient outside of a given radius containing low frequencies.

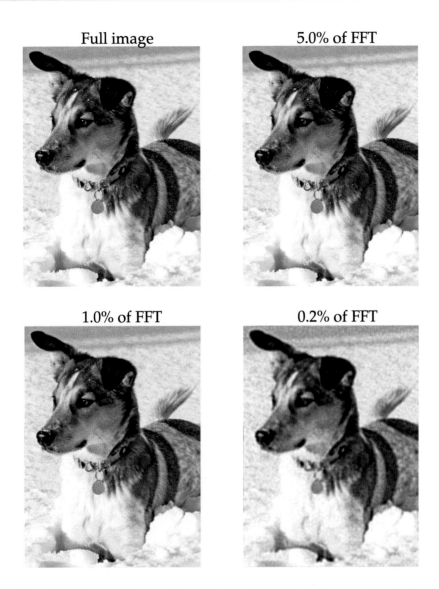

Figure 2.26 Compressed image using various thresholds to keep 5%, 1%, and 0.2% of the largest Fourier coefficients.

Code 2.17 Image denoising via the FFT.

```
Bnoise = B + uint8(200*randn(size(B)));   % Add some noise
Bt=fft2(Bnoise);
F = log(abs(Btshift)+1);            % Put FFT on log-scale

subplot(2,2,1), imagesc(Bnoise)  % Plot image
subplot(2,2,2), imagesc(F)       % Plot FFT

[nx,ny] = size(B);
[X,Y] = meshgrid(-ny/2+1:ny/2,-nx/2+1:nx/2);
R2 = X.^2+Y.^2;
ind = R2<150^2;
```

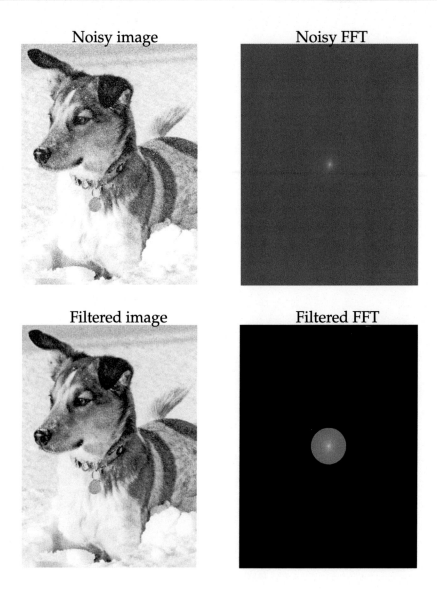

Figure 2.27 Denoising image by eliminating high-frequency Fourier coefficients outside of a given radius (bottom right).

```
Btshiftfilt = Btshift.*ind;
Ffilt = log(abs(Btshiftfilt)+1);    % Put FFT on log-scale
subplot(2,2,4), imagesc(Ffilt)      % Plot filtered FFT

Btfilt = ifftshift(Btshiftfilt);
Bfilt = ifft2(Btfilt);
subplot(2,2,3), imagesc(uint8(real(Bfilt))) % Filtered image
```

2D wavelet Transform for Images

Similar to the FFT, the discrete wavelet transform is extensively used for image processing and compression. Code 2.18 computes the wavelet transform of an image, and the first

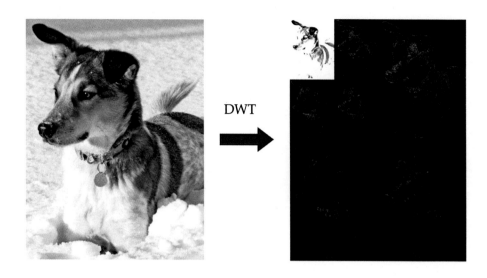

Figure 2.28 Illustration of three level discrete wavelet transform.

three levels are illustrated in Fig. 2.28. In this figure, the hierarchical nature of the wavelet decomposition is seen. The upper left corner of the DWT image is a low-resolution version of the image, and the subsequent features add fine details to the image.

Code 2.18 Example of a two level wavelet decomposition.

```
%% Wavelet decomposition (2 level)
n = 2; w = 'db1'; [C,S] = wavedec2(B,n,w);

% LEVEL 1
A1 = appcoef2(C,S,w,1); % Approximation
[H1 V1 D1] = detcoef2('a',C,S,k); % Details
A1 = wcodemat(A1,128);
H1 = wcodemat(H1,128);
V1 = wcodemat(V1,128);
D1 = wcodemat(D1,128);

% LEVEL 2
A2 = appcoef2(C,S,w,1); % Approximation
[H2 V2 D2] = detcoef2('a',C,S,k); % Details
A2 = wcodemat(A2,128);
H2 = wcodemat(H2,128);
V2 = wcodemat(V2,128);
D2 = wcodemat(D2,128);

dec2 = [A2 H2; V2 D2];
dec1 = [imresize(dec2,size(H1)) H1 ; V1 D1];
image(dec1);
```

Fig. 2.29 shows several versions of the compressed image for various compression ratios, as computed by Code 2.19. The hierarchical representation of data in the wavelet transform is ideal for image compression. Even with an aggressive truncation, retaining only 0.5% of the DWT coefficients, the coarse features of the image are retained. Thus,

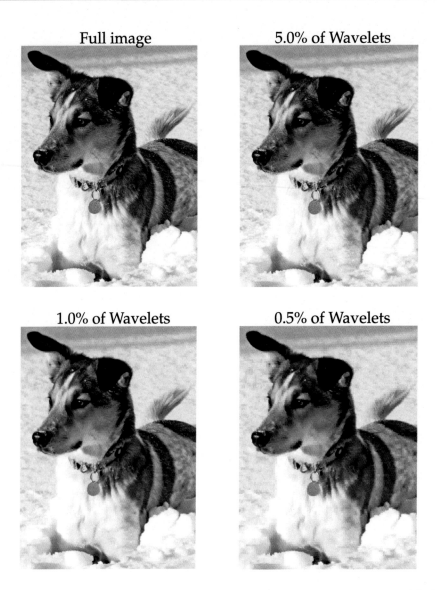

Figure 2.29 Compressed image using various thresholds to keep 5%, 1%, and 0.5% of the largest wavelet coefficients.

when transmitting data, even if bandwidth is limited and much of the DWT information is truncated, the most important features of the data are transferred.

Code 2.19 Wavelet decomposition for image compression.

```
[C,S] = wavedec2(B,4,'db1');
Csort = sort(abs(C(:)));  % Sort by magnitude

for keep =  [.1 .05 .01 .005]
    thresh = Csort(floor((1-keep)*length(Csort)));
    ind = abs(C)>thresh;
    Cfilt = C.*ind;        % Threshold small indices
```

```
% Plot Reconstruction
Arecon=uint8(waverec2(Cfilt,S,'db1'));
figure, imagesc(uint8(Arecon))
end
```

Suggested Reading

Texts
(1) **The analytical theory of heat**, by J.-B. J. Fourier, 1978 [185].
(2) **A wavelet tour of signal processing**, by S. Mallat, 1999 [357].
(3) **Spectral methods in MATLAB**, by L. N. Trefethen, 2000 [523].

Papers and reviews
(1) **An algorithm for the machine calculation of complex Fourier series**, by J. W. Cooley and J. W. Tukey, *Mathematics of Computation*, 1965 [137].
(2) **The wavelet transform, time-frequency localization and signal analysis**, by I. Daubechies, *IEEE Transactions on Information Theory*, 1990 [145].
(3) **An industrial strength audio search algorithm**, by A. Wang et al., *Ismir*, 2003 [545].

3 Sparsity and Compressed Sensing

The inherent structure observed in natural data implies that the data admits a sparse representation in an appropriate coordinate system. In other words, if natural data is expressed in a well-chosen basis, only a few parameters are required to characterize the modes that are active, and in what proportion. All of data compression relies on sparsity, whereby a signal is represented more efficiently in terms of the sparse vector of coefficients in a generic transform basis, such as Fourier or wavelet bases. Recent fundamental advances in mathematics have turned this paradigm upside down. Instead of collecting a high-dimensional measurement and then compressing, it is now possible to acquire *compressed* measurements and solve for the sparsest high-dimensional signal that is consistent with the measurements. This so-called *compressed sensing* is a valuable new perspective that is also relevant for complex systems in engineering, with potential to revolutionize data acquisition and processing. In this chapter, we discuss the fundamental principles of sparsity and compression as well as the mathematical theory that enables compressed sensing, all worked out on motivating examples.

Our discussion on sparsity and compressed sensing will necessarily involve the critically important fields of optimization and statistics. Sparsity is a useful perspective to promote *parsimonious* models that avoid overfitting and remain interpretable because they have the minimal number of terms required to explain the data. This is related to Occam's razor, which states that the simplest explanation is generally the correct one. Sparse optimization is also useful for adding robustness with respect to outliers and missing data, which generally skew the results of least-squares regression, such as the SVD. The topics in this chapter are closely related to randomized linear algebra discussed in Section 1.8, and they will also be used in several subsequent chapters. Sparse regression will be explored further in Chapter 4 and will be used in Section 7.3 to identify interpretable and parsimonious nonlinear dynamical systems models from data.

3.1 Sparsity and Compression

Most natural signals, such as images and audio, are highly compressible. This compressibility means that when the signal is written in an appropriate basis only a few modes are active, thus reducing the number of values that must be stored for an accurate representation. Said another way, a compressible signal $\mathbf{x} \in \mathbb{R}^n$ may be written as a sparse vector $\mathbf{s} \in \mathbb{R}^n$ (containing mostly zeros) in a transform basis $\mathbf{\Psi} \in \mathbb{R}^{n \times n}$:

$$\mathbf{x} = \mathbf{\Psi s}. \tag{3.1}$$

Specifically, the vector **s** is called K-sparse in Ψ if there are exactly K nonzero elements. If the basis Ψ is generic, such as the Fourier or wavelet basis, then only the few active terms in **s** are required to reconstruct the original signal **x**, reducing the data required to store or transmit the signal.

Images and audio signals are both compressible in Fourier or wavelet bases, so that after taking the Fourier or wavelet transform, most coefficients are small and may be set exactly equal to zero with negligible loss of quality. These few active coefficients may be stored and transmitted, instead of the original high-dimensional signal. Then, to reconstruct the original signal in the ambient space (i.e., in pixel space for an image), one need only take the inverse transform. As discussed in Chapter 2, the fast Fourier transform is the enabling technology that makes it possible to efficiently reconstruct an image **x** from the sparse coefficients in **s**. This is the foundation of JPEG compression for images and MP3 compression for audio.

The Fourier modes and wavelets are *generic* or *universal* bases, in the sense that nearly all natural images or audio signals are sparse in these bases. Therefore, once a signal is compressed, one needs only store or transmit the sparse vector **s** rather than the entire matrix Ψ, since the Fourier and wavelet transforms are already hard-coded on most machines. In Chapter 1 we found that it is also possible to compress signals using the SVD, resulting in a *tailored* basis. In fact, there are two ways that the SVD can be used to compress an image: 1) we may take the SVD of the image directly and only keep the dominant columns of **U** and **V** (Section 1.2), or 2) we may represent the image as a linear combination of *eigen* images, as in the eigenface example (Section 1.6). The first option is relatively inefficient, as the basis vectors **U** and **V** must be stored. However, in the second case, a tailored basis **U** may be computed and stored once, and then used to compress an entire class of images, such as human faces. This tailored basis has the added advantage that the modes are interpretable as correlation features that may be useful for learning. It is important to note that both the Fourier basis $\mathcal{F}$ and the SVD basis **U** are unitary transformations, which will become important in the following sections.

Although the majority of compression theory has been driven by audio, image, and video applications, there are many implications for engineering systems. The solution to a high-dimensional system of differential equations typically evolves on a low-dimensional manifold, indicating the existence of coherent structures that facilitate sparse representation. Even broadband phenomena, such as turbulence, may be instantaneously characterized by a sparse representation. This has a profound impact on how to sense and compute, as will be described throughout this chapter and the remainder of the book.

Example: Image Compression

Compression is relatively simple to implement on images, as described in Section 2.6 and revisited here (see Fig. 3.1). First, we load an image, convert to grayscale, and plot:

```
A=imread('jelly', 'jpeg');   % Load image
Abw=rgb2gray(A);              % Convert image to grayscale
imshow(Abw).                  % Plot image
```

Next, we take the fast Fourier transform and plot the coefficients on a logarithmic scale:

```
At=fft2(Abw);
F = log(abs(fftshift(At))+1);   % put FFT on log-scale
imshow(mat2gray(F),[]);
```

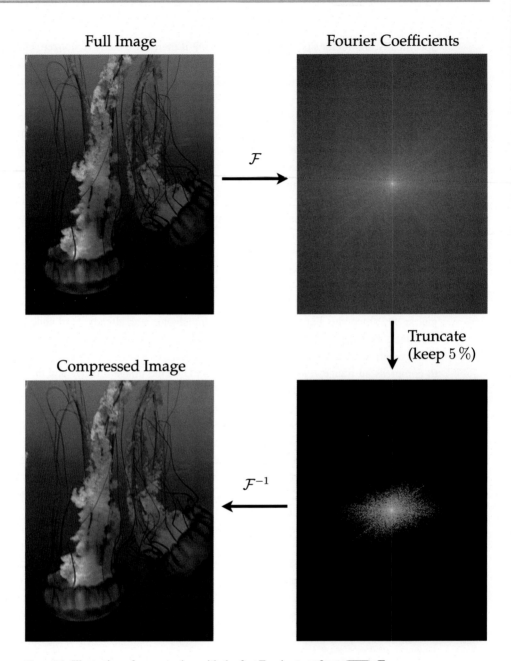

Figure 3.1 Illustration of compression with the fast Fourier transform (FFT) $\mathcal{F}$.

To compress the image, we first arrange all of the Fourier coefficients in order of magnitude and decide what percentage to keep (in this case 5 %). This sets the threshold for truncation:

```
Bt = sort(abs(At(:)));
keep = 0.05;
thresh = Bt(floor((1-keep)*length(Bt)));
ind = abs(At)>thresh;
Atlow = At.*ind;
```

Figure 3.2 Compressed image (left), and viewed as a surface (right).

Finally, we plot the compressed image by taking the inverse FFT (iFFT):

```
Alow=uint8(ifft2(Atlow));
imshow(Alow)
```

To understand the role of the sparse Fourier coefficients in a compressed image, it helps to view the image as a surface, where the height of a point is given by the brightness of the corresponding pixel. This is shown in Fig. 3.2. Here we see that the surface is relatively simple, and may be represented as a sum of a few spatial Fourier modes.

```
Anew = imresize(Abw,.2);
surf(double(Anew));
shading flat, view(-168,86)
```

Why Signals Are Compressible: The Vastness of Image Space

It is important to note that the compressibility of images is related to the overwhelming dimensionality of image space. For even a simple 20×20 pixel black and white image, there are 2^{400} distinct possible images, which is larger than the number of nucleons in the known universe. The number of images is considerably more staggering for higher resolution images with greater color depth.

In the space of one megapixel images (i.e., 1000×1000 pixels), there is an image of us each being born, of me typing this sentence, and of you reading it. However vast the space of these *natural* images, they occupy a tiny, minuscule fraction of the total image space. The majority of the images in image space represent random noise, resembling television static. For simplicity, consider grayscale images, and imagine drawing a random number for the gray value of each of the pixels. With exceedingly high probability, the resulting image will look like noise, with no apparent significance. You could draw these random images for an

Figure 3.3 Illustration of the vastness of image (pixel) space, with natural images occupying a vanishingly small fraction of the space.

entire lifetime and never find an image of a mountain, or a person, or anything physically recognizable[1].

In other words, natural images are extremely rare in the vastness of image space, as illustrated in Fig. 3.3. Because so many images are unstructured or random, most of the dimensions used to encode images are only necessary for these random images. These dimensions are redundant if all we cared about was encoding natural images. An important implication is that the images we care about (i.e., natural images) are highly compressible, if we find a suitable transformed basis where the redundant dimensions are easily identified.

3.2   Compressed Sensing

Despite the considerable success of compression in real-world applications, it still relies on having access to full high-dimensional measurements. The recent advent of compressed sensing [150, 112, 111, 113, 115, 109, 39, 114, 40] turns the compression paradigm upside down: instead of collecting high-dimensional data just to compress and discard most of the information, it is instead possible to collect surprisingly few *compressed* or *random* measurements and then infer what the sparse representation is in the transformed basis. The idea behind compressed sensing is relatively simple to state mathematically, but until recently finding the sparsest vector consistent with measurements was a non-polynomial (NP) hard problem. The rapid adoption of compressed sensing throughout the engineering and applied sciences rests on the solid mathematical framework[2] that provides conditions

---

[1] The vastness of signal space was described in Borges's "The Library of Babel" in 1944, where he describes a library containing all possible books that could be written, of which actual coherent books occupy a nearly immeasurably small fraction [69]. In Borges's library, there are millions of copies of this very book, with variations on this single sentence. Another famous variation on this theme considers that given enough monkeys typing on enough typewriters, one would eventually recreate the works of Shakespeare. One of the oldest related descriptions of these combinatorially large spaces dates back to Aristotle.

[2] Interestingly, the incredibly important collaboration between Emmanuel Candès and Terrance Tao began with them discussing the odd properties of signal reconstruction at their kids' daycare.

for when it is possible to reconstruct the full signal with high probability using convex algorithms.

Mathematically, compressed sensing exploits the sparsity of a signal in a generic basis to achieve full signal reconstruction from surprisingly few measurements. If a signal $\mathbf{x}$ is K-sparse in $\boldsymbol{\Psi}$, then instead of measuring $\mathbf{x}$ directly (n measurements) and then compressing, it is possible to collect dramatically fewer randomly chosen or *compressed* measurements and then solve for the nonzero elements of $\mathbf{s}$ in the transformed coordinate system. The measurements $\mathbf{y} \in \mathbb{R}^p$, with $K < p \ll n$ are given by

$$\mathbf{y} = \mathbf{C}\mathbf{x}. \tag{3.2}$$

The measurement matrix[3] $\mathbf{C} \in \mathbb{R}^{p \times n}$ represents a set of p linear measurements on the state $\mathbf{x}$. The choice of measurement matrix $\mathbf{C}$ is of critical importance in compressed sensing, and is discussed in Section 3.4. Typically, measurements may consist of random projections of the state, in which case the entries of $\mathbf{C}$ are Gaussian or Bernoulli distributed random variables. It is also possible to measure individual entries of $\mathbf{x}$ (i.e., single pixels if $\mathbf{x}$ is an image), in which case $\mathbf{C}$ consists of random rows of the identity matrix.

With knowledge of the sparse vector $\mathbf{s}$ it is possible to reconstruct the signal $\mathbf{x}$ from (3.1). Thus, the goal of compressed sensing is to find the sparsest vector $\mathbf{s}$ that is consistent with the measurements $\mathbf{y}$:

$$\mathbf{y} = \mathbf{C}\boldsymbol{\Psi}\mathbf{s} = \boldsymbol{\Theta}\mathbf{s}. \tag{3.3}$$

The system of equations in (3.3) is underdetermined since there are infinitely many consistent solutions $\mathbf{s}$. The *sparsest* solution $\hat{\mathbf{s}}$ satisfies the following optimization problem:

$$\hat{\mathbf{s}} = \underset{\mathbf{s}}{\mathrm{argmin}} \, \|\mathbf{s}\|_0 \text{ subject to } \mathbf{y} = \mathbf{C}\boldsymbol{\Psi}\mathbf{s}, \tag{3.4}$$

where $\| \cdot \|_0$ denotes the ℓ_0 pseudo-norm, given by the number of nonzero entries; this is also referred to as the cardinality of $\mathbf{s}$.

The optimization in (3.4) is non-convex, and in general the solution can only be found with a brute-force search that is combinatorial in n and K. In particular, all possible K-sparse vectors in $\mathbb{R}^n$ must be checked; if the exact level of sparsity K is unknown, the search is even broader. Because this search is combinatorial, solving (3.4) is intractable for even moderately large n and K, and the prospect of solving larger problems does not improve with Moore's law of exponentially increasing computational power.

Fortunately, under certain conditions on the measurement matrix $\mathbf{C}$, it is possible to relax the optimization in (3.4) to a convex ℓ_1-minimization [112, 150]:

$$\hat{\mathbf{s}} = \underset{\mathbf{s}}{\mathrm{argmin}} \, \|\mathbf{s}\|_1 \text{ subject to } \mathbf{y} = \mathbf{C}\boldsymbol{\Psi}\mathbf{s}, \tag{3.5}$$

where $\| \cdot \|_1$ is the ℓ_1 norm, given by

$$\|\mathbf{s}\|_1 = \sum_{k=1}^{n} |s_k|. \tag{3.6}$$

---

[3] In the compressed sensing literature, the measurement matrix is often denoted $\boldsymbol{\Phi}$; instead, we use $\mathbf{C}$ to be consistent with the output equation in control theory. $\boldsymbol{\Phi}$ is also already used to denote DMD modes in Chapter 7.

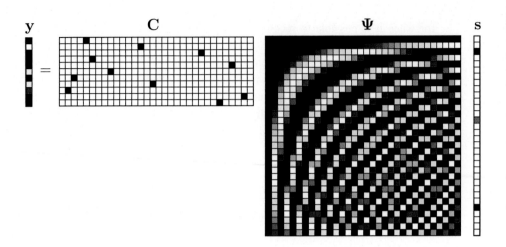

Figure 3.4 Schematic of measurements in the compressed sensing framework.

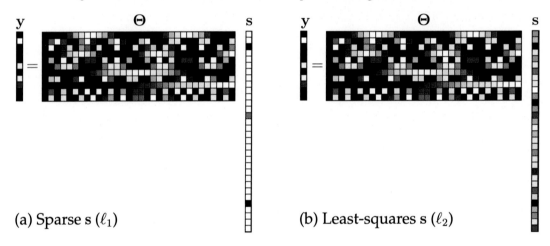

(a) Sparse s (ℓ_1)   (b) Least-squares s (ℓ_2)

Figure 3.5 ℓ_1 and ℓ_2 minimum norm solutions to compressed sensing problem. The difference in solutions for this regression are further considered in Chapter 4.

The ℓ_1 norm is also known as the taxicab or Manhattan norm because it represents the distance a taxi would take between two points on a rectangular grid. The overview of compressed sensing is shown schematically in Fig. 3.4. The ℓ_1 minimum-norm solution is sparse, while the ℓ_2 minimum norm solution is not, as shown in Fig. 3.5.

There are very specific conditions that must be met for the ℓ_1-minimization in (3.5) to converge with high probability to the sparsest solution in (3.4) [109, 111, 39]. These will be discussed in detail in Sec. 3.4, although they may be summarized as:

1.   The measurement matrix $\mathbf{C}$ must be *incoherent* with respect to the sparsifying basis $\boldsymbol{\Psi}$, meaning that the rows of $\mathbf{C}$ are not correlated with the columns of $\boldsymbol{\Psi}$,

2.   The number of measurements p must be sufficiently large, on the order of

$$p \approx \mathcal{O}(K \log(n/K)) \approx k_1 K \log(n/K). \tag{3.7}$$

The constant multiplier k_1 depends on how incoherent $\mathbf{C}$ and $\boldsymbol{\Psi}$ are.

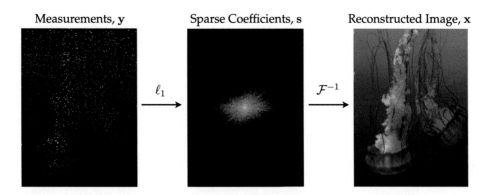

Figure 3.6 Schematic illustration of compressed sensing using ℓ_1 minimization. Note, this is a dramatization, and is not actually based on a compressed sensing calculation. Typically, compressed sensing of images requires a significant number of measurements and is computationally prohibitive.

Roughly speaking, these two conditions guarantee that the matrix $\mathbf{C}\mathbf{\Psi}$ acts as a unitary transformation on K sparse vectors $\mathbf{s}$, preserving relative distances between vectors and enabling almost certain signal reconstruction with ℓ_1 convex minimization. This is formulated precisely in terms of the restricted isometry property (RIP) in Sec. 3.4.

The idea of compressed sensing may be counterintuitive at first, especially given classical results on sampling requirements for exact signal reconstruction. For instance, the Shannon-Nyquist sampling theorem [486, 409] states that perfect signal recovery requires that it is sampled at twice the rate of the highest frequency present. However, this result only provides a strict bound on the required sampling rate for signals with broadband frequency content. Typically, the only signals that are truly broadband are those that have already been compressed. Since an uncompressed signal will generally be sparse in a transform basis, the Shannon-Nyquist theorem may be relaxed, and the signal may be reconstructed with considerably fewer measurements than given by the Nyquist rate. However, even though the number of measurements may be decreased, compressed sensing does still rely on precise *timing* of the measurements, as we will see. Moreover, the signal recovery via compressed sensing is not strictly speaking guaranteed, but is instead possible with high probability, making it foremost a statistical theory. However, the probability of successful recovery becomes astronomically large for moderate sized problems.

Disclaimer

A rough schematic of compressed sensing is shown in Fig. 3.6. However, this schematic is a dramatization, and is not actually based on a compressed sensing calculation since using compressed sensing for image reconstruction is computationally prohibitive. It is important to note that for the majority of applications in imaging, compressed sensing is not practical. However, images are often still used to motivate and explain compressed sensing because of their ease of manipulation and our intuition for pictures. In fact, we are currently guilty of this exact misdirection.

Upon closer inspection of this image example, we are analyzing an image with 1024×768 pixels and approximately 5% of the Fourier coefficients are required for accurate compression. This puts the sparsity level at $K = 0.05 \times 1024 \times 768 \approx 40,000$. Thus, a back of the envelope estimate using (3.7), with a constant multiplier of $k_1 = 3$, indicates that we need $p \approx 350,000$ measurements, which is about 45 % of the original pixels. Even if we had access to these 45 % random measurements, inferring the correct sparse vector of Fourier coefficients is computationally prohibitive, much more so than the efficient FFT based image compression in Section 3.1.

Compressed sensing for images is typically only used in special cases where a reduction of the number of measurements is significant. For example, an early application of compressed sensing technology was for infant MRI (magnetic resonance imaging), where reduction of the time a child must be still could reduce the need for dangerous heavy sedation.

However, it is easy to see that the number of measurements p scales with the sparsity level K, so that if the signal is *more* sparse, then fewer measurements are required. The viewpoint of sparsity is still valuable, and the mathematical innovation of convex relaxation of combinatorially hard ℓ_0 problems to convex ℓ_1 problems may be used much more broadly than for compressed sensing of images.

Alternative Formulations

In addition to the ℓ_1-minimization in (3.5), there are alternative approaches based on *greedy algorithms* [525, 526, 528, 527, 530, 243, 529, 207, 531, 205, 398, 206] that determine the sparse solution of (3.3) through an iterative matching pursuit problem. For instance, the compressed sensing matching pursuit (CoSaMP) [398] is computationally efficient, easy to implement, and freely available.

When the measurements $\mathbf{y}$ have additive noise, say white noise of magnitude ε, there are variants of (3.5) that are more robust:

$$\hat{\mathbf{s}} = \underset{\mathbf{s}}{\operatorname{argmin}} \|\mathbf{s}\|_1, \quad \text{subject to} \quad \|\mathbf{C\Psi s} - \mathbf{y}\|_2 < \varepsilon. \tag{3.8}$$

A related convex optimization is the following:

$$\hat{\mathbf{s}} = \underset{\mathbf{s}}{\operatorname{argmin}} \|\mathbf{C\Psi s} - \mathbf{y}\|_2 + \lambda \|\mathbf{s}\|_1, \tag{3.9}$$

where $\lambda \geq 0$ is a parameter that weights the importance of sparsity. Eqs. (3.8) and (3.9) are closely related [528].

3.3   Compressed Sensing Examples

This section explores concrete examples of compressed sensing for sparse signal recovery. The first example shows that the ℓ_1 norm promotes sparsity when solving a generic underdetermined system of equations, and the second example considers the recovery of a sparse two-tone audio signal with compressed sensing.

ℓ_1 and Sparse Solutions to an Underdetermined System

To see the sparsity promoting effects of the ℓ_1 norm, we consider a generic underdetermined system of equations. We build a matrix system of equations $\mathbf{y} = \boldsymbol{\Theta}\mathbf{s}$ with $p = 200$ rows (measurements) and $n = 1000$ columns (unknowns). In general, there are infinitely many solutions $\mathbf{s}$ that are consistent with these equations, unless we are very unfortunate and the row equations are linearly dependent while the measurements are inconsistent in these rows. In fact, this is an excellent example of the probabilistic thinking used more generally in compressed sensing: if we generate a linear system of equations at random, that has sufficiently many more unknowns than knowns, then the resulting equations will have infinitely many solutions with *high probability*.

In MATLAB, it is straightforward to solve this underdetermined linear system for both the minimum ℓ_1 norm and minimum ℓ_2 norm solutions. The minimum ℓ_2 norm solution is obtained using the pseudo-inverse (related to the SVD from Chapters 1 and 4). The minimum ℓ_1 norm solution is obtained via the **cvx** (ConVeX) optimization package. Fig. 3.7 shows that the ℓ_1-minimum solution is in fact sparse (with most entries being nearly zero), while the ℓ_2-minimum solution is *dense*, with a bit of energy in each vector coefficient.

Code 3.1 Solutions to underdetermined linear system $\mathbf{y} = \mathbf{\Theta s}$.

```
% Solve y = Theta * s for "s"
n = 1000;   % dimension of s
p = 200;    % number of measurements, dim(y)
Theta = randn(p,n);
y = randn(p,1);

% L1 minimum norm solution s_L1
cvx_begin;
    variable s_L1(n);
    minimize( norm(s_L1,1) );
    subject to
        Theta*s_L1 == y;
cvx_end;

s_L2 = pinv(Theta)*y;   % L2 minimum norm solution s_L2
```

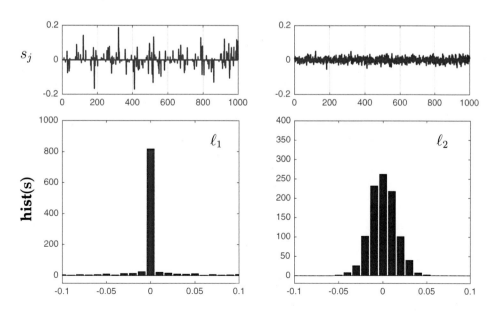

Figure 3.7 Comparison of ℓ_1-minimum (blue, left) and ℓ_2-minimum norm (red, right) solutions to an underdetermined linear system.

Recovering an Audio Signal from Sparse Measurements

To illustrate the use of compressed sensing to reconstruct a high-dimensional signal from a sparse set of random measurements, we consider a signal consisting of a two-tone audio signal:

$$x(t) = \cos(2\pi \times 97t) + \cos(2\pi \times 777t). \tag{3.10}$$

This signal is clearly sparse in the frequency domain, as it is defined by a sum of exactly two cosine waves. The highest frequency present is 777 Hz, so that the Nyquist sampling rate is 1554 Hz. However, leveraging the sparsity of the signal in the frequency domain, we can accurately reconstruct the signal with random samples that are spaced at an average sampling rate of 128 Hz, which is well below the Nyquist sampling rate. Fig. 3.8 shows the result of compressed sensing, as implemented in Code 3.2. In this example, the full signal is generated from $t = 0$ to $t = 1$ with a resolution of $n = 4,096$ and is then randomly sampled at $p = 128$ locations in time. The sparse vector of coefficients in the discrete cosine transform (DCT) basis is solved for using matching pursuit.

Code 3.2 Compressed sensing reconstruction of two-tone cosine signal.

```
%% Generate signal, DCT of signal
n = 4096;    % points in high resolution signal
```

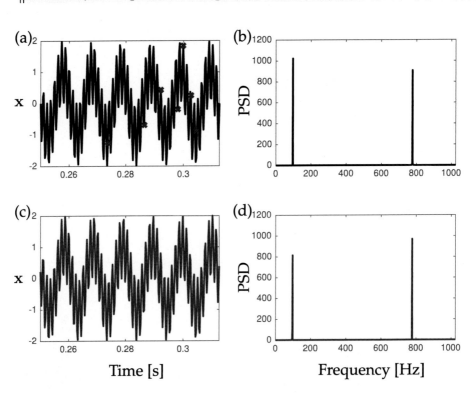

Figure 3.8 Compressed sensing reconstruction of a two-tone audio signal given by $x(t) = \cos(2\pi \times 97t) + \cos(2\pi \times 777t)$. The full signal and power spectral density are shown in panels (a) and (b), respectively. The signal is measured at random sparse locations in time, demarcated by red points in (a), and these measurements are used to build the compressed sensing estimate in (c) and (d). The time series shown in (a) and (c) are a zoom-in of the entire time range, which is from $t = 0$ to $t = 1$.

```
t = linspace(0, 1, n);
x = cos(2* 97 * pi * t) + cos(2* 777 * pi * t);
xt = fft(x); % Fourier transformed signal
PSD = xt.*conj(xt)/n; % Power spectral density

%% Randomly sample signal
p = 128; % num. random samples, p=n/32
perm = round(rand(p, 1) * n);
y = x(perm); % compressed measurement

%% Solve compressed sensing problem
Psi = dct(eye(n, n)); % build Psi
Theta = Psi(perm, :); % Measure rows of Psi

s = cosamp(Theta,y',10,1.e-10,10); % CS via matching pursuit
xrecon = idct(s); % reconstruct full signal
```

It is important to note that the $p = 128$ measurements are randomly chosen from the 4, 096 resolution signal. Thus, we know the precise timing of the sparse measurements at a much higher resolution than our sampling rate. If we chose $p = 128$ measurements uniformly in time, the compressed sensing algorithm fails. Specifically, if we compute the PSD directly from these uniform measurements, the high-frequency signal will be aliased resulting in erroneous frequency peaks.

Finally, it is also possible to replace the matching pursuit algorithm

```
s = cosamp(Theta,y',10,1.e-10,10); % CS via matching pursuit
```

with an ℓ_1 minimization using the **CVX** package [218]:

```
%% L1-Minimization using CVX
cvx_begin;
    variable s(n);
    minimize( norm(s,1) );
    subject to
        Theta*s == y';
cvx_end;
```

In the compressed sensing matching pursuit (CoSaMP) code, the desired level of sparsity K must be specified, and this quantity may not be known ahead of time. The ℓ_1 minimization routine does not require knowledge of the desired sparsity level *a priori*, although convergence to the sparsest solution relies on having sufficiently many measurements p, which indirectly depends on K.

3.4 The Geometry of Compression

Compressed sensing can be summarized in a relatively simple statement: A given signal, if it is sufficiently sparse in a known basis, may be recovered (with high probability) using significantly fewer measurements than the signal length, if there are sufficiently many measurements and these measurements are sufficiently random. Each part of this statement can be made precise and mathematically rigorous in an overarching framework that describes the geometry of sparse vectors, and how these vectors are transformed through random measurements. Specifically, enough good measurements will result in a matrix

$$\mathbf{\Theta} = \mathbf{C}\mathbf{\Psi}$$ (3.11)

that preserves the distance and inner product structure of sparse vectors **s**. In other words, we seek a measurement matrix **C** so that Θ acts as a near isometry map on sparse vectors. Isometry literally means *same distance*, and is closed related to unitarity, which not only preserves distance, but also angles between vectors. When Θ acts as a near isometry, it is possible to solve the following equation for the sparsest vector **s** using convex ℓ_1 minimization:

$$\mathbf{y} = \Theta\mathbf{s}. \tag{3.12}$$

The remainder of this section describes the conditions on the measurement matrix **C** that are required for Θ to act as a near isometry map with high probability. The geometric properties of various norms are shown in Fig. 3.9.

Determining how many measurements to take is relatively simple. If the signal is K-sparse in a basis Ψ, meaning that all but K coefficients are zero, then the number of measurements scales as $p \sim \mathcal{O}(K \log(n/K)) = k_1 K \log(n/K)$, as in (3.7). The constant multiplier k_1, which defines *exactly* how many measurements are needed, depends on the quality of the measurements. Roughly speaking, measurements are good if they are *incoherent* with respect to the columns of the sparsifying basis, meaning that the rows of **C** have small inner product with the columns of Ψ. If the measurements are coherent with columns of the sparsifying basis, then a measurement will provide little information unless that basis mode happens to be non-zero in **s**. In contrast, incoherent measurements are excited by nearly any active mode, making it possible to infer the active modes. Delta functions are incoherent with respect to Fourier modes, as they excite a broadband fre-

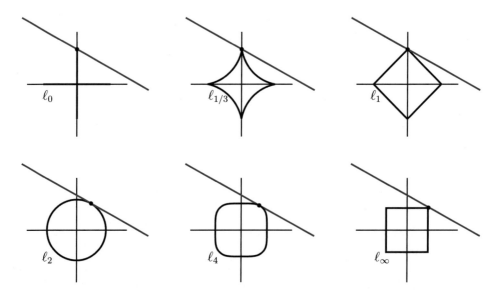

Figure 3.9 The minimum norm point on a line in different ℓ_p norms. The blue line represents the solution set of an under-determined system of equations, and the red curves represent the minimum-norm level sets that intersect this blue line for different norms. In the norms between ℓ_0 and ℓ_1, the minimum-norm solution also corresponds to the sparsest solution, with only one coordinate active. In the ℓ_2 and higher norms, the minimum-norm solution is not sparse, but has all coordinates active.

quency response. The more *incoherent* the measurements, the smaller the required number of measurements p.

The incoherence of measurements $\mathbf{C}$ and the basis $\mathbf{\Psi}$ is given by $\mu(\mathbf{C}, \mathbf{\Psi})$:

$$\mu(\mathbf{C}, \mathbf{\Psi}) = \sqrt{n} \max_{j,k} |\langle \mathbf{c}_k, \mathbf{\psi}_j \rangle|, \tag{3.13}$$

where $\mathbf{c}_k$ is the kth row of the matrix $\mathbf{C}$ and $\mathbf{\psi}_j$ is the jth column of the matrix $\mathbf{\Psi}$. The coherence μ will range between 1 and $\sqrt{n}$.

The Restricted Isometry Property (RIP)

When measurements are incoherent, the matrix $\mathbf{C\Psi}$ satisfies a *restricted isometry property* (RIP) for sparse vectors $\mathbf{s}$,

$$(1 - \delta_K)\|\mathbf{s}\|_2^2 \le \|\mathbf{C\Psi s}\|_2^2 \le (1 + \delta_K)\|\mathbf{s}\|_2^2,$$

with restricted isometry constant δ_K [114]. The constant δ_K is defined as the smallest number that satisfies the above inequality for *all* K-sparse vectors $\mathbf{s}$. When δ_K is small, then $\mathbf{C\Psi}$ acts as a near isometry on K-sparse vectors $\mathbf{s}$. In practice, it is difficult to compute δ_K directly; moreover, the measurement matrix $\mathbf{C}$ may be chosen to be random, so that it is more desirable to derive statistical properties about the bounds on δ_K for a family of measurement matrices $\mathbf{C}$, rather than to compute δ_K for a specific $\mathbf{C}$. Generally, increasing the number of measurements will decrease the constant δ_K, improving the property of $\mathbf{C\Psi}$ to act isometrically on sparse vectors. When there are sufficiently many incoherent measurements, as described above, it is possible to accurately determine the K nonzero elements of the n-length vector $\mathbf{s}$. In this case, there are bounds on the constant δ_K that guarantee exact signal reconstruction for noiseless data. An in-depth discussion of incoherence and the RIP can be found in [39, 114].

Incoherence and Measurement Matrices

Another significant result of compressed sensing is that there are generic sampling matrices $\mathbf{C}$ that are sufficiently incoherent with respect to nearly all transform bases. Specifically, Bernouli and Gaussian random measurement matrices satisfy the RIP for a generic basis $\mathbf{\Psi}$ with high probability [113]. There are additional results generalizing the RIP and investigating incoherence of sparse matrices [205].

In many engineering applications, it is advantageous to represent the signal $\mathbf{x}$ in a generic basis, such as Fourier or wavelets. One key advantage is that single-point measurements are incoherent with respect to these bases, exciting a broadband frequency response. Sampling at random point locations is appealing in applications where individual measurements are expensive, such as in ocean monitoring. Examples of random measurement matrices, including single pixel, Gaussian, Bernoulli, and sparse random, are shown in Fig. 3.10.

A particularly useful transform basis for compressed sensing is obtained by the SVD[4], resulting in a tailored basis in which the data is optimally sparse [316, 80, 81, 31, 98]. A truncated SVD basis may result in a more efficient signal recovery from fewer measurements. Progress has been made developing a compressed SVD and PCA based on the

---

[4] The SVD provides an optimal low-rank matrix approximation, and it is used in principal components analysis (PCA) and proper orthogonal decomposition (POD).

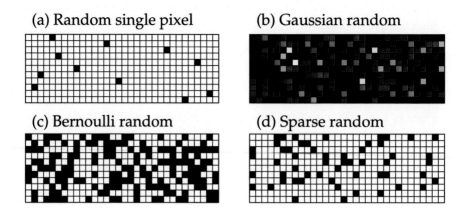

Figure 3.10 Examples of good random measurement matrices **C**.

Johnson-Lindenstrauss (JL) lemma [267, 187, 436, 206]. The JL lemma is closely related to the RIP, indicating when it is possible to embed high-dimensional vectors in a low-dimensional space while preserving spectral properties.

Bad Measurements

So far we have described how to take *good* compressed measurements. Fig. 3.11 shows a particularly poor choice of measurements **C**, corresponding to the last p columns of the sparsifying basis **Ψ**. In this case, the product **Θ** = **CΨ** is a $p \times p$ identity matrix padded with zeros on the left. In this case, any signal **s** that is not active in the last p columns of **Ψ** is in the null-space of **Θ**, and is completely invisible to the measurements **y**. In this case, these measurements incur significant information loss for many sparse vectors.

3.5   Sparse Regression

The use of the ℓ_1 norm to promote sparsity significantly predates compressed sensing. In fact, many benefits of the ℓ_1 norm were well-known and oft-used in statistics decades earlier. In this section, we show that the ℓ_1 norm may be used to *regularize* statistical regression, both to penalize statistical outliers and also to promote *parsimonious* statistical models with as few factors as possible. The role of ℓ_2 versus ℓ_1 in regression is further detailed in Chapter 4.

Outlier Rejection and Robustness

Least squares regression is perhaps the most common statistical model used for data fitting. However, it is well known that the regression fit may be arbitrarily corrupted by a single large outlier in the data; outliers are weighted more heavily in least-squares regression because their distance from the fit-line is squared. This is shown schematically in Fig. 3.12.

In contrast, ℓ_1-minimum solutions give equal weight to all data points, making it potentially more robust to outliers and corrupt data. This procedure is also known as least absolute deviations (LAD) regression, among other names. A script demonstrating the

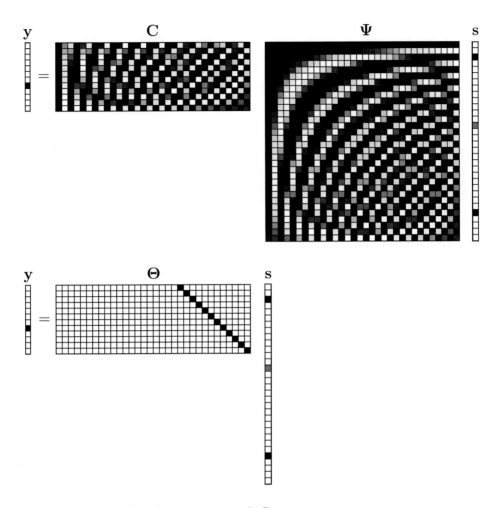

Figure 3.11 Examples of a bad measurement matrix **C**.

use of least-squares (ℓ_2) and LAD (ℓ_1) regression for a dataset with an outlier is given in Code 3.3.

Code 3.3 Use of ℓ_1 norm for robust statistical regression.

```
x = sort(4*(rand(25,1)-.5));  % Random data from [-2,2]
b = .9*x + .1*randn(size(x));  % Line y=.9x with noise
atrue = x\b;            % Least-squares slope (no outliers)

b(end) = -5.5;                   % Introduce outlier
acorrupt = x\b;                  % New slope

cvx_begin;         % L1 optimization to reject outlier
    variable aL1;     % aL1 is slope to be optimized
    minimize( norm(aL1*x-b,1) );      % aL1 is robust
cvx_end;
```

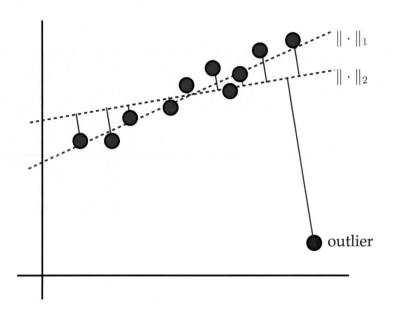

Figure 3.12 Least-squares regression is sensitive to outliers (red), while minimum ℓ_1-norm regression is robust to outliers (blue).

Feature Selection and LASSO Regression

Interpretability is important in statistical models, as these models are often communicated to a non-technical audience, including business leaders and policy makers. Generally, a regression model is more interpretable if it has fewer terms that bear on the outcome, motivating yet another perspective on sparsity.

The least absolute shrinkage and selection operator (LASSO) is an ℓ_1 penalized regression technique that balances model complexity with descriptive capability [518]. This principle of *parsimony* in a model is also a reflection of Occam's razor, stating that among all possible descriptions, the simplest correct model is probably the true one. Since its inception by Tibshirani in 1996 [518], the LASSO has become a cornerstone of statistical modeling, with many modern variants and related techniques [236, 558, 264]. The LASSO is closely related to the earlier nonnegative garrote of Breimen [76], and is also related to earlier work on soft-thresholding by Donoho and Johnstone [153, 154]. LASSO may be thought of as a sparsity-promoting regression that benefits from the stability of the ℓ_2 regularized ridge regression [249], also known as Tikhonov regularization. The elastic net is a frequently used regression technique that combines the ℓ_1 and ℓ_2 penalty terms from LASSO and ridge regression [573]. Sparse regression will be explored in more detail in Chapter 4.

Given a number of observations of the predictors and outcomes of a system, arranged as rows of a matrix $\mathbf{A}$ and a vector $\mathbf{b}$, respectively, regression seeks to find the relationship between the columns of $\mathbf{A}$ that is most consistent with the outcomes in $\mathbf{b}$. Mathematically, this may be written as:

$$\mathbf{Ax} = \mathbf{b}. \tag{3.14}$$

Least-squares regression will tend to result in a vector **x** that has nonzero coefficients for all entries, indicating that *all* columns of **A** must be used to predict **b**. However, we often believe that the statistical model should be *simpler*, indicating that **x** may be sparse. The LASSO adds an ℓ_1 penalty term to *regularize* the least-squares regression problem; i.e., to prevent overfitting:

$$\mathbf{x} = \underset{\mathbf{x}'}{\operatorname{argmin}} \|\mathbf{A}\mathbf{x}' - \mathbf{b}\|_2 + \lambda \|\mathbf{x}\|_1. \tag{3.15}$$

Typically, the parameter λ is varied through a range of values and the fit is *validated* against a test set of holdout data. If there is not enough data to have a sufficiently large training and test set, it is common to repeatedly train and test the model on random selection of the data (often 80 % for training and 20 % for testing), resulting in a *cross-validated* performance. This cross-validation procedure enables the selection of a parsimonious model that has relatively few terms and avoids overfitting.

Many statistical systems are overdetermined, as there are more observations than candidate predictors. Thus, it is not possible to use standard compressed sensing, as measurement noise will guarantee that no exact sparse solution exists that minimizes $\|\mathbf{A}\mathbf{x} - \mathbf{b}\|_2$. However, the LASSO regression works well with overdetermined problems, making it a general regression method. Note that an early version of the geometric picture in Fig. 3.9 to explain the sparsity-promoting nature of the ℓ_1 norm was presented in Tibshirani's 1996 paper [518].

LASSO regression is frequently used to build statistical models for disease, such as cancer and heart failure, since there are many possible predictors, including demographics, lifestyle, biometrics and genetic information. Thus, LASSO represents a clever version of the *kitchen-sink* approach, whereby nearly all possible predictive information is thrown into the mix, and afterwards these are then sifted and sieved through for the truly relevant predictors.

As a simple example, we consider an artificial data set consisting of 100 observations of an outcome, arranged in a vector $\mathbf{b} \in \mathbb{R}^{100}$. Each outcome in **b** is given by a combination of exactly 2 out of 10 candidate predictors, whose observations are arranged in the rows of a matrix $\mathbf{A} \in \mathbb{R}^{100 \times 10}$:

```
A = randn(100,10);      % Matrix of possible predictors
x = [0; 0; 1; 0; 0; 0; -1; 0; 0; 0]; % 2 nonzero predictors
b = A*x + 2*randn(100,1);     % Observations (with noise)
```

The vector **x** is sparse by construction, with only two nonzero entries, and we also add noise to the observations in **b**. The least-squares regression is:

```
>>xL2 = pinv(A)*b

  xL2 =  -0.0232
         -0.3395
          0.9591
         -0.1777
          0.2912
         -0.0525
         -1.2720
         -0.0411
          0.0413
         -0.0500
```

Note that all coefficients are nonzero.

Implementing the LASSO, with 10-fold cross-validation, is a single straightforward command in MATLAB:

```
[XL1 FitInfo] = lasso(A,b,'CV',10);
```

The **lasso** command sweeps through a range of values for λ, and the resulting **x** are each stored as columns of the matrix in **XL1**. To select the most parsimonious model that describes the data while avoiding overfitting, we may plot the cross-validated error as a function of λ, as in Fig. 3.13:

```
lassoPlot(XL1,FitInfo,'PlotType','CV')
```

The green point is at the value of λ that minimizes the cross-validated mean-square error, and the blue point is at the minimum cross-validated error plus one standard deviation. The resulting model is found via **FitInfo.Index1SE**:

```
>> xL1 = XL1(:,FitInfo.Index1SE)

  xL1 =      0
             0
        0.7037
             0
             0
             0
       -0.4929
             0
             0
             0
```

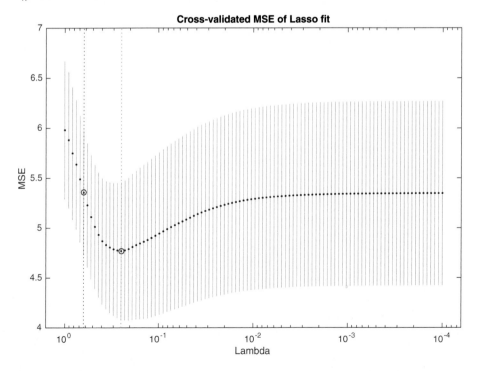

Cross-validated MSE of Lasso fit

Figure 3.13 Output of **lassoPlot** command to visualize cross-validated mean-squared error (MSE) as a function of λ.

Note that the resulting model is sparse and the correct terms are active. However, the regression values for these terms are not accurate, and so it may be necessary to *de-bias* the LASSO by applying a final least-squares regression to the nonzero coefficients identified:

```
>>xL1DeBiased = pinv(A(:,abs(xL1)>0))*b
  xL1DeBiased =   1.0980
                 -1.0671
```

3.6   Sparse Representation

Implicit in our discussion on sparsity is the fact that when high-dimensional signals exhibit low-dimensional structure, they admit a *sparse representation* in an appropriate basis or dictionary. In addition to a signal being sparse in an SVD or Fourier basis, it may also be sparse in an overcomplete dictionary whose columns consist of the training data itself. In essence, in addition to a test signal being sparse in generic feature library $\mathbf{U}$ from the SVD, $\mathbf{X} = \mathbf{U}\boldsymbol{\Sigma}\mathbf{V}^*$, it may also have a sparse representation in the dictionary $\mathbf{X}$.

Wright et al. [560] demonstrated the power of sparse representation in a dictionary of test signals for robust classification of human faces, despite significant noise and occlusions. The so-called sparse representation for classification (SRC) has been widely used in image processing, and more recently to classify dynamical regimes in nonlinear differential equations [98, 433, 191, 308].

The basic schematic of SRC is shown in Fig. 3.14, where a library of images of faces is used to build an overcomplete library $\boldsymbol{\Theta}$. In this example, 30 images are used for each of 20 different people in the Yale B database, resulting in 600 columns in $\boldsymbol{\Theta}$. To use compressed sensing, i.e. ℓ_1-minimization, we need $\boldsymbol{\Theta}$ to be underdetermined, and so we downsample each image from 192×168 to 12×10, so that the flattened images are 120-component vectors. The algorithm used to downsample the images has an impact on the classification accuracy. A new test image $\mathbf{y}$ corresponding to class c, appropriately downsampled to match the columns of $\boldsymbol{\Theta}$, is then sparsely represented as a sum of the columns of $\boldsymbol{\Theta}$ using the compressed sensing algorithm. The resulting vector of coefficients $\mathbf{s}$ should be sparse, and ideally will have large coefficients primarily in the regions of the library corresponding to the correct person in class c. The final classification stage in the algorithm is achieved by computing the ℓ_2 reconstruction error using the coefficients in the $\mathbf{s}$ vector corresponding to each of the categories separately. The category that minimizes the ℓ_2 reconstruction error is chosen for the test image.

Code 3.4 Load Yale faces data and build training and test sets.

```
load ../../CH01_SVD/DATA/allFaces.mat
X = faces;
%% Build Training and Test sets
nTrain = 30;   nTest = 20;   nPeople = 20;
Train = zeros(size(X,1),nTrain*nPeople);
Test = zeros(size(X,1),nTest*nPeople);
for k=1:nPeople
    baseind = 0;
    if(k>1) baseind = sum(nfaces(1:k-1));
    end
    inds = baseind + (1:nfaces(k));
    Train(:,(k-1)*nTrain+1:k*nTrain)=X(:,inds(1:nTrain));
```

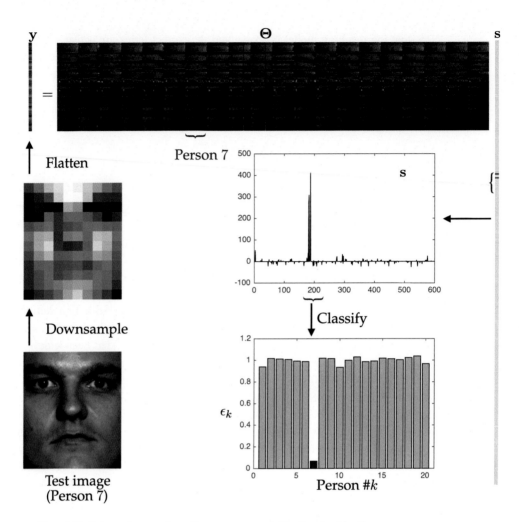

Figure 3.14 Schematic overview of sparse representation for classification.

```
        Test(:,(k-1)*nTest+1:k*nTest)=X(:,inds(nTrain+1:nTrain+nTest
            ));
end
```

Code 3.5 Downsample training images to build Θ library.

```
M = size(Train,2);
Theta = zeros(120,M);
for k=1:M
    temp = reshape(Train(:,k),n,m);
    tempSmall = imresize(temp,[12 10],'lanczos3');
    Theta(:,k) = reshape(tempSmall,120,1);
end
for k=1:M    % Normalize columns of Theta
    Theta(:,k) = Theta(:,k)/norm(Theta(:,k));
end
```

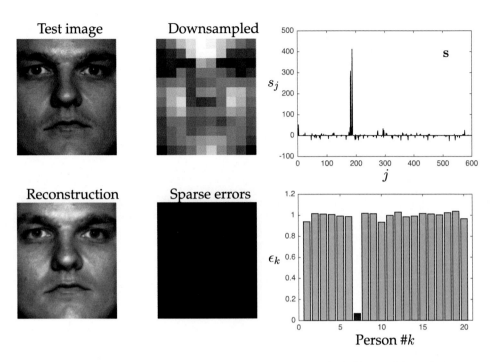

Figure 3.15 Sparse representation for classification demonstrated using a library of faces. A clean test image is correctly identified as the 7*th* person in the library.

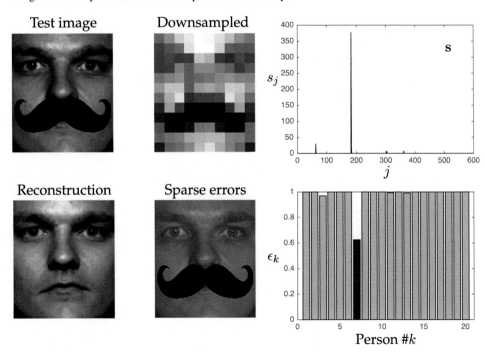

Figure 3.16 Sparse representation for classification demonstrated on example face from person #7 occluded by a fake mustache.

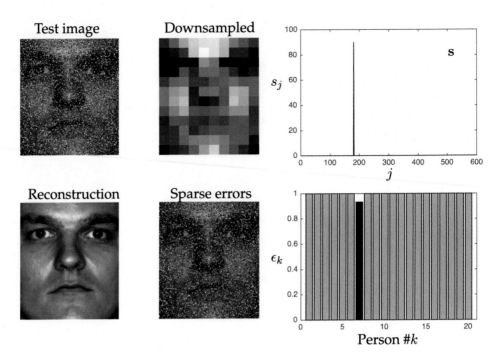

Figure 3.17 Sparse representation for classification demonstrated on example image with 30% occluded pixels (randomly chosen and uniformly distributed).

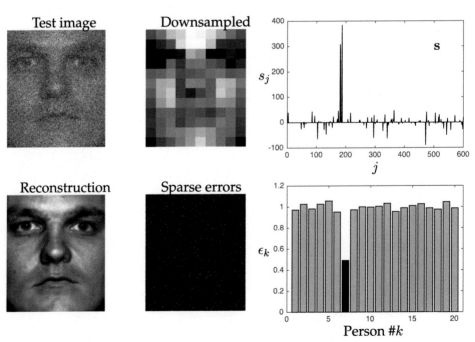

Figure 3.18 Sparse representation for classification demonstrated on example with white noise added to image.

Code 3.6 Build test images and downsample to obtain **y**.

```
x1 = Test(:,126);   % clean image
mustache = double(rgb2gray(imread('mustache.jpg'))/255);
x2 = Test(:,126).*reshape(mustache,n*m,1); % mustache
randvec = randperm(n*m);
first30 = randvec(1:floor(.3*length(randvec)));
vals30 = uint8(255*rand(size(first30)));
x3 = x1;
x3(first30) = vals30; % 30% occluded
x4 = x1 + 50*randn(size(x1));   % random noise

%% DOWNSAMPLE TEST IMAGES
X = [x1 x2 x3 x4];
Y = zeros(120,4);
for k=1:4
    temp = reshape(X(:,k),n,m);
    tempSmall = imresize(temp,[12 10],'lanczos3');
    Y(:,k) = reshape(tempSmall,120,1);
end

%% L1 SEARCH, TESTCLEAN
```

Code 3.7 Search for sparse representation of test image. The same code is used for each of the test images **y**₁ through **y**₄.

```
y1 = Y(:,1);
eps = .01;
cvx_begin;
    variable s1(M);   % sparse vector of coefficients
    minimize( norm(s1,1) );
    subject to
        norm(Theta*s1 - y1,2) < eps;
cvx_end;

plot(s1)
imagesc(reshape(Train*(s1./normTheta'),n,m))
imagesc(reshape(x1-(Train*(s1./normTheta')),n,m))

binErr = zeros(nPeople,1);
for k=1:nPeople
    L = (k-1)*nTrain+1:k*nTrain;
    binErr(k)=norm(x1-(Train(:,L)*(s1(L)./normTheta(L)')))/norm(
        x1)
end
bar(binErr)
```

3.7 Robust Principal Component Analysis (RPCA)

As mentioned earlier in Section 3.5, least-squares regression models are highly susceptible to outliers and corrupted data. Principal component analysis (PCA) suffers from the same weakness, making it *fragile* with respect to outliers. To ameliorate this sensitivity, Candès et al. [110] have developed a robust principal component analysis (RPCA) that seeks to decompose a data matrix **X** into a structured low-rank matrix **L** and a sparse matrix **S** containing outliers and corrupt data:

$$\mathbf{X} = \mathbf{L} + \mathbf{S}. \tag{3.16}$$

The principal components of $\mathbf{L}$ are *robust* to the outliers and corrupt data in $\mathbf{S}$. This decomposition has profound implications for many modern problems of interest, including video surveillance (where the background objects appear in $\mathbf{L}$ and foreground objects appear in $\mathbf{S}$), face recognition (eigenfaces are in $\mathbf{L}$ and shadows, occlusions, etc. are in $\mathbf{S}$), natural language processing and latent semantic indexing, and ranking problems[5].

Mathematically, the goal is to find $\mathbf{L}$ and $\mathbf{S}$ that satisfy the following:

$$\min_{\mathbf{L},\mathbf{S}} \text{rank}(\mathbf{L}) + \|\mathbf{S}\|_0 \text{ subject to } \mathbf{L} + \mathbf{S} = \mathbf{X}. \qquad (3.17)$$

However, neither the rank($\mathbf{L}$) nor the $\|\mathbf{S}\|_0$ terms are convex, and this is not a tractable optimization problem. Similar to the compressed sensing problem, it is possible to solve for the optimal $\mathbf{L}$ and $\mathbf{S}$ with *high probability* using a convex relaxation of (3.17):

$$\min_{\mathbf{L},\mathbf{S}} \|\mathbf{L}\|_* + \lambda\|\mathbf{S}\|_1 \text{ subject to } \mathbf{L} + \mathbf{S} = \mathbf{X}. \qquad (3.18)$$

Here, $\|\cdot\|_*$ denotes the nuclear norm, given by the sum of singular values, which is a proxy for rank. Remarkably, the solution to (3.18) converges to the solution of (3.17) with high probability if $\lambda = 1/\sqrt{\max(n,m)}$, where n and m are the dimensions of $\mathbf{X}$, given that $\mathbf{L}$ and $\mathbf{S}$ satisfy the following conditions:

1. $\mathbf{L}$ is not sparse
2. $\mathbf{S}$ is not low-rank; we assume that the entries are randomly distributed so that they do not have low-dimensional column space.

The convex problem in (3.17) is known as *principal component pursuit* (PCP), and may be solved using the augmented Lagrange multiplier (ALM) algorithm. Specifically, an augmented Lagrangian may be constructed:

$$\mathcal{L}(\mathbf{L},\mathbf{S},\mathbf{Y}) = \|\mathbf{L}\|_* + \lambda\|\mathbf{S}\|_1 + \langle \mathbf{Y}, \mathbf{X} - \mathbf{L} - \mathbf{S}\rangle + \frac{\mu}{2}\|\mathbf{X} - \mathbf{L} - \mathbf{S}\|_F^2. \qquad (3.19)$$

A general solution would solve for the $\mathbf{L}_k$ and $\mathbf{S}_k$ that minimize $\mathcal{L}$, update the Lagrange multipliers $\mathbf{Y}_{k+1} = \mathbf{Y}_k + \mu(\mathbf{X} - \mathbf{L}_k - \mathbf{S}_k)$, and iterate until the solution converges. However, for this specific system, the alternating directions method (ADM) [337, 566] provides a simple procedure to find $\mathbf{L}$ and $\mathbf{S}$.

First, a shrinkage operator $\mathcal{S}_\tau(x) = \text{sign}(x)\max(|x| - \tau, 0)$ is constructed (MATLAB function **shrink** below):

```
function out = shrink(X,tau)
    out = sign(X).*max(abs(X)-tau,0);
end
```

Next, the singular value threshold operator $\text{SVT}_\tau(\mathbf{X}) = \mathbf{U}\mathcal{S}_\tau(\mathbf{\Sigma})\mathbf{V}^*$ is constructed (MATLAB function **SVT** below):

```
function out = SVT(X,tau)
    [U,S,V] = svd(X,'econ');
    out = U*shrink(S,tau)*V';
end
```

---

[5] The ranking problem may be thought of in terms of the Netflix prize for matrix completion. In the Netflix prize, a large matrix of preferences is constructed, with rows corresponding to users and columns corresponding to movies. This matrix is sparse, as most users only rate a handful of movies. The Netflix prize seeks to accurately fill in the missing entries of the matrix, revealing the likely user rating for movies the user has not seen.

Finally, it is possible to use $\mathcal{S}_\tau$ and SVT operators iteratively to solve for **L** and **S**:

Code 3.8 RPCA using alternating directions method (ADM).

```
function [L,S] = RPCA(X)
[n1,n2] = size(X);
mu = n1*n2/(4*sum(abs(X(:))));
lambda = 1/sqrt(max(n1,n2));
thresh = 1e-7*norm(X,'fro');

L = zeros(size(X));
S = zeros(size(X));
Y = zeros(size(X));
count = 0;
while((norm(X-L-S,'fro')>thresh) && (count<1000))
    L = SVT(X-S+(1/mu)*Y,1/mu);
    S = shrink(X-L+(1/mu)*Y,lambda/mu);
    Y = Y + mu*(X-L-S);
    count = count + 1
end
```

This is demonstrated on the eigenface example with the following code:

```
load allFaces.mat
X = faces(:,1:nfaces(1));
[L,S] = RPCA(X);
```

In this example, the original columns of **X**, along with the low-rank and sparse components, are shown in Fig. 3.19. Notice that in this example, RPCA effectively fills in occluded regions of the image, corresponding to shadows. In the low-rank component **L**, shadows are removed and filled in with the most consistent low-rank features from the eigenfaces. This technique can also be used to remove other occlusions such as fake mustaches, sunglasses, or noise.

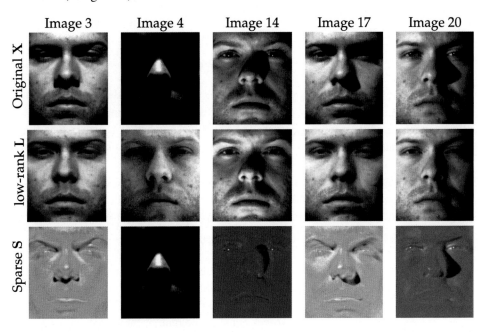

Figure 3.19 Output of RPCA for images in the Yale B database.

3.8   Sparse Sensor Placement

Until now, we have investigated signal reconstruction in a generic basis, such as Fourier or wavelets, with random measurements. This provides considerable flexibility, as no prior structure is assumed, except that the signal is sparse in a known basis. For example, compressed sensing works equally well for reconstructing an image of a mountain, a face, or a cup of coffee. However, if we know that we will be reconstructing a human face, we can dramatically reduce the number of sensors required for reconstruction or classification by optimizing sensors for a particular feature library $\boldsymbol{\Psi}_r = \tilde{\mathbf{U}}$ built from the SVD.

Thus, it is possible to design *tailored* sensors for a particular library, in contrast to the previous approach of random sensors in a generic library. Near-optimal sensor locations may be obtained using fast greedy procedures that scale well with large signal dimension, such as the matrix QR factorization. The following discussion will closely follow Manohar et al. [366] and B. Brunton et al. [89], and the reader is encouraged to find more details there. Similar approaches will be used for efficient sampling of reduced-order models in Chapter 12, where they are termed *hyper-reduction*. There are also extensions of the following for sensor and actuator placement in control [365], based on the balancing transformations discussed in Chapter 9.

Optimizing sensor locations is important for nearly all downstream tasks, including classification, prediction, estimation, modeling, and control. However, identifying optimal locations involves a brute force search through the combinatorial choices of p sensors out of n possible locations in space. Recent greedy and sparse methods are making this search tractable and scalable to large problems. Reducing the number of sensors through principled selection may be critically enabling when sensors are costly, and may also enable faster state estimation for low latency, high bandwidth control.

Sparse Sensor Placement for Reconstruction

The goal of optimized sensor placement in a tailored library $\boldsymbol{\Psi}_r \in \mathbb{R}^{n \times r}$ is to design a sparse measurement matrix $\mathbf{C} \in \mathbb{R}^{p \times n}$, so that inversion of the linear system of equations

$$\mathbf{y} = \mathbf{C}\boldsymbol{\Psi}_r \mathbf{a} = \boldsymbol{\theta}\mathbf{a} \tag{3.20}$$

is as well-conditioned as possible. In other words, we will design $\mathbf{C}$ to minimize the condition number of $\mathbf{C}\boldsymbol{\Psi}_r = \boldsymbol{\theta}$, so that it may be inverted to identify the low-rank coefficients $\mathbf{a}$ given noisy measurements $\mathbf{y}$. The condition number of a matrix $\boldsymbol{\theta}$ is the ratio of its maximum and minimum singular values, indicating how sensitive matrix multiplication or inversion is to errors in the input. Larger condition numbers indicate worse performance inverting a noisy signal. The condition number is a measure of the worst-case error when the signal $\mathbf{a}$ is in the singular vector direction associated with the minimum singular value of $\boldsymbol{\theta}$, and noise is added which is aligned with the maximum singular vector:

$$\boldsymbol{\theta}(\mathbf{a} + \epsilon_{\mathbf{a}}) = \sigma_{\min}\mathbf{a} + \sigma_{\max}\epsilon_{\mathbf{a}}. \tag{3.21}$$

Thus, the signal-to-noise ratio decreases by the condition number after mapping through $\boldsymbol{\theta}$. We therefore seek to minimize the condition number through a principled choice of $\mathbf{C}$. This is shown schematically in Fig. 3.20 for $p = r$.

When the number of sensors is equal to the rank of the library, i.e. $p = r$, then $\boldsymbol{\theta}$ is a square matrix, and we are choosing $\mathbf{C}$ to make this matrix as well-conditioned for inversion

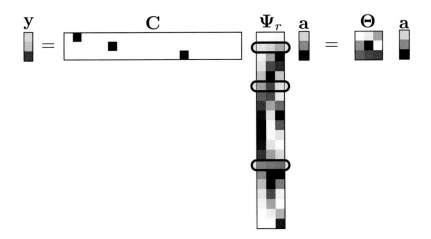

Figure 3.20 Least squares with r sparse sensors provides a unique solution to **a**, hence **x**. *Reproduced with permission from Manohar et al. [366].*

as possible. When $p > r$, we seek to improve the condition of $\mathbf{M} = \boldsymbol{\theta}^T \boldsymbol{\theta}$, which is involved in the pseudo-inverse. It is possible to develop optimization criteria that optimize the minimum singular value, the trace, or the determinant of $\boldsymbol{\theta}$ (resp. $\mathbf{M}$). However, each of these optimization problems is np-hard, requiring a combinatorial search over the possible sensor configurations. Iterative methods exist to solve this problem, such as convex optimization and semidefinite programming [74, 269], although these methods may be expensive, requiring iterative $n \times n$ matrix factorizations. Instead, greedy algorithms are generally used to approximately optimize the sensor placement. These *gappy POD* [179] methods originally relied on random sub-sampling. However, significant performance advances where demonstrated by using principled sampling strategies for reduced order models (ROMs) [53] in fluid dynamics [555] and ocean modeling [565]. More recently, variants of the so-called *empirical interpolation method* (EIM, DEIM and Q-DEIM) [41, 127, 159] have provided near optimal sampling for interpolative reconstruction of nonlinear terms in ROMs.

Random sensors. In general, randomly placed sensors may be used to estimate mode coefficients **a**. However, when $p = r$ and the number of sensors is equal to the number of modes, the condition number is typically very large. In fact, the matrix $\boldsymbol{\Theta}$ is often numerically singular and the condition number is near 10^{16}. Oversampling, as in Sec. 1.8, rapidly improves the condition number, and even $p = r + 10$ usually has much better reconstruction performance.

QR Pivoting for sparse sensors. The greedy matrix QR factorization with column pivoting of $\boldsymbol{\Psi}_r^T$, explored by Drmac and Gugercin [159] for reduced-order modeling, provides a particularly simple and effective sensor optimization. The QR pivoting method is fast, simple to implement, and provides nearly optimal sensors tailored to a specific SVD/POD basis. QR factorization is optimized for most scientific computing libraries, including Matlab, LAPACK, and NumPy. In addition QR can be sped-up by ending the procedure after the first p pivots are obtained.

The reduced matrix QR factorization with column pivoting decomposes a matrix $\mathbf{A} \in \mathbb{R}^{m \times n}$ into a unitary matrix $\mathbf{Q}$, an upper-triangular matrix $\mathbf{R}$ and a column permutation matrix $\mathbf{C}^T$ such that $\mathbf{A}\mathbf{C}^T = \mathbf{Q}\mathbf{R}$. The pivoting procedure provides an approximate greedy solution method to minimize the matrix volume, which is the absolute value of the determinant. QR column pivoting increments the volume of the submatrix constructed from the pivoted columns by selecting a new pivot column with maximal 2-norm, then subtracting from every other column its orthogonal projection onto the pivot column.

Thus QR factorization with column pivoting yields r point sensors (pivots) that best sample the r basis modes $\mathbf{\Psi}_r$

$$\mathbf{\Psi}_r^T \mathbf{C}^T = \mathbf{Q}\mathbf{R}. \tag{3.22}$$

Based on the same principle of pivoted QR, which controls the condition number by minimizing the matrix volume, the oversampled case is handled by the pivoted QR factorization of $\mathbf{\Psi}_r \mathbf{\Psi}_r^T$,

$$(\mathbf{\Psi}_r \mathbf{\Psi}_r^T)\mathbf{C}^T = \mathbf{Q}\mathbf{R}. \tag{3.23}$$

The code for handling both cases is give by

```
if (p==r)      % QR sensor selection, p=r
    [Q,R,pivot] = qr(Psi_r','vector');
elseif (p>r) % Oversampled QR sensors, p>r
    [Q,R,pivot] = qr(Psi_r*Psi_r','vector');
end
C = zeros(p,n);
for j=1:p
    C(j,pivot(j))=1;
end
```

Example: Reconstructing a Face with Sparse Sensors
To demonstrate the concept of signal reconstruction in a tailored basis, we will design optimized sparse sensors in the library of eigenfaces from Section 1.6. Fig. 3.21 shows the QR sensor placement and reconstruction, along with the reconstruction using random sensors. We use $p = 100$ sensors in a $r = 100$ mode library. This code assumes that

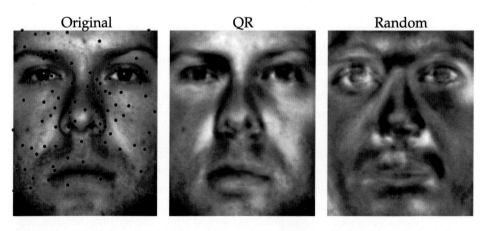

Figure 3.21 (left) Original image and $p = 100$ QR sensors locations in a $r = 100$ mode library. (middle) Reconstruction with QR sensors. (right) Reconstruction with random sensors.

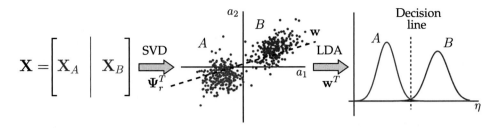

Figure 3.22 Schematic illustrating SVD for feature extraction, followed by LDA for the automatic classification of data into two categories A and B. *Reproduced with permission from Bai et al. [29].*

the faces have been loaded and the singular vectors are in a matrix $\mathbf{U}$. Optimized QR sensors result in a more accurate reconstruction, with about three times less reconstruction error. In addition, the condition number is orders of magnitude smaller than with random sensors. Both QR and random sensors may be improved by oversampling. The following code computes the QR sensors and the approximate reconstruction from these sensors.

```
r = 100; p = 100;   % # of modes r, # of sensors p
Psi = U(:,1:r);
[Q,R,pivot] = qr(Psi','vector');
C = zeros(p,n*m);
for j=1:p
    C(j,pivot(j))=1;
end
%
Theta = C*Psi;
y = faces(pivot(1:p),1);   % Measure at pivot locations
a = Theta\y;               % Estimate coefficients
faceRecon = U(:,1:r)*a;    % Reconstruct face
```

Sparse Classification

For image classification, even fewer sensors may be required than for reconstruction. For example, sparse sensors may be selected that contain the most discriminating information to characterize two categories of data [89]. Given a library of r SVD modes $\mathbf{\Psi}_r$, it is often possible to identify a vector $\mathbf{w} \in \mathbb{R}^r$ in this subspace that maximally distinguishes between two categories of data, as described in Section 5.6 and shown in Fig. 3.22. Sparse sensors $\mathbf{s}$ that map into this discriminating direction, projecting out all other information, are found by:

$$\mathbf{s} = \underset{\mathbf{s}'}{\arg\min} \|\mathbf{s}'\|_1 \quad \text{subject to} \quad \mathbf{\Psi}_r^T \mathbf{s}' = \mathbf{w}. \tag{3.24}$$

This sparse sensor placement optimization for classification (SSPOC) is shown in Fig. 3.23 for an example classifying dogs versus cats. The library $\mathbf{\Psi}_r$ contains the first r *eigenpets* and the vector $\mathbf{w}$ identifies the key differences between dogs and cats. Note that this vector does not care about the degrees of freedom that characterize the various features within the dog or cat clusters, but rather only the differences between the two categories. Optimized sensors are aligned with regions of interest, such as the eyes, nose, mouth, and ears.

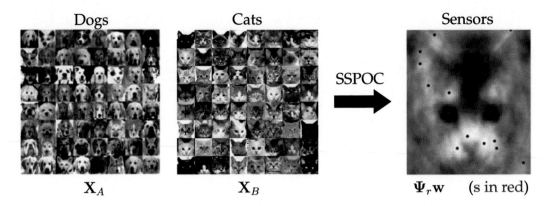

Figure 3.23 Sparse sensor placement optimization for classification (SSPOC) illustrated for optimizing sensors to classify dogs and cats. *Reproduced with permission from B. Brunton et al. [89].*

Suggested Reading
Papers and Reviews

(1) **Regression shrinkage and selection via the lasso**, by R. Tibshirani, *Journal of the Royal Statistical Society B*, 1996 [518].

(2) **Robust uncertainty principles: exact signal reconstruction from highly incomplete frequency information**, by E. J. Candès, J. Romberg, and T. Tao, *IEEE Transactions on Automatic Control*, 2006 [111].

(3) **Compressed sensing**, by D. L. Donoho, *IEEE Transactions on Information Theory*, 2006 [150].

(4) **Compressive sensing**, by R. G. Baraniuk, *IEEE Signal Processing Magazine*, 2007 [39].

(5) **Robust face recognition via sparse representation**, by J. Wright, A. Yang, A. Ganesh, S. Sastry, and Y. Ma, *IEEE Transactions on Pattern Analysis and Machine Intelligence*, 2009 [560].

(6) **Robust principal component analysis?**, by E. J. Candès, X. Li, Y. Ma, and J. Wright, *Journal of the ACM*, 2011 [110].

(7) **Signal recovery from random measurements via orthogonal matching pursuit**, by J. A. Tropp and A. C. Gilbert, *IEEE Transactions on Information Theory*, 2007 [529].

(8) **Data-driven sparse sensor placement**, by K. Manohar, B. W. Brunton, J. N. Kutz, and S. L. Brunton, *IEEE Control Systems Magazine*, 2018 [366].

Part II

Machine Learning and Data Analysis

4 Regression and Model Selection

All of machine learning revolves around optimization. This includes regression and model selection frameworks that aim to provide parsimonious and interpretable models for data [266]. Curve fitting is the most basic of regression techniques, with polynomial and exponential fitting resulting in solutions that come from solving the linear system

$$\mathbf{Ax} = \mathbf{b}. \tag{4.1}$$

When the model is not prescribed, then optimization methods are used to select the best model. This changes the underlying mathematics for function fitting to either an overdetermined or underdetermined optimization problem for linear systems given by:

$$\underset{\mathbf{x}}{\text{argmin}} \left(\|\mathbf{Ax} - \mathbf{b}\|_2 + \lambda g(\mathbf{x}) \right) \qquad \text{or} \tag{4.2a}$$

$$\underset{\mathbf{x}}{\text{argmin}} \, g(\mathbf{x}) \, \text{ subject to } \, \|\mathbf{Ax} - \mathbf{b}\|_2 \leq \epsilon, \tag{4.2b}$$

where $g(\mathbf{x})$ is a given penalization (with penalty parameter λ for overdetermined systems). For over and underdetermined linear systems of equations, which result in either no solutions or an infinite number of solutions of (4.1), a choice of constraint or penalty, which is also known as *regularization*, must be made in order to produce a solution. For instance, one can enforce a solution minimizing the smallest ℓ_2 norm in an underdetermined system so that $\min g(\mathbf{x}) = \min \|\mathbf{x}\|_2$. More generally, when considering regression to nonlinear models, then the overall mathematical framework takes the more general form

$$\underset{\mathbf{x}}{\text{argmin}} \left(f(\mathbf{A}, \mathbf{x}, \mathbf{b}) + \lambda g(\mathbf{x}) \right) \qquad \text{or} \tag{4.3a}$$

$$\underset{\mathbf{x}}{\text{argmin}} \, g(\mathbf{x}) \, \text{ subject to } \, f(\mathbf{A}, \mathbf{x}, \mathbf{b}) \leq \epsilon \tag{4.3b}$$

which are often solved using gradient descent algorithms. Indeed, this general framework is also at the center of deep learning algorithms.

In addition to optimization strategies, a central concern in data science is understanding if a proposed model has over-fit or under-fit the data. Thus *cross-validation* strategies are critical for evaluating any proposed model. Cross-validation will be discussed in detail in what follows, but the main concepts can be understood from Fig. 4.1. A given data set must be partitioned into a training, validation and withhold set. A model is constructed from the training and validation data and finally tested on the withhold set. For over-fitting, increasing the model complexity or training epochs (iterations) improves the error on the training set while leading to increased error on the withhold set. Fig. 4.1(a) shows the canonical behavior of data over-fitting, suggesting that the model complexity and/or training epochs be limited in order to avoid the over-fitting. In contrast, under-fitting limits

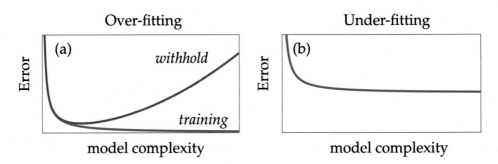

Figure 4.1 Prototypical behavior of over- and under-fitting of data. (a) For over-fitting, increasing the model complexity or training epochs (iterations) leads to improved reduction of error on training data while increasing the error on the withheld data. (b) For under-fitting, the error performance is limited due to restrictions on model complexity. These canonical graphs are ubiquitous in data science and of paramount importance when evaluating a model.

the ability to achieve a good model as shown in Fig. 4.1(b). However, it is not always clear if you are under-fitting or if the model can be improved. Cross-validation is of such paramount importance that it is automatically included in most machine learning algorithms in MATLAB. Importantly, the following mantra holds: *if you don't cross-validate, you is dumb.*

The next few chapters will outline how optimization and cross-validation arise in practice, and will highlight the choices that need to be made in applying meaningful constraints and structure to $g(\mathbf{x})$ so as to achieve interpretable solutions. Indeed, the objective (loss) function $f(\cdot)$ and regularization $g(\cdot)$ are equally important in determining computationally tractable optimization strategies. Often times, proxy loss and regularization functions are chosen in order to achieve approximations to the true objective of the optimization. Such choices depend strongly upon the application area and data under consideration.

4.1   Classic Curve Fitting

Curve fitting is one of the most basic and foundational tools in data science. From our earliest educational experiences in the engineering and physical sciences, least-square polynomial fitting was advocated for understanding the dominant trends in real data. Andrien-Marie Legendre used least-squares as early as 1805 to fit astronomical data [328], with Gauss more fully developing the theory of least squares as an optimization problem in a seminal contribution of 1821 [197]. Curve fitting in such astronomical applications was highly effective given the simple elliptical orbits (quadratic polynomial functions) manifest by planets and comets. Thus one can argue that data science has long been a cornerstone of our scientific efforts. Indeed, it was through Kepler's access to Tycho Brahe's state-of-the art astronomical data that he was able, after eleven years of research, to produce the foundations for the laws of planetary motion, positing the elliptical nature of planetary orbits, which were clearly best-fit solutions to the available data [285].

A broader mathematical viewpoint of curve fitting, which we will advocate throughout this text, is *regression*. Like curve fitting, regression attempts to estimate the relationship among variables using a variety of statistical tools. Specifically, one can consider the general relationship between independent variables $\mathbf{X}$, dependent variables $\mathbf{Y}$, and some unknown parameters $\boldsymbol{\beta}$:

$$\mathbf{Y} = f(\mathbf{X}, \boldsymbol{\beta}) \tag{4.4}$$

where the regression function $f(\cdot)$ is typically prescribed and the parameters $\boldsymbol{\beta}$ are found by optimizing the *goodness-of-fit* of this function to data. In what follows, we will consider curve fitting as a special case of regression. Importantly, regression and curve fitting discover relationships among variables by optimization. Broadly speaking, machine learning is framed around regression techniques, which are themselves framed around optimization based on data. Thus, at its absolute mathematical core, machine learning and data science revolve around positing an optimization problem. Of course, the success of optimization itself depends critically on defining an *objective function* to be optimized.

Least-Squares Fitting Methods

To illustrate the concepts of regression, we will consider classic least-squarespolynomial fitting for characterizing trends in data. The concept is straightforward and simple: use a simple function to describe a trend by minimizing the sum-square error between the selected function $f(\cdot)$ and its fit to the data. As we show here, classical curve fitting is formulated as a simple solution of $\mathbf{Ax} = \mathbf{b}$.

Consider a set of n data points

$$(x_1, y_1), \ (x_2, y_2), \ (x_3, y_3), \ \cdots, (x_n, y_n). \tag{4.5}$$

Further, assume that we would like to find a best fit line through these points. We can approximate the line by the function

$$f(x) = \beta_1 x + \beta_2 \tag{4.6}$$

where the constants β_1 and β_2, which are the parameters of the vector $\boldsymbol{\beta}$ of (4.4), are chosen to minimize some error associated with the fit. The line fit gives the *linear regression* model $\mathbf{Y} = f(\mathbf{A}, \boldsymbol{\beta}) = \beta_1 \mathbf{X} + \beta_2$. Thus the function gives a linear model which approximates the data, with the approximation error at each point given by

$$f(x_k) = y_k + E_k \tag{4.7}$$

where y_k is the true value of the data and E_k is the error of the fit from this value.

Various error metrics can be minimized when approximating with a given function $f(x)$. The choice of error metric, or norm, used to compute a goodness-of-fit will be critical in this chapter. Three standard possibilities are often considered which are associated with the ℓ_2 (least-squares), ℓ_1, and ℓ_∞ norms. These are defined as follows:

$$E_\infty(f) = \max_{1 < k < n} |f(x_k) - y_k| \qquad \text{Maximum Error } (\ell_\infty) \tag{4.8a}$$

$$E_1(f) = \frac{1}{n} \sum_{k=1}^{n} |f(x_k) - y_k| \qquad \text{Mean Absolute Error } (\ell_1) \tag{4.8b}$$

$$E_2(f) = \left(\frac{1}{n} \sum_{k=1}^{n} |f(x_k) - y_k|^2 \right)^{1/2} \qquad \text{Least-squares Error } (\ell_2). \tag{4.8c}$$

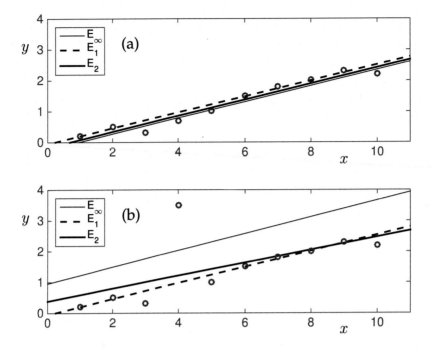

Figure 4.2 Line fits for the three different error metrics E_∞, E_1 and E_2. In (a), the data has not outliers and the three linear models, although different, produce approximately the same model. With outliers, (b) shows that the predictions are significantly different.

Such regression error metrics have been previously considered in Chapter 1, but they will be considered once again here in the framework of model selection. In addition to the above norms, one can more broadly consider the error based on the ℓ_p-norm

$$E_p(f) = \left(\frac{1}{n} \sum_{k=1}^{n} |f(x_k) - y_k|^p \right)^{1/p}. \tag{4.9}$$

For different values of p, the best fit line will be different. In most cases, the differences are small. However, when there are outliers in the data, the choice of norm can have a significant impact.

When fitting a curve to a set of data, the root-mean square (RMS) error (4.8c) is often chosen to be minimized. This is called a *least-squares fit*. Fig. 4.2 depicts three line fits that minimize the errors E_∞, E_1 and E_2 listed previously. The E_∞ error line fit is strongly influenced by the one data point which does not fit the trend. The E_1 and E_2 line fit nicely through the bulk of the data, although their slopes are quite different in comparison to when the data has no outliers. The linear models for these three error metrics are constructed using MATLAB's **fminsearch** command. The code for all three is given as follows:

Code 4.1 Regression for linear fit.

```
% The data
x=[1 2 3 4 5 6 7 8 9 10]
y=[0.2 0.5 0.3 3.5 1.0 1.5 1.8 2.0 2.3 2.2]

p1=fminsearch('fit1',[1 1],[],x,y);
```

```
p2=fminsearch('fit2',[1 1],[],x,y);
p3=fminsearch('fit3',[1 1],[],x,y);

xf=0:0.1:11
y1=polyval(p1,xf); y2=polyval(p2,xf); y3=polyval(p3,xf);

subplot(2,1,2)
plot(xf,y1,'k'), hold on
plot(xf,y2,'k--','Linewidth',[2])
plot(xf,y3,'k','Linewidth',[2])
plot(x,y,'ro','Linewidth',[2]), hold on
```

For each error metric, the computation of the error metrics (4.8) must be computed. The **fminsearch** command requires that the objective function for minimization be given. For the three error metrics considered, this results in the following set of functions for **fminsearch**:

Code 4.2 Maximum error ℓ_∞.

```
function E=fit1(x0,x,y)
E=max(abs( x0(1)*x+x0(2)-y ));
```

Code 4.3 Sum of absolute error ℓ_1.

```
function E=fit2(x0,x,y)
E=sum(abs( x0(1)*x+x0(2)-y ));
```

Code 4.4 Least-squares error ℓ_2.

```
function E=fit3(x0,x,y)
E=sum(abs( x0(1)*x+x0(2)-y ).^2 );
```

Finally, for the outlier data, an additional point is added to the data in order to help illustrate the influence of the error metrics on producing a linear regression model.

Code 4.5 Data which includes an outlier.

```
x=[1 2 3 4 5 6 7 8 9 10]
y=[0.2 0.5 0.3 0.7 1.0 1.5 1.8 2.0 2.3 2.2]
```

Least-Squares Line

Least-squares fitting to linear models has critical advantages over other norms and metrics. Specifically, the optimization is inexpensive, since the error can be computed analytically. To show this explicitly, consider applying the least-square fit criteria to the data points (x_k, y_k) where $k = 1, 2, 3, \cdots, n$. To fit the curve

$$f(x) = \beta_1 x + \beta_2 \tag{4.10}$$

to this data, the error E_2 is found by minimizing the sum

$$E_2(f) = \sum_{k=1}^{n} |f(x_k) - y_k|^2 = \sum_{k=1}^{n} (\beta_1 x_k + \beta_2 - y_k)^2. \tag{4.11}$$

Minimizing this sum requires differentiation. Specifically, the constants β_1 and β_2 are chosen so that a minimum occurs. Thus we require: $\partial E_2/\partial \beta_1 = 0$ and $\partial E_2/\partial \beta_2 = 0$. Note that although a zero derivative can indicate either a minimum or maximum, we know this must be a minimum of the error since there is no maximum error, i.e. we can always choose a line that has a larger error. The minimization condition gives:

$$\frac{\partial E_2}{\partial \beta_1} = 0: \quad \sum_{k=1}^{n} 2(\beta_1 x_k + \beta_2 - y_k) x_k = 0 \tag{4.12a}$$

$$\frac{\partial E_2}{\partial \beta_2} = 0: \quad \sum_{k=1}^{n} 2(\beta_1 x_k + \beta_2 - y_k) = 0. \tag{4.12b}$$

Upon rearranging, a 2×2 system of linear equations is found for A and B

$$\left(\begin{array}{cc} \sum_{k=1}^{n} x_k^2 & \sum_{k=1}^{n} x_k \\ \sum_{k=1}^{n} x_k & n \end{array} \right) \left(\begin{array}{c} \beta_1 \\ \beta_2 \end{array} \right) = \left(\begin{array}{c} \sum_{k=1}^{n} x_k y_k \\ \sum_{k=1}^{n} y_k \end{array} \right) \quad \longrightarrow \quad \mathbf{Ax} = \mathbf{b}. \tag{4.13}$$

This linear system of equations can be solved using the backslash command in MATLAB. Thus an optimization procedure is unnecessary since the solution is computed exactly from a 2×2 matrix.

This method can be easily generalized to higher polynomial fits. In particular, a parabolic fit to a set of data requires the fitting function

$$f(x) = \beta_1 x^2 + \beta_2 x + \beta_3 \tag{4.14}$$

where now the three constants β_1, β_2, and β_3 must be found. These can be solved for with the 3×3 system resulting from minimizing the error $E_2(\beta_1, \beta_2, \beta_3)$ by taking

$$\frac{\partial E_2}{\partial \beta_1} = 0 \tag{4.15a}$$

$$\frac{\partial E_2}{\partial \beta_2} = 0 \tag{4.15b}$$

$$\frac{\partial E_2}{\partial \beta_3} = 0. \tag{4.15c}$$

In fact, any polynomial fit of degree k will yield a $(k + 1) \times (k + 1)$ linear system of equations $\mathbf{Ax} = \mathbf{b}$ whose solution can be found.

Data Linearization
Although a powerful method, the minimization procedure for general fitting of arbitrary functions results in equations which are nontrivial to solve. Specifically, consider fitting data to the exponential function

$$f(x) = \beta_2 \exp(\beta_1 x). \tag{4.16}$$

The error to be minimized is

$$E_2(\beta_1, \beta_2) = \sum_{k=1}^{n} (\beta_2 \exp(\beta_1 x_k) - y_k)^2. \tag{4.17}$$

Applying the minimizing conditions leads to

$$\frac{\partial E_2}{\partial \beta_1} = 0: \quad \sum_{k=1}^{n} 2(\beta_2 \exp(\beta_1 x_k) - y_k)\beta_2 x_k \exp(\beta_1 x_k) = 0 \tag{4.18a}$$

$$\frac{\partial E_2}{\partial \beta_2} = 0 : \quad \sum_{k=1}^{n} 2(\beta_2 \exp(\beta_1 x_k) - y_k) \exp(\beta_1 x_k) = 0. \quad (4.18b)$$

This in turn leads to the 2×2 system

$$\beta_2 \sum_{k=1}^{n} x_k \exp(2\beta_1 x_k) - \sum_{k=1}^{n} x_k y_k \exp(\beta_1 x_k) = 0 \quad (4.19a)$$

$$\beta_2 \sum_{k=1}^{n} \exp(2\beta_1 x_k) - \sum_{k=1}^{n} y_k \exp(\beta_1 x_k) = 0. \quad (4.19b)$$

This system of equations is nonlinear and cannot be solved in a straightforward fashion. Indeed, a solution may not even exist. Or many solution may exist. Section 4.2 describes a possible iterative procedure, called gradient descent, for solving this nonlinear system of equations.

To avoid the difficulty of solving this nonlinear system, the exponential fit can be *linearized* by the transformation

$$Y = \ln(y) \quad (4.20a)$$
$$X = x \quad (4.20b)$$
$$\beta_3 = \ln \beta_2. \quad (4.20c)$$

Then the fit function

$$f(x) = y = \beta_2 \exp(\beta_1 x) \quad (4.21)$$

can be linearized by taking the natural log of both sides so that

$$\ln y = \ln(\beta_2 \exp(\beta_1 x)) = \ln \beta_2 + \ln(\exp(\beta_1 x)) = \beta_3 + \beta_1 x \implies Y = \beta_1 X + \beta_3. \quad (4.22)$$

By fitting to the natural log of the y-data

$$(x_i, y_i) \rightarrow (x_i, \ln y_i) = (X_i, Y_i) \quad (4.23)$$

the curve fit for the exponential function becomes a linear fitting problem which is easily handled. Thus, if a transform exists that linearizes the data, then standard polynomial fitting methods can be used to solve the resulting linear system $\mathbf{Ax} = \mathbf{b}$.

4.2 Nonlinear Regression and Gradient Descent

Polynomial and exponential curve fitting admit analytically tractable, best-fit least-squares solutions. However, such curve fits are highly specialized and a more general mathematical framework is necessary for solving a broader set of problems. For instance, one may wish to fit a nonlinear function of the form $f(x) = \beta_1 \cos(\beta_2 x + \beta_3) + \beta_4$ to a data set. Instead of solving a linear system of equations, general nonlinear curve fitting leads to a system of nonlinear equations. The general theory of nonlinear regression assumes that the fitting function takes the general form

$$f(x) = f(x, \boldsymbol{\beta}) \quad (4.24)$$

where the $m < n$ fitting coefficients $\boldsymbol{\beta} \in \mathbb{R}^m$ are used to minimize the error. The root-mean square error is then defined as

$$E_2(\boldsymbol{\beta}) = \sum_{k=1}^{n}(f(x_k, \boldsymbol{\beta}) - y_k)^2 \tag{4.25}$$

which can be minimized by considering the $m \times m$ system generated from minimizing with respect to each parameter β_j

$$\frac{\partial E_2}{\partial \beta_j} = 0 \quad j = 1, 2, \cdots, m. \tag{4.26}$$

In general, this gives the *nonlinear* set of equations

$$\sum_{k=1}^{n}(f(x_k, \boldsymbol{\beta}) - y_k)\frac{\partial f}{\partial \beta_j} = 0 \quad j = 1, 2, 3, \cdots, m. \tag{4.27}$$

There are no general methods available for solving such nonlinear systems. Indeed, nonlinear systems can have no solutions, several solutions, or even an infinite number of solutions. Most attempts at solving nonlinear systems are based on iterative schemes which require a good initial guesse to converge to the global minimum error. Regardless, the general fitting procedure is straightforward and allows for the construction of a best fit curve to match the data. In such a solution procedure, it is imperative that a reasonable initial guess be provided for by the user. Otherwise, rapid convergence to the desired root may not be achieved.

Fig. 4.3 shows two example functions to be minimized. The first is a convex function (Fig. 4.3(a)). Convex functions are ideal in that guarantees of convergence exist for many algorithms, and gradient descent can be tuned to perform exceptionally well for such functions. The second illustrates a nonconvex function and shows many of the typical problems associated with gradient descent, including the fact that the function has multiple local minima as well as flat regions where gradients are difficult to actually compute, i.e. the gradient is near zero. Optimizing this nonconvex function requires a good guess for the initial conditions of the gradient descent algorithm, although there are many advances

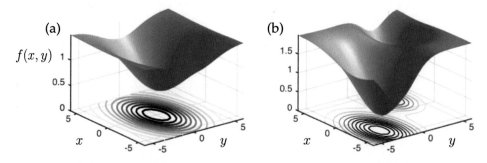

Figure 4.3 Two objective function landscapes representing (a) a convex function and (b) a nonconvex function. Convex functions have many guarantees of convergence, while nonconvex functions have a variety of pitfalls that can limit the success of gradient descent. For nonconvex functions, local minima and an inability to compute gradient directions (derivatives that are near zero) make it challenging for optimization.

around gradient descent for restarting and ensuring that one is not stuck in a local minima. Recent training algorithms for deep neural networks have greatly advanced gradient descent innovations. This will be further considered in Chapter 6 on neural networks.

Gradient Descent

For high-dimensional systems, we generalize the concept of a minimum or maximum, i.e. an extremum of a multi-dimensional function $f(\mathbf{x})$. At an extremum, the gradient must be zero, so that

$$\nabla f(\mathbf{x}) = \mathbf{0}. \tag{4.28}$$

Since saddles exist in higher-dimensional spaces, one must test if the extremum point is a minimum or maximum. The idea behind gradient descent, or steepest descent, is to use the derivative information as the basis of an iterative algorithm that progressively converges to a local minimum point of $f(\mathbf{x})$.

To illustrate how to proceed in practice, consider the simple two-dimensional surface

$$f(x, y) = x^2 + 3y^2 \tag{4.29}$$

which has a single minimum located at the origin $(x, y) = 0$. The gradient for this function is

$$\nabla f(\mathbf{x}) = \frac{\partial f}{\partial x}\hat{\mathbf{x}} + \frac{\partial f}{\partial y}\hat{\mathbf{y}} = 2x\hat{\mathbf{x}} + 6y\hat{\mathbf{y}} \tag{4.30}$$

where $\hat{\mathbf{x}}$ and $\hat{\mathbf{y}}$ are unit vectors in the x and y directions, respectively.

Fig. 4.4 illustrates the gradient steepest descent algorithm. At the initial guess point, the gradient $\nabla f(\mathbf{x})$ is computed. This gives the direction of steepest descent towards the minimum point of $f(\mathbf{x})$, i.e. the minimum is located in the direction given by $-\nabla f(\mathbf{x})$. Note that the gradient does not point at the minimum, but rather gives the locally steepest path for minimizing $f(\mathbf{x})$. The geometry of the steepest descent suggests the construction of an algorithm whereby the next point in the iteration is picked by following the steepest descent so that

$$\mathbf{x}_{k+1}(\delta) = \mathbf{x}_k - \delta \nabla f(\mathbf{x}_k) \tag{4.31}$$

where the parameter δ dictates how far to move along the gradient descent curve. This formula represents a generalization of a Newton method where the derivative is used to compute an update in the iteration scheme. In gradient descent, it is crucial to determine how much to step forward according to the computed gradient, so that the algorithm is always is *going downhill* in an optimal way. This requires the determination of the correct value of δ in the algorithm.

To compute the value of δ, consider the construction of a new function

$$F(\delta) = f(\mathbf{x}_{k+1}(\delta)) \tag{4.32}$$

which must be minimized now as a function of δ. This is accomplished by computing $\partial F/\partial \delta = 0$. Thus one finds

$$\frac{\partial F}{\partial \delta} = -\nabla f(\mathbf{x}_{k+1})\nabla f(\mathbf{x}_k) = 0. \tag{4.33}$$

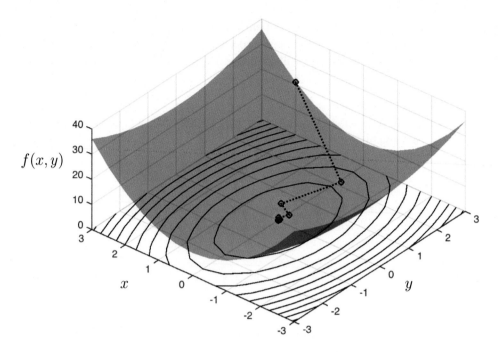

Figure 4.4 Gradient descent algorithm applied to the function $f(x, y) = x^2 + 3y^2$. In the top panel, the contours are plotted for each successive value (x, y) in the iteration algorithm given the initial guess $(x, y) = (3, 2)$. Note the orthogonality of each successive gradient in the steepest descent algorithm. The bottom panel demonstrates the rapid convergence and error (E) to the minimum (optimal) solution.

The geometrical interpretation of this result is the following: $\nabla f(\mathbf{x}_k)$ is the gradient direction of the current iteration point and $\nabla f(\mathbf{x}_{k+1})$ is the gradient direction of the future point, thus δ is chosen so that the two gradient directions are orthogonal.

For the example given above with $f(x, y) = x^2 + 3y^2$, we can compute this conditions as follows:

$$\mathbf{x}_{k+1} = \mathbf{x}_k - \delta \nabla f(\mathbf{x}_k) = (1 - 2\delta)x\, \hat{\mathbf{x}} + (1 - 6\delta)y\, \hat{\mathbf{y}}. \tag{4.34}$$

This expression is used to compute

$$F(\delta) = f(\mathbf{x}_{k+1}(\delta)) = (1 - 2\delta)^2 x^2 + 3(1 - 6\delta)^2 y^2 \tag{4.35}$$

whereby its derivative with respect to δ gives

$$F'(\delta) = -4(1 - 2\delta)x^2 - 36(1 - 6\delta)y^2. \tag{4.36}$$

Setting $F'(\delta) = 0$ then gives

$$\delta = \frac{x^2 + 9y^2}{2x^2 + 54y^2} \tag{4.37}$$

as the optimal descent step length. Note that the length of δ is updated as the algorithm progresses. This gives us all the information necessary to perform the steepest descent search for the minimum of the given function.

Code 4.6 Gradient descent example.

```
x(1)=3; y(1)=2; % initial guess
f(1)=x(1)^2+3*y(1)^2; % initial function value
for j=1:10
    del=(x(j)^2 +9*y(j)^2)/(2*x(j)^2 + 54*y(j)^2);
    x(j+1)=(1-2*del)*x(j); % update values
    y(j+1)=(1-6*del)*y(j);
    f(j+1)=x(j+1)^2+3*y(j+1)^2;

    if abs(f(j+1)-f(j))<10^(-6) % check convergence
        break
    end
end
```

As is clearly evident, this descent search algorithm based on derivative information is similar to Newton's method for root finding both in one-dimension as well as higher-dimensions. Fig. 4.4 shows the rapid convergence to the minimum for this convex function. Moreover, the gradient descent algorithm is the core algorithm of advanced iterative solvers such as the bi-conjugate gradient descent method (**bicgstab**) and the generalized method of residuals (**gmres**) [220].

In the example above, the gradient could be computed analytically. More generally, given just data itself, the gradient can be computed with numerical algorithms. The **gradient** command can be used to compute local or global gradients. Fig. 4.5 shows the gradient terms $\partial f/\partial x$ and $\partial f/\partial y$ for the two functions shown in Fig. 4.3. The code used to produce these critical terms for the gradient descent algorithm is given by

```
[dfx,dfy]=gradient(f,dx,dy);
```

where the function $f(x, y)$ is a two-dimensional function computed from a known function or directly from data. The output are matrices containing the values of $\partial f/\partial x$ and $\partial f/\partial y$ over the discretized domain. The gradient can then be used to approximate either local or global gradients to execute the gradient descent. The following code, whose results are shown in Fig. 4.6, uses the **interp2** function to extract the values of the function and gradient of the function in Fig. 4.3(b).

Code 4.7 Gradient descent example using interpolation.

```
x(1)=x0(jj); y(1)=y0(jj);
f(1)=interp2(X,Y,F,x(1),y(1));
dfx=interp2(X,Y,dFx,x(1),y(1));
dfy=interp2(X,Y,dFy,x(1),y(1));

for j=1:10
    del=fminsearch('delsearch',0.2,[],x(end),y(end),dfx,dfy,X,Y,
        F); % optimal tau
    x(j+1)=x(j)-del*dfx; % update x, y, and f
    y(j+1)=y(j)-del*dfy;
    f(j+1)=interp2(X,Y,F,x(j+1),y(j+1));
    dfx=interp2(X,Y,dFx,x(j+1),y(j+1));
    dfy=interp2(X,Y,dFy,x(j+1),y(j+1));

    if abs(f(j+1)-f(j))<10^(-6) % check convergence
        break
    end
end
```

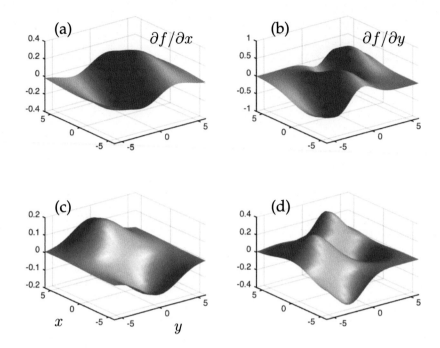

Figure 4.5 Computation of the gradient for the two functions illustrated in Fig. 4.3. In the left panels, the gradient terms (a) $\partial f/\partial x$ and (c) $\partial f/\partial y$ are computed for Fig. 4.3(a), while the right panels compute these same terms for Fig. 4.3(b) in (b) and (d), respectively. The **gradient** command numerically generates the gradient.

In this code, the **fminsearch** command is used to find the correct value of δ. The function to optimize the size of the iterative step is given by

```
function mindel=delsearch(del,x,y,dfx,dfy,X,Y,F)
x0=x-del*dfx;
y0=y-del*dfy;
mindel=interp2(X,Y,F,x0,y0);
```

This discussion provides a rudimentary introduction to gradient descent. A wide range of innovations have attempted to speed up this dominant nonlinear optimization procedure, including alternating descent methods. Some of these will be discussed further in the neural network chapter where gradient descent plays a critical role in training a network. For now, one can see that there are a number of issues for this nonlinear optimization procedure including determining the initial guess, step size δ, and computing the gradient efficiently.

Alternating Descent
Another common technique for optimizing nonlinear functions of several variables is the *alternating descent method* (ADM). Instead of computing the gradient in several variables, optimization is done iteratively in one variable at a time. For the example just demonstrated, this would make the computation of the gradient unnecessary. The basic strategy is simple: optimize along one variable at a time, seeking the minimum while holding all other variables fixed. After passing through each variable once, the process is repeated until a desired convergence is reached. The following code shows a portion of the iteration

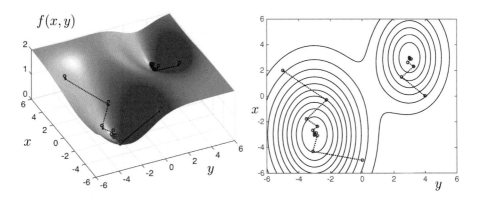

Figure 4.6 Gradient descent applied to the function featured in Fig. 4.3(b). Three initial conditions are shown: $(x_0, y_0) = \{(4, 0), (0, -5), (-5, 2)\}$. The first of these (red circles) gets stuck in a local minima while the other two initial conditions (blue and magenta) find the global minima. Interpolation of the gradient functions of Fig. 4.5 are used to update the solutions.

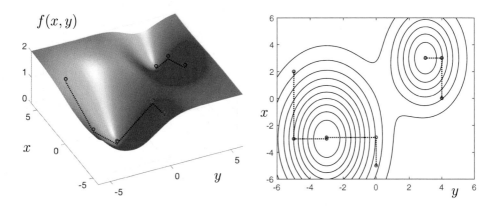

Figure 4.7 Alternating descent applied to the function in Fig. 4.3(b). Three initial conditions are shown: $(x_0, y_0) = \{(4, 0), (0, -5), (-5, 2)\}$. The first of these (red circles) gets stuck in a local minima while the other two initial conditions (blue and magenta) find the global minima. No gradients are computed to update the solution. Note the rapid convergence in comparison with Fig. 4.6.

procedure for the example of Fig. 4.6. This replaces the gradient computation to produce an iterative update.

Code 4.8 Alternating descent algorithm for updating solution.

```
fx=interp2(X,Y,F,xa(1),y); xa(2)=xa(1); [~,ind]=min(fx); ya(2)=y
    (ind);
fy=interp2(X,Y,F,x,ya(2)); ya(3)=ya(2); [~,ind]=min(fy); xa(3)=x
    (ind);
```

Note that the alternating descent only requires a line search along one variable at a time, thus potentially speeding up computations. Moreover, the method is derivative free, which is attractive in many applications.

4.3   Regression and Ax = b: Over- and Under-Determined Systems

Curve fitting, as shown in the previous two sections, results in a optimization problem. In many cases, the optimization can be mathematically framed as solving the linear system of equations $\mathbf{Ax} = \mathbf{b}$. Before proceeding to discuss model selection and the various optimization methods available for this problem, it is instructive to consider that in many circumstances in modern data science, the linear system $\mathbf{Ax} = \mathbf{b}$ is typically massively over- or under-determined. Over-determined systems have more constraints (equations) than unknown variables while under-determined systems have more unknowns than constraints. Thus in the former case, there are generally no solutions satisfying the linear system, and instead, approximate solutions are found to minimize a given error. In the latter case, there are an infinite number of solutions, and some choice of constraint must be made in order to select an appropriate and unique solution. The goal of this section is to highlight two different norms (ℓ_2 and ℓ_1) used for optimization that are used to solve $\mathbf{Ax} = \mathbf{b}$ for over- and under-determined systems. The choice of norm has a profound impact on the optimal solution achieved.

Before proceeding further, it should be noted that the system $\mathbf{Ax} = \mathbf{b}$ considered here is a restricted instance of $\mathbf{Y} = f(\mathbf{X}, \boldsymbol{\beta})$ in (4.4). Thus the solution $\mathbf{x}$ contains the *loadings* or *leverage scores* relating the relationship between the input data $\mathbf{A}$ and outcome data $\mathbf{b}$. A simple solution for this linear problem uses the Moose-Penrose pseudo inverse $\mathbf{A}^\dagger$ from Sec. 1.4:

$$\mathbf{x} = \mathbf{A}^\dagger \mathbf{b}. \tag{4.38}$$

This operator is computed with the **pinv(A)** command in MATLAB. However, such a solution is restrictive, and a greater degree of flexibility is sought for computing solutions. Our particular aim in this section is to demonstrate the interplay in solving over- and under-determined systems using the ℓ_1 and ℓ_2 norms.

Over-Determined Systems

Fig. 4.8 shows the general structure of an over-determined system. As already stated, there are generally no solutions that satisfy $\mathbf{Ax} = \mathbf{b}$. Thus, the optimization problem to be solved involves minimizing the error, for example the least-squares ℓ_2 error E_2, by finding an appropriate value of $\hat{\mathbf{x}}$:

$$\hat{\mathbf{x}} = \underset{\mathbf{x}}{\text{argmin}} \, \|\mathbf{Ax} - \mathbf{b}\|_2. \tag{4.39}$$

This basic architecture does not explicitly enforce any constraints on the loadings $\mathbf{x}$. In order to both minimize the error and enforce a constraint on the solution, the basic optimization architecture can be modified to the following

$$\hat{\mathbf{x}} = \underset{\mathbf{x}}{\text{argmin}} \, \|\mathbf{Ax} - \mathbf{b}\|_2 + \lambda_1 \|\mathbf{x}\|_1 + \lambda_2 \|\mathbf{x}\|_2 \tag{4.40}$$

where the parameters λ_1 and λ_2 control the penalization of the ℓ_1 and ℓ_2 norms, respectively. This now explicitly enforces a constraint on the solution vector itself, not just the error. The ability to design the penalty by adding regularizing constraints is critical for understanding *model selection* in the following.

In the examples that follow, a particular focus will be given to the role of the ℓ_1 norm. The ℓ_1 norm, as already shown in Chapter 3, promotes sparsity so that many of the loadings

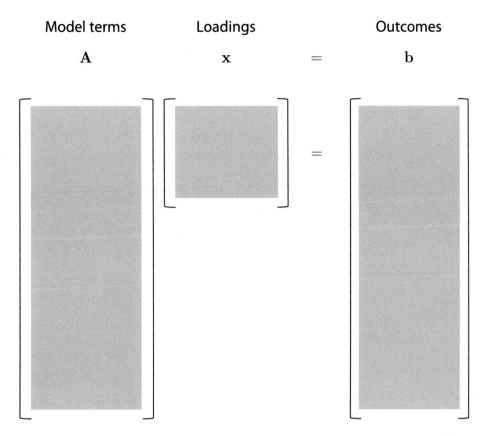

Figure 4.8 Regression framework for overdetermined systems. In this case, $\mathbf{Ax} = \mathbf{b}$ cannot be satisfied in general. Thus, finding solutions for this system involves minimizing, for instance, the least-square error $\|\mathbf{Ax} - \mathbf{b}\|_2$ subject to a constraint on the solution $\mathbf{x}$, such as minimizing the ℓ_2 norm $\|\mathbf{x}\|_2$.

of the solution $\mathbf{x}$ are zero. This will play an important role in variable and model selection in the next section. For now, consider solving the optimization problem (4.40) with $\lambda_2 = 0$. We use the open-source convex optimization package **cvx** in MATLAB [218], to compute our solution to (4.40). The following code considers various values of the ℓ_1 penalization in producing solutions to an over-determined systems with 500 constraints and 100 unknowns.

Code 4.9 Solutions for an over-determined system.

```
n=500; m=100;
A=rand(n,m);
b=rand(n,1);
xdag=pinv(A)*b;

lam=[0 0.1 0.5];
for j=1:3

    cvx_begin;
    variable x(m)
    minimize( norm(A*x-b,2) + lam(j)*norm(x,1) );
    cvx_end;
```

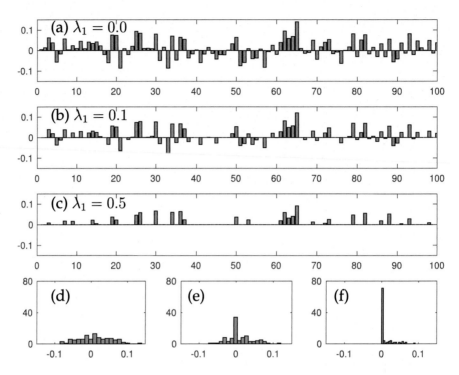

Figure 4.9 Solutions to an overdetermined system with 500 constraints and 100 unknowns. Panels (a)-(c) show a bar plot of the values of the loadings of the vectors **x**. Note that as the ℓ_1 penalty is increased from (a) $\lambda_1 = 0$ to (b) $\lambda_1 = 0.1$ to (c) $\lambda_1 = 0.5$, the number of zero elements of the vector increases, i.e. it becomes more sparse. A histogram of the loading values for (a)-(c) is shown in the panels (d)-(f), respectively. This highlights the role that the ℓ_1 norm plays in promoting sparsity in the solution.

```
    subplot(4,1,j),bar(x)
    subplot(4,3,9+j), hist(x,20)
end
```

Fig. 4.9 highlights the results of the optimization process as a function of the parameter λ_1. It should be noted that the solution with $\lambda_1 = 0$ is equivalent to the solution **xdag** produced by computing the pseudo-inverse of the matrix **A**. Note that the ℓ_1 norm promotes a sparse solution where many of the components of the solution vector **x** are zero. The histograms of the solution values of **x** in Fig. 4.9(d)-(f) are particularly revealing as they show the sparsification process for increasing λ_1.

The regression for over-determined systems can be generalized to matrix systems as shown in Fig. 4.8. In this case, the **cvx** command structure simply modifies the size of the matrix **b** and solution matrix **x**. Consider the two solutions of an over-determined system generated from the following code.

Code 4.10 Solutions for over-determined matrix system.

```
n=300; m=60; p=20;
A=rand(n,m); b=rand(n,p);

lam=[0 0.1];
```

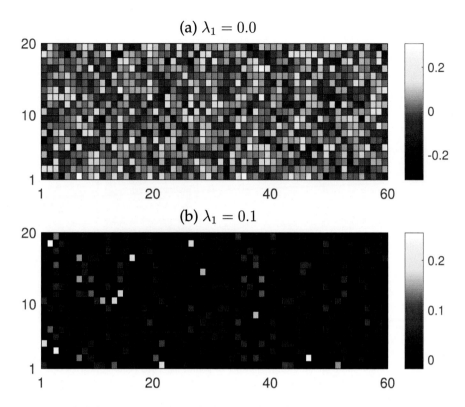

Figure 4.10 Solutions to an overdetermined system $\mathbf{Ax} = \mathbf{b}$ with 300 constraints and 60×20 unknowns. Panels (a) and (b) show a plot of the values of the loadings of the matrix $\mathbf{x}$ with ℓ_1 penalty (a) $\lambda_1 = 0$ to (b) $\lambda_1 = 0.1$.

```
for j=1:2
    cvx_begin;
    variable x(m,p)
    minimize(norm(A*x-b,2) + lam(j)*norm(x,1));
    cvx_end;
    subplot(2,1,j), pcolor(x.'), colormap(hot), colorbar
end
```

Fig. 4.10 shows the results of this matrix over-determined systems for two different values of the added ℓ_1 penalty. Note that the addition of the ℓ_1 norm sparsifies the solution and produces a matrix which is dominated by zero entries. The two examples in Figs. 4.9 and 4.10 show the important role that the ℓ_2 and ℓ_1 norms have in generating different types of solutions. In the following sections of this book, these norms will be exploited to produce parsimonious models from data.

Under-Determined Systems

For undetermined systems, there are an infinite number of possible solutions satisfying $\mathbf{Ax} = \mathbf{b}$. The goal in this case is to impose an additional constraint, or set of constraints, whereby a unique solution is generated from the infinite possibilities. The basic mathemati-

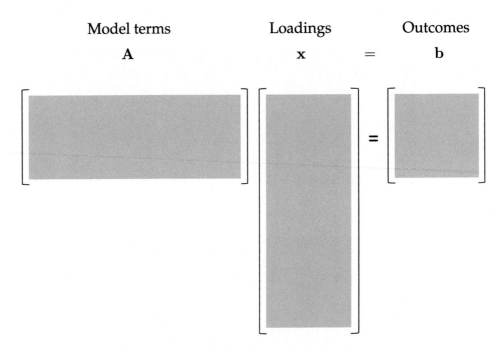

Model terms   Loadings   Outcomes

Figure 4.11 Regression framework for underdetermined systems. In this case, $\mathbf{Ax} = \mathbf{b}$ can be satisfied. In fact, there are an infinite number of solutions. Thus pinning down a unique solution for this system involves minimizing a constraint. For instance, from an infinite number of solutions, we choose the one that minimizes the ℓ_2 norm $\|\mathbf{x}\|_2$, which is subject to the constraint $\mathbf{Ax} = \mathbf{b}$.

cal structure is shown in Fig. 4.11. As an optimization, the solution to the under-determined system can be stated as

$$\min \|\mathbf{x}\|_p \text{ subject to } \mathbf{Ax} = \mathbf{b} \qquad (4.41)$$

where the p denotes the p-norm of the vector $\mathbf{x}$. For simplicity, we consider the ℓ_2 and ℓ_1 norms only. As has already been shown for over-determined systems, the ℓ_1 norm promotes sparsity of the solution.

We again use the convex optimization package **cvx** to compute our solution to (4.41). The following code considers both ℓ_2 and ℓ_1 penalization in producing solutions to an under-determined systems with 20 constraints and 100 unknowns.

Code 4.11 Solutions for an under-determined matrix systems.

```
n=20; m=100
A=rand(n,m); b=rand(n,1);

cvx_begin;
variable x2(m)
minimize( norm(x2,2) );
subject to
A*x2 == b;
cvx_end;

cvx_begin;
variable x1(m)
minimize( norm(x1,1) );
```

```
subject to
A*x1 == b;
cvx_end;
```

This code produces two solution vectors **x2** and **x1** which minimize the ℓ_2 and ℓ_1 norm respectively. Note the way that **cvx** allows one to impose constraints in the optimization routine. Fig. 4.12 shows a bar plot and histogram of the two solutions produced. As before, the sparsity promoting ℓ_1 norm yields a solution vector dominated be zeros. In fact, for this case, there are exactly 80 zeros for this linear system since there are only 20 constraints for the 100 unknowns.

As with the over-determined system, the optimization can be modified to handle more general under-determined matrix equations as shown in Fig. 4.11. The **cvx** optimization package may be used for this case as before with over-determined systems. The software engine can also work with more general p-norms as well as minimize with both ℓ_1 an ℓ_2 penalties simultaneously. For instance, a common optimization modifies (4.41) to the following

$$\min \left(\lambda_1 \|\mathbf{x}\|_1 + \lambda_2 \|\mathbf{x}\|_2 \right) \quad \text{subject to} \quad \mathbf{Ax} = \mathbf{b} \tag{4.42}$$

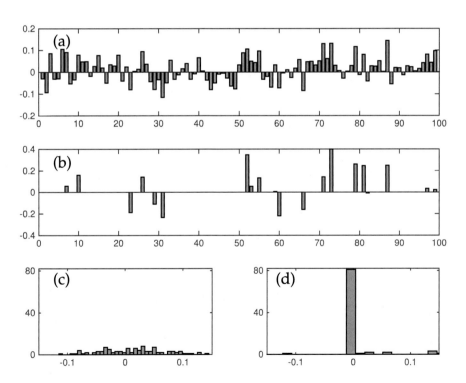

Figure 4.12 Solutions to an under-determined system with 20 constraints and 100 unknowns. Panels (a) and (b) show a bar plot of the values of the loadings of the vectors **x**. In the former panel, the optimization is subject to minimizing the ℓ_2 norm of the solution, while the latter panel is subject to minimizing the ℓ_1 norm. Note that the ℓ_1 penalization produces a sparse solution vector. A histogram of the loading values for (a) and (b) is shown in the panels (c) and (d) respectively.

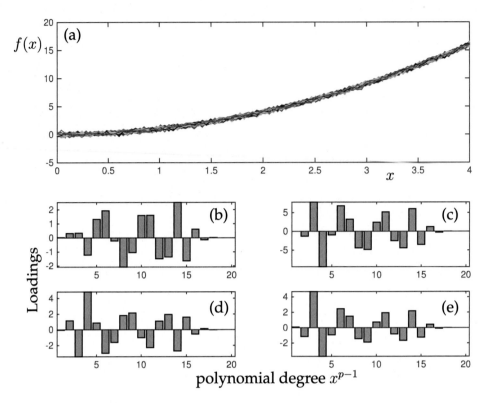

Figure 4.13 (a) One hundred realizations of the parabolic function (4.43) with additive white noise parametrized by $\sigma = 0.1$. Although the noise is small, the least-square fitting procedure produces significant variability when fitting to a polynomial of degree twenty. Panels (b)-(e) demonstrate the loadings (coefficients) for the various polynomial coefficients for four different noise realizations. This demonstrated model variability frames the model selection architecture.

where the weighting between λ_1 and λ_2 can be used to promote a desired sparsification of the solution. These different optimization strategies are common and will be considered further in the following.

4.4   Optimization as the Cornerstone of Regression

In the previous two sections of this chapter, the fitting function $f(x)$ was specified. For instance, it may be desirable to produce a line fit so that $f(x) = \beta_1 x + \beta_2$. The coefficients are then found by the regression and optimization methods already discussed. In what follows, our objective is to develop techniques which allow us to objectively select a good model for fitting the data, i.e. should one use a quadratic or cubic fit? The error metric alone does not dictate a good model selection as the more terms that are chosen for fitting, the more parameters are available for lowering the error, regardless of whether the additional terms have any meaning or interpretability.

Optimization strategies will play a foundational role in extracting interpretable results and meaningful models from data. As already shown in previous sections, the interplay of the ℓ_2 and ℓ_1 norms has a critical impact on the optimization outcomes. To illustrate further the role of optimization and the variety of possible outcomes, consider the simple example of data generated from noisy measurements of a parabola

$$f(x) = x^2 + \mathcal{N}(0, \sigma) \tag{4.43}$$

where $\mathcal{N}(0, \sigma)$ is a normally distributed random variable with mean zero and standard deviation σ. Fig. 4.13(a) shows an example of 100 random measurements of (4.43). The parabolic structure is clearly evident despite the noise added to the measurement. Indeed, a parabolic fit is trivial to compute using classic least-square fitting methods outlined in the first section of this chapter.

The goal is to *discover* the best model for the data given. So instead of specifying a model *a priori*, in practice, we do not know what the function is and need to discover it. We can begin by positing a regression to a set of polynomial models. In particular, consider framing the model selection problem $\mathbf{Y} = f(\mathbf{X}, \boldsymbol{\beta})$ of (4.4) as the following system $\mathbf{Ax} = \mathbf{b}$:

$$\begin{bmatrix} | & | & | & \cdots & | \\ 1 & x_j & x_j^2 & \cdots & x_j^{p-1} \\ | & | & | & \cdots & | \end{bmatrix} \begin{bmatrix} \beta_1 \\ \vdots \\ \beta_p \end{bmatrix} = \begin{bmatrix} f(x_1) \\ f(x_2) \\ \vdots \\ f(x_{100}) \end{bmatrix} \tag{4.44}$$

where the matrix $\mathbf{A}$ contains polynomial models up to degree $p - 1$ with each row representing a measurement, the β_k are the coefficients for each polynomial, and the matrix $\mathbf{b}$ contains the outcomes (data) $f(x_j)$. In what follows, we will consider a scenario where 100 measurements are taken and 20 term (19th order) polynomial is fit. Thus the matrix system $\mathbf{Ax} = \mathbf{b}$ results in an over-determined system as illustrated in Fig. 4.8.

The following code solves the over-determined system (4.44) using least-square regression via the **pinv** function. For this case, four realizations are run in order to illustrate the impact that a small amount of noise has on the regression procedure.

Code 4.12 Least-squares polynomial fit to parabola with noise.

```
n=100; L=4;
x=linspace(0,L,n);
f=(x.^2).';                    % parabola with 100 data points

M=20;                          % polynomial degree
for j=1:M
   phi(:,j)=(x.').^(j-1);      % build matrix A
end

for j=1:4
    fn=(x.^2+0.1*randn(1,n)).';
    an=pinv(phi)*fn; fna=phi*an;   % least-square fit
    En=norm(f-fna)/norm(f);
    subplot(4,2,4+j),bar(an)
end
```

Fig. 4.13(b)-(e) shows four typical loadings $\boldsymbol{\beta}$ computed from the regression procedure. Note that despite the low-level of noise added, the loadings are significantly different from one another. Thus each noise realization produces a very different model to explain the data.

The variability of the regression results are problematic for model selection. It suggests that even a small amount of measurement noise can lead to significantly different conclusions about the underlying model. In what follows, we quantify this variability while also considering various regression procedures for solving the over-determined linear system $\mathbf{Ax} = \mathbf{b}$. Highlighted here are five standard methods: least-square regression (**pinv**), the backslash operator (\\), LASSO (least absolute shrinkage and selection operator) (**lasso**), robust fit (**robustfit**), and ridge regression (**ridge**). Returning to the last section, and specifically (4.40), helps frame the mathematical architecture for these various $\mathbf{Ax} = \mathbf{b}$ solvers. Specifically, the Moore-Penrose pseudo-inverse (**pinv**) solves (4.40) with $\lambda_1 = \lambda_2 = 0$. The backslash command (\\) for over-determined systems solves the linear system via a QR decomposition [524]. The LASSO (**lasso**) solves (4.40) with $\lambda_1 > 0$ and $\lambda_2 = 0$. Ridge regression (**ridge**) solves (4.40) with $\lambda_1 = 0$ and $\lambda_2 > 0$. However, the modern implementation of ridge in MATLAB is a bit more nuanced. The popular elastic net algorithm weights both the ℓ_2 and ℓ_1 penalty, thus providing a tunable hybrid model regression between ridge and LASSO. Robust fit (**robustfit**) solves (4.40) by a weighted least-squares fitting. Moreover, it allows one to leverage robust statistics methods and penalize according to the Huber norm so as to promote outlier rejection [260]. In the data considered here, no outliers are imposed on the data so that the power of robust fit is not properly leveraged. Regardless, it is an important technique one should consider.

Fig. 4.14 shows a series of box plots for 100 realizations of data that illustrate the differences with the various regression techniques considered. It also highlights critically important differences with optimization strategies based on the ℓ_2 and ℓ_1 norm. From a model selection point of view, the least-square fitting procedure produces significant variability in the loading parameters $\boldsymbol{\beta}$ as illustrated in Fig. 4.14, panels (a), (b) and (e). The least-square fitting was produced by the Moore-Penrose pseudo-inverse or QR decomposition respectively. If some ℓ_1 penalty (regularization) is allowed, then Fig. 4.14, panels (d), (d) and (f), show that a more parsimonious model is selected with low variability. This is expected as the ℓ_1 norm sparsifies the solution vector of loading values $\boldsymbol{\beta}$. Indeed, the standard LASSO regression correctly selects the quadratic polynomial as the dominant contribution to the data. The following code was used to generate this data.

Code 4.13 Comparison of regression methods.

```
lambda=0.1; phi2=phi(:,2:end);
for jj=1:100
    f=(x.^2+0.2*randn(1,n)).';
    a1=pinv(phi)*f; f1=phi*a1; E1(jj)=norm(f-f1)/norm(f);
    a2=phi\f; f2=phi*a2; E2(jj)=norm(f-f2)/norm(f);
    [a3,stats]=lasso(phi,f,'Lambda',lambda); f3=phi*a3; E3(jj)=
        norm(f-f3)/norm(f);
    [a4,stats]=lasso(phi,f,'Lambda',lambda,'Alpha',0.8); f4=phi*a4
        ; E4(jj)=norm(f-f4)/norm(f);
a5=robustfit(phi2,f);f5=phi*a5;E5(jj)=norm(f-f5)/norm(f);
a6=ridge(f,phi2,0.5,0);f6=phi*a6;E6(jj)=norm(f-f6)/norm(f);

    A1(:,jj)=a1;A2(:,jj)=a2;A3(:,jj)=a3;A4(:,jj)=a4;A5(:,jj)=a5;A6
        (:,jj)=a6;
    plot(x,f), hold on
end
Err=[E1; E2; E3; E4; E5; E6];
Err2=[E1; E2; E3; E4; E5];
```

This code also produces the 100 realizations visualized in Fig. 4.13(a).

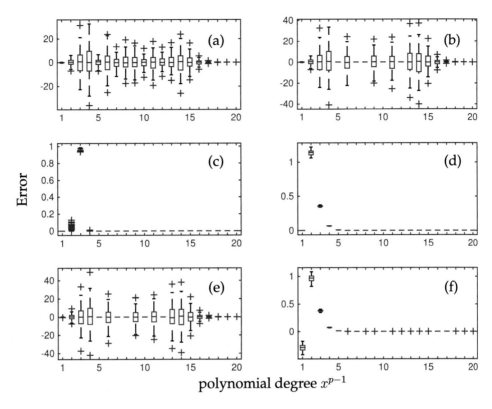

Figure 4.14 Comparison of regression methods for $\mathbf{Ax} = \mathbf{b}$ for an over-determined system of linear equations. The 100 realizations of data are generated from a simple parabola (4.43) that is fit to a 20th degree polynomial via (4.44). The box plots show (a) least-square regression via the Moore-Penrose pseudo-inverse (**pinv**), (b) the backslash command (\), (c) LASSO regression (**lasso**), (d) LASSO regression with different ℓ_2 versus ℓ_1 penalization, (e) robust fit, and (f) ridge regression. Note the significant variability in the loading values for the strictly ℓ_2 based methods ((a), (b) and (e)), and the low-variability for ℓ_1 weighted methods ((c), (d) and (f)). Only the standard LASSO (c) identifies the dominance of the parabolic term.

Despite the significant variability exhibited in Fig. 4.14 for most of the loading values by the different regression techniques, the error produced in the fitting procedure has little variability. Moreover, the various methods all produce regressions that have comparable error. Thus despite their differences in optimization frameworks, the error from fitting is relatively agnostic to the underlying method. This suggests that using the error alone as a metric for model selection is potentially problematic since almost any method can produce a reliable, low-error model. Fig. 4.15(a) shows a box plot of the error produced using the regression methods of Fig. 4.14. All of the regression techniques produce comparably low error and low variability results using significantly different strategies.

As a final note to this section and the code provided, we can consider instead the regression procedure as a function of the number of polynomials in (4.44). In our example of Fig. 4.14, polynomials up to degree 20 were considered. If instead, we sweep through polynomial degrees, then something interesting and important occurs as illustrated in Fig. 4.15(b)-(c). Specifically, the error of the regression collapses to 10^{-3} after the

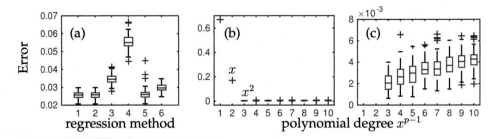

Figure 4.15 (a) Comparison of the error for the six regression methods used in Fig. 4.14. Despite the variability across the optimization methods, all of them produce low-error solutions. (b) Error using least-square regression as a function of increasing degree of polynomial. The error drops rapidly until the quadratic term is used in the regression. (c) Detail of the error showing that the error actually increases slightly by using a higher-degree of polynomial to fit the data.

quadratic term is added as shown in panel (b). This is expected since the original model was a quadratic function with a small amount of noise. Remarkably, as more polynomial terms are added, the ensemble error actually increases in the regression procedure as highlighted in panel (c). Thus simply adding more terms does not improve the error, which is counter-intuitive at first. The code to produce these results are given by the following:

Code 4.14 Model fitting with polynomials of varying degree.

```
En=zeros(100,M);
for jj=1:M
    for j=1:jj
        phi(:,j)=(x.').^(j-1);
    end
    f=(x.^2).';
    for j=1:100
        fn=(x.^2+0.1*randn(1,n)).';
        an=pinv(phi)*fn; fna=phi*an;
        En(j,jj)=norm(f-fna)/norm(f);
    end
end
```

Note that we have only swept through polynomials up to degree 10. Note further that panel (c) of Fig. 4.15 is a detail of panel (b). The error produced by a simple parabolic fit is approximately twice as good as a polynomial with degree 10. These results will help frame our model selection framework of the remaining sections.

4.5   The Pareto Front and *Lex Parsimoniae*

The preceding chapters show that regression is more nuanced than simply choosing a model and performing a least-square fit. Not only are there numerous metrics for constraining the solution, the model itself should be carefully selected in order to achieve a better, more interpretable description of the data. Such considerations on an appropriate model date back to William of Occam (c. 1287–1347), who was an English Franciscan friar, scholastic philosopher, and theologian. Occam proposed his law of parsimony (in latin *lex parsimoniae*), commonly known as Occam's razor, whereby he stated that among competing hypotheses, the one with the fewest assumptions should be selected, or when you have two competing theories that make exactly the same predictions, the simpler one is the more likely. The philosophy of Occam's razor has been used extensively throughout the physical and biological sciences for developing governing equations to model observed phenomena.

Parsimony also plays a central role in the mathematical work of Vilfredo Pareo (c. 1848–1923). Pareto was an Italian engineer, sociologist, economist, political scientist, and philosopher. He made several important contributions to economics, specifically in the study of income distribution and in the analysis of individuals' choices. He was also responsible for popularizing the use of the term *elite* in social analysis. In more recent times, he has become known for the popular 80/20 rule which is qualitatively illustrated in Fig. 4.16, named after him as the Pareto principle by management consultant Joseph M. Juran in 1941. Stated simply, it is a common principle in business and consulting management that, for instance, observes that 80% of sales come from 20% of clients. This concept was popularized by Richard Koch's book *The 80/20 Principle* [294] (along with several follow-up books [295, 296, 297]), which illustrated a number of practical applications of the Pareto principle in business management and life.

Pareto and Occam ultimately advocated the same philosophy: explain the majority of observed data with a parsimonious model. Importantly, model selection is not simply about reducing error, it is about producing a model that has a high degree of interpretability, generalization and predictive capabilities. Fig. 4.16 shows the basic concept of the *Pareto*

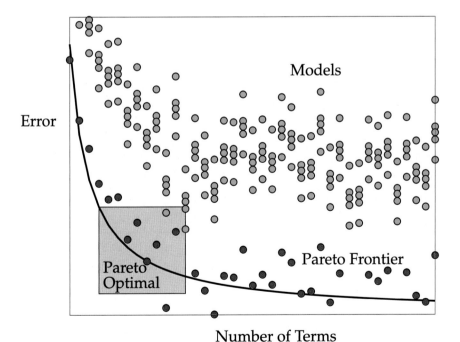

Figure 4.16 For model selection, the criteria of accuracy (low error) is balanced against parsimony. There can be a variety of models with the same number of terms (green and magenta points), but the *Pareto Frontier* (magenta points) is defined by the envelope of models that produce the lowest error for a given number of terms. The solid line provides an approximation to the Pareto frontier. The *Pareto optimal* solutions (shaded region) are those models that produce accurate models while remaining parsimonious.

Frontier and *Pareto Optimal* solutions. Specifically, for each model considered, the number of terms and the error in matching the data is computed. The solutions with the lowest error for a given number of terms define the Pareto frontier. Those parsimonious solutions that optimally balance error and complexity are in the shaded region and represent the Pareto optimal solutions. In game theory, the Pareto optimal solution is thought of as a strategy that cannot be made to perform better against one opposing strategy without performing less well against another (in this case error and complexity). In economics, it describes a situation in which the profit of one party cannot be increased without reducing the profit of another. Our objective is to select, in an principled way, the best model from the space of Pareto optimal solutions. To this end, information criteria, which will be discussed in subsequent sections, will be used to select from candidate modes in the Pareto optimal region.

Overfitting

The Pareto concept needs amending when considering application to real data. Specifically, when building models with many free parameters, it is often the case in machine learning applications with high-dimensional data, it is easy to overfit a model to the data. Indeed, the increase in error illustrated in Fig. 4.15(c) as a function of increasing model complexity illustrates this point. Thus, unlike what is depicted in Fig. 4.16 where the error goes towards zero as the number of model terms (parameters) is increased, the error may actually increase when considering models with a higher number of terms and/or parameters. To determine the correct model, various cross-validation and model selection algorithms are necessary.

To illustrate the overfitting that occurs with real data, consider the simple example of the last section. In this example, we are simply trying to find the correct parabolic model measured with additive noise (4.43). The results of Figs. 4.15(b) and 4.15(c) already indicate that overfitting is occurring for polynomial models beyond second order. The following MATLAB example will highlight the effects of overfitting. Consider the following code that produces a training and test set for the parabola of (4.43). The training set is on the region $x \in [0, 4]$ while the test set (extrapolation region) will be for $x \in [4, 8]$.

Code 4.15 Parabolic model with training and test data.

```
n=200; L=8;
x=linspace(0,L,n);
x1=x(1:100);    % train
x2=x(101:200);  % test
n1=length(x1);
n2=length(x2);
ftrain=(x1.^2).';    % train parabola x=[0,4]
ftest=(x2.^2).';     % test parbola x=[4,5]
figure(1), subplot(3,1,1),
plot(x1,ftrain,'r',x2,ftest,'b','Linewidth',[2])
```

This code produces the ideal model on two distinct regions: $x \in [0, 4]$ and $x \in [4, 8]$. Once measurement noise is added to the model, then the parameters for a polynomial fit no longer produce the perfect parabolic model. We can compute for given noisy measurements both an interpolation error, where measurements are taken in the data regime of $x \in [0, 4]$, and extrapolation error, where measurements are taken in the data regime of $x \in [4, 8]$. For this example, a least squares regression is performed using the pseudo-inverse (**pinv**) from MATLAB.

Code 4.16 Overfitting a quadratic model.

```
M=30; % number of model terms
Eni=zeros(100,M); Ene=zeros(100,M);
for jj=1:M
    for j=1:jj
        phi_i(:,j)=(x1.').^(j-1); % interpolation key
        phi_e(:,j)=(x2.').^(j-1); % extrapolation key
    end

    f=(x.^2).';
    for j=1:100
        fni=(x1.^2+0.1*randn(1,n1)).'; % interpolation
        fne=(x2.^2+0.1*randn(1,n2)).'; % extrapolation

        ani=pinv(phi_i)*fni; fnai=phi_i*ani;
        Eni(j,jj)=norm(ftrain-fnai)/norm(ftrain);

        fnae=phi_e*ani;  % use loadings from x in [0,4]
        Ene(j,jj)=norm(ftest-fnae)/norm(ftest);
    end
end
```

This simple example shows some of the most basic and common features associated with overfitting of models. Specifically, overfitting does not allow for generalization. Consider the results of Fig. 4.17 generated from the above code. In this example, the least-square loadings (4.44) for a polynomial are computed using the pseudo-inverse for data in the range $x \in [0, 4]$. The interpolation error for these loadings are demonstrated in Figs. 4.17(b) and (c). Note the impact of overfitting by polynomials for this interpolation of the data. Specifically, the error of the interpolated fit increases from beyond a second degree polynomial. Extrapolation for an overfit model produces significant errors. Figs. 4.17(d) and (e) show the error growth as a function of the least-square fit pth degree polynomial model. The error in Fig. 4.17(d) is on a logarithmic plot since it grows to 10^{13}. This demonstrates a clear inability of the overfit model to generalize to the range $x \in [4, 8]$. Indeed, only a parsimonious model with a 2nd degree polynomial can easily generalize to the range $x \in [4, 8]$ while keeping the error small.

The above example shows that some form of model selection to systematically deduce a parsimonious model is critical for producing viable models that can generalize outside of where data is collected. Much of machine learning revolves around (i) using data to generate predictive models, and (ii) cross-validation techniques to remove the most deleterious effects of overfitting. Without a cross-validation strategy, one will almost certainly produce a nongeneralizable model such as that exhibited in Fig. 4.17. In what follows, we will consider some standard strategies for producing reasonable models.

4.6 Model Selection: Cross-Validation

The previous section highlights many of the fundamental problems with regression. Specifically, it is easy to overfit a model to the data, thus leading to a model that is incapable of generalizing for extrapolation. This is an especially pernicious issue in training deep

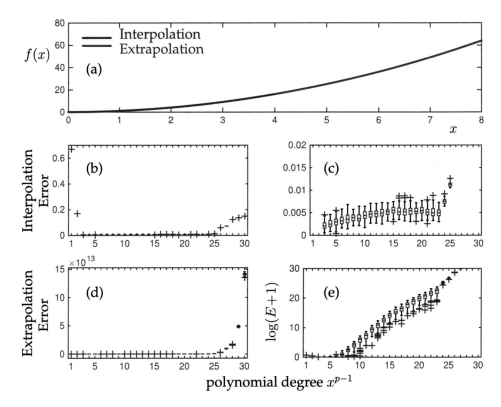

Figure 4.17 (a) The ideal model $f(x) = x^2$ over the domain $x \in [0, 8]$. Data is collected in the region $x \in [0, 4]$ in order to build a polynomial regression model (4.44) with increasing polynomial degree. In the interpolation regime $x \in [0, 4]$, the model error stays constrained, with increasing error due to overfitting for polynomials of degree greater than 2. The error is shown in panel (b) with a zoom in of the error in panel (c). For extrapolation, $x \in [4, 8]$, the error grows exponentially beyond a parabolic fit. In panel (d), the error is shown to grow to 10^{13}. A zoom in of the region on a logarithmic scale of the error ($\log(E + 1)$ where unity is added so that zero error produces a zero score) shows the exponential growth of error. This clearly shows that the model trained on the interval $x \in [0, 4]$ does not generalize (extrapolate) to the region $x \in [4, 8]$. This example should serve as a serious warning and note of caution in model fitting.

neural nets. To overcome the consequences of overfitting, various techniques have been proposed to more appropriately select a parsimonious model with only a few parameters, thus balancing the error with a model that can more easily generalize, or extrapolate. This provides a reinterpretation of the Pareto front in Fig. 4.16. Specifically, the error increases dramatically with the number of terms due to overfitting, especially when used for extrapolation.

There are two common mathematical strategies for circumventing the effects of overfitting in model selection: *cross-validation* and computing *information criteria*. This section considers the former, while the later method is considered in the next section. Cross-validation strategies are perhaps the most common and critical techniques in almost all machine learning algorithms. Indeed, one should never trust a model unless properly cross-validated. Cross-validation can be stated quite simply: Take random portions of your data and build a model. Do this k times and average the parameter scores (regression loadings) to produce the cross-validated model. Test the model predictions against withheld (extrapolation) data and evaluate whether the model is actually any good. This commonly used strategy is called k-fold cross-validation. It is simple, intuitively appealing, and the k-fold model building procedure produces a statistically based model for evaluation.

To illustrate the concept of cross-validation, we will once again consider fitting polynomial models to the simple function $f(x) = x^2$ (See Fig. 4.18). The previous sections of this chapter have already considered this problem in detail, both from the various regression frameworks available (pseudo-inverse, LASSO, robust fit, etc..), as well as their ability to accurately produce a model for interpolating and extrapolating data. The following MATLAB code considers three regression techniques (least-square fitting of pseudo-inverse, the QR-based backslash, and the sparsity promoting LASSO) for k-fold cross-validation ($k = 2$, 20 and 100). In this case, one can think of the k snapshots of data as trial measurements. As one might expect, there would be an advantage as more trials are taken and $k = 100$ models are averaged for a final model.

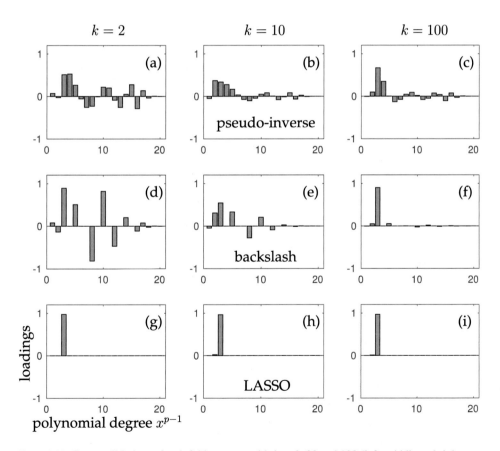

Figure 4.18 Cross-validation using k-fold strategy with $k = 2$, 20 and 100 (left, middle and right columns respectively). Three different regression strategies are cross-validated: least-square fitting of pseudo-inverse, the QR-based backslash, and the sparsity promoting LASSO. Note that the LASSO for this example produces the quadratic model within even a one or two fold validation. The backslash based QR algorithm has a strong signature after 100-fold cross-validation, while the least-square fitting suggests that the quadratic and cubic terms are both important even after 100-fold cross-validation.

Code 4.17 k-fold cross-validation using 100 foldings.

```
n=100; L=4;
x=linspace(0,L,n);
f=(x.^2).';  % parabola with 100 data points

M=21;  % polynomial degree
for j=1:M
    phi(:,j)=(x.').^(j-1);  % build matrix A
end

trials=[2 10 100];
for j=1:3
    for jj=1:trials(j)
        f=(x.^2+0.2*randn(1,n)).';
        a1=pinv(phi)*f; f1=phi*a1; E1(jj)=norm(f-f1)/norm(f);
        a2=phi\f; f2=phi*a2; E2(jj)=norm(f-f2)/norm(f);
        [a3,stats]=lasso(phi,f,'Lambda',0.1); f3=phi*a3; E3(jj)=
            norm(f-f3)/norm(f);
        A1(:,jj)=a1; A2(:,jj)=a2; A3(:,jj)=a3;
    end
    A1m=mean(A1.'); A2m=mean(A2.'); A3m=mean(A3.');
    Err=[E1; E2; E3];

    subplot(3,3,j), bar(A1m), axis([0 21 -1 1.2])
    subplot(3,3,3+j), bar(A2m), axis([0 21 -1 1.2])
    subplot(3,3,6+j), bar(A3m), axis([0 21 -1 1.2])
end
```

Fig. 4.18 shows the results of the k-fold cross-validation computations. By promoting sparsity (parsimony), the LASSO achieves the desired quadratic model after even a single $k = 1$ fold (i.e. thus this is not even cross-validated). In contrast the least-square regression (pseudo-inverse) and QR-based regression both require a significant number of folds to produce the dominant quadratic term. The least-square regression, even after $k = 100$ folds, still includes both a quadratic and cubic term.

The final model selection process under k-fold cross-validation often can involve a *thresholding* of terms that are small in the regression. The above code demonstrates the regression on three regression strategies. Although the LASSO looks almost ideal, it still has a small contributing linear component. The QR strategy of backslash produces a number of small components scattered among the polynomials used in the fit. The least-square regression has the dominant quadratic and cubic terms with a large number of nonzero coefficients scattered across the polynomials. If one thresholds the loadings, then the LASSO and backslash will produce exactly the quadratic model, while the least-square fit produces a quadratic-cubic model. The following code thresholds the loading coefficients and then produces the final cross-validated model. This model can then be evaluated against both the interpolated and extrapolated data regions as in Fig. 4.19.

Code 4.18 Comparison of cross-validated models.

```
Atot=[A1m; A2m; A3m];  % average loadings of three methods
Atot2=(Atot>0.2).*Atot; % threshold
Atot3=[Atot; Atot2];    % combine both thresholded and not

figure(3), bar3(Atot.')
figure(4), bar3(Atot2.')
```

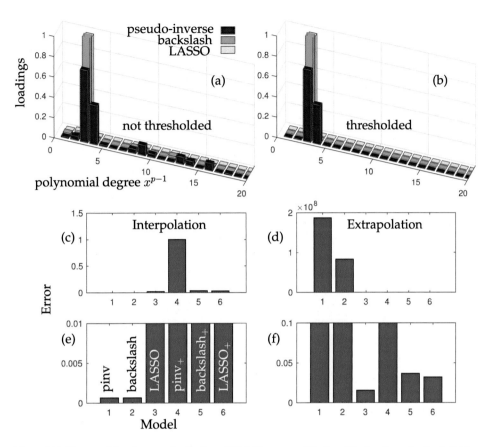

Figure 4.19 Error and loading results for $k = 100$ fold cross-validation. The loadings for the k-fold validation (with thresholding denoted by subscript $+$, (b) and without (a) thresholding) are shown for least-square fitting of pseudo-inverse, the QR-based backslash, and the sparsity promoting LASSO (See Fig. 4.18). Both the (c) interpolation error (and detail in (e)) and (d) extrapolation error (and detail in (f)) are computed. The LASSO performs well for both interpolation and extrapolation while a least-square fit gives poor performance under extrapolation. The 6 models considered are: 1. pseudo-inverse, 2. backslash, 3. LASSO, 4. thresholded pseudo-inverse, 5. thresholded backslash, and 6. thresholded LASSO.

```
n=200; L=8;
x=linspace(0,L,n);
x1=x(1:100);    % train (interpolation)
x2=x(101:200);  % test (extrapolation)

ftrain=(x1.^2).';   % interpolated parabola x=[0,4]
ftest=(x2.^2).';    % extrapolated parbola x=[4,5]

for j=1:M
    phi_i(:,j)=(x1.').^(j-1); % interpolation key
    phi_e(:,j)=(x2.').^(j-1); % extrapolation key
end

for jj=1:6 % compute inter/extra-polation scores
    ani=Atot3(jj,:).';
    fnai=phi_i*ani;
```

```
      Eni(jj)=norm(ftrain-fnai)/norm(ftrain);
      fnae=phi_e*ani;
      Ene(jj)=norm(ftest-fnae)/norm(ftest);
end
```

The results of Fig. 4.19 show that the model selection process, and the regression technique used, makes a critical difference in producing a viable model. It further shows that despite a k-fold cross-validation, the extrapolation error, or generalizability, of the model can still be poor. A good model is one that keeps errors small and also generalizes well, as does the LASSO in the previous example.

k-fold Cross-Validation

The process of k-fold cross validation is highlighted in Fig. 4.20. The concept is to partition a data set into a training set and a test set. The test set, or withhold set, is kept separate from any training procedure for the model. Importantly, the test set is where the model produces an extrapolation approximation, which the figures of the last two sections show to be challenging. In k-fold cross-validation, the training data is further partitioned into k-folds, which are typically randomly selected portions of the data. For instance, in standard 10-fold cross validation, the training data is randomly partitioned into 10 partitions (or folds). Each partition is used to construct a regression model $\mathbf{Y}_j = f(\mathbf{X}_j, \boldsymbol{\beta}_j)$ for $j = 1, 2, \cdots, 10$. One method for constructing the final model is to average the loading values $\bar{\boldsymbol{\beta}} = (1/k) \sum_{j=1}^{k} \boldsymbol{\beta}_j$, which are then used for the final, cross-validated regression model $\mathbf{Y} = f(\mathbf{X}, \bar{\boldsymbol{\beta}})$. This model is then used on the withhold data to test its extrapolation power, or generalizability. The error on this withhold test set is what determines the efficacy of the model. There are a variety of other methods for selecting the best model, including simply choosing the best of the k-fold models. As for partitioning the data, a common strategy is to break the data into 70% training data, 20% validation data, and 10% withheld data. For very large data sets, the validation and withheld can be reduced provided there is enough data to accurately assess the model constructed.

Leave p-out Cross-Validation

Another standard technique for cross-validation involves the so-called *leave p-out cross validation* (LpO CV). In this case, p-samples of the training data are removed from the data and kept as the validation set. A model is built on the remaining training data and the accuracy of the model is tested on the p withheld samples. This is repeated with a new selection of p samples until all the training data has been part of the validation data set. The accuracy of the model is then evaluated on the withheld data from averaging the accuracy of the models and the loadings produced from the various partitions of the data.

4.7   Model Selection: Information Criteria

There is a different approach to model selection than the cross-validation strategies outlined in the previous section. Indeed, model selection has a rigorous set of mathematical innovations starting from the early 1950s. The Kullback-Leibler (KL) divergence [314] measures the distance between two probability density distributions (or data sets which represent the truth and a model) and is the core of modern information theory criteria for evaluating the

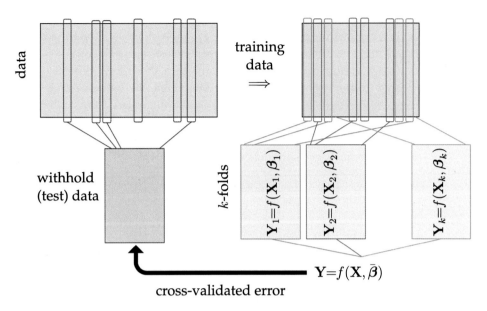

Figure 4.20 Procedure for k-fold cross-validation of models. The data is initially partitioned into a training and test (withold) set. Typically the withold set is generated from a random sample of the overall data. The training data is partitioned into k-folds whereby a random sub-selection of the training data is collected in order to build a regression model $\mathbf{Y}_j = f(\mathbf{X}_j, \boldsymbol{\beta}_j)$. Importantly, each model generates the loading parameters $\boldsymbol{\beta}_j$. After the k-fold models are generated, the best model $\mathbf{Y} = f(\mathbf{X}, \bar{\boldsymbol{\beta}})$ is produced. There are different ways to get the best model, in some cases, it may be appropriate to average the model parameters so that $\bar{\boldsymbol{\beta}} = (1/k) \sum_{j=1}^{k} \boldsymbol{\beta}_j$. One could also simply pick the best parameters from the k-fold set. In either case, the best model is then tested on the withheld data to evaluate its viability.

viability of a model. The KL divergence has deep mathematical connections to statistical methods characterizing entropy as developed by Ludwig E. Boltzmann (c. 1844-1906), as well as a relation to information theory developed by Claude Shannon [486]. Model selection is a well developed field with a large body of literature, most of which is exceptionally well reviewed by Burnham and Anderson [105]. In what follows, only brief highlights will be given to demonstrate some of the standard methods.

The KL divergence between two models $f(\mathbf{X}, \boldsymbol{\beta})$ and $g(\mathbf{X}, \boldsymbol{\mu})$ is defined as

$$I(f, g) = \int f(\mathbf{X}, \boldsymbol{\beta}) \log \left[\frac{f(\mathbf{X}, \boldsymbol{\beta})}{g(\mathbf{X}, \boldsymbol{\mu})} \right] d\mathbf{X} \tag{4.45}$$

where $\boldsymbol{\beta}$ and $\boldsymbol{\mu}$ are parameterizations of the the models $f(\cdot)$ and $g(\cdot)$ respectively. From an information theory perspective, the quantity $I(f, g)$ measures the information lost when g is used to represent f. Note that if $f = g$, then the log term is zero (i.e. $\log(1) = 0$) and $I(f, g) = 0$ so that there is no information lost. In practice, f will represent the *truth*, or measurements of an experiment, while g will be a model proposed to describe f.

Unlike the regression and cross-validation performed previously, when computing KL divergence a model must be specified. Recall that we used cross-validation previously to generate a model using different regression strategies (See Fig. 4.20 for instance). Here a number of models will be posited and the loss of information, or KL divergence, of each model will be computed. The model with the lowest loss of information is generally regarded as the best model. Thus given M proposed models $g_j(\mathbf{X}, \boldsymbol{\mu}_j)$ where $j = 1, 2, \cdots, M$, we can compute $I_j(f, g_j)$ for each model. The correct model, or best model, is the one that minimizes the information loss $\min_j I_j(f, g_j)$.

As a simple example, consider Fig. 4.21 which shows three different models that are compared to the truth data. To generate this figure, the following code was used. The computation of the KL divergence score is also illustrated. Note that in order to avoid division by zero, a constant offset is added to each probability distribution. The truth data generated, $f(x)$, is a simple normally distributed variable. The three models shown are variants of normally and uniformly distributed functions.

Code 4.19 Computation of KL divergence.

```
n=10000;
x1=randn(n,1);   % "truth" model (data)
x2=0.8*randn(n,1)+1; % model 1
x3=0.5*randn(n,1)-1; % model 3 components
x4=0.7*randn(n,1)-3;
x5=5*rand(n,1)-0.5;
x=-6:0.01:6;   % range for data

f=hist(x1,x)+0.01;   % generate PDFs
g1=hist(x2,x)+0.01;
g2a=hist(x3,x); g2b=hist(x4,x); g2=g2a+0.3*g2b+0.01;
```

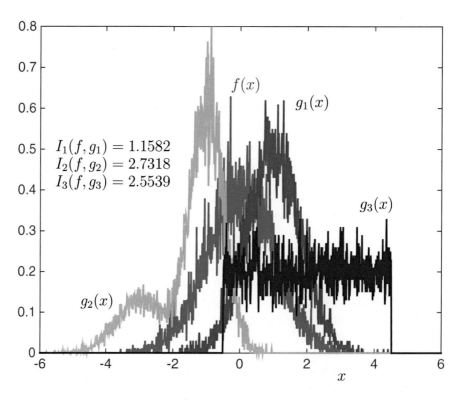

Figure 4.21 Comparison of three models $g_1(x)$, $g_2(x)$ and $g_3(x)$ against the truth model $f(x)$. The KL divergence $I_j(f, g_j)$ for each model is computed, showing that the model $g_1(x)$ is closest to statistically representing the true data.

```
g3=hist(x5,x)+0.01;

f=f/trapz(x,f);   % normalize data
g1=g1/trapz(x,g1); g2=g2/trapz(x,g2); g3=g3/trapz(x,g3);
plot(x,f,x,g1,x,g2,x,g3,'Linewidth',[2])

% compute integrand
Int1=f.*log(f./g1); Int2=f.*log(f./g2); Int3=f.*log(f./g3);

% use if needed
%Int1(isinf(Int1))=0; Int1(isnan(Int1))=0;
%Int2(isinf(Int2))=0; Int2(isnan(Int2))=0;

% KL divergence
I1=trapz(x,Int1); I2=trapz(x,Int2); I3=trapz(x,Int3);
```

Information Criteria: AIC and BIC

This simple example shows the basic ideas behind model selection: compute a distance between a proposed model output $g_j(x)$ and the measured truth $f(x)$. In the early 1970s, Hirotugu Akaike combined Fisher's maximum likelihood computation [183] with the KL divergence score to produce what is now called the *Akaike Information Criterion* (AIC) [7]. The was later modified by Gideon Schwarz to the so-called *Bayesian Information Criterion* BIC [480] which provided an information score that was guaranteed to converge to the correct model in the large data limit, provided the correct model was included in the set of candidate models.

To be more precise, we turn to Akaike's seminal contribution [7]. Akaike was aware that KL divergence cannot be computed in practice since it requires full knowledge of the statistics of the truth model $f(x)$ and of all the parameters in the proposed models $g_j(x)$. Thus, Akaike proposed an alternative way to estimate KL divergence based on the empirical log-likelihood function at its maximum point. This is computable in practice and was a critically enabling insight for rigorous methods of model selection. The technical aspects of Akaike's work connecting log-likelihood estimates and KL divergence [7, 105] was a paradigm shifting mathematical achievement, and thus led to the development of the AIC score

$$AIC = 2K - 2\log\left[\mathcal{L}(\hat{\boldsymbol{\mu}}|\mathbf{x})\right], \tag{4.46}$$

where K is the number of parameters used in the model, $\hat{\boldsymbol{\mu}}$ is an estimate of the best parameters used (i.e. lowest KL divergence) in $g(\mathbf{X}, \boldsymbol{\mu})$ computed from a *maximum likelihood estimate* (MLE), and $\mathbf{x}$ are independent samples of the data to be fit. Thus, instead of a direct measure of the distance between two models, the AIC provides an estimate of the relative distance between the approximating model and the true model or data. As the number of terms gets large in a proposed model, the AIC score increases with slope $2K$, thus providing a penalty for nonparsimonious models. Importantly, due to its relative measure, it will always result in an objective "best" model with the lowest AIC score, but this best model may still be quite poor in prediction and reconstruction of the data.

AIC is one of the standard model selection criteria used today. However, there are others. Highlighted here is the modification of AIC by Gideon Schwarz to construct BIC [480]. BIC is almost identical to AIC aside from the penalization of the information criteria by the number of terms. Specifically, BIC is defined as

$$BIC = \log(n)K - 2\log\left[\mathcal{L}(\hat{\boldsymbol{\mu}}|\mathbf{x})\right], \tag{4.47}$$

where n is the number of data points, or sample size, considered. This slightly different version of the information criteria has one significant consequence. The seminal contribution of Schwarz was to prove that if the correct model was included along with a set of candidate models, then it would be theoretically guaranteed to be selected as the best model based upon BIC for sufficiently large set of data $\mathbf{x}$. This is in contrast to AIC for which in certain pathological cases, it can select the wrong model.

Computing AIC and BIC Scores

MATLAB allows us to directly compute the AIC and/or BIC score from the **aicbic** command. This computational tool is embedded in the econometrics toolbox, and it allows one to evaluate a set of models against one another. The evaluation is made from the log-likelihood estimate of the models under consideration. An arbitrary number of models can be compared.

In the specific example considered here, we consider a ground truth model constructed from the autoregressive model

$$x_n = -4 + 0.2x_{n-1} + 0.5x_{n-2} + \mathcal{N}(0, 2) \tag{4.48}$$

where x_n is the value of the time series at time t_n and $\mathcal{N}(0, 2)$ is a white-noise process with mean zero and variance two. We fit three autoregressive integrated moving average (ARIMA) models to the data. The three ARIMA models have one, two and three time delays in their models. The following code computes their log-likelihood and corresponding AIC and BIC scores.

Code 4.20 Computation of AIC and BIC scores.

```
T = 100; % Sample size
DGP = arima('Constant',-4,'AR',[0.2, 0.5],'Variance',2);
y = simulate(DGP,T);

EstMdl1 = arima('ARLags',1);
EstMdl2 = arima('ARLags',1:2);
EstMdl3 = arima('ARLags',1:3);

logL = zeros(3,1); % Preallocate loglikelihood vector
[~,~,logL(1)] = estimate(EstMdl1,y,'print',false);
[~,~,logL(2)] = estimate(EstMdl2,y,'print',false);
[~,~,logL(3)] = estimate(EstMdl3,y,'print',false);

[aic,bic] = aicbic(logL, [3; 4; 5], T*ones(3,1))
```

Note that the best model, the one with both the lowest AIC and BIC score, is the second model which has two time delays. This is expected as it corresponds to the ground truth model. The output in this case is given by the following.

```
aic =
    381.7732
    358.2422
    358.8479

bic =
    389.5887
```

```
368.6629
371.8737
```

The lowest AIC and BIC score is 358.2422 and 368.6629 respectively. Note that although the correct model was selected, the AIC score provides little distinction between models, especially the two and three time-delay models.

Suggested Reading

Texts

(1) **Model selection and multimodel inference**, by K. P. Burnham and D. R. Anderson [105].

(2) **Multivariate analysis**, by R. A. Johnson and D. Wichern, 2002 [266].

(3) **An introduction to statistical learning**, by G. James, D. Witten, T. Hastie and R. Tibshirani, 2013 [264].

Papers and Reviews

(1) **On the mathematical foundations of theoretical statistics.**, by R. A. Fischer, *Philosophical Transactions of the Royal Society of London*, 1922 [183].

(2) **A new look at the statistical model identification.**, by H. Akaike, *IEEE Transactions on Automatic Control*, 1974 [7].

(3) **Estimating the dimension of a model.**, by G. Schwarz et al., *The annals of statistics*, 1978 [480].

(4) **On information and sufficiency.**, by S. Kullback and R. A. Leibler, *The annals of statistics*, 1951 [314].

(5) **A mathematical theory of communication.**, by C. Shannon, *ACM SIGMOBILE Mobile Computing and Communications Review*, 2001 [480].

5 Clustering and Classification

Machine learning is based upon optimization techniques for data. The goal is to find both a low-rank subspace for optimally embedding the data, as well as regression methods for clustering and classification of different data types. Machine learning thus provides a principled set of mathematical methods for extracting meaningful features from data, i.e. data mining, as well as binning the data into distinct and meaningful patterns that can be exploited for decision making. Specifically, it learns from and makes predictions based on data. For business applications, this is often called *predictive analytics*, and it is at the forefront of modern data-driven decision making. In an integrated system, such as is found in autonomous robotics, various machine learning components (e.g., for processing visual and tactile stimulus) can be integrated to form what we now call *artificial intelligence* (AI). To be explicit: AI is built upon integrated machine learning algorithms, which in turn are fundamentally rooted in optimization.

There are two broad categories for machine learning: *supervised machine learning* and *unsupervised machine learning*. In the former, the algorithm is presented with labelled datasets. The training data, as outlined in the cross-validation method of the last chapter, is labeled by a teacher/expert. Thus examples of the input and output of a desired model are explicitly given, and regression methods are used to find the best model for the given labeled data, via optimization. This model is then used for prediction and classification using new data. There are important variants of supervised methods, including *semi-supervised learning* in which incomplete training is given so that some of the input/output relationships are missing, i.e. for some input data, the actual output is missing. *Active learning* is another common subclass of supervised methods whereby the algorithm can only obtain training labels for a limited set of instances, based on a budget, and also has to optimize its choice of objects to acquire labels for. In an interactive framework, these can be presented to the user for labeling. Finally, in *reinforcement learning*, rewards or punishments are the training labels that help shape the regression architecture in order to build the best model. In contrast, no labels are given for *unsupervised learning* algorithms. Thus, they must find patterns in the data in a principled way in order to determine how to cluster data and generate labels for predicting and classifying new data. In unsupervised learning, the goal itself may be to discover patterns in the data embedded in the low-rank subspaces so that *feature engineering* or *feature extraction* can be used to build an appropriate model.

In this chapter, we will consider some of the most commonly used supervised and unsupervised machine learning methods. As will be seen, our goal is to highlight how data mining can produce important data features (feature engineering) for later use in model building. We will also show that the machine learning methods can be broadly used for clustering and classification, as well as for building regression models for prediction. Critical to all of this machine learning architecture is finding low-rank feature spaces that are informative and interpretable.

5.1   Feature Selection and Data Mining

To exploit data for diagnostics, prediction and control, dominant features of the data must be extracted. In the opening chapter of this book, SVD and PCA were introduced as methods for determining the dominant correlated structures contained within a data set. In the eigenfaces example of Section 1.6, for instance, the dominant features of a large number of cropped face images were shown. These eigenfaces, which are ordered by their ability to account for commonality (correlation) across the data base of faces was guaranteed to give the best set of r features for reconstructing a given face in an ℓ_2 sense with a rank-r truncation. The eigenface modes gave clear and interpretable features for identifying faces, including highlighting the eyes, nose and mouth regions as might be expected. Importantly, instead of working with the high-dimensional measurement space, the feature space allows one to consider a significantly reduced subspace where diagnostics can be performed.

The goal of data mining and machine learning is to construct and exploit the intrinsic low-rank feature space of a given data set. The feature space can be found in an unsupervised fashion by an algorithm, or it can be explicitly constructed by expert knowledge and/or correlations among the data. For eigenfaces, the features are the PCA modes generated by the SVD. Thus each PCA mode is high-dimensional, but the only quantity of importance in feature space is the weight of that particular mode in representing a given face. If one performs an r-rank truncation, then any face needs only r features to represent it in feature space. This ultimately gives a low-rank embedding of the data in an interpretable set of r features that can be leveraged for diagnostics, prediction, reconstruction and/or control.

Several examples will be developed that illustrate how to generate a feature space, starting with a standard data set included with MATLAB. The Fisher iris data set includes measurements of 150 irises of three varieties: setosa, versicolor, and virginica. The 50 samples of each flower include measurements in centimeters of the sepal length, sepal width, petal length, and petal width. For this data set, the four features are already defined in terms of interpretable properties of the biology of the plants. For visualization purposes, Fig. 5.1 considers only the first three of these features. The following code accesses the Fisher iris data set:

Code 5.1 Features of the Fisher irises.

```
load fisheriris;
x1=meas(1:50,:);     % setosa
x2=meas(51:100,:);   % versicolor
x3=meas(101:150,:);  % virginica

plot3(x1(:,1),x1(:,2),x1(:,4),'go'), hold on
plot3(x2(:,1),x2(:,2),x2(:,4),'mo')
plot3(x3(:,1),x3(:,2),x3(:,4),'ro')
```

Fig. 5.1 shows that the properties measured can be used as a good set of features for clustering and classification purposes. Specifically, the three iris varieties are well separated

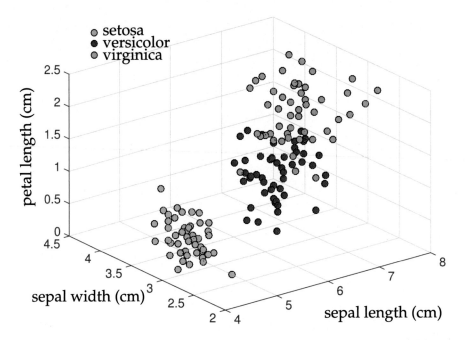

Figure 5.1 Fisher iris data set with 150 measurements over three varieties including 50 measurements each of setosa, versicolor, and virginica. Each flower includes a measurement of sepal length, sepal width, petal length, and petal width. The first three of these are illustrated here showing that these simple biological features are sufficient to show that the data has distinct, quantifiable differences between the species.

in this feature space. The setosa iris is most distinctive in its feature profile, while the versicolor and virginica have a small overlap among the samples taken. For this data set, machine learning is certainly not required to generate a good classification scheme. However, data generally does not so readily reduce down to simple two- and three-dimensional visual cues. Rather, decisions about clustering in feature space occur with many more variables, thus requiring the aid of computational methods to provide good classification schemes.

As a second example, we consider in Fig. 5.2 a selection from an image database of 80 dogs and 80 cats. A specific goal for this data set is to develop an automated classification method whereby the computer can distinguish between cats and dogs. In this case, the data for each cat and dog is the 64×64 pixel space of the image. Thus each image has 4096 measurements, in contrast to the 4 measurements for each example in the iris data set. Like eigenfaces, we will use the SVD to extract the dominant correlations among the images. The following code loads the data and performs a singular value decomposition on the data after the mean is subtracted. The SVD produces an ordered set of modes characterizing the correlation between all the dog and cat images. Fig. 5.3 shows the first four SVD modes of the 160 images (80 dogs and 80 cats).

Code 5.2 Features of dogs and cats.

```
load dogData.mat
load catData.mat
CD=double([dog cat]);
[u,s,v]=svd(CD-mean(CD(:)),'econ');
```

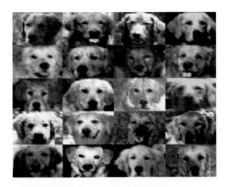 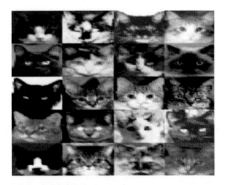

Figure 5.2 Example images of dogs (left) and cats (right). Our goal is to construct a feature space where automated classification of these images can be efficiently computed.

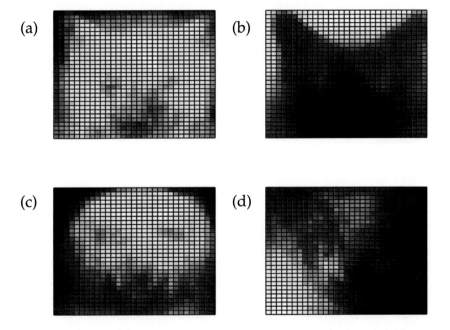

Figure 5.3 First four features (a)-(d) generated from the SVD of the 160 images of dogs and cats, i.e. these are the first four columns of the **U** matrix of the SVD. Typical cat and dog images are shown in Fig. 5.2. Note that the first two modes (a) and (b) show that the triangular ears are important features when images are correlated. This is certainly a distinguishing feature for cats, while dogs tend to lack this feature. Thus in feature space, cats generally add these two dominant modes to promote this feature while dogs tend to subtract these features to remove the triangular ears from their representation.

The original image space, or pixel space, is only one potential set of data to work with. The data can be transformed into a wavelet representation where edges of the images are emphasized. The following code loads in the images in their wavelet representation and computes a new low-rank embedding space.

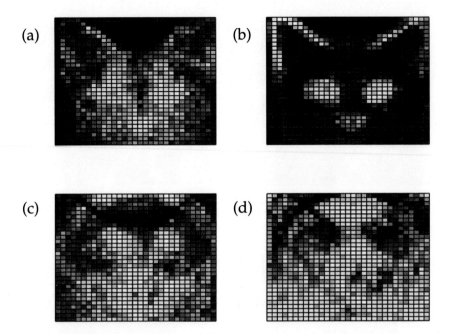

Figure 5.4 First four features (a)-(d) generated from the SVD of the 160 images of dogs and cats in the wavelet domain. As before, the first two modes (a) and (b) show that the triangular ears are important. This is an alternative representation of the dogs and cats that can help better classify dogs versus cats.

Code 5.3 Wavelet features of dogs and cats.

```
load catData_w.mat
load dogData_w.mat
CD2=[dog_wave cat_wave];
[u2,s2,v2]=svd(CD2-mean(CD2(:)),'econ');
```

The equivalent of Fig. 5.3 in wavelet space is shown in Fig. 5.4. Note that the wavelet representation helps emphasize many key features such as the eyes, nose, and ears, potentially making it easier to make a classification decision. Generating a feature space that enables classification is critical for constructing effective machine learning algorithms.

Whether using the image space directly or a wavelet representation, Figs. 5.3 and 5.4 respectively, the goal is to project the data onto the feature space generated by each. A good feature space helps find distinguishing features that allow one to perform a variety of tasks that may include clustering, classification, and prediction. The importance of each feature to an individual image is given by the V matrix in the SVD. Specifically, each column of V determines the loading, or weighting, of each feature onto a specific image. Histograms of these loadings can then be used to visualize how distinguishable cats and dogs are from each other by each feature (See Fig. 5.5). The following code produces a histogram of the distribution of loadings for the dogs and the cats (first 80 images versus second 80 images respectively).

Code 5.4 Feature histograms of dogs and cats.

```
xbin=linspace(-0.25,0.25,20);
for j=1:4
```

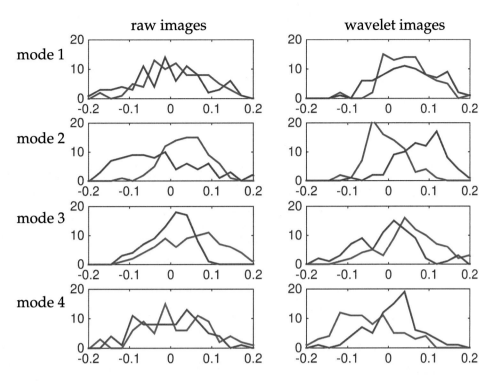

Figure 5.5 Histogram of the distribution of loadings for dogs (blue) and cats (red) on the first four dominant SVD modes. The left panel shows the distributions for the raw images (See Fig. 5.3) while the right panels show the distribution for wavelet transformed data (See Fig. 5.4. The loadings come from the columns of the **V** matrix of the SVD. Note the good separability between dogs and cats using the second mode.

```
    subplot(4,2,2*j-1)
    pdf1=hist(v(1:80,j),xbin)
    pdf2=hist(v(81:160,j),xbin)
    plot(xbin,pdf1,xbin,pdf2,'Linewidth',[2])
end
```

Fig. 5.5 shows the distribution of loading scores for the first four modes for both the raw images as well as the wavelet transformed images. For both the sets of images, the distribution of loadings on the second mode clearly shows a strong separability between dogs and cats. The wavelet processed images also show a nice separability on the fourth mode. Note that the first mode for both shows very little discrimination between the distributions and is thus not useful for classification and clustering objectives.

Features that provide strong separability between different types of data (e.g. dogs and cats) are typically exploited for machine learning tasks. This simple example shows that feature engineering is a process whereby an initial data exploration is used to help identify potential pre-processing methods. These features can then help the computer identify highly distinguishable features in a higher-dimensional space for accurate clustering, classification and prediction. As a final note, consider Fig. 5.6 which projects the dog and cat data onto the first three PCA modes (SVD modes) discovered from the raw images or their

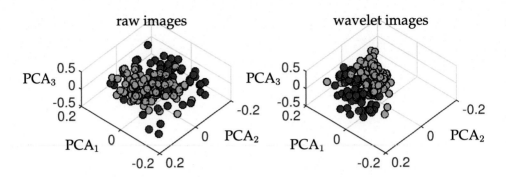

Figure 5.6 Projection of dogs (green) and cats (magenta) into feature space. Note that the raw images and their wavelet counterparts produce different embeddings of the data. Both exhibit clustering around their labeled states of dog and cat. This is exploited in the learning algorithms that follow. The wavelet images are especially good for clustering and classification as this feature space more easily separates the data.

wavelet transformed counterparts. As will be seen later, the wavelet transformed images provide a higher degree of separability, and thus improved classification.

5.2   Supervised versus Unsupervised Learning

As previously stated, the goal of data mining and machine learning is to construct and exploit the intrinsic low-rank feature space of a given data set. Good feature engineering and feature extraction algorithms can then be used to learn classifiers and predictors for the data. Two dominant paradigms exist for learning from data: *supervised methods* and *unsupervised methods*. Supervised data-mining algorithms are presented with labeled data sets, where the training data is labeled by a teacher/expert/supervisor. Thus examples of the input and output of a desired model are explicitly given, and regression methods are used to find the best model via optimization for the given labeled data. This model is then used for prediction and classification using new data. There are important variants of this basic architecture which include semi-supervised learning, active learning and reinforcement learning. For unsupervised learning algorithms, no training labels are given so that an algorithm must find patterns in the data in a principled way in order to determine how to cluster and classify new data. In unsupervised learning, the goal itself may be to discover patterns in the data embedded in the low-rank subspaces so that feature engineering or feature extraction can be used to build an appropriate model.

To illustrate the difference in supervised versus unsupervised learning, consider Fig. 5.7. This shows a scatter plot of two Gaussian distributions. In one case, the data is well separated so that their means are sufficiently far apart and two distinct clusters are observed. In the second case, the two distributions are brought close together so that separating the data is a challenging task. The goal of unsupervised learning is to discover clusters in the data. This is a trivial task by visual inspection, provided the two distributions are sufficiently separated. Otherwise, it becomes very difficult to distinguish clusters in the data. Supervised learning provides labels for some of the data. In this case, points are either labeled with green dots or magenta dots and the task is to classify the unlabeled data (grey dots) as either green or magenta. Much like the unsupervised architecture, if the statistical

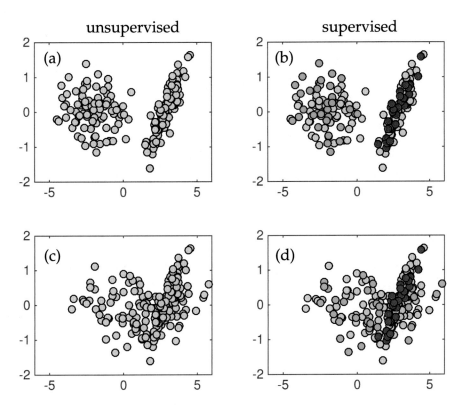

Figure 5.7 Illustration of unsupervised versus supervised learning. In the left panels (a) and (c), unsupervised learning attempts to find clusters for the data in order to classify them into two groups. For well separated data (a), the task is straightforward and labels can easily be produced. For overlapping data (c), it is a very difficult task for an unsupervised algorithm to accomplish. In the right panels (b) and (d), supervised learning provides a number of labels: green balls and magenta balls. The remaining unlabeled data is then classified as green or magenta. For well separated data (b), labeling data is easy, while overlapping data presents significant challenge.

distributions that produced the data are well separated, then using the labels in combination with the data provides a simple way to classify all the unlabeled data points. Supervised algorithms also perform poorly if the data distributions have significant overlap.

Supervised and unsupervised learning can be stated mathematically. Let

$$\mathcal{D} \subset \mathbb{R}^n \tag{5.1}$$

so that $\mathcal{D}$ is an open bounded set of dimension n. Further, let

$$\mathcal{D}' \subset \mathcal{D}. \tag{5.2}$$

The goal of classification is to build a classifier labeling all data in $\mathcal{D}$ given data from $\mathcal{D}'$.

To make our problem statement more precise, consider a set of data points $\mathbf{x}_j \in \mathbb{R}^n$ and labels $\mathbf{y}_j$ for each point where $j = 1, 2, \cdots, m$. Labels for the data can come in many forms, from numeric values, including integer labels, to text strings. For simplicity, we will label the data in a binary way as either plus or minus one so that $\mathbf{y}_j \in \{\pm 1\}$.

For unsupervised learning, the following inputs and outputs are then associated with learning a classification task

Input

$$\text{data } \left\{ \mathbf{x}_j \in \mathbb{R}^n, \ j \in Z := \{1, 2, \cdots, m\} \right\} \tag{5.3a}$$

Output

$$\text{labels } \left\{ \mathbf{y}_j \in \{\pm 1\}, \ j \in Z \right\}. \tag{5.3b}$$

Thus the mathematical framing of unsupervised learning is focused on producing labels $\mathbf{y}_j$ for all the data. Generally, the data $\mathbf{x}_j$ used for training the classifier is from $\mathcal{D}'$. The classifier is then more broadly applied, i.e. it generalizes, to the open bounded domain $\mathcal{D}$. If the data used to build a classifier only samples a small portion of the larger domain, then it is often the case that the classifier will not generalize well.

Supervised learning provides labels for the training stage. The inputs and outputs for this learning classification task can be stated as follows

Input

$$\text{data } \left\{ \mathbf{x}_j \in \mathbb{R}^n, \ j \in Z := \{1, 2, \cdots, m\} \right\} \tag{5.4a}$$

$$\text{labels } \left\{ \mathbf{y}_j \in \{\pm 1\}, \ j \in Z' \subset Z \right\} \tag{5.4b}$$

Output

$$\text{labels } \left\{ \mathbf{y}_j \in \{\pm 1\}, \ j \in Z \right\}. \tag{5.4c}$$

In this case, a subset of the data is labeled and the missing labels are provided for the remaining data. Technically speaking, this is a semi-supervised learning task since some of the training labels are missing. For supervised learning, all the labels are known in order to build the classifier on $\mathcal{D}'$. The classifier is then applied to $\mathcal{D}$. As with unsupervised learning, if the data used to build a classifier only samples a small portion of the larger domain, then it is often the case that the classifier will not generalize well.

For the data sets considered in our feature selection and data mining section, we can consider in more detail the key components required to build a classification model: $\mathbf{x}_j$, $\mathbf{y}_j$, $\mathcal{D}$ and $\mathcal{D}'$. The Fisher iris data of Fig. 5.1 is a classic example for which we can detail these quantities. We begin with the data collected

$$\mathbf{x}_j = \{\text{sepal length, sepal width, petal length, petal width}\}. \tag{5.5}$$

Thus each iris measurement contains four data fields, or features, for our analysis. The labels can be one of the following

$$\mathbf{y}_j = \{\text{setosa, versicolor, virginica}\}. \tag{5.6}$$

In this case the labels are text strings, and there are three of them. Note that in our formulation of supervised and unsupervised learning, there were only two outputs (binary) which were labeled either ± 1. Generally, there can be many labels, and they are often text strings. Finally, there is the domain of the data. For this case

$$\mathcal{D}' \in \{150 \text{ iris samples: } 50 \text{ setosa}, 50 \text{ versicolor, and } 50 \text{ virginica}\} \tag{5.7}$$

and

$$\mathcal{D} \in \{\text{the universe of setosa, versicolor and virginica irises}\}. \tag{5.8}$$

We can similarly assess the dog and cat data as follows:

$$\mathbf{x}_j = \{64 \times 64 \text{ image}= 4096 \text{ pixels}\} \tag{5.9}$$

where each dog and cat is labeled as

$$\mathbf{y}_j = \{\text{dog, cat}\} = \{1, \text{-}1\}. \tag{5.10}$$

In this case the labels are text strings which can also be translated to numeric values. This is consistent with our formulation of supervised and unsupervised learning where there are only two outputs (binary) labeled either ± 1. Finally, there is the domain of the data which is

$$\mathcal{D}' \in \{160 \text{ image samples: 80 dogs and 80 cats}\} \tag{5.11}$$

and

$$\mathcal{D} \in \{\text{the universe of dogs and cats}\}. \tag{5.12}$$

Supervised and unsupervised learning methods aim to either create algorithms for classification, clustering, or regression. The discussion above is a general strategy for classification. The previous chapter discusses regression architectures. For both tasks, the goal is to build a model from data on $\mathcal{D}'$ that can generalize to $\mathcal{D}$. As already shown in the preceding chapter on regression, generalization can be very difficult and cross-validation strategies are critical. Deep neural networks, which are state-of-the-art machine learning algorithms for regression and classification, often have difficulty generalizing. Creating strong generalization schemes is at the forefront of machine learning research.

Some of the difficulties in generalization can be illustrated in Fig. 5.8. These data sets, although easily classified and clustered through visual inspection can be difficulty for many regression and classification schemes. Essentially, the boundary between the data forms a nonlinear manifold that is often difficult to characterize. Moreover, if the sampling data $\mathcal{D}'$ only captures a portion of the manifold, then a classification or regression model will

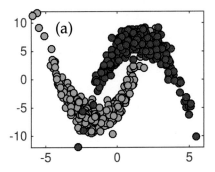 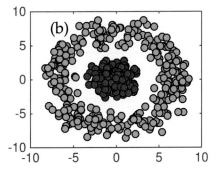

Figure 5.8 Classification and regression models for data can be difficult when the data have nonlinear functions which separate them. In this case, the function separating the green and magenta balls can be difficult to extract. Moreover, if only a small sample of the data $\mathcal{D}'$ is available, then a generalizable model may be impossible to construct for $\mathcal{D}$. The left data set (a) represents two half-moon shapes that are just superimposed while the concentric rings in (b) requires a circle as a separation boundary between the data. Both are challenging to produce.

almost surely fail in characterizing $\mathcal{D}$. These are also only two-dimensional depictions of a classification problem. It is not difficult to imagine how complicated such data embeddings can be in higher dimensional space. Visualization in such cases is essentially impossible and one must rely on algorithms to extract the meaningful boundaries separating data. What follows in this chapter and the next are methods for classification and regression given data on $\mathcal{D}'$ that may or may not be labelled. There is quite a diversity of mathematical methods available for performing such tasks.

5.3 Unsupervised Learning: *k*-means Clustering

A variety of supervised and unsupervised algorithms will be highlighted in this chapter. We will start with one of the most prominent unsupervised algorithms in use today: k-means clustering. The k-means algorithm assumes one is given a set of vector valued data with the goal of partitioning m observations into k clusters. Each observation is labeled as belonging to a cluster with the nearest mean, which serves as a proxy (prototype) for that cluster. This results in a partitioning of the data space into Voronoi cells.

Although the number of observations and dimension of the system are known, the number of partitions k is generally unknown and must also be determined. Alternatively, the user simply chooses a number of clusters to extract from the data. The k-means algorithm is iterative, first assuming initial values for the mean of each cluster and then updating the means until the algorithm has converged. Fig. 5.9 depicts the update rule of the k-means algorithm. The algorithm proceeds as follows: (i) given initial values for k distinct means, compute the distance of each observation $\mathbf{x}_j$ to each of the k means. (ii) Label each observation as belonging to the nearest mean. (iii) Once labeling is completed, find the *center-of-mass* (mean) for each group of labeled points. These new means are then used to

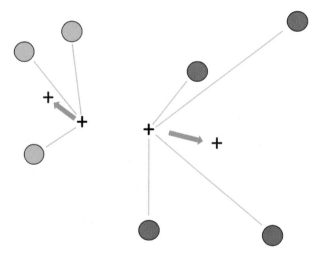

Figure 5.9 Illustration of the k-means algorithm for $k = 2$. Two initial starting values of the man are given (black +). Each point is labeled as belonging to one of the two means. The green balls are thus labeled as part of the cluster with the left + and the magenta balls are labeled as part of the right +. Once labeled, the mean of the two clusters is recomputed (red +). The process is repeated until the means converge.

start back at step (i) in the algorithm. This is a heuristic algorithm that was first proposed by Stuart Lloyd in 1957 [339], although it was not published until 1982.

The *k*-means objective can be stated formally in terms of an optimization problem. Specifically, the following minimization describes this process

$$\underset{\boldsymbol{\mu}_j}{\operatorname{argmin}} \sum_{j=1}^{k} \sum_{\mathbf{x}_j \in \mathcal{D}'_j} \|\mathbf{x}_j - \boldsymbol{\mu}_j\|^2 \tag{5.13}$$

where the $\boldsymbol{\mu}_j$ denote the mean of the jth cluster and $\mathcal{D}'_j$ denotes the subdomain of data associated with that cluster. This minimizes the within-cluster sum of squares. In general, solving the optimization problem as stated is *NP*-hard, making it computationally intractable. However, there a number of heuristic algorithms that provide good performance despite not having a guarantee that they will converge to the globally optimal solution.

Cross-validation of the *k*-means algorithm, as well as any machine learning algorithm, is critical for determining its effectiveness. Without labels the cross validation procedure is more nuanced as there is no ground truth to compare with. The cross-validation methods of the last section, however, can still be used to test the robustness of the classifier to different sub-selections of the data through *k*-fold cross-validation. The following portions of code generate Lloyd's algorithm for *k*-means clustering. We first consider making two clusters of data and partitioning the data into a training and test set.

Code 5.5 *k*-means data generation.

```
% training & testing set sizes
n1=100;   % training set size
n2=50;    % test set size

% random ellipse 1 centered at (0,0)
x=randn(n1+n2,1); y=0.5*randn(n1+n2,1);

% random ellipse 2 centered at (1,-2) and rotated by theta
x2=randn(n1+n2,1)+1; y2=0.2*randn(n1+n2,1)-2; theta=pi/4;
A=[cos(theta) -sin(theta); sin(theta) cos(theta)];
x3=A(1,1)*x2+A(1,2)*y2; y3=A(2,1)*x2+A(2,2)*y2;
subplot(2,2,1)
plot(x(1:n1),y(1:n1),'ro'), hold on
plot(x3(1:n1),y3(1:n1),'bo')

% training set:  first 200 of 240 points
X1=[x3(1:n1) y3(1:n1)];
X2=[x(1:n1) y(1:n1)];

Y=[X1; X2]; Z=[ones(n1,1); 2*ones(n1,1)];

% test set:  remaining 40 points
x1test=[x3(n1+1:end) y3(n1+1:end)];
x2test=[x(n1+1:end) y(n1+1:end)];
```

Fig. 5.11 shows the data generated from two distinct Gaussian distributions. In this case, we have ground truth data to check the *k*-means clustering against. In general, this is not the case. The Lloyd algorithm guesses the number of clusters and the initial cluster means and then proceeds to update them in an iterative fashion. *k*-means is sensitive to the initial guess and many modern versions of the algorithm also provide principled strategies for initialization.

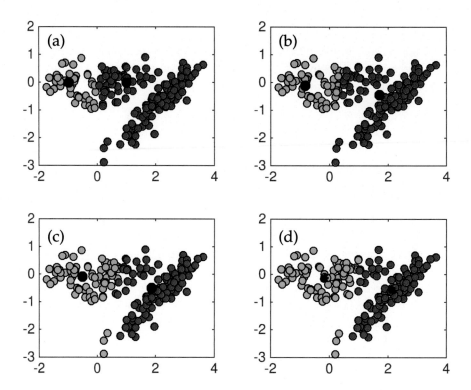

Figure 5.10 Illustration of the k-means iteration procedure based upon Lloyd's algorithm [339]. Two clusters are sought so that $k = 2$. The initial guesses (black circles in panel (a)) are used to initially label all the data according to their distance from each initial guess for the mean. The means are then updated by computing the means of the newly labeled data. This two-stage heuristic converges after approximately four iterations.

Code 5.6 Lloyd algorithm for k-means.

```
g1=[-1 0]; g2=[1 0]; %  Initial guess
for j=1:4
    class1=[]; class2=[];
    for jj=1:length(Y)
        d1=norm(g1-Y(jj,:));
        d2=norm(g2-Y(jj,:));
        if d1<d2
            class1=[class1; [Y(jj,1) Y(jj,2)]];
        else
            class2=[class2; [Y(jj,1) Y(jj,2)]];
        end
    end
    g1=[mean(class1(1:end,1)) mean(class1(1:end,2))];
    g2=[mean(class2(1:end,1)) mean(class2(1:end,2))];
end
```

Fig. 5.10 shows the iterative procedure of the k-means clustering. The two initial guesses are used to initially label all the data points (Fig. 5.10(a)). New means are computed and the data relabeled. After only four iterations, the clusters converge. This algorithm was explicitly developed here to show how the iteration procedure rapidly provides an unsupervised labeling of all of the data. MATLAB has a built in k-means algorithm that only requires a

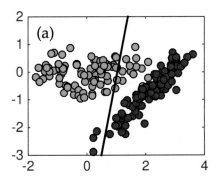 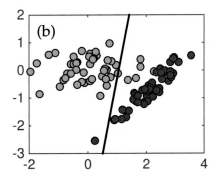

Figure 5.11 *k*-means clustering of the data using MATLAB's **means** command. Only the data and number of clusters need be specified. (a) The training data is used to produce a decision line (black line) separating the clusters. Note that the line is clearly not optimal. The classification line can then be used on withheld data to test the accuracy of the algorithm. For the test data, one (of 50) magenta ball would be mislabeled while six (of 50) green balls are mislabeled.

data matrix and the number of clusters desired. It is simple to use and provides a valuable diagnostic tool for data. The following code uses the MATLAB command **mean** and also extracts the *decision line* generated from the algorithm separating the two clusters.

Code 5.7 *k*-means using MATLAB.

```
% kmeans code
[ind,c]=kmeans(Y,2);
plot(c(1,1),c(1,2),'k*','Linewidth',[2])
plot(c(2,1),c(2,2),'k*','Linewidth',[2])

midx=(c(1,1)+c(2,1))/2; midy=(c(1,2)+c(2,2))/2;
slope=(c(2,2)-c(1,2))/(c(2,1)-c(1,1)); % rise/run
b=midy+(1/slope)*midx;
xsep=-1:0.1:2; ysep=-(1/slope)*xsep+b;

figure(1), subplot(2,2,1), hold on
plot(xsep,ysep,'k','Linewidth',[2]),axis([-2 4 -3 2])

% error on test data
figure(1), subplot(2,2,2)
plot(x(n1+1:end),y(n1+1:end),'ro'), hold on
plot(x3(n1+1:end),y3(n1+1:end),'bo')
plot(xsep,ysep,'k','Linewidth',[2]), axis([-2 4 -3 2])
```

Fig. 5.11 shows the results of the *k*-means algorithm and depicts the decision line separating the data into two clusters. The green and magenta balls denote the true labels of the data, showing that the *k*-means line does not correctly extract the labels. Indeed, a supervised algorithm is more proficient in extracting the ground truth results, as will be shown later in this chapter. Regardless, the algorithm does get a majority of the data labeled correctly.

The success of *k*-means is based on two factors: (i) no supervision is required, and (ii) it is a fast heuristic algorithm. The example here shows that the method is not very accurate, but this is often the case in unsupervised methods as the algorithm has limited knowledge of the data. Cross-validation efforts, such as *k*-fold cross-validation, can help improve the model and make the unsupervised learning more accurate, but it will generally be less accurate than a supervised algorithm that has labeled data.

5.4   Unsupervised Hierarchical Clustering: Dendrogram

Another commonly used unsupervised algorithm for clustering data is a *dendrogram*. Like k-means clustering, dendrograms are created from a simple hierarchical algorithm, allowing one to efficiently visualize if data is clustered without any labeling or supervision. This hierarchical approach will be applied to the data illustrated in Fig. 5.12 where a ground truth is known. Hierarchical clustering methods are generated either from a top-down or a bottom-up approach. Specifically, they are one of two types:

Agglomerative: Each data point $\mathbf{x}_j$ is its own cluster initially. The data is merged in pairs as one creates a hierarchy of clusters. The merging of data eventually stops once all the data has been merged into a single über cluster. This is the bottom-up approach in hierarchical clustering.

Divisive: In this case, all the observations $\mathbf{x}_j$ are initially part of a single giant cluster. The data is then recursively split into smaller and smaller clusters. The splitting continues until the algorithm stops according to a user specified objective. The divisive method can split the data until each data point is its own node.

In general, the merging and splitting of data is accomplished with a heuristic, greedy algorithm which is easy to execute computationally. The results of hierarchical clustering are usually presented in a dendrogram.

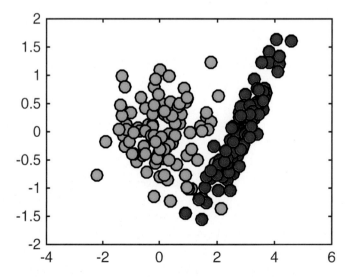

Figure 5.12 Example data used for construction of a dendrogram. The data is constructed from two Gaussian distributions (50 points each) that are easy to discern through a visual inspection. The dendrogram will produce a hierarchy that ideally would separate green balls from magenta balls.

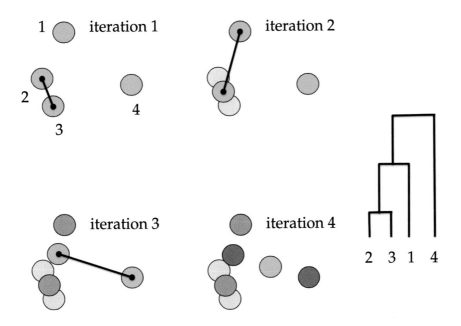

Figure 5.13 Illustration of the agglomerative hierarchical clustering scheme applied to four data points. In the algorithm, the distance between the four data points is computed. Initially the Euclidian distance between points 2 and 3 is closest. Points 2 and 3 are now merged into a point mid-way between them and the distances are once again computed. The dendrogram on the right shows how the process generates a summary (dendrogram) of the hierarchical clustering. Note that the length of the branches of the dendrogram tree are directly related to the distance between the merged points.

In this section, we will focus on agglomerative hierarchical clustering and the dendrogram command from MATLAB. Like the Lloyd algorithm for k-means clustering, building the dendrogram proceeds from a simple algorithmic structure based on computing the distance between data points. Although we typically use a Euclidean distance, there are a number of important distance metrics one might consider for different types of data. Some typical distances are given as follows:

$$\text{Euclidean distance } \|\mathbf{x}_j - \mathbf{x}_k\|_2 \tag{5.14a}$$

$$\text{Squared Euclidean distance } \|\mathbf{x}_j - \mathbf{x}_k\|_2^2 \tag{5.14b}$$

$$\text{Manhattan distance } \|\mathbf{x}_j - \mathbf{x}_k\|_1 \tag{5.14c}$$

$$\text{Maximum distance } \|\mathbf{x}_j - \mathbf{x}_k\|_\infty \tag{5.14d}$$

$$\text{Mahalanobis distance } \sqrt{(\mathbf{x}_j - \mathbf{x}_k)^T \mathbf{C}^{-1}(\mathbf{x}_j - \mathbf{x}_k)} \tag{5.14e}$$

where $\mathbf{C}^{-1}$ is the covariance matrix. As already illustrated in the previous chapter, the choice of norm can make a tremendous difference for exposing patterns in the data that can be exploited for clustering and classification.

The dendrogram algorithm is shown in Fig. 5.13. The algorithm is as follows: (i) the distance between all m data points $\mathbf{x}_j$ is computed (the figure illustrates the use of a Euclidean distance), (ii) the closest two data points are merged into a single new data point midway between their original locations, and (iii) repeat the calculation with the new $m - 1$ points.

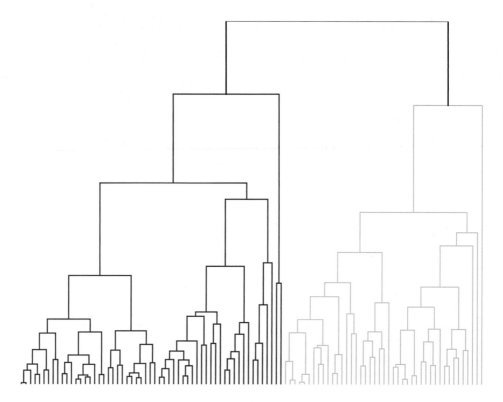

Figure 5.14 Dendrogram structure produced from the data in Fig. 5.12. The dendrogram shows which points are merged as well as the distance between points. Two clusters are generated for this level of threshold.

The algorithm continues until the data has been hierarchically merged into a single data point.

The following code performs a hierarchical clustering using the **dendrogram** command from MATLAB. The example we use is the same as that considered for k-means clustering. Fig. 5.12 shows the data under consideration. Visual inspection shows two clear clusters that are easily discernible. As with k-means, our goal is to see how well a dendrogram can extract the two clusters.

Code 5.8 Dendrogram for unsupervised clustering.

```
Y3=[X1(1:50,:); X2(1:50,:)];
Y2 = pdist(Y3,'euclidean');
Z = linkage(Y2,'average');
thresh=0.85*max(Z(:,3));
[H,T,O]=dendrogram(Z,100,'ColorThreshold',thresh);
```

Fig. 5.14 shows the dendrogram associated with the data in Fig. 5.12. The structure of the algorithm shows which points are merged as well as the distance between points. The threshold command is important in labeling where each point belongs in the hierarchical scheme. By setting the threshold at different levels, there can be more or fewer clusters in the dendrogram. The following code uses the output of the dendrogram to show how

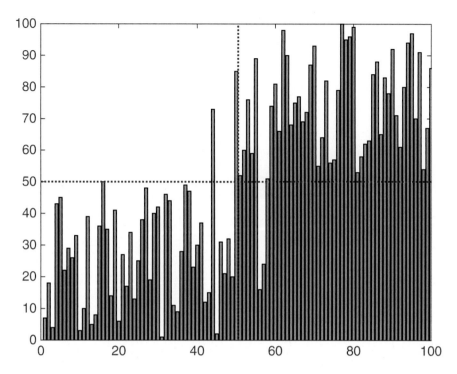

Figure 5.15 Clustering outcome from dendrogram routine. This is a summary of Fig. 5.14, showing how each of the points was clustered through the distance metric. The horizontal red dotted line shows where the ideal separation should occur. The first 50 points (green dots of Fig. 5.12) should be grouped so that they are below the red horizontal line in the lower left quadrant. The second 50 points (magenta dots of Fig. 5.12) should be grouped above the red horizontal line in the upper right quadrant. In summary, the dendrogram only misclassified two green points and two magenta points.

the data was labeled. Recall that the first 50 data points are from the green cluster and the second 50 data points are from the magenta cluster.

Code 5.9 Dendrogram labels for cats and dogs.

```
bar(O), hold on
plot([0 100],[50 50],'r:','Linewidth',2)
plot([50.5 50.5],[0 100],'r:','Linewidth',2)
```

Fig. 5.15 shows how the data was clustered in the dendrogram. If perfect clustering had been achieved, then the first 50 points would have been below the horizontal dotted red line while the second 50 points would have been above the horizontal dotted red line. The vertical dotted red line is the line separating the green dots on the left from the magenta dots on the right.

The following code shows how a greater number of clusters are generated by adjusting the threshold in the **dendrogram** command. This is equivalent to setting the number of clusters in k-means to something greater than two. Recall that one rarely has a ground truth to compare with when doing unsupervised clustering, so tuning the threshold becomes important.

```
thresh=0.25*max(Z(:,3));
[H,T,O]=dendrogram(Z,100,'ColorThreshold',thresh);
```

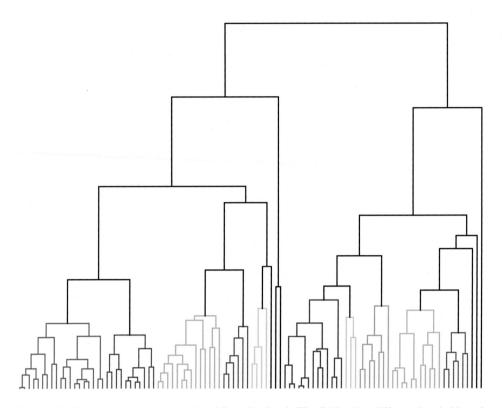

Figure 5.16 Dendrogram structure produced from the data in Fig. 5.12 with a different threshold used than in Fig. 5.14. The dendrogram shows which points are merged as well as the distance between points. In this case, more than a dozen clusters are generated.

Fig. 5.16 shows a new dendrogram with a different threshold. Note that in this case, the hierarchical clustering produces more than a dozen clusters. The tuning parameter can be seen to be critical for unsupervised clustering, much like choosing the number of clusters in k-means. In summary, both k-means and hierarchical clustering provide a method whereby data can be parsed automatically into clusters. This provides a starting point for interpretations and analysis in data mining.

5.5   Mixture Models and the Expectation-Maximization Algorithm

The third unsupervised method we consider is known as *finite mixture models*. Often the models are assumed to be Gaussian distributions in which case this method is known as *Gaussian mixture models* (GMM). The basic assumption in this method is that data observations $\mathbf{x}_j$ are a mixture of a set of k processes that combine to form the measurement. Like k-means and hierarchical clustering, the GMM model we fit to the data requires that we specify the number of mixtures k and the individual statistical properties of each mixture that best fit the data. GMMs are especially useful since the assumption that each mixture model has a Gaussian distribution implies that it can be completely characterized by two parameters: the mean and the variance.

The algorithm that enables the GMM computes the maximum-likelihood using the famous *Expectation-Maximization* (EM) algorithm of Dempster, Laird and Rubin [148]. The EM algorithm is designed to find maximum likelihood parameters of statistical models. Generally, the iterative structure of the algorithm finds a local maximum-likelihood, which estimates the true parameters that cannot be directly solved for. As with most data, the observed data involves many latent or unmeasured variables and unknown parameters. Regardless, the alternating and iterative construction of the algorithm recursively estimates the best parameters possible from an initial guess. The EM algorithm proceeds like the *k*-means algorithm in that initial guesses for the mean and variance are given for the assumed *k*-distributions. The algorithm then recursively updates the weights of the mixtures versus the parameters of each mixture. One alternates between these two until convergence is achieved.

In any such iteration scheme, it is not obvious that the solution will converge, or that the solution is good, since it typically falls into a local value of the maximum-likelihood. But it can be proven that in this context it does converge, and that the derivative of the likelihood is arbitrarily close to zero at that point, which in turn means that the point is either a maximum or a saddle point [561]. In general, multiple maxima may occur, with no guarantee that the global maximum will be found. Some likelihoods also have singularities, i.e., nonsensical maxima. For example, one of the solutions that may be found by EM in a mixture model involves setting one of the components to have zero variance and the mean equal to one of the data points. Cross-validation can often alleviate some of the common pitfalls that can occur by initializing the algorithm with some bad initial guesses.

The fundamental assumption of the mixture model is that the probability density function (PDF) for observations of data $\mathbf{x}_j$ is a weighted linear sum of a set of unknown distributions

$$f(\mathbf{x}_j, \mathbf{\Theta}) = \sum_{p=1}^{k} \alpha_p f_p(\mathbf{x}_j, \mathbf{\Theta}_p) \tag{5.15}$$

where $f(\cdot)$ is the measured PDF, $f_p(\cdot)$ is the PDF of the mixture j, and k is the total number of mixtures. Each of the PDFs $f_j(\cdot)$ is weighted by α_p ($\alpha_1 + \alpha_2 + \cdots + \alpha_k = 1$) and parametrized by an unknown vector of parameters $\mathbf{\Theta}_p$. To state the objective of mixture models more precisely then: *Given the observed PDF $f(\mathbf{x}_j, \mathbf{\Theta})$, estimate the mixture weights α_p and the parameters of the distribution $\mathbf{\Theta}_p$.* Note that $\mathbf{\Theta}$ is a vector containing all the parameters $\mathbf{\Theta}_p$. Making this task somewhat easier is the fact that we assume the form of the PDF distribution $f_p(\cdot)$.

For GMM, the parameters in the vector $\mathbf{\Theta}_p$ are known to include only two variables: the mean μ_p and variance σ_p. Moreover, the distribution $f_p(\cdot)$ is normally distributed so that (5.15) becomes

$$f(\mathbf{x}_j, \mathbf{\Theta}) = \sum_{p=1}^{k} \alpha_p \mathcal{N}_p(\mathbf{x}_j, \mu_p, \sigma_p). \tag{5.16}$$

This gives a much more tractable framework since there are now a limited set of parameters. Thus once one assumes a number of mixtures k, then the task is to determine α_p along with μ_p and σ_p for each mixture. It should be noted that there are many other distributions besides Gaussian that can be imposed, but GMM are common since without prior knowledge, an assumption of Gaussian distribution is typically assumed.

An estimate of the parameter vector $\boldsymbol{\Theta}$ can be computed using the *maximum likelihood estimate* (MLE) of Fisher. The MLE computes the value of $\boldsymbol{\Theta}$ from the roots of

$$\frac{\partial L(\boldsymbol{\Theta})}{\partial \boldsymbol{\Theta}} = 0 \tag{5.17}$$

where the log-likelihood function L is

$$L(\boldsymbol{\Theta}) = \sum_{j=1}^{n} \log f(\mathbf{x}_j | \boldsymbol{\Theta}) \tag{5.18}$$

and the sum is over all the n data vectors $\mathbf{x}_j$. The solution to this optimization problem, i.e. when the derivative is zero, produces a local maximizer. This maximizer can be computed using the EM algorithm since derivatives cannot be explicitly computed without an analytic form.

The EM algorithm starts by assuming an initial estimate (guess) of the parameter vector $\boldsymbol{\Theta}$. This estimate can be used to estimate

$$\tau_p(\mathbf{x}_j, \boldsymbol{\Theta}) = \frac{\alpha_p f_p(\mathbf{x}_j, \boldsymbol{\Theta}_p)}{f(\mathbf{x}_j, \boldsymbol{\Theta})} \tag{5.19}$$

which is the posterior probability of component membership of $\mathbf{x}_j$ in the pth distribution. In other words, does $\mathbf{x}_j$ belong to the pth mixture? The E-step of the EM algorithm uses this posterior to compute memberships. For GMM, the algorithm proceeds as follows: Given an initial parametrization of $\boldsymbol{\Theta}$ and α_p, compute

$$\tau_p^{(k)}(\mathbf{x}_j) = \frac{\alpha_p^{(k)} \mathcal{N}_p(\mathbf{x}_j, \mu_p^{(k)}, \sigma_p^{(k)})}{\mathcal{N}(\mathbf{x}_j, \boldsymbol{\Theta}^{(k)})}. \tag{5.20}$$

With an estimated posterior probability, the M-step of the algorithm then updates the parameters and mixture weights

$$\alpha_p^{(k+1)} = \frac{1}{n} \sum_{j=1}^{n} \tau_p^{(k)}(\mathbf{x}_j) \tag{5.21a}$$

$$\mu_p^{(k+1)} = \frac{\sum_{j=1}^{n} \mathbf{x}_j \tau_p^{(k)}(\mathbf{x}_j)}{\sum_{j=1}^{n} \tau_p^{(k)}(\mathbf{x}_j)} \tag{5.21b}$$

$$\Sigma_p^{(k+1)} = \frac{\sum_{j=1}^{n} \tau_p^{(k)}(\mathbf{x}_j) \left(\mathbf{x}_j - \mu_p^{(k+1)}\right) \left(\mathbf{x}_j - \mu_p^{(k+1)}\right)^T}{\sum_{j=1}^{n} \tau_p^{(k)}(\mathbf{x}_j)} \tag{5.21c}$$

where the matrix $\Sigma_p^{(k+1)}$ is the covariance matrix containing the variance parameters. The E- and M-steps are alternated until convergence within a specified tolerance. Recall that to initialize the algorithm, the number of mixture models k must be specified and initial parametrization (guesses) of the distributions given. This is similar to the k-means algorithm where the number of clusters k is prescribed and an initial guess for the cluster centers is specified.

The GMM is popular since it simply fits k Gaussian distributions to data, which is reasonable for unsupervised learning. The GMM algorithm also has a stronger theoretical base than most unsupervised methods as both k-means and hierarchical clustering are

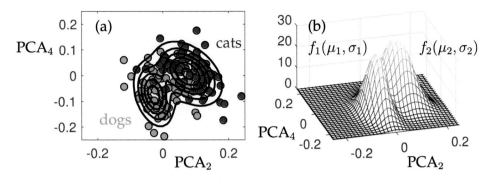

Figure 5.17 GMM fit of the second and fourth principal components of the dog and cat wavelet image data. The two Gaussians are well placed over the distinct dog and cat features as shown in (a). The PDF of the Gaussian models extracted are highlighted in (b) in arbitrary units.

simply defined as algorithms. The primary assumption in GMM is the number of clusters and the form of the distribution $f(\cdot)$.

The following code executes a GMM model on the second and fourth principal components of the dog and cat wavelet image data introduced previously in Figs. 5.4-5.6. Thus the features are the second and fourth columns of the right singular vector of the SVD. The **fitgmdist** command is used to extract the mixture model.

Code 5.10 Gaussian mixture model for cats versus dogs.

```
dogcat=v(:,2:2:4);
GMMModel=fitgmdist(dogcat,2)
AIC= GMMModel.AIC

subplot(2,2,1)
h=ezcontour(@(x1,x2)pdf(GMMModel,[x1 x2]));
subplot(2,2,2)
h=ezmesh(@(x1,x2)pdf(GMMModel,[x1 x2]));
```

The results of the algorithm can be plotted for visual inspection, and the parameters associated with each Gaussian are given. Specifically, the mixing proportion of each model along with the mean in each of the two dimensions of the feature space. The following is displayed to the screen.

```
Component 1:
Mixing proportion: 0.355535
Mean:    -0.0290   -0.0753

Component 2:
Mixing proportion: 0.644465
Mean:    0.0758    0.0076

AIC =

 -792.8105
```

The code can also produce an AIC score for how well the mixture of Gaussians explain the data. This gives a principled method for cross-validating in order to determine the number of mixtures required to describe the data.

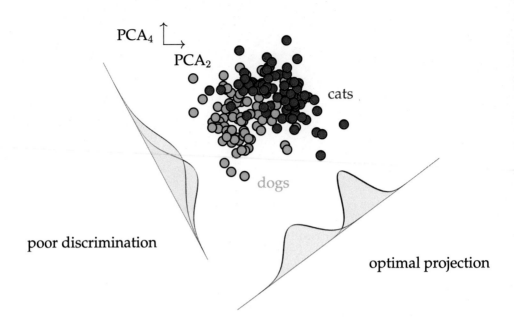

Figure 5.18 Illustration of linear discriminant analysis (LDA). The LDA optimization method produces an optimal dimensionality reduction to a decision line for classification. The figure illustrates the projection of data onto the second and fourth principal component modes of the dog and cat wavelet data considered in Fig. 5.4. Without optimization, a general projection can lead to very poor discrimination between the data. However, the LDA separates the probability distribution functions in an optimal way.

Fig. 5.17 shows the results of the GMM fitting procedure along with the original data of cats and dogs. The Gaussians produced from the fitting procedure are also illustrated. The **fitgmdist** command can also be used with **cluster** to label new data from the feature separation discovered by GMM.

5.6   Supervised Learning and Linear Discriminants

We now turn our attention to supervised learning methods. One of the earliest supervised methods for classification of data was developed by Fisher in 1936 in the context of taxonomy [182]. His *linear discriminant analysis* (LDA) is still one of the standard techniques for classification. It was generalized by C. R. Rao for multi-class data in 1948 [446]. The goal of these algorithms is to find a linear combination of features that characterizes or separates two or more classes of objects or events in the data. Importantly, for this supervised technique we have labeled data which guides the classification algorithm. Fig. 5.18 illustrates the concept of finding an optimal low-dimensional embedding of the data for classification. The LDA algorithm aims to solve an optimization problem to find a subspace whereby the different labeled data have clear separation between their distribution of points. This then makes classification easier because an optimal feature space has been selected.

The supervised learning architecture includes a training and withhold set of data. The withhold set is never used to train the classifier. However, the training data can be partitioned into k-folds, for instance, to help build a better classification model. The last chapter details how cross-validation should be appropriately used. The goal here is to train an algorithm that uses feature space to make a decision about how to classify data. Fig. 5.18 gives a cartoon of the key idea involved in LDA. In our example, two data sets are considered and projected onto new bases. In the left figure, the projection shows that the data is completely mixed, making it difficult to separate the data. In the right figure, which is the ideal charicature for LDA, the data are well separated with the means μ_1 and μ_2 being well apart when projected onto the chosen subspace. Thus the goal of LDA is two-fold: *find a suitable projection that maximizes the distance between the inter-class data while minimizing the intra-class data.*

For a two-class LDA, this results in the following mathematical formulation. Construct a projection $\mathbf{w}$ such that

$$\mathbf{w} = \arg\max_{\mathbf{w}} \frac{\mathbf{w}^T \mathbf{S}_B \mathbf{w}}{\mathbf{w}^T \mathbf{S}_W \mathbf{w}} \tag{5.22}$$

where the scatter matrices for between-class $\mathbf{S}_B$ and within-class $\mathbf{S}_W$ data are given by

$$\mathbf{S}_B = (\mu_2 - \mu_1)(\mu_2 - \mu_1)^T \tag{5.23}$$

$$\mathbf{S}_W = \sum_{j=1}^{2} \sum_{\mathbf{x}} (\mathbf{x} - \mu_j)(\mathbf{x} - \mu_j)^T . \tag{5.24}$$

These quantities essentially measure the variance of the data sets as well as the variance of the difference in the means. The criterion in (5.22) is commonly known as the generalized Rayleigh quotient whose solution can be found via the generalized eigenvalue problem

$$\mathbf{S}_B \mathbf{w} = \lambda \mathbf{S}_W \mathbf{w} \tag{5.25}$$

where the maximum eigenvalue λ and its associated eigenvector gives the quantity of interest and the projection basis. Thus, once the scatter matrices are constructed, the generalized eigenvectors can be constructed with MATLAB.

Performing an LDA analysis in MATLAB is simple. One needs only to organize the data into a training set with labels, which can then be applied to a test data set. Given a set of data $\mathbf{x}_j$ for $j = 1, 2, \cdots, m$ with corresponding labels $\mathbf{y}_j$, the algorithm will find an optimal classification space as shown in Fig. 5.18. New data $\mathbf{x}_k$ with $k = m+1, m+2, \cdots, m+n$ can then be evaluated and labeled. We illustrate the classification of data using the dog and cat data set introduced in the feature section of this chapter. Specifically, we consider the dog and cat images in the wavelet domain and label them so that $\mathbf{y}_j \in \{\pm 1\}$ ($\mathbf{y}_j = 1$ is a dog and $\mathbf{y}_j = -1$ is a cat). The following code trains on the first 60 images of dogs and cats, and then tests the classifier on the remaining 20 dog and cat images. For simplicity, we train on the second and fourth principal components as these show good discrimination between dogs and cats (See Fig. 5.5).

Code 5.11 LDA analysis of dogs versus cats.

```
load catData_w.mat
load dogData_w.mat
CD=[dog_wave cat_wave];
[u,s,v]=svd(CD-mean(CD(:)));

xtrain=[v(1:60,2:2:4); v(81:140,2:2:4)];
```

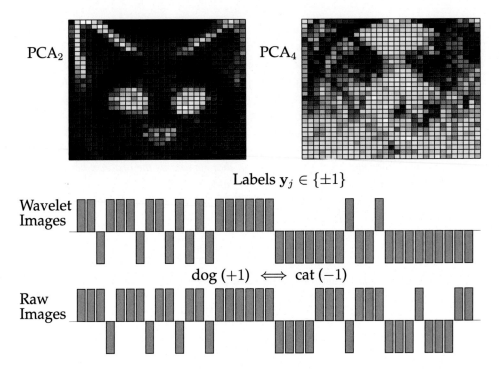

Figure 5.19 Depiction of the performance achieved for classification using the second and fourth principal component modes. The top two panels are PCA modes (features) used to build a classifier. The labels returned are either $y_j \in \{\pm 1\}$. The ground truth answer in this case should produce a vector of 20 ones followed by 20 negative ones.

```
label=[ones(60,1); -1*ones(60,1)];
test=[v(61:80,2:2:4); v(141:160,2:2:4)];

class=classify(test,xtrain,label);
truth=[ones(20,1); -1*ones(20,1)];
E=100-sum(0.5*abs(class-truth))/40*100
```

Note that the **classify** command in MATLAB takes in the three matrices of interest: the training data, the test data, and the labels for the training data. What is produced are the labels for the test set. One can also extract from this command the decision line for online use. Fig. 5.19 shows the results of the classification on the 40 test data samples. Recall that this classification is performed using only the second and fourth PCA modes which cluster as shown in Fig. 5.18. The returned labels are either ±1 depending on whether a cat or dog is labeled. The ground truth labels for the test data should return a +1 (dogs) for the first 20 test sets and a −1 (cats) for the second test set. The accuracy of classification for this realization is 82.5% (2/20 cats are mislabeled while 5/20 dogs are mislabeled). Comparing the wavelet images to the raw images we see that the feature selection in the raw images is not as good. In particular, for the same two principal components, 9/20 cats are mislabeled and 4/20 dogs are mislabeled.

Of course, the data is fairly limited and cross-validation should always be performed to evaluate the classifier. The following code runs 100 trials of the **classify** command where 60 dog and cat images are randomly selected and tested against the remaining 20 images.

Code 5.12 Cross-validation of the LDA analysis.

```
for jj=1:100;
    r1=randperm(80); r2=randperm(80);
    ind1=r1(1:60); ind2=r2(1:60)+60;
    ind1t=r1(61:80); ind2t=r2(61:80)+60;

    xtrain=[v(ind1,2:2:4); v(ind2,2:2:4)];
    test=[v(ind1t,2:2:4); v(ind2t,2:2:4)];

    label=[ones(60,1); -1*ones(60,1)];
    truth=[ones(20,1); -1*ones(20,1)];
    class=classify(test,xtrain,label);
    E(jj)=sum(abs(class-truth))/40*100;
end
```

Fig. 5.20 shows the results of the cross-validation over 100 trials. Note the variability that can occur from trial to trial. Specifically, the performance can achieve 100%, but can also be as low as 40%, which is worse than a coin flip. The average classification score (red dotted line) is around 70%. Cross-validation, as already highlighted in the regression chapter, is critical for testing and robustifying the model. Recall that the methods for producing a classifier are based on optimization and regression, so that all the cross-validation methods can be ported to the clustering and classification problem.

In addition to a linear discriminant line, a quadratic discriminant line can be found to separate the data. Indeed, the **classify** command in MATLAB allows one to not only produce the classifier, but also extract the line of separation between the data. The following

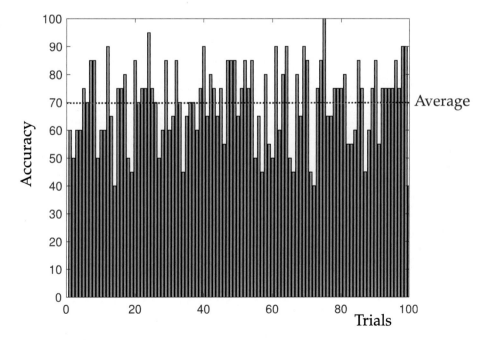

Figure 5.20 Performance of the LDA over 100 trials. Note the variability that can occur in the classifier depending on which data is selected for training and testing. This highlights the importance of cross-validation for building a robust classifier.

commands are used to produce labels for new data as well as the discrimination line between the dogs and cats.

Code 5.13 Plotting the linear and quadratic discrimination lines.

```
subplot(2,2,1)
[class,~,~,~,coeff]=classify(test,xtrain,label);
K = coeff(1,2).const;
L = coeff(1,2).linear;
f = @(x,y) K + [x y]*L;
h2 = ezplot(f,[-.15 0.25 -.3 0.2]);
subplot(2,2,2)
[class,~,~,~,coeff]=classify(test,xtrain,label,'quadratic');
K = coeff(1,2).const;
L = coeff(1,2).linear;
Q = coeff(1,2).quadratic;
f = @(x,y) K + [x y]*L + sum(([x y]*Q) .* [x y], 2);
h2 = ezplot(f,[-.15 0.25 -.3 0.2]);
```

Fig. 5.21 shows the dog and cat data along with the linear and quadratic lines separating them. This linear or quadratic fit is found in the structured variable **coeff** which is returned with classify. The quadratic line of separation can often offer a little more flexibility when trying to fit boundaries separating data. A major advantage of LDA based methods: they are easily interpretable and easy to compute. Thus, they are widely used across many branches of the sciences for classification of data.

5.7   Support Vector Machines (SVM)

One of the most successful data mining methods developed to date is the *support vector machine* (SVM). It is a core machine learning tool that is used widely in industry and science, often providing results that are better than competing methods. Along with the *random forest* algorithm, they have been pillars of machine learning in the last few decades. With enough training data, the SVM can now be replaced with deep neural nets. But

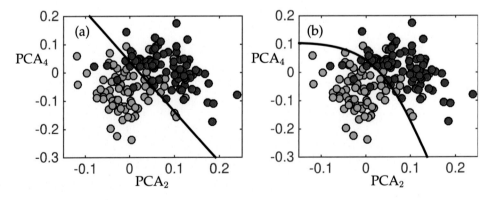

Figure 5.21 Classification line for (a) linear discriminant (LDA) and (b) quadratic discriminant (QDA) for dog (green dots) versus cat (magenta dots) data projected onto the second and fourth principal components. This two dimensional feature space allows for a good discrimination in the data. The two lines represent the best line and parabola for separating the data for a given training sample.

otherwise, SVM and random forest are frequently used algorithms for applications where the best classification scores are required.

The original SVM algorithm by Vapnik and Chervonenkis evolved out of the statistical learning literature in 1963, where hyperplanes are optimized to split the data into distinct clusters. Nearly three decades later, Boser, Guyon and Vapnik created nonlinear classifiers by applying the kernel trick to maximum-margin hyperplanes [70]. The current standard incarnation (soft margin) was proposed by Cortes and Vapnik in the mid-1990s [138].

Linear SVM

The key idea of the linear SVM method is to construct a hyperplane

$$\mathbf{w} \cdot \mathbf{x} + b = 0 \tag{5.26}$$

where the vector $\mathbf{w}$ and constant b parametrize the hyperplane. Fig. 5.22 shows two potential hyperplanes splitting a set of data. Each has a different value of $\mathbf{w}$ and constant b. The optimization problem associated with SVM is to not only optimize a decision line which makes the fewest labeling errors for the data, but also optimizes the largest margin between the data, shown in the gray region of Fig. 5.22. The vectors that determine the boundaries of the margin, i.e. the vectors touching the edge of the gray regions, are termed the *support vectors*. Given the hyperplane (5.26), a new data point $\mathbf{x}_j$ can be classified by simply computing the sign of $(\mathbf{w} \cdot \mathbf{x}_j + b)$. Specifically, for classification labels $\mathbf{y}_j \in \{\pm 1\}$,

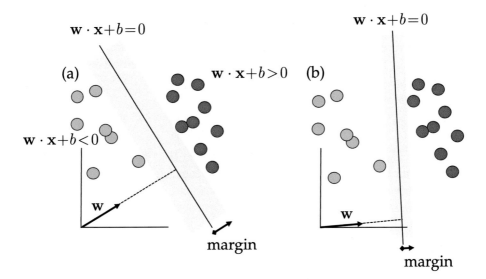

Figure 5.22 The SVM classification scheme constructs a hyperplane $\mathbf{w} \cdot \mathbf{x} + b = 0$ that optimally separates the labeled data. The area of the margin separating the labeled data is maximal in (a) and much less in (b). Determining the vector $\mathbf{w}$ and parameter b is the goal of the SVM optimization. Note that for data to the right of the hyperplane $\mathbf{w} \cdot \mathbf{x} + b > 0$, while for data to the left $\mathbf{w} \cdot \mathbf{x} + b < 0$. Thus the classification labels $\mathbf{y}_j \in \{\pm 1\}$ for the data to the left or right of the hyperplane is given by $\mathbf{y}_j(\mathbf{w} \cdot \mathbf{x}_j + b) = \text{sign}(\mathbf{w} \cdot \mathbf{x}_j + b)$. So only the sign of $\mathbf{w} \cdot \mathbf{x} + b$ needs to be determined in order to label the data. The vectors touching the edge of the gray regions of are termed the *support vectors*.

the data to the left or right of the hyperplane is given by

$$\mathbf{y}_j(\mathbf{w} \cdot \mathbf{x}_j + b) = \text{sign}(\mathbf{w} \cdot \mathbf{x}_j + b) = \begin{cases} +1 & \text{magenta ball} \\ -1 & \text{green ball.} \end{cases} \tag{5.27}$$

Thus the classifier $\mathbf{y}_j$ is explicitly dependent on the position of $\mathbf{x}_j$.

Critical to the success of the SVM is determining $\mathbf{w}$ and b in a principled way. As with all machine learning methods, an appropriate optimization must be formulated. The optimization is aimed at both minimizing the number of misclassified data points as well as creating the largest margin possible. To construct the optimization objective function, we define a loss function

$$\ell(\mathbf{y}_j, \bar{\mathbf{y}}_j) = \ell(\mathbf{y}_j, \text{sign}(\mathbf{w} \cdot \mathbf{x}_j + b)) = \begin{cases} 0 & \text{if } \mathbf{y}_j = \text{sign}(\mathbf{w} \cdot \mathbf{x}_j + b) \\ +1 & \text{if } \mathbf{y}_j \neq \text{sign}(\mathbf{w} \cdot \mathbf{x}_j + b) \end{cases}. \tag{5.28}$$

Stated more simply

$$\ell(\mathbf{y}_j, \bar{\mathbf{y}}_j) = \begin{cases} 0 & \text{if data is correctly labeled} \\ +1 & \text{if data is incorrectly labeled} \end{cases}. \tag{5.29}$$

Thus each mislabeled point produces a loss of unity. The training error over m data points is the sum of the loss functions $\ell(\mathbf{y}_j, \bar{\mathbf{y}}_j)$.

In addition to minimizing the loss function, the goal is also to make the margin as large as possible. We can then frame the linear SVM optimization problem as

$$\underset{\mathbf{w}, b}{\text{argmin}} \sum_{j=1}^{m} \ell(\mathbf{y}_j, \bar{\mathbf{y}}_j) + \frac{1}{2} \|\mathbf{w}\|^2 \quad \text{subject to} \quad \min_j |\mathbf{x}_j \cdot \mathbf{w}| = 1. \tag{5.30}$$

Although this is a concise statement of the optimization problem, the fact that the loss function is discrete and constructed from ones and zeros makes it very difficult to actually optimize. Most optimization algorithms are based on some form of gradient descent which requires smooth objective functions in order to compute derivatives or gradients to update the solution. A more common formulation then is given by

$$\underset{\mathbf{w}, b}{\text{argmin}} \sum_{j=1}^{m} H(\mathbf{y}_j, \bar{\mathbf{y}}_j) + \frac{1}{2} \|\mathbf{w}\|^2 \quad \text{subject to} \quad \min_j |\mathbf{x}_j \cdot \mathbf{w}| = 1 \tag{5.31}$$

where α is the weighting of the loss function and $H(z) = \max(0, 1 - z)$ is called a Hinge loss function. This is a smooth function that counts the number of errors in a linear way and that allows for piecewise differentiation so that standard optimization routines can be employed.

Nonlinear SVM

Although easily interpretable, linear classifiers are of limited value. They are simply too restrictive for data embedded in a high-dimensional space and which may have the structured separation as illustrated in Fig. 5.8. To build more sophisticated classification curves, the feature space for SVM must be enriched. SVM does this by included nonlinear features and then building hyperplanes in this new space. To do this, one simply maps the data into a nonlinear, higher-dimensional space

$$\mathbf{x} \mapsto \boldsymbol{\Phi}(\mathbf{x}). \tag{5.32}$$

We can call the $\mathbf{\Phi}(\mathbf{x})$ new *observables* of the data. The SVM algorithm now learns the hyperplanes that optimally split the data into distinct clusters in a new space. Thus one now considers the hyperplane function

$$f(\mathbf{x}) = \mathbf{w} \cdot \mathbf{\Phi}(\mathbf{x}) + b \tag{5.33}$$

with corresponding labels $\mathbf{y}_j \in \{\pm 1\}$ for each point $f(\mathbf{x}_j)$.

This simple idea, of enriching feature space by defining new functions of the data $\mathbf{x}$, is exceptionally powerful for clustering and classification. As a simple example, consider two dimensional data $\mathbf{x} = (x_1, x_2)$. One can easily enrich the space by considering polynomials of the data.

$$(x_1, x_2) \mapsto (z_1, z_2, z_3) := (x_1, x_2, x_1^2 + x_2^2). \tag{5.34}$$

This gives a new set of polynomial coordinates in x_1 and x_2 that can be used to embed the data. This philosophy is simple: by embedding the data in a higher dimensional space, it is much more likely to be separable by hyperplanes. As a simple example, consider the data illustrated in Fig. 5.8(b). A linear classifier (or hyperplane) in the x_1-x_2 plane will clearly not be able to separate the data. However, the embedding (5.34) projects into a three dimensional space which can be easily separated by a hyperplane as illustrated in Fig. 5.23.

The ability of SVM to embed in higher-dimensional nonlinear spaces makes it one of the most successful machine learning algorithms developed. The underlying optimization algorithm (5.31) remains unchanged, except that the previous labeling function $\bar{\mathbf{y}}_j = \text{sign}(\mathbf{w} \cdot \mathbf{x}_j + b)$ is now

$$\bar{\mathbf{y}}_j = \text{sign}(\mathbf{w} \cdot \mathbf{\Phi}(\mathbf{x}_j) + b). \tag{5.35}$$

The function $\mathbf{\Phi}(\mathbf{x})$ specifies the enriched space of observables. As a general rule, more features are better for classification.

Kernel Methods for SVM

Despite its promise, the SVM method of building nonlinear classifiers by enriching in higher-dimensions leads to a computationally intractable optimization. Specifically, the large number of additional features leads to the *curse of dimensionality*. Thus computing the vectors $\mathbf{w}$ is prohibitively expensive and may not even be represented explicitly in memory. The *kernel trick* solves this problem. In this scenario, the $\mathbf{w}$ vector is represented as follows

$$\mathbf{w} = \sum_{j=1}^{m} \alpha_j \mathbf{\Phi}(\mathbf{x}_j) \tag{5.36}$$

where α_j are parameters that weight the different nonlinear observable functions $\mathbf{\Phi}(\mathbf{x}_j)$. Thus the vector $\mathbf{w}$ is expanded in the observable set of functions. We can then generalize (5.33) to the following

$$f(\mathbf{x}) = \sum_{j=1}^{m} \alpha_j \mathbf{\Phi}(\mathbf{x}_j) \cdot \mathbf{\Phi}(\mathbf{x}) + b. \tag{5.37}$$

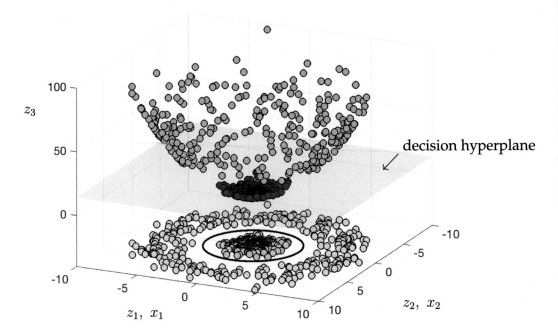

Figure 5.23 The nonlinear embedding of Fig. 5.8(b) using the variables $(x_1, x_2) \mapsto (z_1, z_2, z_3) := (x_1, x_2, x_1^2 + x_2^2)$ in (5.34). A hyperplane can now easily separate the green from magenta balls, showing that linear classification can be accomplished simply be enriching the measurement space of the data. Visual inspection alone suggests that nearly optimal separation can be achieved with the plane $z_3 \approx 14$ (shaded gray plane). In the original coordinate system this gives a circular classification line (black line on the plane x_1 versus x_2) with radius $r = \sqrt{z_3} = \sqrt{x_1^2 + x_2^2} \approx \sqrt{14}$. This example makes it obvious how a hyperplane in higher-dimensions can produce curved classification lines in the original data space.

The *kernel function* [479] is then defined as

$$K(\mathbf{x}_j, \mathbf{x}) = \mathbf{\Phi}(\mathbf{x}_j) \cdot \mathbf{\Phi}(\mathbf{x}). \tag{5.38}$$

With this new definition of **w**, the optimization problem (5.31) becomes

$$\underset{\boldsymbol{\alpha}, b}{\mathrm{argmin}} \sum_{j=1}^{m} H(\mathbf{y}_j, \bar{\mathbf{y}}_j) + \frac{1}{2} \| \sum_{j=1}^{m} \alpha_j \mathbf{\Phi}(\mathbf{x}_j) \|^2 \quad \text{subject to} \quad \min_{j} |\mathbf{x}_j \cdot \mathbf{w}| = 1 \tag{5.39}$$

where $\boldsymbol{\alpha}$ is the vector of α_j coefficients that must be determined in the minimization process. There are different conventions for representing the minimization. However, in this formulation, the minimization is now over $\boldsymbol{\alpha}$ instead of **w**.

In this formulation, the kernel function $K(\mathbf{x}_j, \mathbf{x})$ essentially allows us to represent Taylor series expansions of a large (infinite) number of observables in a compact way [479]. The kernel function enables one to operate in a high-dimensional, implicit feature space without ever computing the coordinates of the data in that space, but rather by simply computing the inner products between all pairs of data in the feature space. For instance, two of the most commonly used kernel functions are

Radial basis functions (RBF): $K(\mathbf{x}_j, \mathbf{x}) = \exp\left(-\gamma \|\mathbf{x}_j - \mathbf{x}\|^2\right)$ (5.40a)

$$\text{Polynomial kernel:} \quad K(\mathbf{x}_j, \mathbf{x}) = (\mathbf{x}_j \cdot \mathbf{x} + 1)^N \tag{5.40b}$$

where N is the degree of polynomials to be considered, which is exceptionally large to evaluate without using the kernel trick, and γ is the width of the Gaussian kernel measuring the distance between individual data points $\mathbf{x}_j$ and the classification line. These functions can be differentiated in order to optimize (5.39).

This represents the major theoretical underpinning of the SVM method. It allows us to construct higher-dimensional spaces using observables generated by kernel functions. Moreover, it results in a computationally tractable optimization. The following code shows the basic workings of the kernel method on the example of dog and cat classification data. In the first example, a standard linear SVM is used, while in the second, the RBF is executed as an option.

Code 5.14 SVM classification.

```
load catData_w.mat
load dogData_w.mat
CD=[dog_wave cat_wave];
[u,s,v]=svd(CD-mean(CD(:)));

features=1:20;
xtrain=[v(1:60,features); v(81:140,features)];
label=[ones(60,1); -1*ones(60,1)];
test=[v(61:80,features); v(141:160,features)];
truth=[ones(20,1); -1*ones(20,1)];

Mdl = fitcsvm(xtrain,label);
test_labels = predict(Mdl,test);

Mdl = fitcsvm(xtrain,label,'KernelFunction','RBF');
test_labels = predict(Mdl,test);
CMdl = crossval(Mdl);          % cross-validate the model
classLoss = kfoldLoss(CMdl)    % compute class loss
```

Note that in this code we have demonstrated some of the diagnostic features of the SVM method in MATLAB, including the cross-validation and class loss scores that are associated with training. This is a superficial treatment of the SVM. Overall, SVM is one of the most sophisticated machine learning tools in MATLAB and there are many options that can be executed in order to tune performance and extract accuracy/cross-validation metrics.

5.8 Classification Trees and Random Forest

Decision trees are common in business. They establish an algorithmic flow chart for making decisions based on criteria that are deemed important and related to a desired outcome. Often the decision trees are constructed by experts with knowledge of the workflow involved in the decision making process. *Decision tree learning* provides a principled method based on data for creating a predictive model for classification and/or regression. Along with SVM, classification and regression trees are core machine learning and data mining algorithms used in industry given their demonstrated success. The work of Leo Breiman and co-workers [79] established many of the theoretical foundations exploited today for data mining.

The decision tree is a hierarchical construct that looks for optimal ways to split the data in order to provide a robust classification and regression. It is the opposite of the unsupervised dendrogram hierarchical clustering previously demonstrated. In this case, our goal is not to move from bottom up in the clustering process, but from top down in order to create the best splits possible for classification. The fact that it is a supervised algorithm, which uses labeled data, allows us to split the data accordingly.

There are significant advantages in developing decision trees for classification and regression: (i) they often produce interpretable results that can be graphically displayed, making them easy to interpret even for nonexperts, (ii) they can handle numerical or categorical data equally well, (iii) they can be statistically validated so that the reliability of the model can be assessed, (iv) they perform well with large data sets at scale, and (v) the algorithms mirror human decision making, again making them more interpretable and useful.

As one might expect, the success of decision tree learning has produced a large number of innovations and algorithms for how to best split the data. The coverage here will be limited, but we will highlight the basic architecture for data splitting and tree construction. Recall that we have the following:

$$\text{data } \{\mathbf{x}_j \in \mathbb{R}^n, \ j \in Z := \{1, 2, \cdots, m\}\} \tag{5.41a}$$

$$\text{labels } \{\mathbf{y}_j \in \{\pm 1\}, \ j \in Z' \subset Z\}. \tag{5.41b}$$

The basic decision tree algorithm is fairly simple: (i) scan through each component (feature) x_k ($k = 1, 2, \cdots, n$) of the vector $\mathbf{x}_j$ to identify the value of x_j that gives the best labeling prediction for $\mathbf{y}_j$. (ii) Compare the prediction accuracy for each split on the feature x_j. The feature giving the best segmentation of the data is selected as the split for the tree. (iii) With the two new branches of the tree created, this process is repeated on each branch. The algorithm terminates once the each individual data point is a unique cluster, known as a *leaf*, on a new branch of the tree. This is essentially the inverse of the dendrogram.

As a specific example, consider the Fisher iris data set from Fig. 5.1. For this data, each flower had four features (petal width and length, sepal width and length), and three labels (setosa, versicolor and virginica). There were fifty flowers of each variety for a total of 150 data points. Thus for this data the vector $\mathbf{x}_j$ has the four components

$$x_1 = \text{sepal width} \tag{5.42a}$$

$$x_2 = \text{sepal length} \tag{5.42b}$$

$$x_3 = \text{petal width} \tag{5.42c}$$

$$x_4 = \text{petal length.} \tag{5.42d}$$

The decision tree algorithm scans over these four features in order to decide how to best split the data. Fig. 5.24 shows the splitting process in the space of the four variables x_1 through x_4. Illustrated are two data planes containing x_1 versus x_2 (panel (b)) and x_3 versus x_4 (panel (a)). By visual inspection, one can see that the x_3 (petal length) variable maximally separates the data. In fact, the decision tree performs the first split of the data at $x_3 = 2.35$. No further splitting is required to predict setosa, as this first split is sufficient. The variable x_4 then provides the next most promising split at $x_4 = 1.75$. Finally, a third split is performed at $x_3 = 4.95$. Only three splits are shown. This process shows that the splitting procedure is has an intuitive appeal as the data splits optimally separating the data

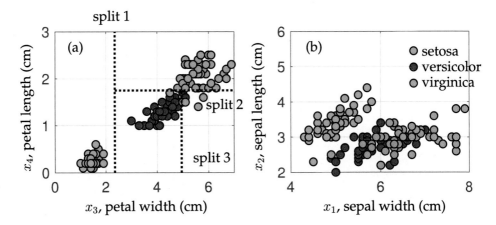

Figure 5.24 Illustration of the splitting procedure for decision tree learning performed on the Fisher iris data set. Each variable x_1 through x_4 is scanned over to determine the best split of data which retains the best correct classification of the labeled data in the split. The variable $x_3 = 2.35$ provides the first split in the data for building a classification tree. This is followed by a second split at $x_4 = 1.75$ and a third split at $x_3 = 4.95$. Only three splits are shown. The classification tree after three splits is shown in Fig. 5.25. Note that although the setosa data in the x_1 and x_2 direction seems to be well separated along a diagonal line, the decision tree can only split along horizontal and vertical lines.

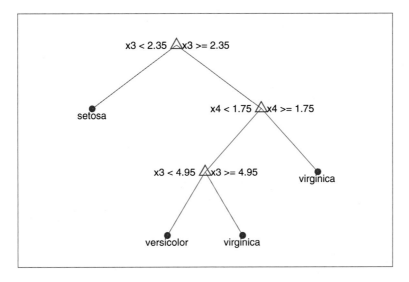

Figure 5.25 Tree structure generated by the MATLAB **fitctree** command. Note that only three splits are conducted, creating a classification tree that produces a class error of 4.67%

are clear visible. Moreover, the splitting does not occur on the x_1 and x_2 (width and length) variables as they do not provide a clear separation of the data. Fig. 5.25 shows the tree used for Fig. 5.24.

The following code fits a tree to the Fisher iris data. Note that the **fitctree** command allows for many options, including a cross-validation procedure (used in the code) and parameter tuning (not used in the code).

Code 5.15 Decision tree classification of Fisher iris data.

```
load fisheriris;
tree=fitctree(meas,species,'MaxNumSplits',3,'CrossVal','on')
view(tree.Trained{1},'Mode','graph');
classError = kfoldLoss(tree)

x1=meas(1:50,:);    % setosa
x2=meas(51:100,:);  % versicolor
x3=meas(101:150,:); % virginica
```

The results of the splitting procedure are demonstrated in Fig. 5.25. The **view** command generates an interactive window showing the tree structure. The tree can be pruned and other diagnostics are shown in this interactive graphic format. The class error achieved for the Fisher iris data is 4.67%.

As a second example, we construct a decision tree to the classify dogs versus cats using our previously considered wavelet images. The following code loads and splits the data.

Code 5.16 Decision tree classification of dogs versus cats.

```
load catData_w.mat
load dogData_w.mat
CD=[dog_wave cat_wave];
[u,s,v]=svd(CD-mean(CD(:)));

features=1:20;
xtrain=[v(1:60,features); v(81:140,features)];
label=[ones(60,1); -1*ones(60,1)];
test=[v(61:80,features); v(141:160,features)];
truth=[ones(20,1); -1*ones(20,1)];

Mdl = fitctree(xtrain,label,'MaxNumSplits',2,'CrossVal','on');
classError = kfoldLoss(Mdl)
view(Mdl.Trained{1},'Mode','graph');
classError = kfoldLoss(Mdl)
```

Fig. 5.26 shows the resulting classification tree. Note that the decision tree learning algorithm identifies the first two splits as occurring along the x_2 and x_4 variables respectively. These two variables have been considered previously since their histograms show them to be more distinguishable than the other PCA components (See Fig. 5.5). For this splitting, which has been cross-validated, the class error achieved is approximately 16%, which can be compared with the 30% error of LDA.

As a final example, we consider census data that is included in MATLAB. The following code shows some important uses of the classification and regression tree architecture. In particular, the variables included can be used to make associations between relationships. In this case, the various data is used to predict the salary data. Thus, salary is the outcome of the classification. Moreover, the importance of each variable and its relation to salary can be computed, as shown in Fig. 5.27. The following code highlights some of the functionality of the tree architecture.

Code 5.17 Decision tree classification of census data.

```
load census1994
X = adultdata(:,{'age','workClass','education_num','
   marital_status','race','sex','capital_gain',...
   'capital_loss','hours_per_week','salary'});
```

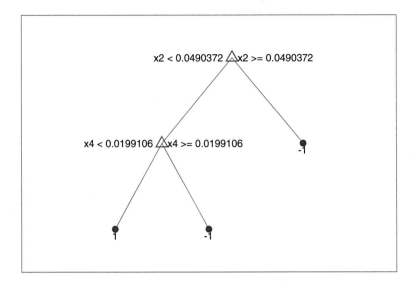

Figure 5.26 Tree structure generated by the MATLAB **fitctree** command for dog versus cat data. Note that only two splits are conducted, creating a classification tree that produces a class error of approximately 16%

```
Mdl = fitctree(X,'salary','PredictorSelection','curvature','
    Surrogate','on');

imp = predictorImportance(Mdl);

bar(imp,'FaceColor',[.6 .6 .6],'EdgeColor','k');
title('Predictor Importance Estimates');
ylabel('Estimates'); xlabel('Predictors'); h = gca;
h.XTickLabel = Mdl.PredictorNames;
h.XTickLabelRotation = 45;
```

As with the SVM algorithm, there exists a wide variety of tuning parameters for classification trees, and this is a superficial treatment. Overall, such trees are one of the most sophisticated machine learning tools in MATLAB and there are many options that can be executed to tune performance and extract accuracy/cross-validation metrics.

Random Forest Algorithms

Before closing this section, it is important to mention Breiman's *random forest* [77] innovations for decision learning trees. Random forests, or random decision forests, are an ensemble learning method for classification and regression. This is an important innovation since the decision trees created by splitting are generally not robust to different samples of the data. Thus one can generate two significantly different classification trees with two subsamples of the data. This presents significant challenges for cross-validation. In ensemble learning, a multitude of decision trees are constructed in the training process. The random decision forests correct for a decision trees' habit of overfitting to their training set, thus providing a more robust framework for classification.

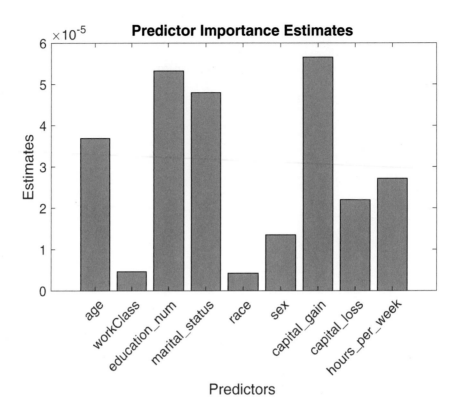

Figure 5.27 Importance of variables for prediction of salary data for the US census of 1994. The classification tree architecture allows for sophisticated treatment of data, including understanding how each variable contributes statistically to predicting a classification outcome.

There are many variants of the random forest architecture, including variants with *boosting* and *bagging*. These will not be considered here except to mention that the MATLAB **figctree** exploits many of these techniques through its options. One way to think about ensemble learning is that it allows for robust classification trees. It often does this by focusing its training efforts on hard-to-classify data instead of easy-to-classify data. Random forests, bagging and boosting are all extensive subjects in their own right, but have already been incorporated into leading software which build decision learning trees.

5.9   Top 10 Algorithms in Data Mining 2008

This chapter has illustrated the tremendous diversity of supervised and unsupervised methods available for the analysis of data. Although the algorithms are now easily accessible through many commercial and open-source software packages, the difficulty is now evaluating which method(s) should be used on a given problem. In December 2006, various machine learning experts attending the IEEE International Conference on Data Mining (ICDM) identified the top 10 algorithms for data mining [562]. The identified algorithms where the following: C4.5, *k*-Means, SVM, Apriori, EM, PageRank, AdaBoost, kNN, Naive Bayes, and CART. These top 10 algorithms were identified at the time as being among the most influential data mining algorithms in the research community. In the summary article, each algorithm was briefly described along with its impact and potential future directions of research. The 10 algorithms covered classification, clustering, statistical learning, association analysis, and link mining, which are all among the most important topics in data mining research and development. Interestingly, deep learning and neural networks, which are the topic of the next chapter, are not mentioned in the article. The landscape of data science would change significantly in 2012 with the ImageNET data set, and deep convolutional neural networks began to dominate almost any meaningful metric for classification and regression accuracy.

In this section, we highlight their identified top 10 algorithms and the basic mathematical structure of each. Many of them have already been covered in this chapter. This list is not exhaustive, nor does it rank them beyond their inclusion in the top 10 list. Our objective is simply to highlight what was considered by the community as the state-of-the-art data mining tools in 2008. We begin with those algorithms already considered previously in this chapter.

k-means

This is one of the workhorse unsupervised algorithms. As already demonstrated, the goal of k-means is simply to cluster by proximity to a set of k points. By updating the locations of the k points according to the mean of the points closest to them, the algorithm iterates to the k-means. The structure of the MATLAB command is as follows

```
[labels,centers]=kmeans(X,k)
```

The **means** command takes in data **X** and the number of prescribed clusters k. It returns labels for each point **labels** along with their location **centers**.

EM (mixture models)

Mixture models are the second workhorse algorithm for unsupervised learning. The assumption underlying the mixture models is that the observed data is produced by a mixture of different probability distribution functions whose weightings are unknown. Moreover, the parameters must be estimated, thus requiring the Expectation-Maximization (EM) algorithm. The structure of the MATLAB command is as follows

```
Model=fitgmdist(X,k)
```

where the **fitgmdist** by default fits Gaussian mixtures to the data **X** in k clusters. The **Model** output is a structured variable containing information on the probability distributions (mean, variance, etc.) along with the goodness-of-fit.

Support Vector Machine (SVM)

One of the most powerful and flexible supervised learning algorithms used for most of the 90s and 2000s, the SVM is an exceptional off-the-shelf method for classification and regression. The main idea: project the data into higher dimensions and split the data with hyperplanes. Critical to making this work in practice was the kernel trick for efficiently evaluating inner products of functions in higher-dimensional space. The structure of the MATLAB command is as follows

```
Model = fitcsvm(xtrain,label);
```

```
test_labels = predict(Model,test);
```

where the **fitcsvm** command takes in labeled training data denoted by **train** and **label**, and it produces a structured output **Model**. The structured output can be used along with the **predict** command to take test data **test** and produce labels (**test**$_{labels}$). There exist many options and tuning parameters for **fitcsvm**, making it one of the best off-the-shelf methods.

CART (Classification and Regression Tree)

This was the subject of the last section and was demonstrated to provide another powerful technique of supervised learning. The underlying idea was to split the data in a principled and informed way so as to produce an interpretable clustering of the data. The data splitting occurs along a single variable at a time to produce branches of the tree structure. The structure of the MATLAB command is as follows

```
tree = fitctree(xtrain,label);
```

where the **fitctree** command takes in labeled training data denoted by **train** and **label**, and it produces a structured output **tree**. There are many options and tuning parameters for **fitctree**, making it one of the best off-the-shelf methods.

k-nearest Neighbors (kNN)

This is perhaps the simplest supervised algorithm to understand. It is highly interpretable and easy to execute. Given a new data point x_k which does not have a label, simply find the k nearest neighbors x_j with labels y_j. The label of the new point x_k is determined by a majority vote of the kNN. Given a model for the data, the MATLAB command to execute the kNN search is the following

```
label = knnsearch(Mdl,test)
```

where the **knnsearch** uses the **Mdl** to label the test data **test**.

Naive Bayes

The Naive Bayes algorithm provides an intuitive framework for supervised learning. It is simple to construct and does not require any complicated parameter estimation, similar to SVM and/or classification trees. It further gives highly interpretable results that are remarkably good in practice. The method is based upon Bayes's theorem and the computation of conditional probabilities. Thus one can estimate the label of a new data point based on the prior probability distributions of the labeled data. The MATLAB command structure for constructing a Naive Bayes model is the following

```
Model = fitNaiveBayes(xtrain,label)
```

where the **fitcNativeBayes** command takes in labeled training data denoted by **train** and **label**, and it produces a structured output **Model**. The structured output can be used with the **predict** command to label test data **test**.

AdaBoost (Ensemble Learning and Boosting)

AdaBoost is an example of an *ensemble learning* algorithm [188]. Broadly speaking, AdaBoost is a form of random forest [77] which takes into account an ensemble of decision tree models. The way all boosting algorithms work is to first consider an equal weighting for all training data $\mathbf{x}_j$. Boosting re-weights the importance of the data according to how difficult they are to classify. Thus the algorithm focuses on harder to classify data. Thus a family of weak learners can be trained to yield a strong learner by boosting the importance of hard to classify data [470]. This concept and its usefulness are based upon a seminal theoretical contribution by Kearns and Valiant [283]. The structure of the MATLAB command is as follows

```
ada = fitcensemble(xtrain,label,'Method','AdaBoostM1')
```

where the **fitcensemble** command is a general ensemble learner that can do many more things than AdaBoost, including robust boosting and gradient boosting. Gradient boosting is one of the most powerful techniques [189].

C4.5 (Ensemble Learning of Decision Trees)
This algorithm is another variant of decision tree learning developed by J. R. Quinlan [443, 444]. At its core, the algorithm splits the data according to an information entropy score. In its latest versions, it supports boosting as well as many other well known functionalities to improve performance. Broadly, we can think of this as a strong performing version of CART. The **fitcensemble** algorithm highlighted with AdaBoost gives a generic ensemble learning architecture that can incorporate decision trees, allowing for a C4.5-like algorithm.

Apriori Algorithm
The last two methods highlighted here tend to focus on different aspects of data mining. In the Apriori algorithm, the goal is to find frequent itemsets from data. Although this may sound trivial, it is not since data sets tend to be very large and can easily produce NP-hard computations because of the combinatorial nature of the algorithms. The Apriori algorithm provides an efficient algorithm for finding frequent itemsets using a candidate generation architecture [4]. This algorithm can then be used for fast learning of associate rules in the data.

PageRank
The founding of Google by Sergey Brin and Larry Page revolved around the PageRank algorithm [82]. PageRank produces a static ranking of variables, such as web pages, by computing an off-line value for each variable that does not depend on search queries. The PageRank is associated with graph theory as it originally interpreted a hyperlink from one page to another as a vote. From this, and various modifications of the original algorithm, one can then compute an importance score for each variable and provide an ordered rank list. The number of enhancements for this algorithm is quite large. Producing accurate orderings of variables (web pages) and their importance remains an active topic of research.

Suggested Reading

Texts

(1) **Machine learning: a probabilistic perspective**, by K. P. Murphy, 2012 [396].

(2) **Pattern recognition and machine learning**, by C. M. Bishop, 2006 [64].

(3) **Pattern classification**, by R. O. Duda, P. E. Hart, and D. G. Stork, 2000 [161].

(4) **An introduction to statistical learning**, by G. James, D. Witten, T. Hastie and R. Tibshirani, 2013 [264].

(5) **Learning with kernels: support vector machines, regularization, optimization, and beyond**, by B. Schölkopf and A. J. Smola, 2002 [479].

(6) **Classification and regression trees**, by L. Breiman, J. Friedman, C. J. Stone and R. A. Olshen, 1984 [79].

(7) **Random forests**, by L. Breiman, 2001 [77].

Papers and Reviews

(1) **Top 10 algorithms in data mining**, by X. Wu et al., *Knowledge and information systems*, 2008 [562].

(2) **The strength of weak learnability**, by R. E. Schapire, *Machine Learning*, 1990 [470].

(3) **Greedy function approximation: a gradient boosting machine**, by J. H. Friedman, *Annals of Statistics*, 2001 [189].

6 Neural Networks and Deep Learning

Neural networks (NNs) were inspired by the Nobel prize winning work of Hubel and Wiesel on the primary visual cortex of cats [259]. Their seminal experiments showed that neuronal networks were organized in hierarchical layers of cells for processing visual stimulus. The first mathematical model of the NN, termed the Neocognitron in 1980 [193], had many of the characteristic features of today's deep convolutional NNs (or DCNNs), including a multi-layer structure, convolution, max pooling and nonlinear dynamical nodes. The recent success of DCNNs in computer vision has been enabled by two critical components: (i) the continued growth of computational power, and (ii) exceptionally large labeled data sets which take advantage of the power of a *deep* multi-layer architecture. Indeed, although the theoretical inception of NNs has an almost four-decade history, the analysis of the ImageNet data set in 2012 [310] provided a watershed moment for NNs and deep learning [324]. Prior to this data set, there were a number of data sets available with approximately tens of thousands of labeled images. ImageNet provided over 15 million labeled, high-resolution images with over 22,000 categories. DCNNs, which are only one potential category of NNs, have since transformed the field of computer vision by dominating the performance metrics in almost every meaningful computer vision task intended for classification and identification.

Although ImageNet has been critically enabling for the field, NNs were textbook material in the early 1990s with a focus typically on a small number of layers. Critical machine learning tasks such as principal component analysis (PCA) were shown to be intimately connected with networks which included back propagation. Importantly, there were a number of critical innovations which established multilayer feedforward networks as a class of universal approximators [255]. The past five years have seen tremendous advances in NN architectures, many designed and tailored for specific application areas. Innovations have come from algorithmic modifications that have led to significant performance gains in a variety of fields. These innovations include pretraining, dropout, inception modules, data augmentation with virtual examples, batch normalization, and/or residual learning (See Ref. [216] for a detailed exposition of NNs). This is only a partial list of potential algorithmic innovations, thus highlighting the continuing and rapid pace of progress in the field. Remarkably, NNs were not even listed as one of the top 10 algorithms of data mining in 2008 [562]. But a decade later, its undeniable and growing list of successes on challenge data sets make it perhaps the most important data mining tool for our emerging generation of scientists and engineers.

As already shown in the last two chapters, all of machine learning revolves fundamentally around optimization. NNs specifically optimize over a compositional function

$$\underset{\mathbf{A}_j}{\mathrm{argmin}} \left(f_M(\mathbf{A}_M, \cdots, f_2(\mathbf{A}_2, f_1(\mathbf{A}_1, \mathbf{x})) \cdots) + \lambda g(\mathbf{A}_j) \right) \tag{6.1}$$

which is often solved using stochastic gradient descent and back propagation algorithms. Each matrix $\mathbf{A}_k$ denotes the weights connecting the neural network from the kth to $(k+1)$th layer. It is a massively underdetermined system which is regularized by $g(\mathbf{A}_j)$. Composition and regularization are critical for generating expressive representations of the data and preventing overfitting, respectively. This general optimization framework is at the center of deep learning algorithms, and its solution will be considered in this chapter. Importantly, NNs have significant potential for overfitting of data so that cross-validation must be carefully considered. Recall that *if you don't cross-validate, you is dumb*.

6.1   Neural Networks: 1-Layer Networks

The generic architecture of a multi-layer NN is shown in Fig. 6.1. For classification tasks, the goal of the NN is to map a set of input data to a classification. Specifically, we train the NN to accurately map the data $\mathbf{x}_j$ to their correct label $\mathbf{y}_j$. As shown in Fig. 6.1, the input space has the dimension of the raw data $\mathbf{x}_j \in \mathbb{R}^n$. The output layer has the dimension of the designed classification space. Constructing the output layer will be discussed further in the following.

Immediately, one can see that there are a great number of design questions regarding NNs. How many layers should be used? What should be the dimension of the layers? How should the output layer be designed? Should one use all-to-all or sparsified connections between layers? How should the mapping between layers be performed: a *linear mapping* or a *nonlinear mapping*? Much like the tuning options on SVM and classification trees, NNs have a significant number of design options that can be tuned to improve performance.

Initially, we consider the mapping between layers of Fig. 6.1. We denote the various layers between input and output as $\mathbf{x}^{(k)}$ where k is the layer number. For a linear mapping between layers, the following relations hold

$$\mathbf{x}^{(1)} = \mathbf{A}_1 \mathbf{x} \tag{6.2a}$$

$$\mathbf{x}^{(2)} = \mathbf{A}_2 \mathbf{x}^{(1)} \tag{6.2b}$$

$$\mathbf{y} = \mathbf{A}_3 \mathbf{x}^{(2)}. \tag{6.2c}$$

This forms a compositional structure so that the mapping between input and output can be represented as

$$\mathbf{y} = \mathbf{A}_3 \mathbf{A}_2 \mathbf{A}_1 \mathbf{x}. \tag{6.3}$$

This basic architecture can scale to M layers so that a general representation between input data and the output layer for a linear NN is given by

$$\mathbf{y} = \mathbf{A}_M \mathbf{A}_{M-1} \cdots \mathbf{A}_2 \mathbf{A}_1 \mathbf{x}. \tag{6.4}$$

This is generally a highly underdetermined system that requires some constraints on the solution in order to select a unique solution. One constraint is immediately obvious: The mapping must generate M distinct matrices that give the best mapping. It should be noted

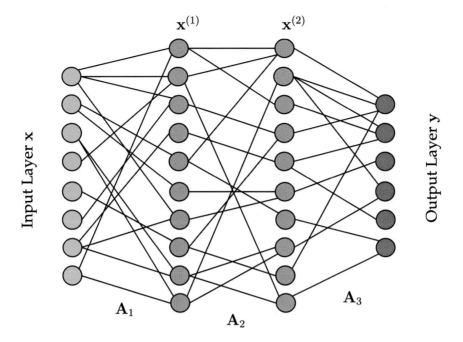

Figure 6.1 Illustration of a neural net architecture mapping an input layer **x** to an output layer **y**. The middle (hidden) layers are denoted $\mathbf{x}^{(j)}$ where j determines their sequential ordering. The matrices $\mathbf{A}_j$ contain the coefficients that map each variable from one layer to the next. Although the dimensionality of the input layer $\mathbf{x} \in \mathbb{R}^n$ is known, there is great flexibility in choosing the dimension of the inner layers as well as how to structure the output layer. The number of layers and how to map between layers is also selected by the user. This flexible architecture gives great freedom in building a good classifier.

that linear mappings, even with a compositional structure, can only produce a limited range of functional responses due to the limitations of the linearity.

Nonlinear mappings are also possible, and generally used, in constructing the NN. Indeed, nonlinear activation functions allow for a richer set of functional responses than their linear counterparts. In this case, the connections between layers are given by

$$\mathbf{x}^{(1)} = f_1(\mathbf{A}_1, \mathbf{x}) \tag{6.5a}$$

$$\mathbf{x}^{(2)} = f_2(\mathbf{A}_2, \mathbf{x}^{(1)}) \tag{6.5b}$$

$$\mathbf{y} = f_3(\mathbf{A}_3, \mathbf{x}^{(2)}). \tag{6.5c}$$

Note that we have used different nonlinear functions $f_j(\cdot)$ between layers. Often a single function is used; however, there is no constraint that this is necessary. In terms of mapping the data between input and output over M layers, the following is derived

$$\mathbf{y} = f_M(\mathbf{A}_M, \cdots, f_2(\mathbf{A}_2, f_1(\mathbf{A}_1, \mathbf{x})) \cdots) \tag{6.6}$$

which can be compared with (6.1) for the general optimization which constructs the NN. As a highly underdetermined system, constraints should be imposed in order to extract a desired solution type, as in (6.1). For big data applications such as ImageNET and computer vision tasks, the optimization associated with this compositional framework is expensive given the number of variables that must be determined. However, for moderate sized networks, it can be performed on workstation and laptop computers. Modern stochastic gradient descent and back propagation algorithms enable this optimization, and both are covered in later sections.

A One-Layer Network

To gain insight into how an NN might be constructed, we will consider a single layer network that is optimized to build a classifier between dogs and cats. The dog and cat example was considered extensively in the previous chapter. Recall that we were given images of dogs and cats, or a wavelet version of dogs and cats. Fig. 6.2 shows our construction. To make this as simple as possible, we consider the simple NN output

$$\mathbf{y} = \{\text{dog, cat}\} = \{+1, -1\} \tag{6.7}$$

which labels each data vector with an output $\mathbf{y} \in \{\pm 1\}$. In this case the output layer is a single node. As in previous supervised learning algorithms the goal is to determine a mapping so that each data vector $\mathbf{x}_j$ is labeled correctly by $\mathbf{y}_j$.

The easiest mapping is a linear mapping between the input images $\mathbf{x}_j \in \mathbb{R}^n$ and the output layer. This gives a linear system $\mathbf{AX} = \mathbf{Y}$ of the form

$$\mathbf{AX} = \mathbf{Y} \rightarrow [a_1\ a_2\ \cdots\ a_n] \begin{bmatrix} | & | & & | \\ \mathbf{x}_1 & \mathbf{x}_2 & \cdots & \mathbf{x}_p \\ | & | & & | \end{bmatrix} = [+1\ +1\ \cdots\ -1\ -1] \tag{6.8}$$

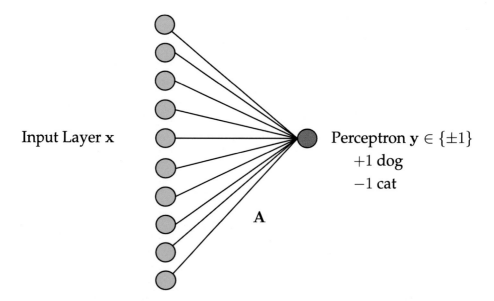

Figure 6.2 Single layer network for binary classification between dogs and cats. The output layer for this case is a perceptron with $\mathbf{y} \in \{\pm 1\}$. A linear mapping between the input image space and output output layer can be constructed for training data by solving $\mathbf{A} = \mathbf{Y}\mathbf{X}^\dagger$. This gives a least square regression for the matrix $\mathbf{A}$ mapping the images to label space.

where each column of the matrix $\mathbf{X}$ is a dog or cat image and the columns of $\mathbf{Y}$ are its corresponding labels. Since the output layer is a single node, both $\mathbf{A}$ and $\mathbf{Y}$ reduce to vectors. In this case, our goal is to determine the matrix (vector) $\mathbf{A}$ with components a_j. The simplest solution is to take the pseudo-inverse of the data matrix $\mathbf{X}$

$$\mathbf{A} = \mathbf{Y}\mathbf{X}^{\dagger}. \tag{6.9}$$

Thus a single output layer allows us to build a NN using least-square fitting. Of course, we could also solve this linear system in a variety of other ways, including with sparsity-promoting methods. The following code solves this problem through both least-square fitting (**pinv**) and the LASSO.

Code 6.1 1-layer, linear neural network.

```
load catData_w.mat; load dogData_w.mat; CD=[dog_wave cat_wave];
train=[dog_wave(:,1:60) cat_wave(:,1:60)];
test=[dog_wave(:,61:80) cat_wave(:,61:80)];
label=[ones(60,1); -1*ones(60,1)].';

A=label*pinv(train); test_labels=sign(A*test);
subplot(4,1,1), bar(test_labels)
subplot(4,1,2), bar(A)
figure(2), subplot(2,2,1)
A2=flipud(reshape(A,32,32)); pcolor(A2), colormap(gray)

figure(1), subplot(4,1,3)
A=lasso(train.',label.','Lambda',0.1).';
test_labels=sign(A*test);
bar(test_labels)
subplot(4,1,4)
bar(A)
figure(2), subplot(2,2,2)
A2=flipud(reshape(A,32,32)); pcolor(A2), colormap(gray)
```

Figs. 6.3 and 6.4 show the results of this linear single-layer NN with single node output layer. Specifically, the four rows of Fig. 6.3 show the output layer on the withheld test data for both the pseudo-inverse and LASSO methods along with a bar graph of the 32×32 (1024 pixels) weightings of the matrix $\mathbf{A}$. Note that all matrix elements are nonzero in the pseudo-inverse solution, while the LASSO highlights a small number of pixels that can classify the pictures as well as using all pixels. Fig. 6.4 shows the matrix $\mathbf{A}$ for the two solution strategies reshaped into 32×32 images. Note that for the pseudo-inverse, the weightings of the matrix elements $\mathbf{A}$ show many features of the cat and dog face. For the LASSO method, only a few pixels are required that are clustered near the eyes and ears. Thus for this single layer network, interpretable results are achieved by looking at the weights generated in the matrix $\mathbf{A}$.

6.2   Multi-Layer Networks and Activation Functions

The previous section constructed what is perhaps the simplest NN possible. It was linear, had a single layer, and a single output layer neuron. The potential generalizations are endless, but we will focus on two simple extensions of the NN in this section. The first extension concerns the assumption of linearity in which we assumed that there is a linear

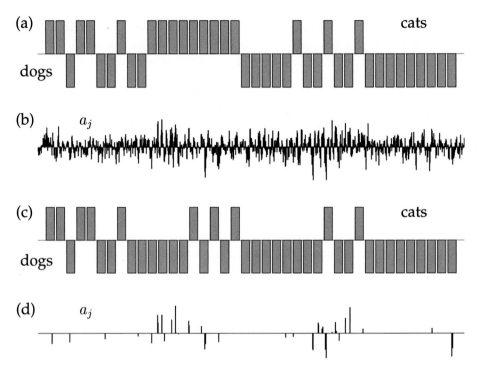

Figure 6.3 Classification of withheld data tested on a trained, single-layer network with linear mapping between inputs (pixel space) and a single output. (a) and (c) are the bar graph of the output layer score $\mathbf{y} \in \{\pm 1\}$ achieved for the withheld data using a pseudo-inverse for training and the LASSO for training respectively. The results show in both cases that dogs are more often misclassified than cats are misclassified. (b) and (d) show the coefficients of the matrix $\mathbf{A}$ for the pseudo-inverse and LASSO respectively. Note that the LASSO has only a small number of nonzero elements, thus suggesting the NN is highly sparse.

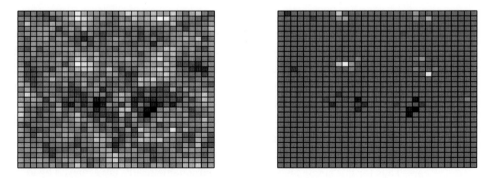

Figure 6.4 Weightings of the matrix $\mathbf{A}$ reshaped into 32×32 arrays. The left matrix shows the matrix $\mathbf{A}$ computed by least-square regression (the pseudo-inverse) while the right matrix shows the matrix $\mathbf{A}$ computed by LASSO. Both matrices provide similar classification scores on withheld data. They further provide interpretability in the sense that the results from the pseudo-inverse show many of the features of dogs and cats while the LASSO shows that measuring near the eyes and ears alone can give the features required for distinguishing between dogs and cats.

transform from the image space to the output layer: $\mathbf{A}\mathbf{x} = \mathbf{y}$ in (6.8). We highlight here common nonlinear transformations from input-to-output space represented by

$$\mathbf{y} = f(\mathbf{A}, \mathbf{x}) \tag{6.10}$$

where $f(\cdot)$ is a specified *activation function* (transfer function) for our mapping.

The linear mapping used previously, although simple, does not offer the flexibility and performance that other mappings offer. Some standard activation functions are given by

$$f(x) = x \qquad\qquad\quad - \quad \text{linear} \tag{6.11a}$$

$$f(x) = \begin{cases} 0 & x \le 0 \\ 1 & x > 0 \end{cases} \quad - \quad \text{binary step} \tag{6.11b}$$

$$f(x) = \frac{1}{1 + \exp(-x)} \quad - \quad \text{logistic (soft step)} \tag{6.11c}$$

$$f(x) = \tanh(x) \qquad\quad - \quad \text{TanH} \tag{6.11d}$$

$$f(x) = \begin{cases} 0 & x \le 0 \\ x & x > 0 \end{cases} \quad - \quad \text{rectified linear unit (ReLU).} \tag{6.11e}$$

There are other possibilities, but these are perhaps the most commonly considered in practice and they will serve for our purposes. Importantly, the chosen function $f(x)$ will be differentiated in order to be used in gradient descent algorithms for optimization. Each of the functions above is either differentiable or piecewise differentiable. Perhaps the most commonly used activation function is currently the ReLU, which we denote $f(x) = \text{ReLU}(x)$.

With a nonlinear activation function $f(x)$, or if there are more than one layer, then standard linear optimization routines such as the pseudo-inverse and LASSO can no longer be used. Although this may not seem immediately significant, recall that we are optimizing in a high-dimensional space where each entry of the matrix $\mathbf{A}$ needs to be found through optimization. Even moderate to small problems can be computationally expensive to solve without using specialty optimization methods. Fortunately, the two dominant optimization components for training NNs, stochastic gradient descent and backpropagation, are included with the neural network function calls in MATLAB. As these methods are critically enabling, both of them are considered in detail in the next two sections of this chapter.

Multiple layers can also be considered as shown in (6.4) and (6.5c). In this case, the optimization must simultaneously identify multiple connectivity matrices $\mathbf{A}_1, \mathbf{A}_2, \cdots \mathbf{A}_M$, in contrast to the linear case where only a single matrix is determined $\bar{\mathbf{A}} = \mathbf{A}_M \cdots \mathbf{A}_2 \mathbf{A}_M$. The multiple layer structure significantly increases the size of the optimization problem as each matrix element of the M matrices must be determined. Even for a one layer structure, an optimization routine such as **fminsearch** will be severely challenged when considering a nonlinear transfer function and one needs to move to a gradient descent-based algorithm.

MATLAB's neural network toolbox, much like TensorFlow in python, has a wide range of features which makes it exceptionally powerful and convenient for building NNs. In the following code, we will train a NN to classify between dogs and cats as in the previous example. However, in this case, we allow the single layer to have a nonlinear transfer function that maps the input to the output layer. The output layer for this example will be modified to the following

$$y = \begin{bmatrix} 1 \\ 0 \end{bmatrix} = \{\text{dog}\} \quad \text{and} \quad y = \begin{bmatrix} 0 \\ 1 \end{bmatrix} = \{\text{cat}\}. \tag{6.12}$$

Half of the data is extracted for training, while the other half is used for testing the results. The following code builds a network using the **train** command to classify between our images.

Code 6.2 Neural network with nonlinear transfer functions.

```
load catData_w.mat; load dogData_w.mat;
CD=[dog_wave cat_wave];

x=[dog_wave(:,1:40) cat_wave(:,1:40)];
x2=[dog_wave(:,41:80) cat_wave(:,41:80)];
label=[ones(40,1)    zeros(40,1);
        zeros(40,1)  ones(40,1)].';

net = patternnet(2,'trainscg');
net.layers{1}.transferFcn = 'tansig';

net = train(net,x,label);
view(net)
y = net(x);
y2= net(x2);
perf = perform(net,label,y);
classes2 = vec2ind(y);
classes3 = vec2ind(y2);
```

In the code above, the **patternnet** command builds a classification network with two outputs (6.12). It also optimizes with the option **trainscg** which is a *scaled conjugate gradient backpropagation*. The **net.layers** also allows us to specify the transfer function, in this case hyperbolic tangent functions (6.11d). The **view(net)** command produces a diagnostic tool shown in Fig. 6.5 that summarizes the optimization and NN.

The results of the classification for a cross-validated training set as well as a withhold set are shown in Fig. 6.6. Specifically, the desired outputs are given by the vectors (6.12). For both the training and withhold sets, the two components of the vector are shown for the 80 training images (40 cats and 40 dogs) and the 80 withheld images (40 cats and 40 dogs). The training set produces a perfect classifier using a one layer network with a hyperbolic tangent transfer function (6.11d). On the withheld data, it incorrectly identifies 6 of 40 dogs and cats, yielding an accuracy of $\approx 85\%$ on new data.

The diagnostic tool shown in Fig. 6.5 allows access to a number of features critical for evaluating the NN. Fig. 6.7 is a summary of the performance achieved by the NN training tool. In this figure, the training algorithm automatically breaks the data into a training, validation and test set. The backpropagation enabled, stochastic gradient descent optimization algorithm then iterates through a number of training epochs until the cross-validated error achieves a minimum. In this case, twenty-two epochs is sufficient to achieve a minimum. The error on the test set is significantly higher than what is achieved for cross-validation. For this case, only a limited amount of data is used for training (40 dogs and 40 cats), thus making it difficult to achieve great performance. Regardless, as already shown, once the algorithm has been trained it can be used to evaluate new data as shown in Fig. 6.6.

There are two other features easily available with the NN diagnostic tool of Fig. 6.5. Fig. 6.8 shows an error histogram associated with the trained network. As with Fig. 6.7, the

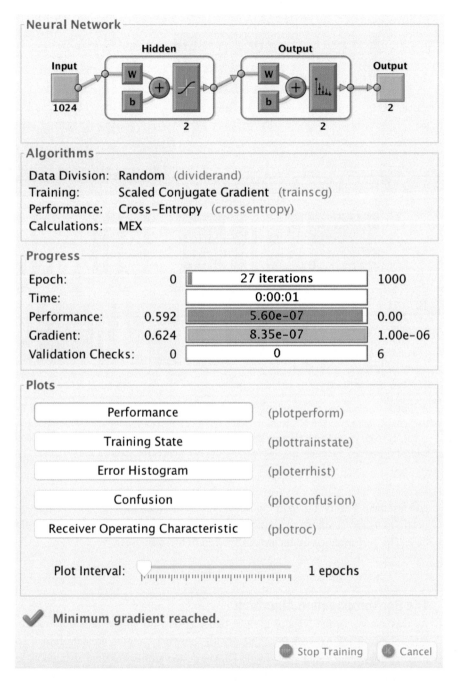

Figure 6.5 MATLAB neural network visualization tool. The number of iterations along with the performance can all be accessed from the interactive graphical tool. The performance, error histogram and confusion buttons produce Figs. 6.7-6.9 respectively.

data is divided into training, validation, and test sets. This provides an overall assessment of the classification quality that can be achieved by the NN training algorithm. Another view of the performance can be seen in the confusion matrices for the training, validation,

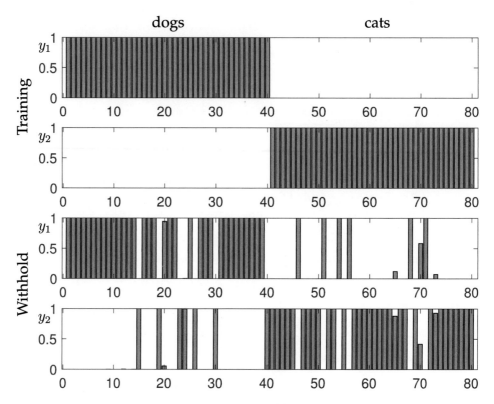

Figure 6.6 Comparison of the output vectors $\mathbf{y} = [y_1 \; y_2]^T$ which are ideally (6.12) for the dogs and cats considered here. The NN training stage produces a cross-validated classifier that achieves 100% accuracy in classifying the training data (top two panels for 40 dogs and 40 cats). When applied to a withheld set, 85% accuracy is achieved (bottom two panels for 40 dogs and 40 cats).

and test data. This is shown in Fig. 6.9. Overall, between Figs. 6.7 to 6.9, high-quality diagnostic tools are available to evaluate how well the NN is able to achieve its classification task. The performance limits are easily seen in these figures.

6.3   The Backpropagation Algorithm

As was shown for the NNs of the last two sections, training data is required to determine the weights of the network. Specifically, the network weights are determined so as to best classify dog versus cat images. In the 1-layer network, this was done using both least-square regression and LASSO. This shows that at its core, an optimization routine and objective function is required to determine the weights. The objective function should minimize a measure of the misclassified images. The optimization, however, can be modified by imposing a regularizer or constraints, such as the ℓ_1 penalization in LASSO.

In practice, the objective function chosen for optimization is not the true objective function desired, but rather a proxy for it. Proxies are chosen largely due to the ability to differentiate the objective function in a computationally tractable manner. There are also many different objective functions for different tasks. Instead, one often considers a suitably

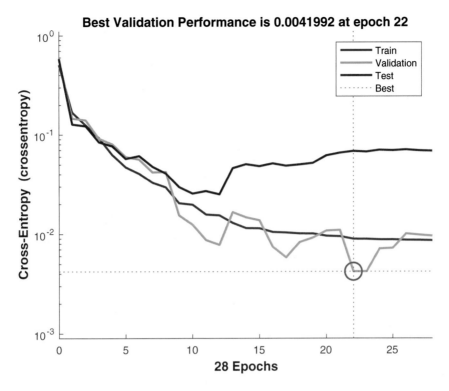

Figure 6.7 Summary of training of the NN over a number of epochs. The NN architecture automatically separates the data into training, validation and test sets. The training continues (with a maximum of 1000 epochs) until the validation error curve hits a minimum. The training then stops and the trained algorithm is then used on the test set to evaluate performance. The NN trained here has only a limited amount of data (40 dogs and 40 cats), thus limiting the performance. This figure is accessed with the **performance** button on the NN interactive tool of Fig. 6.6.

chosen loss function so as to approximate the true objective. Ultimately, computational tractability is critical for training NNs.

The backpropagation algorithm (backprop) exploits the compositional nature of NNs in order to frame an optimization problem for determining the weights of the network. Specifically, it produces a formulation amenable to standard gradient descent optimization (See Section 4.2). Backprop relies on a simple mathematical principle: the chain rule for differentiation. Moreover, it can be proven that the computational time required to evaluate the gradient is within a factor of five of the time required for computing the actual function itself [44]. This is known as the Baur-Strassen theorem. Fig. 6.10 gives the simplest example of backprop and how the gradient descent is to be performed. The input-to-output relationship for this single node, one hidden layer network, is given by

$$y = g(z, b) = g(f(x, a), b). \tag{6.13}$$

Thus given a function $f(\cdot)$ and $g(\cdot)$ with weighting constants a and b, the output error produce by the network can be computed against the ground truth as

$$E = \frac{1}{2}(y_0 - y)^2 \tag{6.14}$$

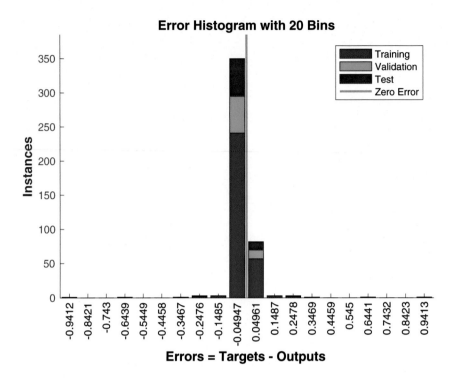

Figure 6.8 Summary of the error performance of the NN architecture for training, validation and test sets. This figure is accessed with the **errorhistogram** button on the NN interactive tool of Fig. 6.6.

where y_0 is the correct output and y is the NN approximation to the output. The goal is to find a and b to minimize the error. The minimization requires

$$\frac{\partial E}{\partial a} = -(y_0 - y)\frac{dy}{dz}\frac{dz}{da} = 0 \, . \tag{6.15}$$

A critical observation is that the compositional nature of the network along with the chain rule forces the optimization to backpropagate error through the network. In particular, the terms $dy/dz \; dz/da$ show how this backprop occurs. Given functions $f(\cdot)$ and $g(\cdot)$, the chain rule can be explicitly computed.

Backprop results in an iterative, gradient descent update rule

$$a_{k+1} = a_k + \delta\frac{\partial E}{\partial a_k} \tag{6.16a}$$

$$b_{k+1} = b_k + \delta\frac{\partial E}{\partial b_k} \tag{6.16b}$$

where δ is the so-called learning rate and $\partial E/\partial a$ along with $\partial E/\partial b$ can be explicitly computed using (6.15). The iteration algorithm is executed to convergence. As with all iterative optimization, a good initial guess is critical to achieve a good solution in a reasonable amount of computational time.

Backprop proceeds as follows: (i) A NN is specified along with a labeled training set. (ii) The initial weights of the network are set to random values. Importantly, one must not initialize the weights to zero, similar to what may be done in other machine learning

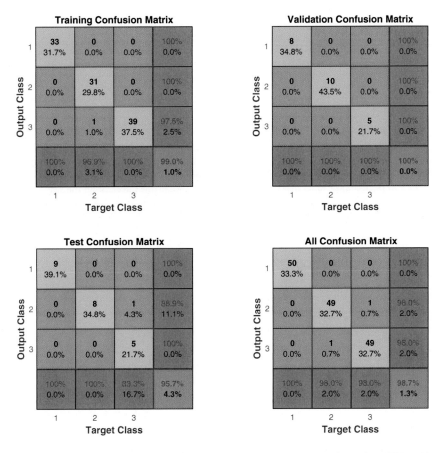

Figure 6.9 Summary of the error performance through confusion matrices of the NN architecture for training, validation and test sets. This figure is accessed with the **confusion** button on the NN interactive tool of Fig. 6.6.

algorithms. If weights are initialized to zero, after each update, the outgoing weights of each neuron will be identical, because the gradients will be identical. Moreover, NNs often get stuck at local optima where the gradient is zero but that are not global minima, so random weight initialization allows one to have a chance of circumventing this by starting at many different random values. (iii) The training data is run through the network to produce an output **y**, whose ideal ground-truth output is $\mathbf{y}_0$. The derivatives with respect to each network weight is then computed using backprop formulas (6.15). (iv) For a given learning rate δ, the network weights are updated as in (6.16). (v) We return to step (iii) and continue iterating until a maximum number of iterations is reached or convergence is achieved.

As a simple example, consider the linear activation function

$$f(\xi, \alpha) = g(\xi, \alpha) = \alpha\xi. \tag{6.17}$$

In this case we have in Fig. 6.10

$$z = ax \tag{6.18a}$$

$$y = bz. \tag{6.18b}$$

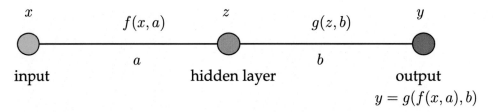

Figure 6.10 Illustration of the backpropagation algorithm on a one-node, one hidden layer network. The compositional nature of the network gives the input-output relationship $y = g(z, b) = g(f(x, a), b)$. By minimizing the error between the output y and its desired output y_0, the composition along with the chain rule produces an explicit formula (6.15) for updating the values of the weights. Note that the chain rule backpropagates the error all the way through the network. Thus by minimizing the output, the chain rule acts on the compositional function to produce a product of derivative terms that advance backward through the network.

We can now explicitly compute the gradients such as (6.15). This gives

$$\frac{\partial E}{\partial a} = -(y_0 - y)\frac{dy}{dz}\frac{dz}{da} = -(y_0 - y) \cdot b \cdot x \tag{6.19a}$$

$$\frac{\partial E}{\partial b} = -(y_0 - y)\frac{dy}{db} = -(y_0 - y)z = -(y_0 - y) \cdot a \cdot x. \tag{6.19b}$$

Thus with the current values of a and b, along with the input-output pair x and y and target truth y_0, each derivative can be evaluated. This provides the required information to perform the update (6.16).

The backprop for a deeper net follows in a similar fashion. Consider a network with M hidden layers labeled z_1 to z_m with the first connection weight a between x and z_1. The generalization of Fig. 6.10 and (6.15) is given by

$$\frac{\partial E}{\partial a} = -(y_0 - y)\frac{dy}{dz_m}\frac{dz_m}{dz_{m-1}} \cdots \frac{dz_2}{dz_1}\frac{dz_1}{da}. \tag{6.20}$$

The cascade of derivates induced by the composition and chain rule highlights the backpropagation of errors that occurs when minimizing the classification error.

A full generalization of backprop involves multiple layers as well multiple nodes per layer. The general situation is illustrated in Fig. 6.1. The objective is to determine the matrix elements of each matrix $\mathbf{A}_j$. Thus a significant number of network parameters need to be updated in gradient descent. Indeed, training a network can often be computationally infeasible even though the update rules for individual weights is not difficult. NNs can thus suffer from the curse of dimensionality as each matrix from one layer to another requires updating n^2 coefficients for an n-dimensional input, assuming the two connected layers are both n-dimensional.

Denoting all the weights to be updated by the vector $\mathbf{w}$, where $\mathbf{w}$ contains all the elements of the matrices $\mathbf{A}_j$ illustrated in Fig. 6.1, then

$$\mathbf{w}_{k+1} = \mathbf{w}_k + \delta\nabla E \tag{6.21}$$

where the gradient of the error ∇E, through the composition and chain rule, produces the backpropagation algorithm for updating the weights and reducing the error. Expressed in a component-by-component way

$$w_{k+1}^j = w_k^j + \delta \frac{\partial E}{\partial w_k^j} \tag{6.22}$$

where this equation holds for the jth component of the vector $\mathbf{w}$. The term $\partial E / \partial w^j$ produces the backpropagation through the chain rule, i.e. it produces the sequential set of functions to evaluate as in (6.20). Methods for solving this optimization more quickly, or even simply enabling the computation to be tractable, remain of active research interest. Perhaps the most important method is stochastic gradient descent which is considered in the next section.

6.4 The Stochastic Gradient Descent Algorithm

Training neural networks is computationally expensive due to the size of the NNs being trained. Even NNs of modest size can become prohibitively expensive if the optimization routines used for training are not well informed. Two algorithms have been especially critical for enabling the training of NNs: *stochastic gradient descent* (SGD) and backprop. Backprop allows for an efficient computation of the objective function's gradient while SGD provides a more rapid evaluation of the optimal network weights. Although alternative optimization methods for training NNs continue to provide computational improvements, backprop and SGD are both considered here in detail so as to give the reader an idea of the core architecture for building NNs.

Gradient descent was considered in Section 4.2. Recall that this algorithm was developed for nonlinear regression where the data fit takes the general form

$$f(x) = f(x, \boldsymbol{\beta}) \tag{6.23}$$

where $\boldsymbol{\beta}$ are fitting coefficients used to minimize the error. In NNs, the parameters $\boldsymbol{\beta}$ are the network weights, thus we can rewrite this in the form

$$f(\mathbf{x}) = f(\mathbf{x}, \mathbf{A}_1, \mathbf{A}_2, \cdots, \mathbf{A}_M) \tag{6.24}$$

where the $\mathbf{A}_j$ are the connectivity matrices from one layer to the next in the NN. Thus $\mathbf{A}_1$ connects the first and second layers, and there are M hidden layers.

The goal of training the NN is to minimize the error between the network and the data. The standard root-mean square error for this case is defined as

$$\underset{\mathbf{A}_j}{\operatorname{argmin}} E(\mathbf{A}_1, \mathbf{A}_2, \cdots, \mathbf{A}_M) = \underset{\mathbf{A}_j}{\operatorname{argmin}} \sum_{k=1}^{n} (f(\mathbf{x}_k, \mathbf{A}_1, \mathbf{A}_2, \cdots, \mathbf{A}_M) - \mathbf{y}_k)^2 \tag{6.25}$$

which can be minimized by setting the partial derivative with respect to each matrix component to zero, i.e. we require $\partial E / \partial (a_{ij})_k = 0$ where $(a_{ij})_k$ is the ith row and jth column of the kth matrix ($k = 1, 2, \cdots M$). Recall that the zero derivate is a minimum since there is no maximum error. This gives the gradient $\nabla f(\mathbf{x})$ of the function with respect to the NN parameters. Note further that $f(\cdot)$ is the function evaluated at each of the n data points.

As was shown in Section 4.2, this leads to a Newton-Raphson iteration scheme for finding the minima

$$\mathbf{x}_{j+1}(\delta) = \mathbf{x}_j - \delta \nabla f(\mathbf{x}_j) \tag{6.26}$$

where δ is a parameter determining how far a step should be taken along the gradient direction. In NNs, this parameter is called the *learning rate*. Unlike standard gradient descent, it can be computationally prohibitive to compute an optimal learning rate.

Although the optimization formulation is easily constructed, evaluating (6.25) is often computationally intractable for NNs. This due to two reasons: (i) the number of matrix weighting parameters for each $\mathbf{A}_j$ is quite large, and (ii) the number of data points n is generally also large.

To render the computation (6.25) potentially tractable, SGD does not estimate the gradient in (6.26) using all n data points. Rather, a single, randomly chosen data point, or a subset for *batch gradient descent*, is used to approximate the gradient at each step of the iteration. In this case, we can reformulate the least-square fitting of (6.25) so that

$$E(\mathbf{A}_1, \mathbf{A}_2, \cdots, \mathbf{A}_M) = \sum_{k=1}^{n} E_k(\mathbf{A}_1, \mathbf{A}_2, \cdots, \mathbf{A}_M) \tag{6.27}$$

and

$$E_k(\mathbf{A}_1, \mathbf{A}_2, \cdots, \mathbf{A}_M) = (f_k(\mathbf{x}_k, \mathbf{A}_1, \mathbf{A}_2, \cdots, \mathbf{A}_M) - \mathbf{y}_k)^2 \tag{6.28}$$

where $f_k(\cdot)$ is now the fitting function for each data point, and the entries of the matrices $\mathbf{A}_j$ are determined from the optimization process.

The gradient descent iteration algorithm (6.26) is now updated as follows

$$\mathbf{w}_{j+1}(\delta) = \mathbf{w}_j - \delta \nabla f_k(\mathbf{w}_j) \tag{6.29}$$

where $\mathbf{w}_j$ is the vector of all the network weights from $\mathbf{A}_j$ ($j = 1, 2, \cdots, M$) at the jth iteration, and the gradient is computed using only the kth data point and $f_k(\cdot)$. Thus instead of computing the gradient with all n points, only a single data point is randomly selected and used. At the next iteration, another randomly selected point is used to compute the gradient and update the solution. The algorithm may require multiple passes through all the data to converge, but each step is now easy to evaluate versus the expensive computation of the Jacobian which is required for the gradient. If instead of a single point, a subset of points is used, then we have the following batch gradient descent algorithm

$$\mathbf{w}_{j+1}(\delta) = \mathbf{w}_j - \delta \nabla f_K(\mathbf{w}_j) \tag{6.30}$$

where $K \in [k_1, k_2, \cdots k_p]$ denotes the p randomly selected data points k_j used to approximate the gradient.

The following code is a modification of the code shown in Section 4.2 for gradient descent. The modification here involves taking a significant subsampling of the data to approximate the gradient. Specifically, a batch gradient descent is illustrated with a fixed learning rate of $\delta = 2$. Ten points are used to approximate the gradient of the function at each step.

Code 6.3 Stochastic gradient descent algorithm.

```
h=0.1; x=-6:h:6; y=-6:h:6; n=length(x);
[X,Y]=meshgrid(x,y); clear x, clear y

F1=1.5-1.6*exp(-0.05*(3*(X+3).^2+(Y+3).^2));
F=F1 + (0.5-exp(-0.1*(3*(X-3).^2+(Y-3).^2)));
[dFx,dFy]=gradient(F,h,h);
```

```
x0=[4   0 -5]; y0=[0 -5   2]; col=['ro','bo','mo'];
for jj=1:3
   q=randperm(n); i1=sort(q(1:10));
   q2=randperm(n); i2=sort(q2(1:10));
   x(1)=x0(jj); y(1)=y0(jj);
   f(1)=interp2(X(i1,i2),Y(i1,i2),F(i1,i2),x(1),y(1));
   dfx=interp2(X(i1,i2),Y(i1,i2),dFx(i1,i2),x(1),y(1));
   dfy=interp2(X(i1,i2),Y(i1,i2),dFy(i1,i2),x(1),y(1));

   tau=2;
   for j=1:50
      x(j+1)=x(j)-tau*dfx; % update x, y, and f
      y(j+1)=y(j)-tau*dfy;
      q=randperm(n); ind1=sort(q(1:10));
      q2=randperm(n); ind2=sort(q2(1:10));
      f(j+1)=interp2(X(i1,i2),Y(i1,i2),F(i1,i2),x(j+1),y(j+1))
      dfx=interp2(X(i1,i2),Y(i1,i2),dFx(i1,i2),x(j+1),y(j+1));
      dfy=interp2(X(i1,i2),Y(i1,i2),dFy(i1,i2),x(j+1),y(j+1));
      if abs(f(j+1)-f(j))<10^(-6) % check convergence
          break
      end
   end
   if jj==1; x1=x; y1=y; f1=f; end
   if jj==2; x2=x; y2=y; f2=f; end
   if jj==3; x3=x; y3=y; f3=f; end
   clear x, clear y, clear f
end
```

Fig. 6.11 shows the convergence of SGD for three initial conditions. As with gradient descent, the algorithm can get stuck in local minima. However, the SGD now approximates the gradient with only 100 points instead of the full 10^4 points, thus allowing for a computation which is three orders of magnitude smaller. Importantly, the SGD is a scalable algorithm, allowing for significant computational savings even as the data grows to be high-

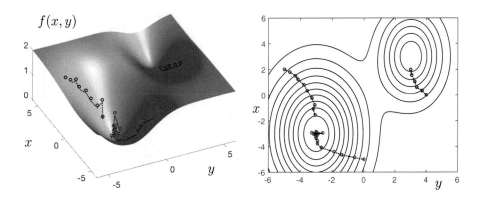

Figure 6.11 Stochastic gradient descent applied to the function featured in Fig. 4.3(b). The convergence can be compared to a full gradient descent algorithm as shown in Fig. 4.6. Each step of the stochastic (batch) gradient descent selects 100 data points for approximating the gradient, instead of the 10^4 data points of the data. Three initial conditions are shown: $(x_0, y_0) = \{(4, 0), (0, -5), (-5, 2)\}$. The first of these (red circles) gets stuck in a local minima while the other two initial conditions (blue and magenta) find the global minima. Interpolation of the gradient functions of Fig. 4.5 are used to update the solutions.

dimensional. For this reason, SGD has become a critically enabling part of NN training. Note that the learning rate, batch size, and data sampling play an important role in the convergence of the method.

6.5   Deep Convolutional Neural Networks

With the basics of the NN architecture in hand, along with an understanding of how to formulate an optimization framework (backprop) and actually compute the gradient descent efficiently (SGD), we are ready to construct *deep convolution neural nets* (DCNN) which are the fundamental building blocks of *deep learning* methods. Indeed, today when practitioners generally talk about NNs for practical use, they are typically talking about DCNNs. But as much as we would like to have a principled approach to building DCNNs, there remains a great deal of artistry and expert intuition for producing the highest performing networks. Moreover, DCNNs are especially prone to overtraining, thus requiring special care to cross-validate the results. The recent textbook on deep learning by Goodfellow et al. [216] provides a detailed an extensive account of the state-of-the-art in DCNNs. It is especially useful for highlighting many rules-of-thumb and tricks for training effective DCNNs.

Like SVM and random forest algorithms, the MATLAB package for building NNs has a tremendous number of features and tuning parameters. This flexibility is both advantageous and overwhelming at the same time. As was pointed out at the beginning of this chapter, it is immediately evident that there are a great number of design questions regarding NNs. How many layers should be used? What should be the dimension of the layers? How should the output layer be designed? Should one use all-to-all or sparsified connections between layers? How should the mapping between layers be performed: a *linear mapping* or a *nonlinear mapping*?

The prototypical structure of a DCNN is illustrated in Fig. 6.12. Included in the visualization is a number of commonly used convolutional and pooling layers. Also illustrated is the fact that each layer can be used to build multiple downstream layers, or *feature* spaces, that can be engineered by the choice of activation functions and/or network parametrizations. All of these layers are ultimately combined into the output layer. The number of connections that require updating through backprop and SGD can be extraordinarily high, thus even modest networks and training data may require signifiant computational resources. A typical DCNN is constructed of a number of layers, with DCNNs typically having between 7-10 layers. More recent efforts have considered the advantages of a truly deep network with approximately 100 layers, but the merits of such architectures are still not fully known. The following paragraphs highlight some of the more prominent elements that comprise DCNNs, including convolutional layers, pooling layers, fully-connected layers and dropout.

Convolutional Layers

Convolutional layers are similar to windowed (Gabor) Fourier transforms or wavelets from Chapter 2, in that a small selection of the full high-dimensional input space is extracted and used for feature engineering. Fig. 6.12 shows the convolutional windows (dark gray boxes) that are slid across the entire layer (light gray boxes). Each convolution window transforms

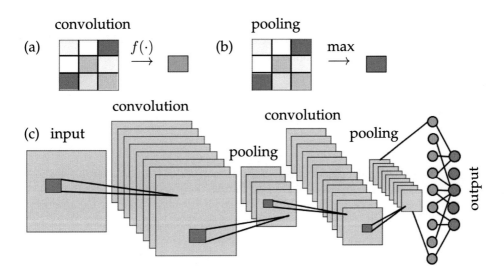

Figure 6.12 Prototypical DCNN architecture which includes commonly used convolutional and pooling layers. The dark gray boxes show the convolutional sampling from layer to layer. Note that for each layer, many functional transformations can be used to produce a variety of feature spaces. The network ultimately integrates all this information into the output layer.

the data into a new node through a given activation function, as shown in Fig. 6.12(a). The feature spaces are thus built from the smaller patches of the data. Convolutional layers are especially useful for images as they can extract important features such as edges. Wavelets are also known to efficiently extract such features and there are deep mathematical connections between wavelets and DCNNs as shown by Mallat and co-workers [358, 12]. Note that in Fig. 6.12, the input layer can be used to construct many layers by simply manipulating the activation function $f(\cdot)$ to the next layer as well the size of the convolutional window.

Pooling Layers

It is common to periodically insert a Pooling layer between successive convolutional layers in a DCNN architecture. Its function is to progressively reduce the spatial size of the representation in order to reduce the number of parameters and computation in the network. This is an effective strategy to (i) help control overfitting and (ii) fit the computation in memory. Pooling layers operate independently on every depth slice of the input and resize them spatially. Using the max operation, i.e. the maximum value for all the nodes in its convolutional window, is called *max pooling*. In image processing, the most common form of max pooling is a pooling layer with filters of size 2×2 applied with a stride of 2 down-samples every depth slice in the input by 2 along both width and height, discarding 75% of the activations. Every max pooling operation would in this case be taking a max over 4 numbers (a 2x2 region in some depth slice). The depth dimension remains unchanged. An example max pooling operation is shown in Fig. 6.12(b), where a 3×3 convolutional cell is transformed to a single number which is the maximum of the 9 numbers.

Fully-Connected Layers

Occasionally, fully-connected layers are inserted into the DCNN so that different regions can be connected. The pooling and convolutional layers are *local* connections only, while the fully-connected layer restores *global* connectivity. This is another commonly used layer in the DCNN architecture, providing a potentially important feature space to improve performance.

Dropout

Overfitting is a serious problem in DCNNs. Indeed, overfitting is at the core of why DCNNs often fail to demonstrate good generalizability properties (See Chapter 4 on regression). Large DCNNs are also slow to use, making it difficult to deal with overfitting by combining the predictions of many different large neural nets for online implementation. Dropout is a technique which helps address this problem. The key idea is to randomly drop nodes in the network (along with their connections) from the DCNN during training, i.e. during SGD/backprop updates of the network weights. This prevents units from co-adapting too much. During training, dropout samples form an exponential number of different "thinned" networks. This idea is similar to the ensemble methods for building random forests. At test time, it is easy to approximate the effect of averaging the predictions of all these thinned networks by simply using a single unthinned network that has smaller weights. This significantly reduces overfitting and has shown to give major improvements over other regularization methods [499].

There are many other techniques that have been devised for training DCNNs, but the above methods highlight some of the most commonly used. The most successful applications of these techniques tend to be in computer vision tasks where DCNNs offer unparalleled performance in comparison to other machine learning methods. Importantly, the ImageNET data set is what allowed these DCNN layers to be maximally leveraged for human level recognition performance.

To illustrate how to train and execute a DCNN, we use data from MATLAB. Specifically, we use a data set that has a training and test set with the alphabet characters A, B, and C. The following code loads the data set and plots a representative sample of the characters in Fig. 6.13.

Code 6.4 Loading alphabet images.

```
load lettersTrainSet
perm = randperm(1500,20);
for j = 1:20
    subplot(4,5,j);
    imshow(XTrain(:,:,:,perm(j)));
end
```

This code loads the training data, XTrain, that contains 1500 28×28 grayscale images of the letters A, B, and C in a 4-D array. There are equal numbers of each letter in the data set. The variable TTrain contains the categorical array of the letter labels, i.e. the truth labels. The following code constructs and trains a DCNN.

Code 6.5 Train a DCNN.

```
layers = [imageInputLayer([28 28 1]);
          convolution2dLayer(5,16);
```

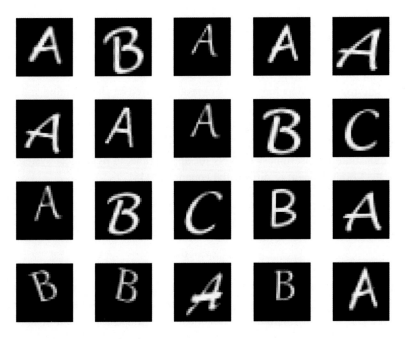

Figure 6.13 Representative images of the alphabet characters A, B, and C. There are a total of 1500 28×28 grayscale images (XTrain) of the letters that are labeled (TTrain).

```
            reluLayer();
            maxPooling2dLayer(2,'Stride',2);
            fullyConnectedLayer(3);
            softmaxLayer();
            classificationLayer()];
options = trainingOptions('sgdm');
rng('default') % For reproducibility
net = trainNetwork(XTrain,TTrain,layers,options);
```

Note the simplicity in how diverse network layers are easily put together. In addition, a ReLu activation layer is specified along with the training method of stochastic gradient descent (sgdm). The **trainNetwork** command integrates the options and layer specifications to build the best classifier possible. The resulting trained network can now be used on a test data set.

Code 6.6 Test the DCNN performance.

```
load lettersTestSet;
YTest = classify(net,XTest);
accuracy = sum(YTest == TTest)/numel(TTest)
```

The resulting classification performance is approximately 93%. One can see by this code structure that modifying the network architecture and specifications is trivial. Indeed, one can probably easily engineer a network to outperform the illustrated DCNN. As already mentioned, artistry and expert intuition are critical for producing the highest performing networks.

6.6   Neural Networks for Dynamical Systems

Neural networks offer an amazingly flexible architecture for performing a diverse set of mathematical tasks. To return to S. Mallat: *Supervised learning is a high-dimensional interpolation problem [358]*. Thus if sufficiently rich data can be acquired, NNs offer the ability to interrogate the data for a variety of tasks centered on classification and prediction. To this point, the tasks demonstrated have primarily been concerned with computer vision. However, NNs can also be used for future state predictions of dynamical systems (See Chapter 7).

To demonstrate the usefulness of NNs for applications in dynamical systems, we will consider the Lorenz system of differential equations [345]

$$\dot{x} = \sigma(y - x) \tag{6.31a}$$

$$\dot{y} = x(\rho - z) - y \tag{6.31b}$$

$$\dot{z} = xy - \beta z, \tag{6.31c}$$

where the state of the system is given by $\mathbf{x} = [x \ y \ z]^T$ with the parameters $\sigma = 10$, $\rho = 28$, and $\beta = 8/3$. This system will be considered in further detail in the next chapter. For the present, we will simulate this nonlinear system and use it as a demonstration of how NNs can be trained to characterize dynamical systems. Specifically, the goal of this section is to demonstrate that we can train a NN to learn an update rule which advances the state space from $\mathbf{x}_k$ to $\mathbf{x}_{k+1}$, where k denotes the state of the system at time t_k. Accurately advancing the solution in time requires a nonlinear transfer function since Lorenz itself is nonlinear.

The training data required for the NN is constructed from high-accuracy simulations of the Lorenz system. The following code generates a diverse set of initial conditions. One hundred initial conditions are considered in order to generate one hundred trajectories. The sampling time is fixed at $\Delta t = 0.01$. Note that the sampling time is not the same as the time-steps taken by the 4th-order Runge-Kutta method [316]. The time-steps are adaptively chosen to meet the stringent tolerances of accuracy chosen for this example.

Code 6.7 Create training data of Lorenz trajectories.

```
% Simulate Lorenz system
dt=0.01; T=8; t=0:dt:T;
b=8/3; sig=10; r=28;

Lorenz = @(t,x)([ sig * (x(2) - x(1))          ; ...
                  r * x(1)-x(1) * x(3) - x(2) ; ...
                  x(1) * x(2) - b*x(3)        ]);
ode_options = odeset('RelTol',1e-10, 'AbsTol',1e-11);

input=[]; output=[];
for j=1:100   % training trajectories
    x0=30*(rand(3,1)-0.5);
    [t,y] = ode45(Lorenz,t,x0);
    input=[input; y(1:end-1,:)];
    output=[output; y(2:end,:)];
    plot3(y(:,1),y(:,2),y(:,3)), hold on
    plot3(x0(1),x0(2),x0(3),'ro')
end
```

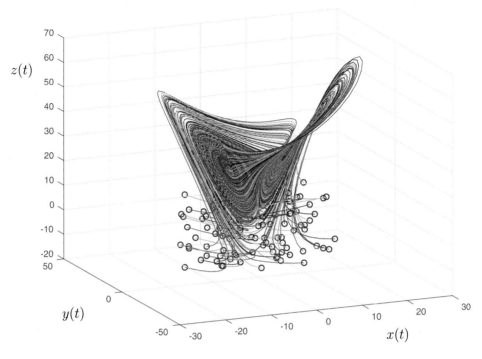

Figure 6.14 Evolution of the Lorenz dynamical equations for one hundred randomly chosen initial conditions (red circles). For the parameters $\sigma = 10$, $\rho = 28$, and $\beta = 8/3$, all trajectories collapse to an attractor. These trajectories, generated from a diverse set of initial data, are used to train a neural network to learn the nonlinear mapping from $\mathbf{x}_k$ to $\mathbf{x}_{k+1}$.

The simulation of the Lorenz system produces to key matrices: **input** and **output**. The former is a matrix of the system at $\mathbf{x}_k$, while the latter is the corresponding state of the system $\mathbf{x}_{k+1}$ advanced $\Delta t = 0.01$.

The NN must learn the nonlinear mapping from $\mathbf{x}_k$ to $\mathbf{x}_{k+1}$. Fig. 6.14 shows the various trajectories used to train the NN. Note the diversity of initial conditions and the underlying attractor of the Lorenz system.

We now build a NN trained on trajectories of Fig. 6.14 to advance the solution $\Delta t = 0.01$ into the future for an arbitrary initial condition. Here, a three-layer network is constructed with ten nodes in each layer and a different activation unit for each layer. The choice of activation types, nodes in the layer and number of layers are arbitrary. It is trivial to make the network deeper and wider and enforce different activation units. The performance of the NN for the arbitrary choices made is quite remarkable and does not require additional tuning. The NN is build with the following few lines of code.

Code 6.8 Build a neural network for Lorenz system.

```
net = feedforwardnet([10 10 10]);
net.layers{1}.transferFcn = 'logsig';
net.layers{2}.transferFcn = 'radbas';
net.layers{3}.transferFcn = 'purelin';
net = train(net,input.',output.');
```

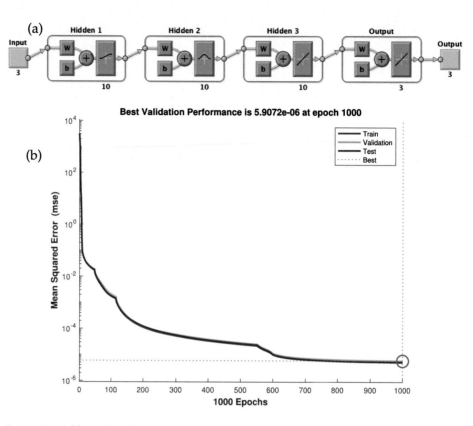

Figure 6.15 (a) Network architecture used to train the NN on the trajectory data of Fig. 6.14. A three-layer network is constructed with ten nodes in each layer and a different activation unit for each layer. (b) Performance summary of the NN optimization algorithm. Over 1000 epochs of training, accuracies on the order of 10^{-5} are produced. The NN is also cross-validated in the process.

The code produces a function **net** which can be used with a new set of data to produce predictions of the future. Specifically, the function **net** gives the nonlinear mapping from $\mathbf{x}_k$ to $\mathbf{x}_{k+1}$. Fig. 6.15 shows the structure of the network along with the performance of the training over 1000 epochs of training. The results of the cross-validation are also demonstrated. The NN converges steadily to a network that produces accuracies on the order of 10^{-5}.

Once the NN is trained on the trajectory data, the nonlinear model mapping $\mathbf{x}_k$ to $\mathbf{x}_{k+1}$ can be used to predict the future state of the system from an initial condition. In the following code, the trained function **net** is used to take an initial condition and advance the solution Δt. The output can be re-inserted into the **net** function to estimate the solution $2\Delta t$ into the future. This iterative mapping can produce a prediction for the future state as far into the future as desired. In what follows, the mapping is used to predict the Lorenz solutions eight time units into the future from for a given initial condition. This can then be compared against the ground truth simulation of the evolution using a 4th-order Runge-Kutta method. The following iteration scheme gives the NN approximation to the dynamics.

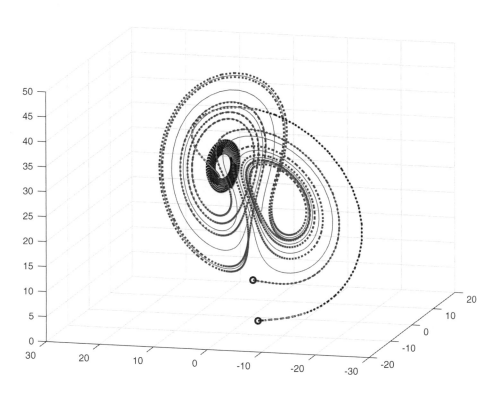

Figure 6.16 Comparison of the time evolution of the Lorenz system (solid line) with the NN prediction (dotted line) for two randomly chosen initial conditions (red dots). The NN prediction stays close to the dynamical trajectory of the Lorenz model. A more detailed comparison is given in Fig. 6.17.

Code 6.9 Neural network for prediction.

```
ynn(1,:)=x0;
for jj=2:length(t)
    y0=net(x0);
    ynn(jj,:)=y0.'; x0=y0;
end
plot3(ynn(:,1),ynn(:,2),ynn(:,3),':','Linewidth',[2])
```

Fig. 6.16 shows the evolution of two randomly drawn trajectories (solid lines) compared against the NN prediction of the trajectories (dotted lines). The NN prediction is remarkably accurate in producing an approximation to the high-accuracy simulations. This shows that the data used for training is capable of producing a high-quality nonlinear model mapping x_k to x_{k+1}. The quality of the approximation is more clearly seen in Fig. 6.17 where the time evolution of the individual components of x are shown against the NN predictions. See Section 7.5 for further details.

In conclusion, the NN can be trained to learn dynamics. More precisely, the NN seems to learn an algorithm which is approximately equivalent to a 4th-order Runge-Kutta scheme for advancing the solution a time-step Δt. Indeed, NNs have been used to model dynamical systems [215] and other physical processes [381] for decades. However, great strides have been made recently in using DNNs to learn Koopman embeddings, resulting in several excellent papers [550, 368, 513, 564, 412, 332]. For example, the VAMPnet architec-

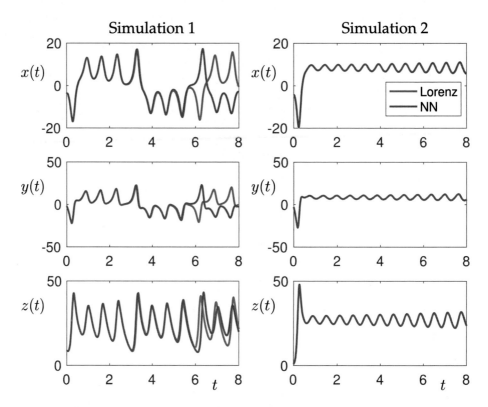

Figure 6.17 Comparison of the time evolution of the Lorenz system for two randomly chosen initial conditions (Also shown in Fig. 6.16). The left column shows that the evolution of the Lorenz differential equations and the NN mapping gives identical results until $t \approx 5.5$, at which point they diverge. In contrast, the NN prediction stays on the trajectory of the second initial condition for the entire time window.

ture [550, 368] uses a time-lagged auto-encoder and a custom variational score to identify Koopman coordinates on an impressive protein folding example. In an alternative formulation, variational auto-encoders can build low-rank models that are efficient and compact representations of the Koopman operator from data [349]. By construction, the resulting network is both parsimonious and interpretable, retaining the flexibility of neural networks and the physical interpretation of Koopman theory. In all of these recent studies, DNN representations have been shown to be more flexible and exhibit higher accuracy than other leading methods on challenging problems.

6.7   The Diversity of Neural Networks

There are a wide variety of NN architectures, with only a few of the most dominant architectures considered thus far. This chapter and book does not attempt to give a comprehensive assessment of the state-of-the-art in neural networks. Rather, our focus is on illustrating some of the key concepts and enabling mathematical architectures that have led NNs to a dominant position in modern data science. For a more in-depth review, please see [216]. However, to conclude this chapter, we would like to highlight some of the

NN architectures that are used in practice for various data science tasks. This overview is inspired by the *neural network zoo* as highlighted by Fjodor Van Veen of the Asimov Institute (http://www.asimovinstitute.org).

The neural network zoo highlights some of the different architectural structures around NNs. Some of the networks highlighted are commonly used across industry, while others serve niche roles for specific applications. Regardless, it demonstrates that tremendous variability and research effort focused on NNs as a core data science tool. Fig. 6.18 highlights the prototype structures to be discussed in what follows. Note that the bottom panel has a key to the different type of nodes in the network, including input cells, output cells, and hidden cells. Additionally, the hidden layer NN cells can have memory effects, kernel structures and/or convolution/pooling. For each NN architecture, a brief description is given along with the original paper proposing the technique.

Perceptron

The first mathematical model of NNs by Fukushima was termed the Neocognitron in 1980 [193]. His model had a single layer with a single output cell called the perceptron, which made a categorial decision based on the sign of the output. Fig. 6.2 shows this architecture to classify between dogs and cats. The perceptron is an algorithm for supervised learning of binary classifiers.

Feed Forward (FF)

Feed forward networks connect the input layer to output layer by forming connections between the units so that they do not form a cycle. Fig. 6.1 has already shown a version of this architecture where the information simply propagates from left to right in the network. It is often the workhorse of supervised learning where the weights are trained so as to best classify a given set of data. A feedforward network was used in Figs. 6.5 and 6.15 for training a classifier for dogs versus cats and predicting time-steps of the Lorenz attractor respectively. An important subclass of feed forward networks is *deep feed forward* (DFF) NNs. DFFs simply put together a larger number of hidden layers, typically 7-10 layers, to form the NN. A second important class of FF is the *radial basis network*, which uses radial basis functions as the activation units [87]. Like any FF network, radial basis function networks have many uses, including function approximation, time series prediction, classification, and control.

Recurrent Neural Network (RNN)

Illustrated in Fig. 6.18(a), RNNs are characterized by connections between units that form a directed graph along a sequence. This allows it to exhibit dynamic temporal behavior for a time sequence [172]. Unlike feedforward neural networks, RNNs can use their internal state (memory) to process sequences of inputs. The prototypical architecture in Fig. 6.18(a) shows that each cell feeds back on itself. This self-interaction, which is not part of the FF architecture, allows for a variety of innovations. Specifically, it allows for time delays and/or feedback loops. Such controlled states are referred to as gated state or gated memory, and are part of two key innovations: *long-short term memory* (LSTM)networks [248] and

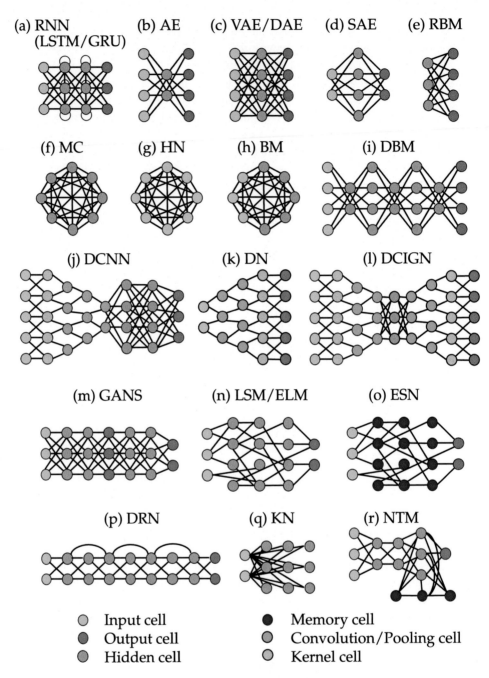

Figure 6.18 Neural network architectures commonly considered in the literature. The NNs are comprised of input nodes, output nodes, and hidden nodes. Additionally, the nodes can have memory, perform convolution and/or pooling, and perform a kernel transformation. Each network, and their acronym is explained in the text.

gated recurrent units (GRU) [132]. LSTM is of particular importance as it revolutionized speech recognition, setting a variety of performance records and outperforming traditional models in a variety of speech applications. GRUs are a variation of LSTMs which have been demonstrated to exhibit better performance on smaller datasets.

Auto Encoder (AE)

The aim of an auto encoder, represented in Fig. 6.18(b), is to learn a representation (encoding) for a set of data, typically for the purpose of dimensionality reduction. For AEs, the input and output cells are matched so that the AE is essentially constructed to be a nonlinear transform into and out of a new representation, acting as an approximate identity map on the data. Thus AEs can be thought of as a generalization of linear dimensionality reduction techniques such as PCA. AEs can potentially produce nonlinear PCA representations of the data, or nonlinear manifolds on which the data should be embedded [71]. Since most data lives in nonlinear subspaces, AEs are an important class of NN for data science, with many innovations and modifications. Three important modifications of the standard AE are commonly used. The *variational auto encoder* (VAE) [290] (shown in Fig. 6.18(c)) is a popular approach to unsupervised learning of complicated distributions. By making strong assumptions concerning the distribution of latent variables, it can be trained using standard gradient descent algorithms to provide a good assessments of data in an unsupervised fashion. The *denoising auto encoder* (DAE) [541] (shown in Fig. 6.18(c)) takes a partially corrupted input during training to recover the original undistorted input. Thus noise is intentionally added to the input in order to learn the nonlinear embedding. Finally, the *sparse auto encoder* (SAE) [432] (shown in Fig. 6.18(d)) imposes sparsity on the hidden units during training, while having a larger number of hidden units than inputs, so that an autoencoder can learn useful structures in the input data. Sparsity is typically imposed by thresholding all but the few strongest hidden unit activations.

Markov Chain (MC)

A Markov chain is a stochastic model describing a sequence of possible events in which the probability of each event depends only on the state attained in the previous event. So although not formally a NN, it shares many common features with RNNs. Markov chains are standard even in undergraduate probability and statistics courses. Fig. 6.18(f) shows the basic architecture where each cell is connected to the other cells by a probability model for a transition.

Hopfield Network (HN)

A Hopfield network is a form of a RNN which was popularized by John Hopfield in 1982 for understanding human memory [254]. Fig. 6.18(g) shows the basic architecture of an all-to-all connected network where each node can act as an input cell. The network serves as a trainable content-addressable *associative* memory system with binary threshold nodes. Given an input, it is iterated on the network with a guarantee to converge to a local minimum. Sometimes it converge to a false pattern, or memory (wrong local minimum), rather than the stored pattern (expected local minimum).

Boltzmann Machine (BM)

The Boltzmann machine, sometimes called a stochastic Hopfield network with hidden units, is a stochastic, generative counterpart of the Hopfield network. They were one of the first neural networks capable of learning internal representations, and are able to represent and (given sufficient time) solve difficult combinatoric problems [246]. Fig. 6.18(h) shows the structure of the BM. Note that unlike Markov chains (which have no input units) or

Hopfield networks (where all cells are inputs), the BM is a hybrid which has a mixture of input cells and hidden units. Boltzmann machines are intuitively appealing due to their resemblance to the dynamics of simple physical processes. They are named after the Boltzmann distribution in statistical mechanics, which is used in their sampling function.

Restricted Boltzmann Machine (RBM)

Introduced under the name *Harmonium* by Paul Smolensky in 1986 [493], RBMs have been proposed for dimensionality reduction, classification, collaborative filtering, feature learning, and topic modeling. They can be trained for either supervised or unsupervised tasks. G. Hinton helped bring them to prominence by developing fast algorithms for evaluating them [397]. RBMs are a subset of BMs where restrictions are imposed on the NN such that nodes in the NN must form a bipartite graph (See Fig. 6.18(e)). Thus a pair of nodes from each of the two groups of units (commonly referred to as the "visible" and "hidden" units, respectively) may have a symmetric connection between them; there are no connections between nodes within a group. RBMs can be used in deep learning networks and deep belief networks by stacking RBMs and optionally fine-tuning the resulting deep network with gradient descent and backpropagation.

Deep Belief Network (DBN)

DBNs are a generative graphical model that are composed of multiple layers of latent hidden variables, with connections between the layers but not between units within each layer [52]. Fig. 6.18(i) shows the architecture of the DBN. The training of the DBNs can be done stack by stack from AE or RBM layers. Thus each of these layers only has to learn to encode the previous network, which is effectively a greedy training algorithm for finding locally optimal solutions. Thus DBNs can be viewed as a composition of simple, unsupervised networks such as RBMs and AEs where each sub-network's hidden layer serves as the visible layer for the next.

Deep Convolutional Neural Network (DCNN)

DCNNs are the workhorse of computer vision and have already been considered in this chapter. They are abstractly represented in Fig. 6.18(j), and in a more specific fashion in Fig. 6.12. Their impact and influence on computer vision cannot be overestimated. They were originally developed for document recognition [325].

Deconvolutional Network (DN)

Deconvolutional Networks, shown in Fig. 6.18(k), are essentially a reverse of DCNNs [567]. The mathematical structure of DNs permit the unsupervised construction of hierarchical image representations. These representations can be used for both low-level tasks such as denoising, as well as providing features for object recognition. Each level of the hierarchy groups information from the level beneath to form more complex features that exist over a larger scale in the image. As with DCNNs, it is well suited for computer vision tasks.

Deep Convolutional Inverse Graphics Network (DCIGN)

The DCIGN is a form of a VAE that uses DCNNs for the encoding and decoding [313]. As with the AE/VAE/SAE structures, the output layer shown in Fig. 6.18(l) is constrained to match the input layer. DCIGN combine the power of DCNNs with VAEs, which provides a formative mathematical architecture for computer visions and image processing.

Generative Adversarial Network (GAN)

In an innovative modification of NNs, the GAN architecture of Fig. 6.18(m) trains two networks simultaneously [217]. The networks, often which are a combination of DCNNs and/or FFs, train by one of the networks generating content which the other attempts to judge. Specifically, one network generates candidates and the other evaluates them. Typically, the generative network learns to map from a latent space to a particular data distribution of interest, while the discriminative network discriminates between instances from the true data distribution and candidates produced by the generator. The generative network's training objective is to increase the error rate of the discriminative network (i.e., "fool" the discriminator network by producing novel synthesized instances that appear to have come from the true data distribution). The GAN architecture has produced interesting results in computer vision for producing synthetic data, such as images and movies.

Liquid State Machine (LSM)

The LSM shown in Fig. 6.18(n) is a particular kind of spiking neural network [352]. An LSM consists of a large collection of nodes, each of which receives time varying input from external sources (the inputs) as well as from other nodes. Nodes are randomly connected to each other. The recurrent nature of the connections turns the time varying input into a spatio-temporal pattern of activations in the network nodes. The spatio-temporal patterns of activation are read out by linear discriminant units. This architecture is motivated by spiking neurons in the brain, thus helping understand how information processing and discrimination might happen using spiking neurons.

Extreme Learning Machine (ELM)

With the same underlying architecture of an LSM shown in Fig. 6.18(n), the ELM is a FF network for classification, regression, clustering, sparse approximation, compression and feature learning with a single layer or multiple layers of hidden nodes, where the parameters of hidden nodes (not just the weights connecting inputs to hidden nodes) need not be tuned. These hidden nodes can be randomly assigned and never updated, or can be inherited from their ancestors without being changed. In most cases, the output weights of hidden nodes are usually learned in a single step, which essentially amounts to learning a linear model [108].

Echo State Network (ESN)

ESNs are RNNs with a sparsely connected hidden layer (with typically 1% connectivity). The connectivity and weights of hidden neurons have memory and are fixed and randomly assigned (See Fig. 6.18(o)). Thus like LSMs and ELMs they are not fixed into a well-ordered layered structure. The weights of output neurons can be learned so that the network can generate specific temporal patterns [263].

Deep Residual Network (DRN)

DRNs took the deep learning world by storm when Microsoft Research released Deep Residual Learning for Image Recognition [237]. These networks led to 1st-place winning entries in all five main tracks of the ImageNet and COCO 2015 competitions, which covered image classification, object detection, and semantic segmentation. The robustness of ResNets has since been proven by various visual recognition tasks and by nonvisual tasks involving speech and language. DRNs are very deep FF networks where there are extra connections that pass from one layer to a layer two to five layers downstream. This then carries input from an earlier stage to a future stage. These networks can be 150 layers deep, which is only abstractly represented in Fig. 6.18(p).

Kohonen Network (KN)

Kohonen networks are also known as self-organizing feature maps [298]. KNs use competitive learning to classify data without supervision. Input is presented to the KN as in Fig. 6.18(q), after which the network assesses which of the neurons closely match that input. These self-organizing maps differ from other NNs as they apply competitive learning as opposed to error-correction learning (such as backpropagation with gradient descent), and in the sense that they use a neighborhood function to preserve the topological properties of the input space. This makes KNs useful for low-dimensional visualization of high-dimensional data.

Neural Turing Machine (NTM)

An NTM implements a NN controller coupled to an external memory resource (See Fig. 6.18(r)), which it interacts with through attentional mechanisms [219]. The memory interactions are differentiable end-to-end, making it possible to optimize them using gradient descent. An NTM with a LSTM controller can infer simple algorithms such as copying, sorting, and associative recall from input and output examples.

Suggested Reading

Texts
(1) **Deep learning**, by I. Goodfellow, Y. Bengio and A. Courville, 2016 [216].
(2) **Neural networks for pattern recognition**, by C. M. Bishop, 1995 [63].

Papers and Reviews
(1) **Deep learning**, by Y. LeCun, Y. Bengio and G. Hinton, *Nature*, 2015 [324].
(2) **Understanding deep convolutional networks**, by S. Mallat, *Phil. Trans. R. Soc. A*, 2016 [358].
(3) **Deep learning: mathematics and neuroscience**, by T. Poggio, *Views & Reviews, McGovern Center for Brains, Minds and Machines*, 2016 [430].
(4) **Imagenet classification with deep convolutional neural**, by A. Krizhevsky, I. Sutskever and G. Hinton, *Advances in neural information processing systems*, 2012 [310].

Part III

Dynamics and Control

7 Data-Driven Dynamical Systems

Dynamical systems provide a mathematical framework to describe the world around us, modeling the rich interactions between quantities that co-evolve in time. Formally, dynamical systems concerns the analysis, prediction, and understanding of the behavior of systems of differential equations or iterative mappings that describe the evolution of the state of a system. This formulation is general enough to encompass a staggering range of phenomena, including those observed in classical mechanical systems, electrical circuits, turbulent fluids, climate science, finance, ecology, social systems, neuroscience, epidemiology, and nearly every other system that evolves in time.

Modern dynamical systems began with the seminal work of Poincaré on the chaotic motion of planets. It is rooted in classical mechanics, and may be viewed as the culmination of hundreds of years of mathematical modeling, beginning with Newton and Leibniz. The full history of dynamical systems is too rich for these few pages, having captured the interest and attention of the greatest minds for centuries, and having been applied to countless fields and challenging problems. Dynamical systems provides one of the most complete and well-connected fields of mathematics, bridging diverse topics from linear algebra and differential equations, to topology, numerical analysis, and geometry. Dynamical systems has become central in the modeling and analysis of systems in nearly every field of the engineering, physical, and life sciences.

Modern dynamical systems is currently undergoing a renaissance, with analytical derivations and first principles models giving way to data-driven approaches. The confluence of big data and machine learning is driving a paradigm shift in the analysis and understanding of dynamical systems in science and engineering. Data are abundant, while physical laws or governing equations remain elusive, as is true for problems in climate science, finance, epidemiology, and neuroscience. Even in classical fields, such as optics and turbulence, where governing equations do exist, researchers are increasingly turning toward data-driven analysis. Many critical data-driven problems, such as predicting climate change, understanding cognition from neural recordings, predicting and suppressing the spread of disease, or controlling turbulence for energy efficient power production and transportation, are primed to take advantage of progress in the data-driven discovery of dynamics.

In addition, the classical geometric and statistical perspectives on dynamical systems are being complemented by a third *operator-theoretic* perspective, based on the evolution of measurements of the system. This so-called *Koopman* operator theory is poised to capitalize on the increasing availability of measurement data from complex systems. Moreover, Koopman theory provides a path to identify intrinsic coordinate systems to represent nonlinear dynamics in a linear framework. Obtaining linear representations of strongly nonlinear systems has the potential to revolutionize our ability to predict and control these systems.

This chapter presents a modern perspective on dynamical systems in the context of current goals and open challenges. Data-driven dynamical systems is a rapidly evolving field, and therefore, we focus on a mix of established and emerging methods that are driving current developments. In particular, we will focus on the key challenges of discovering dynamics from data and finding data-driven representations that make nonlinear systems amenable to linear analysis.

7.1   Overview, Motivations, and Challenges

Before summarizing recent developments in data-driven dynamical systems, it is important to first provide a mathematical introduction to the notation and summarize key motivations and open challenges in dynamical systems.

Dynamical Systems

Throughout this chapter, we will consider dynamical systems of the form:

$$\frac{d}{dt}\mathbf{x}(t) = \mathbf{f}(\mathbf{x}(t), t; \boldsymbol{\beta}), \tag{7.1}$$

where $\mathbf{x}$ is the state of the system and $\mathbf{f}$ is a vector field that possibly depends on the state $\mathbf{x}$, time t, and a set of parameters $\boldsymbol{\beta}$.

For example, consider the Lorenz equations [345]

$$\dot{x} = \sigma(y - x) \tag{7.2a}$$

$$\dot{y} = x(\rho - z) - y \tag{7.2b}$$

$$\dot{z} = xy - \beta z, \tag{7.2c}$$

with parameters $\sigma = 10$, $\rho = 28$, and $\beta = 8/3$. A trajectory of the Lorenz system is shown in Fig. 7.1. In this case, the state vector is $\mathbf{x} = \begin{bmatrix} x & y & z \end{bmatrix}^T$ and the parameter vector is $\boldsymbol{\beta} = \begin{bmatrix} \sigma & \rho & \beta \end{bmatrix}^T$.

The Lorenz system is among the simplest and most well-studied dynamical systems that exhibits chaos, which is characterized as a sensitive dependence on initial conditions. Two trajectories with nearby initial conditions will rapidly diverge in behavior, and after long times, only statistical statements can be made.

It is simple to simulate dynamical systems, such as the Lorenz system. First, the vector field $\mathbf{f}(\mathbf{x}, t; \boldsymbol{\beta})$ is defined in the function **lorenz**:

```
function dx = lorenz(t,x,Beta)
dx = [
Beta(1)*(x(2)-x(1));
x(1)*(Beta(2)-x(3))-x(2);
x(1)*x(2)-Beta(3)*x(3);
];
```

Next, we define the system parameters $\boldsymbol{\beta}$, initial condition $\mathbf{x}_0$, and time span:

```
Beta = [10; 28; 8/3]; % Lorenz's parameters (chaotic)

x0=[0; 1; 20];  % Initial condition
```

Figure 7.1 Chaotic trajectory of the Lorenz system from (7.2).

```
dt = 0.001;
tspan=dt:dt:50;
options = odeset('RelTol',1e-12,'AbsTol',1e-12*ones(1,3));
```

Finally, we simulate the equations with **ode45**, which implements a fourth-order Runge Kutta integration scheme with adaptive time step:

```
[t,x]=ode45(@(t,x) lorenz(t,x,Beta),tspan,x0,options);
plot3(x(:,1),x(:,2),x(:,3));
```

We will often consider the simpler case of an autonomous system without time dependence or parameters:

$$\frac{d}{dt}\mathbf{x}(t) = \mathbf{f}(\mathbf{x}(t)). \tag{7.3}$$

In general, $\mathbf{x}(t) \in \mathbf{M}$ is an n-dimensional state that lives on a smooth manifold $\mathbf{M}$, and $\mathbf{f}$ is an element of the tangent bundle $\mathbf{TM}$ of $\mathbf{M}$ so that $\mathbf{f}(\mathbf{x}(t)) \in \mathbf{T}_{\mathbf{x}(t)}\mathbf{M}$. However, we will typically consider the simpler case where $\mathbf{x}$ is a vector, $\mathbf{M} = \mathbb{R}^n$, and $\mathbf{f}$ is a Lipschitz continuous function, guaranteeing existence and uniqueness of solutions to (7.3). For the more general formulation, see [1].

Discrete-Time Systems
We will also consider the discrete-time dynamical system

$$\mathbf{x}_{k+1} = \mathbf{F}(\mathbf{x}_k). \tag{7.4}$$

Also known as a *map*, the discrete-time dynamics are more general than the continuous-time formulation in (7.3), encompassing discontinuous and hybrid systems as well.

For example, consider the logistic map:

$$x_{k+1} = \beta x_k(1 - x_k). \tag{7.5}$$

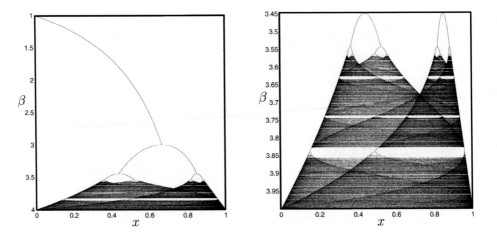

Figure 7.2   Attracting sets of the logistic map for varying parameter β.

As the parameter β is increased, the attracting set becomes increasingly complex, shown in Fig. 7.2. A series of period-doubling bifurcations occur until the attracting set becomes fractal.

Discrete-time dynamics may be induced from continuous-time dynamics, where $\mathbf{x}_k$ is obtained by sampling the trajectory in (7.3) discretely in time, so that $\mathbf{x}_k = \mathbf{x}(k\Delta t)$. The discrete-time propagator $\mathbf{F}_{\Delta t}$ is now parameterized by the time step Δt. For an arbitrary time t, the *flow map* $\mathbf{F}_t$ is defined as

$$\mathbf{F}_t(\mathbf{x}(t_0)) = \mathbf{x}(t_0) + \int_{t_0}^{t_0+t} \mathbf{f}(\mathbf{x}(\tau))\, d\tau. \qquad (7.6)$$

The discrete-time perspective is often more natural when considering experimental data and digital control.

Linear Dynamics and Spectral Decomposition
Whenever possible, it is desirable to work with linear dynamics of the form

$$\frac{d}{dt}\mathbf{x} = \mathbf{A}\mathbf{x}. \qquad (7.7)$$

Linear dynamical systems admit closed-form solutions, and there are a wealth of techniques for the analysis, prediction, numerical simulation, estimation, and control of such systems. The solution of (7.7) is given by

$$\mathbf{x}(t_0 + t) = e^{\mathbf{A}t}\mathbf{x}(t_0). \qquad (7.8)$$

The dynamics are entirely characterized by the eigenvalues and eigenvectors of the matrix $\mathbf{A}$, given by the *spectral decomposition* (eigen-decomposition) of $\mathbf{A}$:

$$\mathbf{A}\mathbf{T} = \mathbf{T}\mathbf{\Lambda}. \qquad (7.9)$$

When $\mathbf{A}$ has n distinct eigenvalues, then $\mathbf{\Lambda}$ is a diagonal matrix containing the eigenvalues λ_j and $\mathbf{T}$ is a matrix whose columns are the linearly independent eigenvectors $\boldsymbol{\xi}_j$ associated with eigenvalues λ_j. In this case, it is possible to write $\mathbf{A} = \mathbf{T}\mathbf{\Lambda}\mathbf{T}^{-1}$, and the solution in (7.8) becomes

$$\mathbf{x}(t_0 + t) = \mathbf{T}e^{\mathbf{\Lambda}t}\mathbf{T}^{-1}\mathbf{x}(t_0). \qquad (7.10)$$

More generally, in the case of repeated eigenvalues, the matrix $\mathbf{\Lambda}$ will consist of Jordan blocks [427]. See Section 8.2 for a detailed derivation of the above arguments for control systems. Note that the continuous-time system gives rise to a discrete-time dynamical system, with $\mathbf{F}_t$ given by the solution map $\exp(\mathbf{A}t)$ in (7.8). In this case, the discrete-time eigenvalues are given by $e^{\lambda t}$.

The matrix $\mathbf{T}^{-1}$ defines a transformation, $\mathbf{z} = \mathbf{T}^{-1}\mathbf{x}$, into intrinsic eigenvector coordinates, $\mathbf{z}$, where the dynamics become decoupled:

$$\frac{d}{dt}\mathbf{z} = \mathbf{\Lambda}\mathbf{z}. \qquad (7.11)$$

In other words, each coordinate, z_j, only depends on itself, with simple dynamics given by

$$\frac{d}{dt}z_j = \lambda_j z_j. \qquad (7.12)$$

Thus, it is highly desirable to work with linear systems, since it is possible to easily transform the system into eigenvector coordinates where the dynamics become decoupled. No such closed-form solution or simple linear change of coordinates exist in general for nonlinear systems, motivating many of the directions described in this chapter.

Goals and Challenges in Modern Dynamical Systems

As we generally use dynamical systems to model real-world phenomena, there are a number of high-priority goals associated with the analysis of dynamical systems:

1. **Future state prediction.** In many cases, such as meteorology and climatology, we seek predictions of the future state of a system. Long-time predictions may still be challenging.
2. **Design and optimization.** We may seek to tune the parameters of a system for improved performance or stability, for example through the placement of fins on a rocket.
3. **Estimation and control.** It is often possible to actively control a dynamical system through feedback, using measurements of the system to inform actuation to modify the behavior. In this case, it is often necessary to estimate the full state of the system from limited measurements.
4. **Interpretability and physical understanding.** Perhaps a more fundamental goal of dynamical systems is to provide physical insight and interpretability into a system's behavior through analyzing trajectories and solutions to the governing equations of motion.

Real-world systems are generally nonlinear and exhibit multi-scale behavior in both space and time. It must also be assumed that there is uncertainty in the equations of motion, in the specification of parameters, and in the measurements of the system. Some systems are more sensitive to this uncertainty than others, and probabilistic approaches must be used. Increasingly, it is also the case that the basic equations of motion are not specified and they might be intractable to derive from first principles.

This chapter will cover recent data-driven techniques to identify and analyze dynamical systems. The majority of this chapter addresses two primary challenges of modern dynamical systems:

1. **Nonlinearity.** Nonlinearity remains a primary challenge in analyzing and controlling dynamical systems, giving rise to complex global dynamics. We saw above that linear systems may be completely characterized in terms of the spectral decomposition (i.e., eigenvalues and eigenvectors) of the matrix $\mathbf{A}$, leading to general procedures for prediction, estimation, and control. No such overarching framework exists for nonlinear systems, and developing this general framework is a mathematical grand challenge of the 21st century.

   The leading perspective on nonlinear dynamical systems considers the geometry of subspaces of local linearizations around fixed points and periodic orbits, global heteroclinic and homoclinic orbits connecting these structures, and more general attractors [252]. This geometric theory, originating with Poincaré, has transformed how we model complex systems, and its success can be largely attributed to theoretical results, such as the Hartman-Grobman theorem, which establish when and where it is possible to approximate a nonlinear system with linear dynamics. Thus, it is often possible to apply the wealth of linear analysis techniques in a small neighborhood of a fixed point or periodic orbit. Although the geometric perspective provides quantitative locally linear models, global analysis has remained largely qualitative and computational, limiting the theory of nonlinear prediction, estimation, and control away from fixed points and periodic orbits.

2. **Unknown dynamics.** Perhaps an even more central challenge arises from the lack of known governing equations for many modern systems of interest. Increasingly, researchers are tackling more complex and realistic systems, such as are found in neuroscience, epidemiology, and ecology. In these fields, there is a basic lack of known *physical laws* that provide first principles from which it is possible to derive equations of motion. Even in systems where we do know the governing equations, such as turbulence, protein folding, and combustion, we struggle to find patterns in these high-dimensional systems to uncover intrinsic coordinates and coarse-grained variables along which the dominant behavior evolves.

   Traditionally, physical systems were analyzed by making ideal approximations and then deriving simple differential equation models via Newton's second law. Dramatic simplifications could often be made by exploiting symmetries and clever coordinate systems, as highlighted by the success of Lagrangian and Hamiltonian dynamics [2, 369]. With increasingly complex systems, the paradigm is shifting from this classical approach to data-driven methods to discover governing equations.

   All models are approximations, and with increasing complexity, these approximations often become suspect. Determining what is the correct model is becoming more subjective, and there is a growing need for automated model discovery techniques that illuminate underlying physical mechanisms. There are also often latent variables that are relevant to the dynamics but may go unmeasured. Uncovering these hidden effects is a major challenge for data-driven methods.

Identifying unknown dynamics from data and learning intrinsic coordinates that enable the linear representation of nonlinear systems are two of the most pressing goals of modern dynamical systems. Overcoming the challenges of unknown dynamics and nonlinearity has the promise of transforming our understanding of complex systems, with tremendous potential benefit to nearly all fields of science and engineering.

Throughout this chapter we will explore these issues in further detail and describe a number of the emerging techniques to address these challenges. In particular, there are two key approaches that are defining modern data-driven dynamical systems:

1. **Operator theoretic representations.** To address the issue of nonlinearity, operator-theoretic approaches to dynamical systems are becoming increasingly used. As we will show, it is possible to represent nonlinear dynamical systems in terms of infinite-dimensional but linear operators, such as the Koopman operator from Section 7.4 that advances measurement functions, and the Perron-Frobenius operator that advances probability densities and ensembles through the dynamics.

2. **Data-driven regression and machine learning.** As data becomes increasingly abundant, and we continue to investigate systems that are not amenable to first-principles analysis, regression and machine learning are becoming vital tools to discover dynamical systems from data. This is the basis of many of the techniques described in this chapter, including the dynamic mode decomposition (DMD) in Section 7.2, the sparse identification of nonlinear dynamics (SINDy) in Section 7.3, the data-driven Koopman methods in Section 7.5, as well as the use of genetic programming to identify dynamics from data [68, 477].

It is important to note that many of the methods and perspectives described in this chapter are interrelated, and continuing to strengthen and uncover these relationships is the subject of ongoing research. It is also worth mentioning that a third major challenge is the high-dimensionality associated with many modern dynamical systems, such as are found in population dynamics, brain simulations, and high-fidelity numerical discretizations of partial differential equations. High-dimensionality is addressed extensively in the subsequent chapters on reduced-order models (ROMs).

7.2   Dynamic Mode Decomposition (DMD)

Dynamic mode decomposition was developed by Schmid [474, 472] in the fluid dynamics community to identify spatio-temporal coherent structures from high-dimensional data. DMD is based on proper orthogonal decomposition (POD), which utilizes the computationally efficient singular value decomposition (SVD), so that it scales well to provide effective dimensionality reduction in high-dimensional systems. In contrast to SVD/POD, which results in a hierarchy of modes based entirely on spatial correlation and energy content, while largely ignoring temporal information, DMD provides a modal decomposition where each mode consists of spatially correlated structures that have the same linear behavior in time (e.g., oscillations at a given frequency with growth or decay). Thus, DMD not only provides dimensionality reduction in terms of a reduced set of modes, but also provides a model for how these modes evolve in time.

Soon after the development of the original DMD algorithm [474, 472], Rowley, Mezic, and collaborators established an important connection between DMD and Koopman theory [456] (see Section 7.4). DMD may be formulated as an algorithm to identify the best-fit linear dynamical system that advances high-dimensional measurements forward in time [535]. In this way, DMD approximates the Koopman operator restricted to the set of direct measurements of the state of a high-dimensional system. This connection between the computationally straightforward and linear DMD framework and nonlinear dynamical systems has generated considerable interest in these methods [317].

Within a short amount of time, DMD has become a workhorse algorithm for the data-driven characterization of high-dimensional systems. DMD is equally valid for experimental and numerical data, as it is not based on knowledge of the governing equations, but is instead based purely on measurement data. The DMD algorithm may also be seen as connecting the favorable aspects of the SVD (see Chapter 1) for spatial dimensionality reduction and the FFT (see Chapter 2) for temporal frequency identification [129, 317]. Thus, each DMD mode is associated with a particular *eigenvalue* $\lambda = a + ib$, with a particular frequency of oscillation b and growth or decay rate a.

There are many variants of DMD and it is connected to existing techniques from system identification and modal extraction. DMD has become especially popular in recent years in large part due to its simple numerical implementation and strong connections to nonlinear dynamical systems via Koopman spectral theory. Finally, DMD is an extremely flexible platform, both mathematically and numerically, facilitating innovations related to compressed sensing, control theory, and multi-resolution techniques. These connections and extensions will be discussed at the end of this section.

The DMD Algorithm

Several algorithms have been proposed for DMD, although here we present the *exact* DMD framework developed by Tu et al. [535]. Whereas earlier formulations required uniform sampling of the dynamics in time, the approach presented here works with irregularly sampled data and with concatenated data from several different experiments or numerical simulations. Moreover, the exact formulation of Tu et al. provides a precise mathematical definition of DMD that allows for rigorous theoretical results. Finally, exact DMD is based on the efficient and numerically well-conditioned singular value decomposition, as is the original formulation by Schmid [472].

DMD is inherently data-driven, and the first step is to collect a number of pairs of snapshots of the state of a system as it evolves in time. These snapshot pairs may be denoted by $\{(\mathbf{x}(t_k), \mathbf{x}(t_k'))\}_{k=1}^{m}$, where $t_k' = t_k + \Delta t$, and the timestep Δt is sufficiently small to resolve the highest frequencies in the dynamics. As before, a snapshot may be the state of a system, such as a three-dimensional fluid velocity field sampled at a number of discretized locations, that is reshaped into a high-dimensional column vector. These snapshots are then arranged into two data matrices, $\mathbf{X}$ and $\mathbf{X}'$:

$$\mathbf{X} = \begin{bmatrix} | & | & & | \\ \mathbf{x}(t_1) & \mathbf{x}(t_2) & \cdots & \mathbf{x}(t_m) \\ | & | & & | \end{bmatrix} \tag{7.13a}$$

$$\mathbf{X}' = \begin{bmatrix} | & | & & | \\ \mathbf{x}(t_1') & \mathbf{x}(t_2') & \cdots & \mathbf{x}(t_m') \\ | & | & & | \end{bmatrix}. \tag{7.13b}$$

The original formulations of Schmid [472] and Rowley et al. [456] assumed uniform sampling in time, so that $t_k = k\Delta t$ and $t'_k = t_k + \Delta t = t_{k+1}$. If we assume uniform sampling in time, we will adopt the notation $\mathbf{x}_k = \mathbf{x}(k\Delta t)$.

The DMD algorithm seeks the leading spectral decomposition (i.e., eigenvalues and eigenvectors) of the best-fit linear operator $\mathbf{A}$ that relates the two snapshot matrices in time:

$$\mathbf{X}' \approx \mathbf{A}\mathbf{X}. \tag{7.14}$$

The best fit operator $\mathbf{A}$ then establishes a linear dynamical system that best advances snapshot measurements forward in time. If we assume uniform sampling in time, this becomes:

$$\mathbf{x}_{k+1} \approx \mathbf{A}\mathbf{x}_k. \tag{7.15}$$

Mathematically, the best-fit operator $\mathbf{A}$ is defined as

$$\mathbf{A} = \underset{\mathbf{A}}{\operatorname{argmin}} \|\mathbf{X}' - \mathbf{A}\mathbf{X}\|_F = \mathbf{X}'\mathbf{X}^\dagger \tag{7.16}$$

where $\|\cdot\|_F$ is the Frobenius norm and † denotes the pseudo-inverse. The optimized DMD algorithm generalizes the optimization framework of exact DMD to perform a regression to exponential time dynamics, thus providing an improved computation of the DMD modes and their eigenvalues [20].

It is worth noting at this point that the matrix $\mathbf{A}$ in (7.15) closely resembles the Koopman operator in (7.53), if we choose direct linear measurements of the state, so that $\mathbf{g}(\mathbf{x}) = \mathbf{x}$. This connection was originally established by Rowley, Mezic and collaborators [456], and has sparked considerable interest in both DMD and Koopman theory. These connections will be explored in more depth below.

For a high-dimensional state vector $\mathbf{x} \in \mathbb{R}^n$, the matrix $\mathbf{A}$ has n^2 elements, and representing this operator, let alone computing its spectral decomposition, may be intractable. Instead, the DMD algorithm leverages dimensionality reduction to compute the dominant eigenvalues and eigenvectors of $\mathbf{A}$ without requiring any explicit computations using $\mathbf{A}$ directly. In particular, the pseudo-inverse $\mathbf{X}^\dagger$ in (7.16) is computed via the singular value decomposition of the matrix $\mathbf{X}$. Since this matrix typically has far fewer columns than rows, i.e. $m \ll n$, there are at most m nonzero singular values and corresponding singular vectors, and hence the matrix $\mathbf{A}$ will have at most rank m. Instead of computing $\mathbf{A}$ directly, we compute the projection of $\mathbf{A}$ onto these leading singular vectors, resulting in a small matrix $\tilde{\mathbf{A}}$ of size at most $m \times m$. A major contribution of Schmid [472] was a procedure to approximate the high-dimensional DMD modes (eigenvectors of $\mathbf{A}$) from the reduced matrix $\tilde{\mathbf{A}}$ and the data matrix $\mathbf{X}$ without ever resorting to computations on the full $\mathbf{A}$. Tu et al. [535] later proved that these approximate modes are in fact exact eigenvectors of the full $\mathbf{A}$ matrix under certain conditions. Thus, the exact DMD algorithm of Tu et al. [535] is given by the following steps:

Step 1. Compute the singular value decomposition of $\mathbf{X}$ (see Chapter 1):

$$\mathbf{X} \approx \tilde{\mathbf{U}}\tilde{\mathbf{\Sigma}}\tilde{\mathbf{V}}^*, \tag{7.17}$$

where $\tilde{\mathbf{U}} \in \mathbb{C}^{n \times r}$, $\tilde{\mathbf{\Sigma}} \in \mathbb{C}^{r \times r}$, and $\tilde{\mathbf{V}} \in \mathbb{C}^{m \times r}$ and $r \leq m$ denotes either the exact or approximate rank of the data matrix $\mathbf{X}$. In practice, choosing the approximate rank r is one of the most important and subjective steps in DMD, and in dimensionality reduction in general. We advocate the principled hard-thresholding algorithm of Gavish and Donoho [200] to determine r from noisy data (see Section 1.7). The columns of the matrix $\tilde{\mathbf{U}}$ are also known as POD modes, and they satisfy $\tilde{\mathbf{U}}^* \tilde{\mathbf{U}} = \mathbf{I}$. Similarly, columns of $\tilde{\mathbf{V}}$ are orthonormal and satisfy $\tilde{\mathbf{V}}^* \tilde{\mathbf{V}} = \mathbf{I}$.

Step 2.   According to (7.16), the full matrix $\mathbf{A}$ may be obtained by computing the pseudo-inverse of $\mathbf{X}$:

$$\mathbf{A} = \mathbf{X}' \tilde{\mathbf{V}} \tilde{\mathbf{\Sigma}}^{-1} \tilde{\mathbf{U}}^*. \tag{7.18}$$

However, we are only interested in the leading r eigenvalues and eigenvectors of $\mathbf{A}$, and we may thus project $\mathbf{A}$ onto the POD modes in $\mathbf{U}$:

$$\tilde{\mathbf{A}} = \tilde{\mathbf{U}}^* \mathbf{A} \tilde{\mathbf{U}} = \tilde{\mathbf{U}}^* \mathbf{X}' \tilde{\mathbf{V}} \tilde{\mathbf{\Sigma}}^{-1}. \tag{7.19}$$

The key observation here is that the reduced matrix $\tilde{\mathbf{A}}$ has the same nonzero eigenvalues as the full matrix $\mathbf{A}$. Thus, we need only compute the reduced $\tilde{\mathbf{A}}$ directly, without ever working with the high-dimensional $\mathbf{A}$ matrix. The reduced-order matrix $\tilde{\mathbf{A}}$ defines a linear model for the dynamics of the vector of POD coefficients $\tilde{\mathbf{x}}$:

$$\tilde{\mathbf{x}}_{k+1} = \tilde{\mathbf{A}} \tilde{\mathbf{x}}_k. \tag{7.20}$$

Note that the matrix $\tilde{\mathbf{U}}$ provides a map to reconstruct the full state $\mathbf{x}$ from the reduced state $\tilde{\mathbf{x}}$: $\mathbf{x} = \tilde{\mathbf{U}} \tilde{\mathbf{x}}$.

Step 3.   The spectral decomposition of $\tilde{\mathbf{A}}$ is computed:

$$\tilde{\mathbf{A}} \mathbf{W} = \mathbf{W} \mathbf{\Lambda}. \tag{7.21}$$

The entries of the diagonal matrix $\mathbf{\Lambda}$ are the DMD eigenvalues, which also correspond to eigenvalues of the full $\mathbf{A}$ matrix. The columns of $\mathbf{W}$ are eigenvectors of $\tilde{\mathbf{A}}$, and provide a coordinate transformation that diagonalizes the matrix. These columns may be thought of as linear combinations of POD mode amplitudes that behave linearly with a single temporal pattern given by λ.

Step 4.   The high-dimensional DMD modes $\mathbf{\Phi}$ are reconstructed using the eigenvectors $\mathbf{W}$ of the reduced system and the time-shifted snapshot matrix $\mathbf{X}'$ according to:

$$\mathbf{\Phi} = \mathbf{X}' \tilde{\mathbf{V}} \tilde{\mathbf{\Sigma}}^{-1} \mathbf{W}. \tag{7.22}$$

Remarkably, these DMD modes are eigenvectors of the high-dimensional $\mathbf{A}$ matrix corresponding to the eigenvalues in $\mathbf{\Lambda}$, as shown in Tu et al. [535]:

$$\mathbf{A}\mathbf{\Phi} = (\mathbf{X}' \tilde{\mathbf{V}} \tilde{\mathbf{\Sigma}}^{-1} \underbrace{\tilde{\mathbf{U}}^*)(\mathbf{X}' \tilde{\mathbf{V}} \tilde{\mathbf{\Sigma}}^{-1}}_{\tilde{\mathbf{A}}} \mathbf{W})$$

$$= \mathbf{X}' \tilde{\mathbf{V}} \tilde{\mathbf{\Sigma}}^{-1} \tilde{\mathbf{A}} \mathbf{W}$$

$$= \mathbf{X}' \tilde{\mathbf{V}} \tilde{\mathbf{\Sigma}}^{-1} \mathbf{W} \mathbf{\Lambda}$$

$$= \mathbf{\Phi} \mathbf{\Lambda}.$$

In the original paper by Schmid [472], DMD modes are computed using $\boldsymbol{\Phi} = \tilde{\mathbf{U}}\mathbf{W}$, which are known as *projected modes*; however, these modes are not guaranteed to be exact eigenvectors of $\mathbf{A}$. Because $\mathbf{A}$ is defined as $\mathbf{A} = \mathbf{X}'\mathbf{X}^{\dagger}$, eigenvectors of $\mathbf{A}$ should be in the column space of $\mathbf{X}'$, as in the exact DMD definition, instead of the column space of $\mathbf{X}$ in the original DMD algorithm. In practice, the column spaces of $\mathbf{X}$ and $\mathbf{X}'$ will tend to be nearly identical for dynamical systems with low-rank structure, so that the projected and exact DMD modes often converge.

To find a DMD mode corresponding to a zero eigenvalue, $\lambda = 0$, it is possible to use the exact formulation if $\boldsymbol{\phi} = \mathbf{X}'\tilde{\mathbf{V}}\tilde{\boldsymbol{\Sigma}}^{-1}\mathbf{w} \neq 0$. However, if this expression is null, then the projected mode $\boldsymbol{\phi} = \tilde{\mathbf{U}}\mathbf{w}$ should be used.

Historical Perspective

In the original formulation, the snapshot matrices $\mathbf{X}$ and $\mathbf{X}'$ were formed with a collection of sequential snapshots, evenly spaced in time:

$$\mathbf{X} = \begin{bmatrix} | & | & & | \\ \mathbf{x}_1 & \mathbf{x}_2 & \cdots & \mathbf{x}_m \\ | & | & & | \end{bmatrix} \tag{7.23a}$$

$$\mathbf{X}' = \begin{bmatrix} | & | & & | \\ \mathbf{x}_2 & \mathbf{x}_3 & \cdots & \mathbf{x}_{m+1} \\ | & | & & | \end{bmatrix}. \tag{7.23b}$$

Thus, the matrix $\mathbf{X}$ can be written in terms of iterations of the matrix $\mathbf{A}$ as:

$$\mathbf{X} \approx \begin{bmatrix} | & | & & | \\ \mathbf{x}_1 & \mathbf{A}\mathbf{x}_1 & \cdots & \mathbf{A}^{m-1}\mathbf{x}_1 \\ | & | & & | \end{bmatrix}. \tag{7.24}$$

Thus, the columns of the matrix $\mathbf{X}$ belong to a Krylov subspace generated by the propagator $\mathbf{A}$ and the initial condition $\mathbf{x}_1$. In addition, the matrix $\mathbf{X}'$ may be related to $\mathbf{X}$ through the *shift* operator as:

$$\mathbf{X}' = \mathbf{X}\mathbf{S}, \tag{7.25}$$

where $\mathbf{S}$ is defined as

$$\mathbf{S} = \begin{bmatrix} 0 & 0 & 0 & \cdots & 0 & a_1 \\ 1 & 0 & 0 & \cdots & 0 & a_2 \\ 0 & 1 & 0 & \cdots & 0 & a_3 \\ \vdots & \vdots & \vdots & \ddots & \vdots & \vdots \\ 0 & 0 & 0 & \cdots & 1 & a_m \end{bmatrix}. \tag{7.26}$$

Thus, the first $m - 1$ columns of $\mathbf{X}'$ are obtained directly by shifting the corresponding columns of $\mathbf{X}$, and the last column is obtained as a best-fit combination of the m columns of $\mathbf{X}$ that minimizes the residual. In this way, the DMD algorithm resembles an Arnoldi algorithm used to find the dominant eigenvalues and eigenvectors of a matrix $\mathbf{A}$ through iteration. The matrix $\mathbf{S}$ will share eigenvalues with the high-dimensional $\mathbf{A}$ matrix, so that decomposition of $\mathbf{S}$ may be used to obtain dynamic modes and eigenvalues. However, computations based on $\mathbf{S}$ is not as numerically stable as the exact algorithm above.

Spectral Decomposition and DMD Expansion

One of the most important aspects of the DMD is the ability to expand the system state in terms of a data-driven spectral decomposition:

$$\mathbf{x}_k = \sum_{j=1}^{r} \boldsymbol{\phi}_j \lambda_j^{k-1} b_j = \boldsymbol{\Phi} \boldsymbol{\Lambda}^{k-1} \mathbf{b}, \tag{7.27}$$

where $\boldsymbol{\phi}_j$ are DMD modes (eigenvectors of the $\mathbf{A}$ matrix), λ_j are DMD eigenvalues (eigenvalues of the $\mathbf{A}$ matrix), and b_j is the mode amplitude. The vector $\mathbf{b}$ of mode amplitudes is generally computed as

$$\mathbf{b} = \boldsymbol{\Phi}^\dagger \mathbf{x}_1. \tag{7.28}$$

More principled approaches to select dominant and sparse modes have been considered [129, 270]. However, computing the mode amplitudes is generally quite expensive, even using the straightforward definition in (7.28). Instead, it is possible to compute these amplitudes using POD projected data:

$$\mathbf{x}_1 = \boldsymbol{\Phi} \mathbf{b} \tag{7.29a}$$

$$\implies \quad \tilde{\mathbf{U}} \tilde{\mathbf{x}}_1 = \mathbf{X}' \tilde{\mathbf{V}} \tilde{\boldsymbol{\Sigma}}^{-1} \mathbf{W} \mathbf{b} \tag{7.29b}$$

$$\implies \quad \tilde{\mathbf{x}}_1 = \tilde{\mathbf{U}}^* \mathbf{X}' \tilde{\mathbf{V}} \tilde{\boldsymbol{\Sigma}}^{-1} \mathbf{W} \mathbf{b} \tag{7.29c}$$

$$\implies \quad \tilde{\mathbf{x}}_1 = \tilde{\mathbf{A}} \mathbf{W} \mathbf{b} \tag{7.29d}$$

$$\implies \quad \tilde{\mathbf{x}}_1 = \mathbf{W} \boldsymbol{\Lambda} \mathbf{b} \tag{7.29e}$$

$$\implies \quad \mathbf{b} = (\mathbf{W} \boldsymbol{\Lambda})^{-1} \tilde{\mathbf{x}}_1. \tag{7.29f}$$

The matrices $\mathbf{W}$ and $\boldsymbol{\Lambda}$ are both size $r \times r$, as opposed to the large $\boldsymbol{\Phi}$ matrix that is $n \times r$.

The spectral expansion above may also be written in continuous time by introducing the continuous eigenvalues $\omega = \log(\lambda)/\Delta t$:

$$\mathbf{x}(t) = \sum_{j=1}^{r} \boldsymbol{\phi}_j e^{\omega_j t} b_j = \boldsymbol{\Phi} \exp(\boldsymbol{\Omega} t) \mathbf{b}, \tag{7.30}$$

where $\boldsymbol{\Omega}$ is a diagonal matrix containing the continuous-time eigenvalues ω_j.

Example and Code

A basic DMD code is provided here:

```
function [Phi, Lambda, b] = DMD(X,Xprime,r)

[U,Sigma,V] = svd(X,'econ');        % Step 1
Ur = U(:,1:r);
Sigmar = Sigma(1:r,1:r);
Vr = V(:,1:r);

Atilde = Ur'*Xprime*Vr/Sigmar;      % Step 2
[W,Lambda] = eig(Atilde);           % Step 3

Phi = Xprime*(Vr/Sigmar)*W;         % Step 4
alpha1 = Sigmar*Vr(1,:)';
b = (W*Lambda)\alpha1;
```

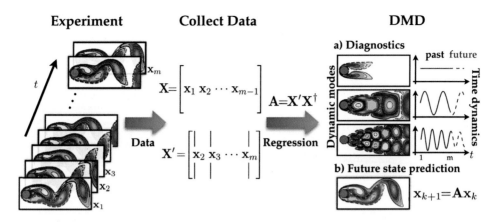

Figure 7.3 Overview of DMD illustrated on the fluid flow past a circular cylinder at Reynolds number 100. *Reproduced from [317].*

This DMD code is demonstrated in Fig. 7.3 for the fluid flow past a circular cylinder at Reynolds number 100, based on the cylinder diameter. The two-dimensional Navier-Stokes equations are simulated using the immersed boundary projection method (IBPM) solver[1] based on the fast multi-domain method of Taira and Colonius [511, 135]. The data required for this example may be downloaded without running the IBPM code at *dmdbook.com*.

With this data, it is simple to compute the dynamic mode decomposition:

```
% VORTALL contains flow fields reshaped into column vectors
X = VORTALL;
[Phi, Lambda, b] = DMD(X(:,1:end-1),X(:,2:end),21);
```

Extensions, Applications, and Limitations

One of the major advantages of dynamic mode decomposition is its simple framing in terms of linear regression. DMD does not require knowledge of governing equations. For this reason, DMD has been rapidly extended to include several methodological innovations and has been widely applied beyond fluid dynamics [317], where it originated. Here, we present a number of the leading algorithmic extensions and promising domain applications, and we also present current limitations of the DMD theory that must be addressed in future research.

Methodological Extensions

- **Compression and randomized linear algebra.** DMD was originally designed for high-dimensional data sets in fluid dynamics, such as a fluid velocity or vorticity field, which may contain millions of degrees of freedom. However, the fact that DMD often uncovers low-dimensional structure in these high dimensional data implies that there may be more efficient measurement and computational strategies based on principles of *sparsity* (see Chapter 3). There have been several independent and highly successful extensions and modifications of DMD to exploit low-rank structure and sparsity.

---

[1] The IBPM code is publicly available at: *https://github.com/cwrowley/ibpm*.

In 2014, Jovanovic et al. [270] used sparsity promoting optimization to identify the fewest DMD modes required to describe a data set, essentially identifying a few dominant DMD mode amplitudes in **b**. The alternative approach, of testing and comparing all subsets of DMD modes, represents a computationally intractable brute force search.

Another line of work is based on the fact that DMD modes generally admit a sparse representation in Fourier or wavelet bases. Moreover, the time dynamics of each mode are simple pure tone harmonics, which are the definition of sparse in a Fourier basis. This sparsity has facilitated several efficient measurement strategies that reduce the number of measurements required in time [536] and space [96, 225, 174], based on compressed sensing. This has the broad potential to enable high-resolution characterization of systems from under-resolved measurements.

Related to the use of compressed sensing, randomized linear algebra has recently been used to accelerate DMD computations when full-state data is available. Instead of collecting subsampled measurements and using compressed sensing to infer high-dimensional structures, randomized methods start with full data and then randomly project into a lower-dimensional subspace, where computations may be performed more efficiently. Bistrian and Navon [66] have successfully accelerated DMD using a randomized singular value decomposition, and Erichson et al. [175] demonstrates how all of the expensive DMD computations may be performed in a projected subspace.

Finally, libraries of DMD modes have also been used to identify dynamical regimes [308], based on the sparse representation for classification [560] (see Section 3.6), which was used earlier to identify dynamical regimes using libraries of POD modes [80, 98].

- **Inputs and control.** A major strength of DMD is the ability to describe complex and high-dimensional dynamical systems in terms of a small number of dominant modes, which represent spatio-temporal coherent structures. Reducing the dimensionality of the system from n (often millions or billions) to r (tens or hundreds) enables faster and lower-latency prediction and estimation. Lower-latency predictions generally translate directly into controllers with higher performance and robustness. Thus, compact and efficient representations of complex systems such as fluid flows have been long-sought, resulting in the field of reduced order modeling. However, the original DMD algorithm was designed to characterize naturally evolving systems, without accounting for the effect of actuation and control.

  Shortly after the original DMD algorithm, Proctor et al. [434] extended the algorithm to disambiguate between the natural unforced dynamics and the effect of actuation. This essentially amounts to a generalized evolution equation

$$\mathbf{x}_{k+1} \approx \mathbf{A}\mathbf{x}_k + \mathbf{B}\mathbf{u}_k, \tag{7.31}$$

which results in another linear regression problem (see Section 10.1).

The original motivation for DMD with control (DMDc) was the use of DMD to characterize epidemiological systems (e.g., malaria spreading across a continent), where it is not possible to stop intervention efforts, such as vaccinations and bed nets, in order to characterize the unforced dynamics [433].

Since the original DMDc algorithm, the compressed sensing DMD and DMDc algorithms have been combined, resulting in a new framework for compressive system identification [30]. In this framework, it is possible to collect undersampled measurements of an actuated system and identify an accurate and efficient low-order model, related to DMD and the eigensystem realization algorithm (ERA; see Section 9.3) [272].

DMDc models, based on linear and nonlinear measurements of the system, have recently been used with model predictive control (MPC) for enhanced control of nonlinear systems by Korda and Mezić [302]. Model predictive control using DMDc models were subsequently used as a benchmark comparison for MPC based on fully nonlinear models in the work of Kaiser et al. [277], and the DMDc models performed surprisingly well, even for strongly nonlinear systems.

- **Nonlinear measurements.** Much of the excitement around DMD is due to the strong connection to nonlinear dynamics via the Koopman operator [456]. Indeed, DMD is able to accurately characterize periodic and quasi-periodic behavior, even in nonlinear systems, as long as a sufficient amount of data is collected. However, the basic DMD algorithm uses linear measurements of the system, which are generally not rich enough to characterize truly nonlinear phenomena, such as transients, intermittent phenomena, or broadband frequency cross-talk. In Williams et al. [556], DMD measurements were augmented to include nonlinear measurements of the system, enriching the basis used to represent the Koopman operator. The so-called *extended DMD* (eDMD) algorithm then seeks to obtain a linear model $\mathbf{A_Y}$ advancing nonlinear measurements $\mathbf{y} = \mathbf{g}(\mathbf{x})$:

$$\mathbf{y}_{k+1} \approx \mathbf{A_Y}\mathbf{y}_k. \tag{7.32}$$

For high-dimensional systems, this augmented state $\mathbf{y}$ may be intractably large, motivating the use of kernel methods to approximate the evolution operator $\mathbf{A_Y}$ [557]. This kernel DMD has since been extended to include dictionary learning techniques [332].

It has recently been shown that eDMD is equivalent to the variational approach of conformation dynamics (VAC) [405, 407, 408], first derived by Noé and Nüske in 2013 to simulate molecular dynamics with a broad separation of timescales. Further connections between eDMD and VAC and between DMD and the time lagged independent component analysis (TICA) are explored in a recent review [293]. A key contribution of VAC is a variational score enabling the objective assessment of Koopman models via cross-validation.

Following the extended DMD, it was shown that there are relatively restrictive conditions for obtaining a linear regression model that includes the original state of the system [92]. For nonlinear systems with multiple fixed points, periodic orbits, and other attracting structures, there is no finite-dimensional linear system including the state $\mathbf{x}$ that is topologically conjugate to the nonlinear system. Instead, it is important to identify Koopman invariant subspaces, spanned by eigenfunctions of the Koopman operator; in general, it will not be possible to directly write the state $\mathbf{x}$ in the span of these eigenvectors, although it may be possible to identify $\mathbf{x}$ through a unique inverse. A practical algorithm for identifying eigenfunctions is provided by Kaiser et al. [276].

- **De-noising.** The DMD algorithm is purely data-driven, and is thus equally applicable to experimental and numerical data. When characterizing experimental data with DMD, the effects of sensor noise and stochastic disturbances must be accounted for. The original DMD algorithm is particularly sensitive to noise, and it was shown that significant and systematic biases are introduced to the eigenvalue distribution [164, 28, 147, 241]. Although increased sampling decreases the variance of the eigenvalue distribution, it does not remove the bias [241].

  There are several approaches to correct for the effect of sensor noise and disturbances. Hemati et al. [241] use the total least-squares regression to account for the possibility of noisy measurements and disturbances to the state, replacing the original least-squares regression. Dawson et al. [147] compute DMD on the data in forward and backward time and then average the resulting operator, removing the systematic bias. This work also provides an excellent discussion on the sources of noise and a comparison of various denoising algorithms.

  More recently, Askham and Kutz [20] introduced the optimized DMD algorithm, which uses a variable projection method for nonlinear least squares to compute the DMD for unevenly timed samples, significantly mitigating the bias due to noise. The subspace DMD algorithm of Takeishi et al. [514] also compensates for measurement noise by computing an orthogonal projection of future snapshots onto the space of previous snapshots and then constructing a linear model. Extensions that combine DMD with Bayesian approaches have also been developed [512].

- **Multiresolution.** DMD is often applied to complex, high-dimensional dynamical systems, such as fluid turbulence or epidemiological systems, that exhibit multiscale dynamics in both space and time. Many multiscale systems exhibit transient or intermittent phenomena, such as the El Niño observed in global climate data. These transient dynamics are not captured accurately by DMD, which seeks spatio-temporal modes that are globally coherent across the entire time series of data. To address this challenge, the multiresolution DMD (mrDMD) algorithm was introduced [318], which effectively decomposes the dynamics into different timescales, isolating transient and intermittent patterns. Multiresolution DMD modes were recently shown to be advantageous for sparse sensor placement by Manohar et al. [367].

- **Delay measurements.** Although DMD was developed for high-dimensional data where it is assumed that one has access to the full-state of a system, it is often desirable to characterize spatio-temporal coherent structures for systems with incomplete measurements. As an extreme example, consider a single measurement that oscillates as a sinusoid, $x(t) = \sin(\omega t)$. Although this would appear to be a perfect candidate for DMD, the algorithm incorrectly identifies a real eigenvalue because the data does not have sufficient rank to extract a complex conjugate pair of eigenvalues $\pm i\omega$. This paradox was first explored by Tu et al. [535], where it was discovered that a solution is to stack delayed measurements into a larger matrix to augment the rank of the data matrix and extract phase information. Delay coordinates have been used effectively to extract coherent patterns in neural recordings [90]. The connections between delay DMD and Koopman [91, 18, 144] will be discussed more in Section 7.5.

- **Streaming and parallelized codes.** Because of the computational burden of computing the DMD on high-resolution data, several advances have been made to accelerate DMD in streaming applications and with parallelized algorithms. DMD is often used in a streaming setting, where a moving window of snapshots are processed continuously, resulting in redundant computations when new data becomes available. Several algorithms exist for streaming DMD, based on the incremental SVD [242], a streaming method of snapshots SVD [424], and rank-one updates to the DMD matrix [569]. The DMD algorithm is also readily parallelized, as it is based on the SVD. Several parallelized codes are available, based on the QR [466] and SVD [175, 177, 176].

Applications

- **Fluid dynamics.** DMD originated in the fluid dynamics community [472], and has since been applied to a wide range of flow geometries (jets, cavity flow, wakes, channel flow, boundary layers, etc.), to study mixing, acoustics, and combustion, among other phenomena. In the original paper of Schmid [474, 472], both a cavity flow and a jet were considered. In the original paper of Rowley *et al.* [456], a jet in cross-flow was investigated. It is no surprise that DMD has subsequently been used widely in both cavity flows [472, 350, 481, 43, 42] and jets [473, 49, 483, 475].

  DMD has also been applied to wake flows, including to investigate frequency lock-on [534], the wake past a gurney flap [415], the cylinder wake [28], and dynamic stall [166]. Boundary layers have also been extensively studied with DMD [411, 465, 383]. In acoustics, DMD has been used to capture the near-field and far-field acoustics that result from instabilities observed in shear flows [495]. In combustion, DMD has been used to understand the coherent heat release in turbulent swirl flames [387] and to analyze a rocket combustor [258]. DMD has also been used to analyze non-normal growth mechanisms in thermoacoustic interactions in a Rijke tube. DMD has been compared with POD for reacting flows [459]. DMD has also been used to analyze more exotic flows, including a simulated model of a high-speed train [392]. Shock turbulent boundary layer interaction (STBLI) has also been investigated, and DMD was used to identify a pulsating separation bubble that is accompanied by shockwave motion [222]. DMD has also been used to study self-excited fluctuations in detonation waves [373]. Other problems include identifying hairpin vortices [516], decomposing the flow past a surface mounted cube [393], modeling shallow water equations [65], studying nano fluids past a square cylinder [463], and measuring the growth rate of instabilities in annular liquid sheets [163].

- **Epidemiology.** DMD has recently been applied to investigate epidemiological systems by Proctor and Eckhoff [435]. This is a particularly interpretable application, as modal frequencies often correspond to yearly or seasonal fluctuations. Moreover, the phase of DMD modes gives insight into how disease fronts propagate spatially, potentially informing future intervention efforts. The application of DMD to disease systems also motivated the DMD with control [434], since it is infeasible to stop vaccinations in order to identify the unforced dynamics.

- **Neuroscience.** Complex signals from neural recordings are increasingly high-fidelity and high dimensional, with advances in hardware pushing the frontiers of data collection. DMD has the potential to transform the analysis of such neural recordings, as evidenced in a recent study that identified dynamically relevant features in ECOG data of sleeping patients [90]. Since then, several works have applied DMD to neural recordings or suggested possible implementation in hardware [3, 85, 520].

- **Video processing.** Separating foreground and background objects in video is a common task in surveillance applications. Real-time separation is a challenge that is only exacerbated by ever increasing video resolutions. DMD provides a flexible platform for video separation, as the background may be approximated by a DMD mode with zero eigenvalue [223, 174, 424].

- **Other applications.** DMD has been applied to an increasingly diverse array of problems, including robotics [56], finance [363], and plasma physics [517]. It is expected that this trend will increase.

Challenges

- **Traveling waves.** DMD is based on the SVD of a data matrix $\mathbf{X} = \mathbf{U}\boldsymbol{\Sigma}\mathbf{V}^*$ whose columns are spatial measurements evolving in time. In this case, the SVD is a space-time separation of variables into spatial modes, given by the columns of $\mathbf{U}$, and time dynamics, given by the columns of $\mathbf{V}$. As in POD, DMD thus has limitations for problems that exhibit traveling waves, where separation of variables is known to fail.

- **Transients.** Many systems of interest are characterized by transients and intermittent phenomena. Several methods have been proposed to identify these events, such as the multi-resolution DMD and the use of delay coordinates. However, it is still necessary to formalize the choice of relevant timescales and the window size to compute DMD.

- **Continuous spectrum.** Related to the above, many systems are characterized by broadband frequency content, as opposed to a few distinct and discrete frequencies. This broadband frequency content is also known as a *continuous spectrum*, where every frequency in a continuous range is observed. For example, the simple pendulum exhibits a continuous spectrum, as the system has a natural frequency for small deflections, and this frequency continuously deforms and slows as energy is added to the pendulum. Other systems include nonlinear optics and broadband turbulence. These systems pose a serious challenge for DMD, as they result in a large number of modes, even though the dynamics are likely generated by the nonlinear interactions of a few dominant modes.

  Several data-driven approaches have been recently proposed to handle systems with continuous spectra. Applying DMD to a vector of delayed measurements of a system, the so-called *HAVOK* analysis in Section 7.5, has been shown to approximate the dynamics of chaotic systems, such as the Lorenz system, which exhibits a continuous spectrum. In addition, Lusch et al. [349] showed that it is possible to design a deep learning architecture with an auxiliary network to parameterize the continuous frequency.

- **Strong nonlinearity and choice of measurements.** Although significant progress has been made connecting DMD to nonlinear systems [557], choosing nonlinear measurements to augment the DMD regression is still not an exact science. Identifying measurement subspaces that remain closed under the Koopman operator is an ongoing challenge [92]. Recent progress in deep learning has the potential to enable the representation of extremely complex eigenfunctions from data [550, 368, 513, 564, 412, 349].

7.3   Sparse Identification of Nonlinear Dynamics (SINDy)

Discovering dynamical systems models from data is a central challenge in mathematical physics, with a rich history going back at least as far as the time of Kepler and Newton and the discovery of the laws of planetary motion. Historically, this process relied on a combination of high-quality measurements and expert intuition. With vast quantities of data and increasing computational power, the *automated* discovery of governing equations and dynamical systems is a new and exciting scientific paradigm.

Typically, the form of a candidate model is either constrained via prior knowledge of the governing equations, as in Galerkin projection [402, 455, 471, 404, 119, 549, 32, 118] (see Chapter 12), or a handful of heuristic models are tested and parameters are optimized to fit data. Alternatively, best-fit linear models may be obtained using DMD or ERA. Simultaneously identifying the nonlinear structure and parameters of a model from data is considerably more challenging, as there are combinatorially many possible model structures.

The sparse identification of nonlinear dynamics (SINDy) algorithm [95] bypasses the intractable combinatorial search through all possible model structures, leveraging the fact that many dynamical systems

$$\frac{d}{dt}\mathbf{x} = \mathbf{f}(\mathbf{x}) \tag{7.33}$$

have dynamics $\mathbf{f}$ with only a few active terms in the space of possible right-hand side functions; for example, the Lorenz equations in (7.2) only have a few linear and quadratic interaction terms per equation.

We then seek to approximate $\mathbf{f}$ by a generalized linear model

$$\mathbf{f}(\mathbf{x}) \approx \sum_{k=1}^{p} \theta_k(\mathbf{x})\xi_k = \mathbf{\Theta}(\mathbf{x})\boldsymbol{\xi}, \tag{7.34}$$

with the fewest nonzero terms in $\boldsymbol{\xi}$ as possible. It is then possible to solve for the relevant terms that are active in the dynamics using sparse regression [518, 573, 236, 264] that penalizes the number of terms in the dynamics and scales well to large problems.

First, time-series data is collected from (7.33) and formed into a data matrix:

$$\mathbf{X} = \begin{bmatrix} \mathbf{x}(t_1) & \mathbf{x}(t_2) & \cdots \mathbf{x}(t_m) \end{bmatrix}^T. \tag{7.35}$$

A similar matrix of derivatives is formed:

$$\dot{\mathbf{X}} = \begin{bmatrix} \dot{\mathbf{x}}(t_1) & \dot{\mathbf{x}}(t_2) & \cdots \dot{\mathbf{x}}(t_m) \end{bmatrix}^T. \tag{7.36}$$

In practice, this may be computed directly from the data in $\mathbf{X}$; for noisy data, the total-variation regularized derivative tends to provide numerically robust derivatives [125]. Alternatively, it is possible to formulate the SINDy algorithm for discrete-time systems $\mathbf{x}_{k+1} = \mathbf{F}(\mathbf{x}_k)$, as in the DMD algorithm, and avoid derivatives entirely.

A library of candidate nonlinear functions $\mathbf{\Theta}(\mathbf{X})$ may be constructed from the data in $\mathbf{X}$:

$$\mathbf{\Theta}(\mathbf{X}) = \begin{bmatrix} \mathbf{1} & \mathbf{X} & \mathbf{X}^2 & \cdots & \mathbf{X}^d & \cdots & \sin(\mathbf{X}) & \cdots \end{bmatrix}. \tag{7.37}$$

Here, the matrix $\mathbf{X}^d$ denotes a matrix with column vectors given by all possible time-series of d-th degree polynomials in the state $\mathbf{x}$. In general, this library of candidate functions is only limited by one's imagination.

The dynamical system in (7.33) may now be represented in terms of the data matrices in (7.36) and (7.37) as

$$\dot{\mathbf{X}} = \mathbf{\Theta}(\mathbf{X})\,\mathbf{\Xi}. \tag{7.38}$$

Each column $\boldsymbol{\xi}_k$ in $\mathbf{\Xi}$ is a vector of coefficients determining the active terms in the k-th row in (7.33). A parsimonious model will provide an accurate model fit in (7.38) with as few terms as possible in $\mathbf{\Xi}$. Such a model may be identified using a convex ℓ_1-regularized sparse regression:

$$\boldsymbol{\xi}_k = \mathrm{argmin}_{\boldsymbol{\xi}'_k}\, \|\dot{\mathbf{X}}_k - \mathbf{\Theta}(\mathbf{X})\boldsymbol{\xi}'_k\|_2 + \lambda\|\boldsymbol{\xi}'_k\|_1. \tag{7.39}$$

Here, $\dot{\mathbf{X}}_k$ is the k-th column of $\dot{\mathbf{X}}$, and λ is a sparsity-promoting knob. Sparse regression, such as the LASSO [518] or the sequential thresholded least-squares (STLS) algorithm used in SINDy [95], improves the numerical robustness of this identification for noisy overdetermined problems, in contrast to earlier methods [548] that used compressed sensing [150, 109, 112, 111, 113, 39, 529]. We advocate the STLS (Code 7.1) to select active terms.

Code 7.1 Sequentially thresholded least-squares.

```
function Xi = sparsifyDynamics(Theta,dXdt,lambda,n)
% Compute Sparse regression: sequential least squares
Xi = Theta\dXdt;   % Initial guess: Least-squares

% Lambda is our sparsification knob.
for k=1:10
    smallinds = (abs(Xi)<lambda);    % Find small coefficients
    Xi(smallinds)=0;                 % and threshold
    for ind = 1:n                    % n is state dimension
        biginds = ~smallinds(:,ind);
% Regress dynamics onto remaining terms to find sparse Xi
        Xi(biginds,ind) = Theta(:,biginds)\dXdt(:,ind);
    end
end
```

The sparse vectors $\boldsymbol{\xi}_k$ may be synthesized into a dynamical system:

$$\dot{x}_k = \mathbf{\Theta}(\mathbf{x})\boldsymbol{\xi}_k. \tag{7.40}$$

Note that x_k is the k-th element of $\mathbf{x}$ and $\mathbf{\Theta}(\mathbf{x})$ is a row vector of symbolic functions of $\mathbf{x}$, as opposed to the data matrix $\mathbf{\Theta}(\mathbf{X})$. Fig. 7.4 shows how SINDy may be used to discover the Lorenz equations from data. Code 7.2 generates data and performs the SINDy regression for the Lorenz system.

Code 7.2 SINDy regression to identify the Lorenz system from data.

```
%% Generate Data
Beta = [10; 28; 8/3]; % Lorenz's parameters (chaotic)
n = 3;
x0=[-8; 8; 27];  % Initial condition
tspan=[.01:.01:50];
options = odeset('RelTol',1e-12,'AbsTol',1e-12*ones(1,n));
[t,x]=ode45(@(t,x) lorenz(t,x,Beta),tspan,x0,options);

%% Compute Derivative
for i=1:length(x)
```

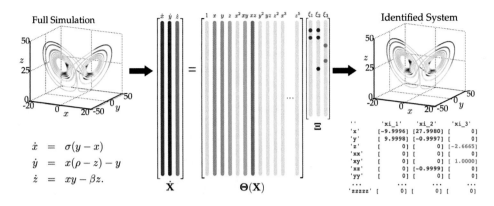

$$\dot{x} = \sigma(y - x)$$
$$\dot{y} = x(\rho - z) - y$$
$$\dot{z} = xy - \beta z.$$

Figure 7.4 Schematic of the sparse identification of nonlinear dynamics (SINDy) algorithm [95]. Parsimonious models are selected from a library of candidate nonlinear terms using sparse regression. This library $\Theta(\mathbf{X})$ may be constructed purely from measurement data. *Modified from Brunton et al. [95].*

```
      dx(i,:) = lorenz(0,x(i,:),Beta);
end

%% Build library and compute sparse regression
Theta = poolData(x,n,3);   % up to third order polynomials
lambda = 0.025;            % lambda is our sparsification knob.
Xi = sparsifyDynamics(Theta,dx,lambda,n)
```

This code also relies on a function **poolData** that generates the library Θ. In this case, polynomials up to third order are used. This code is available online.

The output of the SINDy algorithm is a sparse matrix of coefficients Ξ:

' '	'xdot'	'ydot'	'zdot'
'1'	[0]	[0]	[0]
'x'	[-10.0000]	[28.0000]	[0]
'y'	[10.0000]	[-1.0000]	[0]
'z'	[0]	[0]	[-2.6667]
'xx'	[0]	[0]	[0]
'xy'	[0]	[0]	[1.0000]
'xz'	[0]	[-1.0000]	[0]
'yy'	[0]	[0]	[0]
'yz'	[0]	[0]	[0]
'zz'	[0]	[0]	[0]
'xxx'	[0]	[0]	[0]
'xxy'	[0]	[0]	[0]
'xxz'	[0]	[0]	[0]
'xyy'	[0]	[0]	[0]
'xyz'	[0]	[0]	[0]
'xzz'	[0]	[0]	[0]
'yyy'	[0]	[0]	[0]
'yyz'	[0]	[0]	[0]
'yzz'	[0]	[0]	[0]
'zzz'	[0]	[0]	[0]

The result of the SINDy regression is a parsimonious model that includes only the most important terms required to explain the observed behavior. The sparse regression procedure used to identify the most parsimonious nonlinear model is a convex procedure.

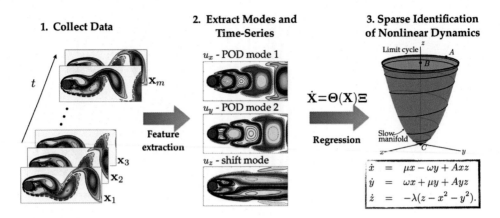

Figure 7.5 Schematic overview of nonlinear model identification from high-dimensional data using the sparse identification of nonlinear dynamics (SINDy) [95]. This procedure is modular, so that different techniques can be used for the feature extraction and regression steps. In this example of flow past a cylinder, SINDy discovers the model of Noack et al. [402]. *Modified from Brunton et al. [95].*

The alternative approach, which involves regression onto every possible sparse nonlinear structure, constitutes an intractable brute-force search through the combinatorially many candidate model forms. SINDy bypasses this combinatorial search with modern convex optimization and machine learning. It is interesting to note that for discrete-time dynamics, if $\Theta(\mathbf{X})$ consists only of linear terms, and if we remove the sparsity promoting term by setting $\lambda = 0$, then this algorithm reduces to the dynamic mode decomposition [472, 456, 535, 317]. If a least-squares regression is used, as in DMD, then even a small amount of measurement error or numerical round-off will lead to every term in the library being active in the dynamics, which is non-physical. A major benefit of the SINDy architecture is the ability to identify parsimonious models that contain only the required nonlinear terms, resulting in interpretable models that avoid overfitting.

Applications, Extensions, and Historical Context

The SINDy algorithm has recently been applied to identify high-dimensional dynamical systems, such as fluid flows, based on POD coefficients [95, 341, 342]. Fig. 7.5 illustrates the application of SINDy to the flow past a cylinder, where the generalized mean-field model of Noack et al. [402] was discovered from data. SINDy has also been applied to identify models in nonlinear optics [497] and plasma physics [141].

Because SINDy is formulated in terms of linear regression in a nonlinear library, it is highly extensible. The SINDy framework has been recently generalized by Loiseau and Brunton [341] to incorporate known physical constraints and symmetries in the equations by implementing a constrained sequentially thresholded least-squares optimization. In particular, energy preserving constraints on the quadratic nonlinearities in the Navier-Stokes equations were imposed to identify fluid systems [341], where it is known that these constraints promote stability [355, 32, 118]. This work also showed that polynomial libraries are particularly useful for building models of fluid flows in terms of POD coefficients, yielding interpretable models that are related to classical Galerkin projection [95, 341].

Loiseau et al. [342] also demonstrated the ability of SINDy to identify dynamical systems models of high-dimensional systems, such as fluid flows, from a few physical sensor measurements, such as lift and drag measurements on the cylinder in Fig. 7.5. For actuated systems, SINDy has been generalized to include inputs and control [100], and these models are highly effective for model predictive control [277]. It is also possible to extend the SINDy algorithm to identify dynamics with rational function nonlinearities [361], integral terms [469], and based on highly corrupt and incomplete data [522]. SINDy was also recently extended to incorporate information criteria for objective model selection [362], and to identify models with hidden variables using delay coordinates [91]. Finally, the SINDy framework was generalized to include partial derivatives, enabling the identification of partial differential equation models [460, 468]. Several of these recent innovations will be explored in more detail below.

More generally, the use of sparsity-promoting methods in dynamics is quite recent [548, 467, 414, 353, 98, 433, 31, 29, 89, 364, 366]. Other techniques for dynamical system discovery include methods to discover equations from time-series [140], equation-free modeling [288], empirical dynamic modeling [503, 563], modeling emergent behavior [452], the nonlinear autoregressive model with exogenous inputs (NARMAX) [208, 571, 59, 484], and automated inference of dynamics [478, 142, 143]. Broadly speaking, these techniques may be classified as system identification, where methods from statistics and machine learning are used to identify dynamical systems from data. Nearly all methods of system identification involve some form of regression of data onto dynamics, and the main distinction between the various techniques is the degree to which this regression is constrained. For example, the dynamic mode decomposition generates best-fit linear models. Recent nonlinear regression techniques have produced nonlinear dynamic models that preserve physical constraints, such as conservation of energy. A major breakthrough in automated nonlinear system identification was made by Bongard and Lipson [68] and Schmidt and Lipson [477], where they used genetic programming to identify the structure of nonlinear dynamics. These methods are highly flexible and impose very few constraints on the form of the dynamics identified. In addition, SINDy is closely related to NARMAX [59], which identifies the structure of models from time-series data through an orthogonal least squares procedure.

Discovering Partial Differential Equations

A major extension of the SINDy modeling framework generalized the library to include partial derivatives, enabling the identification of partial differential equations [460, 468]. The resulting algorithm, called the partial differential equation functional identification of nonlinear dynamics (PDE-FIND), has been demonstrated to successfully identify several canonical PDEs from classical physics, purely from noisy data. These PDEs include Navier-Stokes, Kuramoto-Sivashinsky, Schrödinger, reaction diffusion, Burgers, Korteweg–de Vries, and the diffusion equation for Brownian motion [460].

PDE-FIND is similar to SINDy, in that it is based on sparse regression in a library constructed from measurement data. The sparse regression and discovery method is shown in Fig. 7.6. PDE-FIND is outlined below for PDEs in a single variable, although the theory is readily generalized to higher dimensional PDEs. The spatial time-series data is arranged into a single column vector $\Upsilon \in \mathbb{C}^{mn}$, representing data collected over m time points

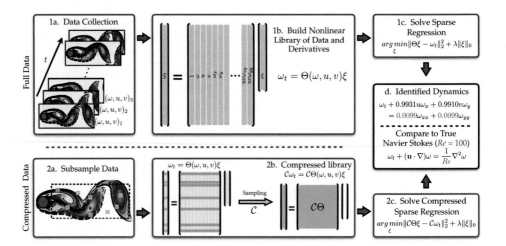

Figure 7.6 Steps in the PDE functional identification of nonlinear dynamics (PDE-FIND) algorithm, applied to infer the Navier-Stokes equations from data (*reproduced from Rudy et al. [460]*). **1a.** Data is collected as snapshots of a solution to a PDE. **1b.** Numerical derivatives are taken and data is compiled into a large matrix Θ, incorporating candidate terms for the PDE. **1c.** Sparse regressions is used to identify active terms in the PDE. **2a.** For large datasets, sparse sampling may be used to reduce the size of the problem. **2b.** Subsampling the dataset is equivalent to taking a subset of rows from the linear system in (7.42). **2c.** An identical sparse regression problem is formed but with fewer rows. **d.** Active terms in $\boldsymbol{\xi}$ are synthesized into a PDE.

and n spatial locations. Additional inputs, such as a known potential for the Schrödinger equation, or the magnitude of complex data, is arranged into a column vector $\mathbf{Q} \in \mathbb{C}^{mn}$. Next, a library $\boldsymbol{\Theta}(\boldsymbol{\Upsilon}, \mathbf{Q}) \in \mathbb{C}^{mn \times D}$ of D candidate linear and nonlinear terms and partial derivatives for the PDE is constructed. Derivatives are taken either using finite differences for clean data, or when noise is added, with polynomial interpolation. The candidate linear and nonlinear terms and partial derivatives are then combined into a matrix $\boldsymbol{\Theta}(\boldsymbol{\Upsilon}, \mathbf{Q})$ which takes the form:

$$\boldsymbol{\Theta}(\boldsymbol{\Upsilon}, \mathbf{Q}) = \begin{bmatrix} \mathbf{1} & \boldsymbol{\Upsilon} & \boldsymbol{\Upsilon}^2 & \dots & \mathbf{Q} & \dots & \boldsymbol{\Upsilon}_x & \boldsymbol{\Upsilon}\boldsymbol{\Upsilon}_x & \dots \end{bmatrix}. \qquad (7.41)$$

Each column of $\boldsymbol{\Theta}$ contains all of the values of a particular candidate function across all of the mn space-time grid points on which data is collected. The time derivative $\boldsymbol{\Upsilon}_t$ is also computed and reshaped into a column vector. Fig. 7.6 demonstrates the data collection and processing. As an example, a column of $\boldsymbol{\Theta}(\boldsymbol{\Upsilon}, \mathbf{Q})$ may be qu_x^2.

The PDE evolution can be expressed in this library as follows:

$$\boldsymbol{\Upsilon}_t = \boldsymbol{\Theta}(\boldsymbol{\Upsilon}, \mathbf{Q})\boldsymbol{\xi}. \qquad (7.42)$$

Each entry in $\boldsymbol{\xi}$ is a coefficient corresponding to a term in the PDE, and for canonical PDEs, the vector $\boldsymbol{\xi}$ is *sparse*, meaning that only a few terms are active.

If the library $\boldsymbol{\Theta}$ has a sufficiently rich column space that the dynamics are in it's span, then the PDE should be well-represented by (7.42) with a sparse vector of coefficients $\boldsymbol{\xi}$. To identify the few active terms in the dynamics, a sparsity-promoting regression is employed, as in SINDy. Importantly, the regression problem in (7.42) may be poorly conditioned.

Algorithm 1 STRidge(Θ, Υ_t, λ, *tol*, iters)

$\hat{\xi} = arg\,min_\xi \|\Theta\xi - \Upsilon_t\|_2^2 + \lambda\|\xi\|_2^2$ % ridge regression

bigcoeffs = $\{j : |\hat{\xi}_j| \geq tol\}$ % select large coefficients

$\hat{\xi}[\sim \text{bigcoeffs}] = 0$ % apply hard threshold

$\hat{\xi}[\text{bigcoeffs}] = \text{STRidge}(\Theta[:, \text{bigcoeffs}], \Upsilon_t, tol, \text{iters} - 1)$

                 % recursive call with fewer coefficients

return $\hat{\xi}$

Error in computing the derivatives will be magnified by numerical errors when inverting Θ. Thus a least squares regression radically changes the qualitative nature of the inferred dynamics.

In general, we seek the sparsest vector ξ that satisfies (7.42) with a small residual. Instead of an intractable combinatorial search through all possible sparse vector structures, a common technique is to relax the problem to a convex ℓ_1 regularized least squares [518]; however, this tends to perform poorly with highly correlated data. Instead, we use ridge regression with hard thresholding, which we call sequential threshold ridge regression (STRidge in Algorithm 1, reproduced from Rudy et al. [460]). For a given tolerance and threshold λ, this gives a sparse approximation to ξ. We iteratively refine the tolerance of Algorithm 1 to find the best predictor based on the selection criteria,

$$\hat{\xi} = \text{argmin}_\xi \|\Theta(\Upsilon, Q)\xi - \Upsilon_t\|_2^2 + \epsilon\kappa(\Theta(\Upsilon, Q))\|\xi\|_0 \tag{7.43}$$

where $\kappa(\Theta)$ is the condition number of the matrix Θ, providing stronger regularization for ill-posed problems. Penalizing $\|\xi\|_0$ discourages over fitting by selecting from the optimal position in a Pareto front.

As in the SINDy algorithm, it is important to provide sufficiently rich training data to disambiguate between several different models. For example, Fig. 7.7 illustrates the use of PDE-FIND algorithm identifying the Korteweg–de Vries (KdV) equation. If only a single traveling wave is analyzed, the method incorrectly identifies the standard linear advection equation, as this is the simplest equation that describes a single traveling wave. However, if two traveling waves of different amplitudes are analyzed, the KdV equation is correctly identified, as it describes the different amplitude-dependent wave speeds.

The PDE-FIND algorithm can also be used to identify PDEs based on Lagrangian measurements that follow the path of individual particles. For example, Fig. 7.8 illustrates the identification of the diffusion equation describing Brownian motion of a particle based on a single long time-series measurement of the particle position. In this example, the time series is broken up into several short sequences, and the evolution of the distribution of these positions is used to identify the diffusion equation.

Extension of SINDy for Rational Function Nonlinearities

Many dynamical systems, such as metabolic and regulatory networks in biology, contain rational function nonlinearities in the dynamics. Often, these rational function nonlinearities arise because of a separation of time scales. Although the original SINDy algorithm is highly flexible in terms of the choice of the library of nonlinearities, it is not straightforward to identify rational functions, since general rational functions are not sparse linear combi-

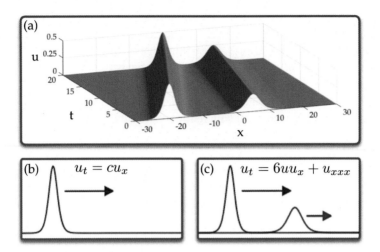

Figure 7.7 Inferring nonlinearity via observing solutions at multiple amplitudes (*reproduced from Rudy et al. [460]*). (**a**) An example 2-soliton solution to the KdV equation. (**b**) Applying our method to a single soliton solution determines that it solves the standard advection equation. (**c**) Looking at two completely separate solutions reveals nonlinearity.

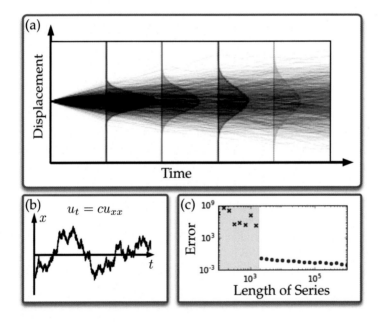

Figure 7.8 Inferring the diffusion equation from a single Brownian motion (*reproduced from Rudy et al. [460]*). (**a**) Time series is broken into many short random walks that are used to construct histograms of the displacement. (**b**) The Brownian motion trajectory, following the diffusion equation. (**c**) Parameter error ($\|\boldsymbol{\xi}^* - \hat{\boldsymbol{\xi}}\|_1$) vs. length of known time series. Blue symbols correspond to correct identification of the structure of the diffusion model, $u_t = cu_{xx}$.

nations of a few basis functions. Instead, it is necessary to reformulate the dynamics in an *implicit* ordinary differential equation and modify the optimization procedure accordingly, as in Mangan et al. [361].

We consider dynamical systems with rational nonlinearities:

$$\dot{x}_k = \frac{f_N(\mathbf{x})}{f_D(\mathbf{x})} \qquad (7.44)$$

where x_k is the k-th variable, and $f_N(\mathbf{x})$ and $f_D(\mathbf{x})$ represent numerator and denominator polynomials in the state variable $\mathbf{x}$. For each index k, it is possible to multiply both sides by the denominator f_D, resulting in the equation:

$$f_N(\mathbf{x}) - f_D(\mathbf{x})\dot{x}_k = 0. \qquad (7.45)$$

The implicit form of (7.45) motivates a generalization of the function library Θ in (7.37) in terms of the state $\mathbf{x}$ and the derivative $\dot{x}_k$:

$$\Theta(\mathbf{X}, \dot{x}_k(\mathbf{t})) = \begin{bmatrix} \Theta_N(\mathbf{X}) & \text{diag}(\dot{x}_k(\mathbf{t}))\,\Theta_D(\mathbf{X}) \end{bmatrix}. \qquad (7.46)$$

The first term, $\Theta_N(\mathbf{X})$, is the library of numerator monomials in $\mathbf{x}$, as in (7.37). The second term, $\text{diag}(\dot{x}_k(\mathbf{t}))\,\Theta_D(\mathbf{X})$, is obtained by multiplying each column of the library of denominator polynomials $\Theta_D(\mathbf{X})$ with the vector $\dot{x}_k(\mathbf{t})$ in an element-wise fashion. For a single variable x_k, this would give the following:

$$\text{diag}(\dot{x}_k(\mathbf{t}))\Theta(\mathbf{X}) = \begin{bmatrix} \dot{x}_k(\mathbf{t}) & (\dot{x}_k x_k)(\mathbf{t}) & (\dot{x}_k x_k^2)(\mathbf{t}) & \dots \end{bmatrix}. \qquad (7.47)$$

In most cases, we will use the same polynomial degree for both the numerator and denominator library, so that $\Theta_N(\mathbf{X}) = \Theta_D(\mathbf{X})$. Thus, the augmented library in (7.46) is only twice the size of the original library in (7.37).

We may now write the dynamics in (7.45) in terms of the augmented library in (7.46):

$$\Theta(\mathbf{X}, \dot{x}_k(\mathbf{t}))\boldsymbol{\xi}_k = \mathbf{0}. \qquad (7.48)$$

The sparse vector of coefficients $\boldsymbol{\xi}_k$ will have nonzero entries for the active terms in the dynamics. However, it is not possible to use the same sparse regression procedure as in SINDy, since the sparsest vector $\boldsymbol{\xi}_k$ that satisfies (7.48) is the trivial zero vector.

Instead, the sparsest nonzero vector $\boldsymbol{\xi}_k$ that satisfies (7.48) is identified as the sparsest vector in the null space of Θ. This is generally a nonconvex problem, although there are recent algorithms developed by Qu et al. [440], based on the alternating directions method (ADM), to identify the sparsest vector in a subspace. Unlike the original SINDy algorithm, this procedure is quite sensitive to noise, as the null-space is numerically approximated as the span of the singular vectors corresponding to small singular value. When noise is added to the data matrix $\mathbf{X}$, and hence to Θ, the noise floor of the singular value decomposition goes up, increasing the rank of the numerical null space.

General Formulation for Implicit ODEs

The optimization procedure above may be generalized to include a larger class of implicit ordinary differential equations, in addition to those containing rational function nonlinearities. The library $\Theta(\mathbf{X}, \dot{x}_k(\mathbf{t}))$ contains a subset of the columns of the library $\Theta([\mathbf{X} \quad \dot{\mathbf{X}}])$, which is obtained by building nonlinear functions of the state $\mathbf{x}$ and derivative $\dot{\mathbf{x}}$. Identifying the sparsest vector in the null space of $\Theta([\mathbf{X} \quad \dot{\mathbf{X}}])$ provides more flexibility in identifying

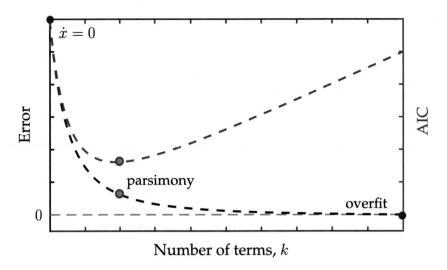

Figure 7.9 Illustration of model selection using SINDy and information criteria, as in Mangan et al. [362]. The most parsimonious model on the Pareto front is chosen to minimize the AIC score (blue circle), preventing overfitting.

nonlinear equations with mixed terms containing various powers of any combination of derivatives and states. For example, the system given by

$$\dot{x}^2 x^2 - \dot{x} x - x^2 = 0 \tag{7.49}$$

may be represented as a sparse vector in the null space of $\Theta([\mathbf{X} \quad \dot{\mathbf{X}}])$. This formulation may be extended to include higher order derivatives in the library Θ library, for example to identify second-order implicit differential equations:

$$\Theta\left([\mathbf{X} \quad \dot{\mathbf{X}} \quad \ddot{\mathbf{X}}]\right). \tag{7.50}$$

The generality of this approach enables the identification of many systems of interest, including those systems with rational function nonlinearities.

Information Criteria for Model Selection

When performing the sparse regression in the SINDy algorithm, the sparsity-promoting parameter λ is a free variable. In practice, different values of λ will result in different models with various levels of sparsity, ranging from the trivial model $\dot{x} = 0$ for very large λ to the simple least-squares solution for $\lambda = 0$. Thus, by varying λ, it is possible to sweep out a Pareto front, balancing error versus complexity, as in Fig. 7.9. To identify the most parsimonious model, with low error and a reasonable complexity, it is possible to leverage information criteria for model selection, as described in Mangan et al. [362]. In particular, if we compute the Akaike information criterion (AIC) [6, 7], which penalizes the number of terms in the model, then the most parsimonious model minimizes the AIC. This procedure has been applied to several sparse identification problems, and in every case, the true model was correctly identified [362].

7.4   Koopman Operator Theory

Koopman operator theory has recently emerged as an alternative perspective for dynamical systems in terms of the evolution of measurements $g(\mathbf{x})$. In 1931, Bernard O. Koopman demonstrated that it is possible to represent a nonlinear dynamical system in terms of an infinite-dimensional linear operator acting on a Hilbert space of measurement functions of the state of the system. This so-called *Koopman operator* is linear, and its spectral decomposition completely characterizes the behavior of a nonlinear system, analogous to (7.7). However, it is also infinite-dimensional, as there are infinitely many degrees of freedom required to describe the space of all possible measurement functions g of the state. This poses new challenges. Obtaining finite-dimensional, matrix approximations of the Koopman operator is the focus of intense research efforts and holds the promise of enabling globally linear representations of nonlinear dynamical systems. Expressing nonlinear dynamics in a linear framework is appealing because of the wealth of optimal estimation and control techniques available for linear systems (see Chapter 8) and the ability to analytically predict the future state of the system. Obtaining a finite-dimensional approximation of the Koopman operator has been challenging in practice, as it involves identifying a subspace spanned by a subset of eigenfunctions of the Koopman operator.

Mathematical Formulation of Koopman Theory

The Koopman operator advances measurement functions of the state with the flow of the dynamics. We consider real-valued measurement functions $g : \mathbf{M} \to \mathbb{R}$, which are elements of an infinite-dimensional Hilbert space. The functions g are also commonly known as *observables*, although this may be confused with the unrelated *observability* from control theory. Typically, the Hilbert space is given by the Lebesgue square-integrable functions on $\mathbf{M}$; other choices of a measure space are also valid.

The Koopman operator $\mathcal{K}_t$ is an infinite-dimensional linear operator that acts on measurement functions g as:

$$\mathcal{K}_t g = g \circ \mathbf{F}_t \tag{7.51}$$

where $\circ$ is the composition operator. For a discrete-time system with timestep Δt, this becomes:

$$\mathcal{K}_{\Delta t} g(\mathbf{x}_k) = g(\mathbf{F}_{\Delta t}(\mathbf{x}_k)) = g(\mathbf{x}_{k+1}). \tag{7.52}$$

In other words, the Koopman operator defines an infinite-dimensional linear dynamical system that advances the observation of the state $g_k = g(\mathbf{x}_k)$ to the next time step:

$$g(\mathbf{x}_{k+1}) = \mathcal{K}_{\Delta t} g(\mathbf{x}_k). \tag{7.53}$$

Note that this is true for *any* observable function g and for any state $\mathbf{x}_k$.

The Koopman operator is linear, a property which is inherited from the linearity of the addition operation in function spaces:

$$\mathcal{K}_t \left(\alpha_1 g_1(\mathbf{x}) + \alpha_2 g_2(\mathbf{x}) \right) = \alpha_1 g_1 \left(\mathbf{F}_t(\mathbf{x}) \right) + \alpha_2 g_2 \left(\mathbf{F}_t(\mathbf{x}) \right) \tag{7.54a}$$

$$= \alpha_1 \mathcal{K}_t g_1(\mathbf{x}) + \alpha_2 \mathcal{K}_t g_2(\mathbf{x}). \tag{7.54b}$$

For sufficiently smooth dynamical systems, it is also possible to define the continuous-time analogue of the Koopman dynamical system in (7.53):

$$\frac{d}{dt}g = \mathcal{K}g. \tag{7.55}$$

The operator $\mathcal{K}$ is the infinitesimal generator of the one-parameter family of transformations $\mathcal{K}_t$ [1]. It is defined by its action on an observable function g:

$$\mathcal{K}g = \lim_{t \to 0} \frac{\mathcal{K}_{tg} - g}{t} = \lim_{t \to 0} \frac{g \circ \mathbf{F}_t - g}{t}. \tag{7.56}$$

The linear dynamical systems in (7.55) and (7.53) are analogous to the dynamical systems in (7.3) and (7.4), respectively. It is important to note that the original state $\mathbf{x}$ may be the observable, and the infinite-dimensional operator $\mathcal{K}_t$ will advance this function. However, the simple representation of the observable $g = \mathbf{x}$ in a chosen basis for Hilbert space may become arbitrarily complex once iterated through the dynamics. In other words, finding a representation for $\mathcal{K}\mathbf{x}$ may not be simple or straightforward.

Koopman Eigenfunctions and Intrinsic Coordinates

The Koopman operator is linear, which is appealing, but is infinite dimensional, posing issues for representation and computation. Instead of capturing the evolution of all measurement functions in a Hilbert space, applied Koopman analysis attempts to identify key measurement functions that evolve linearly with the flow of the dynamics. Eigenfunctions of the Koopman operator provide just such a set of special measurements that behave linearly in time. In fact, a primary motivation to adopt the Koopman framework is the ability to simplify the dynamics through the eigen-decomposition of the operator.

A discrete-time Koopman eigenfunction $\varphi(\mathbf{x})$ corresponding to eigenvalue λ satisfies

$$\varphi(\mathbf{x}_{k+1}) = \mathcal{K}_{\Delta t}\varphi(\mathbf{x}_k) = \lambda\varphi(\mathbf{x}_k). \tag{7.57}$$

In continuous-time, a Koopman eigenfunction $\varphi(\mathbf{x})$ satisfies

$$\frac{d}{dt}\varphi(\mathbf{x}) = \mathcal{K}\varphi(\mathbf{x}) = \lambda\varphi(\mathbf{x}). \tag{7.58}$$

Obtaining Koopman eigenfunctions from data or from analytic expressions is a central applied challenge in modern dynamical systems. Discovering these eigenfunctions enables globally linear representations of strongly nonlinear systems.

Applying the chain rule to the time derivative of the Koopman eigenfunction $\varphi(\mathbf{x})$ yields

$$\frac{d}{dt}\varphi(\mathbf{x}) = \nabla\varphi(\mathbf{x}) \cdot \dot{\mathbf{x}} = \nabla\varphi(\mathbf{x}) \cdot \mathbf{f}(\mathbf{x}). \tag{7.59}$$

Combined with (7.58), this results in a partial differential equation (PDE) for the eigenfunction $\varphi(\mathbf{x})$:

$$\nabla\varphi(\mathbf{x}) \cdot \mathbf{f}(\mathbf{x}) = \lambda\varphi(\mathbf{x}). \tag{7.60}$$

With this nonlinear PDE, it is possible to approximate the eigenfunctions, either by solving for the Laurent series or with data via regression, both of which are explored below. This formulation assumes that the dynamics are both continuous and differentiable. The discrete-time dynamics in (7.4) are more general, although in many examples the continuous-time dynamics have a simpler representation than the discrete-time map for long times. For example, the simple Lorenz system has a simple continuous-time representation, yet is generally unrepresentable for even moderately long discrete-time updates.

The key takeaway from (7.57) and (7.58) is that the nonlinear dynamics become completely linear in eigenfunction coordinates, given by $\varphi(\mathbf{x})$. As a simple example, any conserved quantity of a dynamical system is a Koopman eigenfunction corresponding to eigenvalue $\lambda = 0$. This establishes a Koopman extension of the famous Noether's theorem [406], implying that any symmetry in the governing equations gives rise to a new Koopman eigenfunction with eigenvalue $\lambda = 0$. For example, the Hamiltonian energy function is a Koopman eigenfunction for a conservative system. In addition, the constant function $\varphi = 1$ is always a trivial eigenfunction corresponding to $\lambda = 0$ for every dynamical system.

Eigenvalue lattices Interestingly, a set of Koopman eigenfunctions may be used to generate more eigenfunctions. In discrete time, we find that the product of two eigenfunctions $\varphi_1(\mathbf{x})$ and $\varphi_2(\mathbf{x})$ is also an eigenfunction

$$\mathcal{K}_t \left(\varphi_1(\mathbf{x}) \varphi_2(\mathbf{x}) \right) = \varphi_1(\mathbf{F}_t(\mathbf{x})) \varphi_2(\mathbf{F}_t(\mathbf{x})) \tag{7.61a}$$

$$= \lambda_1 \lambda_2 \varphi_1(\mathbf{x}) \varphi_2(\mathbf{x}) \tag{7.61b}$$

corresponding to a new eigenvalue $\lambda_1 \lambda_2$ given by the product of the two eigenvalues of $\varphi_1(\mathbf{x})$ and $\varphi_2(\mathbf{x})$.

In continuous time, the relationship becomes:

$$\mathcal{K} (\varphi_1 \varphi_2) = \frac{d}{dt} (\varphi_1 \varphi_2) \tag{7.62a}$$

$$= \dot{\varphi}_1 \varphi_2 + \varphi_1 \dot{\varphi}_2 \tag{7.62b}$$

$$= \lambda_1 \varphi_1 \varphi_2 + \lambda_2 \varphi_1 \varphi_2 \tag{7.62c}$$

$$= (\lambda_1 + \lambda_2) \varphi_1 \varphi_2. \tag{7.62d}$$

Interestingly, this means that the set of Koopman eigenfunctions establishes a commutative monoid under point-wise multiplication; a monoid has the structure of a group, except that the elements need not have inverses. Thus, depending on the dynamical system, there may be a finite set of *generator* eigenfunction elements that may be used to construct all other eigenfunctions. The corresponding eigenvalues similarly form a lattice, based on the product $\lambda_1 \lambda_2$ or sum $\lambda_1 + \lambda_2$, depending on whether the dynamics are in discrete time or continuous time. For example, given a linear system $\dot{x} = \lambda x$, then $\varphi(x) = x$ is an eigenfunction with eigenvalue λ. Moreover, $\varphi^\alpha = x^\alpha$ is also an eigenfunction with eigenvalue $\alpha \lambda$ for any α.

The continuous time and discrete time lattices are related in a simple way. If the continuous-time eigenvalues are given by λ, then the corresponding discrete-time eigenvalues are given by $e^{\lambda t}$. Thus, the eigenvalue expressions in (7.61b) and (7.62d) are related as:

$$e^{\lambda_1 t} e^{\lambda_2 t} \varphi_1(\mathbf{x}) \varphi_2(\mathbf{x}) = e^{(\lambda_1 + \lambda_2)t} \varphi_1(\mathbf{x}) \varphi_2(\mathbf{x}). \tag{7.63}$$

As another simple demonstration of the relationship between continuous-time and discrete-time eigenvalues, consider the continuous-time definition in (7.56) applied to an eigenfunction:

$$\lim_{t \to 0} \frac{\mathcal{K}_t \varphi(\mathbf{x}) - \varphi(\mathbf{x})}{t} = \lim_{t \to 0} \frac{e^{\lambda t} \varphi(\mathbf{x}) - \varphi(\mathbf{x})}{t} = \lambda \varphi(\mathbf{x}). \tag{7.64}$$

Koopman Mode Decomposition and Finite Representations

Until now, we have considered scalar measurements of a system, and we uncovered special *eigen*-measurements that evolve linearly in time. However, we often take multiple measurements of a system. In extreme cases, we may measure the entire state of a high-dimensional spatial system, such as an evolving fluid flow. These measurements may then be arranged in a vector $\mathbf{g}$:

$$\mathbf{g}(\mathbf{x}) = \begin{bmatrix} g_1(\mathbf{x}) \\ g_2(\mathbf{x}) \\ \vdots \\ g_p(\mathbf{x}) \end{bmatrix}. \tag{7.65}$$

Each of the individual measurements may be expanded in terms of the eigenfunctions $\varphi_j(\mathbf{x})$, which provide a basis for Hilbert space:

$$g_i(\mathbf{x}) = \sum_{j=1}^{\infty} v_{ij}\varphi_j(\mathbf{x}). \tag{7.66}$$

Thus, the vector of observables, $\mathbf{g}$, may be similarly expanded:

$$\mathbf{g}(\mathbf{x}) = \begin{bmatrix} g_1(\mathbf{x}) \\ g_2(\mathbf{x}) \\ \vdots \\ g_p(\mathbf{x}) \end{bmatrix} = \sum_{j=1}^{\infty} \varphi_j(\mathbf{x})\mathbf{v}_j, \tag{7.67}$$

where $\mathbf{v}_j$ is the j-th *Koopman mode* associated with the eigenfunction φ_j.

For conservative dynamical systems, such as those governed by Hamiltonian dynamics, the Koopman operator is unitary. Thus, the Koopman eigenfunctions are orthonormal for conservative systems, and it is possible to compute the Koopman modes $\mathbf{v}_j$ directly by projection:

$$\mathbf{v}_j = \begin{bmatrix} \langle \varphi_j, g_1 \rangle \\ \langle \varphi_j, g_2 \rangle \\ \vdots \\ \langle \varphi_j, g_p \rangle \end{bmatrix}, \tag{7.68}$$

where $\langle \cdot, \cdot \rangle$ is the standard inner product of functions in Hilbert space. These modes have a physical interpretation in the case of direct spatial measurements of a system, $\mathbf{g}(\mathbf{x}) = \mathbf{x}$, in which case the modes are coherent *spatial* modes that behave linearly with the same temporal dynamics (i.e., oscillations, possibly with linear growth or decay).

Given the decomposition in (7.67), it is possible to represent the dynamics of the measurements $\mathbf{g}$ as follows:

$$\mathbf{g}(\mathbf{x}_k) = \mathcal{K}_{\Delta t}^k \mathbf{g}(\mathbf{x}_0) = \mathcal{K}_{\Delta t}^k \sum_{j=0}^{\infty} \varphi_j(\mathbf{x}_0)\mathbf{v}_j \tag{7.69a}$$

$$= \sum_{j=0}^{\infty} \mathcal{K}_{\Delta t}^k \varphi_j(\mathbf{x}_0)\mathbf{v}_j \tag{7.69b}$$

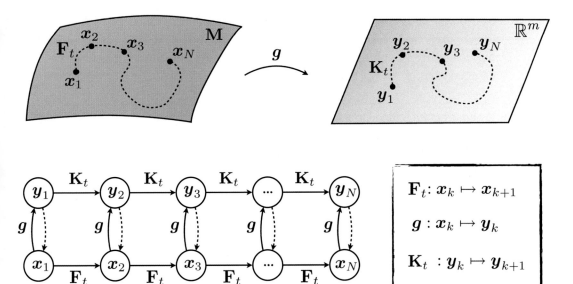

Figure 7.10 Schematic illustrating the Koopman operator for nonlinear dynamical systems. The dashed lines from $\mathbf{y}_k \to \mathbf{x}_k$ indicate that we would like to be able to recover the original state.

$$= \sum_{j=0}^{\infty} \lambda_j^k \varphi_j(\mathbf{x}_0) \mathbf{v}_j. \tag{7.69c}$$

This sequence of triples, $\{(\lambda_j, \varphi_j, \mathbf{v}_j)\}_{j=0}^{\infty}$ is known as the *Koopman mode decomposition*, and was introduced by Mezic in 2005 [376]. The Koopman mode decomposition was later connected to data-driven regression via the dynamic mode decomposition [456], which will be discussed in Section 7.2.

Invariant Eigenspaces and Finite-Dimensional Models

Instead of capturing the evolution of all measurement functions in a Hilbert space, applied Koopman analysis approximates the evolution on an invariant subspace spanned by a finite set of measurement functions.

A *Koopman-invariant subspace* is defined as the span of a set of functions $\{g_1, g_2, \cdots, g_p\}$ if all functions g in this subspace

$$g = \alpha_1 g_1 + \alpha_2 g_2 + \cdots + \alpha_p g_p \tag{7.70}$$

remain in this subspace after being acted on by the Koopman operator $\mathcal{K}$:

$$\mathcal{K}g = \beta_1 g_1 + \beta_2 g_2 + \cdots + \beta_p g_p. \tag{7.71}$$

It is possible to obtain a finite-dimensional matrix representation of the Koopman operator by restricting it to an invariant subspace spanned by a finite number of functions $\{g_j\}_{j=0}^{p}$. The matrix representation $\mathbf{K}$ acts on a vector space $\mathbb{R}^p$, with the coordinates given by the values of $g_j(\mathbf{x})$. This induces a finite-dimensional linear system, as in (7.53) and (7.55).

Any finite set of eigenfunctions of the Koopman operator will span an invariant subspace. Discovering these eigenfunction coordinates is, therefore, a central challenge, as they provide intrinsic coordinates along which the dynamics behave linearly. In practice, it is more likely that we will identify an *approximately* invariant subspace, given by a set of functions $\{g_j\}_{j=0}^{P}$, where each of the functions g_j is well approximated by a finite sum of eigenfunctions: $g_j \approx \sum_{k=0}^{P} \alpha_k \varphi_k$.

Examples of Koopman Embeddings

Nonlinear System with Single Fixed Point and a Slow Manifold

Here, we consider an example system with a single fixed point, given by:

$$\dot{x}_1 = \mu x_1 \tag{7.72a}$$

$$\dot{x}_2 = \lambda(x_2 - x_1^2). \tag{7.72b}$$

For $\lambda < \mu < 0$, the system exhibits a slow attracting manifold given by $x_2 = x_1^2$. It is possible to augment the state $\mathbf{x}$ with the nonlinear measurement $g = x_1^2$, to define a three-dimensional Koopman invariant subspace. In these coordinates, the dynamics become linear:

$$\frac{d}{dt}\begin{bmatrix} y_1 \\ y_2 \\ y_3 \end{bmatrix} = \begin{bmatrix} \mu & 0 & 0 \\ 0 & \lambda & -\lambda \\ 0 & 0 & 2\mu \end{bmatrix} \begin{bmatrix} y_1 \\ y_2 \\ y_3 \end{bmatrix} \quad \text{for} \quad \begin{bmatrix} y_1 \\ y_2 \\ y_3 \end{bmatrix} = \begin{bmatrix} x_1 \\ x_2 \\ x_1^2 \end{bmatrix}. \tag{7.73a}$$

The full three-dimensional Koopman observable vector space is visualized in Fig. 7.11. Trajectories that start on the invariant manifold $y_3 = y_1^2$, visualized by the blue surface, are constrained to stay on this manifold. There is a *slow* subspace, spanned by the eigenvectors corresponding to the slow eigenvalues μ and 2μ; this subspace is visualized by the green surface. Finally, there is the original asymptotically attracting manifold of the original system, $y_2 = y_1^2$, which is visualized as the red surface. The blue and red parabolic surfaces always intersect in a parabola that is inclined at a $45°$ angle in the y_2-y_3 direction. The green surface approaches this $45°$ inclination as the ratio of fast to slow dynamics become increasingly large. In the full three-dimensional Koopman observable space, the dynamics produce a single stable node, with trajectories rapidly attracting onto the green subspace and then slowly approaching the fixed point.

Intrinsic coordinates defined by eigenfunctions of the Koopman operator The left eigenvectors of the Koopman operator yield Koopman eigenfunctions (i.e., eigenobservables). The Koopman eigenfunctions of (7.73a) corresponding to eigenvalues μ and λ are:

$$\varphi_\mu = x_1, \quad \text{and} \quad \varphi_\lambda = x_2 - bx_1^2 \quad \text{with} \quad b = \frac{\lambda}{\lambda - 2\mu}. \tag{7.74}$$

The constant b in φ_λ captures the fact that for a finite ratio λ/μ, the dynamics only shadow the asymptotically attracting slow manifold $x_2 = x_1^2$, but in fact follow neighboring parabolic trajectories. This is illustrated more clearly by the various surfaces in Fig. 7.11 for different ratios λ/μ.

In this way, a set of intrinsic coordinates may be determined from the observable functions defined by the left eigenvectors of the Koopman operator on an invariant subspace. Explicitly,

$$\varphi_\alpha(\mathbf{x}) = \boldsymbol{\xi}_\alpha \mathbf{y}(\mathbf{x}), \quad \text{where} \quad \boldsymbol{\xi}_\alpha \mathbf{K} = \alpha \boldsymbol{\xi}_\alpha. \tag{7.75}$$

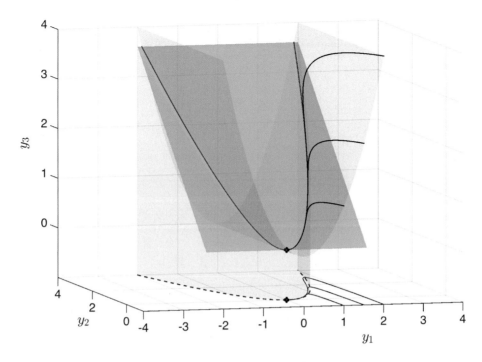

Figure 7.11 Visualization of three-dimensional linear Koopman system from (7.73a) along with projection of dynamics onto the x_1-x_2 plane. The attracting slow manifold is shown in red, the constraint $y_3 = y_1^2$ is shown in blue, and the slow unstable subspace of (7.73a) is shown in green. Black trajectories of the linear Koopman system in **y** project onto trajectories of the full nonlinear system in **x** in the y_1-y_2 plane. Here, $\mu = -0.05$ and $\lambda = 1$. *Reproduced from Brunton et al. [92].*

These eigen-observables define observable subspaces that remain invariant under the Koopman operator, even after coordinate transformations. As such, they may be regarded as intrinsic coordinates [556] on the Koopman-invariant subspace.

Example of Intractable Representation

Consider the logistic map, given by:

$$x_{k+1} = \beta x_k (1 - x_k). \tag{7.76}$$

Let our observable subspace include x and x^2:

$$\mathbf{y}_k = \begin{bmatrix} x \\ x^2 \end{bmatrix}_k \triangleq \begin{bmatrix} x_k \\ x_k^2 \end{bmatrix}. \tag{7.77}$$

Writing out the Koopman operator, the first row equation is simple:

$$\mathbf{y}_{k+1} = \begin{bmatrix} x \\ x^2 \end{bmatrix}_{k+1} = \begin{bmatrix} \beta & -\beta \\ ? & ? \end{bmatrix} \begin{bmatrix} x \\ x^2 \end{bmatrix}_k, \tag{7.78}$$

but the second row is not obvious. To find this expression, expand x_{k+1}^2:

$$x_{k+1}^2 = (\beta x_k (1 - x_k))^2 = \beta^2 \left(x_k^2 - 2x_k^3 + x_k^4 \right). \tag{7.79}$$

Thus, cubic and quartic polynomial terms are required to advance x^2. Similarly, these terms need polynomials up to sixth and eighth order, respectively, and so on, ad infinitum:

$$
\begin{bmatrix} x \\ x^2 \\ x^3 \\ x^4 \\ x^5 \\ \vdots \end{bmatrix}_{k+1}
=
\begin{array}{ccccccccccc}
 & x & x^2 & x^3 & x^4 & x^5 & x^6 & x^7 & x^8 & x^9 & x^{10} \\
\end{array}
\begin{bmatrix}
\beta & -\beta & 0 & 0 & 0 & 0 & 0 & 0 & 0 & 0 & \cdots \\
0 & \beta^2 & -2\beta^2 & r^2 & 0 & 0 & 0 & 0 & 0 & 0 & \cdots \\
0 & 0 & \beta^3 & -3\beta^3 & 3\beta^3 & \beta^3 & 0 & 0 & 0 & 0 & \cdots \\
0 & 0 & 0 & \beta^4 & -4\beta^4 & 6\beta^4 & -4\beta^4 & \beta^4 & 0 & 0 & \cdots \\
0 & 0 & 0 & 0 & \beta^5 & -5\beta^5 & 10\beta^5 & -10\beta^5 & 5\beta^5 & -\beta^5 & \cdots \\
\vdots & \vdots & \vdots & \vdots & \vdots & \vdots & \vdots & \vdots & \vdots & \vdots & \ddots
\end{bmatrix}
\begin{bmatrix} x \\ x^2 \\ x^3 \\ x^4 \\ x^5 \\ \vdots \end{bmatrix}_{k}.
$$

It is interesting to note that the rows of this equation are related to the rows of Pascal's triangle, with the n-th row scaled by r^n, and with the omission of the first row:

$$
\left[x^0\right]_{k+1} = \left[0\right]\left[x^0\right]_k. \tag{7.80}
$$

The above representation of the Koopman operator in a polynomial basis is somewhat troubling. Not only is there no closure, but the determinant of any finite-rank truncation is very large for $\beta > 1$. This illustrates a pitfall associated with naive representation of the infinite dimensional Koopman operator for a simple chaotic system. Truncating the system, or performing a least squares fit on an augmented observable vector (i.e., DMD on a nonlinear measurement; see Section 7.5) yields poor results, with the truncated system only agreeing with the true dynamics for a small handful of iterations, as the complexity of the representation grows quickly:

$$
\begin{array}{c}
1 \\ x \\ x^2 \\ x^3 \\ x^4 \\ x^5 \\ x^6 \\ x^7 \\ x^8 \\ \vdots
\end{array}
\begin{bmatrix} 0 \\ 1 \\ 0 \\ 0 \\ 0 \\ 0 \\ 0 \\ 0 \\ 0 \\ \vdots \end{bmatrix}
\overset{\mathcal{K}}{\Longrightarrow}
\begin{bmatrix} 0 \\ \beta \\ -\beta \\ 0 \\ 0 \\ 0 \\ 0 \\ 0 \\ 0 \\ \vdots \end{bmatrix}
\overset{\mathcal{K}}{\Longrightarrow}
\begin{bmatrix} 0 \\ \beta^2 \\ -\beta^2 - \beta^3 \\ 2\beta^3 \\ -\beta^3 \\ 0 \\ 0 \\ 0 \\ 0 \\ \vdots \end{bmatrix}
\overset{\mathcal{K}}{\Longrightarrow}
\begin{bmatrix} 0 \\ \beta^3 \\ -\beta^3 - \beta^4 - \beta^5 \\ 2\beta^4 + 2\beta^5 + 2\beta^6 \\ -\beta^4 - \beta^5 - 6\beta^6 - \beta^7 \\ 6\beta^6 + 4\beta^7 \\ -2\beta^6 - 6\beta^7 \\ 4\beta^7 \\ -\beta^7 \\ \vdots \end{bmatrix}. \tag{7.81}
$$

Analytic Series Expansions for Eigenfunctions

Given the dynamics in (7.1), it is possible to solve the PDE in (7.60) using standard techniques, such as recursively solving for the terms in a Taylor or Laurent series. A number of simple examples are explored below.

Linear Dynamics

Consider the simple linear dynamics

$$
\frac{d}{dt}x = x. \tag{7.82}
$$

Assuming a Taylor series expansion for $\varphi(x)$:

$$\varphi(x) = c_0 + c_1 x + c_2 x^2 + c_3 x^3 + \cdots$$

then the gradient and directional derivatives are given by:

$$\nabla \varphi = c_1 + 2c_2 x + 3c_3 x^2 + 4c_4 x^3 + \cdots$$

$$\nabla \varphi \cdot f = c_1 x + 2c_2 x^2 + 3c_3 x^3 + 4c_4 x^4 + \cdots$$

Solving for terms in the Koopman eigenfunction PDE (7.60), we see that $c_0 = 0$ must hold. For any positive integer λ in (7.60), only one of the coefficients may be nonzero. Specifically, for $\lambda = k \in \mathbb{Z}^+$, then $\varphi(x) = cx^k$ is an eigenfunction for any constant c. For instance, if $\lambda = 1$, then $\varphi(x) = x$.

Quadratic Nonlinear Dynamics

Consider a nonlinear dynamical system

$$\frac{d}{dt} = x^2. \tag{7.83}$$

There is no Taylor series that satisfies (7.60), except the trivial solution $\varphi = 0$ for $\lambda = 0$. Instead, we assume a Laurent series:

$$\varphi(x) = \cdots + c_{-3} x^{-3} + c_{-2} x^{-2} + c_{-1} x^{-1} + c_0$$
$$+ c_1 x + c_2 x^2 + c_3 x^3 + \cdots.$$

The gradient and directional derivatives are given by:

$$\nabla \varphi = \cdots - 3c_{-3} x^{-4} - 2c_{-2} x^{-3} - c_{-1} x^{-2} + c_1 + 2c_2 x$$
$$+ 3c_3 x^2 + 4c_4 x^3 + \cdots$$

$$\nabla \varphi \cdot f = \cdots - 3c_{-3} x^{-2} - 2c_{-2} x^{-1} - c_{-1} + c_1 x^2 + 2c_2 x^3$$
$$+ 3c_3 x^4 + 4c_4 x^5 + \cdots.$$

Solving for the coefficients of the Laurent series that satisfy (7.60), we find that all coefficients with positive index are zero, i.e. $c_k = 0$ for all $k \geq 1$. However, the nonpositive index coefficients are given by the recursion $\lambda c_{k+1} = k c_k$, for negative $k \leq -1$. Thus, the Laurent series is

$$\varphi(x) = c_0 \left(1 - \lambda x^{-1} + \frac{\lambda^2}{2} x^{-2} - \frac{\lambda^3}{3} x^{-3} + \cdots \right) = c_0 e^{-\lambda/x}.$$

This holds for all values of $\lambda \in \mathbb{C}$. There are also other Koopman eigenfunctions that can be identified from the Laurent series.

Polynomial Nonlinear Dynamics

For a more general nonlinear dynamical system

$$\frac{d}{dt} = a x^n, \tag{7.84}$$

$\varphi(x) = e^{\frac{\lambda}{(1-n)a} x^{1-n}}$ is an eigenfunction for all $\lambda \in \mathbb{C}$.

As mentioned above, it is also possible to generate new eigenfunctions by taking powers of these primitive eigenfunctions; the resulting eigenvalues generate a *lattice* in the complex plane.

History and Recent Developments

The original analysis of Koopman in 1931 was introduced to describe the evolution of measurements of Hamiltonian systems [300], and this theory was generalized by Koopman and von Neumann to systems with continuous eigenvalue spectrum in 1932 [301]. In the case of Hamiltonian flows, the Koopman operator $\mathcal{K}_t$ is unitary, and forms a one-parameter family of unitary transformations in Hilbert space. Unitary operators should be familiar by now, as the discrete Fourier transform (DFT) and the singular value decomposition (SVD) both provide unitary coordinate transformations. Unitarity implies that the inner product of any two observable functions remains unchanged through action of the Koopman operator, which is intuitively related to the phase-space volume preserving property of Hamiltonian systems. In the original paper [300], Koopman drew connections between the Koopman eigenvalue spectrum and conserved quantities, integrability, and ergodicity. Interestingly, Koopman's 1931 paper was central in the celebrated proofs of the ergodic theorem by Birkhoff and von Neumann [62, 399, 61, 389].

Koopman analysis has recently gained renewed interest with the pioneering work of Mezic and collaborators [379, 376, 102, 104, 103, 377, 322]. The Koopman operator is also known as the composition operator, which is formally the pull-back operator on the space of scalar observable functions [1], and it is the dual, or left-adjoint, of the Perron-Frobenius operator, or transfer operator, which is the push-forward operator on the space of probability density functions. When a polynomial basis is chosen to represent the Koopman operator, then it is closely related to Carleman linearization [121, 122, 123], which has been used extensively in nonlinear control [500, 305, 38, 509]. Koopman analysis is also connected to the resolvent operator theory from fluid dynamics [487].

Recently, it has been shown that the operator theoretic framework complements the traditional geometric and probabilistic perspectives. For example, level sets of Koopman eigenfunctions form invariant partitions of the state-space of a dynamical system [103]; in particular, eigenfunctions of the Koopman operator may be used to analyze the ergodic partition [380, 102]. Koopman analysis has also been recently shown to generalize the Hartman-Grobman theorem to the entire basin of attraction of a stable or unstable equilibrium point or periodic orbit [322].

At the time of this writing, representing Koopman eigenfunctions for general dynamical systems remains a central unsolved challenge. Significant research efforts are focused on developing data-driven techniques to identify Koopman eigenfunctions and use these for control, which will be discussed in the following sections and chapters. Recently, new work has emerged that attempts to leverage the power of deep learning to discover and represent eigenfunctions from data [550, 368, 513, 564, 412, 349].

7.5   Data-Driven Koopman Analysis

Obtaining linear representations for strongly nonlinear systems has the potential to revolutionize our ability to predict and control these systems. The linearization of dynamics near fixed points or periodic orbits has long been employed for *local* linear representation of the dynamics [252]. The Koopman operator is appealing because it provides a *global* linear representation, valid far away from fixed points and periodic orbits. However, previous attempts to obtain finite-dimensional approximations of the Koopman operator have had limited success. Dynamic mode decomposition [472, 456, 317] seeks to approximate the Koopman operator with a best-fit linear model advancing spatial measurements from one time to the next, although these linear measurements are not rich enough for many non-linear systems. Augmenting DMD with nonlinear measurements may enrich the model, but there is no guarantee that the resulting models will be closed under the Koopman operator [92]. Here, we describe several approaches for identifying Koopman embeddings and eigenfunctions from data. These methods include the extended dynamic mode decomposition [556], extensions based on SINDy [276], and the use of delay coordinates [91].

Extended DMD

The extended DMD algorithm [556] is essentially the same as standard DMD [535], except that instead of performing regression on direct measurements of the state, regression is performed on an augmented vector containing nonlinear measurements of the state. As discussed earlier, eDMD is equivalent to the variational approach of conformation dynamics [405, 407, 408], which was developed in 2013 by Noé and Nüske.

Here, we will modify the notation slightly to conform to related methods. In eDMD, an augmented state is constructed:

$$\mathbf{y} = \mathbf{\Theta}^T(\mathbf{x}) = \begin{bmatrix} \theta_1(\mathbf{x}) \\ \theta_2(\mathbf{x}) \\ \vdots \\ \theta_p(\mathbf{x}) \end{bmatrix}. \tag{7.85}$$

$\mathbf{\Theta}$ may contain the original state $\mathbf{x}$ as well as nonlinear measurements, so often $p \gg n$. Next, two data matrices are constructed, as in DMD:

$$\mathbf{Y} = \begin{bmatrix} | & | & & | \\ \mathbf{y}_1 & \mathbf{y}_2 & \cdots & \mathbf{y}_m \\ | & | & & | \end{bmatrix}, \qquad \mathbf{Y}' = \begin{bmatrix} | & | & & | \\ \mathbf{y}_2 & \mathbf{y}_3 & \cdots & \mathbf{y}_{m+1} \\ | & | & & | \end{bmatrix}. \tag{7.86a}$$

Finally, a best-fit linear operator $\mathbf{A_Y}$ is constructed that maps $\mathbf{Y}$ into $\mathbf{Y}'$:

$$\mathbf{A_Y} = \underset{\mathbf{A_Y}}{\operatorname{argmin}} \|\mathbf{Y}' - \mathbf{A_Y}\mathbf{Y}\| = \mathbf{Y}'\mathbf{Y}^\dagger. \tag{7.87}$$

This regression may be written in terms of the data matrices $\mathbf{\Theta}(\mathbf{X})$ and $\mathbf{\Theta}(\mathbf{X}')$:

$$\mathbf{A_Y} = \underset{\mathbf{A_Y}}{\operatorname{argmin}} \|\mathbf{\Theta}^T(\mathbf{X}') - \mathbf{A_Y}\mathbf{\Theta}^T(\mathbf{X})\| = \mathbf{\Theta}^T(\mathbf{X})\left(\mathbf{\Theta}^T(\mathbf{X})\right)^\dagger. \tag{7.88}$$

Because the augmented vector $\mathbf{y}$ may be significantly larger than the state $\mathbf{x}$, kernel methods are often employed to compute this regression [557]. In principle, the enriched library $\mathbf{\Theta}$ provides a larger basis in which to approximate the Koopman operator. It has been shown recently that in the limit of infinite snapshots, the extended DMD operator converges to the Koopman operator projected onto the subspace spanned by $\mathbf{\Theta}$ [303]. However, if $\mathbf{\Theta}$ does not span a Koopman invariant subspace, then the projected operator may not have any resemblance to the original Koopman operator, as all of the eigenvalues and eigenvectors may be different. In fact, it was shown that the extended DMD operator will have spurious eigenvalues and eigenvectors unless it is represented in terms of a Koopman invariant subspace [92]. Therefore, it is essential to use validation and cross-validation techniques to ensure that eDMD models are not overfit, as discussed below. For example, it was shown that eDMD cannot contain the original state $\mathbf{x}$ as a measurement and represent a system that has multiple fixed points, periodic orbits, or other attractors, because these systems cannot be topologically conjugate to a finite-dimensional linear system [92].

Approximating Koopman Eigenfunctions from Data

In discrete-time, a Koopman eigenfunction $\varphi(\mathbf{x})$ evaluated at a number of data points in $\mathbf{X}$ will satisfy:

$$
\begin{bmatrix} \lambda\varphi(\mathbf{x}_1) \\ \lambda\varphi(\mathbf{x}_2) \\ \vdots \\ \lambda\varphi(\mathbf{x}_m) \end{bmatrix} = \begin{bmatrix} \varphi(\mathbf{x}_2) \\ \varphi(\mathbf{x}_3) \\ \vdots \\ \varphi(\mathbf{x}_{m+1}) \end{bmatrix}. \tag{7.89}
$$

It is possible to approximate this eigenfunction as an expansion in terms of a set of candidate functions,

$$
\mathbf{\Theta}(\mathbf{x}) = \begin{bmatrix} \theta_1(\mathbf{x}) & \theta_2(\mathbf{x}) & \cdots & \theta_p(\mathbf{x}) \end{bmatrix}. \tag{7.90}
$$

The Koopman eigenfunction may be approximated in this basis as:

$$
\varphi(\mathbf{x}) \approx \sum_{k=1}^{p} \theta_k(\mathbf{x})\xi_k = \mathbf{\Theta}(\mathbf{x})\boldsymbol{\xi}. \tag{7.91}
$$

Writing (7.89) in terms of this expansion yields the matrix system:

$$
\left(\lambda\mathbf{\Theta}(\mathbf{X}) - \mathbf{\Theta}(\mathbf{X}') \right) \boldsymbol{\xi} = \mathbf{0}. \tag{7.92}
$$

If we seek the best *least-squares* fit to (7.92), this reduces to the extended DMD [557, 556] formulation:

$$
\lambda\boldsymbol{\xi} = \mathbf{\Theta}(\mathbf{X})^{\dagger}\mathbf{\Theta}(\mathbf{X}')\boldsymbol{\xi}. \tag{7.93}
$$

Note that (7.93) is the transpose of (7.88), so that left eigenvectors become right eigenvectors. Thus, eigenvectors $\boldsymbol{\xi}$ of $\mathbf{\Theta}^{\dagger}\mathbf{\Theta}'$ yield the coefficients of the eigenfunction $\varphi(\mathbf{x})$ represented in the basis $\mathbf{\Theta}(\mathbf{x})$. It is absolutely essential to then confirm that predicted eigenfunctions actually behave linearly on trajectories, by comparing them with the predicted dynamics $\varphi_{k+1} = \lambda\varphi_k$, because the regression above will result in spurious eigenvalues and eigenvectors unless the basis elements θ_j span a Koopman invariant subspace [92].

Sparse Identification of Eigenfunctions

It is possible to leverage the SINDy regression [95] to identify Koopman eigenfunctions corresponding to a particular eigenvalue λ, selecting only the few active terms in the library $\mathbf{\Theta}(\mathbf{x})$ to avoid overfitting. Given the data matrices, $\mathbf{X}$ and $\dot{\mathbf{X}}$ from above it is possible to construct the library of basis functions $\mathbf{\Theta}(\mathbf{X})$ as well as a library of directional derivatives, representing the possible terms in $\nabla\varphi(\mathbf{x}) \cdot \mathbf{f}(\mathbf{x})$ from (7.60):

$$\boldsymbol{\Gamma}(\mathbf{x}, \dot{\mathbf{x}}) = \begin{bmatrix} \nabla\theta_1(\mathbf{x}) \cdot \dot{\mathbf{x}} & \nabla\theta_2(\mathbf{x}) \cdot \dot{\mathbf{x}} & \cdots & \nabla\theta_p(\mathbf{x}) \cdot \dot{\mathbf{x}} \end{bmatrix}. \tag{7.94}$$

It is then possible to construct $\boldsymbol{\Gamma}$ from data:

$$\boldsymbol{\Gamma}(\mathbf{X}, \dot{\mathbf{X}}) = \begin{bmatrix} \nabla\theta_1(\mathbf{x}_1) \cdot \dot{\mathbf{x}}_1 & \nabla\theta_2(\mathbf{x}_1) \cdot \dot{\mathbf{x}}_1 & \cdots & \nabla\theta_p(\mathbf{x}_1) \cdot \dot{\mathbf{x}}_1 \\ \nabla\theta_1(\mathbf{x}_2) \cdot \dot{\mathbf{x}}_2 & \nabla\theta_2(\mathbf{x}_2) \cdot \dot{\mathbf{x}}_2 & \cdots & \nabla\theta_p(\mathbf{x}_2) \cdot \dot{\mathbf{x}}_2 \\ \vdots & \vdots & \ddots & \vdots \\ \nabla\theta_1(\mathbf{x}_m) \cdot \dot{\mathbf{x}}_m & \nabla\theta_2(\mathbf{x}_m) \cdot \dot{\mathbf{x}}_m & \cdots & \nabla\theta_p(\mathbf{x}_m) \cdot \dot{\mathbf{x}}_m \end{bmatrix}.$$

For a given eigenvalue λ, the Koopman PDE in (7.60) may be evaluated on data:

$$\left(\lambda\boldsymbol{\Theta}(\mathbf{X}) - \boldsymbol{\Gamma}(\mathbf{X}, \dot{\mathbf{X}}) \right) \boldsymbol{\xi} = \mathbf{0}. \tag{7.95}$$

The formulation in (7.95) is implicit, so that $\boldsymbol{\xi}$ will be in the null-space of $\lambda\boldsymbol{\Theta}(\mathbf{X}) - \boldsymbol{\Gamma}(\mathbf{X}, \dot{\mathbf{X}})$. The right null-space of (7.95) for a given λ is spanned by the right singular vectors of $\lambda\boldsymbol{\Theta}(\mathbf{X}) - \boldsymbol{\Gamma}(\mathbf{X}, \dot{\mathbf{X}}) = \mathbf{U}\boldsymbol{\Sigma}\mathbf{V}^*$ (i.e., columns of $\mathbf{V}$) corresponding to zero-valued singular values. It may be possible to identify the few active terms in an eigenfunction by finding the sparsest vector in the null-space [440], as in the implicit-SINDy algorithm [361] described in Section 7.3. In this formulation, the eigenvalues λ are not known *a priori*, and must be learned with the approximate eigenfunction. Koopman eigenfuntions and eigenvalues can also be determined as the solution to the eigenvalue problem $\mathbf{A}_{\mathbf{Y}}\boldsymbol{\xi}_\alpha = \lambda_\alpha\boldsymbol{\xi}_\alpha$, where $\mathbf{A}_{\mathbf{Y}} = \boldsymbol{\Theta}^\dagger\boldsymbol{\Gamma}$ is obtained via least-squares regression, as in the continuous-time version of eDMD. While many eigenfunctions are spurious, those corresponding to lightly damped eigenvalues can be well approximated.

From a practical standpoint, data in $\mathbf{X}$ does not need to be sampled from full trajectories, but can be obtained using more sophisticated strategies such as latin hypercube sampling or sampling from a distribution over the phase space. Moreover, reproducing kernel Hilbert spaces (RKHS) can be employed to describe $\varphi(\mathbf{x})$ *locally* in patches of state space.

Example: Duffing System (Kaiser et al [276])

We demonstrate the sparse identification of Koopman eigenfunctions on the undamped Duffing oscillator:

$$\frac{d}{dt}\begin{bmatrix} x_1 \\ x_2 \end{bmatrix} = \begin{bmatrix} x_2 \\ x_1 - x_1^3 \end{bmatrix}$$

where x_1 is the position and x_2 is the velocity of a particle in a double well potential with equilibria $(0, 0)$ and $(\pm 1, 0)$. This system is conservative, with Hamiltonian $\mathcal{H} = \frac{1}{2}x_2^2 - \frac{1}{2}x_1^2 + \frac{1}{4}x_1^4$. The Hamiltonian, and in general any conserved quantity, is a Koopman eigenfunction with zero eigenvalue.

For the eigenvalue $\lambda = 0$, (7.95) becomes $-\boldsymbol{\Gamma}(\mathbf{X}, \dot{\mathbf{X}})\boldsymbol{\xi} = \mathbf{0}$, and hence a sparse $\boldsymbol{\xi}$ is sought in the null-space of $-\boldsymbol{\Gamma}(\mathbf{X}, \dot{\mathbf{X}})$. A library of candidate functions is constructed from data, employing polynomials up to fourth order:

$$\boldsymbol{\Theta}(\mathbf{X}) = \begin{bmatrix} | & | & | & | & & | \\ x_1(t) & x_2(t) & x_1^2(t) & x_1(t)x_2(t) & \cdots & x_2^4(t) \\ | & | & | & | & & | \end{bmatrix}$$

and

$$\Gamma(\mathbf{X}, \dot{\mathbf{X}}) = \begin{bmatrix} | & | & | & | & & | \\ \dot{x}_1(t) & \dot{x}_2(t) & 2x_1(t)\dot{x}_1(t) & x_2(t)\dot{x}_1(t) + x_1(t) + \dot{x}_2(t) & \cdots & 4x_2(t)^3\dot{x}_2(t) \\ | & | & | & | & & | \end{bmatrix}.$$

A sparse vector of coefficients $\boldsymbol{\xi}$ may be identified, with the few nonzero entries determining the active terms in the Koopman eigenfunction. The identified Koopman eigenfunction associated with $\lambda = 0$ is

$$\varphi(\mathbf{x}) = -2/3x_1^2 + 2/3x_2^2 + 1/3x_1^4. \tag{7.96}$$

This eigenfunction matches the Hamiltonian perfectly up to a constant scaling.

Data-Driven Koopman and Delay Coordinates

Instead of advancing instantaneous linear or nonlinear measurements of the state of a system directly, as in DMD, it may be possible to obtain intrinsic measurement coordinates for Koopman based on time-delayed measurements of the system [506, 91, 18, 144]. This perspective is data-driven, relying on the wealth of information from previous measurements to inform the future. Unlike a linear or weakly nonlinear system, where trajectories may get trapped at fixed points or on periodic orbits, chaotic dynamics are particularly well-suited to this analysis: trajectories evolve to densely fill an attractor, so more data provides more information. The use of delay coordinates may be especially important for systems with long-term memory effects, where the Koopman approach has recently been shown to provide a successful analysis tool [508]. Interestingly, a connection between the Koopman operator and the Takens embedding was explored as early as 2004 [379], where a stochastic Koopman operator is defined and a statistical Takens theorem is proven.

The time-delay measurement scheme is shown schematically in Fig. 7.12, as illustrated on the Lorenz system for a single time-series measurement of the first variable, $x(t)$. The conditions of the Takens embedding theorem are satisfied [515], so it is possible to obtain a diffeomorphism between a delay embedded attractor and the attractor in the original coordinates. We then obtain eigen-time-delay coordinates from a time-series of a single measurement $x(t)$ by taking the SVD of the Hankel matrix $\mathbf{H}$:

$$\mathbf{H} = \begin{bmatrix} x(t_1) & x(t_2) & \cdots & x(t_{m_c}) \\ x(t_2) & x(t_3) & \cdots & x(t_{m_c+1}) \\ \vdots & \vdots & \ddots & \vdots \\ x(t_{m_o}) & x(t_{m_o+1}) & \cdots & x(t_m) \end{bmatrix} = \mathbf{U}\boldsymbol{\Sigma}\mathbf{V}^*. \tag{7.97}$$

The columns of $\mathbf{U}$ and $\mathbf{V}$ from the SVD are arranged hierarchically by their ability to model the columns and rows of $\mathbf{H}$, respectively. Often, $\mathbf{H}$ may admit a low-rank approximation by the first r columns of $\mathbf{U}$ and $\mathbf{V}$. Note that the Hankel matrix in (7.97) is the basis of the eigensystem realization algorithm [272] in linear system identification (see Section 9.3) and singular spectrum analysis (SSA) [88] in climate time-series analysis.

The low-rank approximation to (7.97) provides a *data-driven* measurement system that is approximately invariant to the Koopman operator for states on the attractor. By definition, the dynamics map the attractor into itself, making it *invariant* to the flow. In other words, the columns of $\mathbf{U}$ form a Koopman invariant subspace. We may re-write (7.97) with the

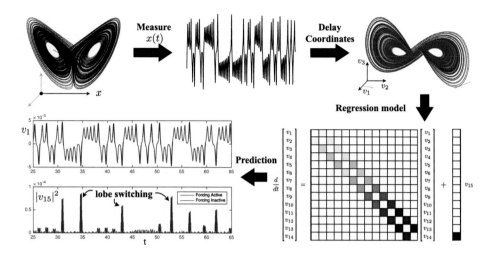

Figure 7.12 Decomposition of chaos into a linear system with forcing. A time series $x(t)$ is stacked into a Hankel matrix **H**. The SVD of **H** yields a hierarchy of *eigen* time series that produce a delay-embedded attractor. A best-fit linear regression model is obtained on the delay coordinates **v**; the linear fit for the first $r - 1$ variables is excellent, but the last coordinate v_r is not well-modeled as linear. Instead, v_r is an input that forces the first $r - 1$ variables. Rare forcing events correspond to lobe switching in the chaotic dynamics. This architecture is called the Hankel alternative view of Koopman (HAVOK) analysis, from [91]. *Figure modified from Brunton et al. [91].*

Koopman operator $\mathcal{K} \triangleq \mathcal{K}_{\Delta t}$:

$$
\mathbf{H} = \begin{bmatrix} x(t_1) & \mathcal{K}x(t_1) & \cdots & \mathcal{K}^{m_c-1}x(t_1) \\ \mathcal{K}x(t_1) & \mathcal{K}^2 x(t_1) & \cdots & \mathcal{K}^{m_c}x(t_1) \\ \vdots & \vdots & \ddots & \vdots \\ \mathcal{K}^{m_o-1}x(t_1) & \mathcal{K}^{m_o}x(t_1) & \cdots & \mathcal{K}^{m-1}x(t_1) \end{bmatrix}.
\tag{7.98}
$$

The columns of (7.97) are well-approximated by the first r columns of **U**. The first r columns of **V** provide a time series of the magnitude of each of the columns of $\mathbf{U\Sigma}$ in the data. By plotting the first three columns of **V**, we obtain an embedded attractor for the Lorenz system (See Fig. 7.12).

The connection between eigen-time-delay coordinates from (7.97) and the Koopman operator motivates a linear regression model on the variables in **V**. Even with an approximately Koopman-invariant measurement system, there remain challenges to identifying a linear model for a chaotic system. A linear model, however detailed, cannot capture multiple fixed points or the unpredictable behavior characteristic of chaos with a positive Lyapunov exponent [92]. Instead of constructing a closed linear model for the first r variables in **V**, we build a linear model on the first $r - 1$ variables and recast the last variable, v_r, as a forcing term:

$$
\frac{d}{dt}\mathbf{v}(t) = \mathbf{Av}(t) + \mathbf{B}v_r(t),
\tag{7.99}
$$

where $\mathbf{v} = \begin{bmatrix} v_1 & v_2 & \cdots & v_{r-1} \end{bmatrix}^T$ is a vector of the first $r-1$ eigen-time-delay coordinates. Other work has investigated the splitting of dynamics into deterministic linear, and chaotic stochastic dynamics [376].

In all of the examples explored in [91], the linear model on the first $r-1$ terms is accurate, while no linear model represents v_r. Instead, v_r is an input forcing to the linear dynamics in (7.99), which approximates the nonlinear dynamics. The statistics of $v_r(t)$ are non-Gaussian, with long tails correspond to rare-event forcing that drives lobe switching in the Lorenz system; this is related to rare-event forcing distributions observed and modeled by others [355, 461, 356]. The forced linear system in (7.99) was discovered after applying the SINDy algorithm [95] to delay coordinates of the Lorenz system. Continuing to develop Koopman on delay coordinates has significant promise in the context of closed-loop feedback control, where it may be possible to manipulate the behavior of a chaotic system by treating v_r as a disturbance.

In addition, the use of delay coordinates as intrinsic measurements for Koopman analysis suggests that Koopman theory may also be used to improve spatially distributed sensor technologies. A spatial array of sensors, for example the $\mathcal{O}(100)$ strain sensors on the wings of flying insects, may use phase delay coordinates to provide nearly optimal embeddings to detect and control convective structures (e.g., stall from a gust, leading edge vortex formation and convection, etc.).

HAVOK Code for Lorenz System

Below is the code to generate a HAVOK model for the same Lorenz system data generated in Code 7.2. Here we use $\Delta t = 0.01$, $m_o = 10$, and $r = 10$, although the results would be more accurate for $\Delta t = 0.001$, $m_o = 100$, and $r = 15$.

Code 7.3 HAVOK code for Lorenz data generated in Section 7.1.

```
%% EIGEN-TIME DELAY COORDINATES
stackmax = 10;      %  Number of shift-stacked rows
r=10;               %  Rank of HAVOK Model
H = zeros(stackmax,size(x,1)-stackmax);
for k=1:stackmax
    H(k,:) = x(k:end-stackmax-1+k,1);
end
[U,S,V] = svd(H,'econ'); % Eigen delay coordinates

%% COMPUTE DERIVATIVES (4TH ORDER CENTRAL DIFFERENCE)
dV = zeros(length(V)-5,r);
for i=3:length(V)-3
    for k=1:r
        dV(i-2,k) = (1/(12*dt))*(-V(i+2,k)+8*V(i+1,k)-8*V(i-1,k)
            +V(i-2,k));
    end
end
% trim first and last two that are lost in derivative
V = V(3:end-3,1:r);

%% BUILD HAVOK REGRESSION MODEL ON TIME DELAY COORDINATES
Xi = V\dV;
A = Xi(1:r-1,1:r-1)';
B = Xi(end,1:r-1)';
```

Neural Networks for Koopman Embeddings

Despite the promise of Koopman embeddings, obtaining tractable representations has remained a central challenge. Recall that even for relatively simple dynamical systems, the eigenfunctions of the Koopman operator may be arbitrarily complex. Deep learning, which is well-suited for representing arbitrary functions, has recently emerged as a promising approach for discovering and representing Koopman eigenfunctions [550, 368, 513, 564, 412, 332, 349], providing a data-driven embedding of strongly nonlinear systems into intrinsic linear coordinates. In particular, the Koopman perspective fits naturally with the deep auto-encoder structure discussed in Chapter 6, where a few key latent variables $\mathbf{y} = \varphi(\mathbf{x})$ are discovered to parameterize the dynamics. In a Koopman network, an additional constraint is enforced so that the dynamics must be linear on these latent variables, forcing the functions $\varphi(\mathbf{x})$ to be Koopman eigenfunctions, as illustrated in Fig. 7.13. The constraint of linear dynamics is enforced by the loss function $\|\varphi(\mathbf{x}_{k+1}) - \mathbf{K}\varphi(\mathbf{x}_k)\|$, where $\mathbf{K}$ is a matrix. In general, linearity is enforced over multiple time steps, so that a trajectory is captured by iterating $\mathbf{K}$ on the latent variables. In addition, it is important to be able to map back to physical variables $\mathbf{x}$, which is why the autoencoder structure is favorable [349]. Variational autoencoders are also used for stochastic dynamical systems, such as molecular dynamics, where the map back to physical configuration space from the latent variables is probabilistic [550, 368].

For simple systems with a discrete eigenvalue spectrum, a compact representation may be obtained in terms of a few autoencoder variables. However, dynamical systems with continuous eigenvalue spectra defy low-dimensional representations using many existing neural network or Koopman representations. Continuous spectrum dynamics are ubiquitous, ranging from the simple pendulum to nonlinear optics and broadband turbulence. For example, the classical pendulum, given by

$$\ddot{x} = -\sin(\omega x) \tag{7.100}$$

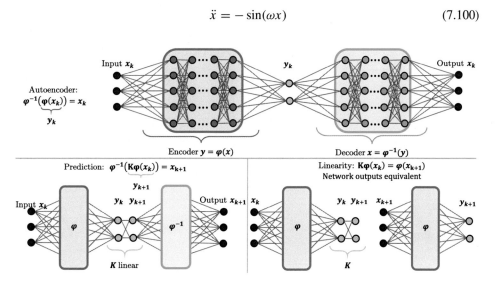

Figure 7.13 Deep neural network architecture used to identify Koopman eigenfunctions $\varphi(\mathbf{x})$. The network is based on a deep auto-encoder (a), which identifies intrinsic coordinates $\mathbf{y} = \varphi(\mathbf{x})$. Additional loss functions are included to enforce linear dynamics in the auto-encoder variables (b,c). *Reproduced with permission from Lusch et al. [349].*

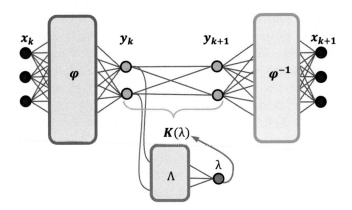

Figure 7.14 Modified network architecture with auxiliary network to parameterize the continuous eigenvalue spectrum. A continuous eigenvalue λ enables aggressive dimensionality reduction in the auto-encoder, avoiding the need for higher harmonics of the fundamental frequency that are generated by the nonlinearity. *Reproduced with permission from Lusch et al. [349].*

exhibits a continuous range of frequencies, from ω to 0, as the amplitude of the pendulum oscillation is increased. Thus, the continuous spectrum confounds a simple description in terms of a few Koopman eigenfunctions [378]. Indeed, away from the linear regime, an infinite Fourier sum is required to approximate the shift in frequency.

In a recent work by Lusch et al. [349], an auxiliary network is used to parameterize the continuously varying eigenvalue, enabling a network structure that is both parsimonious and interpretable. This parameterized network is depicted schematically in Fig. 7.14 and illustrated on the simple pendulum in Fig. 7.15. In contrast to other network structures, which require a large autoencoder layer to encode the continuous frequency shift with an asymptotic expansion in terms of harmonics of the natural frequency, the parameterized network is able to identify a single complex conjugate pair of eigenfunctions with a varying imaginary eigenvalue pair. If this explicit frequency dependence is unaccounted for, then a high-dimensional network is necessary to account for the shifting frequency and eigenvalues.

It is expected that neural network representations of dynamical systems, and Koopman embeddings in particular, will remain a growing area of interest in data-driven dynamics. Combining the representational power of deep learning with the elegance and simplicity of Koopman embeddings has the potential to transform the analysis and control of complex systems.

Suggested Reading
Texts
(1)   **Nonlinear oscillations, dynamical systems, and bifurcations of vector fields**, by P. Holmes and J. Guckenheimer, 1983 [252].
(2)   **Dynamic mode decomposition: Data-driven modeling of complex systems**, by J. N. Kutz, S. L. Brunton, B. W. Brunton, and J. L. Proctor, 2016 [317].
(3)   **Differential equations and dynamical systems**, by L. Perko, 2013 [427].

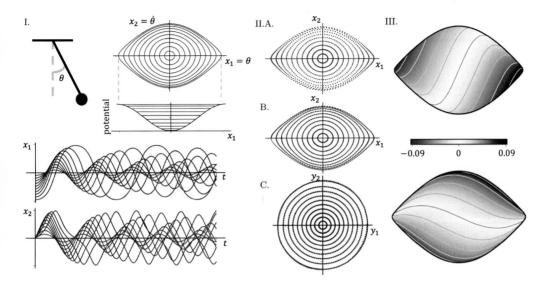

Figure 7.15 Neural network embedding of the nonlinear pendulum, using the parameterized network in Fig. 7.14. As the pendulum amplitude increases, the frequency continuously changes (I). In the Koopman eigenfunction coordinates (III), the dynamics become linear, given by perfect circles (IIIC). *Reproduced with permission from Lusch et al. [349].*

Papers and reviews

(1)   **Distilling free-form natural laws from experimental data**, by M. Schmidt and H. Lipson, *Science*, 2009 [477].

(2)   **Discovering governing equations from data by sparse identification of nonlinear dynamical systems**, by S. L. Brunton, J. L. Proctor, and J. N. Kutz, *Proceedings of the National Academy of Sciences*, 2016 [95].

(3)   **On dynamic mode decomposition: theory and applications**, by J. H. Tu, C. W. Rowley, D. M. Luchtenburg, S. L. Brunton, J. N. Kutz, *Journal of Computational Dynamics*, 2014 [535].

(4)   **Hamiltonian systems and transformation in Hilbert Space**, by B. O. Koopman, *Proceedings of the National Academy of Sciences*, 1931 [300].

(5)   **Spectral properties of dynamical systems, model reduction and decompositions**, by I. Mezić, *Nonlinear Dynamics*, 2005 [376].

(6)   **Data-driven model reduction and transfer operator approximation**, by S. Klus, F. Nuske, P. Koltai, H. Wu, I. Kevrekidis, C. Schutte, and F. Noe, *Journal of Nonlinear Dynamics*, 2018 [293].

(7)   **Hidden physics models: Machine learning of nonlinear partial differential equations**, by M. Raissi and G. E. Karniadakis, *Journal of Computational Physics*, 2018 [445].

8 Linear Control Theory

The focus of this book has largely been on characterizing complex systems through dimensionality reduction, sparse sampling, and dynamical systems modeling. However, an overarching goal for many systems is the ability to actively manipulate their behavior for a given engineering objective. The study and practice of manipulating dynamical systems is broadly known as control theory, and it is one of the most successful fields at the interface of applied mathematics and practical engineering. Control theory is inseparable from data science, as it relies on sensor measurements (data) obtained from a system to achieve a given objective. In fact, control theory deals with living data, as successful application modifies the dynamics of the system, thus changing the characteristics of the measurements. Control theory forces the reader to confront reality, as simplifying assumptions and model approximations are tested.

Control theory has helped shape the modern technological and industrial landscape. Examples abound, including cruise control in automobiles, position control in construction equipment, fly-by-wire autopilots in aircraft, industrial automation, packet routing in the internet, commercial heating ventilation and cooling systems, stabilization of rockets, and PID temperature and pressure control in modern espresso machines, to name only a few of the many applications. In the future, control will be increasingly applied to high-dimensional, strongly nonlinear and multiscale problems, such as turbulence, neuroscience, finance, epidemiology, autonomous robots, and self driving cars. In these future applications, data-driven modeling and control will be vitally important; this is be the subject of Chapters 7 and 10.

This chapter will introduce the key concepts from closed-loop feedback control. The goal is to build intuition for how and when to use feedback control, motivated by practical real-world challenges. Most of the theory will be developed for linear systems, where a wealth of powerful techniques exist [165, 492]. This theory will then be demonstrated on simple and intuitive examples, such as to develop a cruise controller for an automobile or stabilize an inverted pendulum on a moving cart.

Types of Control

There are many ways to manipulate the behavior of a dynamical system, and these control approaches are organized schematically in Fig. 8.1. Passive control does not require input energy, and when sufficient, it is desirable because of its simplicity, reliability, and low cost. For example, stop signs at a traffic intersection regulate the flow of traffic. Active control requires input energy, and these controllers are divided into two broad categories based on whether or not sensors are used to inform the controller. In the first category, open-loop

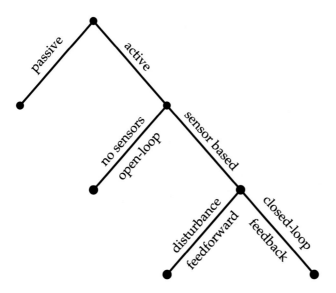

Figure 8.1 Schematic illustrating the various types of control. Most of this chapter will focus on closed-loop feedback control.

control relies on a pre-programmed control sequence; in the traffic example, signals may be pre-programmed to regulate traffic dynamically at different times of day. In the second category, active control uses sensors to inform the control law. Disturbance feedforward control measures exogenous disturbances to the system and then feeds this into an open-loop control law; an example of feedforward control would be to preemptively change the direction of the flow of traffic near a stadium when a large crowd of people are expected to leave. Finally, the last category is closed-loop feedback control, which will be the main focus of this chapter. Closed-loop control uses sensors to measure the system directly and then shapes the control in response to whether the system is actually achieving the desired goal. Many modern traffic systems have smart traffic lights with a control logic informed by inductive sensors in the roadbed that measure traffic density.

8.1 Closed-Loop Feedback Control

The main focus of this chapter is closed-loop feedback control, which is the method of choice for systems with uncertainty, instability, and/or external disturbances. Fig. 8.2 depicts the general feedback control framework, where sensor measurements, $\mathbf{y}$, of a system are fed back into a controller, which then decides on an actuation signal, $\mathbf{u}$, to manipulate the dynamics and provide robust performance despite model uncertainty and exogenous disturbances. In all of the examples discussed in this chapter, the vector of exogenous disturbances may be decomposed as $\mathbf{w} = \begin{bmatrix} \mathbf{w}_d^T & \mathbf{w}_n^T & \mathbf{w}_r^T \end{bmatrix}^T$, where $\mathbf{w}_d$ are disturbances to the state of the system, $\mathbf{w}_n$ is measurement noise, and $\mathbf{w}_r$ is a reference trajectory that should be tracked by the closed-loop system.

Mathematically, the system and measurements are typically described by a dynamical system:

$$\frac{d}{dt}\mathbf{x} = \mathbf{f}(\mathbf{x}, \mathbf{u}, \mathbf{w}_d) \tag{8.1a}$$

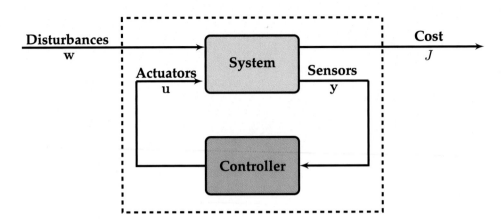

Figure 8.2 Standard framework for feedback control. Measurements of the system, $\mathbf{y}(t)$, are fed back into a controller, which then decides on the appropriate actuation signal $\mathbf{u}(t)$ to control the system. The control law is designed to modify the system dynamics and provide good performance, quantified by the cost J, despite exogenous disturbances and noise in $\mathbf{w}$. The exogenous input $\mathbf{w}$ may also include a reference trajectory $\mathbf{w}_r$ that should be tracked.

$$\mathbf{y} = \mathbf{g}(\mathbf{x}, \mathbf{u}, \mathbf{w}_n). \qquad (8.1b)$$

The goal is to construct a control law

$$\mathbf{u} = \mathbf{k}(\mathbf{y}, \mathbf{w}_r) \qquad (8.2)$$

that minimizes a cost function

$$J \triangleq J(\mathbf{x}, \mathbf{u}, \mathbf{w}_r). \qquad (8.3)$$

Thus, modern control relies heavily on techniques from optimization [74]. In general, the controller in (8.2) will be a dynamical system, rather than a static function of the inputs. For example, the Kalman filter in Section 8.5 dynamically estimates the full state $\mathbf{x}$ from measurements of $\mathbf{u}$ and $\mathbf{y}$. In this case, the control law will become $\mathbf{u} = \mathbf{k}(\mathbf{y}, \hat{\mathbf{x}}, \mathbf{w}_r)$, where $\hat{\mathbf{x}}$ is the full-state estimate.

To motivate the added cost and complexity of sensor-based feedback control, it is helpful to compare with open-loop control. For reference tracking problems, the controller is designed to steer the output of a system towards a desired reference output value $\mathbf{w}_r$, thus minimizing the error $\epsilon = \mathbf{y} - \mathbf{w}_r$. Open-loop control, shown in Fig. 8.3, uses a model of the system to design an actuation signal $\mathbf{u}$ that produces the desired reference output. However, this pre-planned strategy cannot correct for external disturbances to the system and is fundamentally incapable of changing the dynamics. Thus, it is impossible to stabilize an unstable system, such as an inverted pendulum, with open-loop control, since the system model would have to be known perfectly and the system would need to be perfectly isolated from disturbances. Moreover, any model uncertainty will directly contribute to open-loop tracking error.

In contrast, closed-loop feedback control, shown in Fig. 8.4 uses sensor measurements of the system to inform the controller about how the system is actually responding. These sensor measurements provide information about unmodeled dynamics and disturbances that would degrade the performance in open-loop control. Further, with feedback it is

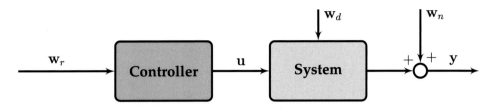

Figure 8.3 Open-loop control diagram. Given a desired reference signal $\mathbf{w}_r$, the open-loop control law constructs a control protocol $\mathbf{u}$ to drive the system based on a model. External disturbances ($\mathbf{w}_d$) and sensor noise ($\mathbf{w}_n$), as well as unmodeled system dynamics and uncertainty, are not accounted for and degrade performance.

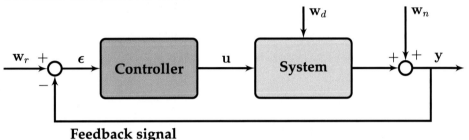

Figure 8.4 Closed-loop feedback control diagram. The sensor signal $\mathbf{y}$ is fed back and subtracted from the reference signal $\mathbf{w}_r$, providing information about how the system is responding to actuation and external disturbances. The controller uses the resulting error $\boldsymbol{\varepsilon}$ to determine the correct actuation signal $\mathbf{u}$ for the desired response. Feedback is often able to stabilize unstable dynamics while effectively rejecting disturbances $\mathbf{w}_d$ and attenuating noise $\mathbf{w}_n$.

often possible to modify and stabilize the dynamics of the closed-loop system, something which is not possible with open-loop control. Thus, closed-loop feedback control is often able to maintain high-performance operation for systems with unstable dynamics, model uncertainty, and external disturbances.

Examples of the Benefits of Feedback Control

To summarize, closed-loop feedback control has several benefits over open-loop control:

- It may be possible to stabilize an unstable system;
- It may be possible to compensate for external disturbances;
- It may be possible to correct for unmodeled dynamics and model uncertainty.

These issues are illustrated in the following two simple examples.

Inverted pendulum Consider the unstable inverted pendulum equations, which will be derived later in Section 8.2. The linearized equations are:

$$\frac{d}{dt}\begin{bmatrix} x_1 \\ x_2 \end{bmatrix} = \begin{bmatrix} 0 & 1 \\ g/L & d \end{bmatrix}\begin{bmatrix} x_1 \\ x_2 \end{bmatrix} + \begin{bmatrix} 0 \\ 1 \end{bmatrix} u \tag{8.4}$$

where $x_1 = \theta$, $x_2 = \dot{\theta}$, u is a torque applied to the pendulum arm, g is gravitational acceleration, L is the length of the pendulum arm, and d is damping. We may write this system in standard form as

$$\frac{d}{dt}\mathbf{x} = \mathbf{Ax} + \mathbf{B}u.$$

If we choose constants so that the natural frequency is $\omega_n = \sqrt{g/L} = 1$ and $d = 0$, then the system has eigenvalues $\lambda = \pm 1$, corresponding to an unstable saddle-type fixed point.

No open-loop control strategy can change the dynamics of the system, given by the eigenvalues of $\mathbf{A}$. However, with full-state feedback control, given by $u = -\mathbf{Kx}$, the closed-loop system becomes

$$\frac{d}{dt}\mathbf{x} = \mathbf{Ax} + \mathbf{B}u = (\mathbf{A} - \mathbf{BK})\,\mathbf{x}.$$

Choosing $\mathbf{K} = \begin{bmatrix} 4 & 4 \end{bmatrix}$, corresponding to a control law $u = -4x_1 - 4x_2 = -4\theta - 4\dot{\theta}$, the closed loop system $(\mathbf{A} - \mathbf{BK})$ has stable eigenvalues $\lambda = -1$ and $\lambda = -3$.

Determining when it is possible to change the eigenvalues of the closed-loop system, and determining the appropriate control law $\mathbf{K}$ to achieve this, will be the subject of future sections.

Cruise control To appreciate the ability of closed-loop control to compensate for unmodeled dynamics and disturbances, we will consider a simple model of cruise control in an automobile. Let u be the rate of gas fed into the engine, and let y be the car's speed. Neglecting transients, a crude model[1] is:

$$y = u. \tag{8.5}$$

Thus, if we double the gas input, we double the automobile's speed.

Based on this model, we may design an open-loop cruise controller to track a reference speed w_r by simply commanding an input of $u = w_r$. However, an incorrect automobile model (i.e., in actuality $y = 2u$), or external disturbances, such as rolling hills (i.e., if $y = u + \sin(t)$), are not accounted for in the simple open-loop design.

In contrast, a closed-loop control law, based on measurements of the speed, is able to compensate for unmodeled dynamics and disturbances. Consider the closed-loop control law $u = K(w_r - y)$, so that gas is increased when the measured velocity is too low, and decreased when it is too high. Then if the dynamics are actually $y = 2u$ instead of $y = u$, the open-loop system will have 50% steady-state tracking error, while the performance of the closed-loop system can be significantly improved for large K:

$$y = 2K(w_r - y) \quad \Longrightarrow \quad (1 + 2K)y = 2Kw_r \quad \Longrightarrow \quad y = \frac{2K}{1 + 2K}w_r. \tag{8.6}$$

For $K = 50$, the closed-loop system only has 1% steady-state tracking error. Similarly, an added disturbance w_d will be attenuated by a factor of $1/(2K + 1)$.

As a concrete example, consider a reference tracking problem with a desired reference speed of 60 mph. The model is $y = u$, and the true system is $y = 0.5\,u$. In addition, there is a disturbance in the form of rolling hills that increase and decrease the speed by ± 10 mph at a frequency of 0.5 Hz. An open-loop controller is compared with a closed-loop proportional controller with $K = 50$ in Fig. 8.5 and Code 8.1. Although the closed-loop controller has significantly better performance, we will see later that a large proportional gain may come at the cost of robustness. Adding an integral term will improve performance.

---

[1] A more realistic model would have acceleration dynamics, so that $\dot{x} = -x + u$ and $y = x$.

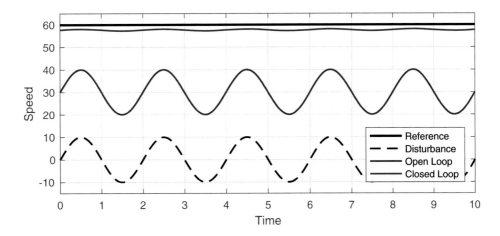

Figure 8.5 Open-loop vs. closed-loop cruise control.

Code 8.1 Compare open-loop and closed-loop cruise control.

```
clear all, close all, clc

t = 0:.01:10;            % time

wr = 60*ones(size(t));   % reference speed
d = 10*sin(pi*t);        % disturbance

aModel = 1;              % y = aModel*u
aTrue = .5;              % y = aTrue*u

uOL = wr/aModel;         % Open-loop u based on model
yOL = aTrue*uOL + d;     % Open-loop response

K = 50;                  % control gain, u=K(wr-y);
yCL = aTrue*K/(1+aTrue*K)*wr + d/(1+aTrue*K);
```

8.2   Linear Time-Invariant Systems

The most complete theory of control has been developed for linear systems [492, 165, 22]. Linear systems are generally obtained by linearizing a nonlinear system about a fixed point or a periodic orbit. However, instability may quickly take a trajectory far away from the fixed point. Fortunately, an effective stabilizing controller will keep the state of the system in a small neighborhood of the fixed point where the linear approximation is valid. For example, in the case of the inverted pendulum, feedback control may keep the pendulum stabilized in the vertical position where the dynamics behave linearly.

Linearization of Nonlinear Dynamics

Given a nonlinear input–output system

$$\frac{d}{dt}\mathbf{x} = \mathbf{f}(\mathbf{x}, \mathbf{u}) \tag{8.7a}$$

$$\mathbf{y} = \mathbf{g}(\mathbf{x}, \mathbf{u}) \qquad (8.7b)$$

it is possible to linearize the dynamics near a fixed point $(\bar{\mathbf{x}}, \bar{\mathbf{u}})$ where $\mathbf{f}(\bar{\mathbf{x}}, \bar{\mathbf{u}}) = \mathbf{0}$. For small $\Delta\mathbf{x} = \mathbf{x} - \bar{\mathbf{x}}$ and $\Delta\mathbf{u} = \mathbf{u} - \bar{\mathbf{u}}$ the dynamics $\mathbf{f}$ may be expanded in a Taylor series about the point $(\bar{\mathbf{x}}, \bar{\mathbf{u}})$:

$$\mathbf{f}(\bar{\mathbf{x}} + \Delta\mathbf{x}, \bar{\mathbf{u}} + \Delta\mathbf{u}) = \mathbf{f}(\bar{\mathbf{x}}, \bar{\mathbf{u}}) + \underbrace{\frac{d\mathbf{f}}{d\mathbf{x}}\bigg|_{(\bar{\mathbf{x}}, \bar{\mathbf{u}})}}_{\mathbf{A}} \cdot \Delta\mathbf{x} + \underbrace{\frac{d\mathbf{f}}{d\mathbf{u}}\bigg|_{(\bar{\mathbf{x}}, \bar{\mathbf{u}})}}_{\mathbf{B}} \cdot \Delta\mathbf{u} + \cdots . \qquad (8.8)$$

Similarly, the output equation $\mathbf{g}$ may be expanded as:

$$\mathbf{g}(\bar{\mathbf{x}} + \Delta\mathbf{x}, \bar{\mathbf{u}} + \Delta\mathbf{u}) = \mathbf{g}(\bar{\mathbf{x}}, \bar{\mathbf{u}}) + \underbrace{\frac{d\mathbf{g}}{d\mathbf{x}}\bigg|_{(\bar{\mathbf{x}}, \bar{\mathbf{u}})}}_{\mathbf{C}} \cdot \Delta\mathbf{x} + \underbrace{\frac{d\mathbf{g}}{d\mathbf{u}}\bigg|_{(\bar{\mathbf{x}}, \bar{\mathbf{u}})}}_{\mathbf{D}} \cdot \Delta\mathbf{u} + \cdots . \qquad (8.9)$$

For small displacements around the fixed point, the higher order terms are negligibly small. Dropping the Δ and shifting to a coordinate system where $\bar{\mathbf{x}}$, $\bar{\mathbf{u}}$, and $\bar{\mathbf{y}}$ are at the origin, the linearized dynamics may be written as:

$$\frac{d}{dt}\mathbf{x} = \mathbf{A}\mathbf{x} + \mathbf{B}\mathbf{u} \qquad (8.10a)$$

$$\mathbf{y} = \mathbf{C}\mathbf{x} + \mathbf{D}\mathbf{u}. \qquad (8.10b)$$

Note that we have neglected the disturbance and noise inputs, $\mathbf{w}_d$ and $\mathbf{w}_n$, respectively; these will be added back in the discussion on Kalman filtering in Section 8.5.

Unforced Linear System
In the absence of control (i.e., $\mathbf{u} = \mathbf{0}$), and with measurements of the full state (i.e., $\mathbf{y} = \mathbf{x}$), the dynamical system in (8.10) becomes

$$\frac{d}{dt}\mathbf{x} = \mathbf{A}\mathbf{x}. \qquad (8.11)$$

The solution $\mathbf{x}(t)$ is given by

$$\mathbf{x}(t) = e^{\mathbf{A}t}\mathbf{x}(0), \qquad (8.12)$$

where the matrix exponential is defined by:

$$e^{\mathbf{A}t} = \mathbf{I} + \mathbf{A}t + \frac{\mathbf{A}^2 t^2}{2} + \frac{\mathbf{A}^3 t^3}{3} + \cdots . \qquad (8.13)$$

The solution in (8.12) is determined entirely by the eigenvalues and eigenvectors of the matrix $\mathbf{A}$. Consider the eigendecomposition of $\mathbf{A}$:

$$\mathbf{A}\mathbf{T} = \mathbf{T}\mathbf{\Lambda}. \qquad (8.14)$$

In the simplest case, $\mathbf{\Lambda}$ is a diagonal matrix of distinct eigenvalues and $\mathbf{T}$ is a matrix whose columns are the corresponding linearly independent eigenvectors of $\mathbf{A}$. For repeated eigenvalues, $\mathbf{\Lambda}$ may be written in Jordan form, with entries above the diagonal for degenerate eigenvalues of multiplicity ≥ 2; the corresponding columns of $\mathbf{T}$ will be generalized eigenvectors.

In either case, it is easier to compute the matrix exponential $e^{\Lambda t}$ than $e^{\mathbf{A}t}$. For diagonal Λ, the matrix exponential is given by:

$$e^{\Lambda t} = \begin{bmatrix} e^{\lambda_1 t} & 0 & \cdots & 0 \\ 0 & e^{\lambda_2 t} & \cdots & 0 \\ \vdots & \vdots & \ddots & \vdots \\ 0 & 0 & \cdots & e^{\lambda_n t} \end{bmatrix}. \tag{8.15}$$

In the case of a nontrivial Jordan block in Λ with entries above the diagonal, simple extensions exist related to nilpotent matrices (for details, see Perko [427]).

Rearranging the terms in (8.14), we find that it is simple to represent powers of $\mathbf{A}$ in terms of the eigenvectors and eigenvalues:

$$\mathbf{A} = \mathbf{T}\Lambda\mathbf{T}^{-1} \tag{8.16a}$$

$$\mathbf{A}^2 = \left(\mathbf{T}\Lambda\mathbf{T}^{-1}\right)\left(\mathbf{T}\Lambda\mathbf{T}^{-1}\right) = \mathbf{T}\Lambda^2\mathbf{T}^{-1} \tag{8.16b}$$

$$\cdots$$

$$\mathbf{A}^k = \left(\mathbf{T}\Lambda\mathbf{T}^{-1}\right)\left(\mathbf{T}\Lambda\mathbf{T}^{-1}\right)\cdots\left(\mathbf{T}\Lambda\mathbf{T}^{-1}\right) = \mathbf{T}\Lambda^k\mathbf{T}^{-1}. \tag{8.16c}$$

Finally, substituting these expressions into (8.13) yields:

$$e^{\mathbf{A}t} = e^{\mathbf{T}\Lambda\mathbf{T}^{-1}t} = \mathbf{T}\mathbf{T}^{-1} + \mathbf{T}\Lambda\mathbf{T}^{-1}t + \frac{\mathbf{T}\Lambda^2\mathbf{T}^{-1}t^2}{2} + \frac{\mathbf{T}\Lambda^3\mathbf{T}^{-1}t^3}{3} + \cdots \tag{8.17a}$$

$$= \mathbf{T}\left[\mathbf{I} + \Lambda t + \frac{\Lambda^2 t^2}{2} + \frac{\Lambda^3 t^3}{3} + \cdots\right]\mathbf{T}^{-1} \tag{8.17b}$$

$$= \mathbf{T}e^{\Lambda t}\mathbf{T}^{-1}. \tag{8.17c}$$

Thus, we see that it is possible to compute the matrix exponential efficiently in terms of the eigendecomposition of $\mathbf{A}$. Moreover, the matrix of eigenvectors $\mathbf{T}$ defines a change of coordinates that dramatically simplifies the dynamics:

$$\mathbf{x} = \mathbf{T}\mathbf{z} \implies \dot{\mathbf{z}} = \mathbf{T}^{-1}\dot{\mathbf{x}} = \mathbf{T}^{-1}\mathbf{A}\mathbf{x} = \mathbf{T}^{-1}\mathbf{A}\mathbf{T}\mathbf{z} \implies \dot{\mathbf{z}} = \Lambda\mathbf{z}. \tag{8.18}$$

In other words, changing to eigenvector coordinates, the dynamics become diagonal. Combining (8.12) with (8.17c), it is possible to write the solution $\mathbf{x}(t)$ as

$$\mathbf{x}(t) = \mathbf{T}\,e^{\Lambda t}\,\underbrace{\underbrace{\mathbf{T}^{-1}\mathbf{x}(0)}_{\mathbf{z}(0)}}_{\mathbf{z}(t)}. \tag{8.19}$$

In the first step, $\mathbf{T}^{-1}$ maps the initial condition in physical coordinates, $\mathbf{x}(0)$, into eigenvector coordinates, $\mathbf{z}(0)$. The next step advances these initial conditions using the diagonal update $e^{\Lambda t}$, which is considerably simpler in eigenvector coordinates $\mathbf{z}$. Finally, multiplying by $\mathbf{T}$ maps $\mathbf{z}(t)$ back to physical coordinates, $\mathbf{x}(t)$.

In addition to making it possible to compute the matrix exponential, and hence the solution $\mathbf{x}(t)$, the eigendecomposition of $\mathbf{A}$ is even more useful to understand the dynamics and stability of the system. We see from (8.19) that the only time-varying portion of the solution is $e^{\Lambda t}$. In general, these eigenvalues $\lambda = a + ib$ may be complex numbers, so that the solutions are given by $e^{\lambda t} = e^{at} (\cos(bt) + i \sin(bt))$. Thus, if all of the eigenvalues λ_k have negative real part (i.e., $\text{Re}(\lambda) = a < 0$), then the system is stable, and solutions all decay to $\mathbf{x} = \mathbf{0}$ as $t \to \infty$. However, if even a single eigenvalue has positive real part, then the system is unstable and will diverge from the fixed point along the corresponding unstable eigenvector direction. Any random initial condition is likely to have a component in this unstable direction, and moreover, disturbances will likely excite all eigenvectors of the system.

Forced Linear System

With forcing, and for zero initial condition, $\mathbf{x}(0) = \mathbf{0}$, the solution to (8.10a) is

$$\mathbf{x}(t) = \int_0^t e^{\mathbf{A}(t-\tau)} \mathbf{B} \mathbf{u}(\tau) d\tau \triangleq e^{\mathbf{A}t} \mathbf{B} * \mathbf{u}(t). \tag{8.20}$$

The control input $\mathbf{u}(t)$ is convolved with the kernel $e^{\mathbf{A}t}\mathbf{B}$. With an output $\mathbf{y} = \mathbf{Cx}$, we have $\mathbf{y}(t) = \mathbf{C}e^{\mathbf{A}t}\mathbf{B} * \mathbf{u}(t)$. This convolution is illustrated in Fig. 8.6 for a single-input, single-output (SISO) system in terms of the impulse response $g(t) = \mathbf{C}e^{\mathbf{A}t}\mathbf{B} = \int_0^t \mathbf{C}e^{\mathbf{A}(t-\tau)}\mathbf{B}\delta(\tau) d\tau$ given a Dirac delta input $u(t) = \delta(t)$.

Discrete-Time Systems

In many real-world applications, systems are sampled at discrete instances in time. Thus, digital control systems are typically formulated in terms of discrete-time dynamical systems:

$$\mathbf{x}_{k+1} = \mathbf{A}_d \mathbf{x}_k + \mathbf{B}_d \mathbf{u}_k \tag{8.21a}$$

$$\mathbf{y}_k = \mathbf{C}_d \mathbf{x}_k + \mathbf{D}_d \mathbf{u}_k, \tag{8.21b}$$

where $\mathbf{x}_k = \mathbf{x}(k\Delta t)$. The system matrices in (8.21) can be obtained from the continuous-time system in (8.10) as

$$\mathbf{A}_d = e^{\mathbf{A}\Delta t} \tag{8.22a}$$

$$\mathbf{B}_d = \int_0^{\Delta t} e^{\mathbf{A}\tau} \mathbf{B} \, d\tau \tag{8.22b}$$

$$\mathbf{C}_d = \mathbf{C} \tag{8.22c}$$

$$\mathbf{D}_d = \mathbf{D}. \tag{8.22d}$$

The stability of the discrete-time system in (8.21) is still determined by the eigenvalues of $\mathbf{A}_d$, although now a system is stable if and only if all discrete-time eigenvalues are inside the unit circle in the complex plane. Thus, $\exp(\mathbf{A}\Delta t)$ defines a conformal mapping on the complex plane from continuous-time to discrete-time, where eigenvalues in the left-half plane map to eigenvalues inside the unit circle.

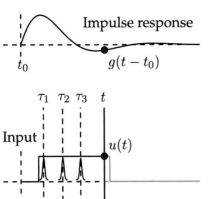

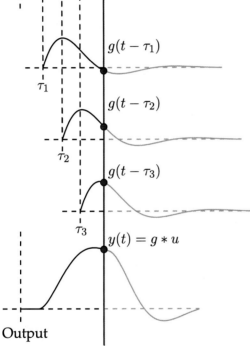

Figure 8.6 Convolution for a single-input, single-output (SISO) system.

Example: Inverted Pendulum

Consider the inverted pendulum in Fig. 8.8 with a torque input u at the base. The equation of motion, derived using the Euler–Lagrange equations[2], is:

$$\ddot{\theta} = -\frac{g}{L}\sin(\theta) + u. \tag{8.23}$$

Introducing the state $\mathbf{x}$, given by the angular position and velocity, we can write this second order differential equation as a system of first order equations:

$$\mathbf{x} = \begin{bmatrix} x_1 \\ x_2 \end{bmatrix} = \begin{bmatrix} \theta \\ \dot{\theta} \end{bmatrix} \quad \Longrightarrow \quad \frac{d}{dt}\begin{bmatrix} x_1 \\ x_2 \end{bmatrix} = \begin{bmatrix} x_2 \\ -\frac{g}{L}\sin(x_1) + u \end{bmatrix}. \tag{8.24}$$

---

[2] The Lagrangian is $\mathcal{L} = \frac{m}{2}L^2\dot{\theta}^2 - mgL\cos(\theta)$, and the Euler–Lagrange equation is $\frac{d}{dt}\partial\mathcal{L}/\partial\dot{\theta} - \partial\mathcal{L}/\partial\theta = \tau$, where τ is the input torque.

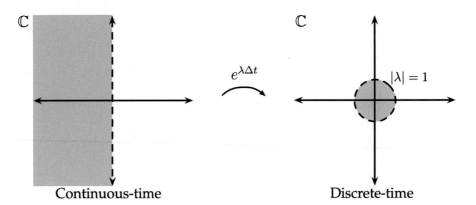

Figure 8.7 The matrix exponential defines a conformal map on the complex plane, mapping stable eigenvalues in the left half plane into eigenvalues inside the unit circle.

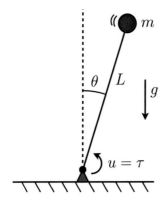

Figure 8.8 Schematic of inverted pendulum system.

Taking the Jacobian of $\mathbf{f}(\mathbf{x}, \mathbf{u})$ yields

$$\frac{\mathbf{df}}{\mathbf{dx}} = \begin{bmatrix} 0 & 1 \\ -\frac{g}{L}\cos(x_1) & 0 \end{bmatrix}, \qquad \frac{\mathbf{df}}{\mathbf{du}} = \begin{bmatrix} 0 \\ 1 \end{bmatrix}. \tag{8.25}$$

Linearizing at the pendulum up ($x_1 = \pi$, $x_2 = 0$) and down ($x_1 = 0$, $x_2 = 0$) equilibria gives

$$\underbrace{\frac{d}{dt}\begin{bmatrix} x_1 \\ x_2 \end{bmatrix} = \begin{bmatrix} 0 & 1 \\ \frac{g}{L} & 0 \end{bmatrix}\begin{bmatrix} x_1 \\ x_2 \end{bmatrix} + \begin{bmatrix} 0 \\ 1 \end{bmatrix}u}_{\text{Pendulum up,}\quad \lambda = \pm\sqrt{g/L}} \qquad \underbrace{\frac{d}{dt}\begin{bmatrix} x_1 \\ x_2 \end{bmatrix} = \begin{bmatrix} 0 & 1 \\ -\frac{g}{L} & 0 \end{bmatrix}\begin{bmatrix} x_1 \\ x_2 \end{bmatrix} + \begin{bmatrix} 0 \\ 1 \end{bmatrix}u}_{\text{Pendulum down,}\quad \lambda = \pm i\sqrt{g/L}}.$$

Thus, we see that the down position is a stable center with eigenvalues $\lambda = \pm i\sqrt{g/L}$ corresponding to oscillations at a natural frequency of $\sqrt{g/L}$. The pendulum up position is an unstable saddle with eigenvalues $\lambda = \pm\sqrt{g/L}$.

8.3   Controllability and Observability

A natural question arises in linear control theory: To what extent can closed-loop feedback $\mathbf{u} = -\mathbf{Kx}$ manipulate the behavior of the system in (8.10a)? We already saw in Section 8.1 that it was possible to modify the eigenvalues of the unstable inverted pendulum system via closed-loop feedback, resulting in a new system matrix $(\mathbf{A} - \mathbf{BK})$ with stable eigenvalues. This section will provide concrete conditions on when and how the system dynamics may be manipulated through feedback control. The dual question, of when it is possible to estimate the full state $\mathbf{x}$ from measurements $\mathbf{y}$, will also be addressed.

Controllability

The ability to design the eigenvalues of the closed-loop system with the choice of $\mathbf{K}$ relies on the system in (8.10a) being *controllable*. The controllability of a linear system is determined entirely by the column space of the *controllability* matrix $\mathcal{C}$:

$$\mathcal{C} = \begin{bmatrix} \mathbf{B} & \mathbf{AB} & \mathbf{A}^2\mathbf{B} & \cdots & \mathbf{A}^{n-1}\mathbf{B} \end{bmatrix}. \tag{8.26}$$

If the matrix $\mathcal{C}$ has n linearly independent columns, so that it spans all of $\mathbb{R}^n$, then the system in (8.10a) is controllable. The span of the columns of the controllability matrix $\mathcal{C}$ forms a Krylov subspace that determines which state vector directions in $\mathbb{R}^n$ may be manipulated with control. Thus, in addition to controllability implying arbitrary eigenvalue placement, it also implies that any state $\boldsymbol{\xi} \in \mathbb{R}^n$ is reachable in a finite time with some actuation signal $\mathbf{u}(t)$.

The following three conditions are equivalent:

1.   *Controllability.* The span of $\mathcal{C}$ is $\mathbb{R}^n$. The matrix $\mathcal{C}$ may be generated by

     ```
     >> ctrb(A,B)
     ```

     and the rank may be tested to see if it is equal to n, by

     ```
     >> rank(ctrb(A,B))
     ```

2.   *Arbitrary eigenvalue placement.* It is possible to design the eigenvalues of the closed-loop system through choice of feedback $\mathbf{u} = -\mathbf{Kx}$:

     $$\frac{d}{dt}\mathbf{x} = \mathbf{Ax} + \mathbf{Bu} = (\mathbf{A} - \mathbf{BK})\,\mathbf{x}. \tag{8.27}$$

     Given a set of desired eigenvalues, the gain $\mathbf{K}$ can be determined by

     ```
     >> K = place(A,B,neweigs);
     ```

     Designing $\mathbf{K}$ for the best performance will be discussed in Section 8.4.

3.   *Reachability of* $\mathbb{R}^n$. It is possible to steer the system to any arbitrary state $\mathbf{x}(t) = \boldsymbol{\xi} \in \mathbb{R}^n$ in a finite time with some actuation signal $\mathbf{u}(t)$.

Note that reachability also applies to open-loop systems. In particular, if a direction $\boldsymbol{\xi}$ is not in the span of $\mathcal{C}$, then it is impossible for control to push in this direction in either open-loop or closed-loop.

Examples The notion of controllability is more easily understood by investigating a few simple examples. First, consider the following system

$$\frac{d}{dt}\begin{bmatrix} x_1 \\ x_2 \end{bmatrix} = \begin{bmatrix} 1 & 0 \\ 0 & 2 \end{bmatrix}\begin{bmatrix} x_1 \\ x_2 \end{bmatrix} + \begin{bmatrix} 0 \\ 1 \end{bmatrix}u \quad \Longrightarrow \quad \mathcal{C} = \begin{bmatrix} 0 & 0 \\ 1 & 2 \end{bmatrix}. \qquad (8.28)$$

This system is not controllable, because the controllability matrix $\mathcal{C}$ consists of two linearly dependent vectors and does not span $\mathbb{R}^2$. Even before checking the rank of the controllability matrix, it is easy to see that the system won't be controllable since the states x_1 and x_2 are completely decoupled and the actuation input u only effects the second state.

Modifying this example to include two actuation inputs makes the system controllable by increasing the control authority:

$$\frac{d}{dt}\begin{bmatrix} x_1 \\ x_2 \end{bmatrix} = \begin{bmatrix} 1 & 0 \\ 0 & 2 \end{bmatrix}\begin{bmatrix} x_1 \\ x_2 \end{bmatrix} + \begin{bmatrix} 1 & 0 \\ 0 & 1 \end{bmatrix}\begin{bmatrix} u_1 \\ u_2 \end{bmatrix} \quad \Longrightarrow \quad \mathcal{C} = \begin{bmatrix} 1 & 0 & 1 & 0 \\ 0 & 1 & 0 & 2 \end{bmatrix}. \qquad (8.29)$$

This *fully actuated* system is clearly controllable because x_1 and x_2 may be independently controlled with u_1 and u_2. The controllability of this system is confirmed by checking that the columns of $\mathcal{C}$ do span $\mathbb{R}^2$.

The most interesting cases are less obvious than these two examples. Consider the system

$$\frac{d}{dt}\begin{bmatrix} x_1 \\ x_2 \end{bmatrix} = \begin{bmatrix} 1 & 1 \\ 0 & 2 \end{bmatrix}\begin{bmatrix} x_1 \\ x_2 \end{bmatrix} + \begin{bmatrix} 0 \\ 1 \end{bmatrix}u \quad \Longrightarrow \quad \mathcal{C} = \begin{bmatrix} 0 & 1 \\ 1 & 2 \end{bmatrix}. \qquad (8.30)$$

This two-state system is controllable with a single actuation input because the states x_1 and x_2 are now coupled through the dynamics. Similarly,

$$\frac{d}{dt}\begin{bmatrix} x_1 \\ x_2 \end{bmatrix} = \begin{bmatrix} 1 & 0 \\ 0 & 2 \end{bmatrix}\begin{bmatrix} x_1 \\ x_2 \end{bmatrix} + \begin{bmatrix} 1 \\ 1 \end{bmatrix}u \quad \Longrightarrow \quad \mathcal{C} = \begin{bmatrix} 1 & 1 \\ 1 & 2 \end{bmatrix}. \qquad (8.31)$$

is controllable even though the dynamics of x_1 and x_2 are decoupled, because the actuator $\mathbf{B} = \begin{bmatrix} 1 & 1 \end{bmatrix}^T$ is able to simultaneously affect both states and they have different timescales.

We will see in Section 8.3 that controllability is intimately related to the alignment of the columns of $\mathbf{B}$ with the eigenvector directions of $\mathbf{A}$.

Observability

Mathematically, observability of the system in (8.10) is nearly identical to controllability, although the physical interpretation differs somewhat. A system is *observable* if it is possible to estimate any state $\boldsymbol{\xi} \in \mathbb{R}^n$ from a time-history of the measurements $\mathbf{y}(t)$.

Again, the observability of a system is entirely determined by the row space of the *observability* matrix $\mathcal{O}$:

$$\mathcal{O} = \begin{bmatrix} \mathbf{C} \\ \mathbf{CA} \\ \mathbf{CA}^2 \\ \vdots \\ \mathbf{CA}^{n-1} \end{bmatrix}. \qquad (8.32)$$

In particular, if the rows of the matrix $\mathcal{O}$ span $\mathbb{R}^n$, then it is possible to estimate any full-dimensional state $\mathbf{x} \in \mathbb{R}^n$ from the time-history of $\mathbf{y}(t)$. The matrix $\mathcal{O}$ may be generated by

```
|| >> obsv(A,C);
```

The motivation for full-state estimation is relatively straightforward. We have already seen that with full-state feedback, $\mathbf{u} = -\mathbf{Kx}$, it is possible to modify the behavior of a controllable system. However, if full-state measurements of $\mathbf{x}$ are not available, it is necessary to *estimate* $\mathbf{x}$ from the measurements. This is possible when the system is observable. In Section 8.5, we will see that it is possible to design an observer dynamical system to estimate the full-state from noisy measurements. As in the case of a controllable system, if a system is observable, it is possible to design the eigenvalues of the estimator dynamical system to have desirable characteristics, such as fast estimation and effective noise attenuation.

Interestingly, the observability criterion is mathematically the dual of the controllability criterion. In fact, the observability matrix is the transpose of the controllability matrix for the pair $(\mathbf{A}^T, \mathbf{C}^T)$:

```
|| >> O = ctrb(A',C')';  % 'obsv' is dual of 'crtb'
```

The PBH Test for Controllability

There are many tests to determine whether or not a system is controllable. One of the most useful and illuminating is the Popov–Belevitch–Hautus (PBH) test. The PBH test states that the pair $(\mathbf{A}, \mathbf{B})$ is controllable if and only if the column rank of the matrix $\begin{bmatrix} (\mathbf{A} - \lambda\mathbf{I}) & \mathbf{B} \end{bmatrix}$ is equal to n for all $\lambda \in \mathbb{C}$. This test is particularly fascinating because it connects controllability[3] to a relationship between the columns of $\mathbf{B}$ and the eigenspace of $\mathbf{A}$.

First, the PBH test only needs to be checked at λ that are eigenvalues of $\mathbf{A}$, since the rank of $\mathbf{A} - \lambda\mathbf{I}$ is equal to n except when λ is an eigenvalue of $\mathbf{A}$. In fact, the characteristic equation $\det(\mathbf{A} - \lambda\mathbf{I}) = 0$ is used to determine the eigenvalues of $\mathbf{A}$ as exactly those values where the matrix $\mathbf{A} - \lambda\mathbf{I}$ becomes rank deficient, or degenerate.

Now, given that $(\mathbf{A} - \lambda\mathbf{I})$ is only rank deficient for eigenvalues λ, it also follows that the null-space, or kernel, of $\mathbf{A} - \lambda\mathbf{I}$ is given by the span of the eigenvectors corresponding to that particular eigenvalue. Thus, for $\begin{bmatrix} (\mathbf{A} - \lambda\mathbf{I}) & \mathbf{B} \end{bmatrix}$ to have rank n, the columns in $\mathbf{B}$ must have some component in each of the eigenvector directions associated with $\mathbf{A}$ to complement the null-space of $\mathbf{A} - \lambda\mathbf{I}$.

If $\mathbf{A}$ has n distinct eigenvalues, then the system will be controllable with a single actuation input, since the matrix $\mathbf{A} - \lambda\mathbf{I}$ will have at most one eigenvector direction in the null-space. In particular, we may choose $\mathbf{B}$ as the sum of all of the n linearly independent eigenvectors, and it will be guaranteed to have some component in each direction. It is also interesting to note that if $\mathbf{B}$ is a random vector ($>>$**B=randn(n,1);**), then $(\mathbf{A}, \mathbf{B})$ will be controllable with high probability, since it will be exceedingly unlikely that $\mathbf{B}$ will be randomly chosen so that it has zero contribution from any given eigenvector.

If there are degenerate eigenvalues with multiplicity ≥ 2, so that the null-space of $\mathbf{A} - \lambda\mathbf{I}$ is multidimensional, then the actuation input must have as many degrees of freedom. In other words, the only time that multiple actuators (columns of $\mathbf{B}$) are strictly required is for

---

[3] There is an equivalent PBH test for observability that states that $\begin{bmatrix} (\mathbf{A} - \lambda\mathbf{I}) \\ \mathbf{C} \end{bmatrix}$ must have row rank n for all $\lambda \in \mathbb{C}$ for the system to be observable.

systems that have degenerate eigenvalues. However, if a system is highly nonnormal, it may helpful to have multiple actuators in practice for better control authority. Such nonnormal systems are characterized by large transient growth due to destructive interference between nearly parallel eigenvectors, often with similar eigenvalues.

The Cayley–Hamilton Theorem and Reachability

To provide insight into the relationship between the controllability of the pair $(\mathbf{A}, \mathbf{B})$ and the reachability of any vector $\boldsymbol{\xi} \in \mathbb{R}^n$ via the actuation input $\mathbf{u}(t)$, we will leverage the Cayley–Hamilton theorem. This is a gem of linear algebra that provides an elegant way to represent solutions of $\dot{\mathbf{x}} = \mathbf{A}\mathbf{x}$ in terms of a finite sum of powers of $\mathbf{A}$, rather than the infinite sum required for the matrix exponential in (8.13).

The Cayley–Hamilton theorem states that every matrix $\mathbf{A}$ satisfies its own characteristic (eigenvalue) equation, $\det(\mathbf{A} - \lambda\mathbf{I}) = 0$:

$$\det(\mathbf{A} - \lambda\mathbf{I}) = \lambda^n + a_{n-1}\lambda^{n-1} + \cdots + a_2\lambda^2 + a_1\lambda + a_0 = 0 \tag{8.33a}$$

$$\implies \quad \mathbf{A}^n + a_{n-1}\mathbf{A}^{n-1} + \cdots + a_2\mathbf{A}^2 + a_1\mathbf{A} + a_0\mathbf{I} = \mathbf{0}. \tag{8.33b}$$

Although this is relatively simple to state, it has profound consequences. In particular, it is possible to express $\mathbf{A}^n$ as a linear combination of smaller powers of $\mathbf{A}$:

$$\mathbf{A}^n = -a_0\mathbf{I} - a_1\mathbf{A} - a_2\mathbf{A}^2 - \cdots - a_{n-1}\mathbf{A}^{n-1}. \tag{8.34}$$

It is straightforward to see that this also implies that any higher power $\mathbf{A}^{k \geq n}$ may also be expressed as a sum of the matrices $\{\mathbf{I}, \mathbf{A}, \cdots, \mathbf{A}^{n-1}\}$:

$$\mathbf{A}^{k \geq n} = \sum_{j=0}^{n-1} \alpha_j \mathbf{A}^j. \tag{8.35}$$

Thus, it is possible to express the infinite sum in the exponential $e^{\mathbf{A}t}$ as:

$$e^{\mathbf{A}t} = \mathbf{I} + \mathbf{A}t + \frac{\mathbf{A}^2 t^2}{2} + \cdots \tag{8.36a}$$

$$= \beta_0(t)\mathbf{I} + \beta_1(t)\mathbf{A} + \beta_2(t)\mathbf{A}^2 + \cdots + \beta_{n-1}(t)\mathbf{A}^{n-1}. \tag{8.36b}$$

We are now equipped to see how controllability relates to the reachability of an arbitrary vector $\boldsymbol{\xi} \in \mathbb{R}^n$. From (8.20), we see that a state $\boldsymbol{\xi}$ is reachable if there is some $\mathbf{u}(t)$ so that:

$$\boldsymbol{\xi} = \int_0^t e^{\mathbf{A}(t-\tau)}\mathbf{B}\mathbf{u}(\tau)\, d\tau. \tag{8.37}$$

Expanding the exponential in the right hand side in terms of (8.36b), we have:

$$\boldsymbol{\xi} = \int_0^t [\beta_0(t-\tau)\mathbf{I}\mathbf{B}\mathbf{u}(\tau) + \beta_1(t-\tau)\mathbf{A}\mathbf{B}\mathbf{u}(\tau) + \cdots$$

$$\cdots + \beta_{n-1}(t-\tau)\mathbf{A}^{n-1}\mathbf{B}\mathbf{u}(\tau)]d\tau$$

$$= \mathbf{B}\int_0^t \beta_0(t-\tau)\mathbf{u}(\tau)\, d\tau + \mathbf{A}\mathbf{B}\int_0^t \beta_1(t-\tau)\mathbf{u}(\tau)\, d\tau + \cdots$$

$$\cdots + \mathbf{A}^{n-1}\mathbf{B}\int_0^t \beta_{n-1}(t-\tau)\mathbf{u}(\tau)\, d\tau$$

$$
= \begin{bmatrix} \mathbf{B} & \mathbf{AB} & \cdots & \mathbf{A}^{n-1}\mathbf{B} \end{bmatrix}
\begin{bmatrix}
\int_0^t \beta_0(t-\tau)\mathbf{u}(\tau)\,d\tau \\
\int_0^t \beta_1(t-\tau)\mathbf{u}(\tau)\,d\tau \\
\vdots \\
\int_0^t \beta_{n-1}(t-\tau)\mathbf{u}(\tau)\,d\tau
\end{bmatrix}.
$$

Note that the matrix on the left is the controllability matrix $\mathcal{C}$, and we see that the only way that all of $\mathbb{R}^n$ is reachable is if the column space of $\mathcal{C}$ spans all of $\mathbb{R}^n$. It is somewhat more difficult to see that if $\mathcal{C}$ has rank n then it is possible to design a $\mathbf{u}(t)$ to reach any arbitrary state $\boldsymbol{\xi} \in \mathbb{R}^n$, but this relies on the fact that the n functions $\{\beta_j(t)\}_{j=0}^{n-1}$ are linearly independent functions. It is also the case that there is not a *unique* actuation input $\mathbf{u}(t)$ to reach a given state $\boldsymbol{\xi}$, as there are many different paths one may take.

Gramians and Degrees of Controllability/Observability

The previous tests for controllability and observability are binary, in the sense that the rank of $\mathcal{C}$ (resp. $\mathcal{O}$) is either n, or it isn't. However, there are *degrees* of controllability and observability, as some states $\mathbf{x}$ may be easier to control or estimate than others.

To identify which states are more or less controllable, one must analyze the eigendecomposition of the controllability Gramian:

$$
\mathbf{W}_c(t) = \int_0^t e^{\mathbf{A}\tau}\mathbf{B}\mathbf{B}^* e^{\mathbf{A}^*\tau}\,d\tau. \tag{8.38}
$$

Similarly, the observability Gramian is given by:

$$
\mathbf{W}_o(t) = \int_0^t e^{\mathbf{A}^*\tau}\mathbf{C}^*\mathbf{C} e^{\mathbf{A}\tau}\,d\tau. \tag{8.39}
$$

These Gramians are often evaluated at infinite time, and unless otherwise stated, we refer to $\mathbf{W}_c = \lim_{t\to\infty}\mathbf{W}_c(t)$ and $\mathbf{W}_o = \lim_{t\to\infty}\mathbf{W}_o(t)$.

The controllability of a state $\mathbf{x}$ is measured by $\mathbf{x}^*\mathbf{W}_c\mathbf{x}$, which will be larger for more controllable states. If the value of $\mathbf{x}^*\mathbf{W}_c\mathbf{x}$ is large, then it is possible to navigate the system far in the $\mathbf{x}$ direction with a unit control input. The observability of a state is similarly measured by $\mathbf{x}^*\mathbf{W}_o\mathbf{x}$. Both Gramians are symmetric and positive semi-definite, having nonnegative eigenvalues. Thus, the eigenvalues and eigenvectors may be ordered hierarchically, with eigenvectors corresponding to large eigenvalues being more easily controllable or observable. In this way, the Gramians induce a new inner-product over state-space in terms of the controllability or observability of the states.

Gramians may be visualized by ellipsoids in state-space, with the principal axes given by directions that are hierarchically ordered in terms of controllability or observability. An example of this visualization is shown in Fig. 9.2 in Chapter 9. In fact, Gramians may be used to design reduced-order models for high-dimensional systems. Through a balancing transformation, a key subspace is identified with the most jointly controllable and observable modes. These modes then define a good projection basis to define a model that captures the dominant input–output dynamics. This form of balanced model reduction will be investigated further in Section 9.2.

Gramians are also useful to determine the minimum-energy control $\mathbf{u}(t)$ required to navigate the system to $\mathbf{x}(t_f)$ at time t_f from $\mathbf{x}(0) = \mathbf{0}$:

$$\mathbf{u}(t) = \mathbf{B}^* \left(e^{\mathbf{A}(t_f - t)} \right)^* \mathbf{W}_c(t_f)^{-1} \mathbf{x}(t_f). \tag{8.40}$$

The total energy expended by this control law is given by

$$\int_0^{t_f} \|\mathbf{u}(\tau)\|^2 \, d\tau = \mathbf{x}^* \mathbf{W}_c(t_f)^{-1} \mathbf{x}. \tag{8.41}$$

It can now be seen that if the controllability matrix is nearly singular, then there are directions that require extreme actuation energy to manipulate. Conversely, if the eigenvalues of $\mathbf{W}_c$ are all large, then the system is easily controlled.

It is generally impractical to compute the Gramians directly using (8.38) and (8.39). Instead, the controllablity Gramian is the solution to the following Lyapunov equation:

$$\mathbf{A}\mathbf{W}_c + \mathbf{W}_c \mathbf{A}^* + \mathbf{B}\mathbf{B}^* = \mathbf{0}, \tag{8.42}$$

while the observability Gramian is the solution to

$$\mathbf{A}^* \mathbf{W}_o + \mathbf{W}_o \mathbf{A} + \mathbf{C}^* \mathbf{C} = \mathbf{0}. \tag{8.43}$$

Obtaining Gramians by solving a Lyapunov equation is typically quite expensive for high-dimensional systems [213, 231, 496, 489, 55]. Instead, Gramians are often approximated empirically using snapshot data from the direct and adjoint systems, as will be discussed in Section 9.2.

Stabilizability and Detectability

In practice, full-state controllability and observability may be too much to expect in high-dimensional systems. For example, in a high-dimensional fluid system, it may be unrealistic to manipulate every minor fluid vortex; instead control authority over the large, energy-containing coherent structures is often enough.

Stabilizability refers to the ability to control all unstable eigenvector directions of $\mathbf{A}$, so that they are in the span of $\mathcal{C}$. In practice, we might relax this definition to include lightly damped eigenvector modes, corresponding to eigenvalues with a small, negative real part. Similarly, if all unstable eigenvectors of $\mathbf{A}$ are in the span of $\mathcal{O}^*$, then the system is detectable.

There may also be states in the model description that are superfluous for control. As an example, consider the control system for a commercial passenger jet. The state of the system may include the passenger seat positions, although this will surely not be controllable by the pilot, nor should it be.

8.4   Optimal Full-State Control: Linear Quadratic Regulator (LQR)

We have seen in the previous sections that if $(\mathbf{A}, \mathbf{B})$ is controllable, then it is possible to arbitrarily manipulate the eigenvalues of the closed-loop system $(\mathbf{A} - \mathbf{B}\mathbf{K})$ through choice of a full-state feedback control law $\mathbf{u} = -\mathbf{K}\mathbf{x}$. This implicitly assumes that full-state measurements are available (i.e., $\mathbf{C} = \mathbf{I}$ and $\mathbf{D} = \mathbf{0}$, so that $\mathbf{y} = \mathbf{x}$). Although full-state measurements are not always available, especially for high-dimensional systems, we will show in the next section that if the system is observable, it is possible to build a full-state estimate from the sensor measurements.

Given a controllable system, and either measurements of the full-state or an observable system with a full-state estimate, there are many choices of stabilizing control laws $\mathbf{u} = -\mathbf{Kx}$. It is possible to make the eigenvalues of the closed-loop system $(\mathbf{A} - \mathbf{BK})$ arbitrarily stable, placing them as far as desired in the left-half of the complex plane. However, overly stable eigenvalues may require exceedingly expensive control expenditure and might also result in actuation signals that exceed maximum allowable values. Choosing very stable eigenvalues may also cause the control system to over-react to noise and disturbances, much as a new driver will over-react to vibrations in the steering wheel, causing the closed-loop system to jitter. Over stabilization can counterintuitively degrade robustness and may lead to instability if there are small time delays or unmodeled dynamics. Robustness will be discussed in Section 8.8.

Choosing the best gain matrix $\mathbf{K}$ to stabilize the system without expending too much control effort is an important goal in *optimal* control. A balance must be struck between the stability of the closed-loop system and the aggressiveness of control. It is important to take control expenditure into account 1) to prevent the controller from over-reacting to high-frequency noise and disturbances, 2) so that actuation does not exceed maximum allowed amplitudes, and 3) so that control is not prohibitively expensive. In particular, the cost function

$$J(t) = \int_0^t \mathbf{x}(\tau)^*\mathbf{Q}\mathbf{x}(\tau) + \mathbf{u}(\tau)^*\mathbf{R}\mathbf{u}(\tau)\,d\tau \tag{8.44}$$

balances the cost of effective regulation of the state with the cost of control. The matrices $\mathbf{Q}$ and $\mathbf{R}$ weight the cost of deviations of the state from zero and the cost of actuation, respectively. The matrix $\mathbf{Q}$ is positive semi-definite, and $\mathbf{R}$ is positive definite; these matrices are often diagonal, and the diagonal elements may be tuned to change the relative importance of the control objectives.

Adding such a cost function makes choosing the control law a well-posed optimization problem, for which there is a wealth of theoretical and numerical techniques [74]. The linear-quadratic-regulator (LQR) control law $\mathbf{u} = -\mathbf{K}_r\mathbf{x}$ is designed to minimize $J = \lim_{t\to\infty} J(t)$. LQR is so-named because it is a linear control law, designed for a linear system, minimizing a quadratic cost function, that regulates the state of the system to $\lim_{t\to\infty} \mathbf{x}(t) = \mathbf{0}$. Because the cost-function in (8.44) is quadratic, there is an analytical solution for the optimal controller gains $\mathbf{K}_r$, given by

$$\mathbf{K}_r = \mathbf{R}^{-1}\mathbf{B}^*\mathbf{X}, \tag{8.45}$$

where $\mathbf{X}$ is the solution to an algebraic Riccati equation:

$$\mathbf{A}^*\mathbf{X} + \mathbf{X}\mathbf{A} - \mathbf{X}\mathbf{B}\mathbf{R}^{-1}\mathbf{B}^*\mathbf{X} + \mathbf{Q} = \mathbf{0}. \tag{8.46}$$

Solving the above Riccati equation for $\mathbf{X}$, and hence for $\mathbf{K}_r$, is numerically robust and already implemented in many programming languages [323, 55]. In Matlab, $\mathbf{K}_r$ is obtained via

```
>> Kr = lqr(A,B,Q,R);
```

However, solving the Riccati equation scales as $\mathcal{O}(n^3)$ in the state-dimension n, making it prohibitively expensive for large systems or for online computations for slowly changing

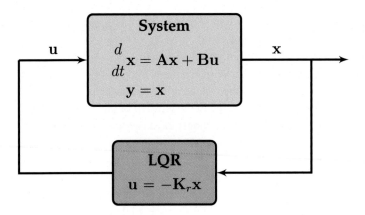

Figure 8.9 Schematic of the linear quadratic regulator (LQR) for optimal full-state feedback. The optimal controller for a linear system given measurements of the full state, $\mathbf{y} = \mathbf{x}$, is given by proportional control $\mathbf{u} = -\mathbf{K}_r\mathbf{x}$ where $\mathbf{K}_r$ is a constant gain matrix obtained by solving an algebraic Riccati equation.

state equations or linear parameter varying (LPV) control. This motivates the development of reduced-order models that capture the same dominant behavior with many fewer states. Control-oriented reduced-order models will be developed more in Chapter 9.

The LQR controller is shown schematically in Fig. 8.9. Out of all possible control laws $\mathbf{u} = \mathbf{K}(\mathbf{x})$, including nonlinear controllers, the LQR controller $\mathbf{u} = -\mathbf{K}_r\mathbf{x}$ is optimal, as we will show in Section 8.4. However, it may be the case that a linearized system is linearly uncontrollable while the full nonlinear system in (8.7) is controllable with a nonlinear control law $\mathbf{u} = \mathbf{K}(\mathbf{x})$.

Derivation of the Riccati Equation for Optimal Control

It is worth taking a theoretical detour here to derive the Riccati equation in (8.46) for the problem of optimal full-state regulation. This derivation will provide an example of how to solve convex optimization problems using the calculus of variations, and it will also provide a template for computing the optimal control solution for *nonlinear* systems. Because of the similarity of optimal control to the formulation of Lagrangian and Hamiltonian classical mechanics in terms of the variational principal, we adopt similar language and notation.

First, we will add a terminal cost to our LQR cost function in (8.44), and also introduce a factor of $1/2$ to simplify computations:

$$J = \int_0^{t_f} \underbrace{\frac{1}{2}\left(\mathbf{x}^*\mathbf{Q}\mathbf{x} + \mathbf{u}^*\mathbf{R}\mathbf{u}\right)}_{\text{Lagrangian, } \mathcal{L}} d\tau + \underbrace{\frac{1}{2}\mathbf{x}(t_f)^*\mathbf{Q}_f\mathbf{x}(t_f)}_{\text{Terminal cost}}. \tag{8.47}$$

The goal is to minimize the quadratic cost function J subject to the dynamical constraint:

$$\dot{\mathbf{x}} = \mathbf{Ax} + \mathbf{Bu}. \tag{8.48}$$

We may solve this using the calculus of variations by introducing the following augmented cost function

$$J_{\text{aug}} = \int_0^{t_f} \left[\frac{1}{2} \left(\mathbf{x}^* \mathbf{Q} \mathbf{x} + \mathbf{u}^* \mathbf{R} \mathbf{u} \right) + \boldsymbol{\lambda}^* \left(\mathbf{A}\mathbf{x} + \mathbf{B}\mathbf{u} - \dot{\mathbf{x}} \right) \right] d\tau + \frac{1}{2}\mathbf{x}(t_f)^* \mathbf{Q}_f \mathbf{x}(t_f). \quad (8.49)$$

The variable $\boldsymbol{\lambda}$ is a Lagrange multiplier, called the *co-state*, that enforces the dynamic constraints. $\boldsymbol{\lambda}$ may take any value and $J_{\text{aug}} = J$ will hold.

Taking the total variation of J_{aug} in (8.49) yields:

$$\delta J_{\text{aug}} = \int_0^{t_f} \left[\frac{\partial \mathcal{L}}{\partial \mathbf{x}} \delta \mathbf{x} + \frac{\partial \mathcal{L}}{\partial \mathbf{u}} \delta \mathbf{u} + \boldsymbol{\lambda}^* \mathbf{A} \delta \mathbf{x} + \boldsymbol{\lambda}^* \mathbf{B} \delta \mathbf{u} - \boldsymbol{\lambda}^* \delta \dot{\mathbf{x}} \right] d\tau + \mathbf{Q}_f \mathbf{x}(t_f) \delta \mathbf{x}(t_f). \quad (8.50)$$

The partial derivatives[4] of the Lagrangian are $\partial \mathcal{L}/\partial \mathbf{x} = \mathbf{x}^* \mathbf{Q}$ and $\partial \mathcal{L}/\partial \mathbf{u} = \mathbf{u}^* \mathbf{R}$. The last term in the integral may be modified using integration by parts:

$$-\int_0^{t_f} \boldsymbol{\lambda}^* \delta \dot{\mathbf{x}} \, d\tau = -\boldsymbol{\lambda}^*(t_f) \delta \mathbf{x}(t_f) + \boldsymbol{\lambda}^*(0) \delta \mathbf{x}(0) + \int_0^{t_f} \dot{\boldsymbol{\lambda}}^* \delta \mathbf{x} \, d\tau.$$

The term $\boldsymbol{\lambda}^*(0)\delta\mathbf{x}(0)$ is equal to zero, or else the control system would be non-causal (i.e., then future control could change the initial condition of the system).

Finally, the total variation of the augmented cost function in (8.50) simplifies as follows:

$$\delta J_{\text{aug}} = \int_0^{t_f} \left(\mathbf{x}^* \mathbf{Q} + \boldsymbol{\lambda}^* \mathbf{A} + \dot{\boldsymbol{\lambda}}^* \right) \delta \mathbf{x} \, d\tau + \int_0^{t_f} \left(\mathbf{u}^* \mathbf{R} + \boldsymbol{\lambda}^* \mathbf{B} \right) \delta \mathbf{u} \, d\tau$$
$$+ \left(\mathbf{x}(t_f)^* \mathbf{Q}_f - \boldsymbol{\lambda}^*(t_f) \right) \delta \mathbf{x}(t_f). \quad (8.51)$$

Each variation term in (8.51) must equal zero for an optimal control solution that minimizes J. Thus, we may break this up into three equations:

$$\mathbf{x}^* \mathbf{Q} + \boldsymbol{\lambda}^* \mathbf{A} + \dot{\boldsymbol{\lambda}}^* = \mathbf{0} \quad (8.52a)$$

$$\mathbf{u}^* \mathbf{R} + \boldsymbol{\lambda}^* \mathbf{B} = \mathbf{0} \quad (8.52b)$$

$$\mathbf{x}(t_f)^* \mathbf{Q}_f - \boldsymbol{\lambda}^*(t_f) = \mathbf{0}. \quad (8.52c)$$

Note that the constraint in (8.52c) represents an initial condition for the reverse-time equation for $\boldsymbol{\lambda}$ starting at t_f. Thus, the dynamics in (8.48) with initial condition $\mathbf{x}(0) = \mathbf{x}_0$ and (8.52) with the final-time condition $\boldsymbol{\lambda}(t_f) = \mathbf{Q}_f \mathbf{x}(t_f)$ form a two-point boundary value problem. This may be integrated numerically to find the optimal control solution, even for nonlinear systems.

Because the dynamics are linear, it is possible to *posit* the form $\boldsymbol{\lambda} = \mathbf{P}\mathbf{x}$, and substitute into (8.52) above. The first equation becomes:

$$\left(\dot{\mathbf{P}}\mathbf{x} + \mathbf{P}\dot{\mathbf{x}} \right)^* + \mathbf{x}^* \mathbf{Q} + \boldsymbol{\lambda}^* \mathbf{A} = \mathbf{0}.$$

Taking the transpose, and substituting (8.48) in for $\dot{\mathbf{x}}$, yields:

$$\dot{\mathbf{P}}\mathbf{x} + \mathbf{P}(\mathbf{A}\mathbf{x} + \mathbf{B}\mathbf{u}) + \mathbf{Q}\mathbf{x} + \mathbf{A}^* \mathbf{P}\mathbf{x} = \mathbf{0}.$$

From (8.52b), we have

$$\mathbf{u} = -\mathbf{R}^{-1}\mathbf{B}^* \boldsymbol{\lambda} = -\mathbf{R}^{-1}\mathbf{B}^* \mathbf{P}\mathbf{x}.$$

---

[4] The derivative of a matrix expression $\mathbf{A}\mathbf{x}$ with respect to $\mathbf{x}$ is $\mathbf{A}$, and the derivative of $\mathbf{x}^* \mathbf{A}$ with respect to $\mathbf{x}$ is $\mathbf{A}^*$.

Finally, combining yields:

$$\dot{\mathbf{P}}\mathbf{x} + \mathbf{P}\mathbf{A}\mathbf{x} + \mathbf{A}^*\mathbf{P}\mathbf{x} - \mathbf{P}\mathbf{B}\mathbf{R}^{-1}\mathbf{B}^*\mathbf{P}\mathbf{x} + \mathbf{Q}\mathbf{x} = \mathbf{0}. \tag{8.53}$$

This equation must be true for all **x**, and so it may also be written as a matrix equation. Dropping the terminal cost and letting time go to infinity, the $\dot{\mathbf{P}}$ term disappears, and we recover the algebraic Riccati equation:

$$\mathbf{P}\mathbf{A} + \mathbf{A}\mathbf{P}^* - \mathbf{P}\mathbf{B}\mathbf{R}^{-1}\mathbf{B}^*\mathbf{P} + \mathbf{Q} = \mathbf{0}.$$

Although this procedure is somewhat involved, each step is relatively straightforward. In addition, the dynamics in Eq (8.48) may be replaced with nonlinear dynamics $\dot{\mathbf{x}} = \mathbf{f}(\mathbf{x}, \mathbf{u})$, and a similar nonlinear two-point boundary value problem may be formulated with $\partial \mathbf{f}/\partial \mathbf{x}$ replacing **A** and $\partial \mathbf{f}/\partial \mathbf{u}$ replacing **B**. This procedure is extremely general, and may be used to numerically obtain nonlinear optimal control trajectories.

Hamiltonian Formulation Similar to the Lagrangian formulation above, it is also possible to solve the optimization problem by introducing the following Hamiltonian:

$$\mathcal{H} = \underbrace{\frac{1}{2}\left(\mathbf{x}^*\mathbf{Q}\mathbf{x} + \mathbf{u}^*\mathbf{R}\mathbf{u}\right)}_{\mathcal{L}} + \boldsymbol{\lambda}^*\left(\mathbf{A}\mathbf{x} + \mathbf{B}\mathbf{u}\right). \tag{8.54}$$

Then Hamilton's equations become:

$$\dot{\mathbf{x}} = \left(\frac{\partial \mathcal{H}}{\partial \boldsymbol{\lambda}}\right)^* = \mathbf{A}\mathbf{x} + \mathbf{B}\mathbf{u} \qquad\qquad \mathbf{x}(0) = \mathbf{x}_0$$

$$-\dot{\boldsymbol{\lambda}} = \left(\frac{\partial \mathcal{H}}{\partial \mathbf{x}}\right)^* = \mathbf{Q}\mathbf{x} + \mathbf{A}^*\boldsymbol{\lambda} \qquad\qquad \boldsymbol{\lambda}(t_f) = \mathbf{Q}_f\mathbf{x}(t_f).$$

Again, this is a two-point boundary value problem in **x** and $\boldsymbol{\lambda}$. Plugging in the same expression $\boldsymbol{\lambda} = \mathbf{P}\mathbf{x}$ will result in the same Riccati equation as above.

8.5   Optimal Full-State Estimation: The Kalman Filter

The optimal LQR controller from Section 8.4 relies on full-state measurements of the system. However, full-state measurements may either be prohibitively expensive or technologically infeasible to obtain, especially for high-dimensional systems. The computational burden of collecting and processing full-state measurements may also introduce unacceptable time delays that will limit robust performance.

Instead of measuring the full state **x**, it may be possible to estimate the state from limited noisy measurements **y**. In fact, full-state estimation is mathematically possible as long as the pair $(\mathbf{A}, \mathbf{C})$ are observable, although the effectiveness of estimation depends on the degree of observability as quantified by the observability Gramian. The Kalman filter [279, 551, 221] is the most commonly used full-state estimator, as it optimally balances the competing effects of measurement noise, disturbances, and model uncertainty. As will be shown in the next section, it is possible to use the full-state estimate from a Kalman filter in conjunction with the optimal full-state LQR feedback law.

When deriving the optimal full-state estimator, it is necessary to re-introduce disturbances to the state, $\mathbf{w}_d$, and sensor noise, $\mathbf{w}_n$:

$$\frac{d}{dt}\mathbf{x} = \mathbf{A}\mathbf{x} + \mathbf{B}\mathbf{u} + \mathbf{w}_d \tag{8.56a}$$

$$\mathbf{y} = \mathbf{C}\mathbf{x} + \mathbf{D}\mathbf{u} + \mathbf{w}_n. \tag{8.56b}$$

The Kalman filter assumes that both the disturbance and noise are zero-mean Gaussian processes with known covariances:

$$\mathbb{E}\left(\mathbf{w}_d(t)\mathbf{w}_d(\tau)^*\right) = \mathbf{V}_d\delta(t - \tau), \tag{8.57a}$$

$$\mathbb{E}\left(\mathbf{w}_n(t)\mathbf{w}_n(\tau)^*\right) = \mathbf{V}_n\delta(t - \tau). \tag{8.57b}$$

Here $\mathbb{E}$ is the expected value and $\delta(\cdot)$ is the Dirac delta function. The matrices $\mathbf{V}_d$ and $\mathbf{V}_n$ are positive semi-definite with entries containing the covariances of the disturbance and noise terms. Extensions to the Kalman filter exist for correlated, biased, and unknown noise and disturbance terms [498, 372].

It is possible to obtain an estimate $\hat{\mathbf{x}}$ of the full-state $\mathbf{x}$ from measurements of the input $\mathbf{u}$ and output $\mathbf{y}$, via the following estimator dynamical system:

$$\frac{d}{dt}\hat{\mathbf{x}} = \mathbf{A}\hat{\mathbf{x}} + \mathbf{B}\mathbf{u} + \mathbf{K}_f\left(\mathbf{y} - \hat{\mathbf{y}}\right) \tag{8.58a}$$

$$\hat{\mathbf{y}} = \mathbf{C}\hat{\mathbf{x}} + \mathbf{D}\mathbf{u}. \tag{8.58b}$$

The matrices $\mathbf{A}$, $\mathbf{B}$, $\mathbf{C}$, and $\mathbf{D}$ are obtained from the system model, and the filter gain $\mathbf{K}_f$ is determined via a similar procedure as in LQR. $\mathbf{K}_f$ is given by

$$\mathbf{K}_f = \mathbf{Y}\mathbf{C}^*\mathbf{V}_n, \tag{8.59}$$

where $\mathbf{y}$ is the solution to another algebraic Riccati equation:

$$\mathbf{Y}\mathbf{A}^* + \mathbf{A}\mathbf{Y} - \mathbf{Y}\mathbf{C}^*\mathbf{V}_n^{-1}\mathbf{C}\mathbf{Y} + \mathbf{V}_d = \mathbf{0}. \tag{8.60}$$

This solution is commonly referred to as the Kalman filter, and it is the optimal full-state estimator with respect to the following cost function:

$$J = \lim_{t\to\infty}\mathbb{E}\left((\mathbf{x}(t) - \hat{\mathbf{x}}(t))^*(\mathbf{x}(t) - \hat{\mathbf{x}}(t))\right). \tag{8.61}$$

This cost function implicitly includes the effects of disturbance and noise, which are required to determine the optimal balance between aggressive estimation and noise attenuation. Thus, the Kalman filter is referred to as *linear quadratic estimation* (LQE), and has a dual formulation to the LQR optimization. The cost in (8.61) is computed as an ensemble average over many realizations.

The filter gain $\mathbf{K}_f$ may be determined in Matlab via

```
>> Kf = lqe(A,Vd,C,Vd,Vn);  % design Kalman filter gain
```

Optimal control and estimation are mathematical dual problems, as are controllability and observability, so the Kalman filter may also be found using LQR:

```
>> Kf = (lqr(A',C',Vd,Vn))';  % LQR and LQE are dual problems
```

The Kalman filter is shown schematically in Fig. 8.10.

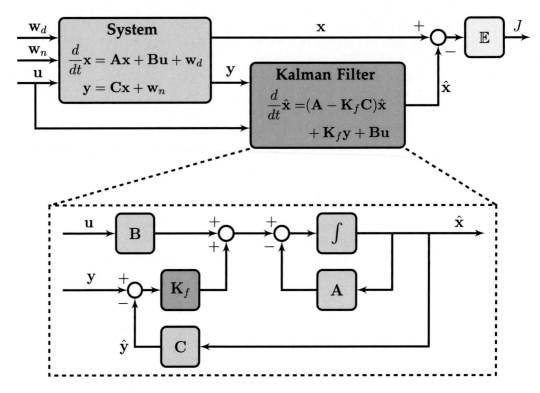

Figure 8.10 Schematic of the Kalman filter for full-state estimation from noisy measurements $\mathbf{y} = \mathbf{C}\mathbf{x} + \mathbf{w}_n$ with process noise (disturbances) $\mathbf{w}_d$. This diagram does not have a feedthrough term $\mathbf{D}$, although it may be included.

Substituting the output estimate $\hat{\mathbf{y}}$ from (8.58b) into (8.58a) yields:

$$\frac{d}{dt}\hat{\mathbf{x}} = \left(\mathbf{A} - \mathbf{K}_f\mathbf{C}\right)\hat{\mathbf{x}} + \mathbf{K}_f\mathbf{y} + \left(\mathbf{B} - \mathbf{K}_f\mathbf{D}\right)\mathbf{u} \tag{8.62a}$$

$$= \left(\mathbf{A} - \mathbf{K}_f\mathbf{C}\right)\hat{\mathbf{x}} + \begin{bmatrix}\mathbf{K}_f, & \left(\mathbf{B} - \mathbf{K}_f\mathbf{D}\right)\end{bmatrix}\begin{bmatrix}\mathbf{y}\\\mathbf{u}\end{bmatrix}. \tag{8.62b}$$

The estimator dynamical system is expressed in terms of the estimate $\hat{\mathbf{x}}$ with inputs $\mathbf{y}$ and $\mathbf{u}$. If the system is observable it is possible to place the eigenvalues of $\mathbf{A} - \mathbf{K}_f\mathbf{C}$ arbitrarily with choice of $\mathbf{K}_f$. When the eigenvalues of the estimator are stable, then the state estimate $\hat{\mathbf{x}}$ converges to the full-state $\mathbf{x}$ asymptotically, as long as the model faithfully captures the true system dynamics. To see this convergence, consider the dynamics of the estimation error $\boldsymbol{\epsilon} = \mathbf{x} - \hat{\mathbf{x}}$:

$$\frac{d}{dt}\boldsymbol{\epsilon} = \frac{d}{dt}\mathbf{x} - \frac{d}{dt}\hat{\mathbf{x}}$$

$$= [\mathbf{A}\mathbf{x} + \mathbf{B}\mathbf{u} + \mathbf{w}_d] - \left[(\mathbf{A} - \mathbf{K}_f\mathbf{C})\hat{\mathbf{x}} + \mathbf{K}_f\mathbf{y} + (\mathbf{B} - \mathbf{K}_f\mathbf{D})\mathbf{u}\right]$$

$$= \mathbf{A}\boldsymbol{\epsilon} + \mathbf{w}_d + \mathbf{K}_f\mathbf{C}\hat{\mathbf{x}} - \mathbf{K}_f\mathbf{y} + \mathbf{K}_f\mathbf{D}\mathbf{u}$$

$$= \mathbf{A}\boldsymbol{\epsilon} + \mathbf{w}_d + \mathbf{K}_f\mathbf{C}\hat{\mathbf{x}} - \mathbf{K}_f\underbrace{[\mathbf{C}\mathbf{x} + \mathbf{D}\mathbf{u} + \mathbf{w}_n]}_{\mathbf{y}} + \mathbf{K}_f\mathbf{D}\mathbf{u}$$

$$= (\mathbf{A} - \mathbf{K}_f\mathbf{C})\boldsymbol{\epsilon} + \mathbf{w}_d - \mathbf{K}_f\mathbf{w}_n.$$

Therefore, the estimate $\hat{\mathbf{x}}$ will converge to the true full state when $\mathbf{A} - \mathbf{K}_f\mathbf{C}$ has stable eigenvalues. As with LQR, there is a tradeoff between over-stabilization of these eigenvalues and the amplification of sensor noise. This is similar to the behavior of an inexperienced driver who may hold the steering wheel too tightly and will overreact to every minor bump and disturbance on the road.

There are many variants of the Kalman filter for nonlinear systems [274, 275, 538], including the extended and unscented Kalman filters. The ensemble Kalman filter [14] is an extension that works well for high-dimensional systems, such as in geophysical data assimilation [449]. All of these methods still assume Gaussian noise processes, and the particle filter provides a more general, although more computationally intensive, alternative that can handle arbitrary noise distributions [226, 451]. The unscented Kalman filter balances the efficiency of the Kalman filter and accuracy of the particle filter.

8.6 Optimal Sensor-Based Control: Linear Quadratic Gaussian (LQG)

The full-state estimate from the Kalman filter is generally used in conjunction with the full-state feedback control law from LQR, resulting in optimal sensor-based feedback. Remarkably, the LQR gain $\mathbf{K}_r$ and the Kalman filter gain $\mathbf{K}_f$ may be designed separately, and the resulting sensor-based feedback will remain optimal and retain the closed-loop eigenvalues when combined.

Combining the LQR full-state feedback with the Kalman fitler full-state estimator results in the linear-quadratic Gaussian (LQG) controller. The LQG controller is a dynamical system with input $\mathbf{y}$, output $\mathbf{u}$, and internal state $\hat{\mathbf{x}}$:

$$\frac{d}{dt}\hat{\mathbf{x}} = \left(\mathbf{A} - \mathbf{K}_f\mathbf{C} - \mathbf{B}\mathbf{K}_r\right)\hat{\mathbf{x}} + \mathbf{K}_f\mathbf{y} \tag{8.63a}$$

$$\mathbf{u} = -\mathbf{K}_r\hat{\mathbf{x}}. \tag{8.63b}$$

The LQG controller is optimal with respect to the following ensemble-averaged version of the cost function from (8.44):

$$J(t) = \left\langle \int_0^t \left[\mathbf{x}(\tau)^*\mathbf{Q}\mathbf{x}(\tau) + \mathbf{u}(\tau)^*\mathbf{R}\mathbf{u}(\tau)\right] d\tau \right\rangle. \tag{8.64}$$

The controller $\mathbf{u} = -\mathbf{K}_r\hat{\mathbf{x}}$ is in terms of the state estimate, and so this cost function must be averaged over many realizations of the disturbance and noise. Applying LQR to $\hat{\mathbf{x}}$ results in the following state dynamics:

$$\frac{d}{dt}\mathbf{x} = \mathbf{A}\mathbf{x} - \mathbf{B}\mathbf{K}_r\hat{\mathbf{x}} + \mathbf{w}_d \tag{8.65a}$$

$$= \mathbf{A}\mathbf{x} - \mathbf{B}\mathbf{K}_r\mathbf{x} + \mathbf{B}\mathbf{K}_r\left(\mathbf{x} - \hat{\mathbf{x}}\right) + \mathbf{w}_d \tag{8.65b}$$

$$= \mathbf{A}\mathbf{x} - \mathbf{B}\mathbf{K}_r\mathbf{x} + \mathbf{B}\mathbf{K}_r\boldsymbol{\epsilon} + \mathbf{w}_d. \tag{8.65c}$$

Again $\boldsymbol{\epsilon} = \mathbf{x} - \hat{\mathbf{x}}$ as before. Finally, the closed-loop system may be written as

$$\frac{d}{dt}\begin{bmatrix}\mathbf{x} \\ \boldsymbol{\epsilon}\end{bmatrix} = \begin{bmatrix}\mathbf{A} - \mathbf{B}\mathbf{K}_r & \mathbf{B}\mathbf{K}_r \\ \mathbf{0} & \mathbf{A} - \mathbf{K}_f\mathbf{C}\end{bmatrix}\begin{bmatrix}\mathbf{x} \\ \boldsymbol{\epsilon}\end{bmatrix} + \begin{bmatrix}\mathbf{I} & \mathbf{0} \\ \mathbf{I} & -\mathbf{K}_f\end{bmatrix}\begin{bmatrix}\mathbf{w}_d \\ \mathbf{w}_n\end{bmatrix}. \tag{8.66}$$

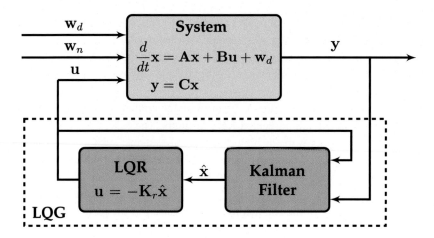

Figure 8.11 Schematic illustrating the linear quadratic Gaussian (LQG) controller for optimal closed-loop feedback based on noisy measurements **y**. The optimal LQR and Kalman filter gain matrices $\mathbf{K}_r$ and $\mathbf{K}_f$ may be designed independently, based on two different algebraic Riccati equations. When combined, the resulting sensor-based feedback remains optimal.

Thus, the closed-loop eigenvalues of the LQG regulated system are given by the eigenvalues of $\mathbf{A} - \mathbf{B}\mathbf{K}_r$ and $\mathbf{A} - \mathbf{K}_f\mathbf{C}$, which were optimally chosen by the LQR and Kalman filter gain matrices, respectively.

The LQG framework, shown in Fig. 8.11, relies on an accurate model of the system and knowledge of the magnitudes of the disturbances and measurement noise, which are assumed to be Gaussian processes. In real-world systems, each of these assumptions may be invalid, and even small time delays and model uncertainty may destroy the robustness of LQG and result in instability [155]. The lack of robustness of LQG regulators to model uncertainty motivates the introduction of robust control in Section 8.8. For example, it is possible to *robustify* LQG regulators through a process known as loop-transfer recovery. However, despite robustness issues, LQG control is extremely effective for many systems, and is among the most common control paradigms.

In contrast to classical control approaches, such as proportional-integral-derivative (PID) control and designing faster inner-loop control and slow outer-loop control assuming a separation of timescales, LQG is able to handle multiple-input, multiple output (MIMO) systems with overlapping timescales and multi-objective cost functions with no additional complexity in the algorithm or implementation.

8.7   Case Study: Inverted Pendulum on a Cart

To consolidate the concepts of optimal control, we will implement a stabilizing controller for the inverted pendulum on the cart, shown in Fig. 8.12. The full nonlinear dynamics are given by

$$\dot{x} = v \tag{8.67a}$$

$$\dot{v} = \frac{-m^2 L^2 g \cos(\theta) \sin(\theta) + mL^2(mL\omega^2 \sin(\theta) - \delta v) + mL^2 u}{mL^2(M + m(1 - \cos(\theta)^2))} \tag{8.67b}$$

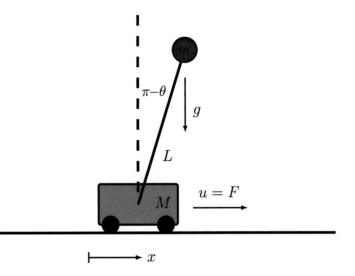

Figure 8.12 Schematic of inverted pendulum on a cart. The control forcing acts to accelerate or decelerate cart. For this example, we assume the following parameter values: pendulum mass ($m = 1$), cart mass ($M = 5$), pendulum length ($L = 2$), gravitational acceleration ($g = -10$), and cart damping ($\delta = 1$).

$$\dot{\theta} = \omega \tag{8.67c}$$

$$\dot{\omega} = \frac{(m + M)mgL\sin(\theta) - mL\cos(\theta)(mL\omega^2\sin(\theta) - \delta v) + mL\cos(\theta)u}{mL^2(M + m(1 - \cos(\theta)^2))} \tag{8.67d}$$

where x is the cart position, v is the velocity, θ is the pendulum angle, ω is the angular velocity, m is the pendulum mass, M is the cart mass, L is the pendulum arm, g is the gravitational acceleration, δ is a friction damping on the dart, and u is a control force applied to the cart.

The following Matlab function, **pendcart**, may be used to simulate the full nonlinear system in (8.67):

Code 8.2 Right-hand side function for inverted pendulum on cart.

```
function dx = pendcart(x,m,M,L,g,d,u)

Sx = sin(x(3));
Cx = cos(x(3));
D = m*L*L*(M+m*(1-Cx^2));

dx(1,1) = x(2);
dx(2,1) = (1/D)*(-m^2*L^2*g*Cx*Sx + m*L^2*(m*L*x(4)^2*Sx - d*x
    (2))) + m*L*L*(1/D)*u;
dx(3,1) = x(4);
dx(4,1) = (1/D)*((m+M)*m*g*L*Sx - m*L*Cx*(m*L*x(4)^2*Sx - d*x(2)
    )) - m*L*Cx*(1/D)*u;
```

There are two fixed points, corresponding to either the pendulum down ($\theta = 0$) or pendulum up ($\theta = \pi$) configuration; in both cases, $v = \omega = 0$ for the fixed point, and the cart position x is a free variable, as the equations do not depend explicitly on x. It is possible to linearize the equations in (8.67) about either the up or down solutions, yielding the following linearized dynamics:

$$
\frac{d}{dt}\begin{bmatrix} x_1 \\ x_2 \\ x_3 \\ x_4 \end{bmatrix} = \begin{bmatrix} 0 & 1 & 0 & 0 \\ 0 & -\frac{\delta}{M} & b\frac{mg}{M} & 0 \\ 0 & 0 & 0 & 1 \\ 0 & -b\frac{\delta}{ML} & -b\frac{(m+M)g}{ML} & 0 \end{bmatrix}\begin{bmatrix} x_1 \\ x_2 \\ x_3 \\ x_4 \end{bmatrix} + \begin{bmatrix} 0 \\ \frac{1}{M} \\ 0 \\ b\frac{1}{ML} \end{bmatrix} u, \quad \text{for} \quad \begin{bmatrix} x_1 \\ x_2 \\ x_3 \\ x_4 \end{bmatrix} = \begin{bmatrix} x \\ v \\ \theta \\ \omega \end{bmatrix},
$$

$$(8.68)$$

where $b = 1$ for the pendulum up fixed point, and $b = -1$ for the pendulum down fixed point. The system matrices **A** and **B** may be entered in Matlab using the values for the constants given in Fig. 8.12:

Code 8.3 Construct system matrices for inverted pendulum on a cart.

```
clear all, close all, clc

m = 1;  M = 5;  L = 2;  g = -10;  d = 1;

b = 1; % Pendulum up (b=1)

A = [0 1 0 0;
     0 -d/M b*m*g/M 0;
     0 0 0 1;
     0 -b*d/(M*L) -b*(m+M)*g/(M*L) 0];
B = [0; 1/M; 0; b*1/(M*L)];
```

We may also confirm that the open-loop system is unstable by checking the eigenvalues of **A**:

```
>> lambda = eig(A)

lambda =
          0
    -2.4311
    -0.2336
     2.4648
```

In the following, we will test for controllability and observability, develop full-state feedback (LQR), full-state estimation (Kalman filter), and sensor-based feedback (LQG) solutions.

Full-state Feedback Control of the Cart-Pendulum

In this section, we will design an LQR controller to stabilize the inverted pendulum configuration ($\theta = \pi$) assuming full-state measurements, $\mathbf{y} = \mathbf{x}$. Before any control design, we must confirm that the system is linearly controllable with the given **A** and **B** matrices:

```
>> rank(ctrb(A,B))

ans =
     4
```

Thus, the pair $(\mathbf{A}, \mathbf{B})$ is controllable, since the controllability matrix has full rank. It is then possible to specify given **Q** and **R** matrices for the cost function and design the LQR controller gain matrix **K**:

Code 8.4 Design LQR controller to stabilize inverted pendulum on a cart.

```
%% Design LQR controller
Q = eye(4);  % 4x4 identify matrix
```

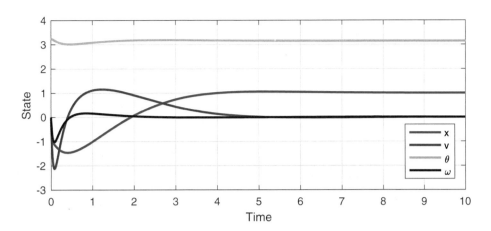

Figure 8.13 Closed-loop system response of inverted pendulum on a cart stabilized with an LQR controller.

```
R = .0001;

K = lqr(A,B,Q,R);
```

We may then simulate the closed-loop system response of the full nonlinear system. We will initialize our simulation slightly off equilibrium, at $\mathbf{x}_0 = \begin{bmatrix} -1 & 0 & \pi + .1 & 0 \end{bmatrix}^T$, and we also impose a desired step change in the reference position of the cart, from $x = -1$ to $x = 1$.

Code 8.5 Simulate closed-loop inverted pendulum on a cart system.

```
%% Simulate closed-loop system
tspan = 0:.001:10;
x0 = [-1; 0; pi+.1; 0];    % initial condition
wr = [1; 0; pi; 0];        % reference position
u=@(x)-K*(x - wr);         % control law
[t,x] = ode45(@(t,x)pendcart(x,m,M,L,g,d,u(x)),tspan,x0);
```

In this code, the actuation is set to:

$$u = -\mathbf{K}\left(\mathbf{x} - \mathbf{w}_r\right), \tag{8.69}$$

where $\mathbf{w}_r = \begin{bmatrix} 1 & 0 & \pi & 0 \end{bmatrix}^T$ is the reference position. The closed-loop response is shown in Fig. 8.13.

In the above procedure, specifying the system dynamics and simulating the closed-loop system response is considerably more involved than actually designing the controller, which amounts to a single function call in Matlab. It is also helpful to compare the LQR response to the response obtained by nonoptimal eigenvalue placement. In particular, Fig. 8.14 shows the system response and cost function for 100 randomly generated sets of stable eigenvalues, chosen in the interval $[-3.5, -.5]$. The LQR controller has the lowest overall cost, as it is chosen to minimize J. The code to plot the pendulum–cart system is provided online.

Non-minimum phase systems It can be seen from the response that in order to move from $x = -1$ to $x = 1$, the system initially moves in the wrong direction. This behavior

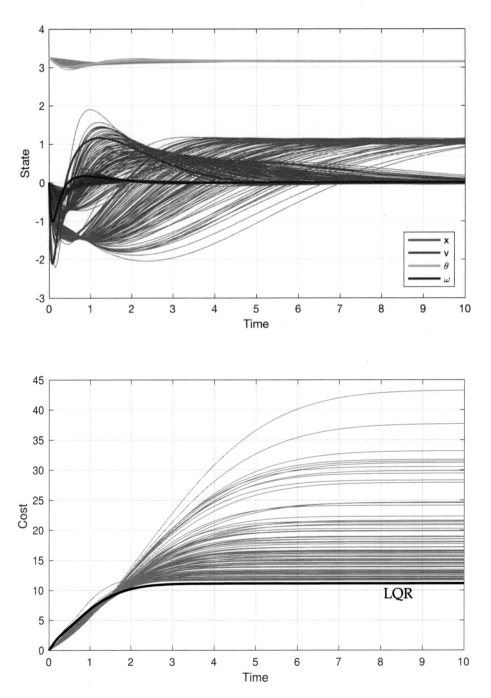

Figure 8.14 Comparison of LQR controller response and cost function with other pole placement locations. Bold lines represent the LQR solutions.

indicates that the system is *non-minimum phase*, which introduces challenges for robust control, as we will soon see. There are many examples of non-minimum phase systems in control. For instance, parallel parking an automobile first involves moving the center of mass of the car away from the curb before it then moves closer. Other examples include increasing altitude in an aircraft, where the elevators must first move the center of mass down to increase the angle of attack on the main wings before lift increases the altitude. Adding cold fuel to a turbine may also initially drop the temperature before it eventually increases.

Full-State Estimation of the Cart-Pendulum

Now we turn to the full-state estimation problem based on limited noisy measurements **y**. For this example, we will develop the Kalman filter for the pendulum-down condition ($\theta = 0$), since without feedback the system in the pendulum-up condition will quickly leave the fixed point where the linear model is valid. When we combine the Kalman filter with LQR in the next example, it will be possible to control to the unstable inverted pendulum configuration. Switching to the pendulum-down configuration is simple in the code:

```
b = -1; % pendulum down (b=-1)
```

Before designing a Kalman filter, we must choose a sensor and test for observability. If we measure the cart position, $y = x_1$,

```
C = [1 0 0 0];        % measure cart position, x
```

then the observability matrix has full rank:

```
>> rank(obsv(A,C))

ans =
     4
```

Because the cart position x_1 does not appear explicitly in the dynamics, the system is not fully observable for any measurement that doesn't include x_1. Thus, it is impossible to estimate the cart position with a measurement of the pendulum angle. However, if the cart position is not important for the cost function (i.e., if we only want to stabilize the pendulum, and don't care where the cart is located), then other choices of sensor will be admissible.

Now we design the Kalman filter, specifying disturbance and noise covariances:

```
%% Specify disturbance and noise magnitude
Vd = eye(4);    % disturbance covariance
Vn = 1;         % noise covariance

% Build Kalman filter
[Kf,P,E] = lqe(A,eye(4),C,Vd,Vn);   % design Kalman filter
% alternatively, possible to design using "LQR" code
Kf = (lqr(A',C',Vd,Vn))';
```

The Kalman filter gain matrix is given by

```
Kf =
    1.9222
    1.3474
   -0.6182
   -1.8016
```

Finally, to simulate the system and Kalman filter, we must augment the original system to include disturbance and noise inputs:

```
%% Augment system with additional inputs
B_aug = [B eye(4) 0*B];    % [u I*wd 0*wn]
D_aug = [0 0 0 0 0 1];     % D matrix passes noise through

sysC = ss(A,B_aug,C,D_aug);    % single-measurement system

% "true" system w/ full-state output, disturbance, no noise
sysTruth = ss(A,B_aug,eye(4),zeros(4,size(B_aug,2)));

sysKF = ss(A-Kf*C,[B Kf],eye(4),0*[B Kf]);    % Kalman filter
```

We now simulate the system with a single output measurement, including additive disturbances and noise, and we use this as the input to a Kalman filter estimator. At time $t = 1$ and $t = 15$, we give the system a large positive and negative impulse in the actuation, respectively.

```
%% Estimate linearized system in "down" position
dt = .01;
t = dt:dt:50;

uDIST = sqrt(Vd)*randn(4,size(t,2));  % random disturbance
uNOISE = sqrt(Vn)*randn(size(t));      % random noise
u = 0*t;
u(1/dt) = 20/dt;     % positive impulse
u(15/dt) = -20/dt;   % negative impulse

u_aug = [u; uDIST; uNOISE];  % input w/ disturbance and noise

[y,t] = lsim(sysC,u_aug,t);          % noisy measurement
[xtrue,t] = lsim(sysTruth,u_aug,t);  % true state
[xhat,t] = lsim(sysKF,[u; y'],t);    % state estimate
```

Fig. 8.15 shows the noisy measurement signal used by the Kalman filter, and Fig. 8.16 shows the full noiseless state, with disturbances, along with the Kalman filter estimate.

To build intuition, it is recommended that the reader investigate the performance of the Kalman filter when the model is an imperfect representation of the simulated dynamics. When combined with full-state control in the next section, small time delays and changes to the system model may cause fragility.

Sensor-Based Feedback Control of the Cart-Pendulum

To apply an LQG regulator to the inverted pendulum on a cart, we will simulate the full nonlinear system in Simulink, as shown in Fig. 8.17. The nonlinear dynamics are encapsulated in the block '**cartpend_sim**', and the inputs consist of the actuation signal u and disturbance $\mathbf{w}_d$. We record the full state for performance analysis, although only noisy measurements $y = \mathbf{C}x + w_n$ and the actuation signal u are passed to the Kalman filter. The full-state estimate is then passed to the LQR block, which commands the desired actuation signal. For this example, we use the following LQR and LQE weighting matrices:

```
Q = eye(4);      % state cost
R = .000001;     % actuation cost

Vd = .04*eye(4); % disturbance covariance
Vn = .0002;      % noise covariance
```

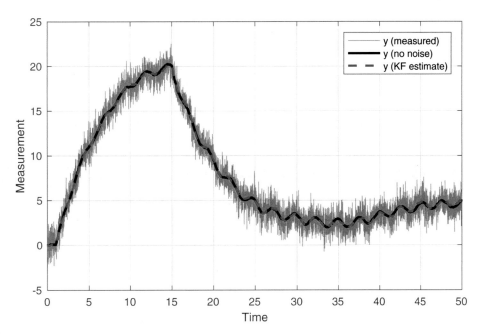

Figure 8.15 Noisy measurement that is used for the Kalman filter, along with the underlying noiseless signal and the Kalman filter estimate.

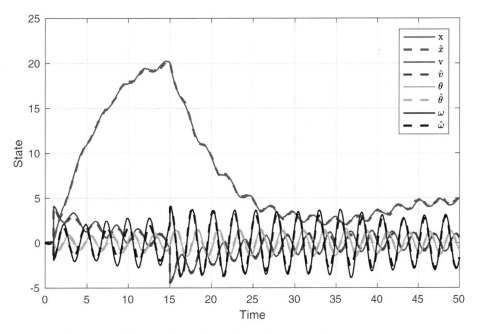

Figure 8.16 The true and Kalman filter estimated states for the pendulum on a cart system.

The system starts near the vertical equilibrium, at $\mathbf{x}_0 = \begin{bmatrix} 0 & 0 & 3.14 & 0 \end{bmatrix}^T$, and we command a step in the cart position from $x = 0$ to $x = 1$ at $t = 10$. The resulting response is shown in Fig. 8.18. Despite noisy measurements (Fig. 8.19) and disturbances (Fig. 8.20), the controller is able to effectively track the reference cart position while stabilizing the inverted pendulum.

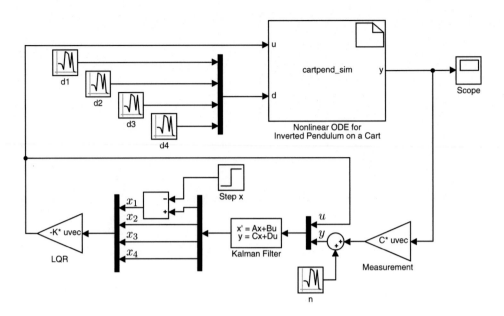

Figure 8.17 Matlab Simulink model for sensor-based LQG feedback control.

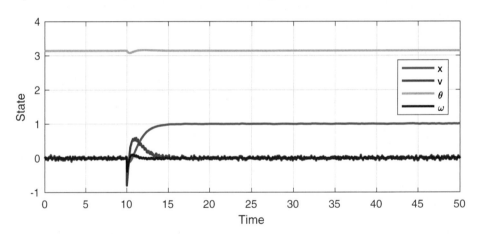

Figure 8.18 Output response using LQG feedback control.

8.8   Robust Control and Frequency Domain Techniques

Until now, we have described control systems in terms of state-space systems of ordinary differential equations. This perspective readily lends itself to stability analysis and design via placement of closed-loop eigenvalues. However, in a seminal paper by John Doyle in 1978 [155][5], it was shown that LQG regulators can have arbitrarily small stability margins, making them *fragile* to model uncertainties, time delays, and other model imperfections.

Fortunately, a short time after Doyle's famous 1978 paper, a rigorous mathematical theory was developed to design controllers that promote robustness. Indeed, this new theory

---

[5] Title: Guaranteed margins for LQG regulators; Abstract: There are none.

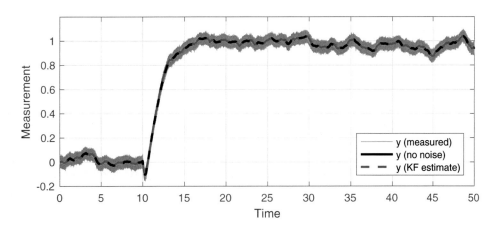

Figure 8.19 Noisy measurement used for the Kalman filter, along with the underlying noiseless signal and the Kalman filter estimate.

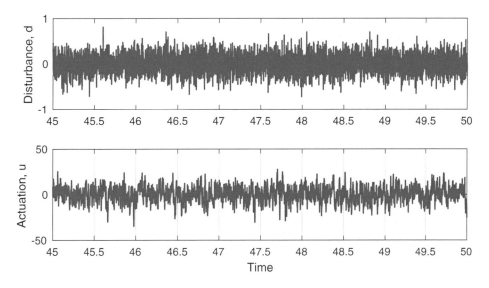

Figure 8.20 Noisy measurement used for the Kalman filter, along with the underlying noiseless signal and the Kalman filter estimate.

of robust control generalizes the optimal control framework used to develop LQR/LQG, by incorporating a different cost function that penalizes *worse-case scenario* performance.

To understand and design controllers for robust performance, it will be helpful to look at frequency domain *transfer functions* of various signals. In particular, we will consider the sensitivity, complementary sensitivity, and loop transfer functions. These enable quantitative and visual approaches to assess robust performance, and they enable intuitive and compact representations of control systems.

Robust control is a natural perspective when considering uncertain models obtained from noisy or incomplete data. Moreover, it may be possible to manage system nonlinearity as a form of structured model uncertainty. Finally, we will discuss known factors that limit robust performance, including time delays and non-minimum phase behavior.

Frequency Domain Techniques

To understand and manage the tradeoffs between robustness and performance in a control system, it is helpful to design and analyze controllers using frequency domain techniques.

The Laplace transform allows us to go between the time-domain (state-space) and frequency domain:

$$\mathcal{L}\{f(t)\} = f(s) = \int_{0^-}^{\infty} f(t)e^{-st}dt. \tag{8.70}$$

Here, s is the complex-valued Laplace variable. The Laplace transform may be thought of as a one-sided generalized Fourier transform that is valid for functions that don't converge to zero as $t \rightarrow \infty$. The Laplace transform is particularly useful because it transforms differential equations into algebraic equations, and convolution integrals in the time domain become simple products in the frequency domain. To see how time derivatives pass through the Laplace transform, we use integration by parts:

$$\mathcal{L}\left\{\frac{d}{dt}f(t)\right\} = \int_{0^-}^{\infty} \underbrace{\frac{d}{dt}f(t)}_{dv} \underbrace{e^{-st}}_{u} dt$$

$$= \left[f(t)e^{-st}\right]_{t=0^-}^{t=\infty} - \int_{0^-}^{\infty} f(t)(-se^{-st})dt$$

$$= f(0^-) + s\mathcal{L}\{f(t)\}.$$

Thus, for zero initial conditions, $\mathcal{L}\{df/dt\} = sf(s)$.

Taking the Laplace transform of the control system in (8.10) yields

$$s\mathbf{x}(s) = \mathbf{A}\mathbf{x}(s) + \mathbf{B}\mathbf{u}(s) \tag{8.71a}$$

$$\mathbf{y}(s) = \mathbf{C}\mathbf{x}(s) + \mathbf{D}\mathbf{u}(s). \tag{8.71b}$$

It is possible to solve for $\mathbf{x}(s)$ in the first equation, as

$$(s\mathbf{I} - \mathbf{A})\mathbf{x}(s) = \mathbf{B}\mathbf{u}(s) \quad \Longrightarrow \quad \mathbf{x}(s) = (s\mathbf{I} - \mathbf{A})^{-1}\mathbf{B}\mathbf{u}(s). \tag{8.72}$$

Substituting this into the second equation we arrive at a mapping from inputs $\mathbf{u}$ to outputs $\mathbf{y}$:

$$\mathbf{y}(s) = \left[\mathbf{C}(s\mathbf{I} - \mathbf{A})^{-1}\mathbf{C} + \mathbf{D}\right]\mathbf{u}(s). \tag{8.73}$$

We define this mapping as the *transfer function*:

$$\mathbf{G}(s) = \frac{\mathbf{y}(s)}{\mathbf{u}(s)} = \mathbf{C}(s\mathbf{I} - \mathbf{A})^{-1}\mathbf{B} + \mathbf{D}. \tag{8.74}$$

For linear systems, there are three equivalent representations: 1) time-domain, in terms of the impulse response; 2) frequency domain, in terms of the transfer function; and 3) state-space, in terms of a system of differential equations. These representations are shown schematically in Fig. 8.21. As we will see, there are many benefits to analyzing control systems in the frequency domain.

Frequency Response

The transfer function in (8.74) is particularly useful because it gives rise to the frequency response, which is a graphical representation of the control system in terms of measurable data. To illustrate this, we will consider a single-input, single-output (SISO) system. It is a

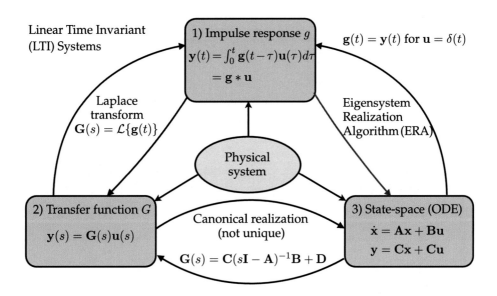

Figure 8.21 Three equivalent representations of linear time invariant systems.

property of linear systems with zero initial conditions, that a sinusoidal input will give rise to a sinusoidal output with the same frequency, perhaps with a different magnitude A and phase ϕ:

$$u(t) = \sin(\omega t) \quad \Longrightarrow \quad y(t) = A\sin(\omega t + \phi). \tag{8.75}$$

This is true for long-times, after initial transients die out. The amplitude A and phase ϕ of the output sinusoid depend on the input frequency ω. These functions $A(\omega)$ and $\phi(\omega)$ may be mapped out by running a number of experiments with sinusoidal input at different frequencies ω. Alternatively, this information is obtained from the complex-valued transfer function $G(s)$:

$$A(\omega) = |G(i\omega)|, \qquad\qquad \phi(\omega) = \angle G(i\omega). \tag{8.76}$$

Thus, the amplitude and phase angle for input $\sin(\omega t)$ may be obtained by evaluating the transfer function at $s = i\omega$ (i.e., along the imaginary axis in the complex plane). These quantities may then be plotted, resulting in the *frequency response* or *Bode plot*.

For a concrete example, consider the spring-mass-damper system, shown in Fig. 8.22. The equations of motion are given by:

$$m\ddot{x} = -\delta\dot{x} - kx + u. \tag{8.77}$$

Choosing values $m = 1$, $\delta = 1$, $k = 2$, and taking the Laplace transform yields:

$$G(s) = \frac{1}{s^2 + s + 2}. \tag{8.78}$$

Here we are assuming that the output y is a measurement of the position of the mass, x. Note that the denominator of the transfer function $G(s)$ is the characteristic equation of (8.77), written in state-space form. Thus, the poles of the complex function $G(s)$ are eigenvalues of the state-space system.

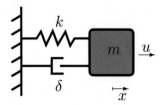

Figure 8.22 Spring-mass-damper system.

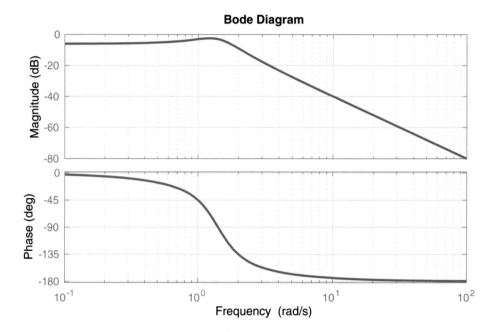

Figure 8.23 Frequency response of spring-mass-damper system. The magnitude is plotted on a logarithmic scale, in units of decibel (dB), and the frequency is likewise on a log-scale.

It is now possible to create this system in Matlab and plot the frequency response, as shown in Fig. 8.23. Note that the frequency response is readily interpretable and provides physical intuition. For example, the zero slope of the magnitude at low frequencies indicates that slow forcing translates directly into motion of the mass, while the roll-off of the magnitude at high frequencies indicates that fast forcing is attenuated and doesn't significantly effect the motion of the mass. Moreover, the resonance frequency is seen as a peak in the magnitude, indicating an amplification of forcing at this frequency.

Code 8.6 Create transfer function and plot frequency response (Bode) plot.

```
s = tf('s');              % Laplace variable
G = 1/(s^2 + s + 2);      % Transfer function

bode(G);                  % Frequency response
```

Given a state-space realization,

```
>> A = [0 1; -2 -1];
>> B = [0; 1];
```

```
>> C = [1 0];
>> D = 0;
```

it is simple to obtain a frequency domain representation:

```
>> [num,den] = ss2tf(A,B,C,D);  % State space to transf. fun.
>> G = tf(num,den)              % Create transfer function

G =
        1
   -----------
   s^2 + s + 2
```

Similarly, it is possible to obtain a state-space system from a transfer function, although this representation is not unique:

```
>> [A,B,C,D] = tf2ss(G.num{1},G.den{1})

A =
   -1.0000    -2.0000
    1.0000         0
B =
     1
     0
C =
     0     1
D =
     0
```

Notice that this representation has switched the ordering of our variables to $\mathbf{x} = \begin{bmatrix} v & x \end{bmatrix}^T$, although it still has the correct input–output characteristics.

The frequency-domain is also useful because impulsive or step inputs are particularly simple to represent with the Laplace transform. These are also simple in Matlab. The impulse response (Fig. 8.24) is given by

```
>> impulse(G);     % Impulse response
```

and the step response (Fig. 8.25) is given by

```
>> step(G);        % Step response
```

Performance and the Loop Transfer Function: Sensitivity and Complementary Sensitivity

Consider a slightly modified version of Fig. 8.4, where the disturbance has a model, $\mathbf{P}_d$. This new diagram, shown in Fig. 8.26, will be used to derive the important transfer functions relevant for assessing robust performance.

$$\mathbf{y} = \mathbf{GK}(\mathbf{w}_r - \mathbf{y} - \mathbf{w}_n) + \mathbf{G}_d\mathbf{w}_d \tag{8.79a}$$

$$\implies (\mathbf{I} + \mathbf{GK})\mathbf{y} = \mathbf{GKw}_r - \mathbf{GKw}_n + \mathbf{G}_d\mathbf{w}_d. \tag{8.79b}$$

$$\implies \mathbf{y} = \underbrace{(\mathbf{I} + \mathbf{GK})^{-1}\mathbf{GK}}_{\mathbf{T}}\mathbf{w}_r - \underbrace{(\mathbf{I} + \mathbf{GK})^{-1}\mathbf{GK}}_{\mathbf{T}}\mathbf{w}_n + \underbrace{(\mathbf{I} + \mathbf{GK})^{-1}}_{\mathbf{S}}\mathbf{G}_d\mathbf{w}_d. \tag{8.79c}$$

Here, $\mathbf{S}$ is the *sensitivity function*, and $\mathbf{T}$ is the *complementary sensitivity function*. We may denote $\mathbf{L} = \mathbf{GK}$ the *loop transfer function*, which is the open-loop transfer function in the

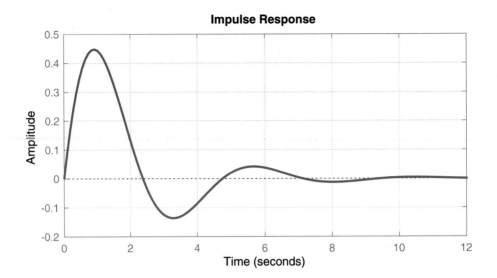

Figure 8.24 Impulse response of spring-mass-damper system.

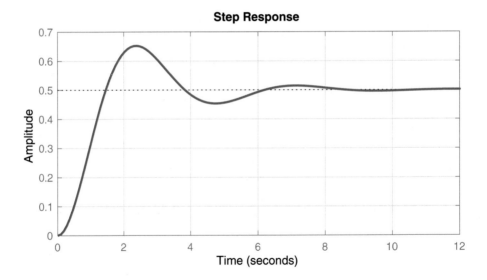

Figure 8.25 Step response of spring-mass-damper system.

absence of feedback. Both $\mathbf{S}$ and $\mathbf{T}$ may be simplified in terms of $\mathbf{L}$:

$$\mathbf{S} = (\mathbf{I} + \mathbf{L})^{-1} \tag{8.80a}$$

$$\mathbf{T} = (\mathbf{I} + \mathbf{L})^{-1}\mathbf{L}. \tag{8.80b}$$

Conveniently, the sensitivity and complementary sensitivity functions must add up to the identity: $\mathbf{S} + \mathbf{T} = \mathbf{I}$.

In practice, the transfer function from the exogenous inputs to the noiseless error ϵ is more useful for design:

$$\epsilon = \mathbf{w}_r - \mathbf{y} = \mathbf{S}\mathbf{w}_r + \mathbf{T}\mathbf{w}_n - \mathbf{S}\mathbf{G}_d\mathbf{w}_d. \tag{8.81}$$

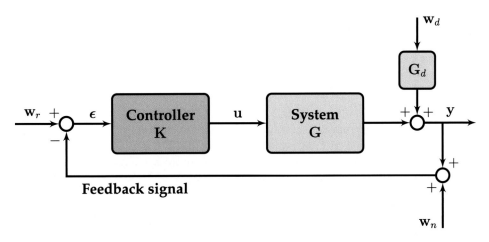

Figure 8.26 Closed-loop feedback control diagram with reference input, noise, and disturbance. We will consider the various transfer functions from exogenous inputs to the error ϵ, thus deriving the loop transfer function, as well as the sensitivity and complementary sensitivity functions.

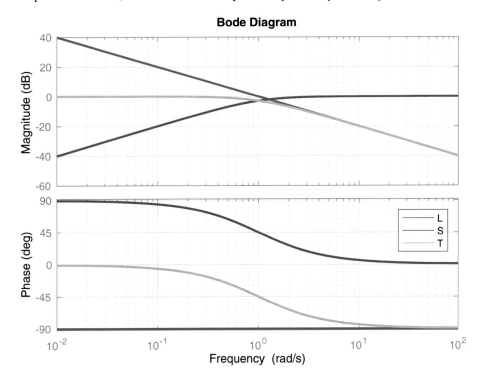

Figure 8.27 Loop transfer function along with sensitivity and complementary sensitivity functions.

Thus, we see that the sensitivity and complementary sensitivity functions provide the maps from reference, disturbance, and noise inputs to the tracking error. Since we desire small tracking error, we may then specify $\mathbf{S}$ and $\mathbf{T}$ to have desirable properties, and ideally we will be able to achieve these specifications by designing the loop transfer function $\mathbf{L}$. In practice, we will choose the controller $\mathbf{K}$ with knowledge of the model $\mathbf{G}$ so that the loop transfer function has beneficial properties in the frequency domain. For example, small gain at high frequencies will attenuate sensor noise, since this will result in **T** being small. Similarly, high gain at low frequencies will provide good reference tracking performance, as **S** will be small at low frequencies. However, **S** and **T** cannot both be small everywhere, since $\mathbf{S} + \mathbf{T} = \mathbf{I}$, from (8.80), and so these design objectives may compete.

For performance and robustness, we want the maximum peak of **S**, $M_\mathbf{S} = \|\mathbf{S}\|_\infty$, to be as small as possible. From (8.81), it is clear that in the absence of noise, feedback control improves performance (i.e. reduces error) for all frequencies where $|\mathbf{S}| < 1$; thus control is effective when $\mathbf{T} \approx \mathbf{1}$. As explained in [492] (pg. 37), all real systems will have a range of frequencies where $|\mathbf{S}| > 1$, in which case performance is degraded. Minimizing the peak $M_\mathbf{S}$ mitigates the amount of degradation experienced with feedback at these frequencies, improving performance. In addition, the minimum distance of the loop transfer function **L** to the point -1 in the complex plane is given by $M_\mathbf{S}^{-1}$. By the Nyquist stability theorem, the larger this distance, the greater the stability margin of the closed-loop system, improving robustness. These are the two major reasons to minimize $M_\mathbf{S}$.

The controller *bandwidth* ω_B is the frequency below which feedback control is effective. This is a subjective definition. Often, ω_B is the frequency where $|\mathbf{S}(j\omega)|$ first crosses -3 dB from below. We would ideally like the controller bandwidth to be as large as possible without amplifying sensor noise, which typically has a high frequency. However, there are fundamental bandwidth limitations that are imposed for systems that have time delays or right half plane zeros [492].

Inverting the Dynamics

With a model of the form in (8.10) or (8.73), it may be possible to design an open-loop control law to achieve some desired specification without the use of measurement-based feedback or feedforward control. For instance, if perfect tracking of the reference input $\mathbf{w}_r$ is desired in Fig. 8.3, under certain circumstances it may be possible to design a controller by inverting the system dynamics **G**: $\mathbf{K}(s) = \mathbf{G}^{-1}(s)$. In this case, the transfer function from reference $\mathbf{w}_r$ to output **s** is given by $\mathbf{GG}^{-1} = \mathbf{1}$, so that the output perfectly matches the reference. However, perfect control is never possible in real-world systems, and this strategy should be used with caution, since it generally relies on a number of significant assumptions on the system **G**. First, effective control based on inversion requires extremely precise knowledge of **G** and well-characterized, predictable disturbances; there is little room for model errors or uncertainties, as there are no sensor measurements to determine if performance is as expected and no corrective feedback mechanisms to modify the actuation strategy to compensate.

For open-loop control using system inversion, **G** must also be stable. It is impossible to fundamentally change the dynamics of a linear system through open-loop control, and thus an unstable system cannot be stabilized without feedback. Attempting to stabilize an unstable system by inverting the dynamics will typically have disastrous consequences. For instance, consider the following unstable system with a pole at $s = 5$ and a zero at $s = -10$: $G(s) = (s + 10)/(s - 5)$. Inverting the dynamics would result in a controller $K = (s - 5)/(s + 10)$; however, if there is even the slightest uncertainty in the model, so that the true pole is at $5 - \epsilon$, then the open-loop system will be:

$$G_{\text{true}}(s)K(s) = \frac{s - 5}{s - 5 + \epsilon}.$$

This system is still unstable, despite the attempted pole cancelation. Moreover, the unstable mode is now nearly unobservable.

In addition to stability, **G** must not have any time delays or zeros in the right-half plane, and it must have the same number of poles as zeros. If **G** has any zeros in the right-half plane, then the inverted controller **K** will be unstable, since it will have right-half plane poles. These systems are called *non-minimum phase*, and there have been generalizations to dynamic inversion that provide bounded inverses to these systems [149]. Similarly, time delays are not invertible, and if **G** has more poles than zeros, then the resulting controller will not be realizable and may have extremely large actuation signals **b**. There are also generalizations that provide *regularized* model inversion, where optimization schemes are applied with penalty terms added to keep the resulting actuation signal **b** bounded. These regularized open-loop controllers are often significantly more effective, with improved robustness.

Combined, these restrictions on **G** imply that model-based open-loop control should only be used when the system is well-behaved, accurately characterized by a model, when disturbances are characterized, and when the additional feedback control hardware is unnecessarily expensive. Otherwise, performance goals must be modest. Open-loop model inversion is often used in manufacturing and robotics, where systems are well-characterized and constrained in a standard operating environment.

Robust Control

As discussed previously, LQG controllers are known to have arbitrarily poor robustness margins. This is a serious problem in systems such as turbulence control, neuromechanical systems, and epidemiology, where the dynamics are wrought with uncertainty and time delays.

Fig. 8.2 shows the most general schematic for closed-loop feedback control, encompassing both optimal and robust control strategies. In the generalized theory of modern control, the goal is to minimize the transfer function from exogenous inputs **w** (reference, disturbances, noise, etc.) to a multi-objective cost function **J** (accuracy, actuation cost, time-domain performance, etc.). Optimal control (e.g., LQR, LQE, LQG) is optimal with respect to the $\mathcal{H}_2$ norm, a bounded two-norm on a Hardy space, consisting of stable and strictly proper transfer functions (meaning gain rolls off at high frequency). Robust control is similarly optimal with respect to the $\mathcal{H}_\infty$ bounded infinity-norm, consisting of stable and proper transfer functions (gain does not grow infinite at high frequencies). The infinity norm is defined as:

$$\|\mathbf{G}\|_\infty \triangleq \max_\omega \sigma_1 \left(\mathbf{G}(i\omega) \right). \tag{8.82}$$

Here, σ_1 denotes the maximum singular value. Since the $\| \cdot \|_\infty$ norm is the maximum value of the transfer function at any frequency, it is often called a *worst-case scenario norm*; therefore, minimizing the infinity norm provides robustness to worst-case exogenous inputs. $\mathcal{H}_\infty$ robust controllers are used when robustness is important. There are many connections between $\mathcal{H}_2$ and $\mathcal{H}_\infty$ control, as they exist within the same framework and simply optimize different norms. We refer the reader to the excellent reference books expanding on this theory [492, 165].

If we let $\mathbf{G}_{\mathbf{w} \rightarrow \mathbf{J}}$ denote the transfer function from $\mathbf{w}$ to $\mathbf{J}$, then the goal of $\mathcal{H}_\infty$ control is to construct a controller to minimize the infinity norm: min $\|\mathbf{G}_{\mathbf{w} \rightarrow \mathbf{J}}\|_\infty$. This is typically difficult, and no analytic closed-form solution exists for the optimal controller in general. However, there are relatively efficient iterative methods to find a controller such that $\|\mathbf{G}_{\mathbf{w} \rightarrow \mathbf{J}}\|_\infty < \gamma$, as described in [156]. There are numerous conditions and caveats that describe when this method can be used. In addition, there are computationally efficient algorithms implemented in both Matlab and Python, and these methods require relatively low overhead from the user.

Selecting the cost function $\mathbf{J}$ to meet design specifications is a critically important part of robust control design. Considerations such as disturbance rejection, noise attenuation, controller bandwidth, and actuation cost may be accounted for by a weighted sum of the transfer functions $\mathbf{S}$, $\mathbf{T}$, and $\mathbf{KS}$. In the *mixed sensitivity* control problem, various weighting transfer function are used to balance the relative importance of these considerations at various frequency ranges. For instance, we may weight $\mathbf{S}$ by a low-pass filter and $\mathbf{KS}$ by a high-pass filter, so that disturbance rejection at low frequency is promoted and control response at high-frequency is discouraged. A general cost function may consist of three weighting filters $\mathbf{F}_k$ multiplying $\mathbf{S}$, $\mathbf{T}$, and $\mathbf{KS}$:

$$\left\| \begin{bmatrix} \mathbf{F}_1 \mathbf{S} \\ \mathbf{F}_2 \mathbf{T} \\ \mathbf{F}_3 \mathbf{KS} \end{bmatrix} \right\|_\infty .$$

Another possible robust control design is called $\mathcal{H}_\infty$ loop-shaping. This procedure may be more straightforward than mixed sensitivity synthesis for many problems. The loop-shaping method consists of two major steps. First, a desired open-loop transfer function is specified based on performance goals and classical control design. Second, the shaped loop is made robust with respect to a large class of model uncertainty. Indeed, the procedure of $\mathcal{H}_\infty$ loop shaping allows the user to design an ideal controller to meet performance specifications, such as rise-time, band-width, settling-time, etc. Typically, a loop shape should have large gain at low frequency to guarantee accurate reference tracking and slow disturbance rejection, low gain at high frequencies to attenuate sensor noise, and a cross-over frequency that ensures desirable bandwidth. The loop transfer function is then robustified so that there are improved gain and phase margins.

$\mathcal{H}_2$ optimal control (e.g., LQR, LQE, LQG) has been an extremely popular control paradigm because of its simple mathematical formulation and its tunability by user input. However, the advantages of $\mathcal{H}_\infty$ control are being increasingly realized. Additionally, there are numerous consumer software solutions that make implementation relatively straightforward. In Matlab, mixed sensitivity is accomplished using the **mixsyn** command in the robust control toolbox. Similarly, loop-shaping is accomplished using the **loopsyn** command in the robust control toolbox.

Fundamental Limitations on Robust Performance
As discussed above, we want to minimize the peaks of $\mathbf{S}$ and $\mathbf{T}$ to improve robustness. Some peakedness is inevitable, and there are certain system characteristics that significantly limit performance and robustness. Most notably, time delays and right-half plane zeros of the open-loop system will limit the effective control bandwidth and will increase the attainable

lower-bound for peaks of **S** and **T**. This contributes to both degrading performance and decreasing robustness.

Similarly, a system will suffer from robust performance limitations if the number of poles exceeds the number of zeros by more than 2. These fundamental limitations are quantified in the *waterbed* integrals, which are so named because if you push a waterbed down in one location, it must rise in a another. Thus, there are limits to how much one can push down peaks in **S** without causing other peaks to pop up.

Time delays are relatively easy to understand, since a time delay τ will introduce an additional phase lag of $\tau\omega$ at the frequency ω, limiting how fast the controller can respond effectively (i.e. bandwidth). Thus, the bandwidth for a controller with acceptable phase margins is typically $\omega_B < 1/\tau$.

Following the discussion in [492], these fundamental limitations may be understood in relation to the limitations of open-loop control based on model inversion. If we consider high-gain feedback $\mathbf{u} = \mathbf{K}(\mathbf{w}_r - \mathbf{y})$ for a system as in Fig. 8.26 and (8.81), but without disturbances or noise, we have

$$\mathbf{u} = \mathbf{K}\epsilon = \mathbf{KSw}_r. \tag{8.83}$$

We may write this in terms of the complementary sensitivity **T**, by noting that since $\mathbf{T} = \mathbf{I} - \mathbf{S}$, we have $\mathbf{T} = \mathbf{L}(\mathbf{I} + \mathbf{L})^{-1} = \mathbf{GKS}$:

$$\mathbf{u} = \mathbf{G}^{-1}\mathbf{Tw}_r. \tag{8.84}$$

Thus, at frequencies where **T** is nearly the identity **I** and control is effective, the actuation is effectively inverting **G**. Even with sensor-based feedback, perfect control is unattainable. For example, if **G** has right-half plane zeros, then the actuation signal will become unbounded if the gain **K** is too aggressive. Similarly, limitations arise with time delays and when the number of poles of **G** exceed the number of zeros, as in the case of open-loop model-based inversion.

As a final illustration of the limitation of right-half plane zeros, we consider the case of proportional control $u = Ky$ in a single-input, single output system with $G(s) = N(s)/D(s)$. Here, roots of the numerator $N(s)$ are zeros and roots of the denominator $D(s)$ are poles. The closed-loop transfer function from reference w_r to sensors s is given by:

$$\frac{y(s)}{w_r(s)} = \frac{GK}{1 + GK} = \frac{NK/D}{1 + NK/D} = \frac{NK}{D + NK}. \tag{8.85}$$

For small control gain K, the term NK in the denominator is small, and the poles of the closed-loop system are near the poles of G, given by roots of D. As K is increased, the NK term in the denominator begins to dominate, and closed-loop poles are attracted to the roots of N, which are the open-loop zeros of G. Thus, if there are right-half plane zeros of the open-loop system G, then high-gain proportional control will drive the system unstable. These effects are often observed in the root locus plot from classical control theory. In this way, we see that right-half plane zeros will directly impose limitations on the gain margin of the controller.

Suggested Reading

Texts

(1) **Feedback Systems: An Introduction for Scientists and Engineers**, by K. J. Aström and R. M. Murray, 2010 [22].

(2) **Feedback Control Theory**, by J. C. Doyle, B. A. Francis, and A. R. Tannenbaum, 2013 [157].

(3) **Multivariable Feedback Control: Analysis and Design**, by S. Skogestad and I. Postlethwaite, 2005 [492].

(4) **A Course in Robust Control Theory: A Convex Approach**, by G. E. Dullerud and F. Paganini, 2000 [165].

(5) **Optimal Control and Estimation**, by R. F. Stengel, 2012 [501].

Papers and Reviews

(1) **Guaranteed margins for LQG regulators**, by J. C. Doyle, *IEEE Transactions on Automatic Control*, 1978 [155].

9 Balanced Models for Control

Many systems of interest are exceedingly high dimensional, making them difficult to characterize. High dimensionality also limits controller robustness due to significant computational time delays. For example, for the governing equations of fluid dynamics, the resulting discretized equations may have millions or billions of degrees of freedom, making them expensive to simulate. Thus, significant effort has gone into obtaining reduced-order models that capture the most relevant mechanisms and are suitable for feedback control.

Unlike reduced-order models based on proper orthogonal decomposition (see Chapters 11 and 12), which order modes based on energy content in the data, here we will discuss a class of *balanced* reduced-order models that employ a different inner product to order modes based on input–output energy. Thus, only modes that are both highly controllable and highly observable are selected, making balanced models ideal for control applications. In this chapter we also describe related procedures for model reduction and system identification, depending on whether or not the user starts with a high-fidelity model or simply has access to measurement data.

9.1 Model Reduction and System Identification

In many nonlinear systems, it is still possible to use linear control techniques. For example, in fluid dynamics there are numerous success stories of linear model-based flow control [27, 180, 94], for example to delay transition from laminar to turbulent flow in a spatially developing boundary layer, to reduce skin-friction drag in wall turbulence, and to stabilize the flow past an open cavity. However, many linear control approaches do not scale well to large state spaces, and they may be prohibitively expensive to enact for real-time control on short timescales. Thus, it is often necessary to develop low-dimensional approximations of the system for use in real-time feedback control.

There are two broad approaches to obtain reduced-order models (ROMs): First, it is possible to start with a high-dimensional system, such as the discretized Navier–Stokes equations, and project the dynamics onto a low-dimensional subspace identified, for example, using proper orthogonal decomposition (POD; Chapter 11) [57, 251] and Galerkin projection [441, 53]. There are numerous variations to this procedure, including the discrete empirical interpolation methods (DEIM; Section 12.5) [127, 419], gappy POD (Section 12.1) [179], balanced proper orthogonal decomposition (BPOD; Section 9.2) [554, 458], and many more. The second approach is to collect data from a simulation or an experiment and identify a low-rank model using data-driven techniques. This approach is typically called system identification, and is often preferred for control design because of the relative ease of implementation. Examples include the dynamic mode decomposition

(DMD; Section 7.2) [472, 456, 535, 317], the eigensystem realization algorithm (ERA; Section 9.3) [272, 351], the observer–Kalman filter identification (OKID; Section 9.3) [273, 428, 271], NARMAX [59], and the sparse identification of nonlinear dynamics (SINDy; Section 7.3) [95].

After a linear model has been identified, either by model reduction or system identification, it may then be used for model-based control design. However, there are a number of issues that may arise in practice, as linear model-based control might not work for a large class of systems. First, the system being modeled may be strongly nonlinear, in which case the linear approximation might only capture a small portion of the dynamic effects. Next, the system may be stochastically driven, so that the linear model will average out the relevant fluctuations. Finally, when control is applied to the full system, the attractor dynamics may change, rendering the linearized model invalid. Exceptions include the stabilization of fixed points, where feedback control rejects nonlinear disturbances and keeps the system in a neighborhood of the fixed point where the linearized model is accurate. There are also methods for system identification and model reduction that are nonlinear, involve stochasticity, and change with the attractor. However, these methods are typically advanced and they also may limit the available machinery from control theory.

9.2   Balanced Model Reduction

The high dimensionality and short timescales associated with complex systems may render the model-based control strategies described in Chapter 8 infeasible for real-time applications. Moreover, obtaining $\mathcal{H}_2$ and $\mathcal{H}_\infty$ optimal controllers may be computationally intractable, as they involve either solving a high-dimensional Riccati equation, or an expensive iterative optimization. As has been demonstrated throughout this book, even if the ambient dimension is large, there may still be a few dominant coherent structures that characterize the system. Reduced-order models provide efficient, low-dimensional representations of these most relevant mechanisms. Low-order models may then be used to design efficient controllers that can be applied in realtime, even for high-dimensional systems. An alternative is to develop controllers based on the full-dimensional model and then apply model reduction techniques directly to the full controller [209, 194, 410, 128].

Model reduction is essentially data reduction that respects the fact that the data is generated by a dynamic process. If the dynamical system is a linear time-invariant (LTI) input–output system, then there is a wealth of machinery available for model reduction, and performance bounds may be quantified. The techniques explored here are based on the singular value decomposition (SVD; Chapter 1) [212, 106, 211], and the minimal realization theory of Ho and Kalman [247, 388]. The general idea is to determine a hierarchical modal decomposition of the system state that may be truncated at some model order, only keeping the coherent structures that are most important for control.

The Goal of Model Reduction

Consider a high-dimensional system, depicted schematically in Fig. 9.1,

$$\frac{d}{dt}\mathbf{x} = \mathbf{A}\mathbf{x} + \mathbf{B}\mathbf{u}, \tag{9.1a}$$

$$\mathbf{y} = \mathbf{C}\mathbf{x} + \mathbf{D}\mathbf{u}, \tag{9.1b}$$

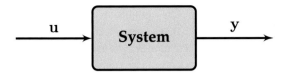

Figure 9.1 Input–output system. A control-oriented reduced-order model will capture the transfer function from **u** to **y**.

for example from a spatially discretized simulation of a PDE. The primary goal of model reduction is to find a coordinate transformation $\mathbf{x} = \boldsymbol{\Psi}\tilde{\mathbf{x}}$ giving rise to a related system $(\tilde{\mathbf{A}}, \tilde{\mathbf{B}}, \tilde{\mathbf{C}}, \tilde{\mathbf{D}})$ with similar input–output characteristics,

$$\frac{d}{dt}\tilde{\mathbf{x}} = \tilde{\mathbf{A}}\tilde{\mathbf{x}} + \tilde{\mathbf{B}}\mathbf{u}, \tag{9.2a}$$

$$\mathbf{y} = \tilde{\mathbf{C}}\tilde{\mathbf{x}} + \tilde{\mathbf{D}}\mathbf{u}, \tag{9.2b}$$

in terms of a state $\tilde{\mathbf{x}} \in \mathbb{R}^r$ with reduced dimension, $r \ll n$. Note that **u** and **y** are the same in (9.1) and (9.2) even though the system states are different. Obtaining the projection operator $\boldsymbol{\Psi}$ will be the focus of this section.

As a motivating example, consider the following simplified model:

$$\frac{d}{dt}\begin{bmatrix} x_1 \\ x_2 \end{bmatrix} = \begin{bmatrix} -2 & 0 \\ 0 & -1 \end{bmatrix}\begin{bmatrix} x_1 \\ x_2 \end{bmatrix} + \begin{bmatrix} 1 \\ 10^{-10} \end{bmatrix} u \tag{9.3a}$$

$$y = \begin{bmatrix} 1 & 10^{-10} \end{bmatrix}\begin{bmatrix} x_1 \\ x_2 \end{bmatrix}. \tag{9.3b}$$

In this case, the state x_2 is barely controllable and barely observable. Simply choosing $\tilde{x} = x_1$ will result in a reduced-order model that faithfully captures the input–output dynamics. Although the choice $\tilde{x} = x_1$ seems intuitive in this extreme case, many model reduction techniques would erroneously favor the state $\tilde{x} = x_2$, since it is more lightly damped. Throughout this section, we will investigate how to accurately and efficiently find the transformation matrix $\boldsymbol{\Psi}$ that best captures the input–output dynamics.

The proper orthogonal decomposition [57, 251] from Chapter 11 provides a transform matrix $\boldsymbol{\Psi}$, the columns of which are modes that are ordered based on energy content.[1] POD has been widely used to generate ROMs of complex systems, many for control, and it is guaranteed to provide an optimal low-rank basis to capture the maximal energy or variance in a data set. However, it may be the case that the most energetic modes are nearly uncontrollable or unobservable, and therefore may not be relevant for control. Similarly, in many cases the most controllable and observable state directions may have very low energy; for example, acoustic modes typically have very low energy, yet they mediate the dominant input–output dynamics in many fluid systems. The rudder on a ship provides a good analogy: although it accounts for a small amount of the total energy, it is dynamically important for control.

---

[1] When the training data consists of velocity fields, for example from a high-dimensional discretized fluid system, then the singular values literally indicate the kinetic energy content of the associated mode. It is common to refer to POD modes as being ordered by *energy* content, even in other applications, although *variance* is more technically correct.

Instead of ordering modes based on energy, it is possible to determine a hierarchy of modes that are most controllable and observable, therefore capturing the most input–output information. These modes give rise to *balanced* models, giving equal weighting to the controllability and observability of a state via a coordinate transformation that makes the controllability and observability Gramians equal and diagonal. These models have been extremely successful, although computing a balanced model using traditional methods is prohibitively expensive for high-dimensional systems. In this section, we describe the balancing procedure, as well as modern methods for efficient computation of balanced models. A computationally efficient suite of algorithms for model reduction and system identification may be found in [50].

A balanced reduced-order model should map inputs to outputs as faithfully as possible for a given model order r. It is therefore important to introduce an *operator norm* to quantify how similarly (9.1) and (9.2) act on a given set of inputs. Typically, we take the infinity norm of the difference between the transfer functions $\mathbf{G}(s)$ and $\mathbf{G}_r(s)$ obtained from the full system (9.1) and reduced system (9.2), respectively. This norm is given by:

$$\|\mathbf{G}\|_\infty \triangleq \max_\omega \sigma_1\left(\mathbf{G}(i\omega)\right). \tag{9.4}$$

See Section 8.8 for a primer on transfer functions. To summarize, we seek a reduced-order model (9.2) of low order, $r \ll n$, so the operator norm $\|\mathbf{G} - \mathbf{G}_r\|_\infty$ is small.

Change of Variables in Control Systems

The balanced model reduction problem may be formulated in terms of first finding a coordinate transformation

$$\mathbf{x} = \mathbf{Tz}, \tag{9.5}$$

that hierarchically orders the states in $\mathbf{z}$ in terms of their ability to capture the input–output characteristics of the system. We will begin by considering an invertible transformation $\mathbf{T} \in \mathbb{R}^{n \times n}$, and then provide a method to compute just the first r columns, which will comprise the transformation $\mathbf{\Psi}$ in (9.2). Thus, it will be possible to retain only the first r most controllable/observable states, while truncating the rest. This is similar to the change of variables into eigenvector coordinates in (8.18), except that we emphasize controllability and observability rather than characteristics of the dynamics.

Substituting $\mathbf{Tz}$ into (9.1) gives:

$$\frac{d}{dt}\mathbf{Tz} = \mathbf{ATz} + \mathbf{Bu} \tag{9.6a}$$

$$\mathbf{y} = \mathbf{CTz} + \mathbf{Du}. \tag{9.6b}$$

Finally, multiplying (9.6a) by $\mathbf{T}^{-1}$ yields:

$$\frac{d}{dt}\mathbf{z} = \mathbf{T}^{-1}\mathbf{ATz} + \mathbf{T}^{-1}\mathbf{Bu} \tag{9.7a}$$

$$\mathbf{y} = \mathbf{CTz} + \mathbf{Du}. \tag{9.7b}$$

This results in the following transformed equations:

$$\frac{d}{dt}\mathbf{z} = \hat{\mathbf{A}}\mathbf{z} + \hat{\mathbf{B}}\mathbf{u} \tag{9.8a}$$

$$y = \hat{\mathbf{C}}\mathbf{z} + \mathbf{D}\mathbf{u}, \tag{9.8b}$$

where $\hat{\mathbf{A}} = \mathbf{T}^{-1}\mathbf{A}\mathbf{T}$, $\hat{\mathbf{B}} = \mathbf{T}^{-1}\mathbf{B}$, and $\hat{\mathbf{C}} = \mathbf{C}\mathbf{T}$. Note that when the columns of $\mathbf{T}$ are orthonormal, the change of coordinates becomes:

$$\frac{d}{dt}\mathbf{z} = \mathbf{T}^*\mathbf{A}\mathbf{T}\mathbf{z} + \mathbf{T}^*\mathbf{B}\mathbf{u} \tag{9.9a}$$

$$y = \mathbf{C}\mathbf{T}\mathbf{z} + \mathbf{D}\mathbf{u}. \tag{9.9b}$$

Gramians and Coordinate Transformations

The controllability and observability Gramians each establish an inner product on state space in terms of how controllable or observable a given state is, respectively. As such, Gramians depend on the particular choice of coordinate system and will transform under a change of coordinates. In the coordinate system $\mathbf{z}$ given by (9.5), the controllability Gramian becomes:

$$\hat{\mathbf{W}}_c = \int_0^\infty e^{\hat{\mathbf{A}}\tau}\hat{\mathbf{B}}\hat{\mathbf{B}}^* e^{\hat{\mathbf{A}}^*\tau}\, d\tau \tag{9.10a}$$

$$= \int_0^\infty e^{\mathbf{T}^{-1}\mathbf{A}\mathbf{T}\tau}\mathbf{T}^{-1}\mathbf{B}\mathbf{B}^*\mathbf{T}^{-*} e^{\mathbf{T}^*\mathbf{A}^*\mathbf{T}^{-*}\tau}\, d\tau \tag{9.10b}$$

$$= \int_0^\infty \mathbf{T}^{-1}e^{\mathbf{A}\tau}\mathbf{T}\mathbf{T}^{-1}\mathbf{B}\mathbf{B}^*\mathbf{T}^{-*}\mathbf{T}^* e^{\mathbf{A}^*\tau}\mathbf{T}^{-*}\, d\tau \tag{9.10c}$$

$$= \mathbf{T}^{-1}\left(\int_0^\infty e^{\mathbf{A}\tau}\mathbf{B}\mathbf{B}^* e^{\mathbf{A}^\tau}\, d\tau\right)\mathbf{T}^{-*} \tag{9.10d}$$

$$= \mathbf{T}^{-1}\mathbf{W}_c\mathbf{T}^{-*}. \tag{9.10e}$$

Note that here we introduce $\mathbf{T}^{-*} := \left(\mathbf{T}^{-1}\right)^* = (\mathbf{T}^*)^{-1}$. The observability Gramian transforms similarly:

$$\hat{\mathbf{W}}_o = \mathbf{T}^*\mathbf{W}_o\mathbf{T}, \tag{9.11}$$

which is an exercise for the reader. Both Gramians transform as tensors (i.e., in terms of the transform matrix $\mathbf{T}$ and its transpose, rather than $\mathbf{T}$ and its inverse), which is consistent with them inducing an inner product on state-space.

Simple Rescaling

This example, modified from Moore 1981 [388], demonstrates the ability to balance a system through a change of coordinates. Consider the system

$$\frac{d}{dt}\begin{bmatrix} x_1 \\ x_2 \end{bmatrix} = \begin{bmatrix} -1 & 0 \\ 0 & -10 \end{bmatrix}\begin{bmatrix} x_1 \\ x_2 \end{bmatrix} + \begin{bmatrix} 10^{-3} \\ 10^3 \end{bmatrix}u \tag{9.12a}$$

$$y = \begin{bmatrix} 10^3 & 10^{-3} \end{bmatrix}\begin{bmatrix} x_1 \\ x_2 \end{bmatrix}. \tag{9.12b}$$

In this example, the first state x_1 is barely controllable, while the second state is barely observable. However, under the change of coordinates $z_1 = 10^3 x_1$ and $z_2 = 10^{-3}x_2$, the system becomes balanced:

$$\frac{d}{dt}\begin{bmatrix} z_1 \\ z_2 \end{bmatrix} = \begin{bmatrix} -1 & 0 \\ 0 & -10 \end{bmatrix}\begin{bmatrix} z_1 \\ z_2 \end{bmatrix} + \begin{bmatrix} 1 \\ 1 \end{bmatrix} u \tag{9.13a}$$

$$y = \begin{bmatrix} 1 & 1 \end{bmatrix}\begin{bmatrix} z_1 \\ z_2 \end{bmatrix}. \tag{9.13b}$$

In this example, the coordinate change simply rescales the state $\mathbf{x}$. For instance, it may be that the first state had units of millimeters while the second state had units of kilometers. Writing both states in meters balances the dynamics; that is, the controllability and observability Gramians are equal and diagonal.

Balancing Transformations

Now we are ready to derive the balancing coordinate transformation $\mathbf{T}$ that makes the controllability and observability Gramians equal and diagonal:

$$\hat{\mathbf{W}}_c = \hat{\mathbf{W}}_o = \mathbf{\Sigma}. \tag{9.14}$$

First, consider the product of the Gramians from (9.10) and (9.11):

$$\hat{\mathbf{W}}_c\hat{\mathbf{W}}_o = \mathbf{T}^{-1}\mathbf{W}_c\mathbf{W}_o\mathbf{T}. \tag{9.15}$$

Plugging in the desired $\hat{\mathbf{W}}_c = \hat{\mathbf{W}}_o = \mathbf{\Sigma}$ yields

$$\mathbf{T}^{-1}\mathbf{W}_c\mathbf{W}_o\mathbf{T} = \mathbf{\Sigma}^2 \implies \mathbf{W}_c\mathbf{W}_o\mathbf{T} = \mathbf{T}\mathbf{\Sigma}^2. \tag{9.16}$$

The latter expression in (9.16) is the equation for the eigendecomposition of $\mathbf{W}_c\mathbf{W}_o$, the product of the Gramians in the original coordinates. Thus, the balancing transformation $\mathbf{T}$ is related to the eigendecomposition of $\mathbf{W}_c\mathbf{W}_o$. The expression 9.16 is valid for any scaling of the eigenvectors, and the correct rescaling must be chosen to exactly balance the Gramians. In other words, there are many such transformations $\mathbf{T}$ that make the product $\hat{\mathbf{W}}_c\hat{\mathbf{W}}_o = \mathbf{\Sigma}^2$, but where the individual Gramians are not equal (for example diagonal Gramians $\hat{\mathbf{W}}_c = \mathbf{\Sigma}_c$ and $\hat{\mathbf{W}}_o = \mathbf{\Sigma}_o$ will satisfy (9.16) if $\mathbf{\Sigma}_c\mathbf{\Sigma}_o = \mathbf{\Sigma}^2$).

We will introduce the matrix $\mathbf{S} = \mathbf{T}^{-1}$ to simplify notation.

Scaling Eigenvectors for the balancing Transformation

To find the correct scaling of eigenvectors to make $\hat{\mathbf{W}}_c = \hat{\mathbf{W}}_o = \mathbf{\Sigma}$, first consider the simplified case of balancing the first diagonal element of $\mathbf{\Sigma}$. Let $\boldsymbol{\xi}_u$ denote the unscaled first column of $\mathbf{T}$, and let $\boldsymbol{\eta}_u$ denote the unscaled first row of $\mathbf{S} = \mathbf{T}^{-1}$. Then

$$\boldsymbol{\eta}_u\mathbf{W}_c\boldsymbol{\eta}_u^* = \sigma_c \tag{9.17a}$$

$$\boldsymbol{\xi}_u^*\mathbf{W}_o\boldsymbol{\xi}_u = \sigma_o. \tag{9.17b}$$

The first element of the diagonalized controllability Gramian is thus σ_c, while the first element of the diagonalized observability Gramian is σ_o. If we scale the eigenvector $\boldsymbol{\xi}_u$ by σ_s, then the inverse eigenvector $\boldsymbol{\eta}_u$ is scaled by σ_s^{-1}. Transforming via the new scaled eigenvectors $\boldsymbol{\xi}_s = \sigma_s\boldsymbol{\xi}_u$ and $\boldsymbol{\eta}_s = \sigma_s^{-1}\boldsymbol{\eta}_u$, yields:

$$\boldsymbol{\eta}_s\mathbf{W}_c\boldsymbol{\eta}_s^* = \sigma_s^{-2}\sigma_c, \tag{9.18a}$$

$$\boldsymbol{\xi}_s^*\mathbf{W}_o\boldsymbol{\xi}_s = \sigma_s^2\sigma_o. \tag{9.18b}$$

Thus, for the two Gramians to be equal,

$$\sigma_s^{-2}\sigma_c = \sigma_s^2\sigma_o \implies \sigma_s = \left(\frac{\sigma_c}{\sigma_o}\right)^{1/4}. \tag{9.19}$$

To balance every diagonal entry of the controllability and observability Gramians, we first consider the unscaled eigenvector transformation $\mathbf{T}_u$ from (9.16); the subscript u simply denotes *unscaled*. As an example, we use the standard scaling in most computational software so that the columns of $\mathbf{T}_u$ have unit norm. Then both Gramians are diagonalized, but are not necessarily equal:

$$\mathbf{T}_u^{-1}\mathbf{W}_c\mathbf{T}_u^{-*} = \mathbf{\Sigma}_c \tag{9.20a}$$

$$\mathbf{T}_u^*\mathbf{W}_o\mathbf{T}_u = \mathbf{\Sigma}_o. \tag{9.20b}$$

The scaling that exactly balances these Gramians is then given by $\mathbf{\Sigma}_s = \mathbf{\Sigma}_c^{1/4}\mathbf{\Sigma}_o^{-1/4}$. Thus, the exact balancing transformation is given by

$$\mathbf{T} = \mathbf{T}_u\mathbf{\Sigma}_s. \tag{9.21}$$

It is possible to directly confirm that this transformation balances the Gramians:

$$(\mathbf{T}_u\mathbf{\Sigma}_s)^{-1}\mathbf{W}_c\,(\mathbf{T}_u\mathbf{\Sigma}_s)^{-*} = \mathbf{\Sigma}_s^{-1}\mathbf{T}_u^{-1}\mathbf{W}_c\mathbf{T}_u^{-*}\mathbf{\Sigma}_s^{-1} = \mathbf{\Sigma}_s^{-1}\mathbf{\Sigma}_c\mathbf{\Sigma}_s^{-1} = \mathbf{\Sigma}_c^{1/2}\mathbf{\Sigma}_o^{1/2} \tag{9.22a}$$

$$(\mathbf{T}_u\mathbf{\Sigma}_s)^*\mathbf{W}_o\,(\mathbf{T}_u\mathbf{\Sigma}_s) = \mathbf{\Sigma}_s\mathbf{T}_u^*\mathbf{W}_o\mathbf{T}_u\mathbf{\Sigma}_s = \mathbf{\Sigma}_s\mathbf{\Sigma}_o\mathbf{\Sigma}_s = \mathbf{\Sigma}_c^{1/2}\mathbf{\Sigma}_o^{1/2}. \tag{9.22b}$$

Manipulations 9.22a and 9.22b rely on the fact that diagonal matrices commute, so that $\mathbf{\Sigma}_c\mathbf{\Sigma}_o = \mathbf{\Sigma}_o\mathbf{\Sigma}_c$, etc.

Example of the Balancing Transform and Gramians
Before confronting the practical challenges associated with accurately and efficiently computing the balancing transformation, it is helpful to consider an illustrative example.

In Matlab, computing the balanced system and the balancing transformation is a simple one-line command:

```
[sysb,g,Ti,T] = balreal(sys); % Balance system
```

In this code, $\mathbf{T}$ is the transformation, $\mathbf{Ti}$ is the inverse transformation, **sysb** is the balanced system, and **g** is a vector containing the diagonal elements of the balanced Gramians.

The following example illustrates the balanced realization for a two-dimensional system. First, we generate a system and compute its balanced realization, along with the Gramians for each system. Next, we visualize the Gramians of the unbalanced and balanced systems in Fig. 9.2.

Code 9.1 Obtaining a balanced realization.

```
A = [-.75 1; -.3 -.75];
B = [2; 1];
C = [1 2];
D = 0;

sys = ss(A,B,C,D);

Wc = gram(sys,'c'); % Controllability Gramian
Wo = gram(sys,'o'); % Observability Gramian
```

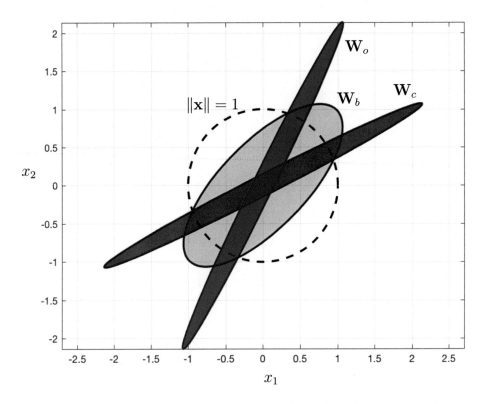

Figure 9.2 Illustration of balancing transformation on Gramians. The reachable set with unit control input is shown in red, given by $\mathbf{W}_c^{1/2}\mathbf{x}$ for $\|\mathbf{x}\| = 1$. The corresponding observable set is shown in blue. Under the balancing transformation $\mathbf{T}$, the Gramians are equal, shown in purple.

```
[sysb,g,Ti,T] = balreal(sys); % Balance the system

BWc = gram(sysb,'c') % Balanced Gramians
BWo = gram(sysb,'o')
```

The resulting balanced Gramians are equal, diagonal, and ordered from most controllable/observable mode to least:

```
>>BWc =
    1.9439   -0.0000
   -0.0000    0.3207

>>BWo =
    1.9439    0.0000
    0.0000    0.3207
```

To visualize the Gramians in Fig. 9.2, we first recall that the distance the system can go in a direction $\mathbf{x}$ with a unit actuation input is given by $\mathbf{x}^*\mathbf{W}_c\mathbf{x}$. Thus, the controllability Gramian may be visualized by plotting $\mathbf{W}_c^{1/2}\mathbf{x}$ for $\mathbf{x}$ on a sphere with $\|\mathbf{x}\| = 1$. The observability Gramian may be similarly visualized.

In this example, we see that the most controllable and observable directions may not be well aligned. However, by a change of coordinates, it is possible to find a new direction that is the most jointly controllable and observable. It is then possible to represent the system in this one-dimensional subspace, while still capturing a significant portion of the input–output energy. If the red and blue Gramians were exactly perpendicular, so that the most controllable direction was the least observable direction, and vice versa, then the balanced Gramian would be a circle. In this case, there is no preferred state direction, and both directions are equally important for the input–output behavior.

Instead of using the **balreal** command, it is possible to manually construct the balancing transformation from the eigendecomposition of $\mathbf{W}_c\mathbf{W}_o$, as described earlier and provided in code available online.

Balanced Truncation

We have now shown that it is possible to define a change of coordinates so that the controllability and observability Gramians are equal and diagonal. Moreover, these new coordinates may be ranked hierarchically in terms of their joint controllability and observability. It may be possible to truncate these coordinates and keep only the most controllable/observable directions, resulting in a reduced-order model that faithfully captures input–output dynamics.

Given the new coordinates $\mathbf{z} = \mathbf{T}^{-1}\mathbf{x} \in \mathbb{R}^n$, it is possible to define a reduced-order state $\tilde{\mathbf{x}} \in \mathbb{R}^r$, as

$$
\mathbf{z} = \left.\begin{bmatrix} z_1 \\ \vdots \\ z_r \\ z_{r+1} \\ \vdots \\ z_n \end{bmatrix}\right\} \tilde{\mathbf{x}}
\tag{9.23}
$$

in terms of the first r most controllable and observable directions. If we partition the balancing transformation $\mathbf{T}$ and inverse transformation $\mathbf{S} = \mathbf{T}^{-1}$ into the first r modes to be retained and the last $n - r$ modes to be truncated,

$$
\mathbf{T} = \begin{bmatrix} \mathbf{\Psi} & \mathbf{T}_t \end{bmatrix}, \quad \mathbf{S} = \begin{bmatrix} \mathbf{\Phi}^* \\ \mathbf{S}_t \end{bmatrix},
\tag{9.24}
$$

then it is possible to rewrite the transformed dynamics in (9.7) as:

$$
\frac{d}{dt}\begin{bmatrix} \tilde{\mathbf{x}} \\ \mathbf{z}_t \end{bmatrix} = \left[\begin{array}{c|c} \mathbf{\Phi}^*\mathbf{A}\mathbf{\Psi} & \mathbf{\Phi}^*\mathbf{A}\mathbf{T}_t \\ \hline \mathbf{S}_t\mathbf{A}\mathbf{\Psi} & \mathbf{S}_t\mathbf{A}\mathbf{T}_t \end{array}\right]\begin{bmatrix} \tilde{\mathbf{x}} \\ \mathbf{z}_t \end{bmatrix} + \begin{bmatrix} \mathbf{\Phi}^*\mathbf{B} \\ \mathbf{S}_t\mathbf{B} \end{bmatrix}\mathbf{u}
\tag{9.25a}
$$

$$
\mathbf{y} = \begin{bmatrix} \mathbf{C}\mathbf{\Psi} & \mathbf{C}\mathbf{T}_t \end{bmatrix}\begin{bmatrix} \tilde{\mathbf{x}} \\ \mathbf{z}_t \end{bmatrix} + \mathbf{D}\mathbf{u}.
\tag{9.25b}
$$

In balanced truncation, the state $\mathbf{z}_t$ is simply truncated (i.e., discarded and set equal to zero), and only the $\tilde{\mathbf{x}}$ equations remain:

$$
\frac{d}{dt}\tilde{\mathbf{x}} = \mathbf{\Phi}^*\mathbf{A}\mathbf{\Psi}\tilde{\mathbf{x}} + \mathbf{\Phi}^*\mathbf{B}\mathbf{u}
\tag{9.26a}
$$

$$
\mathbf{y} = \mathbf{C}\mathbf{\Psi}\tilde{\mathbf{x}} + \mathbf{D}\mathbf{u}.
\tag{9.26b}
$$

Only the first r columns of $\mathbf{T}$ and $\mathbf{S}^* = \mathbf{T}^{-*}$ are required to construct $\boldsymbol{\Psi}$ and $\boldsymbol{\Phi}$, and thus computing the entire balancing transformation $\mathbf{T}$ is unnecessary. Note that the matrix $\boldsymbol{\Phi}$ here is different than the matrix of DMD modes in Section 7.2. The computation of $\boldsymbol{\Psi}$ and $\boldsymbol{\Phi}$ without $\mathbf{T}$ will be discussed in the following sections. A key benefit of balanced truncation is the existence of upper and lower bounds on the error of a given order truncation:

$$\text{Upper bound:} \quad \|\mathbf{G} - \mathbf{G}_r\|_\infty \leq 2 \sum_{j=r+1}^{n} \sigma_j, \tag{9.27a}$$

$$\text{Lower bound:} \quad \|\mathbf{G} - \mathbf{G}_r\|_\infty > \sigma_{r+1}, \tag{9.27b}$$

where σ_j is the jth diagonal entry of the balanced Gramians. The diagonal entries of $\boldsymbol{\Sigma}$ are also known as *Hankel singular values*.

Computing Balanced Realizations

In the previous section we demonstrated the feasibility of obtaining a coordinate transformation that balances the controllability and observability Gramians. However, the computation of this balancing transformation is nontrivial, and significant work has gone into obtaining accurate and efficient methods, starting with Moore in 1981 [388], and continuing with Lall, Marsden, and Glavaški in 2002 [321], Willcox and Peraire in 2002 [554] and Rowley in 2005 [458]. For an excellent and complete treatment of balanced realizations and model reduction, see Antoulas [17].

In practice, computing the Gramians $\mathbf{W}_c$ and $\mathbf{W}_o$ and the eigendecomposition of the product $\mathbf{W}_c \mathbf{W}_o$ in (9.16) may be prohibitively expensive for high-dimensional systems. Instead, the balancing transformation may be approximated from impulse-response data, utilizing the singular value decomposition for efficient extraction of the most relevant subspaces.

We will first show that Gramians may be approximated via a snapshot matrix from impulse-response experiments/simulations. Then, we will show how the balancing transformation may be obtained from this data.

Empirical Gramians

In practice, computing Gramians via the Lyapunov equation is computationally expensive, with computational complexity of $\mathcal{O}(n^3)$. Instead, the Gramians may be approximated by full-state measurements of the discrete-time direct and adjoint systems:

$$\textit{direct:} \quad \mathbf{x}_{k+1} = \mathbf{A}_d \mathbf{x}_k + \mathbf{B}_d \mathbf{u}_k, \tag{9.28a}$$

$$\textit{adjoint:} \quad \mathbf{x}_{k+1} = \mathbf{A}_d^* \mathbf{x}_k + \mathbf{C}_d^* \mathbf{y}_k. \tag{9.28b}$$

(9.28a) is the discrete-time dynamic update equation from (8.21), and (9.28b) is the adjoint equation. The matrices $\mathbf{A}_d$, $\mathbf{B}_d$, and $\mathbf{C}_d$ are the discrete-time system matrices from (8.22). Note that the adjoint equation is generally nonphysical, and must be simulated; thus the methods here apply to analytical equations and simulations, but not to experimental data. An alternative formulation that does not rely on adjoint data, and therefore generalizes to experiments, will be provided in Section 9.3.

Computing the impulse-response of the direct and adjoint systems yields the following discrete-time snapshot matrices:

$$
\mathcal{C}_d = \begin{bmatrix} \mathbf{B}_d & \mathbf{A}_d\mathbf{B}_d & \cdots & \mathbf{A}_d^{m_c-1}\mathbf{B}_d \end{bmatrix} \qquad \mathcal{O}_d = \begin{bmatrix} \mathbf{C}_d \\ \mathbf{C}_d\mathbf{A}_d \\ \vdots \\ \mathbf{C}_d\mathbf{A}_d^{m_o-1} \end{bmatrix}. \tag{9.29}
$$

Note that when $m_c = n$, $\mathcal{C}_d$ is the discrete-time controllability matrix and when $m_o = n$, $\mathcal{O}_d$ is the discrete-time observability matrix; however, we generally consider $m_c, m_o \ll n$. These matrices may also be obtained by sampling the continuous-time direct and adjoint systems at a regular interval Δt.

It is now possible to compute *empirical* Gramians that approximate the true Gramians without solving the Lyapunov equations in (8.42) and (8.43):

$$
\mathbf{W}_c \approx \mathbf{W}_c^e = \mathcal{C}_d\mathcal{C}_d^*, \tag{9.30a}
$$
$$
\mathbf{W}_o \approx \mathbf{W}_o^e = \mathcal{O}_d^*\mathcal{O}_d. \tag{9.30b}
$$

The empirical Gramians essentially comprise a Riemann sum approximation of the integral in the continuous-time Gramians, which becomes exact as the time-step of the discrete-time system becomes arbitrarily small and the duration of the impulse response becomes arbitrarily large. In practice, the impulse-response snapshots should be collected until the lightly-damped transients die out. The method of empirical Gramians is quite efficient, and is widely used [388, 320, 321, 554, 458]. Note that p adjoint impulse responses are required, where p is the number of outputs. This becomes intractable when there are a large number of outputs (e.g., full state measurements), motivating the output projection in the next section.

Balanced POD

Instead of computing the eigendecomposition of $\mathbf{W}_c\mathbf{W}_o$, which is an $n \times n$ matrix, it is possible to compute the balancing transformation via the singular value decomposition of the product of the snapshot matrices,

$$
\mathcal{O}_d\mathcal{C}_d, \tag{9.31}
$$

reminiscent of the method of snapshots from Section 1.3 [490]. This is the approach taken by Rowley [458].

First, define the generalized Hankel matrix as the product of the adjoint ($\mathcal{O}_d$) and direct ($\mathcal{C}_d$) snapshot matrices from (9.29), for the discrete-time system:

$$
\mathbf{H} = \mathcal{O}_d\mathcal{C}_d = \begin{bmatrix} \mathbf{C}_d \\ \mathbf{C}_d\mathbf{A}_d \\ \vdots \\ \mathbf{C}_d\mathbf{A}_d^{m_o-1} \end{bmatrix} \begin{bmatrix} \mathbf{B}_d & \mathbf{A}_d\mathbf{B}_d & \cdots & \mathbf{A}_d^{m_c-1}\mathbf{B}_d \end{bmatrix} \tag{9.32a}
$$

$$= \begin{bmatrix} \mathbf{C}_d \mathbf{B}_d & \mathbf{C}_d \mathbf{A}_d \mathbf{B}_d & \cdots & \mathbf{C}_d \mathbf{A}_d^{m_c-1} \mathbf{B}_d \\ \mathbf{C}_d \mathbf{A}_d \mathbf{B}_d & \mathbf{C}_d \mathbf{A}_d^2 \mathbf{B}_d & \cdots & \mathbf{C}_d \mathbf{A}_d^{m_c} \mathbf{B}_d \\ \vdots & \vdots & \ddots & \vdots \\ \mathbf{C}_d \mathbf{A}_d^{m_o-1} \mathbf{B}_d & \mathbf{C}_d \mathbf{A}_d^{m_o} \mathbf{B}_d & \cdots & \mathbf{C}_d \mathbf{A}_d^{m_c+m_o-2} \mathbf{B}_d \end{bmatrix}. \tag{9.32b}$$

Next, we factor $\mathbf{H}$ using the SVD:

$$\mathbf{H} = \mathbf{U}\boldsymbol{\Sigma}\mathbf{V}^* = \begin{bmatrix} \tilde{\mathbf{U}} & \mathbf{U}_t \end{bmatrix} \begin{bmatrix} \tilde{\boldsymbol{\Sigma}} & \mathbf{0} \\ \mathbf{0} & \boldsymbol{\Sigma}_t \end{bmatrix} \begin{bmatrix} \tilde{\mathbf{V}}^* \\ \mathbf{V}_t^* \end{bmatrix} \approx \tilde{\mathbf{U}}\tilde{\boldsymbol{\Sigma}}\tilde{\mathbf{V}}^*. \tag{9.33}$$

For a given desired model order $r \ll n$, only the first r columns of $\mathbf{U}$ and $\mathbf{V}$ are retained, along with the first $r \times r$ block of $\boldsymbol{\Sigma}$; the remaining contribution from $\mathbf{U}_t \boldsymbol{\Sigma}_t \mathbf{V}_t^*$ may be truncated. This yields a bi-orthogonal set of modes given by:

$$\text{direct modes:} \quad \boldsymbol{\Psi} = \mathcal{C}_d \tilde{\mathbf{V}} \tilde{\boldsymbol{\Sigma}}^{-1/2}, \tag{9.34a}$$

$$\text{adjoint modes:} \quad \boldsymbol{\Phi} = \mathcal{O}_d^* \tilde{\mathbf{U}} \tilde{\boldsymbol{\Sigma}}^{-1/2}. \tag{9.34b}$$

The direct modes $\boldsymbol{\Psi} \in \mathbb{R}^{n \times r}$ and adjoint modes $\boldsymbol{\Phi} \in \mathbb{R}^{n \times r}$ are bi-orthogonal, $\boldsymbol{\Phi}^* \boldsymbol{\Psi} = \mathbf{I}_{r \times r}$, and Rowley [458] showed that they establish the change of coordinates that balance the truncated empirical Gramians. Thus, $\boldsymbol{\Psi}$ approximates the first r-columns of the full $n \times n$ balancing transformation, $\mathbf{T}$, and $\boldsymbol{\Phi}^*$ approximates the first r-rows of the $n \times n$ inverse balancing transformation, $\mathbf{S} = \mathbf{T}^{-1}$.

Now, it is possible to project the original system onto these modes, yielding a balanced reduced-order model of order r:

$$\tilde{\mathbf{A}} = \boldsymbol{\Phi}^* \mathbf{A}_d \boldsymbol{\Psi}, \tag{9.35a}$$

$$\tilde{\mathbf{B}} = \boldsymbol{\Phi}^* \mathbf{B}_d, \tag{9.35b}$$

$$\tilde{\mathbf{C}} = \mathbf{C}_d \boldsymbol{\Psi}. \tag{9.35c}$$

It is possible to compute the reduced system dynamics in (9.35a) without having direct access to $\mathbf{A}_d$. In some cases, $\mathbf{A}_d$ may be exceedingly large and unwieldy, and instead it is only possible to evaluate the action of this matrix on an input vector. For example, in many modern fluid dynamics codes the matrix $\mathbf{A}_d$ is not actually represented, but because it is sparse, it is possible to implement efficient routines to multiply this matrix by a vector.

It is important to note that the reduced-order model in (9.35) is formulated in discrete time, as it is based on discrete-time empirical snapshot matrices. However, it is simple to obtain the corresponding continuous-time system:

```
>>sysD = ss(Atilde,Btilde,Ctilde,D,dt);   % Discrete-time
>>sysC = d2c(sysD);                        % Continuous-time
```

In this example, $\mathbf{D}$ is the same in continuous time and discrete time, and in the full-order and reduced-order models.

Note that a BPOD model may not exactly satisfy the upper bound from balanced truncation (see (9.27)) due to errors in the empirical Gramians.

Output Projection
Often, in high-dimensional simulations, we assume full-state measurements, so that $p = n$ is exceedingly large. To avoid computing $p = n$ adjoint simulations, it is possible instead to solve an output-projected adjoint equation [458]:

$$\mathbf{x}_{k+1} = \mathbf{A}_d^* \mathbf{x}_k + \mathbf{C}_d^* \tilde{\mathbf{U}} \mathbf{y} \qquad (9.36)$$

where $\tilde{\mathbf{U}}$ is a matrix containing the first r singular vectors of $\mathcal{C}_d$. Thus, we first identify a low-dimensional POD subspace $\tilde{\mathbf{U}}$ from a direct impulse response, and then only perform adjoint impulse response simulations by exciting these few *POD coefficient* measurements. More generally, if $\mathbf{y}$ is high dimensional but does not measure the full state, it is possible to use a POD subspace trained on the measurements, given by the first r singular vectors $\tilde{\mathbf{U}}$ of $\mathbf{C}_d \mathcal{C}_d$. Adjoint impulse responses may then be performed in these output POD directions.

Data Collection and Stacking

The powers m_c and m_o in (9.32) signify that data must be collected until the matrices $\mathcal{C}_d$ and $\mathcal{O}_d^*$ are full rank, after which the controllable/observable subspaces have been sampled. Unless we collect data until transients decay, the true Gramians are only approximately balanced. Instead, it is possible to collect data until the Hankel matrix is full rank, balance the resulting model, and then truncate. This more efficient approach is developed in [533] and [346].

The snapshot matrices in (9.29) are generated from impulse-response simulations of the direct (9.28a) and adjoint (9.36) systems. These time-series snapshots are then interleaved to form the snapshot matrices.

Historical Note

The balanced POD method described in the previous subsection originated with the seminal work of Moore in 1981 [388], which provided a data-driven generalization of the minimal realization theory of Ho and Kalman [247]. Until then, minimal realizations were defined in terms of idealized controllable and observable subspaces, which neglected the subtlety of degrees of controllability and observability.

Moore's paper introduced a number of critical concepts that bridged the gap from theory to reality. First, he established a connection between principal component analysis (PCA) and Gramians, showing that information about degrees of controllability and observability may be mined from data via the SVD. Next, Moore showed that a balancing transformation exists that makes the Gramians equal, diagonal, and hierarchically ordered by balanced controllability and observability; moreover, he provides an algorithm to compute this transformation. This set the stage for principled model reduction, whereby states may be truncated based on their joint controllability and observability. Moore further introduced the notion of an empirical Gramian, although he didn't use this terminology. He also realized that computing $\mathbf{W}_c$ and $\mathbf{W}_o$ directly is less accurate than computing the SVD of the empirical snapshot matrices from the direct and adjoint systems, and he avoided directly computing the eigendecomposition of $\mathbf{W}_c \mathbf{W}_o$ by using these SVD transformations. In 2002, Lall, Marsden, and Glavaški in 2002 [321] generalized this theory to nonlinear systems.

One drawback of Moore's approach is that he computed the entire $n \times n$ balancing transformation, which is not suitable for exceedingly high-dimensional systems. In 2002, Willcox and Peraire [554] generalized the method to high-dimensional systems, introducing a variant based on the rank-r decompositions of $\mathbf{W}_c$ and $\mathbf{W}_o$ obtained from the direct and adjoint snapshot matrices. It is then possible to compute the eigendecomposition of $\mathbf{W}_c \mathbf{W}_o$ using efficient eigenvalue solvers without ever actually writing down the full $n \times n$ matrices. However, this approach has the drawback of requiring as many adjoint impulse-response simulations as the number of output equations, which may be exceedingly large for full-state measurements. In 2005, Rowley [458] addressed this issue by introducing the output projection, discussed previously, which limits the number of adjoint simulations to the number of relevant POD modes in the data. He also showed that it is possible to use the eigendecomposition of the product $\mathcal{O}_d \mathcal{C}_d$. The product $\mathcal{O}_d \mathcal{C}_d$ is often smaller, and these computations may be more accurate.

It is interesting to note that a nearly equivalent formulation was developed twenty years earlier in the field of system identification. The so-called eigensystem realization algorithm (ERA) [272], introduced in 1985 by Juang and Pappa, obtains equivalent balanced models without the need for adjoint data, making it useful for system identification in experiments. This connection between ERA and BPOD was established by Ma et al. in 2011 [351].

Balanced Model Reduction Example

In this example we will demonstrate the computation of balanced truncation and balanced POD models on a random state-space system with $n = 100$ states, $q = 2$ inputs, and $p = 2$ outputs. First, we generate a system in Matlab:

```
q = 2;     % Number of inputs
p = 2;     % Number of outputs
n = 100;   % State dimension
sysFull = drss(n,p,q);  % Discrete random system
```

Next, we compute the Hankel singular values, which are plotted in Fig. 9.3. We see that $r = 10$ modes captures over 90% of the input–output energy.

```
hsvs = hsvd(sysFull);  % Hankel singular values
```

Now we construct an exact balanced truncation model with order $r = 10$:

```
%% Exact balanced truncation
sysBT = balred(sysFull,r);  % Balanced truncation
```

The full-order system, and the balanced truncation and balanced POD models are compared in Fig. 9.4. The BPOD model is computed using Code 9.2. It can be seen that the

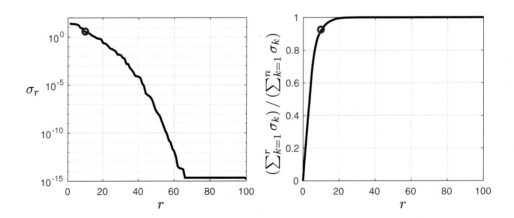

Figure 9.3 Hankel singular values (left) and cumulative energy (right) for random state space system with $n = 100$, $p = q = 2$. The first $r = 10$ HSVs contain 92.9% of the energy.

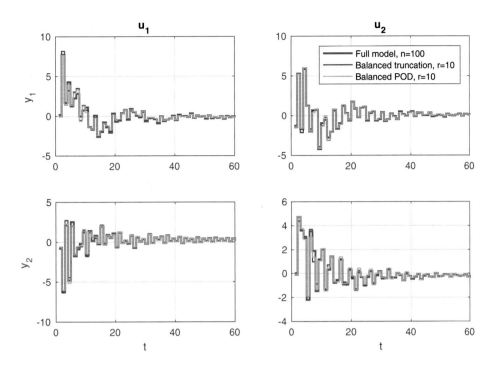

Figure 9.4 Impulse response of full-state model with $n = 100$, $p = q = 2$, along with balanced truncation and balanced POD models with $r = 10$.

balanced model accurately captures the dominant input–output dynamics, even when only 10% of the modes are kept.

Code 9.2 Balanced proper orthogonal decomposition (BPOD).

```
sysBPOD = BPOD(sysFull,sysAdj,r)

[yFull,t,xFull] = impulse(sysFull,0:1:(r*5)+1);
sysAdj = ss(sysFull.A',sysFull.C',sysFull.B',sysFull.D',-1);
[yAdj,t,xAdj] = impulse(sysAdj,0:1:(r*5)+1);
% Not the fastest way to compute, but illustrative
% Both xAdj and xFull are size m x n x 2
HankelOC = [];   % Compute Hankel matrix H=OC
for i=2:size(xAdj,1) % Start at 2 to avoid the D matrix
    Hrow = [];
    for j=2:size(xFull,1)
        Ystar = permute(squeeze(xAdj(i,:,:)),[2 1]);
        MarkovParameter = Ystar*squeeze(xFull(j,:,:));
        Hrow = [Hrow MarkovParameter];
    end
    HankelOC = [HankelOC; Hrow];
end
[U,Sig,V] = svd(HankelOC);
Xdata = [];
Ydata = [];
for i=2:size(xFull,1)   % Start at 2 to avoid the D matrix
    Xdata = [Xdata squeeze(xFull(i,:,:))];
    Ydata = [Ydata squeeze(xAdj(i,:,:))];
end
```

```
Phi = Xdata*V*Sig^(-1/2);
Psi = Ydata*U*Sig^(-1/2);
Ar = Psi(:,1:r)'*sysFull.a*Phi(:,1:r);
Br = Psi(:,1:r)'*sysFull.b;
Cr = sysFull.c*Phi(:,1:r);
Dr = sysFull.d;
sysBPOD = ss(Ar,Br,Cr,Dr,-1);
```

9.3   System Identification

In contrast to model reduction, where the system model $(\mathbf{A}, \mathbf{B}, \mathbf{C}, \mathbf{D})$ was known, system identification is purely data-driven. System identification may be thought of as a form of machine learning, where an input–output map of a system is learned from training data in a representation that generalizes to data that was not in the training set. There is a vast literature on methods for system identification [271, 338], and many of the leading methods are based on a form of dynamic regression that fits models based on data, such as the DMD from Section 7.2. For this section, we consider the eigensystem realization algorithm (ERA) and observer-Kalman filter identification (OKID) methods because of their connection to balanced model reduction [388, 458, 351, 535] and their successful application in high-dimensional systems such as vibration control of aerospace structures and closed-loop flow control [27, 26, 261]. The ERA/OKID procedure is also applicable to multiple-input, multiple-output (MIMO) systems. Other methods include the autoregressive moving average (ARMA) and autoregressive moving average with exogenous inputs (ARMAX) models [552, 72], the nonlinear autoregressive-moving average with exogenous inputs (NARMAX) [59] model, and the SINDy method from Section 7.3.

Eigensystem Realization Algorithm

The eigensystem realization algorithm produces low-dimensional linear input–output models from sensor measurements of an impulse response experiment, based on the "minimal realization" theory of Ho and Kalman [247]. The modern theory was developed to identify structural models for various spacecraft [272], and it has been shown by Ma *et al.* [351] that ERA models are equivalent to BPOD models[2]. However, ERA is based entirely on impulse response measurements and does not require prior knowledge of a model.

We consider a discrete-time system, as described in Section 8.2:

$$\mathbf{x}_{k+1} = \mathbf{A}_d\mathbf{x}_k + \mathbf{B}_d\mathbf{u}_k \tag{9.37a}$$

$$\mathbf{y}_k = \mathbf{C}_d\mathbf{x}_k + \mathbf{D}_d\mathbf{u}_k. \tag{9.37b}$$

A discrete-time delta function input in the actuation $\mathbf{u}$:

$$\mathbf{u}_k^\delta \triangleq \mathbf{u}^\delta(k\Delta t) = \begin{cases} \mathbf{I}, & k = 0 \\ \mathbf{0}, & k = 1, 2, 3, \cdots \end{cases} \tag{9.38}$$

---

[2] BPOD and ERA models both balance the empirical Gramians and approximate balanced truncation [388] for high-dimensional systems, given a sufficient volume of data.

gives rise to a discrete-time impulse response in the sensors **y**:

$$
\mathbf{y}_k^\delta \triangleq \mathbf{y}^\delta (k \Delta t) = \begin{cases} \mathbf{D}_d, & k = 0 \\ \mathbf{C}_d \mathbf{A}_d^{k-1} \mathbf{B}_d, & k = 1, 2, 3, \cdots . \end{cases} \tag{9.39}
$$

In an experiment or simulation, typically q impulse responses are performed, one for each of the q separate input channels. The output responses are collected for each impulsive input, and at a given time-step k, the output vector in response to the j-th impulsive input will form the j-th column of $\mathbf{y}_k^\delta$. Thus, each of the $\mathbf{y}_k^\delta$ is a $p \times q$ matrix $\mathbf{C A}^{k-1} \mathbf{B}$. Note that the system matrices $(\mathbf{A}, \mathbf{B}, \mathbf{C}, \mathbf{D})$ don't actually need to exist, as the method in the next section is purely data-driven.

The Hankel matrix $\mathbf{H}$ from (9.32), is formed by stacking shifted time-series of impulse-response measurements into a matrix, as in the HAVOK method from Section 7.5:

$$
\mathbf{H} = \begin{bmatrix} \mathbf{y}_1^\delta & \mathbf{y}_2^\delta & \cdots & \mathbf{y}_{m_c}^\delta \\ \mathbf{y}_2^\delta & \mathbf{y}_3^\delta & \cdots & \mathbf{y}_{m_c+1}^\delta \\ \vdots & \vdots & \ddots & \vdots \\ \mathbf{y}_{m_o}^\delta & \mathbf{y}_{m_o+1}^\delta & \cdots & \mathbf{y}_{m_c+m_o-1}^\delta \end{bmatrix} \tag{9.40a}
$$

$$
= \begin{bmatrix} \mathbf{C}_d \mathbf{B}_d & \mathbf{C}_d \mathbf{A}_d \mathbf{B}_d & \cdots & \mathbf{C}_d \mathbf{A}_d^{m_c-1} \mathbf{B}_d \\ \mathbf{C}_d \mathbf{A}_d \mathbf{B}_d & \mathbf{C}_d \mathbf{A}_d^2 \mathbf{B}_d & \cdots & \mathbf{C}_d \mathbf{A}_d^{m_c} \mathbf{B}_d \\ \vdots & \vdots & \ddots & \vdots \\ \mathbf{C}_d \mathbf{A}_d^{m_o-1} \mathbf{B}_d & \mathbf{C}_d \mathbf{A}_d^{m_o} \mathbf{B}_d & \cdots & \mathbf{C}_d \mathbf{A}_d^{m_c+m_o-2} \mathbf{B}_d \end{bmatrix}. \tag{9.40b}
$$

The matrix $\mathbf{H}$ may be constructed purely from measurements $\mathbf{y}^\delta$, without separately constructing $\mathcal{O}_d$ and $\mathcal{C}_d$. Thus, we do not need access to adjoint equations.

Taking the SVD of the Hankel matrix yields the dominant temporal patterns in the time-series data:

$$
\mathbf{H} = \mathbf{U} \boldsymbol{\Sigma} \mathbf{V}^* = \begin{bmatrix} \tilde{\mathbf{U}} & \mathbf{U}_t \end{bmatrix} \begin{bmatrix} \tilde{\boldsymbol{\Sigma}} & \mathbf{0} \\ \mathbf{0} & \boldsymbol{\Sigma}_t \end{bmatrix} \begin{bmatrix} \tilde{\mathbf{V}}^* \\ \mathbf{V}_t^* \end{bmatrix} \approx \tilde{\mathbf{U}} \tilde{\boldsymbol{\Sigma}} \tilde{\mathbf{V}}^*. \tag{9.41}
$$

The small small singular values in $\boldsymbol{\Sigma}_t$ are truncated, and only the first r singular values in $\tilde{\boldsymbol{\Sigma}}$ are retained. The columns of $\tilde{\mathbf{U}}$ and $\tilde{\mathbf{V}}$ are *eigen*-time-delay coordinates.

Until this point, the ERA algorithm closely resembles the BPOD procedure from Section 9.2. However, we don't require direct access to $\mathcal{O}_d$ and $\mathcal{C}_d$ or the system $(\mathbf{A}, \mathbf{B}, \mathbf{C}, \mathbf{D})$ to construct the direct and adjoint balancing transformations. Instead, with sensor measurements from an impulse-response experiment, it is also possible to create a second, shifted Hankel matrix $\mathbf{H}'$:

$$
\mathbf{H}' = \begin{bmatrix} \mathbf{y}_2 & \mathbf{y}_3^\delta & \cdots & \mathbf{y}_{m_c+1}^\delta \\ \mathbf{y}_3^\delta & \mathbf{y}_4^\delta & \cdots & \mathbf{y}_{m_c+2}^\delta \\ \vdots & \vdots & \ddots & \vdots \\ \mathbf{y}_{m_o+1}^\delta & \mathbf{y}_{m_o+2}^\delta & \cdots & \mathbf{y}_{m_c+m_o}^\delta \end{bmatrix} \tag{9.42a}
$$

$$= \begin{bmatrix} \mathbf{C}_d \mathbf{A}_d \mathbf{B}_d & \mathbf{C}_d \mathbf{A}_d^2 \mathbf{B}_d & \cdots & \mathbf{C}_d \mathbf{A}_d^{m_c} \mathbf{B}_d \\ \mathbf{C}_d \mathbf{A}_d^2 \mathbf{B}_d & \mathbf{C}_d \mathbf{A}_d^3 \mathbf{B}_d & \cdots & \mathbf{C}_d \mathbf{A}_d^{m_c+1} \mathbf{B}_d \\ \vdots & \vdots & \ddots & \vdots \\ \mathbf{C}_d \mathbf{A}_d^{m_o} \mathbf{B}_d & \mathbf{C}_d \mathbf{A}_d^{m_o+1} \mathbf{B}_d & \cdots & \mathbf{C}_d \mathbf{A}_d^{m_c+m_o-1} \mathbf{B}_d \end{bmatrix} = \mathcal{O}_d \mathbf{A} \mathcal{C}_d. \tag{9.42b}$$

Based on the matrices $\mathbf{H}$ and $\mathbf{H}'$, we are able to construct a reduced-order model as follows:

$$\tilde{\mathbf{A}} = \tilde{\boldsymbol{\Sigma}}^{-1/2} \tilde{\mathbf{U}}^* \mathbf{H}' \tilde{\mathbf{V}} \tilde{\boldsymbol{\Sigma}}^{-1/2}; \tag{9.43a}$$

$$\tilde{\mathbf{B}} = \tilde{\boldsymbol{\Sigma}}^{1/2} \tilde{\mathbf{V}}^* \begin{bmatrix} \mathbf{I}_p & 0 \\ 0 & 0 \end{bmatrix}; \tag{9.43b}$$

$$\tilde{\mathbf{C}} = \begin{bmatrix} \mathbf{I}_q & 0 \\ 0 & 0 \end{bmatrix} \tilde{\mathbf{U}} \tilde{\boldsymbol{\Sigma}}^{1/2}. \tag{9.43c}$$

Here $\mathbf{I}_p$ is the $p \times p$ identity matrix, which extracts the first p columns, and $\mathbf{I}_q$ is the $q \times q$ identity matrix, which extracts the first q rows. Thus, we express the input–output dynamics in terms of a reduced system with a low-dimensional state $\tilde{\mathbf{x}} \in \mathbb{R}^r$:

$$\tilde{\mathbf{x}}_{k+1} = \tilde{\mathbf{A}} \tilde{\mathbf{x}}_k + \tilde{\mathbf{B}} \mathbf{u} \tag{9.44a}$$

$$\mathbf{y} = \tilde{\mathbf{C}} \tilde{\mathbf{x}}_k. \tag{9.44b}$$

$\mathbf{H}$ and $\mathbf{H}'$ are constructed from impulse response simulations/experiments, without the need for storing direct or adjoint snapshots, as in other balanced model reduction techniques. However, if full-state snapshots are available, for example, by collecting velocity fields in simulations or PIV experiments, it is then possible to construct direct modes. These full-state snapshots form $\mathcal{C}_d$, and modes can be constructed by:

$$\boldsymbol{\Psi} = \mathcal{C}_d \tilde{\mathbf{V}} \tilde{\boldsymbol{\Sigma}}^{-1/2}. \tag{9.45}$$

These modes may then be used to approximate the full-state of the high-dimensional system from the low-dimensional model in (9.44) by:

$$\mathbf{x} \approx \boldsymbol{\Psi} \tilde{\mathbf{x}}. \tag{9.46}$$

If enough data is collected when constructing the Hankel matrix $\mathbf{H}$, then ERA balances the empirical controllability and observability Gramians, $\mathcal{O}_d \mathcal{O}_d^*$ and $\mathcal{C}_d^* \mathcal{C}_d$. However, if less data is collected, so that lightly damped transients do not have time to decay, then ERA will only approximately balance the system. It is instead possible to collect just enough data so that the Hankel matrix $\mathbf{H}$ reaches numerical full-rank (i.e., so that remaining singular values are below a threshold tolerance), and compute an ERA model. The resulting ERA model will typically have a relatively low order, given by the numerical rank of the controllability and observability subspaces. It may then be possible to apply exact balanced truncation to this smaller model, as is advocated in [533] and [346].

The code to compute ERA is provided in Code 9.3.

Code 9.3 Eigensystem realization algorithm.

```
function [Ar,Br,Cr,Dr,HSVs] = ERA(YY,m,n,nin,nout,r)
  for i=1:nout
      for j=1:nin
          Dr(i,j) = YY(i,j,1);
          Y(i,j,:) = YY(i,j,2:end);
      end
  end

% Yss = Y(1,1,end);
% Y = Y-Yss;
% Y(i,j,k)::
% i refers to i-th output
% j refers to j-th input
% k refers to k-th timestep

% nin,nout number of inputs and outputs
% m,n dimensions of Hankel matrix
% r, dimensions of reduced model

assert(length(Y(:,1,1))==nout);
assert(length(Y(1,:,1))==nin);
assert(length(Y(1,1,:))>=m+n);

for i=1:m
    for j=1:n
        for Q=1:nout
            for P=1:nin
                H(nout*i-nout+Q,nin*j-nin+P) = Y(Q,P,i+j-1);
                H2(nout*i-nout+Q,nin*j-nin+P) = Y(Q,P,i+j);
            end
        end
    end
end

[U,S,V] = svd(H,'econ');
Sigma = S(1:r,1:r);
Ur = U(:,1:r);
Vr = V(:,1:r);
Ar = Sigma^(-.5)*Ur'*H2*Vr*Sigma^(-.5);
Br = Sigma^(-.5)*Ur'*H(:,1:nin);
Cr = H(1:nout,:)*Vr*Sigma^(-.5);
HSVs = diag(S);
```

Observer Kalman Filter Identification

OKID was developed to complement the ERA for lightly damped experimental systems with noise [273]. In practice, performing isolated impulse response experiments is challenging, and the effect of measurement noise can contaminate results. Moreover, if there is a large separation of timescales, then a tremendous amount of data must be collected to use ERA. This section poses the general problem of approximating the impulse response from arbitrary input–output data. Typically, one would identify reduced-order models according to the following general procedure:

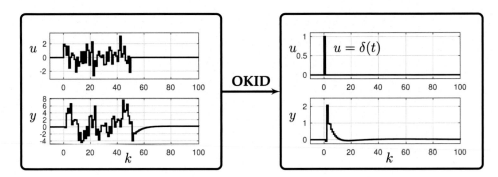

Figure 9.5 Schematic overview of OKID procedure. The output of OKID is an impulse response that can be used for system identification via ERA.

1.   Collect the output in response to a pseudo-random input.
2.   This information is passed through the OKID algorithm to obtain the de-noised linear impulse response.
3.   The impulse response is passed through the ERA to obtain a reduced-order state-space system.

The output $\mathbf{y}_k$ in response to a general input signal $\mathbf{u}_k$, for zero initial condition $\mathbf{x}_0 = \mathbf{0}$, is given by:

$$\mathbf{y}_0 = \mathbf{D}_d \mathbf{u}_0 \tag{9.47a}$$

$$\mathbf{y}_1 = \mathbf{C}_d \mathbf{B}_d \mathbf{u}_0 + \mathbf{D}_d \mathbf{u}_1 \tag{9.47b}$$

$$\mathbf{y}_2 = \mathbf{C}_d \mathbf{A}_d \mathbf{B}_d \mathbf{u}_0 + \mathbf{C}_d \mathbf{B}_d \mathbf{u}_1 + \mathbf{D}_d \mathbf{u}_2 \tag{9.47c}$$

$$\cdots$$

$$\mathbf{y}_k = \mathbf{C}_d \mathbf{A}_d^{k-1} \mathbf{B}_d \mathbf{u}_0 + \mathbf{C}_d \mathbf{A}_d^{k-2} \mathbf{B}_d \mathbf{u}_1 + \cdots + \mathbf{C}_d \mathbf{B}_d \mathbf{u}_{k-1} + \mathbf{D}_d \mathbf{u}_k. \tag{9.47d}$$

Note that there is no $\mathbf{C}$ term in the expression for $\mathbf{y}_0$ since there is zero initial condition $\mathbf{x}_0 = \mathbf{0}$. This progression of measurements $\mathbf{y}_k$ may be further simplified and expressed in terms of impulse-response measurements $\mathbf{y}_k^\delta$:

$$\underbrace{\begin{bmatrix} \mathbf{y}_0 & \mathbf{y}_1 & \cdots & \mathbf{y}_m \end{bmatrix}}_{\mathcal{S}} = \underbrace{\begin{bmatrix} \mathbf{y}_0^\delta & \mathbf{y}_1^\delta & \cdots & \mathbf{y}_m^\delta \end{bmatrix}}_{\mathcal{S}^\delta} \underbrace{\begin{bmatrix} \mathbf{u}_0 & \mathbf{u}_1 & \cdots & \mathbf{u}_m \\ \mathbf{0} & \mathbf{u}_0 & \cdots & \mathbf{u}_{m-1} \\ \vdots & \vdots & \ddots & \vdots \\ \mathbf{0} & \mathbf{0} & \cdots & \mathbf{u}_0 \end{bmatrix}}_{\mathcal{B}} . \tag{9.48}$$

It is often possible to invert the matrix of control inputs, $\mathcal{B}$, to solve for the Markov parameters $\mathcal{S}^\delta$. However, $\mathcal{B}$ may either be un-invertible, or inversion may be ill-conditioned. In addition, $\mathcal{B}$ is large for lightly damped systems, making inversion computationally expensive. Finally, noise is not optimally filtered by simply inverting $\mathcal{B}$ to solve for the Markov parameters.

The OKID method addresses each of these issues. Instead of the original discrete-time system, we now introduce an optimal observer system:

$$\hat{\mathbf{x}}_{k+1} = \mathbf{A}_d \hat{\mathbf{x}}_k + \mathbf{K}_f \left(\mathbf{y}_k - \hat{\mathbf{y}}_k \right) + \mathbf{B}_d \mathbf{u}_k \tag{9.49a}$$

$$\hat{\mathbf{y}}_k = \mathbf{C}_d \hat{\mathbf{x}}_k + \mathbf{D}_d \mathbf{u}_k, \tag{9.49b}$$

which may be re-written as:

$$\hat{\mathbf{x}}_{k+1} = \underbrace{(\mathbf{A}_d - \mathbf{K}_f\mathbf{C}_d)}_{\bar{\mathbf{A}}_d}\hat{\mathbf{x}}_k + \underbrace{[\mathbf{B}_d - \mathbf{K}_f\mathbf{D}_d, \qquad \mathbf{K}_f]}_{\bar{\mathbf{B}}_d}\begin{bmatrix}\mathbf{u}_k \\ \mathbf{y}_k\end{bmatrix}. \tag{9.50}$$

Recall from earlier that if the system is observable, it is possible to place the poles of $\mathbf{A}_d - \mathbf{K}_f\mathbf{C}_d$ anywhere we like. However, depending on the amount of noise in the measurements, the magnitude of process noise, and uncertainty in our model, there are *optimal* pole locations that are given by the *Kalman filter* (recall Section 8.5). We may now solve for the *observer Markov parameters* $\bar{\mathcal{S}}^\delta$ of the system in (9.50) in terms of measured inputs and outputs according to the following algorithm from [273]:

1. Choose the number of observer Markov parameters to identify, l.
2. Construct the data matrices here:

$$\mathcal{S} = \begin{bmatrix}\mathbf{y}_0 & \mathbf{y}_1 & \cdots & \mathbf{y}_l & \cdots & \mathbf{y}_m\end{bmatrix} \tag{9.51}$$

$$\mathcal{V} = \begin{bmatrix}\mathbf{u}_0 & \mathbf{u}_1 & \cdots & \mathbf{u}_l & \cdots & \mathbf{u}_m \\ \mathbf{0} & \mathbf{v}_0 & \cdots & \mathbf{v}_{l-1} & \cdots & \mathbf{v}_{m-1} \\ \vdots & \vdots & \ddots & \vdots & \ddots & \vdots \\ \mathbf{0} & \mathbf{0} & \cdots & \mathbf{v}_0 & \cdots & \mathbf{v}_{m-l}\end{bmatrix} \tag{9.52}$$

where $\mathbf{v}_i = \begin{bmatrix}\mathbf{u}_i^T & \mathbf{y}_i^T\end{bmatrix}^T$.

   The matrix $\mathcal{V}$ resembles $\mathcal{B}$, except that is has been augmented with the outputs $\mathbf{y}_i$. In this way, we are working with a system that is augmented to include a Kalman filter. We are now identifying the observer Markov parameters of the *augmented* system, $\bar{\mathcal{S}}^\delta$, using the equation $\mathcal{S} = \bar{\mathcal{S}}^\delta\mathcal{V}$. It will be possible to identify these observer Markov parameters from the data and then extract the impulse response (Markov parameters) of the original system.

3. Identify the matrix $\bar{\mathcal{S}}^\delta$ of observer Markov parameters by solving $\mathcal{S} = \bar{\mathcal{S}}^\delta\mathcal{V}$ for $\bar{\mathcal{S}}^\delta$ using the right pseudo-inverse of $\mathcal{V}$ (i.e., SVD).
4. Recover system Markov parameters, $\mathcal{S}^\delta$, from the observer Markov parameters, $\bar{\mathcal{S}}^\delta$:

   (a) Order the observer Markov parameters $\bar{\mathcal{S}}^\delta$ as:

$$\bar{\mathcal{S}}_0^\delta = \mathbf{D}, \tag{9.53}$$

$$\bar{\mathcal{S}}_k^\delta = \begin{bmatrix}(\bar{\mathcal{S}}^\delta)_k^{(1)} & (\bar{\mathcal{S}}^\delta)_k^{(2)}\end{bmatrix} \text{ for } k \geq 1, \tag{9.54}$$

   where $(\bar{\mathcal{S}}^\delta)_k^{(1)} \in \mathbb{R}^{q\times p}$, $(\bar{\mathcal{S}}^\delta)_k^{(2)} \in \mathbb{R}^{q\times q}$, and $\mathbf{y}_0^\delta = \bar{\mathcal{S}}_0^\delta = \mathbf{D}$.

   (b) Reconstruct system Markov parameters:

$$\mathbf{y}_k^\delta = (\bar{\mathcal{S}}^\delta)_k^{(1)} + \sum_{i=1}^k (\bar{\mathcal{S}}^\delta)_i^{(2)}\mathbf{y}_{k-i}^\delta \text{ for } k \geq 1. \tag{9.55}$$

Thus, the OKID method identifies the Markov parameters of a system augmented with an asymptotically stable Kalman filter. The system Markov parameters are extracted from the observer Markov parameters by (9.55). These system Markov parameters approximate the impulse response of the system, and may be used directly as inputs to the ERA algorithm. A code to compute OKID is provided in Code 9.4.

ERA/OKID has been widely applied across a range of system identification tasks, including to identify models of aeroelastic structures and fluid dynamic systems. There are numerous extensions of the ERA/OKID methods. For example, there are generalizations for linear parameter varying (LPV) systems and systems linearized about a limit cycle.

Code 9.4 Observer Kalman filter identification (OKID).

```
function H = OKID(y,u,r)
% Inputs: y (sampled output), u (sampled input), r (order)
% Output: H (Markov parameters)

% Step 0, check shapes of y,u
p = size(y,1);   % p is the number of outputs
m = size(y,2);   % m is the number of output samples
q = size(u,1);   % q is the number of inputs

% Step 1, choose impulse length l (5 times system order r)
l = r*5;

% Step 2, form y, V, solve for observer Markov params, Ybar
V = zeros(q + (q+p)*l,m);
for i=1:m
    V(1:q,i) = u(1:q,i);
end
for i=2:l+1
    for j=1:m+1-i
        vtemp = [u(:,j);y(:,j)];
        V(q+(i-2)*(q+p)+1:q+(i-1)*(q+p),i+j-1) = vtemp;
    end
end
Ybar = y*pinv(V,1.e-3);

% Step 3, isolate system Markov parameters H
D = Ybar(:,1:q);   % Feed-through term (D) is first term
for i=1:l
    Ybar1(1:p,1:q,i) = Ybar(:,q+1+(q+p)*(i-1):q+(q+p)*(i-1)+q);
    Ybar2(1:p,1:q,i) = Ybar(:,q+1+(q+p)*(i-1)+q:q+(q+p)*i);
end
Y(:,:,1) = Ybar1(:,:,1) + Ybar2(:,:,1)*D;
for k=2:l
    Y(:,:,k) = Ybar1(:,:,k) + Ybar2(:,:,k)*D;
    for i=1:k-1
        Y(:,:,k) = Y(:,:,k) + Ybar2(:,:,i)*Y(:,:,k-i);
    end
end

H(:,:,1) = D;
for k=2:l+1
    H(:,:,k) = Y(:,:,k-1);
end
```

Combining ERA and OKID

Here we demonstrate ERA and OKID on the same model system from Section 9.2. Because ERA yields the same balanced models as BPOD, the reduced system responses should be the same.

First, we compute an impulse response of the full system, and use this as an input to ERA:

```
%% Obtain impulse response of full system
[yFull,t] = impulse(sysFull,0:1:(r*5)+1);
YY = permute(yFull,[2 3 1]);  % Reorder to be size p x q x m
                              % (default is m x p x q)

%% Compute ERA from impulse response
mco = floor((length(yFull)-1)/2);  % m_c = m_o = (m-1)/2
[Ar,Br,Cr,Dr,HSVs] = ERA(YY,mco,mco,numInputs,numOutputs,r);
sysERA = ss(Ar,Br,Cr,Dr,-1);
```

Next, if an impulse response is unavailable, it is possible to excite the system with a random input signal and use OKID to extract an impulse response. This impulse response is then used by ERA to extract the model.

```
%% Compute random input simulation for OKID
uRandom = randn(numInputs,200);   % Random forcing input
yRandom = lsim(sysFull,uRandom,1:200)';  % Output

%% Compute OKID and then ERA
H = OKID(yRandom,uRandom,r);
mco = floor((length(H)-1)/2);  % m_c = m_o
[Ar,Br,Cr,Dr,HSVs] = ERA(H,mco,mco,numInputs,numOutputs,r);
sysERAOKID = ss(Ar,Br,Cr,Dr,-1);
```

Figure 9.6 shows the input–output data used by OKID to approximate the impulse response. The impulse responses of the resulting systems are computed via

```
[y1,t1] = impulse(sysFull,0:1:200);
[y2,t2] = impulse(sysERA,0:1:100);
[y3,t3] = impulse(sysERAOKID,0:1:100);
```

Finally, the system responses can be seen in Fig. 9.7. The low-order ERA and ERA/OKID models closely match the full model and have similar performance to the BPOD models described previously. Because ERA and BPOD are mathematically equivalent, this agreement is not surprising. However, the ability of ERA/OKID to extract a reduced-order model from the random input data in Fig. 9.6 is quite remarkable. Moreover, unlike BPOD, these methods are readily applicable to experimental measurements, as they do not require nonphysical adjoint equations.

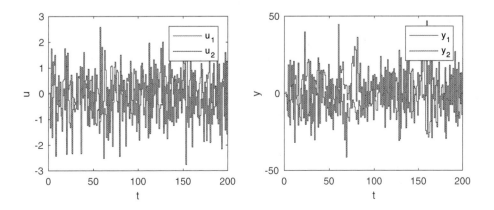

Figure 9.6 Input–output data used by OKID.

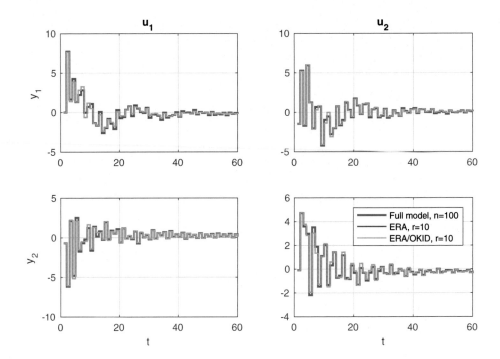

Figure 9.7 Impulse response of full-state model with $n = 100$, $p = q = 2$, along with ERA and ERA/OKID models with $r = 10$.

Suggested Reading
Papers and Reviews
(1)   **Principal component analysis in linear systems: Controllability, observability, and model reduction**, by B. C. Moore, *IEEE Transactions on Automatic Control*, 1981 [388].

(2)   **Identification of linear parameter varying models**, by B. Bamieh and L. Giarré, *International Journal of Robust and Nonlinear Control*, 2002 [34].

(3)   **Balanced model reduction via the proper orthogonal decomposition**, by K. Willcox and J. Peraire, *AIAA Journal*, 2002 [554].

(4)   **Model reduction for fluids using balanced proper orthogonal decomposition**, by C. W. Rowley, *International Journal of Bifurcations and Chaos*, 2005 [458].

(5)   **An eigensystem realization algorithm for modal parameter identification and model reduction**, by J. N. Juang and R. S. Pappa, *Journal of Guidance, Control, and Dynamics*, 1985 [272].

10 Data-Driven Control

As described in Chapter 8, control design often begins with a model of the system being controlled. Notable exceptions include model-free adaptive control strategies and many uses of PID control. For mechanical systems of moderate dimension, it may be possible to write down a model (e.g., based on the Newtonian, Lagrangian, or Hamiltonian formalism) and linearize the dynamics about a fixed point or periodic orbit. However, for modern systems of interest, as are found in neuroscience, turbulence, epidemiology, climate, and finance, typically there are no simple models suitable for control design. Chapter 9 described techniques to obtain control-oriented reduced-order models for high-dimensional systems from data, but these approaches are limited to *linear* systems. Real-world systems are usually nonlinear and the control objective is not readily achieved via linear techniques. Nonlinear control can still be posed as an optimization problem with a high-dimensional, nonconvex cost function landscape with multiple local minima. Machine learning is complementary, as it constitutes a growing set of techniques that may be broadly described as performing nonlinear optimization in a high-dimensional space from data. In this chapter we describe emerging techniques that use machine learning to characterize and control strongly nonlinear, high-dimensional, and multi-scale systems, leveraging the increasing availability of high-quality measurement data.

Broadly speaking, machine learning techniques may be used to 1) characterize a system for later use with model-based control, or 2) directly characterize a control law that effectively interacts with a system. This is illustrated schematically in Fig. 10.1, where data-driven techniques may be applied to either the *System* or *Controller* blocks. In addition, related methods may also be used to identify good sensors and actuators, as discussed previously in Section 3.8. In this chapter, Section 10.1 will explore the use of machine learning to identify nonlinear input–output models for control, based on the methods from Chapter 7. In Section 10.2 we will explore machine learning techniques to directly identify controllers from input–output data. This is a rapidly developing field, with many powerful methods, such as reinforcement learning, iterative learning control, and genetic algorithms. Here we provide a high-level overview of these methods and then explore an example using genetic algorithms. However, it is important to emphasize the breadth and depth of this field, and the fact that any one method may be the subject of an entire book. Finally, in Section 10.3 we describe the adaptive extremum-seeking control strategy, which optimizes the control signal based on how the system responds to perturbations.

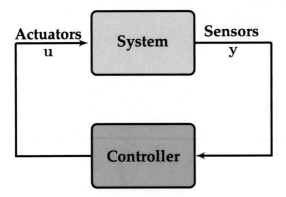

Figure 10.1 In the standard control framework from Chapter 8, machine learning may be used 1) to develop a model of the system or 2) to learn a controller.

10.1   Nonlinear System Identification for Control

The data-driven modeling and control of complex systems is undergoing a revolution, driven by the rise of big data, advanced algorithms in machine learning and optimization, and modern computational hardware. Despite the increasing use of equation-free and adaptive control methods, there remains a wealth of powerful model-based control techniques, such as linear optimal control (see Chapter 8) and model predictive control (MPC) [195, 107]. Increasingly, these model-based control strategies are aided by data-driven techniques that characterize the input–output dynamics of a system of interest from measurements alone, without relying on first principles modeling. Broadly speaking, this is known as *system identification*, which has a long and rich history in control theory going back decades to the time of Kalman. However, with increasingly powerful data-driven techniques, such as those described in Chapter 7, nonlinear system identification is the focus of renewed interest.

The goal of system identification is to identify a low-order model of the input–output dynamics from actuation $\mathbf{u}$ to measurements $\mathbf{y}$. If we are able to measure the full state $\mathbf{x}$ of the system, then this reduces to identifying the dynamics $\mathbf{f}$ that satisfy:

$$\frac{d}{dt}\mathbf{x} = \mathbf{f}(\mathbf{x}, \mathbf{u}). \tag{10.1}$$

This problem may be formulated in discrete-time, since data is typically collected at discrete instances in time and control laws are often implemented digitally. In this case, the dynamics read:

$$\mathbf{x}_{k+1} = \mathbf{F}(\mathbf{x}_k, \mathbf{u}_k). \tag{10.2}$$

When the dynamics are approximately linear, we may identify a linear system

$$\mathbf{x}_{k+1} = \mathbf{A}\mathbf{x}_k + \mathbf{B}\mathbf{u}_k, \tag{10.3}$$

which is the approach taken in the DMD with control (DMDc) algorithm below.

It may also be advantageous to identify a set of measurements $\mathbf{y} = \mathbf{g}(\mathbf{x})$, in which the unforced nonlinear dynamics appear linear:

$$\mathbf{y}_{k+1} = \mathbf{A}_\mathbf{Y}\mathbf{y}_k. \tag{10.4}$$

This is the approach taken in the Koopman control method below. In this way, nonlinear dynamics may be estimated and controlled using standard textbook linear control theory in the intrinsic coordinates **y** [302, 276].

Finally, the nonlinear dynamics in (10.1) or (10.2) may be identified directly using the SINDY with control algorithm. The resulting models may be used with model predictive control for the control of fully nonlinear systems [277].

DMD with Control

Proctor et al. [434] extended the DMD algorithm to include the effect of actuation and control, in the so-called DMD with control (DMDc) algorithm. It was observed that naively applying DMD to data from a system with actuation would often result in incorrect dynamics, as the effects of internal dynamics are confused with the effects of actuation. DMDc was originally motivated by the problem of characterizing and controlling the spread of disease, where it is unreasonable to stop intervention efforts (e.g., vaccinations) just to obtain a characterization of the unforced dynamics [435]. Instead, if the actuation signal is measured, a new DMD regression may be formulated in order to disambiguate the effect of internal dynamics from that of actuation and control. Subsequently, this approach has been extended to perform DMDc on heavily subsampled or compressed measurements by Bai et al. [30].

The DMDc method seeks to identify the best-fit linear operators **A** and **B** that approximately satisfy the following dynamics on measurement data:

$$\mathbf{x}_{k+1} \approx \mathbf{A}\mathbf{x}_k + \mathbf{B}\mathbf{u}_k. \tag{10.5}$$

In addition to the snapshot matrix $\mathbf{X} = \begin{bmatrix} \mathbf{x}_1 & \mathbf{x}_2 & \cdots & \mathbf{x}_m \end{bmatrix}$ and the time-shifted snapshot matrix $\mathbf{X}' = \begin{bmatrix} \mathbf{x}_2 & \mathbf{x}_3 & \cdots & \mathbf{x}_{m+1} \end{bmatrix}$ from (7.23), a matrix of the actuation input history is assembled:

$$\mathbf{\Upsilon} = \begin{bmatrix} | & | & & | \\ \mathbf{u}_1 & \mathbf{u}_2 & \cdots & \mathbf{u}_m \\ | & | & & | \end{bmatrix}. \tag{10.6}$$

The dynamics in (10.5) may be written in terms of the data matrices:

$$\mathbf{X}' \approx \mathbf{A}\mathbf{X} + \mathbf{B}\mathbf{\Upsilon}. \tag{10.7}$$

As in the DMD algorithm (see Section 7.2), the leading eigenvalues and eigenvectors of the best-fit linear operator **A** are obtained via dimensionality reduction and regression. If the actuation matrix **B** is known, then it is straightforward to correct for the actuation and identify the spectral decomposition of **A** by replacing $\mathbf{X}'$ with $\mathbf{X}' - \mathbf{B}\mathbf{\Upsilon}$ in the DMD algorithm:

$$\left(\mathbf{X}' - \mathbf{B}\mathbf{\Upsilon}\right) \approx \mathbf{A}\mathbf{X}. \tag{10.8}$$

When **B** is unknown, both **A** and **B** must be simultaneously identified. In this case, the dynamics in (10.7) may be recast as:

$$\mathbf{X}' \approx \begin{bmatrix} \mathbf{A} & \mathbf{B} \end{bmatrix} \begin{bmatrix} \mathbf{X} \\ \mathbf{\Upsilon} \end{bmatrix} = \mathbf{G}\mathbf{\Omega}, \tag{10.9}$$

and the matrix $\mathbf{G} = \begin{bmatrix} \mathbf{A} & \mathbf{B} \end{bmatrix}$ is obtained via least-squares regression:

$$\mathbf{G} \approx \mathbf{X}'\mathbf{\Omega}^{\dagger}. \tag{10.10}$$

The matrix $\mathbf{\Omega} = \begin{bmatrix} \mathbf{X}^* & \mathbf{\Upsilon}^* \end{bmatrix}^*$ is generally a high-dimensional data matrix, which may be approximated using the SVD:

$$\mathbf{\Omega} = \tilde{\mathbf{U}}\tilde{\mathbf{\Sigma}}\tilde{\mathbf{V}}^*. \tag{10.11}$$

The matrix $\tilde{\mathbf{U}}$ must be split into two matrices, $\tilde{\mathbf{U}} = \begin{bmatrix} \tilde{\mathbf{U}}_1^* & \tilde{\mathbf{U}}_2^* \end{bmatrix}^*$, to provide bases for $\mathbf{X}$ and $\mathbf{\Upsilon}$. Unlike the DMD algorithm, $\tilde{\mathbf{U}}$ provides a reduced basis for the *input space*, while $\hat{\mathbf{U}}$ from

$$\mathbf{X}' = \hat{\mathbf{U}}\hat{\mathbf{\Sigma}}\hat{\mathbf{V}}^* \tag{10.12}$$

defines a reduced basis for the *output space*. It is then possible to approximate $\mathbf{G} = \begin{bmatrix} \mathbf{A} & \mathbf{B} \end{bmatrix}$ by projecting onto this basis:

$$\tilde{\mathbf{G}} = \hat{\mathbf{U}}^*\mathbf{G}\begin{bmatrix} \hat{\mathbf{U}} \\ \mathbf{I} \end{bmatrix}. \tag{10.13}$$

The resulting projected matrices $\tilde{\mathbf{A}}$ and $\tilde{\mathbf{B}}$ in $\tilde{\mathbf{G}}$ are:

$$\tilde{\mathbf{A}} = \hat{\mathbf{U}}^*\mathbf{A}\hat{\mathbf{U}} = \hat{\mathbf{U}}^*\mathbf{X}'\tilde{\mathbf{V}}\tilde{\mathbf{\Sigma}}^{-1}\tilde{\mathbf{U}}_1^*\hat{\mathbf{U}} \tag{10.14a}$$

$$\tilde{\mathbf{B}} = \hat{\mathbf{U}}^*\mathbf{B} \quad = \hat{\mathbf{U}}^*\mathbf{X}'\tilde{\mathbf{V}}\tilde{\mathbf{\Sigma}}^{-1}\tilde{\mathbf{U}}_2^*. \tag{10.14b}$$

More importantly, it is possible to recover the DMD eigenvectors $\mathbf{\Phi}$ from the eigendecomposition $\tilde{\mathbf{A}}\mathbf{W} = \mathbf{W}\mathbf{\Lambda}$:

$$\mathbf{\Phi} = \mathbf{X}'\tilde{\mathbf{V}}\tilde{\mathbf{\Sigma}}^{-1}\tilde{\mathbf{U}}_1^*\hat{\mathbf{U}}\mathbf{W}. \tag{10.15}$$

Ambiguity in Identifying Closed-Loop Systems

For systems that are being actively controlled via feedback, with $\mathbf{u} = \mathbf{K}\mathbf{x}$,

$$\mathbf{x}_{k+1} = \mathbf{A}\mathbf{x}_k + \mathbf{B}\mathbf{u}_k \tag{10.16a}$$

$$= \mathbf{A}\mathbf{x}_k + \mathbf{B}\mathbf{K}\mathbf{x}_k \tag{10.16b}$$

$$= (\mathbf{A} + \mathbf{B}\mathbf{K})\mathbf{x}_k, \tag{10.16c}$$

it is impossible to disambiguate the dynamics $\mathbf{A}$ and the actuation $\mathbf{B}\mathbf{K}$. In this case, it is important to add perturbations to the actuation signal $\mathbf{u}$ to provide additional information. These perturbations may be a white noise process or occasional impulses that provide a kick to the system, providing a signal to disambiguate the dynamics from the feedback signal.

Koopman Operator Nonlinear Control

For nonlinear systems, it may be advantageous to identify data-driven coordinate transformations that make the dynamics appear linear. These coordinate transformations are related to *intrinsic* coordinates defined by eigenfunctions of the Koopman operator (see Section 7.4). Koopman analysis has thus been leveraged for nonlinear estimation [504, 505] and control [302, 276, 423].

It is possible to design estimators and controllers directly from DMD or eDMD models, and Korda et al. [302] used model predictive control (MPC) to control nonlinear systems with eDMD models. MPC performance is also surprisingly good for DMD models, as shown in Kaiser et al. [277]. In addition, Peitz et al. [423] demonstrated the use of MPC for switching control between a small number of actuation values to track a reference value of lift in an unsteady fluid flow; for each constant actuation value, a separate eDMD model was characterized. Surana [504] and Surana and Banaszuk [505] have also demonstrated excellent nonlinear estimators based on Koopman Kalman filters. However, as discussed previously, eDMD models may contain many spurious eigenvalues and eigenvectors because of closure issues related to finding a Koopman-invariant subspace. Instead, it may be advantageous to identify a handful of relevant Koopman eigenfunctions and perform control directly in these coordinates [276].

In Section 7.5, we described several strategies to approximate Koopman eigenfunctions, $\varphi(\mathbf{x})$, where the dynamics become linear:

$$\frac{d}{dt}\varphi(\mathbf{x}) = \lambda\varphi(\mathbf{x}). \tag{10.17}$$

In Kaiser et al. [276] the Koopman eigenfunction equation was extended for control-affine nonlinear systems:

$$\frac{d}{dt}\mathbf{x} = \mathbf{f}(\mathbf{x}) + \mathbf{B}\mathbf{u}. \tag{10.18}$$

For these systems, it is possible to apply the chain rule to $\frac{d}{dt}\varphi(\mathbf{x})$, yielding:

$$\frac{d}{dt}\varphi(\mathbf{x}) = \nabla\varphi(\mathbf{x}) \cdot (\mathbf{f}(\mathbf{x}) + \mathbf{B}\mathbf{u}) \tag{10.19a}$$

$$= \lambda\varphi(\mathbf{x}) + \nabla\varphi(\mathbf{x}) \cdot \mathbf{B}\mathbf{u}. \tag{10.19b}$$

Note that even with actuation, the dynamics of Koopman eigenfunctions remain linear, and the effect of actuation is still additive. However, now the actuation mode $\nabla\varphi(\mathbf{x}) \cdot \mathbf{B}$ may be state dependent. In fact, the actuation *will* be state dependent unless the directional derivative of the eigenfunction is constant in the $\mathbf{B}$ direction. Fortunately, there are many powerful generalizations of standard Riccati-based linear control theory (e.g., LQR, Kalman filters, etc.) for systems with a *state-dependent* Riccati equation.

SINDy with Control

Although it is appealing to identify intrinsic coordinates along which nonlinear dynamics appear linear, these coordinates are challenging to discover, even for relatively simple systems. Instead, it may be beneficial to directly identify the nonlinear actuated dynamical system in (10.1) or (10.2), for use with standard model-based control. Using the sparse identification of nonlinear dynamics (SINDy) method (see Section 7.3) results in computationally efficient models that may be used in real-time with model predictive control [277]. Moreover, these models may be identified from relatively small amounts of training data, compared with neural networks and other leading machine learning methods, so that they may even be characterized online and in response to abrupt changes to the system dynamics.

The SINDy algorithm is readily extended to include the effects of actuation [100, 277]. In addition to collecting measurements of the state snapshots $\mathbf{x}$ in the matrix $\mathbf{X}$, actuation inputs $\mathbf{u}$ are collected in the matrix $\mathbf{\Upsilon}$ from (10.6) as in DMDc. Next, an augmented library of candidate right hand side functions $\mathbf{\Theta}([\mathbf{X} \quad \mathbf{\Upsilon}])$ is constructed:

$$\mathbf{\Theta}([\mathbf{X} \quad \mathbf{\Upsilon}]) = [\mathbf{1} \quad \mathbf{X} \quad \mathbf{\Upsilon} \quad \mathbf{X}^2 \quad \mathbf{X} \otimes \mathbf{\Upsilon} \quad \mathbf{\Upsilon}^2 \quad \cdots]. \qquad (10.20)$$

Here, $\mathbf{X} \otimes \mathbf{\Upsilon}$ denotes quadratic cross-terms between the state $\mathbf{x}$ and the actuation $\mathbf{u}$, evaluated on the data.

In SINDy with control (SINDYc), the same sparse regression is used to determine the fewest active terms in the library required to describe the observed dynamics. As in DMDc, if the system is being actively controlled via feedback $\mathbf{u} = \mathbf{K}(\mathbf{x})$, then it is impossible to disambiguate from the internal dynamics and the actuation, unless an addition perturbation signal is added to the actuation to provide additional information.

Model Predictive Control (MPC) Example

In this example, we will use SINDYc to identify a model of the forced Lorenz equations from data and then control this model using model predictive control (MPC). MPC [107, 195, 438, 391, 447, 439, 196, 326, 173] has become a cornerstone of modern process control and is ubiquitous in the industrial landscape. MPC is used to control strongly nonlinear systems with constraints, time delays, non-minimum phase dynamics, and instability. Most industrial applications of MPC use empirical models based on linear system identification (see Chapter 8), neural networks (see Chapter 6), Volterra series [86, 73], and autoregressive models [6] (e.g., ARX, ARMA, NARX, and NARMAX). Recently, deep learning and reinforcement learning have been combined with MPC [330, 570] with impressive results. However, deep learning requires large volumes of data and may not be readily interpretable. A complementary line of research seeks to identify models for MPC based on limited data to characterize systems in response to abrupt changes.

Model predictive control determines the next immediate control action by solving an optimal control problem over a receding horizon. In particular, the open-loop actuation signal $\mathbf{u}$ is optimized on a receding time-horizon $t_c = m_c \Delta t$ to minimize a cost J over some prediction horizon $t_p = m_p \Delta t$. The control horizon is typically less than or equal to the prediction horizon, and the control is held constant between t_c and t_p. The optimal control is then applied for one time step, and the procedure is repeated and the receding-horizon control re-optimized at each subsequent time step. This results in the control law:

$$\mathbf{K}(\mathbf{x}_j) = \mathbf{u}_{j+1}(\mathbf{x}_j), \qquad (10.21)$$

where $\mathbf{u}_{j+1}$ is the first time step of the optimized actuation starting at $\mathbf{x}_j$. This is shown schematically in Fig. 10.2. It is possible to optimize highly customized cost functions, subject to nonlinear dynamics, with constraints on the actuation and state. However, the computational requirements of re-optimizing at each time-step are considerable, putting limits on the complexity of the model and optimization techniques. Fortunately, rapid advances in computing power and optimization are enabling MPC for real-time nonlinear control.

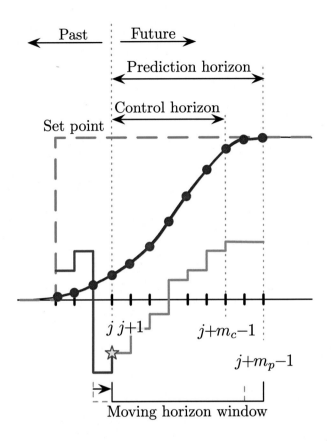

Figure 10.2 Schematic overview of model predictive control, where the actuation input **u** is iteratively optimized over a receding horizon. *Reproduced with permission from Kaiser et al. [277].*

MPC to Control the Lorenz Equations with SINDYc

The following example illustrates how to identify a model with SINDYc for use in MPC. The basic code is the same as SINDy, except that the actuation is included as a variable when building the library Θ.

We test the SINDYc model identification on the forced Lorenz equations:

$$\dot{x} = \sigma(y - x) + g(u) \tag{10.22a}$$

$$\dot{y} = x(\rho - z) - y \tag{10.22b}$$

$$\dot{z} = xy - \beta z. \tag{10.22c}$$

In this example, we train a model using 20 time units of controlled data, and validate it on another 20 time units where we switch the forcing to a periodic signal $u(t) = 50\sin(10t)$. The SINDY algorithm does not capture the effect of actuation, while SINDYc correctly identifies the forced model and predicts the behavior in response to a new actuation that was not used in the training data, as shown in Fig. 10.3.

Finally, SINDYc and neural network models of Lorenz are both used to design model predictive controllers, as shown in Fig. 10.4. Both methods identify accurate models that

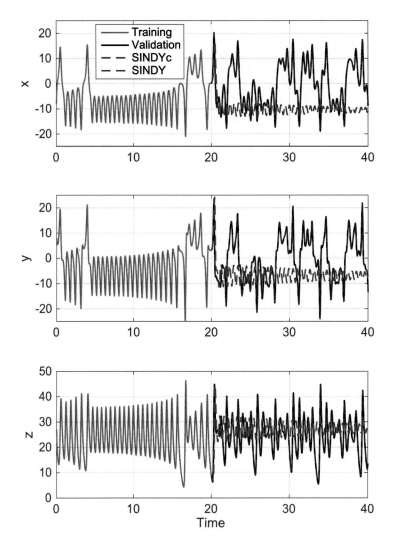

Figure 10.3 SINDY and SINDYc predictions for the controlled Lorenz system in (10.22). Training data consists of the Lorenz system with state feedback. For the training period the input is $u(t) = 26 - x(t) + d(t)$ with a Gaussian disturbance d. Afterward the input u switches to a periodic signal $u(t) = 50\sin(10t)$. *Reproduced with permission from [100].*

capture the dynamics, although the SINDYc procedure requires less data, identifies models more rapidly, and is more robust to noise than the neural network model. This added efficiency and robustness is due to the sparsity promoting optimization, which regularizes the model identification problem. In addition, identifying a sparse model requires less data.

10.2 Machine Learning Control

Machine learning is a rapidly developing field that is transforming our ability to describe complex systems from observational data, rather than first-principles modeling [382, 161, 64, 396]. Until recently, these methods have largely been developed for static data, although

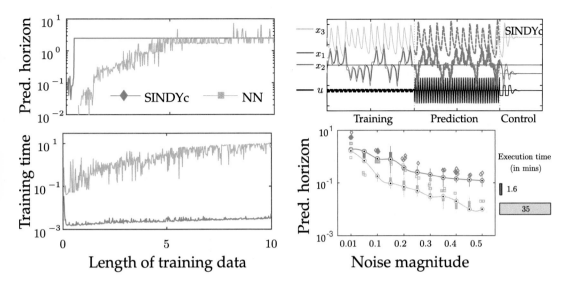

Figure 10.4 Model predictive control of the Lorenz system with a neural network model and a SINDy model. *Reproduced with permission from Kaiser et al. [277].*

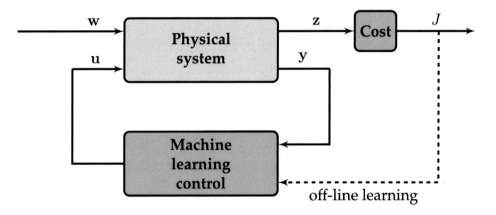

Figure 10.5 Schematic of machine learning control wrapped around a complex system using noisy sensor-based feedback. The control objective is to minimize a well-defined cost function J within the space of possible control laws. An off-line learning loop provides experiential data to train the controller. Genetic programming provides a particularly flexible algorithm to search out effective control laws. The vector z contains all of the information that may factor into the cost.

there is a growing emphasis on using machine learning to characterize dynamical systems. The use of machine learning to learn control laws (i.e., to determine an effective map from sensor outputs to actuation inputs), is even more recent [184]. As machine learning encompasses a broad range of high-dimensional, possibly nonlinear, optimization techniques, it is natural to apply machine learning to the control of complex, nonlinear systems. Specific machine learning methods for control include adaptive neural networks, genetic algorithms, genetic programming, and reinforcement learning. A general machine learning control architecture is shown in Fig. 10.5. Many of these machine learning algorithms are based on biological principles, such as neural networks, reinforcement learning, and evolutionary algorithms.

It is important to note that model-free control methodologies may be applied to numerical or experimental systems with little modification. All of these model-free methods have some sort of macroscopic objective function, typically based on sensor measurements (past and present). Some challenging real-world example objectives in different disciplines include:

Fluid dynamics: In aerodynamic applications, the goal is often some combination of drag reduction, lift increase, and noise reduction, while in pharmaceutical and chemical engineering applications the goal may involve mixing enhancement.

Finance: The goal is often to maximize profit at a given level of risk tolerance, subject to the law.

Epidemiology: The goal may be to effectively suppress a disease with constraints of sensing (e.g., blood samples, clinics, etc.) and actuation (e.g., vaccines, bed nets, etc.).

Industry: The goal of increasing productivity must be balanced with several constraints, including labor and work safety laws, as well as environmental impact, which often have significant uncertainty.

Autonomy and robotics: The goal of self-driving cars and autonomous robots is to achieve a task while interacting safely with a complex environment, including cooperating with human agents.

In the examples above, the objectives involve some minimization or maximization of a given quantity subject to some constraints. These constraints may be hard, as in the case of disease suppression on a fixed budget, or they may involve a complex multi-objective tradeoff. Often, constrained optimizations will result in solutions that live at the boundary of the constraint, which may explain why many companies operate at the fringe of legality. In all of the cases, the optimization must be performed with respect to the underlying dynamics of the system: fluids are governed by the Navier-Stokes equations, finance is governed by human behavior and economics, and disease spread is the result of a complex interaction of biology, human behavior, and geography.

These real-world control problems are extremely challenging for a number of reasons. They are high-dimensional and strongly nonlinear, often with millions or billions of degrees of freedom that evolve according to possibly unknown nonlinear interactions. In addition, it may be exceedingly expensive or infeasible to run different scenarios for system identification; for example, there are serious ethical issues associated with testing different vaccination strategies when human lives are at stake.

Increasingly, challenging optimization problems are being solved with machine learning, leveraging the availability of vast and increasing quantities of data. Many of the recent successes have been on static data (e.g., image classification, speech recognition, etc.), and marketing tasks (e.g., online sales and ad placement). However, current efforts are applying machine learning to analyze and control complex systems with dynamics, with the potential to revolutionize our ability to interact with and manipulate these systems.

The following sections describe a handful of powerful learning techniques that are being widely applied to control complex systems where models may be unavailable. Note that the relative importance of the following methods are not proportional to the amount of space dedicated.

Reinforcement Learning

Reinforcement learning (RL) is an important discipline at the intersection of machine learning and control [507], and it is currently being used heavily by companies such as Google for generalized artificial intelligence, autonomous robots, and self-driving cars. In reinforcement learning, a control policy is refined over time, with improved performance achieved through experience. The most common framework for RL is the Markov decision process, where the dynamics of the system and the control policy are described in a probabilistic setting, so that stochasticity is built into the state dynamics and the actuation strategy. In this way, control policies are probabilistic, promoting a balance of optimization and exploration. Reinforcement learning is closely related to optimal control, although it may be formulated in a more general framework.

Reinforcement learning may be viewed as partially supervised, since it is not always known immediately if a control action was effective or not. In RL, a control policy is enacted by an *agent*, and this agent may only receive partial information about the effectiveness of their control strategy. For example, when learning to play a game like tic-tac-toe or chess, it is not clear if a specific intermediate move is responsible for winning or losing. The player receives binary feedback at the end of the game as to whether or not they win or lose. A major challenge that is addressed by RL is the development of a *value function*, also known as a quality function Q, that describes the value or quality of being in a particular state and making a particular control policy decision. Over time, the agent learns and refines this Q function, improving their ability to make good decisions. In the example of chess, an expert player begins to have intuition for good strategy based on board position, which is a complex value function over an extremely high-dimensional state space (i.e., the space of all possible board configurations). Q-learning is a model-free reinforcement learning strategy, where the value function is learned from experience. Recently, deep learning has been leveraged to dramatically improve the Q-learning process in situations where data is readily available [336, 385, 386, 384]. For example, the Google DeepMind algorithm has been able to master many classic Atari video games and has recently defeated the best players in the world at Go. We leave a more in-depth discussion of reinforcement learning for other books, but emphasize its importance in the growing field of machine learning control.

Iterative Learning Control

Iterative learning control (ILC) [5, 67, 83, 130, 343, 390] is a widely used technique that learns how to refine and optimize repetitive control tasks, such as the motion of a robot arm on a manufacturing line, where the robot arm will be repeating the same motion thousands of times. In contrast to the feedback control methods from Chapter 8 which adjust the actuation signal in real-time based on measurements, ILC refines the entire open-loop actuation sequence after each iteration of a prescribed task. The refinement process may be as simple as a proportional correction based on the measured error, or may involve a more sophisticated update rule. Iterative learning control does not require one to know the system equations and has performance guarantees for linear systems. ILC is therefore a mainstay in industrial control for repetitive tasks in a well-controlled environment, such as trajectory control of a robot arm or printer-head control in additive manufacturing.

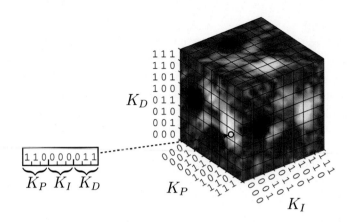

Figure 10.6 Depiction of parameter cube for PID control. The genetic algorithm represents a given parameter value as a *genetic sequence* that concatenates the various parameters. In this example, the parameters are expressed in binary representation that is scaled so that **000** is the minimum bound and **111** is the upper bound. Color indicates the cost associated with each parameter value.

Genetic Algorithms

The genetic algorithm (GA) is one of the earliest and simplest algorithms for parameter optimization, based on the biological principle of optimization through natural selection and fitness [250, 146, 210]. GA is frequently used to tune and adapt the parameters of a controller. In GA, a population comprised of many system realizations with different parameter values compete to minimize a given cost function, and successful parameter values are propagated to future generations through a set of *genetic* rules. The parameters a system are generally represented by a binary sequence, as shown in Fig. 10.6 for a PID control system with three parameters, given by the three control gains K_P, K_I, and K_D. Next, a number of realizations with different parameter values, called *individuals*, are initialized in a population and their performance is evaluated and compared on a given well-defined task. Successful individuals with a lower cost have a higher probability of being selected to advance to the next generation, according to the following genetic operations:

Elitism (optional):   A set number of the most fit individuals with the best performance are advanced directly to the next generation.

Replication: An individual is selected to advance to the next generation.

Crossover: Two individuals are selected to exchange a portion of their code and then advance to the next generation; crossover serves to exploit and enhance existing successful strategies.

Mutation: An individual is selected to have a portion of its code modified with new values; mutation promotes diversity and serves to increase the exploration of parameter space.

For the replication, crossover, and mutation operations, individuals are randomly selected to advance to the next generation with the probability of selection increasing with fitness. The genetic operations are illustrated for the PID control example in Fig. 10.7. These generations are evolved until the fitness of the top individuals converges or other stopping criteria are met.

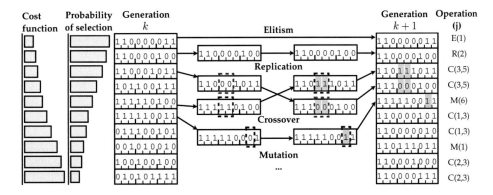

Figure 10.7 Schematic illustrating evolution in a genetic algorithm. The individuals in generation k are each evaluated and ranked in ascending order based on their cost function, which is inversely proportional to their probability of selection for genetic operations. Then, individuals are chosen based on this weighted probability for advancement to generation $k + 1$ using the four operations: elitism, replication, crossover, and mutation. This forms generation $k + 1$, and the sequence is repeated until the population statistics converges or another suitable stopping criterion is reached.

Genetic algorithms are generally used to find nearly globally optimal parameter values, as they are capable of exploring and exploiting local wells in the cost function. GA provides a middle ground between a brute-force search and a convex optimization, and is an alternative to expensive Monte Carlo sampling, which does not scale to high-dimensional parameter spaces. However, there is no guarantee that genetic algorithms will converge to a globally optimal solution. There are also a number of hyper-parameters that may affect performance, including the size of the populations, number of generations, and relative selection rates of the various genetic operations.

Genetic algorithms have been widely used for optimization and control in nonlinear systems [184]. For example, GA was used for parameter tuning in open loop control [394], with applications in jet mixing [304], combustion processes [101], wake control [431, 192], and drag reduction [201]. GA has also been employed to tune an $\mathcal{H}_\infty$ controller in a combustion experiment [233].

Genetic Programming

Genetic programming (GP) [307, 306] is a powerful generalization of genetic algorithms that simultaneously optimizes both the structure and parameters of an input–output map. Recently, genetic programming has also been used to obtain control laws that map sensor outputs to actuation inputs, as shown in Fig. 10.8. The function tree representation in GP is quite flexible, enabling the encoding of complex functions of the sensor signal **y** through a recursive tree structure. Each branch is a signal, and the merging points are mathematical operations. Sensors and constants are the leaves, and the overall control signal u is the root. The genetic operations of crossover, mutation, and replication are shown schematically in Fig. 10.9. This framework is readily generalized to include delay coordinates and temporal filters, as discussed in Duriez et al. [167].

Genetic programming has been recently used with impressive results in turbulence control experiments, led by Bernd Noack and collaborators [403, 417, 199, 168, 169, 416].

Control law

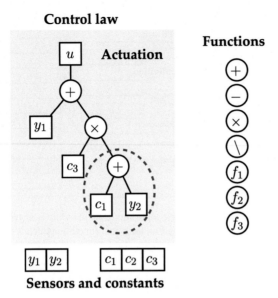

Sensors and constants

Figure 10.8 Illustration of function tree used to represent the control law **u** in genetic programming control.

This provides a new paradigm of control for strongly nonlinear systems, where it is now possible to identify the structure of nonlinear control laws. Genetic programming control is particularly well-suited to experiments where it is possible to rapidly evaluate a given control law, enabling the testing of hundreds or thousands of individuals in a short amount of time. Current demonstrations of genetic programming control in turbulence have produced several macroscopic behaviors, such as drag reduction and mixing enhancement, in an array of flow configurations. Specific flows include the mixing layer [417, 416, 168, 169], the backward facing step [199, 169], and a turbulent separated boundary layer [169].

Example: Genetic Algorithm to Tune PID Control

In this example, we will use the genetic algorithm to tune a proportional-integral-derivative (PID) controller. However, it should be noted that this is just a simple demonstration of evolutionary algorithms, and such heavy machinery is not recommended to tune a PID controller in practice, as there are far simpler techniques.

PID control is among the simplest and most widely used control architectures in industrial control systems, including for motor position and velocity control, for tuning of various sub-systems in an automobile, and for the pressure and temperature controls in modern espresso machines, to name only a few of the myriad applications. As its name suggests, PID control additively combines three terms to form the actuation signal, based on the error signal and its integral and derivative in time. A schematic of PID control is shown in Fig. 10.10.

In the cruise control example in Section 8.1, we saw that it was possible to reduce reference tracking error by increasing the proportional control gain K_P in the control law $u = -K_P(w_r - y)$. However, increasing the gain may eventually cause instability in some systems, and it will not completely eliminate the steady-state tracking error. The addition

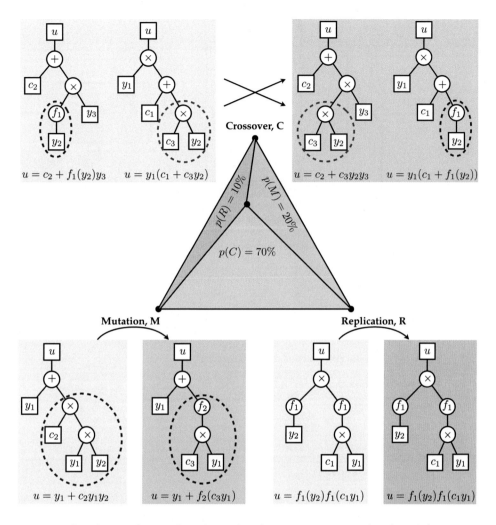

Figure 10.9 Genetic operations used to advance function trees across generations in genetic programming control. The relative selection rates of replication, crossover, and mutation are $p(R) = 0.1$, $p(C) = 0.7$, and $p(M) = 0.2$, respectively.

of an integral control term, $K_I \int_0^t (w_r - y)$ is useful to eliminate steady-state reference tracking error while alleviating the work required by the proportional term.

There are formal rules for how to choose the PID gains for various design specifications, such as fast response and minimal overshoot and ringing. In this example, we explore the use of a genetic algorithm to find effective PID gains to minimize a cost function. We use an LQR cost function

$$J = \int_0^T Q(w_r - y)^2 + Ru^2 \, d\tau$$

with $Q = 1$ and $R = 0.001$ for a step response $w_r = 1$. The system to be controlled will be given by the transfer function

$$G(s) = \frac{1}{s^4 + s}.$$

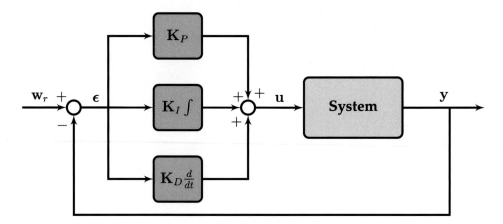

Figure 10.10 Proportional-integral-derivative (PID) control schematic. PID remains ubiquitous in industrial control.

The first step is to write a function that evaluates a given PID controller, as in Code 10.1. The three PID gains are stored in the variable **parms**.

Code 10.1 Evaluate cost function for PID controller.

```
function J = pidtest(G,dt,parms)

s = tf('s');
K = parms(1) + parms(2)/s + parms(3)*s/(1+.001*s);
Loop = series(K,G);
ClosedLoop = feedback(Loop,1);
t = 0:dt:20;
[y,t] = step(ClosedLoop,t);

CTRLtf = K/(1+K*G);
u = lsim(K,1-y,t);
```

Next, it is relatively simple to use a genetic algorithm to optimize the PID control gains, as in Code 10.2. In this example, we run the GA for 10 generations, with a population size of 25 individuals per generation.

Code 10.2 Genetic algorithm to tune PID controller.

```
dt = 0.001;
PopSize = 25;
MaxGenerations = 10;
s = tf('s');
G = 1/(s*(s*s+s+1));

options = optimoptions(@ga,'PopulationSize',PopSize,'
    MaxGenerations',MaxGenerations,'OutputFcn',@myfun);
[x,fval] = ga(@(K)pidtest(G,dt,K),3,-eye(3),zeros(3,1)
    ,[],[],[],[],[],options);
```

The results from intermediate generations are saved using the custom output function in Code 10.3.

Code 10.3 Special output function to save generations.

```
function [state,opts,optchanged]=myfun(opts,state,flag)
persistent history
persistent cost
optchanged = false;

switch flag
  case 'init'
        history(:,:,1) = state.Population;
        cost(:,1) = state.Score;
    case {'iter','interrupt'}
        ss = size(history,3);
        history(:,:,ss+1) = state.Population;
        cost(:,ss+1) = state.Score;
    case 'done'
        ss = size(history,3);
        history(:,:,ss+1) = state.Population;
        cost(:,ss+1) = state.Score;
        save history.mat history cost
end
```

The evolution of the cost function across various generations is shown in Fig. 10.11. As the generations progress, the cost function steadily decreases. The individual gains are shown in Fig. 10.12, with redder dots corresponding to early generations and bluer generations corresponding to later generations. As the genetic algorithm progresses, the PID gains begin to cluster around the optimal solution (black circle).

Fig. 10.13 shows the output in response to the PID controllers from the first generation. It is clear from this plot that many of the controllers fail to stabilize the system, resulting in large deviations in y. In contrast, Fig. 10.14 shows the output in response to the PID controllers from the last generation. Overall, these controllers are more effective at producing a stable step response.

The best controllers from each generation are shown in Fig. 10.15. In this plot, the controllers from early generations are redder, while the controllers from later generations

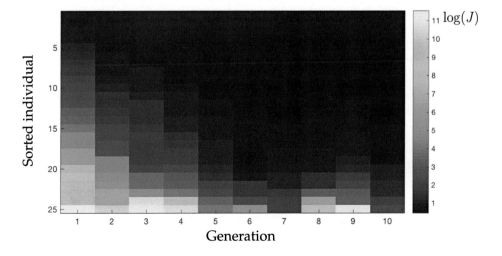

Figure 10.11 Cost function across generations, as GA optimizes PID gains.

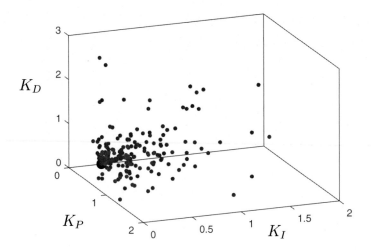

Figure 10.12 PID gains generated from genetic algorithm. Red points correspond to early generations while blue points correspond to later generations. The black point is the best individual found by GA.

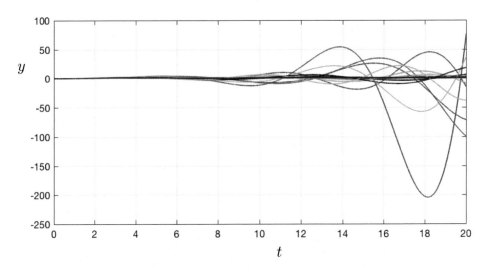

Figure 10.13 PID controller response from first generation of genetic algorithm.

are bluer. As the GA progresses, the controller is able to minimizes output oscillations and achieves fast rise time.

10.3   Adaptive Extremum-Seeking Control

Although there are many powerful techniques for model-based control design, there are also a number of drawbacks. First, in many systems, there may not be access to a model, or the model may not be suitable for control (i.e., there may be strong nonlinearities or the model may be represented in a nontraditional form). Next, even after an attractor has been identified and the dynamics characterized, control may invalidate this model by modifying the attractor, giving rise to new and uncharacterized dynamics. The obvious exception is

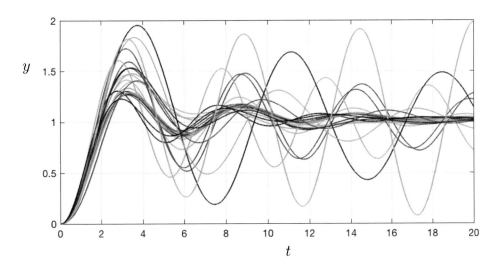

Figure 10.14 PID controller response from last generation of genetic algorithm.

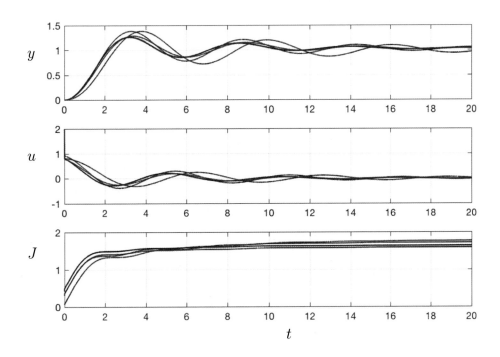

Figure 10.15 Best PID controllers from each generation. Red trajectories are from early generations, and blue trajectories correspond to the last generation.

stabilizing a fixed point or a periodic orbit, in which case effective control keeps the system in a neighborhood where the linearized model remains accurate. Finally, there may be slow changes to the system that modify the underlying dynamics, and it may be difficult to measure and model these effects.

The field of *adaptive* control broadly addresses these challenges, by allowing the control law the flexibility to modify its action based on the changing dynamics of a system. Extremum-seeking control (ESC) [312, 19] is a particularly attractive form of adaptive control for complex systems because it does not rely on an underlying model and it has guaranteed convergence and stability under a set of well-defined conditions. Extremum-seeking may be used to track local maxima of an objective function, despite disturbances, varying system parameters, and nonlinearities. Adaptive control may be implemented for in-time control or used for slow tuning of parameters in a working controller.

Extremum-seeking control may be thought of as an advanced *perturb-and-observe* method, whereby a sinusoidal perturbation is additively injected in the actuation signal and used to estimate the gradient of an objective function J that should be maximized or minimized. The objective function is generally computed based on sensor measurements of the system, although it ultimately depends on the internal dynamics and the choice of the input signal. In extremum-seeking, the control variable **u** may refer either to the actuation signal or a set of parameters that describe the control behavior, such as the frequency of periodic forcing or the gains in a PID controller.

The extremum-seeking control architecture is shown in Fig. 10.16. This schematic depicts ESC for a scalar input u, although the methods readily generalize for vector-valued inputs **u**. A convex objective function $J(u)$, is shown in Fig. 10.17 for static plant dynamics (i.e., for $y = u$). The extremum-seeking controller uses an input perturbation to estimate the gradient of the objective function J and steer the mean actuation signal towards the optimizing value.

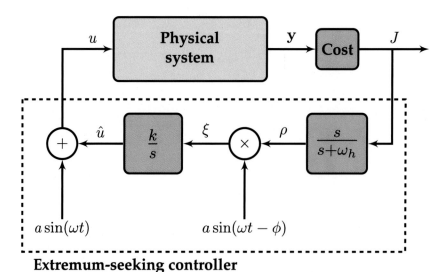

Extremum-seeking controller

Figure 10.16 Schematic illustrating an extremum-seeking controller. A sinusoidal perturbation is added to the best guess of the input $\hat{u}$, and it passes through the plant, resulting in a sinusoidal output perturbation that may be observed in the sensor signal **y** and the cost J. The high-pass filter results in a zero-mean output perturbation, which is then multiplied (demodulated) by the same input perturbation resulting in the signal ξ. This demodulated signal is finally integrated into the best guess $\hat{u}$ for the optimizing input u.

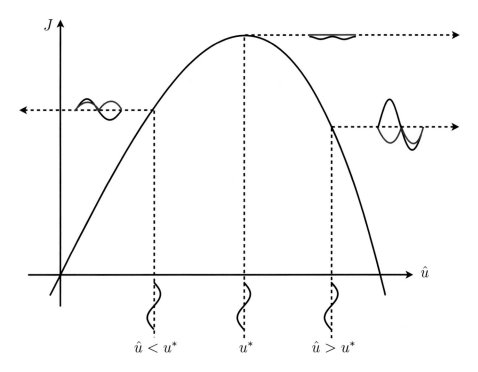

Figure 10.17 Schematic illustrating extremum-seeking control on for a static objective function $J(u)$. The output perturbation (red) is in phase when the input is left of the peak value (i.e. $u < u^*$) and out of phase when the input is to the right of the peak (i.e. $u > u^*$). Thus, integrating the product of input and output sinusoids moves $\hat{u}$ towards u^*.

Three distinct time-scales are relevant for extremum-seeking control:

1. slow – external disturbances and parameter variation;
2. medium – perturbation frequency ω;
3. fast – system dynamics.

In many systems, the internal system dynamics evolve on a fast time-scale. For example, turbulent fluctuations may equilibrate rapidly compared to actuation time-scales. In optical systems, such as a fiber laser [93], the dynamics of light inside the fiber are extremely fast compared to the time-scales of actuation.

In extremum-seeking control, a sinusoidal perturbation is added to the estimate of the input that maximizes the objective function, $\hat{u}$:

$$u = \hat{u} + a \sin(\omega t). \tag{10.23}$$

This input perturbation passes through the system dynamics and output, resulting in an objective function J that varies sinusoidally about some mean value, as shown in Fig. 10.17. The output J is high-pass filtered to remove the mean (DC component), resulting in the oscillatory signal ρ. A simple high-pass filter is represented in the frequency domain as

$$\frac{s}{s + \omega_h} \tag{10.24}$$

where s is the Laplace variable, and ω_h is the filter frequency. The high-pass filter is chosen to pass the perturbation frequency ω. The high-pass filtered output is then multiplied by the input sinusoid, possibly with a phase shift ϕ, resulting in the *demodulated* signal ξ:

$$\xi = a \sin(\omega t - \phi)\rho. \tag{10.25}$$

This signal ξ is mostly positive if the input u is to the left of the optimal value u^* and it is mostly negative if u is to the right of the optimal value u^*, shown as red curves in Fig. 10.17. Thus, the demodulated signal ξ is integrated into $\hat{u}$, the best estimate of the optimizing value

$$\frac{d}{dt}\hat{u} = k\,\xi, \tag{10.26}$$

so that the system estimate $\hat{u}$ is steered towards the optimal input u^*. Here, k is an integral gain, which determines how aggressively the actuation climbs gradients in J.

Roughly speaking, the demodulated signal ξ measures gradients in the objective function, so that the algorithm climbs to the optimum more rapidly when the gradient is larger. This is simple to see for constant plant dynamics, where J is simply a function of the input $J(u) = J(\hat{u} + a\sin(\omega t))$. Expanding $J(u)$ in the perturbation amplitude a, which is assumed to be small, yields:

$$J(u) = J(\hat{u} + a\sin(\omega t)) \tag{10.27a}$$

$$= J(\hat{u}) + \left.\frac{\partial J}{\partial u}\right|_{u=\hat{u}} \cdot a\sin(\omega t) + \mathcal{O}(a^2). \tag{10.27b}$$

The leading-order term in the high-pass filtered signal is $\rho \approx \partial J/\partial u|_{u=\hat{u}} \cdot a\sin(\omega t)$. Averaging $\xi = a\sin(\omega t - \phi)\rho$ over one period yields:

$$\xi_{\text{avg}} = \frac{\omega}{2\pi} \int_0^{2\pi/\omega} a\sin(\omega t - \phi)\rho\, dt \tag{10.28a}$$

$$= \frac{\omega}{2\pi} \int_0^{2\pi/\omega} \left.\frac{\partial J}{\partial u}\right|_{u=\hat{u}} a^2 \sin(\omega t - \phi)\sin(\omega t)\, dt \tag{10.28b}$$

$$= \frac{a^2}{2} \left.\frac{\partial J}{\partial u}\right|_{u=\hat{u}} \cos(\phi). \tag{10.28c}$$

Thus, for the case of trivial plant dynamics, the average signal ξ_{avg} is proportional to the gradient of the objective function J with respect to the input u.

In general, extremum-seeking control may be applied to systems with nonlinear dynamics relating the input u to the outputs $\mathbf{y}$ that act on a faster timescale than the perturbation ω. Thus, J may be time-varying, which complicates the simplistic averaging analysis above. The general case of extremum-seeking control of nonlinear systems is analyzed by Krstić and Wang in [312], where they develop powerful stability guarantees based on a separation of timescales and a singular perturbation analysis. The basic algorithm may also be modified to add a phase ϕ to the sinusoidal input perturbation in (10.25). In [312], there was an additional low-pass filter $\omega_l/(s + \omega_l)$ placed before the integrator to extract the DC component of the demodulated signal ξ. There is also an extension to extremum-seeking called slope-seeking, where a specific slope is sought [19] instead of the standard zero slope corresponding to a maximum or minimum. Slope-seeking is preferred when there is not an extremum, as in the case when control inputs saturate. Extremum-seeking is often

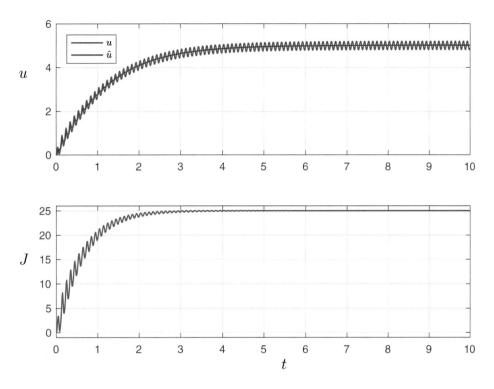

Figure 10.18 Extremum-seeking control response for cost function in (10.29).

used for frequency selection and slope-seeking is used for amplitude selection when tuning an open-loop periodic forcing.

It is important to note that extremum-seeking control will only find local maxima of the objective function, and there are no guarantees that this will correspond to a global maxima. Thus, it is important to start with a good initial condition for the optimization. In a number of studies, extremum-seeking control is used in conjunction with other global optimization techniques, such as a genetic algorithm, or sparse representation for classification [191, 99].

Simple Example of Extremum-Seeking Control

Here we consider a simple application of extremum-seeking control to find the maximum of a static quadratic cost function,

$$J(u) = 25 - (5 - u)^2. \tag{10.29}$$

This function has a single global maxima at $u^* = 5$. Starting at $u = 0$, we apply extremum-seeking control with a perturbation frequency of $\omega = 10\,\text{Hz}$ and an amplitude of $a = 0.2$. Fig. 10.18 shows the controller response and the rapid tracking of the optimal value $u^* = 5$. Code 10.4 shows how extremum-seeking may be implemented using a simple Butterworth high-pass filter.

Notice that when the gradient of the cost function is larger (i.e., closer to $u = 0$), the oscillations in J are larger, and the controller climbs more rapidly. When the input u gets close to the optimum value at $u^* = 5$, even though the input perturbation has the same amplitude a, the output perturbation is nearly zero (on the order of a^2), since the quadratic cost function is flat near the peak. Thus we achieve fast tracking far away from the optimum value and small deviations near the peak.

Code 10.4 Extremum-seeking control code.

```
J = @(u,t)(25-(5-(u)).^2);
y0 = J(0,0);   % u = 0

% Extremum Seeking Control Parameters
freq = 10*2*pi; % sample frequency
dt = 1/freq;
T = 10; % total period of simulation (in seconds)
A = .2;  % amplitude
omega = 10*2*pi; % 10 Hz
phase = 0;
K = 5;    % integration gain

% High pass filter (Butterworth filter)
butterorder=1;
butterfreq=2;   % in Hz for 'high'
[b,a] = butter(butterorder,butterfreq*dt*2,'high')
ys = zeros(1,butterorder+1)+y0;
HPF=zeros(1,butterorder+1);

uhat=u;
for i=1:T/dt
    t = (i-1)*dt;
    yvals(i)=J(u,t);

    for k=1:butterorder
        ys(k) = ys(k+1);
        HPF(k) = HPF(k+1);
    end
    ys(butterorder+1) = yvals(i);
    HPFnew = 0;
    for k=1:butterorder+1
        HPFnew = HPFnew + b(k)*ys(butterorder+2-k);
    end
    for k=2:butterorder+1
        HPFnew = HPFnew - a(k)*HPF(butterorder+2-k);
    end
    HPF(butterorder+1) = HPFnew;

    xi = HPFnew*sin(omega*t + phase);
    uhat = uhat + xi*K*dt;
    u = uhat + A*sin(omega*t + phase);
    uhats(i) = uhat;
    uvals(i) = u;
end
```

To see the ability of extremum-seeking control to handle varying system parameters, consider the time-dependent cost function given by

$$J(u) = 25 - (5 - u - \sin(t))^2. \tag{10.30}$$

The varying parameters, which oscillate at $1/2\pi$ Hz, may be consider slow compared with the perturbation frequency $10\,\mathrm{Hz}$. The response of extremum-seeking control for this slowly varying system is shown in Fig. 10.19. In this response, the actuation signal is able

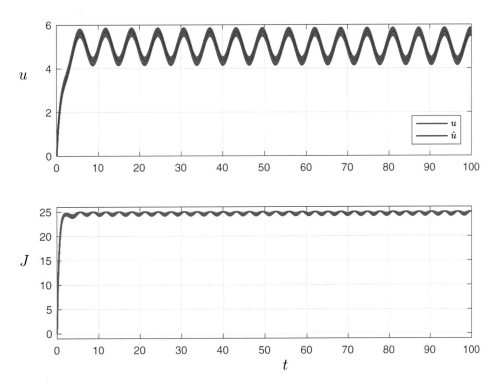

Figure 10.19 Extremum-seeking control response with a slowly changing cost function $J(u, t)$.

to maintain good performance by oscillating back and forth to approximately track the oscillating optimal u^*, which oscillates between 4 and 6. The output function J remains close to the optimal value of 25, despite the unknown varying parameter.

Challenging Example of Extremum-Seeking Control

Here we consider an example inspired by a challenging benchmark problem in Section 1.3 of [19]. This system has a time-varying objective function $J(t)$ and dynamics with a right-half plane zero, making it difficult to control.

In one formulation of extremum-seeking [133, 19], there are additional guidelines for designing the controller if the plant can be split into three blocks that define the input dynamics, a time-varying objective function with no internal dynamics, and the output dynamics, as shown in Fig. 10.20. In this case, there are procedures to design the high-pass filter and integrator blocks.

In this example, the objective function is given by

$$J(\theta) = .05\delta(t - 10) + (\theta - \theta^*(t))^2,$$

where δ is the Dirac delta function, and the optimal value $\theta^*(t)$ is given by

$$\theta^* = .01 + .001t.$$

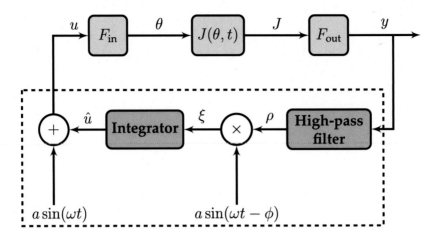

Figure 10.20 Schematic of a specific extremum-seeking control architecture that benefits from a wealth of design techniques [133, 19].

The optimal objective is given by $J^* = .05\delta(t - 10)$. The input and output dynamics are taken from the example in [19], and are given by

$$F_{in}(s) = \frac{s - 1}{(s + 2)(s + 1)}, \qquad F_{out}(s) = \frac{1}{s + 1}.$$

Using the design procedure in [19], one arrives at the high-pass filter $s/(s + 5)$ and an integrator-like block given by $50(s - 4)/(s - .01)$. In addition, a perturbation with $\omega = 5$ and $a = 0.05$ is used, and the demodulating perturbation is phase-shifted by $\phi = .7955$; this phase is obtained by evaluating the input function F_{in} at $i\omega$. The response of this controller is shown in Fig. 10.21, along with the Simulink implementation in Fig. 10.22. The controller is able to accurately track the optimizing input, despite additive sensor noise.

Applications of Extremum-Seeking Control

Because of the lack of assumptions and ease of implementation, extremum-seeking control has been widely applied to a number of complex systems. Although ESC is generally applicable for in-time control of dynamical systems, it is also widely used as an online optimization algorithm that can adapt to slow changes and disturbances. Among the many uses of extremum-seeking control, here we highlight only a few.

Extremum-seeking has been used widely for maximum power point tracking algorithms in photovoltaics [331, 178, 75, 97], and wind energy conversion [395]. In the case of photovoltaics, the voltage or current ripple in power converters due to pulse-width modulation is used for the perturbation signal, and in the case of wind, turbulence is used as the perturbation. Atmospheric turbulent fluctuations were also used as the perturbation signal for the optimization of aircraft control [309]; in this example it is infeasible to add a perturbation signal to the aircraft control surfaces, and a natural perturbation is required. ESC has also been used in optics and electronics for laser pulse shaping [450], tuning high-gain fiber lasers [93, 99], and for beam control in a reconfigurable holographic metamaterial antenna array [265]. Other applications include formation flight optimization [60],

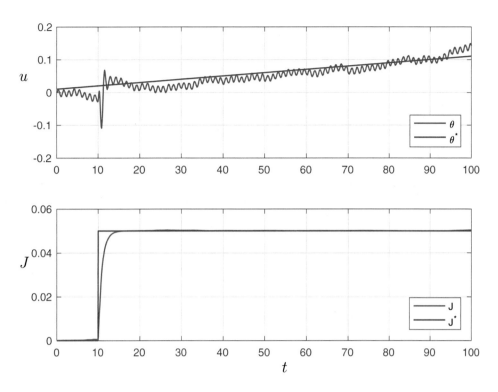

Figure 10.21 Extremum-seeking control response for a challenging test system with a right-half plane zero, inspired by [19].

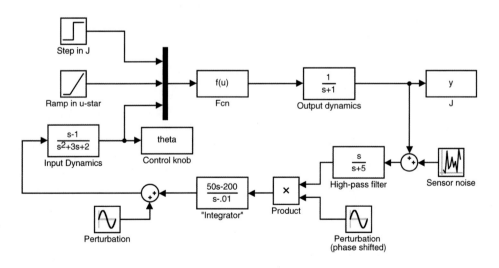

Figure 10.22 Simulink model for extremum-seeking controller used in Fig. 10.21.

bioreactors [546], PID [289] and PI [311] tuning, active braking systems [568], and control of Tokamaks [413].

Extremum-seeking has also been broadly applied in turbulent flow control. Despite the ability to control dynamics in-time with ESC, it is often used as a slow feedback optimization to tune the parameters of a working open-loop controller. This slow feedback has many benefits, such as maintaining performance despite slow changes to environmental conditions. Extremum-seeking has been used to control an axial flow compressor [547], to reduce drag over a bluff-body in an experiment [45, 46] using a rotating cylinder on the upper trailing edge of the rear surface, and for separation control in a high-lift airfoil configuration [47] using pressure sensors and pulsed jets on the leading edge of a single-slotted flap. There have also been impressive industrial-scale uses of extremum-seeking control, for example to control thermoacoustic modes across a range of frequencies in a 4 MW gas turbine combustor [37, 35]. It has also been utilized for separation control in a planar diffusor that is fully turbulent and stalled [36], and to control jet noise [375].

There are numerous extensions to extremum-seeking that improve performance. For example, extended Kalman filters were used as the filters in [202] to control thermoacoustic instabilities in a combustor experiment, reducing pressure fluctuations by nearly 40 dB. Kalman filters were also used with ESC to reduce the flow separation and increase the pressure ratio in a high-pressure axial fan using an injected pulsed air stream [553]. Including the Kalman filter improved the controller bandwidth by a factor of 10 over traditional ESC.

Suggested Reading
Texts
(1)   **Reinforcement learning: An introduction**, by R. S. Sutton and A. G. Barto, 1998 [507].
(2)   **Real-time optimization by extremum-seeking control**, by K. B. Ariyur and M. Krstić, 2003 [19].
(3)   **Machine learning control: Taming nonlinear dynamics and turbulence**, by T. Duriez, S. L. Brunton, and B. R. Noack, 2016 [167].
(4)   **Model predictive control**, by E. F. Camancho, C. B. Alba, 2013 [107].

Papers and Reviews
(1)   **Stability of extremum seeking feedback for general nonlinear dynamic systems**, by M. Krstić and H. H. Wang, *Automatica*, 2000 [312].
(2)   **Dynamic mode decomposition with control**, by J. L. Proctor, S. L. Brunton, and J. N. Kutz, *SIAM Journal on Applied Dynamical Systems*, 2016 [434].
(3)   **Model predictive control: theory and practice – a survey**, by C. E. Garcia, D. M. Prett, and M. Morari, *Automatica*, 1989 [195].
(4)   **Closed-loop turbulence control: Progress and challenges**, by S. L. Brunton and B. R. Noack, *Applied Mechanics Reviews*, 2015 [94].

Part IV

Reduced Order Models

11 Reduced Order Models (ROMs)

The proper orthogonal decomposition (POD) is the SVD algorithm applied to partial differential equations (PDEs). As such, it is one of the most important dimensionality reduction techniques available to study complex, spatio-temporal systems. Such systems are typically exemplified by nonlinear partial differential equations that prescribe the evolution in time and space of the quantities of interest in a given physical, engineering and/or biological system. The success of the POD is related to the seemingly ubiquitous observation that in most complex systems, meaningful behaviors are encoded in low-dimensional patterns of dynamic activity. The POD technique seeks to take advantage of this fact in order to produce low-rank dynamical systems capable of accurately modeling the full spatio-temporal evolution of the governing complex system. Specifically, *reduced order models* (ROMs) leverage POD modes for projecting PDE dynamics to low-rank subspaces where simulations of the governing PDE model can be more readily evaluated. Importantly, the low-rank models produced by the ROM allow for significant improvements in computational speed, potentially enabling prohibitively expensive Monte-Carlo simulations of PDE systems, optimization over parametrized PDE systems, and/or real-time control of PDE-based systems. POD has been extensively used in the fluids dynamics community [251]. It has also found a wide variety of applications in structural mechanics and vibrational analysis [287, 23, 232, 329], optical and MEMS technologies [333, 488], atmospheric sciences (where it is called empirical orthogonal functions (EOFs)) [116, 117], wind engineering applications [494], acoustics [181], and neuroscience [33, 519, 284]. The success of the method relies on its ability to provide physically interpretable spatio-temporal decompositions of data [316, 57, 181, 286, 126, 333].

11.1 POD for Partial Differential Equations

Throughout the engineering, physical and biological sciences, many systems are known to have prescribed relationships between time and space that drive patterns of dynamical activity. Even simple spatio-temporal relationships can lead to highly complex, yet coherent, dynamics that motivate the main thrust of analytic and computational studies. Modeling efforts seek to derive these spatio-temporal relationships either through first principle laws or through well-reasoned conjectures about existing relationships, thus leading generally to an underlying partial differential equation (PDE) that constrains and governs the complex system. Typically, such PDEs are beyond our ability to solve analytically. As a result, two primary solution strategies are pursued: computation and/or asymptotic reduction. In the former, the complex system is discretized in space and time to artificially produce an extremely high-dimensional system of equations which can be solved to a desired level of accuracy, with higher accuracy requiring a larger dimension of the discretized system. In this technique, the high-dimensionality is artificial and simply a consequence of the underlying numerical solution scheme. In contrast, asymptotic reduction seeks to replace the complex system with a simpler set of equations, preferably that are *linear* so as to be amenable to analysis. Before the 1960s and the rise of computation, such asymptotic reductions formed the backbone of applied mathematics in fields such a fluid dynamics. Indeed, asymptotics form the basis of the earliest efforts of dimensionality reduction. Asymptotic methods are not covered in this book, but the computational methods that enable reduced order models are.

To be more mathematically precise about our study of complex systems, we consider generically a system of nonlinear PDEs of a single spatial variable that can be modeled as

$$\mathbf{u}_t = \mathbf{N}\left(\mathbf{u}, \mathbf{u}_x, \mathbf{u}_{xx}, \cdots, x, t; \boldsymbol{\beta}\right) \tag{11.1}$$

where the subscripts denote partial differentiation and $\mathbf{N}(\cdot)$ prescribes the generically nonlinear evolution. The parameter $\boldsymbol{\beta}$ will represent a bifurcation parameter for our later considerations. Further, associated with (11.1) are a set of initial and boundary conditions on a domain $x \in [-L, L]$. Historically, a number of analytic solution techniques have been devised to study (11.1). Typically the aim of such methods is to reduce the PDE (11.1) to a set of ordinary differential equations (ODEs). The standard PDE methods of *separation of variables* and *similarity solutions* are constructed for this express purpose. Once in the form of an ODE, a broader variety of analytic methods can be applied along with a *qualitative theory* in the case of nonlinear behavior [252]. This again highlights the role that *asymptotics* can play in characterizing behavior.

Although a number of potential solution strategies have been mentioned, (11.1) does not admit a closed form solution in general. Even the simplest nonlinearity or a spatially dependent coefficient can render the standard analytic solution strategies useless. However, computational strategies for solving (11.1) are abundant and have provided transformative insights across the physical, engineering and biological sciences. The various computational techniques devised lead to a approximate numerical solution of (11.1), which is of high-dimension. Consider, for instance, a standard spatial discretization of (11.1) whereby the spatial variable x is evaluated at $n \gg 1$ points

$$\mathbf{u}(x_k, t) \quad \text{for} \quad k = 1, 2, \cdots, n \tag{11.2}$$

with spacing $\Delta x = x_{k+1} - x_k = 2L/n$. Using standard finite-difference formulas, spatial derivatives can be evaluated using neighboring spatial points so that, for instance,

$$\mathbf{u}_x = \frac{\mathbf{u}(x_{k+1}, t) - \mathbf{u}(x_{k-1}, t)}{2\Delta x} \tag{11.3a}$$

$$\mathbf{u}_{xx} = \frac{\mathbf{u}(x_{k+1}, t) - 2\mathbf{u}(x_k, t) + \mathbf{u}(x_{k-1}, t)}{\Delta x^2}. \tag{11.3b}$$

Such spatial discretization transforms the governing PDE (11.1) into a set of n ODEs

$$\frac{d\mathbf{u}_k}{dt} = \mathbf{N}\left(\mathbf{u}(x_{k+1}, t), \mathbf{u}(x_k, t), \mathbf{u}(x_{k-1}, t), \cdots, x_k, t, \boldsymbol{\beta}\right), \quad k = 1, 2, \cdots, n. \tag{11.4}$$

This process of discretization produces a more manageable system of equations at the expense of rendering (11.1) high-dimensional. It should be noted that as accuracy requirements become more stringent, the resulting dimension n of the system (11.4) also increases, since $\Delta x = 2L/n$. Thus, the dimension of the underlying computational scheme is artificially determined by the accuracy of the finite-difference differentiation schemes.

The spatial discretization of (11.1) illustrates how high-dimensional systems are rendered. The artificial production of high-dimensional systems is ubiquitous across computational schemes and presents significant challenges for scientific computing efforts. To further illustrate this phenomenon, we consider a second computational scheme for solving (11.1). In particular, we consider the most common technique for analytically solving PDEs: separation of variables. In this method, a solution is assumed, whereby space and time are independent, so that

$$\mathbf{u}(x,t) = \mathbf{a}(t)\psi(x) \tag{11.5}$$

where the variable $\mathbf{a}(t)$ subsumes all the time dependence of (11.1) and $\psi(x)$ characterizes the spatial dependence. Separation of variables is only guaranteed to work analytically if (11.1) is linear with constant coefficients. In that restrictive case, two differential equations can be derived that separately characterize the spatial and temporal dependences of the complex system. The differential equations are related by a constant parameter that is present in each.

For the general form of (11.1), separation of variables can be used to yield a computational algorithm capable of producing accurate solutions. Since the spatial solutions are not known *a priori*, it is typical to assume a set of basis modes which are used to construct $\psi(x)$. Indeed, such assumptions on basis modes underlies the critical ideas of the method of *eigenfunction expansions*. This yields a separation of variables solution ansatz of the form

$$\mathbf{u}(x,t) = \sum_{k=1}^{n} \mathbf{a}_k(t)\psi_k(x) \tag{11.6}$$

where $\psi_k(x)$ form a set of $n \gg 1$ basis modes. As before, this expansion artificially renders a high dimensional system of equations since n modes are required. This separation of variables solution approximates the true solution, provided n is large enough. Increasing the number of modes n is equivalent to increasing the spatial discretization in a finite-difference scheme.

The orthogonality properties of the basis functions $\psi_k(x)$ enable us to make use of (11.6). To illustrate this, consider a scalar version of (11.1) with the associated scalar separable solution $u(x,t) = \sum_{k=1}^{n} a_k(t)\psi_k(x)$. Inserting this solution into the governing equations gives

$$\sum \psi_k \frac{da_k}{dt} = \mathbf{N}\left(\sum a_k\psi_k, \sum a_k(\psi_k)_x, \sum a_k(\psi_k)_{xx}, \cdots, x, t, \boldsymbol{\beta}\right) \tag{11.7}$$

where the sums are from $k = 1, 2, \cdots, n$. Orthogonality of our basis functions implies that

$$\langle\psi_k, \psi_j\rangle = \delta_{kj} = \begin{cases} 0 & j \neq k \\ 1 & j = k \end{cases} \tag{11.8}$$

where δ_{kj} is the Kronecker delta function and $\langle\psi_k, \psi_j\rangle$ is the inner product defined as:

$$\langle\psi_k, \psi_j\rangle = \int_{-L}^{L} \psi_k\psi_j^* dx \tag{11.9}$$

where * denotes complex conjugation.

Once the modal basis is decided on, the governing equations for the $a_k(t)$ can be determined by multiplying (11.7) by $\psi_j(x)$ and integrating from $x \in [-L, L]$. Orthogonality then results in the temporal governing equations, or Galerkin projected dynamics, for each mode

$$\frac{da_k}{dt} = \left\langle \mathbf{N}\left(\sum a_j \psi_j, \sum a_j (\psi_j)_x, \sum a_j (\psi_j)_{xx}, \cdots, x, t, \boldsymbol{\beta}\right), \psi_k \right\rangle \quad k = 1, 2, \cdots, n.$$

$$(11.10)$$

The given form of $\mathbf{N}(\cdot)$ determines the mode-coupling that occurs between the various n modes. Indeed, the hallmark feature of nonlinearity is the production of modal mixing from (11.10).

Numerical schemes based on the Galerkin projection (11.10) are commonly used to perform simulations of the full governing system (11.1). Convergence to the true solution can be accomplished by both judicious choice of the modal basis elements ψ_k as well as the total number of modes n. Interestingly, the separation of variables strategy, which is rooted in *linear* PDEs, works for *nonlinear* and *nonconstant coefficient* PDEs, provided enough modal basis functions are chosen in order to accommodate all the nonlinear mode mixing that occurs in (11.10). A good choice of modal basis elements allows for a smaller set of n modes to be chosen to achieve a desired accuracy. The POD method is designed to specifically address the data-driven selection of a set of basis modes that are tailored to the particular dynamics, geometry, and parameters.

Fourier Mode Expansion

The most prolific basis used for the Galerkin projection technique is Fourier modes. More precisely, the fast Fourier transform (FFT) and its variants have dominated scientific computing applied to the engineering, physical, and biological sciences. There are two primary reasons for this: (i) There is a strong intuition developed around the meaning of Fourier modes as it directly relates to spatial wavelengths and frequencies, and more importantly, (ii) the algorithm necessary to compute the right-hand side of (11.10) can be executed in $O(n \log n)$ operations. The second fact has made the FFT one of the top ten algorithms of the last century and a foundational cornerstone of scientific computing.

The Fourier mode basis elements are given by

$$\psi_k(x) = \frac{1}{L} \exp\left(i\frac{2\pi k x}{L}\right) \quad x \in [0, L] \text{ and } k = -n/2, \cdots, -1, 0, 1, \cdots, n/2 - 1.$$

$$(11.11)$$

It should be noted that in most software packages, including Matlab, the FFT command assumes that the spatial interval is $x \in [0, 2\pi]$. Thus one must rescale a domain of length L to 2π before using the FFT.

Obviously the Fourier modes (11.11) are complex periodic functions on the interval $x \in [0, L]$. However, they are applicable to a much broader class of functions that are not necessarily periodic. For instance, consider a localized Gaussian function

$$u(x, t) = \exp\left(-\sigma x^2\right) \tag{11.12}$$

whose Fourier transform is also a Gaussian. In representing such a function with Fourier modes, a large number of modes are often required since the function itself isn't periodic. Fig. 11.1 shows the Fourier mode representation of the Gaussian for three values of σ. Of note is the fact that a large number of modes is required to represent this simple function,

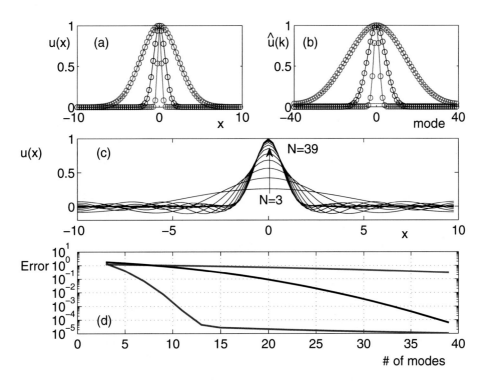

Figure 11.1 Illustration of Fourier modes for representing a localized Gaussian pulse. (a) $n = 80$ Fourier modes are used to represent the Gaussian $u(x) = \exp(-\sigma x^2)$ in the domain $x \in [-10, 10]$ for $\sigma = 0.1$ (red), $\sigma = 1$ (black) and $\sigma = 10$ (blue). (b) The Fourier mode representation of the Gaussian, showing the modes required for an accurate representation of the localized function. (c) The convergence of the n mode solution to the actual Gaussian ($\sigma = 1$) with the (d) L^2 error from the true solution for the three values of σ.

especially as the Gaussian width is decreased. Although the FFT algorithm is extremely fast and widely applied, one can see immediately that a large number of modes are generically required to represent simple functions of interest. Thus, solving problems using the FFT often requires high-dimensional representations (i.e., $n \gg 1$) to accommodate generic, localized spatial behaviors. Ultimately, our aim is to move away from artificially creating such high-dimensional problems.

Special Functions and Sturm-Liouville Theory

In the 1800s and early 1900s, mathematical physics developed many of the governing principles behind heat flow, electromagnetism and quantum mechanics, for instance. Many of the hallmark problems considered were driven by *linear* dynamics, allowing for analytically tractable solutions. And since these problems arose before the advent of computing, nonlinearities were typically treated as perturbations to an underlying linear equation. Thus one often considered complex systems of the form

$$\mathbf{u}_t = \mathbf{L}\mathbf{u} + \epsilon \mathbf{N}(\mathbf{u}, \mathbf{u}_x, \mathbf{u}_{xx}, \cdots, x, t, \boldsymbol{\beta}) \qquad (11.13)$$

where $\mathbf{L}$ is a linear operator and $\epsilon \ll 1$ is a small parameter used for perturbation calculations. Often in mathematical physics, the operator $\mathbf{L}$ is a Sturm-Liouville operator which guarantees many advantageous properties of the eigenvalues and eigenfunctions.

To solve equations of the form in (11.13), special modes are often used that are ideally suited for the problem. Such modes are eigenfunctions of the underlying linear operator L in (11.13):

$$\mathbf{L}\psi_k = \lambda_k \psi_k \qquad (11.14)$$

where $\psi_k(x)$ are orthonormal eigenfunctions of the operator $\mathbf{L}$. The eigenfunctions allow for an *eigenfunction expansion* solution whereby $\mathbf{u}(x, t) = \sum a_k(t)\psi_k(x)$. This leads to the following solution form

$$\frac{da_k}{dt} = \langle \mathbf{Lu}, \psi_k \rangle + \epsilon \langle \mathbf{N}, \psi_k \rangle . \qquad (11.15)$$

The key idea in such an expansion is that the eigenfunctions presumably are ideal for modeling the spatial variations particular to the problem under consideration. Thus, they would seem to be ideal, or perfectly suited, modes for (11.13). This is in contrast to the Fourier mode expansion, as the sinusoidal modes may be unrelated to the particular physics or symmetries in the geometry. For example, the Gaussian example considered can be potentially represented more efficiently by Gauss-Hermite polynomials. Indeed, the wide variety of special functions, including the Sturm-Liouville operators of *Bessel*, *Laguerre*, *Hermite*, *Legendre*, for instance, are aimed at making the representation of solutions more efficient and much more closely related to the underlying physics and geometry. Ultimately, one can think of using such functions as a way of doing *dimensionality reduction* by using an ideally suited set of basis functions.

Dimensionality Reduction

The examples above and solution methods for PDEs illustrate a common problem of scientific computing: the generation of n degree, high-dimensional systems. For many complex PDEs with several spatial dimensions, it is not uncommon for discretization or modal expansion techniques to yield systems of differential equations with millions or billions of degrees of freedom. Such large systems are extremely demanding for even the latest computational architectures, limiting accuracies and run-times in the modeling of many complex systems, such as high Reynolds number fluid flows.

To aid in computation, the selection of a set of optimal basis modes is critical, as it can greatly reduce the number of differential equations generated. Many solution techniques involve the solution of a linear system of size n, which generically involves $O(n^3)$ operations. Thus, reducing n is of paramount importance. One can already see that even in the 1800s and early 1900s, the special functions developed for various problems of mathematical physics were an analytic attempt to generate an ideal set of modes for representing the dynamics of the complex system. However, for strongly nonlinear, complex systems (11.1), even such special functions rarely give the best set of modes. In the next section, we show how one might generate modes ψ_k that are tailored specifically for the dynamics and geometry in (11.1). Based on the SVD algorithm, the *proper orthogonal decomposition* (POD) generates a set of modes that are *optimal* for representing either simulation or measurement data, potentially allowing for significant reduction of the number of modes n required to model the behavior of (11.1) for a given accuracy [57, 542, 543].

11.2 Optimal Basis Elements: The POD Expansion

As illustrated in the previous section, the selection of a good modal basis for solving (11.1) using the Galerkin expansion in (11.6) is critical for efficient scientific computing strategies. Many algorithms for solving PDEs rely on choosing basis modes *a priori* based on (i) computational speed, (ii) accuracy, and/or (iii) constraints on boundary conditions. All these reasons are justified and form the basis of computationally sound methods. However, our primary concern in this chapter is in selecting a method that allows for maximal computational efficiency via *dimensionality reduction*. As already highlighted, many algorithms generate artificially large systems of size n. In what follows, we present a data-driven strategy, whereby optimal modes, also known as POD modes, are selected from numerical and/or experimental observations, thus allowing for a minimal number of modes $r \ll n$ to characterize the dynamics of (11.1).

Two options exist for extracting the optimal basis modes from a given complex system. One can either collect data directly from an experiment, or one can simulate the complex system and sample the state of the system as it evolves according to the dynamics. In both cases, snapshots of the dynamics are taken and optimal modes identified. In the case when the system is simulated to extract modes, one can argue that no computational savings are achieved. However, much like the *LU* decomposition, which has an initial one-time computational cost of $O(n^3)$ before further $O(n^2)$ operations can be applied, the costly modal extraction process is performed only once. The optimal modes can then be used in a computationally efficient manner thereafter.

To proceed with the construction of the optimal POD modes, the dynamics of (11.1) are sampled at some prescribed time interval. In particular, a snapshot $\mathbf{u}_k$ consists of samples of the complex system, with subscript k indicating sampling at time t_k: $\mathbf{u}_k := \begin{bmatrix} \mathbf{u}(x_1, t_k) & \mathbf{u}(x_2, t_k) & \cdots & \mathbf{u}(x_n, t_k) \end{bmatrix}^T$. Now, the continuous functions and modes will be evaluated at n discrete spatial locations, resulting in a high-dimensional vector representation; these will be denoted by bold symbols. We are generally interested in analyzing the computationally or experimentally generated large data set $\mathbf{X}$:

$$\mathbf{X} = \begin{bmatrix} | & | & & | \\ \mathbf{u}_1 & \mathbf{u}_2 & \cdots & \mathbf{u}_m \\ | & | & & | \end{bmatrix} \tag{11.16}$$

where the columns $\mathbf{u}_k = \mathbf{u}(t_k) \in \mathbb{C}^n$ may be measurements from simulations or experiments. $\mathbf{X}$ consists of a *time-series* of data, with m distinct measurement instances in time. Often the *state-dimension* n is very large, on the order of millions or billions in the case of fluid systems. Typically $n \gg m$, resulting in a *tall-skinny* matrix, as opposed to a *short-fat* matrix when $n \ll m$.

As discussed previously, the singular value decomposition (SVD) provides a unique matrix decomposition for any complex valued matrix $\mathbf{X} \in \mathbb{C}^{n \times m}$:

$$\mathbf{X} = \mathbf{U} \mathbf{\Sigma} \mathbf{V}^* \tag{11.17}$$

where $\mathbf{U} \in \mathbb{C}^{n \times n}$ and $\mathbf{V} \in \mathbb{C}^{m \times m}$ are *unitary* matrices and $\mathbf{\Sigma} \in \mathbb{C}^{n \times m}$ is a matrix with nonnegative entries on the diagonal. Here $*$ denotes the complex conjugate transpose. The columns of $\mathbf{U}$ are called *left singular vectors* of $\mathbf{X}$ and the columns of $\mathbf{V}$ are *right singular vectors*. The diagonal elements of $\mathbf{\Sigma}$ are called *singular values* and they are ordered from largest to smallest. The SVD provides critical insight into building an optimal basis set tailored to the specific problem. In particular, the matrix $\mathbf{U}$ is guaranteed to provide the best set of modes to approximate $\mathbf{X}$ in an ℓ_2 sense. Specifically, the columns of this matrix contain the orthogonal modes necessary to form the ideal basis. The matrix $\mathbf{V}$ gives the time-history of each of the modal elements and the diagonal matrix $\mathbf{\Sigma}$ is the weighting of each mode relative to the others. Recall that the modes are arranged with the most dominant first and the least dominant last.

The total number of modes generated is typically determined by the number of snapshots m taken in constructing $\mathbf{X}$ (where normally $n \gg m$). Our objective is to determine the minimal number of modes necessary to accurately represent the dynamics of (11.1) with a Galerkin projection (11.6). Thus we are interested in a rank-r approximation to the true dynamics where typically $r \ll m$. The quantity of interest is then the low-rank decomposition of the SVD given by

$$\tilde{\mathbf{X}} = \tilde{\mathbf{U}}\tilde{\mathbf{\Sigma}}\tilde{\mathbf{V}}^* \tag{11.18}$$

where $\|\mathbf{X} - \tilde{\mathbf{X}}\| < \epsilon$ for a given small value of epsilon. This low-rank truncation allows us to construct the modes of interest $\boldsymbol{\psi}_k$ from the columns of the truncated matrix $\tilde{\mathbf{U}}$. In particular, the optimal basis modes are given by

$$\tilde{\mathbf{U}} = \mathbf{\Psi} = \begin{bmatrix} | & | & & | \\ \boldsymbol{\psi}_1 & \boldsymbol{\psi}_2 & \cdots & \boldsymbol{\psi}_r \\ | & | & & | \end{bmatrix} \tag{11.19}$$

where the truncation preserves the r most dominant modes used in (11.6). The truncated r modes $\{\boldsymbol{\psi}_1, \boldsymbol{\psi}_2, \cdots, \boldsymbol{\psi}_r\}$ are then used as the low-rank, orthogonal basis to represent the dynamics of (11.1).

The above snapshot based method for extracting the low-rank, r-dimensional subspace of dynamic evolution associated with (11.1) is a data-driven computational architecture. Indeed, it provides an equation-free method, i.e. the governing equation (11.1) may actually be unknown. In the event that the underlying dynamics are unknown, then the extraction of the low-rank space allows one to build potential models in an r-dimensional subspace as opposed to remaining in a high-dimensional space where $n \gg r$. These ideas will be explored further in what follows. However, it suffices to highlight at this juncture that an optimal basis representation does not require an underlying knowledge of the complex system (11.1).

Galerkin Projection onto POD Modes

It is possible to approximate the state $\mathbf{u}$ of the PDE using a Galerkin expansion:

$$\mathbf{u}(t) \approx \mathbf{\Psi}\mathbf{a}(t) \tag{11.20}$$

where $\mathbf{a}(t) \in \mathbb{R}^r$ is the time-dependent coefficient vector and $r \ll n$. Plugging this modal expansion into the governing equation (11.13) and applying orthogonality (multiplying by $\mathbf{\Psi}^T$) gives the dimensionally reduced evolution

$$\frac{d\mathbf{a}(t)}{dt} = \mathbf{\Psi}^T \mathbf{L} \mathbf{\Psi} \mathbf{a}(t) + \mathbf{\Psi}^T \mathbf{N}(\mathbf{\Psi}\mathbf{a}(t), \boldsymbol{\beta}). \tag{11.21}$$

By solving this system of much smaller dimension, the solution of a high-dimensional nonlinear dynamical system can be approximated. Of critical importance is evaluating the nonlinear terms in an efficient way using the gappy POD or DEIM mathematical architecture in Chapter 12. Otherwise, the evaluation of the nonlinear terms still requires calculation of functions and inner products with the original dimension n. In certain cases, such as the quadratic nonlinearity of Navier-Stokes, the nonlinear terms can be computed once in an off-line manner. However, parametrized systems generally require repeated evaluation of the nonlinear terms as the POD modes change with $\boldsymbol{\beta}$.

Example: The Harmonic Oscillator

To illustrate the POD method for selecting optimal basis elements, we will consider a classic problem of mathematical physics: the *quantum harmonic oscillator*. Although the ideal basis functions (Gauss-Hermite functions) for this problem are already known, we would like to infer these special functions in a purely data-driven way. In other words, can we deduce these special functions from snapshots of the dynamics alone? The standard harmonic oscillator arises in the study of spring-mass systems. In particular, one often assumes that the restoring force F of a spring is governed by the linear Hooke's law:

$$F(t) = -kx \tag{11.22}$$

where k is the spring constant and $x(t)$ represents the displacement of the spring from its equilibrium position. Such a force gives rise to a potential energy for the spring of the form $V = kx^2/2$.

In considering quantum mechanical systems, such a restoring force (with $k = 1$ without loss of generality) and associated potential energy gives rise to the Schrödinger equation with a parabolic potential

$$iu_t + \frac{1}{2}u_{xx} - \frac{x^2}{2}u = 0 \tag{11.23}$$

where the second term in the partial differential equation represents the kinetic energy of a quantum particle while the last term is the parabolic potential associated with the linear restoring force.

The solution for the quantum harmonic oscillator can be easily computed in terms of special functions. In particular, by assuming a solution of the form

$$u(x, t) = a_k \psi_k(x) \exp\left[-i(k + 1/2)t\right] \tag{11.24}$$

with a_k determined from initial conditions, one finds the following boundary value problem for the eigenmodes of the system

$$\frac{d^2 \psi_k}{dx^2} + (2k + 1 - x^2)\psi_k \tag{11.25}$$

with the boundary conditions $\psi_k \to 0$ as $x \to \pm\infty$. Normalized solutions to this equation can be expressed in terms of *Hermite polynomials*, $H_k(x)$ or the Gaussian-Hermite functions

$$\psi_k = \left(2^k k \sqrt{\pi}\right)^{-1/2} \exp(-x^2/2) H_k(x) \tag{11.26a}$$

$$= (-1)^k \left(2^k k \sqrt{\pi}\right)^{-1/2} \exp(-x^2/2) \frac{d^k}{dx^k} \exp(-x^2). \tag{11.26b}$$

The Gauss-Hermite functions are typically thought of as the optimal basis functions for the harmonic oscillator as they naturally represent the underlying dynamics driven by the Schrödinger equation with parabolic potential. Indeed, solutions of the complex system (11.23) can be represented as the sum

$$u(x, t) = \sum_{k=0}^{\infty} a_k \left(2^k k \sqrt{\pi}\right)^{-1/2} \exp(-x^2/2) H_k(x) \exp\left[-i(k + 1/2)t\right]. \tag{11.27}$$

Such a solution strategy is ubiquitous in mathematical physics as is evidenced by the large number of special functions, often of Sturm-Liouville form, for different geometries and boundary conditions. These include Bessel functions, Laguerre polynomials, Legendre polynomials, parabolic cylinder functions, spherical harmonics, etc.

A numerical solution to the governing PDE (11.23) based on the fast Fourier transform is easy to implement [316]. The following code executes a full numerical solution with the initial conditions $u(x, 0) = \exp(-0.2(x - x_0)^2)$, which is a Gaussian pulse centered at $x = x_0$. This initial condition generically excites a number of Gauss-Hermite functions. In particular, the initial projection onto the eigenmodes is computed from the orthogonality conditions so that

$$a_k = \langle u(x, 0), \psi_k \rangle. \tag{11.28}$$

This inner product projects the initial condition onto each mode ψ_k.

Code 11.1 Harmonic oscillator code.

```
L=30; n=512; x2=linspace(-L/2,L/2,n+1); x=x2(1:n);  % spatial
    discretization
k=(2*pi/L)*[0:n/2-1 -n/2:-1].';      % wavenumbers for FFT
V=x.^2.';                % potential
t=0:0.2:20;              % time domain collection points

u=exp(-0.2*(x-1).^2);  % initial conditions
ut=fft(u);              % FFT initial data
[t,utsol]=ode45('pod_harm_rhs',t,ut,[],k,V);  % integrate PDE
for j=1:length(t)
  usol(j,:)=ifft(utsol(j,:));      % transforming back
end
```

The right-hand side function, **pod_harm_rhs.m** associated with the above code contains the governing equation (11.23) in a three-line MATLAB code:

Code 11.2 Harmonic oscillator right-hand side.

```
function rhs=pod_harm_rhs(t,ut,dummy,k,V)
u=ifft(ut);
rhs=-(i/2)*(k.^2).*ut - 0.5*i*fft(V.*u);
```

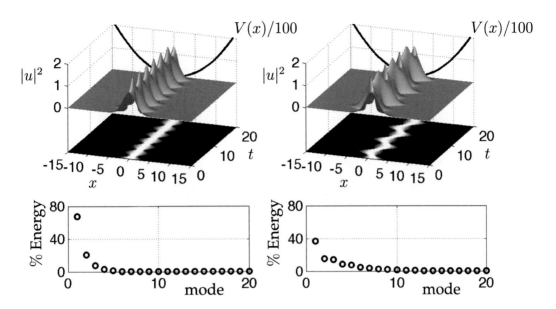

Figure 11.2 Dynamics of the quantum harmonic oscillator (11.23) given the initial condition $u(x, 0) = \exp(-0.2(x - x_0)^2)$ for $x_0 = 0$ (left panel) and $x_0 = 1$ (right panel). The symmetric initial data elicits a dominant five mode response while the initial condition with initial offset $x_0 = 1$ activates ten modes. The bottom panels show the singular values of the SVD of their corresponding top panels along with the percentage of energy (or L^2 norm) in each mode. The dynamics are clearly low-rank given the rapid decay of the singular values.

The two codes together produce dynamics associated with the quantum harmonic oscillator. Fig. 11.2 shows the dynamical evolution of an initial Gaussian $u(x, 0) = \exp(-0.2(x - x_0)^2)$ with $x_0 = 0$ (left panel) and $x_0 = 1$ (right panel). From the simulation, one can see that there are a total of 101 snapshots (the initial condition and an additional 100 measurement times). These snapshots can be organized as in (11.16) and the singular value decomposition performed. The singular values of the decomposition are suggestive of the underlying dimensionality of the dynamics. For the dynamical evolution observed in the top panels of Fig. 11.2, the corresponding singular values of the snapshots are given in the bottom panels. For the symmetric initial condition (symmetric about $x = 0$), five modes dominate the dynamics. In contrast, for an asymmetric initial condition, twice as many modes are required to represent the dynamics with the same precision.

The singular value decomposition not only gives the distribution of energy within the first set of modes, but it also produces the optimal basis elements as columns of the matrix **U**. The distribution of singular values is highly suggestive of how to truncate with a low-rank subspace of r modes, thus allowing us to construct the dimensionally reduced space (11.19) appropriate for a Galerkin-POD expansion.

The modes of the quantum harmonic oscillator are illustrated in Fig. 11.3. Specifically, the first five modes are shown for (i) the Gauss-Hermite functions representing the special function solutions, (ii) the modes of the SVD for the symmetric ($x_0 = 0$) initial conditions, and (iii) the modes of the SVD for the offset (asymmetric, $x_0 = 1$) initial conditions. The Gauss-Hermite functions, by construction, are arranged from lowest eigenvalue

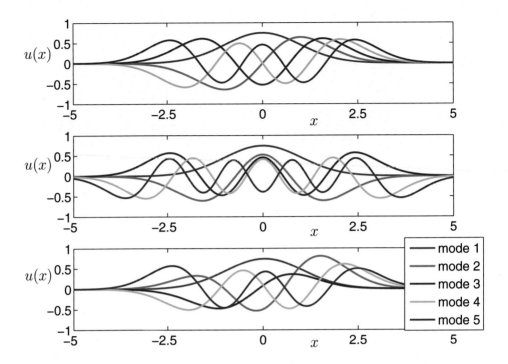

Figure 11.3 First five modes of the quantum harmonic oscillator. In the top panel, the first five Gauss-Hermite modes (11.26), arranged by their Sturm-Liouville eigenvalue, are illustrated. The second panel shows the dominant modes computed from the SVD of the dynamics of the harmonic oscillator with $u(x, 0) = \exp(-0.2x^2)$, illustrated in Fig. 11.2 left panel. Note that the modes are all symmetric since no asymmetric dynamics was actually manifested. For the bottom panel, where the harmonic oscillator was simulated with the offset Gaussian $u(x, 0) = \exp(-0.2(x - 1)^2)$, asymmetry is certainly observed. This also produces modes that are very similar to the Gauss-Hermite functions. Thus a purely snapshot based method is capable of reproducing the nearly ideal basis set for the harmonic oscillator.

of the Sturm-Liouville problem (11.25). The eigenmodes alternate between symmetric and asymmetric modes. For the symmetric (about $x = 0$) initial conditions given by $u(x, 0) = \exp(-0.2x^2)$, the first five modes are all symmetric as the snapshot based method is incapable of producing asymmetric modes since they are actually not part of the dynamics, and thus they are not observable, or manifested in the evolution. In contrast, with a slight offset, $u(x, 0) = \exp(-0.2(x - 1)^2)$, snapshots of the evolution produce asymmetric modes that closely resemble the asymmetric modes of the Gauss-Hermite expansion. Interestingly, in this case, the SVD arranges the modes by the amount of energy exhibited in each mode. Thus the first asymmetric mode (bottom panel in red – third mode) is equivalent to the second mode of the exact Gauss-Hermite polynomials (top panel in green – second mode). The key observation here is that the snapshot based method is capable of generating, or nearly so, the known optimal Gauss-Hermite polynomials characteristic of this system. Importantly, the POD-Galerkin method generalizes to more complex physics and geometries where the solution is not known *a priori*.

11.3   POD and Soliton Dynamics

To illustrate a full implementation of the Galerkin-POD method, we will consider an illustrative complex system whose dynamics are strongly nonlinear. Thus, we consider the nonlinear Schrödinger (NLS) equation

$$iu_t + \frac{1}{2}u_{xx} + |u|^2 u = 0 \qquad (11.29)$$

with the boundary conditions $u \to 0$ as $x \to \pm\infty$. If not for the nonlinear term, this equation could be solved easily in closed form. However, the nonlinearity mixes the eigenfunction components in the expansion (11.6), and it is impossible to derive a simple analytic solution.

To solve the NLS computationally, a Fourier mode expansion is used. Thus the standard fast Fourier transform may be leveraged. Rewriting (11.29) in the Fourier domain, i.e. taking the Fourier transform, gives the set of differential equations

$$\hat{u}_t = -\frac{i}{2}k^2\hat{u} + i\widehat{|u|^2 u} \qquad (11.30)$$

where the Fourier mode mixing occurs due to the nonlinear mixing in the cubic term. This gives the system of differential equations to be solved in order to evaluate the NLS behavior.

The following code formulates the PDE solution as an eigenfunction expansion (11.6) of the NLS (11.29). The first step in the process is to define an appropriate spatial and temporal domain for the solution along with the Fourier frequencies present in the system. The following code produces both the time and space domains of interest:

Code 11.3 Nonlinear Schrödinger equation solver.

```
L=40; n=512; x2=linspace(-L/2,L/2,n+1); x=x2(1:n); % spatial
    discretization
k=(2*pi/L)*[0:n/2-1 -n/2:-1].'; % wavenumbers for FFT
t=linspace(0,2*pi,21); % time domain collection points

N=1;
u=N*sech(x); % initial conditions
ut=fft(u); % FFT initial data
[t,utsol]=ode45('pod_sol_rhs',t,ut,[],k); % integrate PDE
for j=1:length(t)
  usol(j,:)=ifft(utsol(j,:)); % transforming back
end
```

The right-hand side function, **pod_sol_rhs.m** associated with the above code contains the governing equation (11.29) in a three-line MATLAB code:

Code 11.4 NLS right-hand side.

```
function rhs=pod_sol_rhs(t,ut,dummy,k)
u=ifft(ut);
rhs=-(i/2)*(k.^2).*ut + i*fft( (abs(u).^2).*u );
```

It now remains to consider a specific spatial configuration for the initial condition. For the NLS, there are a set of special initial conditions called solitons where the initial conditions are given by

$$u(x,0) = N\text{sech}(x) \qquad (11.31)$$

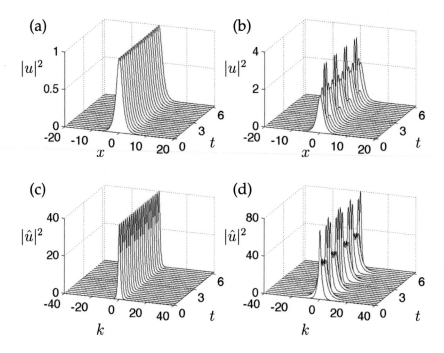

Figure 11.4 Evolution of the (a) $N = 1$ and (b) $N = 2$ solitons. Here steady-state ($N = 1$, left panels (a) and (c)) and periodic ($N = 2$, right panels (b) and (d)) dynamics are observed and approximately 50 and 200 Fourier modes, respectively, are required to model the behaviors.

where N is an integer. We will consider the soliton dynamics with $N = 1$ and $N = 2$. First, the initial condition is projected onto the Fourier modes with the fast Fourier transform.

The dynamics of the $N = 1$ and $N = 2$ solitons are demonstrated in Fig. 11.4. During evolution, the $N = 1$ soliton only undergoes phase changes while its amplitude remains stationary. In contrast, the $N = 2$ soliton undergoes periodic oscillations. In both cases, a large number of Fourier modes, about 50 and 200 respectively, are required to model the simple behaviors illustrated.

The obvious question to ask in light of our dimensionality reduction thinking is this: is the soliton dynamics really a 50 or 200 degrees-of-freedom system as required by the Fourier mode solution technique. The answer is no. Indeed, with the appropriate basis, i.e. the POD modes generated from the SVD, it can be shown that the dynamics is a simple reduction to 1 or 2 modes respectively. Indeed, it can easily be shown that the $N = 1$ and $N = 2$ solitons are truly low dimensional by computing the singular value decomposition of the evolutions shown in Fig. 11.4.

Fig. 11.5 explicitly demonstrates the low-dimensional nature of the numerical solutions by computing the singular values, along with the modes to be used in our new eigenfunction expansion. For both of these cases, the dynamics are truly low dimensional with the $N = 1$ soliton being modeled well by a single POD mode while the $N = 2$ dynamics are modeled quite well with two POD modes. Thus, in performing an eigenfunction expansion, the modes chosen should be the POD modes generated from the simulations themselves. In the next section, we will derive the dynamics of the modal interaction for these two cases, which are low-dimensional and amenable to analysis.

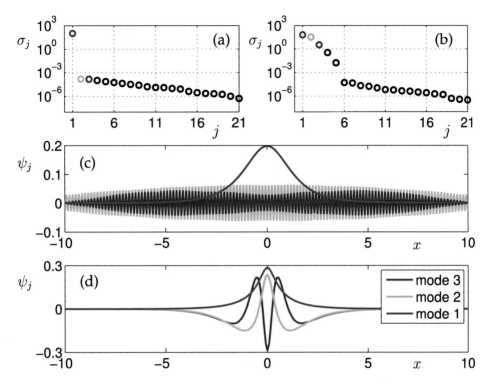

Figure 11.5 Projection of the $N = 1$ and $N = 2$ evolutions onto their POD modes. The top two figures (a) and (b) are the singular values σ_j on a logarithmic scale of the two evolutions demonstrated in (11.4). This demonstrates that the $N = 1$ and $N = 2$ soliton dynamics are primarily low-rank, with the $N = 1$ being a single mode evolution and the $N = 2$ being dominated by two modes that contain approximately 95% of the evolution variance. The first three modes in both cases are shown in the bottom two panels (c) and (d).

Soliton Reduction ($N = 1$)

To take advantage of the low dimensional structure, we first consider the $N = 1$ soliton dynamics. Fig. 11.5 shows that a single mode in the SVD dominates the dynamics. This is the first column of the **U** matrix. Thus the dynamics are recast in a single mode so that

$$u(x, t) = a(t)\psi(x). \tag{11.32}$$

Plugging this into the NLS equation (11.29) yields the following:

$$ia_t\psi + \frac{1}{2}a\psi_{xx} + |a|^2 a|\psi|^2\psi = 0. \tag{11.33}$$

The inner product is now taken with respect to ψ which gives

$$ia_t + \frac{\alpha}{2}a + \beta|a|^2 a = 0 \tag{11.34}$$

where

$$\alpha = \frac{\langle \psi_{xx}, \psi \rangle}{\langle \psi, \psi \rangle} \tag{11.35a}$$

$$\beta = \frac{\langle |\psi|^2 \psi, \psi \rangle}{\langle \psi, \psi \rangle}. \tag{11.35b}$$

This is the low-rank approximation achieved by the POD-Galerkin method.

The differential equation (11.34) for $a(t)$ can be solved explicitly to yield

$$a(t) = a(0) \exp\left(i\frac{\alpha}{2}t + \beta |a(0)|^2 t \right) \tag{11.36}$$

where $a(0)$ is the initial condition for $a(t)$. To find the initial condition, recall that

$$u(x, 0) = \text{sech}(x) = a(0)\psi(x). \tag{11.37}$$

Taking the inner product with respect to $\psi(x)$ gives

$$a(0) = \frac{\langle \text{sech}(x), \psi \rangle}{\langle \psi, \psi \rangle}. \tag{11.38}$$

Thus the one mode expansion gives the approximate PDE solution

$$u(x, t) = a(0) \exp\left(i\frac{\alpha}{2}t + \beta |a(0)|^2 t \right) \psi(x). \tag{11.39}$$

This solution is the low-dimensional POD approximation of the PDE expanded in the best basis possible, i.e. the SVD basis.

For the $N = 1$ soliton, the spatial profile remains constant while its phase undergoes a nonlinear rotation. The POD solution (11.39) can be solved exactly to characterize this phase rotation.

Soliton Reduction ($N = 2$)

The $N = 2$ soliton case is a bit more complicated and interesting. In this case, two modes clearly dominate the behavior of the system, as they contain 96% of the energy. These two modes, ψ_1 and ψ_2, are the first two columns of the matrix $\mathbf{U}$ and are now used to approximate the dynamics observed in Fig. (11.4). In this case, the two mode expansion takes the form

$$u(x, t) = a_1(t)\psi_1(x) + a_2(t)\psi_2(x). \tag{11.40}$$

Inserting this approximation into the governing equation (11.29) gives

$$i\left(a_{1t}\psi_1 + a_{2t}\psi_2\right) + \frac{1}{2}\left(a_1\psi_{1xx} + a_2\psi_{2xx}\right) + (a_1\psi_1 + a_2\psi_2)^2(a_1^*\psi_1^* + a_2^*\psi_2^*) = 0. \tag{11.41}$$

Multiplying out the cubic term gives

$$i\left(a_{1t}\psi_1 + a_{2t}\psi_2\right) + \frac{1}{2}\left(a_1\psi_{1xx} + a_2\psi_{2xx}\right)$$
$$+ \left(|a_1|^2 a_1 |\psi_1|^2 \psi_1 + |a_2|^2 a_2 |\psi_2|^2 \psi_2 + 2|a_1|^2 a_2 |\psi_1|^2 \psi_2 + 2|a_2|^2 a_1 |\psi_2|^2 \psi_1 \right.$$
$$\left. + a_1^2 a_2^* \psi_1^2 \psi_2^* + a_2^2 a_1^* \psi_2^2 \psi_1^* \right). \tag{11.42}$$

All that remains is to take the inner product of this equation with respect to both $\psi_1(x)$ and $\psi_2(x)$. Recall that these two modes are orthogonal, resulting in the following 2×2 system of nonlinear equations:

$$ia_{1t} + \alpha_{11}a_1 + \alpha_{12}a_2 + \left(\beta_{111}|a_1|^2 + 2\beta_{211}|a_2|^2 \right)a_1 \tag{11.43a}$$

$$+ \left(\beta_{121}|a_1|^2 + 2\beta_{221}|a_2|^2 \right) a_2 + \sigma_{121}a_1^2 a_2^* + \sigma_{211}a_2^2 a_1^* = 0$$

$$ia_{2t} + \alpha_{21}a_1 + \alpha_{22}a_2 + \left(\beta_{112}|a_1|^2 + 2\beta_{212}|a_2|^2 \right) a_1 \qquad (11.43b)$$

$$+ \left(\beta_{122}|a_1|^2 + 2\beta_{222}|a_2|^2 \right) a_2 + \sigma_{122}a_1^2 a_2^* + \sigma_{212}a_2^2 a_1^* = 0$$

where

$$\alpha_{jk} = \langle \psi_{j_{xx}}, \psi_k \rangle / 2 \qquad (11.44a)$$

$$\beta_{jkl} = \langle |\psi_j|^2 \psi_k, \psi_l \rangle \qquad (11.44b)$$

$$\sigma_{jkl} = \langle \psi_j^2 \psi_k^*, \psi_l \rangle \qquad (11.44c)$$

and the initial values of the two components are given by

$$a_1(0) = \frac{\langle 2\mathrm{sech}(x), \psi_1 \rangle}{\langle \psi_1, \psi_1 \rangle} \qquad (11.45a)$$

$$a_2(0) = \frac{\langle 2\mathrm{sech}(x), \psi_2 \rangle}{\langle \psi_2, \psi_2 \rangle}. \qquad (11.45b)$$

This gives a complete description of the two mode dynamics predicted from the SVD analysis.

The two mode dynamics accurately approximates the solution. However, there is a phase drift that occurs in the dynamics that would require higher precision in both the time series of the full PDE and more accurate integration of the inner products for the coefficients. Indeed, the most simple trapezoidal rule has been used to compute the inner products and its accuracy is somewhat suspect; this issue will be addressed in the following section. Higher-order schemes could certainly help improve the accuracy. Additionally, incorporating the third or higher modes could also help. In either case, this demonstrates how one would use the low dimensional structures to approximate PDE dynamics in practice.

11.4 Continuous Formulation of POD

Thus far, the POD reduction has been constructed to accommodate discrete data measurement snapshots $\mathbf{X}$ as given by (11.16). The POD reduction generates a set of low-rank basis modes $\mathbf{\Psi}$ so that the following least-squares error is minimized:

$$\underset{\mathbf{\Psi} \text{ s.t. rank}(\mathbf{\Psi})=r}{\mathrm{argmin}} \quad \|\mathbf{X} - \mathbf{\Psi}\mathbf{\Psi}^T\mathbf{X}\|_F. \qquad (11.46)$$

Recall that $\mathbf{X} \in \mathbb{C}^{n \times m}$ and $\mathbf{\Psi} \in \mathbb{C}^{n \times r}$ where r is the rank of the truncation.

In many cases, measurements are performed on a continuous time process over a pre-scribed spatial domain, thus the data we consider are constructed from trajectories

$$u(x, t) \quad t \in [0, T], \; x \in [-L, L]. \qquad (11.47)$$

Such data require a *continuous* time formulation of the POD reduction. In particular, an equivalent of (11.46) must be constructed for these continuous time trajectories. Note that instead of a spatially dependent function $u(x, t)$, one can also consider a vector of trajectories $\mathbf{u}(t) \in \mathbb{C}^n$. This may arise when a PDE is discretized so that the infinite dimensional spatial variable x is finite dimensional. Wolkwein [542, 543] gives an excellent, technical overview of the POD method and its continuous formulation.

To define the continuous formulation, we prescribe the inner product

$$\langle f(x), g(x)\rangle = \int_{-L}^{L} f(x)g^*(x)dx.$$ (11.48)

To find the best fit function through the entire temporal trajectory $u(x, t)$ in (11.47), the following minimization problem must be solved

$$\min_{\psi} \frac{1}{T} \int_0^T \|u(x, t) - \langle u(x, t), \psi(x)\rangle \psi\|^2 \, dt \quad \text{subject to} \quad \|\psi\|^2 = 1$$ (11.49)

where the normalization of the temporal integral by $1/T$ averages the difference between the data and its low-rank approximation using the function ψ over the time $t \in [0, T]$. Equation (11.49) is equivalent to maximizing the inner product between the data $u(x, t)$ and the function $\psi(x)$, i.e. they are maximally parallel in function space. Thus the minimization problem can be restated as

$$\max_{\psi} \frac{1}{T} \int_0^T |\langle u(x, t), \psi(x)\rangle|^2 dt \quad \text{subject to} \quad \|\psi\|^2 = 1.$$ (11.50)

The constrained optimization problem in (11.50) can be reformulated as a Lagrangian functional

$$\mathcal{L}(\psi, \lambda) = \frac{1}{T} \int_0^T |\langle u(x, t), \psi(x)\rangle|^2 dt + \lambda \left(1 - \|\psi\|^2\right)$$ (11.51)

where λ is the Lagrange multiplier that enforces the constraint $\|\psi\|^2 = 1$. This can be rewritten as

$$\mathcal{L}(\psi, \lambda) = \frac{1}{T} \int_0^T \left(\int_{-L}^{L} u(\xi, t)\psi^*(\xi)d\xi \int_{-L}^{L} u^*(x, t)\psi(x)dx \right) dt$$
$$+ \lambda \left(1 - \|\psi\|^2\right) + \lambda \left(1 - \int_{-L}^{L} \psi(x)\psi^*(x)dx\right).$$ (11.52)

The Lagrange multiplier problem requires that the functional derivative be zero:

$$\frac{\partial \mathcal{L}}{\partial \psi^*} = 0.$$ (11.53)

Applying this derivative constraint to (11.52) and interchanging integrals yields

$$\frac{\partial \mathcal{L}}{\partial \psi^*} = \int_{-L}^{L} d\xi \left[\frac{1}{T} \int_0^T \left(u(\xi, t) \int_{-L}^{L} u^*(x, t)\psi(x)dx \right) dt - \lambda \psi(x) \right] = 0.$$ (11.54)

Setting the integrand to zero, the following eigenvalue problem is derived

$$\langle R(\xi, x), \psi\rangle = \lambda \psi$$ (11.55)

where $R(\xi, x)$ is a two-point correlation tensor of the continuous data $u(x, t)$ which is averaged over the time interval where the data is sampled

$$R(\xi, x) = \frac{1}{T} \int_0^T u(\xi, t)u^*(x, t)dt.$$ (11.56)

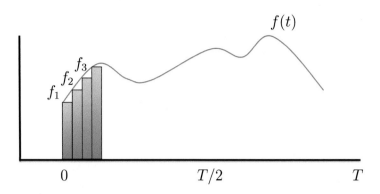

Figure 11.6 Illustration of an implementation of the quadrature rule to evaluate the integrals $\int_0^T f(t)dt$. The rectangles of height $f(t_j) = f_j$ and width δt are summed to approximate the integral.

If the spatial direction x is discretized, resulting in a high-dimensional vector $\mathbf{u}(t) = \begin{bmatrix} u(x_1, t) & u(x_2, t) & \cdots & u(x_n, t) \end{bmatrix}^T$, then $R(\xi, x)$ becomes:

$$\mathbf{R} = \frac{1}{T} \int_0^T \mathbf{u}(t)\mathbf{u}^*(t)dt. \tag{11.57}$$

In practice, the function $\mathbf{R}$ is evaluated using a quadrature rule for integration. This will allow us to connect the method to the snapshot based method discussed thus far.

Quadrature Rules for R: Trapezoidal Rule

The evaluation of the integral (11.57) can be performed by numerical quadrature [316]. The simplest quadrature rule is the trapezoidal rule which evaluates the integral via summation of approximating rectangles. Fig. 11.6 illustrates a version of the trapezoidal rule where the integral is approximated by a summation over a number of rectangles. This gives the approximation of the two-point correlation tensor:

$$\begin{aligned}
\mathbf{R} &= \frac{1}{T} \int_0^T \mathbf{u}(t)\mathbf{u}^*(t)dt \\
&\approx \frac{\Delta t}{T} \left[\mathbf{u}^*(t_1)\mathbf{u}(t_1) + \mathbf{u}^*(t_2)\mathbf{u}(t_2) + \cdots + \mathbf{u}^*(t_m)\mathbf{u}(t_m) \right] \tag{11.58} \\
&= \frac{\Delta t}{T} \left[\mathbf{u}_1^*\mathbf{u}_1 + \mathbf{u}_2^*\mathbf{u}_2 + \cdots + \mathbf{u}_m^*\mathbf{u}_m \right]
\end{aligned}$$

where we have assumed $u(x, t)$ is discretized into a vector $\mathbf{u}_j = \mathbf{u}(t_j)$, and there are m rectangular bins of width Δt so that $(m)\Delta t = T$. Defining a data matrix

$$\mathbf{X} = \begin{bmatrix} \mathbf{u}_1 & \mathbf{u}_2 & \cdots & \mathbf{u}_m \end{bmatrix} \tag{11.59}$$

we can then rewrite the two-point correlation tensor as

$$\mathbf{R} \approx \frac{1}{m}\mathbf{X}^*\mathbf{X} \tag{11.60}$$

which is exactly the definition of the covariance matrix in (1.27), i.e. $\mathbf{C} \approx \mathbf{R}$. Note that the role of $1/T$ is to average over the various trajectories so that the average is subtracted out, giving rise to a definition consistent with the covariance.

Higher-order Quadrature Rules

Numerical integration simply calculates the area under a given curve. The basic ideas for performing such an operation come from the definition of integration

$$\int_a^b f(t)dt = \lim_{\Delta t \to 0} \sum_{j=0}^{m-1} f(t_j)\Delta t \tag{11.61}$$

where $b - a = (m - 1)\Delta t$. The area under the curve is a limiting process of summing up an ever-increasing number of rectangles. This process is known as numerical quadrature. Specifically, any sum can be represented as follows:

$$Q[f] = \sum_{j=0}^{m-1} w_j f(t_j) = w_0 f(t_0) + w_1 f(t_1) + \cdots + w_{m-1} f(t_{m-1}) \tag{11.62}$$

where $a = t_0 < t_1 < t_2 < \cdots < t_{m-1} = b$. Thus the integral is evaluated as

$$\int_a^b f(t)dt = Q[f] + E[f] \tag{11.63}$$

where the term $E[f]$ is the error in approximating the integral by the quadrature sum (11.62). Typically, the error $E[f]$ is due to truncation error. To integrate, we will use polynomial fits to the y-values $f(t_j)$. Thus we assume the function $f(t)$ can be approximated by a polynomial

$$P_n(t) = a_n t^n + a_{n-1} t^{n-1} + \cdots + a_1 t + a_0 \tag{11.64}$$

where the truncation error in this case is proportional to the $(n + 1)^{th}$ derivative $E[f] = A f^{(n+1)}(c)$ and A is a constant. This process of polynomial fitting the data gives the *Newton-Cotes Formulas*.

The following integration approximations result from using a polynomial fit through the data to be integrated. It is assumed that

$$t_k = t_0 + \Delta t k \qquad\qquad f_k = f(t_k). \tag{11.65}$$

This gives the following integration algorithms:

$$\text{Trapezoid Rule} \int_{t_0}^{t_1} f(t)dt = \frac{\Delta t}{2}(f_0 + f_1) - \frac{\Delta t^3}{12} f''(c) \tag{11.66a}$$

$$\text{Simpson's Rule} \int_{t_0}^{t_2} f(t)dt = \frac{\Delta t}{3}(f_0 + 4f_1 + f_2) - \frac{\Delta t^5}{90} f''''(c) \tag{11.66b}$$

$$\text{Simpson's 3/8 Rule} \int_{t_0}^{t_3} f(t)dt = \frac{3\Delta t}{8}(f_0 + 3f_1 + 3f_2 + f_3) - \frac{3\Delta t^5}{80} f''''(c) \tag{11.66c}$$

$$\text{Boole's Rule} \int_{t_0}^{t_4} f(t)dt = \frac{2\Delta t}{45}(7f_0 + 32f_1 + 12f_2 + 32f_3 + 7f_4) - \frac{8\Delta t^7}{945} f^{(6)}(c). \tag{11.66d}$$

These algorithms have varying degrees of accuracy. Specifically, they are $O(\Delta t^2)$, $O(\Delta t^4)$, $O(\Delta t^4)$ and $O(\Delta t^6)$ accurate schemes respectively. The accuracy condition is determined from the truncation terms of the polynomial fit. Note that the *trapezoidal rule* uses a sum of simple trapezoids to approximate the integral. *Simpson's rule* fits a quadratic curve through three points and calculates the area under the quadratic curve. *Simpson's 3/8 rule* uses four points and a cubic polynomial to evaluate the area, while *Boole's rule* uses five points and a quartic polynomial fit to generate an evaluation of the integral.

The integration methods (11.66) give values for the integrals over only a small part of the integration domain. The trapezoidal rule, for instance, only gives a value for $t \in [t_0, t_1]$. However, our fundamental aim is to evaluate the integral over the entire domain $t \in [a, b]$. Assuming once again that our interval is divided as $a = t_0 < t_1 < t_2 < \cdots < t_{m-1} = b$, then the trapezoidal rule applied over the interval gives the total integral

$$\int_a^b f(t)dt \approx Q[f] = \sum_{j=1}^m \frac{\Delta t}{2} \left(f_j + f_{j+1}\right). \tag{11.67}$$

Writing out this sum gives

$$\sum_{j=1}^m \frac{\Delta t}{2} \left(f_j + f_{j+1}\right) = \frac{\Delta t}{2}(f_0 + f_1) + \frac{\Delta t}{2}(f_1 + f_2) + \cdots + \frac{\Delta t}{2}(f_m + f_{m-1})$$

$$= \frac{\Delta t}{2}(f_0 + 2f_1 + 2f_2 + \cdots + 2f_m + f_{m-1}) \tag{11.68}$$

$$= \frac{\Delta t}{2} \left(f_0 + f_{m-1} + 2\sum_{j=1}^m f_j\right).$$

The final expression no longer double counts the values of the points between f_0 and f_{m-1}. Instead, the final sum only counts the intermediate values once, thus making the algorithm about twice as fast as the previous sum expression. These are computational savings which should always be exploited if possible.

POD Modes from Quadrature Rules

Any of these algorithms could be used to approximate the two-point correlation tensor $\mathbf{R}(\xi, x)$. The method of snapshots implicitly uses the trapezoidal rule to produce the snapshot matrix $\mathbf{X}$. Specifically, recall that

$$\mathbf{X} = \begin{bmatrix} | & | & & | \\ \mathbf{u}_1 & \mathbf{u}_2 & \cdots & \mathbf{u}_m \\ | & | & & | \end{bmatrix} \tag{11.69}$$

where the columns $\mathbf{u}_k \in \mathbb{C}^n$ may be measurements from simulations or experiments. The SVD of this matrix produces the modes used to produce a low-rank embedding $\boldsymbol{\Psi}$ of the data.

One could alternatively use a higher-order quadrature rule to produce a low-rank decomposition. Thus the matrix (11.69) would be modified to

$$\mathbf{X} = \begin{bmatrix} | & | & | & | & | & & | & | \\ \mathbf{u}_1 & 4\mathbf{u}_2 & 2\mathbf{u}_3 & 4\mathbf{u}_4 & 2\mathbf{u}_5 & \cdots & 4\mathbf{u}_{m-1} & \mathbf{u}_m \\ | & | & | & | & | & & | & | \end{bmatrix} \tag{11.70}$$

where the Simpson's rule quadrature formula is used. Simpson's rule is commonly used in practice as it is simple to execute and provides significant improvement in accuracy over the trapezoidal rule. Producing this matrix simply involves multiplying the data matrix on the right by $\begin{bmatrix} 1 & 4 & 2 & 4 & \cdots & 2 & 4 & 1 \end{bmatrix}^T$. The SVD can then be used to construct a low-rank embedding $\boldsymbol{\Psi}$. Before approximating the low-rank solution, the quadrature weighting matrix must be undone. To our knowledge, very little work has been done in quantifying the merits of various quadrature rules. However, the interested reader should consider the optimal snapshot sampling strategy developed by Kunisch and Volkwein [315].

11.5   POD with Symmetries: Rotations and Translations

The POD method is not without its shortcomings. It is well known in the POD community that the underlying SVD algorithm does handle invariances in the data in an optimal way. The most common invariances arise from translational or rotational invariances in the data. Translational invariance is observed in the simple phenomenon of wave propagation, making it difficult for correlation to be computed since critical features in the data are no longer aligned snapshot to snapshot.

In what follows, we will consider the effects of both translation and rotation. The examples are motivated from physical problems of practical interest. The important observation is that unless the invariance structure is accounted for, the POD reduction will give an artificially inflated dimension for the underlying dynamics. This challenges our ability to use the POD as a diagnostic tool or as the platform for reduced order models.

Translation: Wave Propagation

To illustrate the impact of translation on a POD analysis, consider a simple translating Gaussian propagating with velocity c.

$$u(x, t) = \exp\left[-(x - ct + 15)^2\right]. \tag{11.71}$$

We consider this solution on the space and time intervals $x \in [-20, 20]$ and $t \in [0, 10]$. The following code produces the representative translating solution and its low-rank representation.

Code 11.5 Translating wave for POD analysis.

```
n=200; L=20; x=linspace(-L,L,n); y=x;    % space
m=41; T=10; t=linspace(0,T,m);           % time
c=3;    % wave speed

X=[];
for j=1:m
    X(:,j)=exp(-(x+15-c*t(j)).^2).';     % data snapshots
end
[U,S,V]=svd(X);    % SVD decomposition
```

Figure 11.7(a) demonstrates the simple evolution to be considered. As is clear from the figure, the translation of the pulse will clearly affect the correlation at a given spatial location. Naive application of the SVD does not account for the translating nature of the data. As a result, the singular values produced by the SVD decay slowly as shown in Fig. 11.7(b) and (c). In fact, the first few modes each contain approximately 8% of the variance.

The slow decay of singular values suggests that a low-rank embedding is not easily constructed. Moreover, there are interesting issues interpreting the POD modes and their

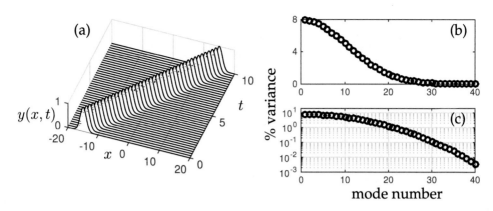

Figure 11.7 (a) Translating Gaussian with speed $c = 3$. The singular value decomposition produces a slow decay of the singular values which is shown on a (b) normal and (c) logarithmic plot.

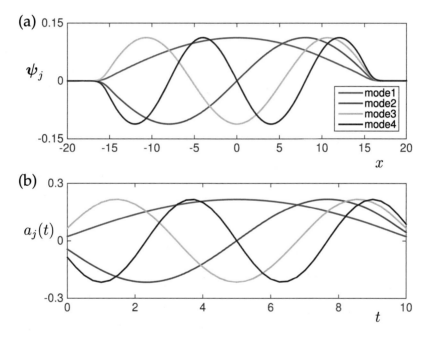

Figure 11.8 First four spatial modes (a) (first four columns of the **U** matrix) and temporal modes (b) (first four columns of the **V** matrix). A wave translating at a constant speed produces Fourier mode structures in both space and time.

time dynamics. Fig. 11.8 shows the first four spatial (**U**) and temporal (**V**) modes generated by the SVD. The spatial modes are global in that they span the entire region where the pulse propagation occurred. Interestingly, they appear to be Fourier modes over the region where the pulse propagated. The temporal modes illustrate a similar Fourier mode basis for this specific example of a translating wave propagating at a constant velocity.

The failure of POD in this case is due simply to the translational invariance. If the invariance is *removed*, or factored out [457], before a data reduction is attempted, then the POD method can once again be used to produce a low-rank approximation. In order

Figure 11.9 Spiral waves (a) $u(x, y)$, (b) $|u(x, y)|$ and (c) $u(x, y)^5$ on the domain $x \in [-20, 20]$ and $y \in [-20, 20]$. The spirals are made to spin clockwise with angular velocity ω.

to remove the invariance, the invariance must first be identified and an auxiliary variable defined. Thus we consider the dynamics rewritten as

$$u(x, t) \rightarrow u(x - c(t)) \tag{11.72}$$

where $c(t)$ corresponds to the translational invariance in the system responsible for limiting the POD method. The parameter c can be found by a number of methods. Rowley and Marsden [457] propose a template based technique for factoring out the invariance. Alternatively, a simple center-of-mass calculation can be used to compute the location of the wave and the variable $c(t)$ [316].

Rotation: Spiral Waves

A second invariance commonly observed in simulations and data is associated with rotation. Much like translation, rotation moves a coherent, low-rank structure in such a way that correlations, which are produced at specific spatial locations, are no longer produced. To illustrate the effects of rotational invariance, a localized spiral wave with rotation will be considered.

A spiral wave centered at the origin can be defined as follows

$$u(x, y) = \tanh\left[\sqrt{x^2 + y^2} \cos\left(A\angle(x + iy) - \sqrt{x^2 + y^2}\right)\right] \tag{11.73}$$

where A is the number of arms of the spiral, and the $\angle$ denotes the phase angle of the quantity $(x + iy)$. To localize the spiral on a spatial domain, it is multiplied by a Gaussian centered at the origin so that our function of interest is given by

$$f(x, y) = u(x, y) \exp\left[-0.01(x^2 + y^2)\right]. \tag{11.74}$$

This function can be produced with the following code.

Code 11.6 Spiral wave for POD analysis.

```
n=100;
L=20; x=linspace(-L,L,n); y=x;
[X,Y]=meshgrid(x,y);

Xd=[];
for j=1:100
    u=tanh(sqrt(X.^2+Y.^2)).*cos(angle(X+i*Y)-(sqrt(X.^2+Y.^2))+
        j/10);
    f=exp(-0.01*(X.^2+Y.^2));
    uf=u.*f;
    Xd(:,j)=reshape(uf,n^2,1);
```

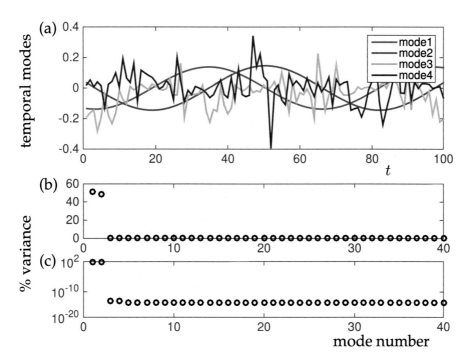

Figure 11.10 (a) First four temporal modes of the matrix **V**. To numerical precision, all the variance is in the first two modes as shown by the singular value decay on a normal (b) and logarithmic (c) plot. Remarkably, the POD extracts exactly two modes (See Fig. 11.11) to represent the rotating spiral wave.

```
      pcolor(x,y,uf), shading interp, colormap(hot)
end
```

Note that the code produces snapshots which advance the phase of the spiral wave by $j/10$ each pass through the for loop. This creates the *rotation* structure we wish to consider. The rate of spin can be made faster or slower by lowering or raising the value of the denominator respectively.

In addition to considering the function $u(x, y)$, we will also consider the closely related functions $|u(x, y)|$ and $u(x, y)^5$ as shown in Fig. 11.9. Although these three functions clearly have the same underlying function that rotates, the change in functional form is shown to produce quite different low-rank approximations for the rotating waves.

To begin our analysis, consider the function $u(x, y)$ illustrated in Fig. 11.9(a). The SVD of this matrix can be computed and its low-rank structure evaluated using the following code.

Code 11.7 SVD decomposition of spiral wave.

```
[U,S,V]=svd(Xd,0);

figure(2)
subplot(4,1,3)
plot(100*diag(S)/sum(diag(S)),'ko','Linewidth',[2])
subplot(4,1,4)
semilogy(100*diag(S)/sum(diag(S)),'ko','Linewidth',[2])
subplot(2,1,1)
```

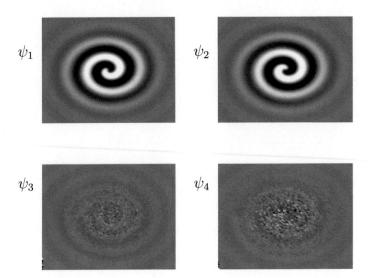

Figure 11.11 First four POD modes associated with the rotating spiral wave $u(x, y)$. The first two modes capture all the variance to numerical precision while the third and fourth mode are noisy due to numerical round-off. The domain considered is $x \in [-20, 20]$ and $y \in [-20, 20]$.

```
plot(V(:,1:4),'Linewidth',[2])
figure(3)
for j=1:4
    subplot(4,4,j)
    mode=reshape(U(:,j),n,n);
    pcolor(X,Y,mode), shading interp,caxis([-0.03 0.03]),
        colormap(gray)
end
```

Two figures are produced. The first assesses the rank of the observed dynamics and the temporal behavior of the first four modes in **V**. Figs. 11.10 (b) and (c) show the decay of singular values on a regular and logarithmic scale respectively. Remarkably, the first two modes capture *all* the variance of the data to numerical precision. This is further illustrated in the time dynamics of the first four modes. Specifically, the first two modes of Fig. 11.10(a) have a clear oscillatory signature associated with the rotation of modes one and two of Fig. 11.11. Modes three and four resemble noise in both time and space as a result of numerical round off.

The spiral wave (11.74) allows for a two-mode truncation that is accurate to numerical precision. This is in part due to the sinusoidal nature of the solution when circumnavigating the solution at a fixed radius. Simply changing the data from $u(x, t)$ to either $|u(x, t)|$ or $u(x, t)^5$ reveals that the low-rank modes and their time dynamics are significantly different. Figs. 11.12 (a) and (b) show the decay of the singular values for these two new functions and demonstrate the significant difference from the two mode evolution previously considered. The dominant time dynamics computed from the matrix **V** are also demonstrated. In the case of the absolute value of the function $|u(x, t)|$, the decay of the singular values is slow and never approaches numerical precision. The quintic function suggests a rank $r = 6$ truncation is capable of producing an approximation to numerical precision. This highlights the fact that rotational invariance complicates the POD reduction procedure.

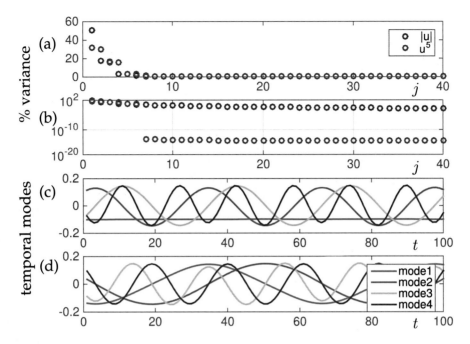

Figure 11.12 Decay of the singular values on a normal (a) and logarithmic (b) scale showing that the function $|u(x, t)|$ produces a slow decay while $u(x, t)^5$ produces an $r = 6$ approximation to numerical accuracy. The first four temporal modes of the matrix $\mathbf{V}$ are shown for these two functions in (c) and (d) respectively.

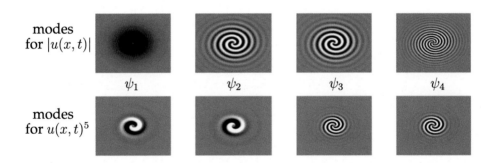

Figure 11.13 First four POD modes associated with the rotating spiral wave $|u(x, y)|$ (top row) and $u(x, t)^5$ (bottom row). Unlike our previous example, the first four modes do not capture all the variance to numerical precision, thus requiring more modes for accurate approximation. The domain considered is $x \in [-20, 20]$ and $y \in [-20, 20]$.

After all, the only difference between the three rotating solutions is the actual shape of the rotating function as they are all rotating with the same speed.

To conclude, invariances can severely limit the POD method. Most notably, it can artificially inflate the dimension of the system and lead to compromised interpretability. Expert knowledge of a given system and its potential invariances can help frame mathematical strategies to remove the invariances, i.e. re-aligning the data [316, 457]. But this strategy also has limitations, especially if two or more invariant structures are present. For instance, if two waves of different speeds are observed in the data, then the methods proposed for removing invariances will fail to capture both wave speeds simultaneously. Ultimately, dealing with invariances remains an open research question.

Suggested Reading

Texts

(1)   **Certified reduced basis methods for parametrized partial differential equations**, by J. Hesthaven, G. Rozza and B. Stamm, 2015 [244].

(2)   **Reduced basis methods for partial differential equations: An introduction**, by A. Quarteroni, A. Manzoni and N. Federico, 2015 [442].

(3)   **Model reduction and approximation: Theory and algorithms**, by P. Benner, A. Cohen, M. Ohlberger and K. Willcox, 2017 [54].

(4)   **Turbulence, coherent structures, dynamical systems and symmetry**, by P. Holmes, J. L. Lumley, G. Berkooz and C. W. Rowley, 2012 [251].

Papers and Reviews

(1)   **A survey of model reduction methods for parametric systems**, by P. Benner, S. Gugercin and K. Willcox, *SIAM Review*, 2015 [53].

(2)   **Model reduction using proper orthogonal decomposition**, by S. Volkwein, *Lecture Notes, Institute of Mathematics and Scientific Computing, University of Graz*, 2011 [542].

(3)   **The proper orthogonal decomposition in the analysis of turbulent flows**, by G. Berkooz, P. Holmes and J. L. Lumley, *Annual Review of Fluid Mechanics*, 1993 [57].

12 Interpolation for Parametric ROMs

In the last chapter, the mathematical framework of ROMs was outlined. Specifically, Chapter 11 has already highlighted the POD method for projecting PDE dynamics to low-rank subspaces where simulations of the governing PDE model can be more readily evaluated. However, the complexity of projecting into the low-rank approximation subspace remains challenging due to the nonlinearity. Interpolation in combination with POD overcomes this difficulty by providing a computationally efficient method for discretely (sparsely) sampling and evaluating the nonlinearity. This chapter leverages the ideas of the sparse and compressive sampling algorithms of Chapter 3 where a small number of samples are capable of reconstructing the low-rank dynamics of PDEs. Ultimately, these methods ensure that the computational complexity of ROMs scale favorably with the rank of the approximation, even for complex nonlinearities. The primary focus of this chapter is to highlight sparse interpolation methods that enable a rapid and low dimensional construction of the ROMs. In practice, these techniques dominate the ROM community since they are critically enabling for evaluating parametrically dependent PDEs where frequent ROM model updates are required.

12.1 Gappy POD

The success of nonlinear model order reduction is largely dependent upon two key innovations: (i) the well-known POD-Galerkin method [251, 57, 542, 543], which is used to project the high-dimensional nonlinear dynamics onto a low-dimensional subspace in a principled way, and (ii) sparse sampling of the state space for interpolating the nonlinear terms required for the subspace projection. Thus sparsity is already established as a critically enabling mathematical framework for model reduction through methods such as gappy POD and its variants [179, 555, 565, 120, 159]. Indeed, efficiently managing the computation of the nonlinearity was recognized early on in the ROMs community, and a variety of techniques were proposed to accomplish this task. Perhaps the first innovation in sparse sampling with POD modes was the technique proposed by Everson and Sirovich for which the gappy POD moniker was derived [179]. In their sparse sampling scheme, random measurements were used to approximate inner products. Principled selection of the interpolation points, through the gappy POD infrastructure [179, 555, 565, 120, 159] or missing point (best points) estimation (MPE) [400, 21], were quickly incorporated into ROMs to improve performance. More recently, the empirical interpolation method (EIM) [41] and its most successful variant, the POD-tailored discrete empirical interpolation method (DEIM) [127], have provided a greedy algorithm that allows for nearly optimal reconstructions of nonlinear terms of the original high-dimensional system. The

DEIM approach combines projection with interpolation. Specifically, DEIM uses selected interpolation indices to specify an interpolation-based projection for a nearly optimal ℓ_2 subspace approximating the nonlinearity.

The low-rank approximation provided by POD allows for a reconstruction of the solution $\mathbf{u}(x, t)$ in (12.9) with r measurements of the n-dimensional state. This viewpoint has profound consequences on how we might consider measuring our dynamical system [179]. In particular, only $r \ll n$ measurements are required for reconstruction, allowing us to define the sparse representation variable $\tilde{\mathbf{u}} \in \mathbb{C}^r$

$$\tilde{\mathbf{u}} = \mathbf{Pu} \tag{12.1}$$

where the measurement matrix $\mathbf{P} \in \mathbb{R}^{r \times n}$ specifies r measurement locations of the full state $\mathbf{u} \in \mathbb{C}^n$. As an example, the measurement matrix might take the form

$$\mathbf{P} = \begin{bmatrix} 1 & 0 & \cdots & & & & & \cdots & 0 \\ 0 & \cdots & 0 & 1 & 0 & \cdots & & \cdots & 0 \\ 0 & \cdots & & & \cdots & 0 & 1 & 0 & \cdots & 0 \\ \vdots & 0 & & & \cdots & 0 & 0 & 1 & \cdots & \vdots \\ 0 & \cdots & & & \cdots & 0 & 0 & 0 & \cdots & 1 \end{bmatrix} \tag{12.2}$$

where measurement locations take on the value of unity and the matrix elements are zero elsewhere. The matrix $\mathbf{P}$ defines a projection onto an r-dimensional space $\tilde{\mathbf{u}}$ that can be used to approximate solutions of a PDE.

The insight and observation of (12.1) forms the basis of the *gappy POD* method introduced by Everson and Sirovich [179]. In particular, one can use a small number of measurements, or gappy data, to reconstruct the full state of the system. In doing so, we can overcome the complexity of evaluating higher-order nonlinear terms in the POD reduction.

Sparse Measurements and Reconstruction

The measurement matrix $\mathbf{P}$ allows for an approximation of the state vector $\mathbf{u}$ from r measurements. The approximation is obtained by using (12.1) with the standard POD projection:

$$\tilde{\mathbf{u}} \approx \mathbf{P} \sum_{k=1}^{r} \tilde{a}_k \boldsymbol{\psi}_k \tag{12.3}$$

where the coefficients $\tilde{a}_k$ minimize the error in approximation: $\|\tilde{\mathbf{u}} - \mathbf{Pu}\|$. The challenge now is how to determine the $\tilde{a}_k$ given that taking inner products of (12.3) can no longer be performed. Specifically, the vector $\tilde{\mathbf{u}}$ has dimension r whereas the POD modes have dimension n, i.e. the inner product requires information from the full range of $\mathbf{x}$, the underlying discretized spatial variable, which is of length n. Thus, the modes $\boldsymbol{\psi}_k(x)$ are in general not orthogonal over the r-dimensional support of $\tilde{\mathbf{u}}$. The support will be denoted as $s[\tilde{\mathbf{u}}]$. More precisely, orthogonality must be considered on the full range versus the support space. Thus the following two relationships hold

$$M_{kj} = \langle \boldsymbol{\psi}_k, \boldsymbol{\psi}_j \rangle = \delta_{kj} \tag{12.4a}$$

$$M_{kj} = \langle \boldsymbol{\psi}_k, \boldsymbol{\psi}_j \rangle_{s[\tilde{\mathbf{u}}]} \neq 0 \quad \text{for all } k, j \tag{12.4b}$$

where M_{kj} are the entries of the Hermitian matrix $\mathbf{M}$ and δ_{kj} is the Kroenecker delta function. The fact that the POD modes are not orthogonal on the support $s[\tilde{\mathbf{u}}]$ leads us to consider alternatives for evaluating the vector $\tilde{\mathbf{a}}$.

To determine the $\tilde{a}_k$, a least-squares algorithm can be used to minimize the error

$$E = \int_{s[\tilde{\mathbf{u}}]} \left[\tilde{\mathbf{u}} - \sum_{k=1}^{r} \tilde{a}_k \boldsymbol{\psi}_k \right]^2 d\mathbf{x} \tag{12.5}$$

where the inner product is evaluated on the support $s[\tilde{\mathbf{u}}]$, thus making the two terms in the integral of the same size r. The minimizing solution to (12.5) requires the residual to be orthogonal to each mode $\boldsymbol{\psi}_k$ so that

$$\left\langle \tilde{\mathbf{u}} - \sum_{k=1}^{r} \tilde{a}_k \boldsymbol{\psi}_k, \boldsymbol{\psi}_j \right\rangle_{s[\tilde{\mathbf{u}}]} = 0 \qquad j \neq k, \ j = 1, 2, \cdots, r. \tag{12.6}$$

In practice, we can project the full state vector $\mathbf{u}$ onto the support space and determine the vector $\tilde{\mathbf{a}}$:

$$\mathbf{M}\tilde{\mathbf{a}} = \mathbf{f} \tag{12.7}$$

where the elements of $\mathbf{M}$ are given by (12.4b) and the components of the vector $\mathbf{f}$ are given by

$$f_k = \langle \mathbf{u}, \boldsymbol{\psi}_k \rangle_{s[\tilde{\mathbf{u}}]} . \tag{12.8}$$

Note that if the measurement space is sufficiently dense, or if the support space is the entire space, then $\mathbf{M} = \mathbf{I}$, implying the eigenvalues of $\mathbf{M}$ approach unity as the number of measurements become dense. Once the vector $\tilde{\mathbf{a}}$ is determined, a reconstruction of the solution can be performed as

$$\mathbf{u}(x, t) \approx \boldsymbol{\Psi}\tilde{\mathbf{a}} . \tag{12.9}$$

As the measurements become dense, not only does the matrix $\mathbf{M}$ converge to the idenity, but $\tilde{\mathbf{a}} \to \mathbf{a}$. Interestingly, these observations lead us to consider the efficacy of the method and/or approximation by considering the condition number of the matrix $\mathbf{M}$ [524]:

$$\kappa(\mathbf{M}) = \|\mathbf{M}\| \|\mathbf{M}^{-1}\| = \frac{\sigma_1}{\sigma_m} . \tag{12.10}$$

Here the 2-norm has been used. If $\kappa(\mathbf{M})$ is small then the matrix is said to be well-conditioned. A minimal value of $\kappa(\mathbf{M})$ is achieved with the identify matrix $\mathbf{M} = \mathbf{I}$. Thus, as the sampling space becomes dense, the condition number also approaches unity. This can be used as a metric for determining how well the sparse sampling is performing. Large condition numbers suggest poor reconstruction while values tending toward unity should perform well.

Harmonic Oscillator Modes

To demonstrate the gappy sampling method and its reconstruction efficacy, we apply the technique to the Gauss-Hermite functions defined by (11.25) and (11.26). In the code that follows, we compute the first ten modes as given by (11.26). To compute the second derivative, we use the fact that the Fourier transform $\mathcal{F}$ can produce a spectrally accurate approximation, i.e. $u_{xx} = \mathcal{F}^{-1}\left[(ik)^2 \mathcal{F}u\right]$. For the sake of producing accurate derivatives, we consider the domain $x \in [-10, 10]$ but then work with the smaller domain of interest $x \in [-4, 4]$. Recall further that the Fourier transform assumes a 2π-periodic domain. This is handled by a scaling factor in the k-wavevectors. The first five modes have been demonstrated in Fig. 11.3. In the code that follows, we view the first 10 modes with a top-view color plot in order highlight the various features of the modes.

Code 12.1 Harmonic oscillator modes.

```
L=10; x3=-L:0.1:L; n=length(x3)-1; % define domain
x2=x3(1:n); k=(2*pi/(2*L))*[0:n/2-1 -n/2:-1]; % k-vector
ye=exp(-(x2.^2)); ye2=exp((x2.^2)/2); % define Gaussians
for j=0:9        % loop through 10 modes
  yd=real(ifft(((i*k).^j).*fft(ye))); % 2nd derivative
  mode=((-1)^(j))*(((2^j)*factorial(j)*sqrt(pi))^(-0.5))*ye2.*yd
     ;
  y(:,j+1)=(mode).';   % store modes as columns
end

x=x2(n/2+1-40:n/2+1+40);   % keep only -4<x<4
yharm=y(n/2+1-40:n/2+1+40,:);
pcolor(flipud((yharm(:,10:-1:1).')))
```

The mode construction is shown in the top panel of Fig. 12.1. Each colored cell represents the discrete value of the mode in the interval $x \in [-4, 4]$ with $\Delta x = 0.1$. Thus there

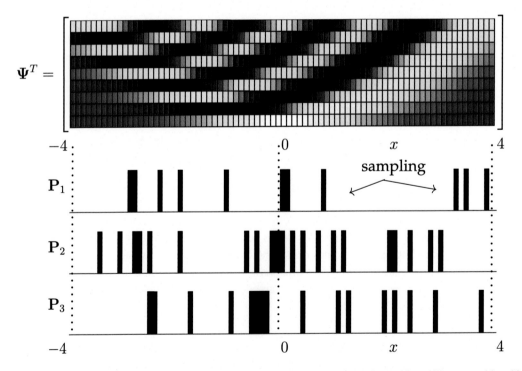

Figure 12.1 The top panel shows the first 10 modes of the quantum harmonic oscillator considered in (11.25) and (11.26). Three randomly generated measurement matrices, $\mathbf{P}_j$ with $j = 1, 2$ and 3, are depicted. There is a 20% chance of performing a measurement at a given spatial location x_j in the interval $x \in [-4, 4]$ with a spacing of $\Delta x = 0.1$.

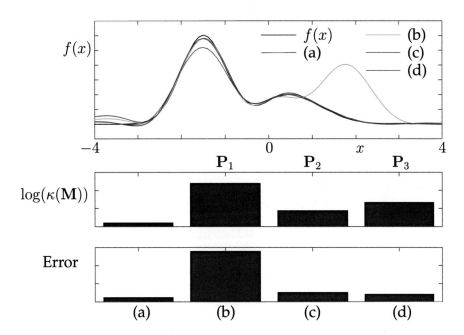

Figure 12.2 The top panel shows the original function (black) along with a 10 mode reconstruction of the test function $f(x) = \exp(-(x - 0.5)^2) + 3\exp(-2(x + 3/2)^2)$ sampled in the full space (red) and three representative support spaces $s[\bar{u}]$ of Fig. 12.1, specifically (b) $\mathbf{P}_1$, (c) $\mathbf{P}_2$, and (d) $\mathbf{P}_3$. Note that the error measurement is specific to the function being considered whereas the condition number metric is independent of the specific function. Although both can serve as proxies for performance, the condition number serves for any function, which is advantageous.

are 81 discrete values for each of the modes $\boldsymbol{\psi}_k$. Our objective is to reconstruct a function outside of the basis modes of the harmonic oscillator. In particular, consider the function

$$f(x) = \exp[-(x - 0.5)^2] + 3\exp[-2(x + 3/2)^2] \tag{12.11}$$

which will be discretized and defined over the same domain as the modal basis of the harmonic oscillator. The following code builds this function and further numerically constructs the projection of the function onto the basis functions $\boldsymbol{\psi}_n$. The original function is plotted in the top panel of Fig. 12.2. Note that the goal now is to reconstruct this function both with a low-rank projection onto the harmonic oscillator modes, and with a gappy reconstruction whereby only a sampling of the data is used, via the measurements $\mathbf{P}_j$. The following code builds the test function and does a basic reconstruction in the 10-mode harmonic oscillator basis. Further, it builds the matrix $\mathbf{M}$ for the full state measurements and computes its condition number.

Code 12.2 Test function and reconstruction.

```
f=(exp(-(x-0.5).^2)+3*exp(-2*(x+1.5).^2))';
for j=1:10  % full reconstruction
  a(j,1)=trapz(x,f.*yharm(:,j));
end
f2=yharm*a;
subplot(2,1,1), plot(x,f2,'r')
Err(1)=norm(f2-f);  % reconstruction error
```

```
for j=1:10   % matrix M reconstruction
    for jj=1:j
        Area=trapz(x,yharm(:,j).*yharm(:,jj));
        M(j,jj)=Area;
        M(jj,j)=Area;
    end
end
cond(M)    % get condition number
```

Results of the low-rank and gappy reconstruction are shown in Fig. 12.2. The low-rank reconstruction is performed using the full measurements projected to the 10 leading harmonic oscillator modes. In this case, the inner product of the measurement matrix is given by (12.4a) and is approximately the identify. The fact that we are working on a limited domain $x \in [-4, 4]$ with a discretization step of $\Delta x = 0.1$ is what makes $\mathbf{M} \approx \mathbf{I}$ versus being exactly the identify. For the three different sparse measurement scenarios $\mathbf{P}_j$ of Fig. 12.1, the reconstruction is also shown along with the least-square error and the logarithm of the condition number $\log[\kappa(\mathbf{M}_j)]$. We also visualize the three matrices $\mathbf{M}_j$ in Fig. 12.3. The condition number of each of these matrices helps determine its reconstruction accuracy.

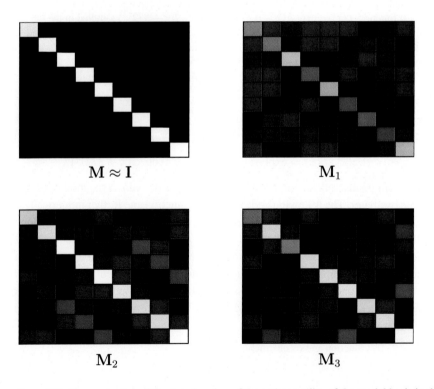

Figure 12.3 Demonstration of the deterioration of the orthogonality of the modal basis in the support space $s[\tilde{\mathbf{u}}]$ as given by the matrix $\mathbf{M}$ defined in (12.4). The top left shows that the identity matrix is produced for full measurements, or nearly so but with errors due to truncation of the domain over $x \in [-4, 4]$. The matrices $\mathbf{M}_j$, which longer look diagonal, correspond to the sparse sampling matrices $\mathbf{P}_j$ in Fig. 12.1. Thus it is clear that the modes are not orthogonal in the support space of the measurements.

Code 12.3 Gappy sampling of harmonic oscillator.

```
c=['g','m','b']; % three different measurement masks
for jloop=1:3
    figure(1), subplot(6,1,3+jloop)
    s=(rand(n,1)>0.8);   % grab 20% random measurements
    bar(x,double(s)), axis([-4.2 4.2 0 1]), axis off

    figure(2)   % construct M_j
    for j=1:10
        for jj=1:j
            Area=trapz(x,s.*(yharm(:,j).*yharm(:,jj)));
            M2(j,jj)=Area; M2(jj,j)=Area;
        end
    end
    subplot(2,2,jloop+1), pcolor(10:-1:1,1:10,(M2'));
    colormap(hot), caxis([-0.1 .3]), axis off
    con(jloop)=cond(M2)

    for j=1:10   % reconstruction using gappy
        ftild(j,1)=trapz(x,s.*(f.*yharm(:,j)));
    end

    atild=M2\ftild;   % compute error
    f2=yharm*atild;
    figure(4),subplot(2,1,1),plot(x,f2,c(jloop))
    Err(jloop+1)=norm(f2-f);
end
```

12.2 Error and Convergence of Gappy POD

As was shown in the previous section, the ability of the gappy sampling strategy to accurately reconstruct a given function depends critically on the placement of the measurement (sensor) locations. Given the importance of this issue, we will discuss a variety of principled methods for placing a limited number of sensors in detail in subsequent sections. Our goal in this section is to investigate the convergence properties and error associated with the gappy method as a function of the percentage of sampling of the full system. Random sampling locations will be used.

Given our random sampling strategy, the results that follow will be statistical in nature, computing averages and variances for batches of randomly selected sampling. The modal basis for our numerical experiments are again the Gauss-Hermite functions defined by (11.25) and (11.26), generated by Code 12.1 and shown in the top panel of Fig. 12.1.

Random Sampling and Convergence

Our study begins with random sampling of the modes at a level of 10%, 20%, 30%, 40%, 50% and 100% respectively. The latter case represents the idealized full sampling of the system. As one would expect, the error and reconstruction are improved as more samples are taken. To show the convergence of the gappy sampling, we consider two error metrics: (i) the ℓ_2 error between our randomly subsampled reconstruction and (ii) the condition number of the matrix $\mathbf{M}$ for a given measurement matrix $\mathbf{P}_j$. Recall that the condition number provides a way to measure the error without knowing the truth, i.e. (12.11).

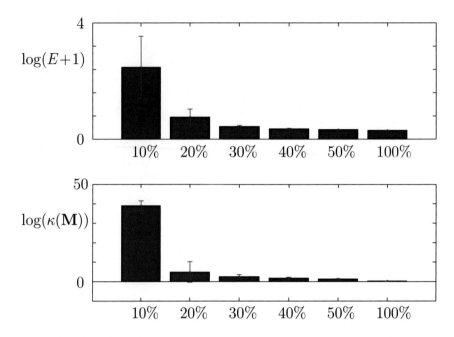

Figure 12.4 Logarithm of the least-square error, $\log(E+1)$ (unity is added to avoid negative numbers), and the log of the condition number, $\log(\kappa(\mathbf{M}))$, as a function of percentage of random measurements. For 10% measurements, the error and condition number are largest as expected. However, the variance of the results, depicted by the red bars is also quite large, suggesting that the performance for a small number of sensors is highly sensitive to their placement.

Fig. 12.4 depicts the average over 1000 trials of the logarithm of the least-square error, $\log(E+1)$ (unity is added to avoid negative numbers), and the log of the condition number, $\log(\kappa(\mathbf{M}))$, as a function of percentage of random measurements. Also depicted is the variance σ with the red bars denoting $\mu \pm \sigma$ where μ is the average value. The error and condition number both perform better as the number of samples increases. Note that the error does not approach zero since only a 10-mode basis expansion is used, thus limiting the accuracy of the POD expansion and reconstruction even with full measurements.

The following code, which is the basis for constructing Fig. 12.4, draws over 1000 random sensor configurations using 10%, 20%, 30%, 40% and 50% sampling. The full reconstruction (100% sampling) is actually performed in Code 12.2 and is used to make the final graphic for Fig. 12.4. Note that as expected, the error and condition number trends are similar, thus supporting the hypothesis that the condition number can be used to evaluate the efficacy of the sparse measurements. Indeed, this clearly shows that the condition number provides an evaluation that does not require knowledge of the function in (12.11).

Code 12.4 Convergence of error and condition number.

```
for thresh=1:5;
  for jloop=1:1000   % 1000 random trials
    n2=randsample(n,8*thresh);   % random sampling
    P=zeros(n,1); P(n2)=1;
    for j=1:10
        for jj=1:j    % compute M matrix
```

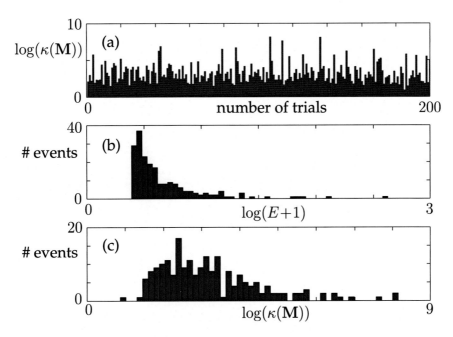

Figure 12.5 Statistics of 20% random measurements considered in Fig. 12.4. The top panel (a) depicts 200 random trials and the condition number $\log(\kappa(\mathbf{M}))$ of each trial. A histogram of (b) the logarithm of the least-square error, $\log(E+1)$, and (c) condition number , $\log(\kappa(\mathbf{M}))$, are also depicted for the 200 trials. The figures illustrate the extremely high variability generated from the random, sparse measurements. In particular, 20% measurements can produce both exceptional results and extremely poor performance depending upon the measurement locations. The measurement vectors $\mathbf{P}$ are generating these statistics are depicted in Fig. 12.6.

```
                Area=trapz(x,P.*(yharm(:,j).*yharm(:,jj)));
                M2(j,jj)=Area; M2(jj,j)=Area;
            end
        end
        for j=1:10  % reconstruction using gappy
            ftild(j,1)=trapz(x,P.*(f.*yharm(:,j)));
        end
        atild=M2\ftild;    % compute error
        f2=yharm*atild;    % compute reconstruction
        Err(jloop)=norm(f2-f);  % L2 error
        con(jloop)=cond(M2);    % condition number
    end
    % mean and variance
    E(thresh)=mean(log(Err+1)); V(thresh)=(var(log(Err+1)));
    Ec(thresh)=mean(log(con)); Vc(thresh)=(var(log(con)));
end
E=[E Efull]; V=[V 0];
Ec=[Ec log(Cfull)]; Vc=[Vc 0];
```

Gappy Measurements and Performance

We can continue this statistical analysis of the gappy reconstruction method by looking more carefully at 200 random trials of 20% measurements. Fig. 12.5 shows three key features of the 200 random trials. In particular, as shown in the top panel of this figure,

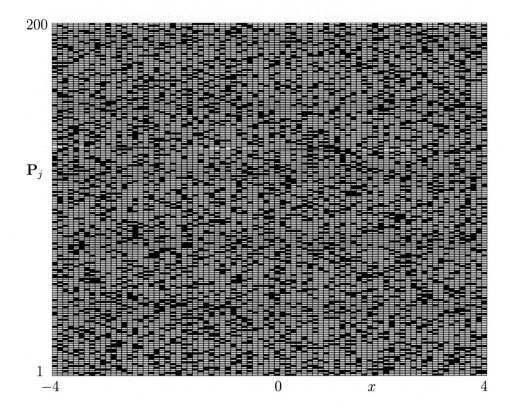

Figure 12.6 Depiction of the 200 random 20% measurement vectors $\mathbf{P}_j$ considered in Fig. 12.5. Each row is a randomly generated measurement trial (from 1 to 200) while the columns represent their spatial location on the domain $x \in [-4, 4]$ with $\Delta x = 0.1$.

there is a large variance in the distribution of the condition number $\kappa(\mathbf{M})$ for 20% sampling. Specifically, the condition number can change by orders of magnitude with the same number of sensors, but simply placed in different locations. A histogram of the distribution of the log error $\log(E+1)$ and the log of the condition number are shown in the bottom two panels. The error appears to be distributed in an exponentially decaying fashion whereas the condition number distribution is closer to a Gaussian. There are distinct outliers whose errors and condition numbers are exceptionally high, suggesting sensor configurations to be avoided.

In order to visualize the random, gappy measurements of the 200 samples used in the statistical analysis of Fig. 12.5, we plot the $\mathbf{P}_j$ measurement masks in each row of the matrix in Fig. 12.6. The white regions represent regions where no measurements occur. The black regions are where the measurements are taken. These are the measurements that generate the orders of magnitude variance in the error and condition number.

As a final analysis, we can sift through the 200 random measurements of Fig. 12.6 and pick out both the ten best and ten worst measurement vectors $\mathbf{P}_j$. Fig. 12.7 shows the results of this sifting process. The top two panels depict the best and worst measurement configurations. Interestingly, the worst measurements have long stretches of missing measurements near the center of the domain where much of the modal variance occurs.

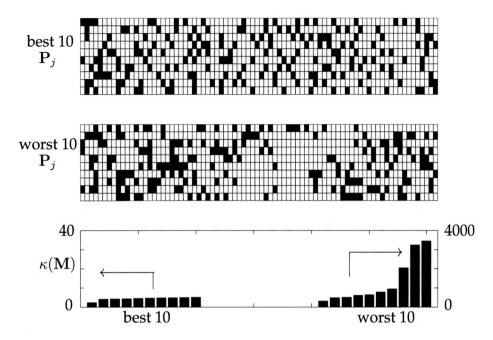

Figure 12.7 Depiction of the 10 best and 10 worst random 20% measurement vectors $\mathbf{P}_j$ considered in Figs. 12.5 and 12.6. The top panel shows that the best measurement vectors sample fairly uniformly across the domain $x \in [-4, 4]$ with $\Delta x = 0.1$. In contrast, the worst randomly generated measurements (middle panel) have large sampling gaps near the center of the domain, leading to a large condition number $\kappa(\mathbf{M})$. The bottom panel shows a bar chart of the best and worst values of the condition number. Note that with 20% sampling, there can be two orders of magnitude difference in the condition number, thus suggesting the importance of prescribing good measurement locations.

In contrast, the best measurements have well sampled domains with few long gaps between measurement locations. The bottom panel shows that the best measurements (on the left) offer an improvement of two orders of magnitude in the condition number over the poor performing counterparts (on the right).

12.3 Gappy Measurements: Minimize Condition Number

The preceding section illustrates that the placement of gappy measurements is critical for accurately reconstructing the POD solution. This suggests that a principled way to determine measurement locations is of great importance. In what follows, we outline a method originally proposed by Willcox [555] for assessing the gappy measurement locations. The method is based on minimizing the condition number $\kappa(\mathbf{M})$ in the placement process. As already shown, the condition number is a good proxy for evaluating the efficacy of the reconstruction. Moreover, it is a measure that is independent of any specific function.

The algorithm proposed [555] is computationally costly, but it can be performed in an offline training stage. Once the sensor locations are determined, they can be used for online reconstruction. The algorithm is as follows:

1. Place sensor k at each spatial location possible and evaluate the condition number $\kappa(\mathbf{M})$. Only points not already containing a sensor are considered.

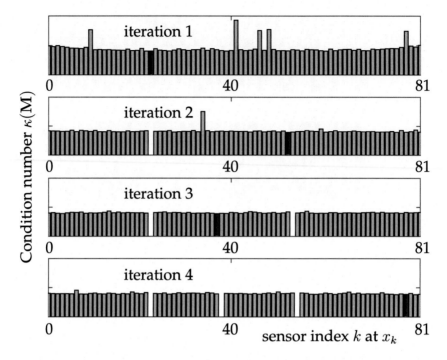

Figure 12.8 Depiction of the first four iterations of the gappy measurement location algorithm of Willcox [555]. The algorithm is applied to a 10-mode expansion given by the Gauss-Hermite functions (11.25) and (11.26) discretized on the interval $x \in [-4, 4]$ with $\Delta x = 0.1$. The top panel shows the condition number $\kappa(\mathbf{M})$ as a single sensor is considered at each of the 81 discrete values x_k. The first sensor minimizes the condition number (shown in red) at x_{23}. A second sensor is now considered at all remaining 80 spatial locations, with the minimal condition number occurring at x_{52} (in red). Repeating this process gives x_{37} and x_{77} for the third and fourth sensor locations for iteration 3 and 4 of the algorithm (highlighted in red). Once a location is selected for a sensor, it is no longer considered in future iterations. This is represented by a gap.

2. Determine the spatial location that minimizes the condition number $\kappa(\mathbf{M})$. This spatial location is now the kth sensor location.
3. Add sensor $k + 1$ and repeat the previous two steps.

The algorithm is not optimal, nor are there guaranteed. However, it works quite well in practice since sensor configurations with low condition number produce good reconstructions with the POD modes.

We apply this algorithm to construct the gappy measurement matrix $\mathbf{P}$. As before, the modal basis for our numerical experiments are the Gauss-Hermite functions defined by (11.25) and (11.26). The gappy measurement matrix algorithm for constructing $\mathbf{P}$ is shown in Note that the algorithm outlined above sets down one sensor at a time, thus with the 10 POD mode expansion, the system is underdetermined until 10 sensors are placed. This gives condition numbers on the order of 10^{16} for the first 9 sensor placements. It also suggests that the first 10 sensor locations may be generated from inaccurate calculations of the condition number.

The following code builds upon Code 12.1 which is used to generate the 10-mode expansion of the Gauss-Hermite functions. The code minimizes the condition number and identifies the first 20 sensor locations. Specifically, the code provides a principled way of producing a measurement matrix **P** that allows for good reconstruction of the POD mode expansion with limited measurements.

Code 12.5 Gappy placement: Minimize condition number.

```
n2=20;      % number of sensors
nall=1:n; ns=[];   %
for jsense=1:n2
    for jloop=1:(n-jsense)
        P=zeros(n,1); P(ns)=1;
        P(nall(jloop))=1;
        for j=1:10
            for jj=1:j    % matrix M
                Area=trapz(x,P.*(yharm(:,j).*yharm(:,jj)));
                M2(j,jj)=Area; M2(jj,j)=Area;
            end
        end
        con(jloop)=cond(M2);   % compute condition number
    end   % end search through all points
    [s1,n1]=min(con); % location to minimize condition #
    kond(jsense)=s1; clear con
    ns=[ns nall(n1)];   % add sensor location
    nall=setdiff(nall,ns);   % new sensor indeces
    P=zeros(n,1);   P(ns)=1;
    Psum(:,jsense)=P;
    for j=1:10
        for jj=1:j
            Area=trapz(x,P.*(yharm(:,j).*yharm(:,jj)));
            M2(j,jj)=Area; M2(jj,j)=Area;
        end
    end
    for j=1:10   % reconstruction using gappy
        ftild(j,1)=trapz(x,P.*(f.*yharm(:,j)));
    end
    atild=M2\ftild;   % compute error
    f1(:,jsense)=yharm*atild;   % iterative reconstruction
    E(jsense)=norm(f1(:,jsense)-f);   % iterative error
end   % end sensor loop
```

In addition to identifying the placement of the first 20 sensors, the code also reconstructs the example function given by (12.11) at each iteration of the routine. Note the use of the **setdiff** command which removes the condition number minimizing sensor location from consideration in the next iteration.

To evaluate the gappy sensor location algorithm, we track the condition number as a function of the number of iterations, up to 20 sensors. Additionally, at each iteration, a reconstruction of the test function (12.11) is computed and a least-square error evaluated. Fig. 12.9 shows the progress of the algorithm as it evaluates the sensor locations for up to 20 sensors. By construction, the algorithm minimizes the condition number $\kappa(\mathbf{M})$ at each step of the iteration, thus as sensors are added, the condition number steadily decreases (top panel of Fig. 12.9). Note that there is a significant decrease in the condition number once 10 sensors are selected since the system is no longer underdetermined with theoretically infinite condition number. The least-square error for the reconstruction of the test function (12.11) follows the same general trend, but the error does not monotonically decrease like the condition number. The least-square error also makes a significant improvement once

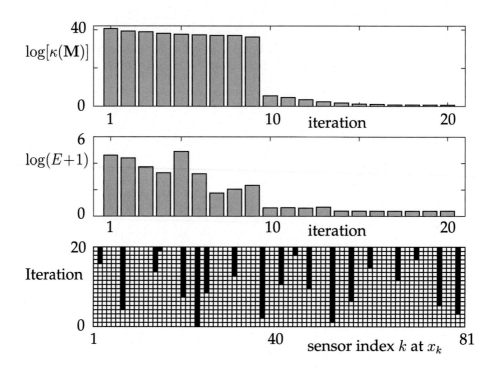

Figure 12.9 Condition number and least-square error (logarithms) as a function of the number of iterations in the gappy sensor placement algorithm. The log of the condition number $\log[\kappa(\mathbf{M})]$ monotonically decreases since this is being minimized at each iteration step. The log of the least-square error in the reconstruction of the test function (12.11) also shows a trend towards improvement as the number of sensors are increased. Once 10 sensors are placed, the system is of full rank and the condition number drops by orders of magnitude. The bottom panel shows the sensors as they turn on (black squares) over the first 20 iterations. The first measurement location is, for instance, at x_{23}.

10 measurements are made. In general, if an r-mode POD expansion is to be considered, then reasonable results using the gappy reconstruction cannot be achieved until r sensors are placed.

We now consider the placement of the sensors as a function of iteration in the bottom panel of Fig. 12.9. Specifically, we depict when sensors are identified in the iteration. The first sensor location is x_{23} followed by x_{52}, x_{37} and x_{77}, respectively. The process is continued until the first 20 sensors are identified. The pattern of sensors depicted is important as it illustrates a fairly uniform sampling of the domain. Alternative schemes will be considered in the following.

As a final illustration of the gappy algorithm, we consider the reconstruction of the test function (12.11) as the number of iterations (sensors) increases. As expected, the more sensors that are used in the gappy framework, the better the reconstruction is, especially if they are placed in a principled way as outlined by Wilcox [555]. Fig. 12.10 shows the reconstructed function with increasing iteration number. In the left panel, iteration one through twenty are shown with the z-axis set to illustrate the extremely poor reconstruction in the early stages of the iteration. The right panel highlights the reconstruction from iteration nine to twenty, and on a more limited z-axis scale, where the reconstruction

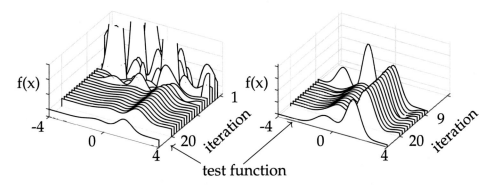

Figure 12.10 Convergence of the reconstruction to the test function (12.11). The left panel shows iterations one through twenty and the significant reconstruction errors of the early iterations and limited number of sensors. Indeed, for the first nine iterations, the condition number and least-square error is quite large since the system is not full rank. The right panel shows a zoom-in of the solution from iteration nine to twenty where the convergence is clearly observed. Comparison in both panels can be made to the test function.

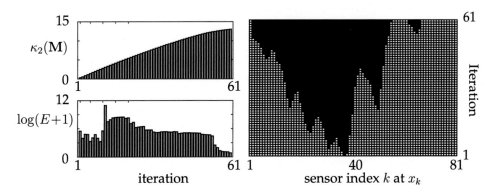

Figure 12.11 Sum of diagonals minus off-diagonals (top left) and least-square error (logarithm) as a function of the number of iterations in the second gappy sensor placement algorithm. The new proxy metric for condition number monotonically increases since this is being maximized at each iteration step. The log of the least-square error in the reconstruction of the test function (12.11) shows a trend towards improvement as the number of sensors are increased, but convergence is extremely slow in comparison to minimizing the condition number. The right panel shows the sensors as they turn on (black squares) over the first 60 iterations. The first measurement location is, for instance, at x_{37}.

converges to the test function. The true test function is also shown in order to visualize the comparison. This illustrates in a tangible way the convergence of the iteration algorithm to the test solution with a principled placement of sensors.

Proxy Measures to the Condition Number

We end this section by considering alternative measures to the condition number $\kappa(\mathbf{M})$. The computation of the condition number itself can be computationally expensive. Moreover, until r sensors are chosen in an r-POD mode expansion, the condition number computation is itself numerically unstable. However, it is clear what the condition number minimization algorithm is trying to achieve: make the measurement matrix $\mathbf{M}$ as near to the identify as possible. This suggests the following alternative algorithm, which was also developed by Willcox [555].

1. Place sensor k at each spatial location possible and evaluate the difference in the sum of the diagonal entries of the matrix $\mathbf{M}$ minus the sum of the off-diagonal components, call this $\kappa_2(\mathbf{M})$. Only points not already containing a sensor are considered.
2. Determine the spatial location that generates the maximum value of the above quantify. This spatial location is now the kth sensor location.
3. Add sensor $k + 1$ and repeat the previous two steps.

This algorithm provides a simple modification of the original algorithm which minimizes the condition number. In particular, the following lines of code provide modifications to Code 12.5. Specifically, where the condition number is computed, the following line is now included:

```
nall=setdiff(nall,ns);   % new sensor indeces
```

Additonally, the sensor locations are now considered at the maximal points so that the following line of code is applied

```
P=zeros(n,1);   P(ns)=1;
```

Thus the modification of two lines of code can enact this new metric which circumvents the computation of the condition number.

To evaluate this new gappy sensor location algorithm, we track the new proxy metric we are trying to maximize as a function of the number of iterations along with the least-square error of our test function (12.11). In this case, up to 60 sensors are considered since the convergence is slower than before. Fig. 12.11 shows the progress of the algorithm as it evaluates the sensor locations for up to 60 sensors. By construction, the algorithm maximizes the sum of the diagonals minus the sum of the off-diagonals at each step of the iteration, thus as sensors are added, this measure steadily increases (top left panel of Fig. 12.11). The least-square error for the reconstruction of the test function (12.11) decreases, but not monotonically. Further, the convergence is very slow. At least for this example, the method does not work as well as the condition number metric. However, it can improve performance in certain cases [555], and it is much more computationally efficient to compute.

As before, we also consider the placement of the sensors as a function of iteration in the right panel of Fig. 12.11. Specifically, we depict the turning on process of the sensors. The first sensor location is x_{37} followed by x_{38}, x_{36} and x_{31} respectively. The process is continued until the first 60 sensors are turned on. The pattern of sensors depicted is significantly different than in the condition number minimization algorithm. Indeed, this algorithm, and with these modes, turns on sensors in local locations without sampling uniformly from the domain.

12.4   Gappy Measurements: Maximal Variance

The previous section developed principled ways to determine the location of sensors for gappy POD measurements. This was a significant improvement over simply choosing sensor locations randomly. Indeed, the minimization of the condition number through location selection performed quite well, quickly improving accuracy and least-square reconstruction error. The drawback to the proposed method was two-fold: the algorithm itself is expensive to implement, requiring a computation of the condition number for every sensor location selected under an exhaustive search. Secondly, the algorithm was ill-conditioned until the rth sensor was chosen in an r-POD mode expansion. Thus the condition number was theoretically infinite, but on the order of 10^{17} for computational purposes.

Karniadakis and co-workers [565] proposed an alternative to the Willcox [555] algorithm to overcome the computational issues outlined. Specifically, instead of placing one sensor at a time, the new algorithm places r sensors, for an r-POD mode expansion, at the first step of the iteration. Thus the matrix generated is no longer ill-conditioned with a theoretically infinite condition number.

The algorithm by Karniadakis further proposes a principled way to select the original r sensor locations. This method selects locations that are extrema points of the POD modes, which are designed to maximally capture variance in the data. Specifically, the following algorithm is suggested:

1. Place r sensors initially.
2. Determine the spatial locations of these first r sensors by considering the maximum of each of the POD modes ψ_k.
3. Add additional sensors at the next largest extrema of the POD modes.

The following code determines the maximum of each mode and constructs a gappy measurement matrix **P** from such locations.

Code 12.6 Gappy placement: Maximize variance.

```
ns=[];
for j=1:10    % walk through the modes
    [s1,n1]=max(yharm(:,j)); % pick max
    ns=[ns n1];
end
P=zeros(n,1);   P(ns)=1;
```

The performance of this algorithm is not strong for only r measurements, but it at least produces stable condition number calculations. To improve performance, one could also use the minimum of each of the modes ψ_k. Thus the maximal value and minimal value of variance are considered. For the harmonic oscillator code, the first mode produces no minimum as the minima are at $x \to \pm\infty$. Thus 19 sensor locations are chosen in the following code:

Code 12.7 Gappy placement: Max and min variance.

```
ns=[];
for j=1:10    % walk through the modes
    [s1,n1]=max(yharm(:,j)); % pick max
    ns=[ns n1];
end
for j=2:10
    [s2,n2]=min(yharm(:,j)); % pick max
    ns=[ns n2];
end
P=zeros(n,1);   P(ns)=1;
```

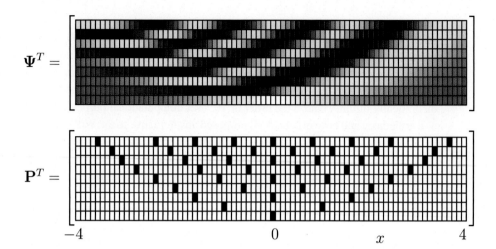

$\boldsymbol{\Psi}^T =$

$\mathbf{P}^T =$

$-4 \qquad\qquad\qquad 0 \qquad\qquad x \qquad 4$

Figure 12.12 The top panel shows the mode structures of the Gauss-Hermite polynomials $\boldsymbol{\Psi}$ in the low-rank approximation of a POD expansion. The discretization interval is $x \in [-4, 4]$ with a spacing of $\Delta x = 0.1$. The color map shows the maximum (white) and minimum (black) that occur in the mode structures. The bottom panel shows the grid cells corresponding to maximum and minimum (extrema) of POD mode variance. The extrema are candidates for sensor locations, or the measurement matrix $\mathbf{P}$, since they represent maximal variance locations. Typically one would take a random subsample of these extrema to begin the evaluation of the gappy placement.

Note that in this case, the number of sensors is almost double that of the previous case. Moreover it only searches for the the locations where variability is highest, which is intuitively appealing for measurements.

More generally, the Karniadakis algorithm [565] advocates randomly selecting p sensors from M potential extrema, and then modifying the search positions with the goal of improving the condition number. In this case, one must identify all the maxima and minima of the POD modes in order to make the selection. The harmonic oscillator modes and their maxima and minima are illustrated in Fig. 12.12. The algorithm used to produce the extrema of each mode, and its potential for use in the gappy algorithm, is as follows:

Code 12.8 Gappy placement: Extrema locations.

```
nmax=[]; nmin=[];
Psum = zeros(n,10);
for j=1:10   % walk through the modes
    nmaxt=[]; nmint=[];
    for jj=2:n-1
        if yharm(jj,j)>yharm(jj-1,j) & yharm(jj,j)>yharm(jj+1,j)
            nmax=[nmax jj];
            nmaxt=[nmaxt jj];
        end
        if yharm(jj,j)<yharm(jj-1,j) & yharm(jj,j)<yharm(jj+1,j)
            nmin=[nmin jj];
            nmint=[nmint jj];
        end
    end
    nst=[nmaxt nmint]
    Psum(nst,j)=1;
end
```

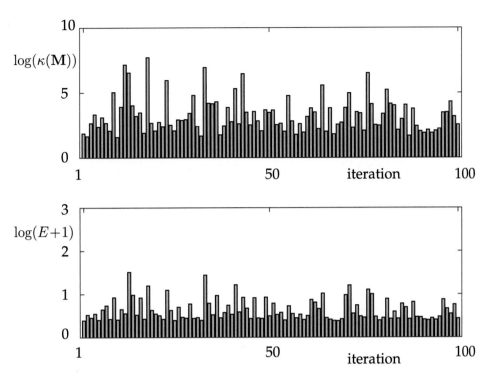

Figure 12.13 Condition number and least-square error to test function (12.11) over 100 random trials that draw 20 sensor locations from the possible 55 extrema depicted in Fig. 12.12. The 100 trials produce a number of sensor configurations that perform close to the level of the condition number minimization algorithm of the last section. However, the computational costs in generating such trials can be significantly lower.

```
ns=[nmax nmin];
ni=randsample(length(ns),20);
nsr=ns(ni);
P=zeros(n,1);  P(nsr)=1;
```

Note that the resulting vector **ns** contains all 55 possible extrema. This computation assumes the data is sufficiently smooth so that extrema are simply found by considering neighboring points, i.e. a maxima exists if its two neighbors have a lower value whereas an minima exists if its neighbors have a higher value.

The maximal variance algorithm suggests trying different configurations of the sensors at the extrema points. In particular, if 20 gappy measurements are desired, then we would need to search through various configurations of the 55 locations using 20 sensors. This combinatorial search is intractable. However, if we simply attempt 100 random trials and select the best performing configuration, it is quite close to the performance of the condition number minimizing algorithm. A full execution of this algorithm, along with a computation of the condition number and least-square fit error with (12.11), is generated by the following code:

Code 12.9 Gappy placement: Random selection.

```
ntot=length(ns);
for jtrials=1:100
```

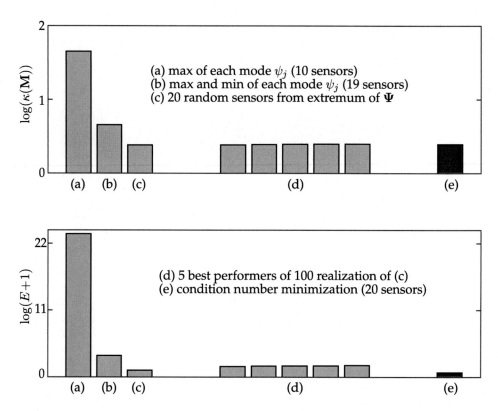

Figure 12.14 Performance metrics for placing sensors based upon the extrema of the variance of the POD modes. Both the least-square error for the reconstruction of the test function (12.11) and the condition number are considered. Illustrated are the results from using (a) the maximum locations of the POD modes, (b) the maximum and minimum locations of each POD mode, and (c) a random selection of 20 of the 55 extremum locations of the POD modes. These are compared against (d) the 5 top selections of 20 sensors from the 100 random trials, and (e) the condition number minimization algorithm (red bar). The random placement of sensors from the extremum locations provides performance close to that of the condition minimization without the same high computational costs.

```
ni=randsample(ntot,20);
nsr=ns(ni);

    P=zeros(n,1);   P(nsr)=1;

    for j=1:10
        for jj=1:j
            Area=trapz(x,P.*(yharm(:,j).*yharm(:,jj)));
            M2(j,jj)=Area; M2(jj,j)=Area;
        end
    end

    for j=1:10  % reconstruction using gappy
        ftild(j,1)=trapz(x,P.*(f.*yharm(:,j)));
    end
    atild=M2\ftild;     % compute error
    f1=yharm*atild;     % iterative reconstruction
    E_tri(jtrials)=norm(f1-f);   % iterative error
    con_tri(jtrials)=cond(M2);
```

```
end
subplot(2,1,1), bar(log(con_tri),'Facecolor',[0.7 0.7 0.7])
subplot(2,1,2), bar(log(E_tri+1),'Facecolor',[0.7 0.7 0.7])
```

The condition number and least-square error for the 100 trials is shown in Fig. 12.13. The configurations perform well compared with random measurements, although some have excellent performance.

A direct comparison of all these methods is shown in Fig. 12.14. Specifically, what is illustrated are the results from using (a) the maximum locations of the POD modes, (b) the maximum and minimum locations of each POD mode, and (c) a random selection of 20 of the 55 extremum locations of the POD modes. These are compared against (d) the best 5 sensor placement locations of 20 sensors selected from the extremum over 100 random trials, and (e) the condition number minimization algorithm in red. The maximal variance algorithm performs approximately as well as the minimum condition number algorithm. However, the algorithm is faster and never computes condition numbers on ill-conditioned matrices. Karniadakis and co-workers [565] also suggest innovations on this basic implementation. Specifically, it is suggested that one consider each sensor, one-by-one, and try placing it in all other available spatial locations. If the condition number is reduced, the sensor is moved to that new location and the next sensor is considered.

12.5 POD and the Discrete Empirical Interpolation Method (DEIM)

The POD method illustrated thus far aims to exploit the underlying low-dimensional dynamics observed in many high-dimensional computations. POD is often used for reduced-order models (ROMs), which are of growing importance in scientific applications and computing. ROMS reduce the computational complexity and time needed to solve large-scale, complex systems [53, 442, 244, 17]. Specifically, ROMs provide a principled approach to approximating high-dimensional spatio-temporal systems [139], typically generated from numerical discretization, by low-dimensional subspaces that produce nearly identical input/output characteristics of the underlying nonlinear dynamical system. However, despite the significant reduction in dimensionality with a POD basis, the complexity of evaluating higher-order nonlinear terms may remain as challenging as the original problem [41, 127]. The empirical interpolation method (EIM), and the simplified discrete empirical interpolation method (DEIM) for the proper orthogonal decomposition (POD) [347, 251], overcome this difficulty by providing a computationally efficient method for discretely (sparsely) sampling and evaluating the nonlinearity. These methods ensure that the computational complexity of ROMs scale favorably with the rank of the approximation, even with complex nonlinearities.

EIM has been developed for the purpose of efficiently managing the computation of the nonlinearity in dimensionality reduction schemes, with DEIM specifically tailored to POD with Galerkin projection. Indeed, DEIM approximates the nonlinearity by using a small, discrete sampling of points that are determined in an algorithmic way. This ensures that the computational cost of evaluating the nonlinearity scales with the rank of the reduced POD basis. As an example, consider the case of an r-mode POD-Galerkin truncation. A simple cubic nonlinearity requires that the POD-Galerkin approximation be cubed, resulting in r^3 operations to evaluate the nonlinear term. DEIM approximates the cubic nonlinearity by using $\mathcal{O}(r)$ discrete sample points of the nonlinearity, thus

Table 12.1 DEIM algorithm for finding approximation basis for the nonlinearity and its interpolation indices. The algorithm first constructs the nonlinear basis modes and initializes the first measurement location, and the matrix $\mathbf{P}_1$, as the maximum of $\boldsymbol{\xi}_1$. The algorithm then successively constructs columns of $\mathbf{P}_j$ by considering the location of the maximum of the residual $\mathbf{R}_j$.

DEIM algorithm

Basis Construction and Initialization

• collect data, construct snapshot matrix	$\mathbf{X} = [\mathbf{u}(t_1)\ \mathbf{u}(t_2)\ \cdots\ \mathbf{u}(t_m)]$
• construct nonlinear snapshot matrix	$\mathbf{N} = [N(\mathbf{u}(t_1))\ N(\mathbf{u}(t_2))\ \cdots\ N(\mathbf{u}(t_m))]$
• singular value decomposition of $\mathbf{N}$	$\mathbf{N} = \Xi \Sigma_{\mathbf{N}} \mathbf{V}_{\mathbf{N}}^*$
• construct rank-p approximating basis	$\Xi_p = [\boldsymbol{\xi}_1\ \boldsymbol{\xi}_2\ \cdots\ \boldsymbol{\xi}_p]$
• choose the first index (initialization)	$[\rho, \gamma_1] = \max |\boldsymbol{\xi}_1|$
• construct first measurement matrix	$\mathbf{P}_1 = [\mathbf{e}_{\gamma_1}]$

Interpolation Indices and Iteration Loop ($j = 2, 3, ..., p$)

• calculate $\mathbf{c}_j$	$\mathbf{P}_j^T \Xi_j \mathbf{c}_j = \mathbf{P}_j^T \boldsymbol{\xi}_{j+1}$
• compute residual	$\mathbf{R}_{j+1} = \boldsymbol{\xi}_{j+1} - \Xi_j \mathbf{c}_j$
• find index of maximum residual	$[\rho, \gamma_j] = \max |\mathbf{R}_{j+1}|$
• add new column to measurement matrix	$\mathbf{P}_{j+1} = [\mathbf{P}_j\ \mathbf{e}_{\gamma_j}]$

preserving a low-dimensional ($\mathcal{O}(r)$) computation, as desired. The DEIM approach combines projection with interpolation. Specifically, DEIM uses selected interpolation indices to specify an interpolation-based projection for a nearly ℓ_2 optimal subspace approximating the nonlinearity. EIM/DEIM are not the only methods developed to reduce the complexity of evaluating nonlinear terms; see for instance the missing point estimation (MPE) [400, 21] or gappy POD [555, 565, 120, 462] methods. However, they have been successful in a large number of diverse applications and models [127]. In any case, the MPE, gappy POD, and EIM/DEIM use a small selected set of spatial grid points to avoid evaluation of the expensive inner products required to evaluate nonlinear terms.

POD and DEIM

Consider a high-dimensional system of nonlinear differential equations that can arise, for example, from the finite difference discretization of a partial differential equation. In addition to constructing a snapshot matrix (12.12) of the solution of the PDE so that POD modes can be extracted, the DEIM algorithm also constructs a snapshot matrix of the nonlinear term of the PDE:

$$\mathbf{N} = \begin{bmatrix} | & | & & | \\ \mathbf{N}_1 & \mathbf{N}_2 & \cdots & \mathbf{N}_m \\ | & | & & | \end{bmatrix} \tag{12.12}$$

where the columns $\mathbf{N}_k \in \mathbb{C}^n$ are evaluations of the nonlinearity at time t_k.

To achieve high accuracy solutions, n is typically very large, making the computation of the solution expensive and/or intractable. The POD-Galerkin method is a principled dimensionality-reduction scheme that approximates the function $\mathbf{u}(t)$ with rank-r optimal

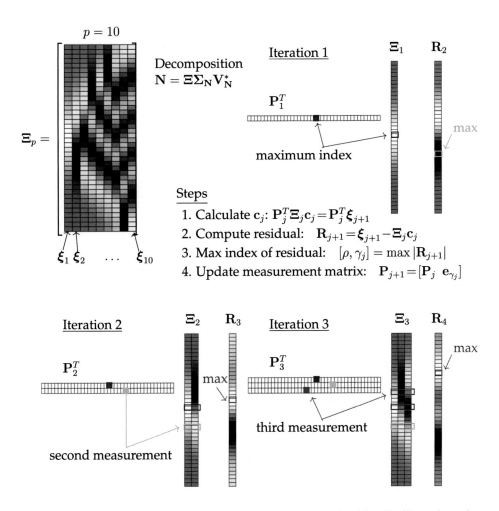

Figure 12.15 Demonstration of the first three iterations of the DEIM algorithm. For illustration only, the nonlinearity matrix $\mathbf{N} = \Xi \Sigma_{\mathbf{N}} \mathbf{V}_{\mathbf{N}}^*$ is assumed to be composed of harmonic oscillator modes with the first ten modes comprising Ξ_p. The initial measurement location is chosen at the maximum of the first mode ξ_1. Afterwards, there is a three step process for selecting subsequent measurement locations based upon the location of the maximum of the residual vector $\mathbf{R}_j$. The first (red), second (green) and third (blue) measurement locations are shown along with the construction of the sampling matrix $\mathbf{P}$

basis functions where $r \ll n$. As shown in the previous chapter, these optimal basis functions are computed from a singular value decomposition of a series of temporal snapshots of the complex system.

The standard POD procedure [251] is a ubiquitous algorithm in the reduced order modeling community. However, it also helps illustrate the need for innovations such as DEIM, Gappy POD and/or MPE. Consider the nonlinear component of the low-dimensional evolution (11.21): $\mathbf{\Psi}^T \mathbf{N}(\mathbf{\Psi}\mathbf{a}(t))$. For a simple nonlinearity such as $N(u(x, t)) = u(x, t)^3$, consider its impact on a spatially-discretized, two-mode POD expansion: $u(x, t) = a_1(t)\psi_1(x) + a_2(t)\psi_2(x)$. The algorithm for computing the nonlinearity requires the evaluation:

$$u(x, t)^3 = a_1^3 \psi_1^3 + 3a_1^2 a_2 \psi_1^2 \psi_2 + 3a_1 a_2^2 \psi_1 \psi_2^2 + a_2^3 \psi_2^3. \tag{12.13}$$

The dynamics of $a_1(t)$ and $a_2(t)$ would then be computed by projecting onto the low-dimensional basis by taking the inner product of this nonlinear term with respect to both ψ_1 and ψ_2. Thus the number of computations not only doubles, but the inner products must be computed with the n-dimensional vectors. Methods such as DEIM overcome this high-dimensional computation.

DEIM

As outlined in the previous section, the shortcomings of the POD-Galerkin method are generally due to the evaluation of the nonlinear term $\mathbf{N}(\mathbf{\Psi}\mathbf{a}(t))$. To avoid this difficulty, DEIM approximates $\mathbf{N}(\mathbf{\Psi}\mathbf{a}(t))$ through projection and interpolation instead of evaluating it directly. Specifically, a low-rank representation of the nonlinearity is computed from the singular value decomposition

$$\mathbf{N} = \Xi \Sigma_{\mathbf{N}} \mathbf{V}_{\mathbf{N}}^* \tag{12.14}$$

where the matrix Ξ contains the optimal basis for spanning the nonlinearity. Specifically, we consider the rank-p basis

$$\Xi_p = [\boldsymbol{\xi}_1 \, \boldsymbol{\xi}_2 \, \cdots \, \boldsymbol{\xi}_p] \tag{12.15}$$

that approximates the nonlinear function ($p \ll n$ and $p \sim r$). The approximation to the nonlinearity $\mathbf{N}$ is given by:

$$\mathbf{N} \approx \Xi_p \mathbf{c}(t) \tag{12.16}$$

where $\mathbf{c}(t)$ is similar to $\mathbf{a}(t)$ in (11.20). Since this is a highly overdetermined system, a suitable vector $\mathbf{c}(t)$ can be found by selecting p rows of the system. The DEIM algorithm was developed to identify which p rows to evaluate.

The DEIM algorithm begins by considering the vectors $\mathbf{e}_{\gamma_j} \in \mathbf{R}^n$ which are the γ_j-th column of the n dimensional identity matrix. We can then construct the projection matrix $\mathbf{P} = [\mathbf{e}_{\gamma_1} \, \mathbf{e}_{\gamma_2} \, \cdots \, \mathbf{e}_{\gamma_p}]$ which is chosen so that $\mathbf{P}^T \Xi_p$ is nonsingular. Then $\mathbf{c}(t)$ is uniquely defined from $\mathbf{P}^T \mathbf{N} = \mathbf{P}^T \Xi_p \mathbf{c}(t)$, and thus,

$$\mathbf{N} \approx \Xi_p (\mathbf{P}^T \Xi_p)^{-1} \mathbf{P}^T \mathbf{N}. \tag{12.17}$$

The tremendous advantage of this result for nonlinear model reduction is that the term $\mathbf{P}^T \mathbf{N}$ requires evaluation of the nonlinearity only at $p \ll n$ indices. DEIM further proposes a principled method for choosing the basis vectors $\boldsymbol{\xi}_j$ and indices γ_j. The DEIM algorithm, which is based on a greedy search, is detailed in [127] and further demonstrated in Table 12.1.

POD and DEIM provide a number of advantages for nonlinear model reduction of complex systems. POD provides a principled way to construct an r-dimensional subspace $\mathbf{\Psi}$ characterizing the dynamics. DEIM augments POD by providing a method to evaluate the problematic nonlinear terms using an p-dimensional subspace Ξ_p that represents the nonlinearity. Thus a small number of points can be sampled to approximate the nonlinear terms in the ROM.

12.6   DEIM Algorithm Implementation

To demonstrate model reduction with DEIM, we again consider the NLS equation (11.29). Recall that the numerical method for solving this equation is given in Codes 11.3 and 11.4.

The output of this code is a matrix **usol** whose rows represent the time snapshots and whose columns represent the spatial discretization points. As in the first section of this chapter, our first step is to transpose this data so that the time snapshots are columns instead of rows. The following code transposes the data and also performs a singular value decomposition to get the POD modes.

Code 12.10 Dimensionality reduction for NLS.

```
X=usol.';   % data matrix X
[U,S,W]=svd(X,0);   % SVD reduction
```

In addition to the standard POD modes, the singular value decomposition of the nonlinear term is also required for the DEIM algorithm. This computes the low-rank representation of $N(u) = |u|^2 u$ directly as $\mathbf{N} = \Xi \Sigma_N \mathbf{V}_N^*$.

Code 12.11 Dimensionality reduction for nonlinearity of NLS.

```
NL=i*(abs(X).^2).*X;
[XI,S_NL,W]=svd(NL,0);
```

Once the low-rank structures are computed, the rank of the system is chosen with the parameter r. In what follows, we choose $r = p = 3$ so that both the standard POD modes and nonlinear modes, Ψ and Ξ_p have three columns each. The following code selects the POD modes for Ψ and projects the initial condition onto the POD subspace.

Code 12.12 Rank selection and POD modes.

```
r=3;   % select rank truncation
Psi=U(:,1:r);   % select POD modes
a=Psi'*u0;   % project initial conditions
```

We now build the interpolation matrix $\mathbf{P}$ by executing the DEIM algorithm outlined in the last section. The algorithm starts by selecting the first interpolation point from the maximum of the first most dominant mode of Ξ_p.

Code 12.13 First DEIM point.

```
[Xi_max,nmax]=max(abs(XI(:,1)));
XI_m=XI(:,1);
z=zeros(n,1);
P=z;  P(nmax)=1;
```

The algorithm iteratively builds $\mathbf{P}$ one column at a time. The next step of the algorithm is to compute the second to rth interpolation point via the greedy DEIM algorithm. Specifically, the vector $\mathbf{c}_j$ is computed from $\mathbf{P}_j^T \Xi_j \mathbf{c}_j = \mathbf{P}_j^T \boldsymbol{\xi}_{j+1}$ where $\boldsymbol{\xi}_j$ are the columns of the nonlinear POD modes matrix Ξ_p. The actual interpolation point comes from looking for the maximum of the residual $\mathbf{R}_{j+1} = \boldsymbol{\xi}_{j+1} - \Xi_j \mathbf{c}_j$. Each iteration of the algorithm produces another column of the sparse interpolation matrix $\mathbf{P}$. The integers **nmax** give the location of the interpolation points.

Code 12.14 DEIM points 2 through r.

```
for j=2:r
    c=(P'*XI_m)\(P'*XI(:,j));
    res=XI(:,j)-XI_m*c;
    [Xi_max,nmax]=max(abs(res));
    XI_m=[XI_m,XI(:,j)];
    P=[P,z];  P(nmax,j)=1;
end
```

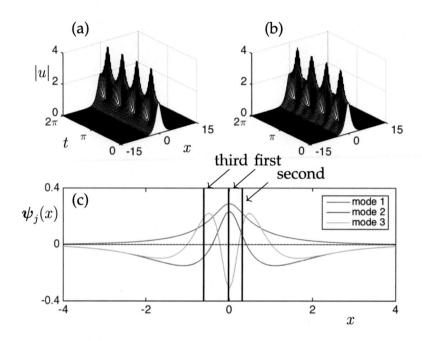

Figure 12.16 Comparison of the (a) full simulation dynamics and (b) rank $r = 3$ ROM using the three DEIM interpolation points. (c) A detail of the three POD modes used for simulation are shown along with the first, second and third DEIM interpolation point location. These three interpolation points are capable of accurately reproducing the evolution dynamics of the full PDE system.

With the interpolation matrix, we are ready to construct the ROM. The first part is to construct the linear term $\boldsymbol{\Psi}^T \mathbf{L} \boldsymbol{\Psi}$ of (11.21) where the linear operator for NLS is the Laplacian. The derivatives are computed using the Fourier transform.

Code 12.15 Projection of linear terms.

```
for j=1:r  % linear derivative terms
    Lxx(:,j)=ifft(-k.^2.*fft(Psi(:,j)));
end
L=(i/2)*(Psi')*Lxx;  % projected linear term
```

The projection of the nonlinearity is accomplished using the interpolation matrix $\mathbf{P}$ with the formula (12.17). Recall that the nonlinear term in (11.21) is multiplied by $\boldsymbol{\Psi}^T$. Also computed is the interpolated version of the low-rank subspace spanned by $\boldsymbol{\Psi}$.

Code 12.16 Projection of nonlinear terms.

```
P_NL=Psi'*( XI_m*inv(P'*XI_m) );  % nonlinear projection
P_Psi=P'*Psi;  % interpolation of Psi
```

It only remains now to advance the solution in time using a numerical time stepper. This is done with a 4th-order Runge-Kutta routine.

Code 12.17 Time stepping of ROM.

```
[tt,a]=ode45('rom_deim_rhs',t,a,[],P_NL,P_Psi,L);
Xtilde=Psi*a';  % DEIM approximation
waterfall(x,t,abs(Xtilde')), shading interp, colormap gray
```

The right hand side of the time stepper is now completely low dimensional.

Code 12.18 Right hand side of ROM.

```
function rhs=rom_deim_rhs(tspan, a,dummy,P_NL,P_Psi,L)
N=P_Psi*a;
rhs=L*a + i*P_NL*((abs(N).^2).*N);
```

A comparison of the full simulation dynamics and rank $r = 3$ ROM using the three DEIM interpolation points is shown in Fig. 12.16. Additionally, the location of the DEIM points relative to the POD modes is shown. Aside from the first DEIM point, the other locations are not on the minima or maxima of the POD modes. Rather, the algorithms places them to maximize the residual.

QDEIM Algorithm

Although DEIM is an efficient greedy algorithm for selecting interpolation points, there are other techniques that are equally efficient. The recently proposed QDEIM algorithm [159] leverages the QR decomposition to provide efficient, greedy interpolation locations. This has been shown to be a robust mathematical architecture for sensor placement in many applications [366]. See Section 3.8 for a more general discussion. The QR decomposition can also provide a greedy strategy to identify interpolation points. In QDEIM, the QR pivot locations are the sensor locations. The following code can replace the DEIM algorithm to produce the interpolation matrix **P**.

Code 12.19 QR based interpolation points

```
[Q,R,pivot]=qr(NL.');
P=pivot(:,1:r);
```

Using this interpolation matrix gives identical interpolation locations as shown in Fig. 12.16. More generally, there are estimates that show that the QDEIM may improve error performance over standard DEIM [159]. The ease of use of the QR algorithm makes this an attractive method for sparse interpolation.

12.7 Machine Learning ROMs

Inspired by machine learning methods, the various POD bases for a parametrized system are merged into a master library of POD modes Ψ_L which contains all the low-rank subspaces exhibited by the dynamical system. This leverages the fact that POD provides a principled way to construct an r-dimensional subspace Ψ_r characterizing the dynamics while sparse sampling augments the POD method by providing a method to evaluate the problematic nonlinear terms using a p-dimensional subspace projection matrix **P**. Thus a small number of points can be sampled to approximate the nonlinear terms in the ROM. Fig. 12.17 illustrates the library building procedure whereby a dynamical regime is sampled in order to construct an appropriate POD basis Ψ.

The method introduced here capitalizes on these methods by building low-dimensional libraries associated with the full nonlinear system dynamics as well as the specific nonlinearities. Interpolation points, as will be shown in what follows, can be used with sparse representation and compressive sensing to (i) identify dynamical regimes, (ii) reconstruct the full state of the system, and (iii) provide an efficient nonlinear model reduction and POD-Galerkin prediction for the future state.

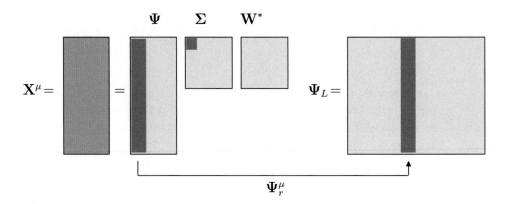

Figure 12.17 Library construction from numerical simulations of the governing equations (11.1). Simulations are performed of the parametrized system for different values of a bifurcation parameter μ. For each regime, low-dimensional POD modes Ψ_r are computed via an SVD decomposition. The various rank-r truncated subspaces are stored in the library of modes matrix Ψ_L. This is the learning stage of the algorithm. (*reproduced from Kutz et al. [319]*)

The concept of library building of low-rank *features* from data is well established in the computer science community. In the reduced-order modeling community, it has recently become an enabling computational strategy for parametric systems. Indeed, a variety of recent works have produced libraries of ROM models [80, 98, 462, 10, 134, 422, 421, 420] that can be selected and/or interpolated through measurement and classification. Alternatively, cluster-based reduced order models use a k-means clustering to build a Markov transition model between dynamical states [278]. These recent innovations are similar to the ideas advocated here. However, our focus is on determining how a suitably chosen **P** can be used across all the libraries for POD mode selection and reconstruction. One can also build two sets of libraries: one for the full dynamics and a second for the nonlinearity so as to make it computationally efficient with the DEIM strategy [462]. Before these more formal techniques based on machine learning were developed, it was already realized that parameter domains could be decomposed into subdomains and a local ROM/POD computed in each subdomain. Patera and co-workers [171] used a partitioning based on a binary tree whereas Amsallem *et al.* [9] used a Voronoi tessellation of the domain. Such methods were closely related to the work of Du and Gunzburger [160] where the data snapshots were partitioned into subsets and multiple reduced bases computed. The multiple bases were then recombined into a single basis, so it doesn't lead to a library, per se. For a review of these domain partitioning strategies, please see Ref. [11].

POD Mode Selection

Although there are a number of techniques for selecting the correct POD library elements to use, including the workhorse k-means clustering algorithm [10, 134, 422, 421, 420], one can also instead make use of sparse sampling and the sparse representation for classification (SRC) innovations outlined in Chapter 3 to characterize the nonlinear dynamical system [80, 98, 462]. Specifically, the goal is to use a limited number of sensors (interpolation points) to classify the dynamical regime of the system from a range of potential POD

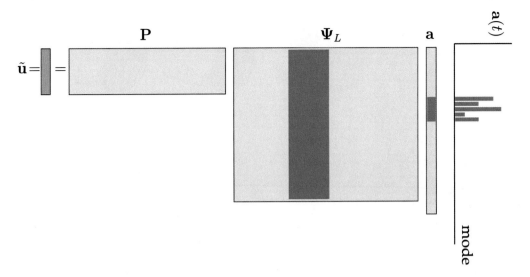

Figure 12.18 The sparse representation for classification (SRC) algorithm for library mode selection; see Section 3.6 for more details. In this mathematical framework, a sparse measurement is taken of the system (11.1) and a highly under-determined system of equations $\mathbf{P}\Psi_L\mathbf{a} = \tilde{\mathbf{u}}$ is solved subject to ℓ_1 penalization so that $\|\mathbf{a}\|_1$ is minimized. Illustrated is the selection of the μth POD modes. The bar plot on the left depicts the nonzero values of the vector $\mathbf{a}$ which correspond to the Ψ_r library elements. Note that the sampling matrix $\mathbf{P}$ that produces the sparse sample $\tilde{\mathbf{u}} = \mathbf{P}\mathbf{u}$ is critical for success in classification of the correct library elements Ψ_r and the corresponding reconstruction. (*reproduced from Kutz et al. [319]*)

library elements characterized by a parameter β. Once a correct classification is a achieved, a standard ℓ_2 reconstruction of the full state space can be accomplished with the selected subset of POD modes, and a POD-Galerkin prediction can be computed for its future.

In general, we will have a sparse measurement vector $\tilde{\mathbf{u}}$ given by (12.1). The full state vector $\mathbf{u}$ can be approximated with the POD library modes ($\mathbf{u} = \Psi_L\mathbf{a}$), therefore

$$\tilde{\mathbf{u}} = \mathbf{P}\Psi_L\mathbf{a}, \tag{12.18}$$

where Ψ_L is the low-rank matrix whose columns are POD basis vectors concatenated across all β regimes and $\mathbf{c}$ is the coefficient vector giving the projection of $\mathbf{u}$ onto these POD modes. If $\mathbf{P}\Psi_L$ obeys the restricted isometry property and $\mathbf{u}$ is sufficiently sparse in Ψ_L, then it is possible to solve the highly-underdetermined system (12.18) with the sparsest vector $\mathbf{a}$. Mathematically, this is equivalent to an ℓ_0 optimization problem which is np-hard. However, under certain conditions, a sparse solution of equation (12.18) can be found (See Chapter 3) by minimizing the l_1 norm instead so that

$$\mathbf{c} = \arg\min_{\mathbf{a}'} \|\mathbf{a}'\|_1, \quad \text{subject to} \quad \tilde{\mathbf{u}} = \mathbf{P}\Psi_L\mathbf{a}. \tag{12.19}$$

The last equation can be solved through standard convex optimization methods. Thus the ℓ_1 norm is a proxy for sparsity. Note that we only use the sparsity for classification, not reconstruction. Fig. 12.18 demonstrates the sparse sampling strategy and prototypical results for the sparse solution $\mathbf{a}$.

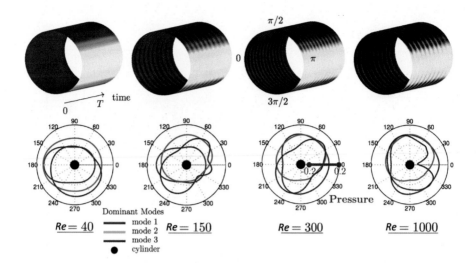

Figure 12.19 Time dynamics of the pressure field (top panels) for flow around a cylinder for Reynolds number $Re = 40, 150, 300$ and 1000. Collecting snapshots of the dynamics reveals low-dimensional structures dominate the dynamics. The dominant three POD pressure modes for each Reynolds number regime are shown in polar coordinates. The pressure scale is in magenta (bottom left). (*reproduced from Kutz et al. [319]*)

Example: Flow around a Cylinder

To demonstrate the sparse classification and reconstruction algorithm developed, we consider the canonical problem of flow around a cylinder. This problem is well understood and has already been the subject of studies concerning sparse spatial measurements [80, 98, 462, 281, 374, 89, 540]. Specifically, it is known that for low to moderate Reynolds numbers, the dynamics are spatially low-dimensional and POD approaches have been successful in quantifying the dynamics. The Reynolds number, Re, plays the role of the bifurcation parameter β in (11.1), i.e. it is a parametrized dynamical system.

The data we consider comes from numerical simulations of the incompressible Navier-Stokes equation:

$$\frac{\partial u}{\partial t} + u \cdot \nabla u + \nabla p - \frac{1}{Re} \nabla^2 u = 0 \tag{12.20a}$$

$$\nabla \cdot u = 0 \tag{12.20b}$$

where $u(x, y, t) \in \mathbb{R}^2$ represents the 2D velocity, and $p(x, y, t) \in \mathbb{R}^2$ the corresponding pressure field. The boundary condition are as follows: (i) Constant flow of $u = (1, 0)^T$ at $x = -15$, i.e., the entry of the channel, (ii) Constant pressure of $p = 0$ at $x = 25$, i.e., the end of the channel, and (iii) Neumann boundary conditions, i.e. $\frac{\partial u}{\partial \mathbf{n}} = 0$ on the boundary of the channel and the cylinder (centered at $(x, y) = (0, 0)$ and of radius unity).

For each relevant value of the parameter Re we perform an SVD on the data matrix in order to extract POD modes. It is well known that for relatively low Reynolds number, a fast decay of the singular values is observed so that only a few POD modes are needed to characterize the dynamics. Fig. 12.19 shows the 3 most dominant POD modes for Reynolds number $Re = 40, 150, 300, 1000$. Note that 99% of the total energy (variance) is selected

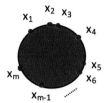 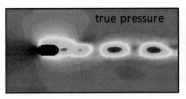 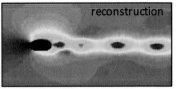

Figure 12.20 Illustration of m sparse sensor locations (left panel) for classification and reconstruction of the flow field. The selection of sensory/interpolation locations can be accomplished by various algorithms [80, 98, 462, 281, 374, 89, 540]. For a selected algorithm, the sensing matrix **P** determines the classification and reconstruction performance. (*reproduced from Kutz et al. [319]*)

for the POD mode selection cut-off, giving a total of 1, 3, 3, and 9 POD modes to represent the dynamics in the regimes shown. For a threshold of 99.9%, more modes are required to account for the variability.

Classification of the Reynolds number is accomplished by solving the optimization problem (12.19) and obtaining the sparse coefficient vector **a**. Note that each entry in **a** corresponds to the energy of a single POD mode from our library. For simplicity, we select a number of local minima and maxima of the POD modes as sampling locations for the matrix **P**. The classification of the Reynolds number is done by summing the absolute value of the coefficient that corresponds to each Reynolds number. To account for the large number of coefficients allocated for the higher Reynolds number (which may be 16 POD modes for 99.9% variance at $Re = 1000$, rather than a single coefficient for Reynolds number 40), we divide by the square root of the number of POD modes allocated in **a** for each Reynolds number. The classified regime is the one that has the largest magnitude after this process.

Although the classification accuracy is high, many of the false classifications are due to categorizing a Reynolds number from a neighboring flow, i.e. Reynolds 1000 is often mistaken for Reynolds number 800. This is due to the fact that these two Reynolds numbers are strikingly similar and the algorithm has a difficult time separating their modal structures. Fig. 12.20 shows a schematic of the sparse sensing configuration along with the reconstruction of the pressure field achieved at $Re = 1000$ with 15 sensors. Classification and reconstruction performance can be improved using other methods for constructing the sensing matrix **P** [80, 98, 462, 281, 374, 89, 540]. Regardless, this example demonstrate the usage of sparsity promoting techniques for POD mode selection (ℓ_1 optimization) and subsequent reconstruction (ℓ_2 projection).

Finally, to visualize the entire sparse sensing and reconstruction process more carefully, Fig. 12.21 shows both the Reynolds number reconstruction for the time-varying flow field along with the pressure field and flow field reconstructions at select locations in time. Note that the SRC scheme along with the supervised ML library provide an effective method for characterizing the flow strictly through sparse measurements. For higher Reynolds numbers, it becomes much more difficult to accurately classify the flow field with such a small number of sensors. However, this does not necessarily jeopardize the ability to reconstruct the pressure field as many of the library elements at higher Reynolds numbers are fairly similar.

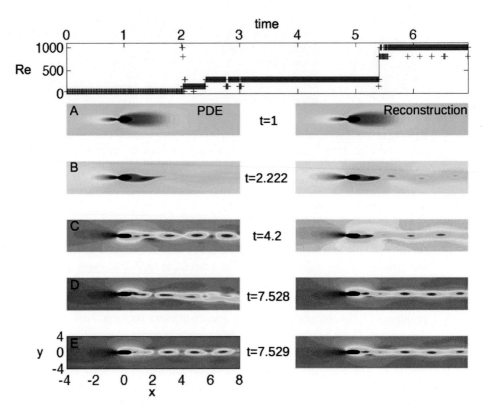

Figure 12.21 Sparse-sensing Reynolds number identification and pressure-field reconstruction for a time-varying flow. The top panel shows the actual Reynolds number used in the full simulation (solid line) along with its compressive sensing identification (crosses). Panels A-D show the reconstruction of the pressure field at four different locations in time (top panel) demonstrating an accurate (qualitatively) reconstruction of the pressure field. (The left side the simulated pressure field is presented, while the right side contains the reconstruction.) Note that for higher Reynolds numbers, the classification becomes more difficult. (*reproduced from Bright et al. [80]*)

Suggested Reading

Texts

(1) **Certified reduced basis methods for parametrized partial differential equations,** by J. Hesthaven, G. Rozza and B. Stamm, 2015 [244].

(2) **Reduced basis methods for partial differential equations: An introduction,** by A. Quarteroni, A. Manzoni and N. Federico, 2015 [442].

(3) **Model reduction and approximation: Theory and algorithms,** by P. Benner, A. Cohen, M. Ohlberger and K. Willcox, 2017 [54].

Papers and Reviews

(1) **A survey of model reduction methods for parametric systems,** by P. Benner, S. Gugercin and K. Willcox, *SIAM Review*, 2015 [53].

(2) **Model reduction using proper orthogonal decomposition,** by S. Volkwein, *Lecture Notes, Institute of Mathematics and Scientific Computing, University of Graz*, 2011 [542].

(3) **Nonlinear model reduction for dynamical systems using sparse sensor locations from learned libraries,** by S. Sargsyan, S. L. Brunton and J. N. Kutz, *Physical Review E*, 2015 [462].

(4) **An online method for interpolating linear parametric reduced-order models,** by D. Amsallem and C. Farhat, *SIAM Journal of Scientific Computing*, 2011 [10].

Glossary

Adjoint – For a finite-dimensional linear map (i.e., a matrix $\mathbf{A}$), the adjoint $\mathbf{A}^*$ is given by the complex conjugate transpose of the matrix. In the infinite-dimensional context, the adjoint $\mathcal{A}^*$ of a linear operator $\mathcal{A}$ is defined so that $\langle \mathcal{A}f, g \rangle = \langle f, \mathcal{A}^*g \rangle$, where $\langle \cdot, \cdot \rangle$ is an inner product.

Akaike information criterion (AIC) – An estimator of the relative quality of statistical models for a given set of data. Given a collection of models for the data, AIC estimates the quality of each model, relative to each of the other models. Thus, AIC provides a means for model selection.

Backpropagation (Backprop) – A method used for computing the gradient descent required for the training of neural networks. Based upon the chain rule, backprop exploits the compositional nature of NNs in order to frame an optimization problem for updating the weights of the network. It is commonly used to train deep neural networks.

Balanced input–output model – A model expressed in a coordinate system where the states are ordered hierarchically in terms of their joint controllability and observability. The controllability and observability Gramians are equal and diagonal for such a system.

Bayesian information criterion (BIC) – An estimator of the relative quality of statistical models for a given set of data. Given a collection of models for the data, BIC estimates the quality of each model, relative to each of the other models. Thus, BIC provides a means for model selection.

Classification – A general process related to categorization, the process in which ideas and objects are recognized, differentiated, and understood. Classification is a common task for machine learning algorithms.

Closed-loop control – A control architecture where the actuation is informed by sensor data about the output of the system.

Clustering – A task of grouping a set of objects in such a way that objects in the same group (called a cluster) are more similar (in some sense) to each other than to those in other groups (clusters). It is a primary goal of exploratory data mining, and a common technique for statistical data analysis.

Coherent structure – A spatial mode that is correlated with the data from a system.

Compression – The process of reducing the size of a high-dimensional vector or array by approximating it as a sparse vector in a transformed basis. For example, MP3 and JPG compression use the Fourier basis or Wavelet basis to compress audio or image signals.

Compressed sensing – The process of reconstructing a high-dimensional vector signal from a random under sampling of the data using the fact that the high-dimensional signal is sparse in a known transform basis, such as the Fourier basis.

Control theory – The framework for modifying a dynamical system to conform to desired engineering specification through sensing and actuation.

Controllability – A system is controllable if it is possible to steer the system to any state with actuation. Degrees of controllability are determined by the controllability Gramian.

Convex optimization – An algorithmic frameworks for minimizing convex functions over convex sets.

Convolutional neural network (CNN) – A class of deep, feed-forward neural networks that is especially amenable to analyzing natural images. The convolution is typically a spatial filter which synthesizes local (neighboring) spatial information.

Cross-validation – A model validation technique for assessing how the results of a statistical analysis will generalize to an independent (withheld) data set.

Data matrix – A matrix where each column vector is a snapshot of the state of a system at a particular instance in time. These snapshots may be *sequential* in time, or they may come from an ensemble of initial conditions or experiments.

Deep learning – A class of machine learning algorithms that typically uses deep CNNs for feature extraction and transformation. Deep learning can leverage supervised (e.g., classification) and/or unsupervised (e.g., pattern analysis) algorithms, learning multiple levels of representations that correspond to different levels of abstraction; the levels form a hierarchy of concepts.

DMD amplitude – The amplitude of a given DMD mode as expressed in the data. These amplitudes may be interpreted as the significance of a given DMD mode, similar to the power spectrum in the FFT.

DMD eigenvalue – Eigenvalues of the best-fit DMD operator $\mathbf{A}$ (see *dynamic mode decomposition*) representing an oscillation frequency and a growth or decay term.

DMD mode (also *dynamic mode*) – An eigenvector of the best-fit DMD operator $\mathbf{A}$ (see *dynamic mode decomposition*). These modes are spatially coherent and oscillate in time at a fixed frequency and a growth or decay rate.

Dynamic mode decomposition (DMD) – The leading eigendecomposition of a best-fit linear operator $\mathbf{A} = \mathbf{X}'\mathbf{X}^{\dagger}$ that propagates the data matrix $\mathbf{X}$ into a future data matrix $\mathbf{X}'$. The eigenvectors of $\mathbf{A}$ are DMD modes and the corresponding eigenvalues determine the time dynamics of these modes.

Dynamical system – A mathematical model for the dynamic evolution of a system. Typically, a dynamical system is formulated in terms of ordinary differential equations on a state-space. The resulting equations may be linear or nonlinear and may also include the effect of actuation inputs and represent outputs as sensor measurements of the state.

Eigensystem realization algorithm (ERA) – A system identification technique that produces balanced input–output models of a system from impulse response data. ERA has been shown to produce equivalent models to balanced proper orthogonal decomposition and dynamic mode decomposition under some circumstances.

Emission – The measurement functions for a hidden Markov model.

Feedback control – Closed-loop control where sensors measure the downstream effect of actuators, so that information is fed back to the actuators. Feedback is essential for robust control where model uncertainty and instability may be counteracted with fast sensor feedback.

Feedforward control – Control where sensors measure the upstream disturbances to a system, so that information is fed forward to actuators to cancel disturbances proactively.

Fast Fourier transform (FFT) – A numerical algorithm to compute the discrete Fourier transform (DFT) in $\mathcal{O}(n \log(n))$ operations. The FFT has revolutionized modern computations, signal processing, compression, and data transmission.

Fourier transform – A change of basis used to represent a function in terms of an infinite series of sines and cosines.

Galerkin projection – A process by which governing partial differential equations are reduced into ordinary differential equations in terms of the dynamics of the coefficients of a set of orthogonal basis modes that are used to approximate the solution.

Gramian – The controllability (resp. observability) Gramian determines the degree to which a state is controllable (resp. observable) via actuation (resp. via estimation). The Gramian establishes an inner product on the state space.

Hidden Markov model (HMM) – A Markov model where there is a hidden state that is only observed through a set of measurements known as emissions.

Hilbert space – A generalized vector space with an inner product. When referred to in this text, a Hilbert space typically refers to an infinite-dimensional function space. These spaces are also complete metric spaces, providing a sufficient mathematical framework to enable calculus on functions.

Incoherent measurements – Measurements that have a small inner product with the basis vectors of a sparsifying transform. For instance, single pixel measurements (i.e., spatial delta functions) are incoherent with respect to the spatial Fourier transform basis, since these single pixel measurements excite all frequencies and do not preferentially align with any single frequency.

Kalman filter – An estimator that reconstructs the full state of a dynamical system from measurements of a time-series of the sensor outputs and actuation inputs. A Kalman filter is itself a dynamical system that is constructed for observable systems to stably converge to the true state of the system. The Kalman filter is optimal for linear systems with Gaussian process and measurement noise of a known magnitude.

Koopman eigenfunction – An eigenfunction of the Koopman operator. These eigenfunctions correspond to measurements on the state-space of a dynamical system that form intrinsic coordinates. In other words, these intrinsic measurements will evolve linearly in time despite the underlying system being nonlinear.

Koopman operator – An infinite-dimensional linear operator that propagates measurement functions from an infinite dimensional Hilbert space through a dynamical system.

Least squares regression – A regression technique where a best-fit line or vector is found by minimizing the sum of squares of the error between the model and the data.

Linear quadratic regulator (LQR) – An optimal proportional feedback controller for full-state feedback, which balances the objectives of regulating the state while not expending too much control energy. The proportional gain matrix is determined by solving an algebraic Riccati equation.

Linear system – A system where superposition of any two inputs results in the superposition of the two corresponding outputs. In other words, doubling the input doubles the output. Linear time-invariant dynamical systems are characterized by linear operators, which are represented as matrices.

Low rank – A property of a matrix where the number of linearly independent rows and columns is small compared with the size of the matrix. Generally, low-rank approximations are sought for large data matrices.

Machine learning – A set of statistical tools and algorithms that are capable of extracting the dominant patterns in data. The data mining can be supervised or unsupervised, with the goal of clustering, classification and prediction.

Markov model – A probabilistic dynamical system where the state vector contains the probability that the system will be in a given state; thus, this state vector must always sum to unity. The dynamics are given by the Markov transition matrix, which is constructed so that each row sums to unity.

Markov parameters – The output measurements of a dynamical system in response to an impulsive input.

Max pooling – A data down-sampling strategy whereby an input representation (image, hidden-layer output matrix, etc.) is reduced in dimensionality, thus allowing for assumptions to be made about features contained in the down-sampled sub-regions.

Model predictive control (MPC) – A form of optimal control that optimizes a control policy over a finite-time horizon, based on a model. The models used for MPC are typically linear and may be determined empirically via system identification.

Moore's law – The observation that transistor density, and hence processor speed, increases exponentially in time. Moore's law is commonly used to predict future computational power and the associated increase in the scale of problem that will be computationally feasible.

Multiscale – The property of having many scales in space and/or time. Many systems, such as turbulence, exhibit spatial and temporal scales that vary across many orders of magnitude.

Observability – A system is observable if it is possible to estimate any system state with a time-history of the available sensors. Degrees of observability are determined by the observability Gramian.

Observable function – A function that measures some property of the state of a system. Observable functions are typically elements of a Hilbert space.

Optimization – Generally a set of algorithms that find the "best available" values of some objective function given a defined domain (or input), including a variety of different types of objective functions and different types of domains. Mathematically, optimization aims to maximize or minimize real function by systematically choosing input values from within an allowed set and computing the value of the function. The generalization of optimization theory and techniques to other formulations constitutes a large area of applied mathematics.

Overdetermined system – A system $\mathbf{Ax} = \mathbf{b}$ where there are more equations than unknowns. Usually there is no exact solution $\mathbf{x}$ to an overdetermined system, unless the vector $\mathbf{b}$ is in the column space of $\mathbf{A}$.

Pareto front – The allocation of resources from which it is impossible to reallocate so as to make any one individual or preference criterion better off without making at least one individual or preference criterion worse off.

Perron-Frobenius operator – The adjoint of the Koopman operator, the Perron-Frobenius operator is an infinite-dimensional operator that advances probability density functions through a dynamical system.

Power spectrum – The squared magnitude of each coefficient of a Fourier transform of a signal. The power corresponds to the amount of each frequency required to reconstruct a given signal.

Principal component – A spatially correlated mode in a given data set, often computed using the singular value decomposition of the data after the mean has been subtracted.

Principal components analysis (PCA) – A decomposition of a data matrix into a hierarchy of principal component vectors that are ordered from most correlated to least correlated with the data. PCA is computed by taking the singular value decomposition of the data after subtracting the mean. In this case, each singular value represents the variance of the corresponding principal component (singular vector) in the data.

Proper orthogonal decomposition (POD) – The decomposition of data from a dynamical system into a hierarchical set of orthogonal modes, often using the singular value decomposition. When the data consists of velocity measurements of a system, such as an incompressible fluid, then the proper orthogonal decomposition orders modes in terms of the amount of energy these modes contain in the given data.

Pseudo-inverse – The pseudo-inverse generalizes the matrix inverse for non-square matrices, and is often used to compute the least-squares solution to a system of equations. The SVD is a common method to compute the pseudo-inverse: given the SVD $\mathbf{X} = \mathbf{U\Sigma V}^*$, the pseudo-inverse is $\mathbf{X}^\dagger = \mathbf{V\Sigma}^{-1}\mathbf{U}^*$.

Recurrent neural network (RNN) – A class of neural networks where connections between units form a directed graph along a sequence. This allows it to exhibit dynamic temporal behavior for a time sequence.

Reduced-order model (ROM) – A model of a high-dimensional system in terms of a low-dimensional state. Typically, a reduced-order model balances accuracy with computational cost of the model.

Regression – A statistical model that represents an outcome variable in terms of indicator variables. Least-squares regression is a linear regression that finds the line of best fit to data; when generalized to higher dimensions and multi-linear regression, this generalizes to principal components regression. Nonlinear regression, dynamic regression, and functional or semantic regression are used in system identification, model reduction, and machine learning.

Restricted isometry property (RIP) – The property that a matrix acts like a unitary matrix, or an isometry map, on sparse vectors. In other words, the distance between any two sparse vectors is preserved if these vectors are mapped through a matrix that satisfies the restricted isometry property.

Robust control – A field of control that penalizes *worst case scenario* control outcomes, thus promoting controllers that are robust to uncertainties, disturbances, and unmodeled dynamics.

Robust statistics – Methods for producing good statistical estimates for data drawn from a wide range of probability distributions, especially for distributions that are not normal and where outliers compromise predictive capabilities.

Singular value decomposition (SVD) – Given a matrix $\mathbf{X} \in \mathbb{C}^{n \times m}$, the SVD is given by $\mathbf{X} = \mathbf{U\Sigma V}^*$ where $\mathbf{U} \in \mathbb{C}^{n \times n}$, $\mathbf{\Sigma} \in \mathbb{C}^{n \times m}$, and $\mathbf{V} \in \mathbb{C}^{m \times m}$. The matrices $\mathbf{U}$ and $\mathbf{V}$ are unitary, so that $\mathbf{UU}^* = \mathbf{U}^*\mathbf{U} = \mathbf{I}$ and $\mathbf{VV}^* = \mathbf{V}^*\mathbf{V} = \mathbf{I}$. The matrix $\mathbf{\Sigma}$ has entries along the diagonal corresponding to the singular values that are ordered from largest to smallest. This produces a hierarchical matrix decomposition that splits a matrix into a sum of rank-1 matrices given by the outer product of a column vector (left singular vector) with a row vector (conjugate transpose of right singular vector). These rank-1 matrices are ordered by the singular value so that the first r rank-1 matrices form the *best* rank-r matrix approximation of the original matrix in a least-squares sense.

Snapshot – A single high-dimensional measurement of a system at a particular time. A number of snapshots collected at a sequence of times may be arranged as column vectors in a data matrix.

Sparse identification of nonlinear dynamics (SINDy) – A nonlinear system identification framework used to simultaneously identify the nonlinear structure and parameters of a dynamical system from data. Various sparse optimization techniques may be used to determine SINDy models.

Sparsity – A vector is *sparse* if most of its entries are zero or nearly zero. Sparsity refers to the observation that most data are sparse when represented as vectors in an appropriate transformed basis, such as Fourier or POD bases.

Spectrogram – A short-time Fourier transform computed on a moving window, which results in a time-frequency plot of which frequencies are active at a given time. The spectrogram is useful for characterizing nonperiodic signals, where the frequency content evolves over time, as in music.

State space – The set of all possible system states. Often the state-space is a vector space, such as $\mathbb{R}^n$, although it may also be a smooth manifold $\mathcal{M}$.

Stochastic gradient descent – Also known as incremental gradient descent, it allows one to approximate the gradient with a single data point instead of all available data. At each step of the gradient descent, a randomly chosen data point is used to compute the gradient direction.

System identification – The process by which a model is constructed for a system from measurement data, possibly after perturbing the system.

Time delay coordinates – An augmented set of coordinates constructed by considering a measurement at the current time along with a number of times in the past at fixed intervals from the current time. Time delay coordinates are often useful in reconstructing attractor dynamics for systems that do not have enough measurements, as in the Takens embedding theorem.

Total least squares – A least-squares regression algorithm that minimizes the error on both the inputs and the outputs. Geometrically, this corresponds to finding the line that minimizes the sum of squares of the total distance to all points, rather than the sum of squares of the vertical distance to all points.

Uncertainty quantification (UQ) – The principled characterization and management of uncertainty in engineering systems. Uncertainty quantification often involves the application of powerful tools from probability and statistics to dynamical systems.

Underdetermined system – A system $\mathbf{Ax} = \mathbf{b}$ where there are fewer equations than unknowns. Generally the system has infinitely many solutions $\mathbf{x}$ unless $\mathbf{b}$ is not in the column space of $\mathbf{A}$.

Unitary matrix – A matrix whose complex conjugate transpose is also its inverse. All eigenvalues of a unitary matrix are on the complex unit circle, and the action of a unitary matrix may be through of as a change of coordinates that preserves the Euclidean distance between any two vectors.

Wavelet – A generalized function, or family of functions, used to generalize the Fourier transform to approximate more complex and multiscale signals.

Bibliography

[1] Ralph Abraham, Jerrold E. Marsden, and Tudor Ratiu. *Manifolds, Tensor Analysis, and Applications*, volume 75 of *Applied Mathematical Sciences*. Springer-Verlag, 1988.

[2] Ralph Abraham and Jerrold E. Marsden. *Foundations of Mechanics*, volume 36. Benjamin/Cummings Publishing Company Reading, Massachusetts, 1978.

[3] Mradul Agrawal, Sandeep Vidyashankar, and Ke Huang. On-chip implementation of ECoG signal data decoding in brain-computer interface. In *Mixed-Signal Testing Workshop (IMSTW), 2016 IEEE 21st International*, pages 1–6. IEEE, 2016.

[4] Rakesh Agrawal, Ramakrishnan Srikant, et al. Fast algorithms for mining association rules. In *Proc. 20th int. conf. very large data bases, VLDB*, volume 1215, pages 487–499, 1994.

[5] Hyo-Sung Ahn, YangQuan Chen, and Kevin L. Moore. Iterative learning control: Brief survey and categorization. *IEEE Transactions on Systems, Man, and Cybernetics, Part C (Applications and Reviews)*, 37(6):1099–1121, 2007.

[6] Hirotugu Akaike. Fitting autoregressive models for prediction. *Annals of the Institute of Statistical Mathematics*, 21(1):243–247, 1969.

[7] Hirotugu Akaike. A new look at the statistical model identification. *Automatic Control, IEEE Transactions on*, 19(6):716–723, 1974.

[8] W. O. Amrein and Anne-Marie Berthier. On support properties of Lp-functions and their Fourier transforms. *Journal of Functional Analysis*, 24(3):258–267, 1977.

[9] David Amsallem, Julien Cortial, and Charbel Farhat. On-demand cfd-based aeroelastic predictions using a database of reduced-order bases and models. In *47th AIAA Aerospace Sciences Meeting Including The New Horizons Forum and Aerospace Exposition*, page 800, 2009.

[10] David Amsallem and Charbel Farhat. An online method for interpolating linear parametric reduced-order models. *SIAM Journal on Scientific Computing*, 33(5):2169–2198, 2011.

[11] David Amsallem, Matthew J. Zahr, and Kyle Washabaugh. Fast local reduced basis updates for the efficient reduction of nonlinear systems with hyper-reduction. *Advances in Computational Mathematics*, 41(5):1187–1230, 2015.

[12] Joakim Andén and Stéphane Mallat. Deep scattering spectrum. *IEEE Transactions on Signal Processing*, 62(16):4114–4128, 2014.

[13] Edward Anderson, Zhaojun Bai, Christian Bischof, Susan Blackford, James Demmel, Jack Dongarra, Jeremy Du Croz, Anne Greenbaum, S. Hammerling, Alan McKenney, et al. *LAPACK Users' Guide*, volume 9. SIAM, 1999.

[14] Jeffrey L. Anderson. An ensemble adjustment Kalman filter for data assimilation. *Monthly Weather Review*, 129(12):2884–2903, 2001.

[15] Claus A. Andersson and Rasmus Bro. The n-way toolbox for matlab. *Chemometrics and Intelligent Laboratory Systems*, 52(1):1–4, 2000.

[16] Marc Antonini, Michel Barlaud, Pierre Mathieu, and Ingrid Daubechies. Image coding using wavelet transform. *IEEE Transactions on Image Processing*, 1(2):205–220, 1992.

[17] Athanasios C. Antoulas. *Approximation of large-scale dynamical systems*. SIAM, 2005.

[18] Hassan Arbabi and Igor Mezić. Ergodic theory, dynamic mode decomposition and computation of spectral properties of the Koopman operator. *SIAM Journal on Applied Dynamical Systems,* 16 (4):2096–2126, 2017.

[19] Kartik B. Ariyur and Miroslav Krstić. *Real-Time Optimization by Extremum-Seeking Control.* Wiley, Hoboken, New Jersey, 2003.

[20] Travis Askham and J. Nathan Kutz. Variable projection methods for an optimized dynamic mode decomposition. *SIAM Journal on Applied Dynamical Systems,* 17 (1):380–416, 2018.

[21] Patricia Astrid. Fast reduced order modeling technique for large scale LTV systems. In *American Control Conference, 2004. Proceedings of the 2004,* volume 1, pages 762–767. IEEE, 2004.

[22] Karl Johan Aström and Richard M. Murray. *Feedback Systems: An Introduction for Scientists and Engineers.* Princeton University Press, 2010.

[23] M. F. A. Azeez and A. F. Vakakis. Proper orthogonal decomposition (POD) of a class of vibroimpact oscillations. *Journal of Sound and Vibration,* 240(5):859–889, 2001.

[24] K. Bache and M. Lichman. UCI machine learning repository, 2013.

[25] Brett W. Bader and Tamara G. Kolda. Efficient MATLAB computations with sparse and factored tensors. *SIAM Journal on Scientific Computing,* 30(1):205–231, December 2007.

[26] S. Bagheri, L. Brandt, and D. S. Henningson. Input-output analysis, model reduction and control of the flat-plate boundary layer. *Journal of Fluid Mechanics,* 620:263–298, 2009.

[27] S. Bagheri, J. Hoepffner, P. J. Schmid, and D. S. Henningson. Input-output analysis and control design applied to a linear model of spatially developing flows. *Applied Mechanics Reviews,* 62(2):020803–1..27, 2009.

[28] Shervin Bagheri. Koopman-mode decomposition of the cylinder wake. *Journal of Fluid Mechanics,* 726:596–623, 2013.

[29] Z. Bai, S. L. Brunton, B. W. Brunton, J. N. Kutz, E. Kaiser, A. Spohn, and B. R. Noack. Data-driven methods in fluid dynamics: Sparse classification from experimental data. In *Invited Chapter for Whither Turbulence and Big Data in the 21st Century,* 2015.

[30] Z. Bai, E. Kaiser, J. L. Proctor, J. N. Kutz, and S. L. Brunton. Dynamic mode decomposition for compressive system identification. *arXiv preprint arXiv:*1710.07737, 2017.

[31] Zhe Bai, Thakshila Wimalajeewa, Zachary Berger, Guannan Wang, Mark Glauser, and Pramod K. Varshney. Low-dimensional approach for reconstruction of airfoil data via compressive sensing. *AIAA Journal,* 53(4):920–933, 2014.

[32] Maciej J. Balajewicz, Earl H. Dowell, and Bernd R. Noack. Low-dimensional modelling of high-Reynolds-number shear flows incorporating constraints from the Navier–Stokes equation. *Journal of Fluid Mechanics,* 729:285–308, 2013.

[33] Madhusudhanan Balasubramanian, Stanislav Zabic, Christopher Bowd, Hilary W. Thompson, Peter Wolenski, S. Sitharama Iyengar, Bijaya B. Karki, and Linda M. Zangwill. A framework for detecting glaucomatous progression in the optic nerve head of an eye using proper orthogonal decomposition. *IEEE Transactions on Information Technology in Biomedicine,* 13(5):781–793, 2009.

[34] B. Bamieh and L. Giarré. Identification of linear parameter varying models. *International Journal of Robust and Nonlinear Control,* 12:841–853, 2002.

[35] Andrzej Banaszuk, Kartik B. Ariyur, Miroslav Krstić, and Clas A. Jacobson. An adaptive algorithm for control of combustion instability. *Automatica,* 40(11):1965–1972, 2004.

[36] Andrzej Banaszuk, Satish Narayanan, and Youping Zhang. Adaptive control of flow separation in a planar diffuser. *AIAA paper,* 617:2003, 2003.

[37] Andrzej Banaszuk, Youping Zhang, and Clas A. Jacobson. Adaptive control of combustion instability using extremum-seeking. In *American Control Conference, 2000. Proceedings of the 2000,* volume 1, pages 416–422. IEEE, 2000.

[38] S. P. Banks. Infinite-dimensional Carleman linearization, the Lie series and optimal control of non-linear partial differential equations. *International Journal of Systems Science*, 23(5):663–675, 1992.

[39] R. G. Baraniuk. Compressive sensing. *IEEE Signal Processing Magazine*, 24(4):118–120, 2007.

[40] R. G. Baraniuk, V. Cevher, M. F. Duarte, and C. Hegde. Model-based compressive sensing. *IEEE Transactions on Information Theory*, 56(4):1982–2001, 2010.

[41] Maxime Barrault, Yvon Maday, Ngoc Cuong Nguyen, and Anthony T. Patera. An empirical interpolation method: application to efficient reduced-basis discretization of partial differential equations. *Comptes Rendus Mathematique*, 339(9):667–672, 2004.

[42] J. Basley, L. R. Pastur, N. Delprat, and F. Lusseyran. Space-time aspects of a three-dimensional multi-modulated open cavity flow. *Physics of Fluids (1994-present)*, 25(6):064105, 2013.

[43] J. Basley, L. R. Pastur, F. Lusseyran, T. M. Faure, and N. Delprat. Experimental investigation of global structures in an incompressible cavity flow using time-resolved PIV. *Experiments in Fluids*, 50(4):905–918, 2011.

[44] Walter Baur and Volker Strassen. The complexity of partial derivatives. *Theoretical Computer Science*, 22(3):317–330, 1983.

[45] J. F. Beaudoin, O. Cadot, J. L. Aider, and J. E. Wesfreid. Bluff-body drag reduction by extremum-seeking control. *Journal of Fluids and Structures*, 22:973–978, 2006.

[46] Jean-Francois Beaudoin, Olivier Cadot, Jean-Luc Aider, and José-Eduardo Wesfreid. Drag reduction of a bluff body using adaptive control methods. *Physics of Fluids*, 18(8):085107, 2006.

[47] R. Becker, R. King, R. Petz, and W. Nitsche. Adaptive closed-loop control on a high-lift configuration using extremum seeking. *AIAA Journal*, 45(6):1382–92, 2007.

[48] P. N. Belhumeur, J. P. Hespanha, and D. J. Kriegman. Eigenfaces vs. Fisherfaces: Recognition using class specific linear projection. *IEEE Transactions on Pattern Analysis and Machine Intelligence (PAMI)*, 19(7):711–720, 1997.

[49] G. Bellani. Experimental studies of complex flows through image-based techniques. 2011.

[50] Brandt A. Belson, Jonathan H. Tu, and Clarence W. Rowley. Algorithm 945: modred—a parallelized model reduction library. *ACM Transactions on Mathematical Software*, 40(4):30, 2014.

[51] Michael Benedicks. On Fourier transforms of functions supported on sets of finite Lebesgue measure. *Journal of Mathematical Analysis and Applications*, 106(1):180–183, 1985.

[52] Yoshua Bengio, Pascal Lamblin, Dan Popovici, and Hugo Larochelle. Greedy layer-wise training of deep networks. In *Advances in Neural Information Processing Systems*, pages 153–160, 2007.

[53] P. Benner, S. Gugercin, and K Willcox. A survey of projection-based model reduction methods for parametric dynamical systems. *SIAM Review*, 57(4):483–531, 2015.

[54] Peter Benner, Albert Cohen, Mario Ohlberger, and Karen Willcox. *Model Reduction and Approximation: Theory and Algorithms*, volume 15. *SIAM*, 2017.

[55] Peter Benner, Jing-Rebecca Li, and Thilo Penzl. Numerical solution of large-scale Lyapunov equations, Riccati equations, and linear-quadratic optimal control problems. *Numerical Linear Algebra with Applications*, 15(9):755–777, 2008.

[56] E. Berger, M. Sastuba, D. Vogt, B. Jung, and H. B. Amor. Estimation of perturbations in robotic behavior using dynamic mode decomposition. *Journal of Advanced Robotics*, 29(5):331–343, 2015.

[57] G. Berkooz, P. Holmes, and J. L. Lumley. The proper orthogonal decomposition in the analysis of turbulent flows. *Annual Review of Fluid Mechanics*, 25:539–575, 1993.

[58] Gregory Beylkin, Ronald Coifman, and Vladimir Rokhlin. Fast wavelet transforms and numerical algorithms i. *Communications on Pure and Applied Mathematics*, 44(2):141–183, 1991.

[59] Stephen A. Billings. *Nonlinear System Identification: NARMAX Methods in the Time, Frequency, and Spatio-Temporal Domains*. John Wiley & Sons, 2013.

[60] P. Binetti, K. B. Ariyur, M. Krstić, and F. Bernelli. Formation flight optimization using extremum seeking feedback. *Journal of Guidance, Control, and Dynamics*, 26(1):132–142, 2003.

[61] G. D. Birkhoff and B. O. Koopman. Recent contributions to the ergodic theory. *Proceedings of the National Academy of Sciences*, 18(3):279–282, 1932.

[62] George D. Birkhoff. Proof of the ergodic theorem. *Proceedings of the National Academy of Sciences*, 17(12):656–660, 1931.

[63] Christopher M. Bishop. *Neural Networks for Pattern Recognition*. Oxford university press, 1995.

[64] Christopher M. Bishop. *Pattern Recognition and Machine Learning*. Springer New York, 2006.

[65] D. A. Bistrian and I. M. Navon. An improved algorithm for the shallow water equations model reduction: Dynamic mode decomposition vs POD. *International Journal for Numerical Methods in Fluids*, 2015.

[66] D. A. Bistrian and I. M. Navon. Randomized dynamic mode decomposition for non-intrusive reduced order modelling. *International Journal for Numerical Methods in Engineering*, 2016.

[67] Paola Bondi, Giuseppe Casalino, and Lucia Gambardella. On the iterative learning control theory for robotic manipulators. *IEEE Journal on Robotics and Automation*, 4(1):14–22, 1988.

[68] Josh Bongard and Hod Lipson. Automated reverse engineering of nonlinear dynamical systems. *Proceedings of the National Academy of Sciences*, 104(24):9943–9948, 2007.

[69] Jorge Luis Borges. The library of Babel. *Collected Fictions*, 1998.

[70] Bernhard E. Boser, Isabelle M. Guyon, and Vladimir N. Vapnik. A training algorithm for optimal margin classifiers. In *Proceedings of the Fifth Annual Workshop on Computational Learning Theory*, pages 144–152. ACM, 1992.

[71] H. Boulard and Y. Kamp. Autoassociative memory by multilayer perceptron and singular values decomposition. *Biol Cybern*, 59:291–294, 1989.

[72] George E. P. Box, Gwilym M. Jenkins, Gregory C. Reinsel, and Greta M. Ljung. *Time Series Analysis: Forecasting and Control*. John Wiley & Sons, 2015.

[73] Stephen Boyd, Leon O. Chua, and Charles A. Desoer. Analytical foundations of Volterra series. *IMA Journal of Mathematical Control and Information*, 1(3):243–282, 1984.

[74] Stephen Boyd and Lieven Vandenberghe. *Convex Pptimization*. Cambridge University Press, 2009.

[75] Antoneta Iuliana Bratcu, Iulian Munteanu, Seddik Bacha, and Bertrand Raison. Maximum power point tracking of grid-connected photovoltaic arrays by using extremum seeking control. *CEAI*, 10(4):3–12, 2008.

[76] Leo Breiman. Better subset regression using the nonnegative garrote. *Technometrics*, 37(4):373–384, 1995.

[77] Leo Breiman. Random forests. *Machine Learning*, 45(1):5–32, 2001.

[78] Leo Breiman et al. Statistical modeling: The two cultures (with comments and a rejoinder by the author). *Statistical Science*, 16(3):199–231, 2001.

[79] Leo Breiman, Jerome Friedman, Charles J. Stone, and Richard A. Olshen. *Classification and Regression Trees*. CRC press, 1984.

[80] I. Bright, G. Lin, and J. N. Kutz. Compressive sensing and machine learning strategies for characterizing the flow around a cylinder with limited pressure measurements. *Physics of Fluids*, 25(127102):1–15, 2013.

[81] Ido Bright, Guang Lin, and J. Nathan Kutz. Classification of spatio-temporal data via asynchronous sparse sampling: Application to flow around a cylinder. *Multiscale Modeling & Simulation*, 14 (2), 823–838, 2016.

[82] Sergey Brin and Lawrence Page. The anatomy of a large-scale hypertextual web search engine. *Computer Networks and ISDN Systems*, 30(1-7):107–117, 1998.

[83] Douglas Bristow, Marina Tharayil, Andrew G. Alleyne, et al. A survey of iterative learning control. *Control Systems, IEEE*, 26(3):96–114, 2006.

[84] Rasmus Bro. Parafac. tutorial and applications. *Chemometrics and Intelligent Laboratory Systems*, 38(2):149–171, 1997.

[85] Alexander Broad, T. D. Murphey, and Brenna Argall. Learning models for shared control of human-machine systems with unknown dynamics. *Robotics: Science and Systems Proceedings*, 2017.

[86] Roger W. Brockett. Volterra series and geometric control theory. *Automatica*, 12(2):167–176, 1976.

[87] David S. Broomhead and David Lowe. Radial basis functions, multi-variable functional interpolation and adaptive networks. Technical report, Royal Signals and Radar Establishment Malvern (United Kingdom), 1988.

[88] D. S. Broomhead and R Jones. Time-series analysis. In *Proceedings of the Royal Society of London A: Mathematical, Physical and Engineering Sciences*, volume 423, pages 103–121. The Royal Society, 1989.

[89] B. W. Brunton, S. L. Brunton, J. L. Proctor, and J. N. Kutz. Sparse sensor placement optimization for classification. *SIAM Journal on Applied Mathematics*, 76(5):2099–2122, 2016.

[90] B. W. Brunton, L. A. Johnson, J. G. Ojemann, and J. N. Kutz. Extracting spatial–temporal coherent patterns in large-scale neural recordings using dynamic mode decomposition. *Journal of Neuroscience Methods*, 258:1–15, 2016.

[91] S. L. Brunton, B. W. Brunton, J. L. Proctor, E. Kaiser, and J. N. Kutz. Chaos as an intermittently forced linear system. *Nature Communications*, 8(19):1–9, 2017.

[92] S. L. Brunton, B. W. Brunton, J. L. Proctor, and J. N Kutz. Koopman invariant subspaces and finite linear representations of nonlinear dynamical systems for control. *PLoS ONE*, 11(2):e0150171, 2016.

[93] S. L. Brunton, X. Fu, and J. N. Kutz. Extremum-seeking control of a mode-locked laser. *IEEE Journal of Quantum Electronics*, 49(10):852–861, 2013.

[94] S. L. Brunton and B. R. Noack. Closed-loop turbulence control: Progress and challenges. *Applied Mechanics Reviews*, 67:050801–1–050801–48, 2015.

[95] S. L. Brunton, J. L. Proctor, and J. N. Kutz. Discovering governing equations from data by sparse identification of nonlinear dynamical systems. *Proceedings of the National Academy of Sciences*, 113(15):3932–3937, 2016.

[96] S. L. Brunton, J. L. Proctor, J. H. Tu, and J. N. Kutz. Compressed sensing and dynamic mode decomposition. *Journal of Computational Dynamics*, 2(2):165–191, 2015.

[97] S. L. Brunton and C. W. Rowley. Maximum power point tracking for photovoltaic optimization using ripple-based extremum seeking control. *IEEE Transactions on Power Electronics*, 25(10):2531–2540, 2010.

[98] S. L. Brunton, J. H. Tu, I. Bright, and J. N. Kutz. Compressive sensing and low-rank libraries for classification of bifurcation regimes in nonlinear dynamical systems. *SIAM Journal on Applied Dynamical Systems*, 13(4):1716–1732, 2014.

[99] Steven L. Brunton, Xing Fu, and J. Nathan Kutz. Self-tuning fiber lasers. *IEEE Journal of Selected Topics in Quantum Electronics*, 20(5), 2014.

[100] Steven L Brunton, Joshua L Proctor, and J Nathan Kutz. Sparse identification of nonlinear dynamics with control (SINDYc). *IFAC NOLCOS*, 49(18):710–715, 2016.

[101] D. Buche, Peter Stoll, Rolf Dornberger, and Petros Koumoutsakos. Multiobjective evolutionary algorithm for the optimization of noisy combustion processes. *Systems, Man, and Cybernetics, Part C: Applications and Reviews, IEEE Transactions on*, 32(4):460–473, 2002.

[102] Marko Budišić and Igor Mezić. An approximate parametrization of the ergodic partition using time averaged observables. In *Decision and Control, 2009 held jointly with the 2009 28th Chinese Control Conference. CDC/CCC 2009. Proceedings of the 48th IEEE Conference on*, pages 3162–3168. IEEE, 2009.

[103] Marko Budišić and Igor Mezić. Geometry of the ergodic quotient reveals coherent structures in flows. *Physica D: Nonlinear Phenomena*, 241(15):1255–1269, 2012.

[104] Marko Budišić, Ryan Mohr, and Igor Mezić. Applied Koopmanism a). *Chaos: An Interdisciplinary Journal of Nonlinear Science*, 22(4):047510, 2012.

[105] Kenneth P. Burnham and David R. Anderson. *Model Selection and Multimodel Inference: A Practical Information-Theoretic Approach*. Springer Science & Business Media, 2003.

[106] Peter A. Businger and Gene H. Golub. Algorithm 358: Singular value decomposition of a complex matrix [f1, 4, 5]. *Communications of the ACM*, 12(10):564–565, 1969.

[107] Eduardo F. Camacho and Carlos Bordons Alba. *Model Predictive Control*. Springer Science & Business Media, 2013.

[108] Erik Cambria, Guang-Bin Huang, Liyanaarachchi Lekamalage Chamara Kasun, Hongming Zhou, Chi Man Vong, Jiarun Lin, Jianping Yin, Zhiping Cai, Qiang Liu, Kuan Li, et al. Extreme learning machines [trends & controversies]. *IEEE Intelligent Systems*, 28(6):30–59, 2013.

[109] E. J. Candès. Compressive sensing. *Proceedings of the International Congress of Mathematics*, 2006.

[110] E. J. Candès, X. Li, Y. Ma, and J. Wright. Robust principal component analysis? *Journal of the ACM*, 58(3):11–1–11–37, 2011.

[111] E. J. Candès, J. Romberg, and T. Tao. Robust uncertainty principles: exact signal reconstruction from highly incomplete frequency information. *IEEE Transactions on Information Theory*, 52(2):489–509, 2006.

[112] E. J. Candès, J. Romberg, and T. Tao. Stable signal recovery from incomplete and inaccurate measurements. *Communications in Pure and Applied Mathematics*, 8(1207–1223), 59.

[113] E. J. Candès and T. Tao. Near optimal signal recovery from random projections: Universal encoding strategies? *IEEE Transactions on Information Theory*, 52(12):5406–5425, 2006.

[114] E. J. Candès and M. B. Wakin. An introduction to compressive sampling. *IEEE Signal Processing Magazine*, pages 21–30, 2008.

[115] Emmanuel J. Candes and Terence Tao. Decoding by linear programming. *Information Theory, IEEE Transactions on*, 51(12):4203–4215, 2005.

[116] Yanhua Cao, Jiang Zhu, Zhendong Luo, and IM Navon. Reduced-order modeling of the upper tropical pacific ocean model using proper orthogonal decomposition. *Computers & Mathematics with Applications*, 52(8):1373–1386, 2006.

[117] Yanhua Cao, Jiang Zhu, I Michael Navon, and Zhendong Luo. A reduced-order approach to four-dimensional variational data assimilation using proper orthogonal decomposition. *International Journal for Numerical Methods in Fluids*, 53(10):1571–1583, 2007.

[118] Kevin Carlberg, Matthew Barone, and Harbir Antil. Galerkin v. least-squares Petrov–Galerkin projection in nonlinear model reduction. *Journal of Computational Physics*, 330:693–734, 2017.

[119] Kevin Carlberg, Charbel Bou-Mosleh, and Charbel Farhat. Efficient non-linear model reduction via a least-squares Petrov–Galerkin projection and compressive tensor approximations. *International Journal for Numerical Methods in Engineering*, 86(2):155–181, 2011.

[120] Kevin Carlberg, Charbel Farhat, Julien Cortial, and David Amsallem. The GNAT method for nonlinear model reduction: effective implementation and application to computational fluid dynamics and turbulent flows. *Journal of Computational Physics*, 242:623–647, 2013.

[121] Torsten Carleman. Application de la théorie des équations intégrales linéaires aux systémes d'équations différentielles non linéaires. *Acta Mathematica*, 59(1):63–87, 1932.

[122] Torsten Carleman. Sur la théorie de l'équation intégrodifférentielle de boltzmann. *Acta Mathematica*, 60(1):91–146, 1933.

[123] Torsten Carleman. Sur les systemes lineaires aux dérivées partielles du premier ordrea deux variables. *CR Acad. Sci. Paris*, 197:471–474, 1933.

[124] J. Douglas Carroll and Jih-Jie Chang. Analysis of individual differences in multidimensional scaling via an N-way generalization of "Eckart-Young" decomposition. *Psychometrika*, 35:283–319, 1970.

[125] Rick Chartrand. Numerical differentiation of noisy, nonsmooth data. *ISRN Applied Mathematics*, 2011, 2011.

[126] Anindya Chatterjee. An introduction to the proper orthogonal decomposition. *Current Science*, 78(7):808–817, 2000.

[127] S. Chaturantabut and D. C. Sorensen. Nonlinear model reduction via discrete empirical interpolation. *SIAM Journal on Scientific Computing*, 32(5):2737–2764, 2010.

[128] K. K. Chen and C. W. Rowley. Normalized coprime robust stability and performance guarantees for reduced-order controllers. *IEEE Transactions on Automatic Control*, 58(4):1068–1073, 2013.

[129] K. K. Chen, J. H. Tu, and C. W. Rowley. Variants of dynamic mode decomposition: Boundary condition, Koopman, and Fourier analyses. *Journal of Nonlinear Science*, 22(6):887–915, 2012.

[130] Yangquan Chen, Kevin L Moore, and Hyo-Sung Ahn. Iterative learning control. In *Encyclopedia of the Sciences of Learning*, pages 1648–1652. Springer, 2012.

[131] Steve Cherry. Singular value decomposition analysis and canonical correlation analysis. *Journal of Climate*, 9(9):2003–2009, 1996.

[132] Kyunghyun Cho, Bart Van Merriënboer, Caglar Gulcehre, Dzmitry Bahdanau, Fethi Bougares, Holger Schwenk, and Yoshua Bengio. Learning phrase representations using rnn encoder-decoder for statistical machine translation. *arXiv preprint arXiv:1406.1078*, 2014.

[133] J. Y. Choi, M. Krstić, K. B. Ariyur, and J. S. Lee. Extremum seeking control for discrete-time systems. *IEEE Transactions on Automatic Control*, 47(2):318–323, FEB 2002.

[134] Youngsoo Choi, David Amsallem, and Charbel Farhat. Gradient-based constrained optimization using a database of linear reduced-order models. *arXiv preprint arXiv:1506.07849*, 2015.

[135] T. Colonius and K. Taira. A fast immersed boundary method using a nullspace approach and multi-domain far-field boundary conditions. *Computer Methods in Applied Mechanics and Engineering*, 197:2131–2146, 2008.

[136] James W. Cooley, Peter A. W. Lewis, and Peter D. Welch. Historical notes on the fast Fourier transform. *Proceedings of the IEEE*, 55(10):1675–1677, 1967.

[137] James W. Cooley and John W Tukey. An algorithm for the machine calculation of complex Fourier series. *Mathematics of Computation*, 19(90):297–301, 1965.

[138] Corinna Cortes and Vladimir Vapnik. Support-vector networks. *Machine Learning*, 20(3):273–297, 1995.

[139] Mark C. Cross and Pierre C. Hohenberg. Pattern formation outside of equilibrium. *Reviews of Modern Physics*, 65(3):851, 1993.

[140] James P. Crutchfield and Bruce S. McNamara. Equations of motion from a data series. *Complex Systems*, 1:417–452, 1987.

[141] Magnus Dam, Morten Brøns, Jens Juul Rasmussen, Volker Naulin, and Jan S. Hesthaven. Sparse identification of a predator-prey system from simulation data of a convection model. *Physics of Plasmas*, 24(2):022310, 2017.

[142] Bryan C. Daniels and Ilya Nemenman. Automated adaptive inference of phenomenological dynamical models. *Nature Communications*, 6, 2015.

[143] Bryan C. Daniels and Ilya Nemenman. Efficient inference of parsimonious phenomenological models of cellular dynamics using s-systems and alternating regression. *PloS one*, 10(3):e0119821, 2015.

[144] Suddhasattwa Das and Dimitrios Giannakis. Delay-coordinate maps and the spectra of Koopman operators. *arXiv preprint arXiv:1706.08544*, 2017.

[145] Ingrid Daubechies. The wavelet transform, time-frequency localization and signal analysis. *IEEE transactions on information theory*, 36(5):961–1005, 1990.

[146] Lawrence Davis et al. *Handbook of Genetic Algorithms*, volume 115. Van Nostrand Reinhold New York, 1991.

[147] Scott T. M. Dawson, Maziar S. Hemati, Matthew O. Williams, and Clarence W. Rowley. Characterizing and correcting for the effect of sensor noise in the dynamic mode decomposition. *Experiments in Fluids*, 57(3):1–19, 2016.

[148] Arthur P. Dempster, Nan M. Laird, and Donald B. Rubin. Maximum likelihood from incomplete data via the EM algorithm. *Journal of the Royal Statistical Society. Series B (methodological)*, pages 1–38, 1977.

[149] Santosh Devasia, Degang Chen, and Brad Paden. Nonlinear inversion-based output tracking. *Automatic Control, IEEE Transactions on*, 41(7):930–942, 1996.

[150] D. L. Donoho. Compressed sensing. *IEEE Transactions on Information Theory*, 52(4):1289–1306, 2006.

[151] D. L. Donoho and M. Gavish. Code supplement to "The optimal hard threshold for singular values is $4/\sqrt{3}$". http://purl.stanford.edu/vg705qn9070, 2014.

[152] David Donoho. 50 years of data science. In *Based on a Presentation at the Tukey Centennial Workshop*. NJ Princeton, 2015.

[153] David L. Donoho, Iain M Johnstone, Jeffrey C Hoch, and Alan S Stern. Maximum entropy and the nearly black object. *Journal of the Royal Statistical Society. Series B (Methodological)*, pages 41–81, 1992.

[154] David L. Donoho and Jain M. Johnstone. Ideal spatial adaptation by wavelet shrinkage. *Biometrika*, 81(3):425–455, 1994.

[155] J. C. Doyle. Guaranteed margins for LQG regulators. *IEEE Transactions on Automatic Control*, 23(4):756–757, 1978.

[156] J. C. Doyle, K. Glover, P. P. Khargonekar, and B. A. Francis. State-space solutions to standard H_2 and H_∞ control problems. *IEEE Transactions on Automatic Control*, 34(8):831–847, 1989.

[157] John C. Doyle, Bruce A. Francis, and Allen R. Tannenbaum. *Feedback Control Theory*. Courier Corporation, 2013.

[158] Petros Drineas and Michael W. Mahoney. A randomized algorithm for a tensor-based generalization of the singular value decomposition. *Linear Algebra and Its Applications*, 420(2-3):553–571, 2007.

[159] Zlatko Drmac and Serkan Gugercin. A new selection operator for the discrete empirical interpolation method—improved a priori error bound and extensions. *SIAM Journal on Scientific Computing*, 38(2):A631–A648, 2016.

[160] Qiang Du and Max Gunzburger.   Model reduction by proper orthogonal decomposition coupled with centroidal voronoi tessellations (keynote). In *ASME 2002 Joint US-European Fluids Engineering Division Conference*, pages 1401–1406. American Society of Mechanical Engineers, 2002.

[161] R. O. Duda, P. E. Hart, and D. G. Stork. *Pattern Classification*. Wiley-Interscience, 2000.

[162] Jed A. Duersch and Ming Gu. Randomized QR with column pivoting. *SIAM Journal on Scientific Computing*, 39(4):C263–C291, 2017.

[163] D. Duke, D. Honnery, and J. Soria. Experimental investigation of nonlinear instabilities in annular liquid sheets. *Journal of Fluid Mechanics*, 691:594–604, 2012.

[164] Daniel Duke, Julio Soria, and Damon Honnery. An error analysis of the dynamic mode decomposition. *Experiments in Fluids*, 52(2):529–542, 2012.

[165] Geir. E. Dullerud and Fernando Paganini. *A Course in Robust Control Theory: A Convex Approach*. Texts in Applied Mathematics. Springer, Berlin, Heidelberg, 2000.

[166] R. Dunne and B. J. McKeon. Dynamic stall on a pitching and surging airfoil. *Experiments in Fluids*, 56(8):1–15, 2015.

[167] T. Duriez, S. L. Brunton, and B. R. Noack. *Machine Learning Control: Taming Nonlinear Dynamics and Turbulence*. Springer, 2016.

[168] Thomas Duriez, Vladimir Parezanović, Laurent Cordier, Bernd R. Noack, Joël Delville, Jean-Paul Bonnet, Marc Segond, and Markus Abel. Closed-loop turbulence control using machine learning. *arXiv preprint arXiv:1404.4589*, 2014.

[169] Thomas Duriez, Vladimir Parezanovic, Jean-Charles Laurentie, Carine Fourment, Joël Delville, Jean-Paul Bonnet, Laurent Cordier, Bernd R Noack, Marc Segond, Markus Abel, Nicolas Gautier, Jean-Luc Aider, Cedric Raibaudo, Christophe Cuvier, Michel Stanislas, and Steven L Brunton. Closed-loop control of experimental shear flows using machine learning. AIAA Paper 2014-2219, 7th Flow Control Conference, 2014.

[170] C. Eckart and G. Young. The approximation of one matrix by another of lower rank. *Psychometrika*, 1(3):211–218, 1936.

[171] Jens L. Eftang, Anthony T. Patera, and Einar M. Rønquist. An" hp" certified reduced basis method for parametrized elliptic partial differential equations. *SIAM Journal on Scientific Computing*, 32(6):3170–3200, 2010.

[172] Jeffrey L. Elman. Finding structure in time. *Cognitive Science*, 14(2):179–211, 1990.

[173] Utku Eren, Anna Prach, Başaran Bahadır Koçer, Saša V. Raković, Erdal Kayacan, and Behçet Açıkmeşe. Model predictive control in aerospace systems: Current state and opportunities. *Journal of Guidance, Control, and Dynamics*, 40(7):1541–1566, 2017.

[174] N. B. Erichson, S. L. Brunton, and J. N. Kutz. Compressed dynamic mode decomposition for real-time object detection. *Journal of Real-Time Image Processing*, 2016.

[175] N. B. Erichson, S. L. Brunton, and J. N. Kutz. Randomized dynamic mode decomposition. *arXiv preprint arXiv:1702.02912*, 2017.

[176] N. B. Erichson, K. Manohar, S. L. Brunton, and J. N. Kutz. Randomized CP tensor decomposition. *arXiv preprint arXiv:1703.09074*.

[177] N. B. Erichson, S. Voronin, S. L. Brunton, and J. N. Kutz. Randomized matrix decompositions using R. *arXiv preprint arXiv:1608.02148*, 2016.

[178] Trishan Esram, Jonathan W. Kimball, Philip T Krein, Patrick L. Chapman, and Pallab Midya. Dynamic maximum power point tracking of photovoltaic arrays using ripple correlation control. *Ieee Transactions On Power Electronics*, 21(5):1282–1291, September 2006.

[179] Richard Everson and Lawrence Sirovich. Karhunen–Loeve procedure for gappy data. *JOSA A*, 12(8):1657–1664, 1995.

[180] N. Fabbiane, O. Semeraro, S. Bagheri, and D. S. Henningson. Adaptive and model-based control theory applied to convectively unstable flows. *Appl. Mech. Rev.*, 66(6):060801–1–20, 2014.

[181] B. F. Feeny. On proper orthogonal co-ordinates as indicators of modal activity. *Journal of Sound and Vibration*, 255(5):805–817, 2002.

[182] Ronald A. Fisher. The use of multiple measurements in taxonomic problems. *Annals of Human Genetics*, 7(2):179–188, 1936.

[183] Ronald Aylmer Fisher. On the mathematical foundations of theoretical statistics. *Philosophical Transactions of the Royal Society of London. Series A, Containing Papers of a Mathematical or Physical Character*, 222:309–368, 1922.

[184] P. J. Fleming and R. C. Purshouse. Evolutionary algorithms in control systems engineering: a survey. *Control Engineering Practice*, 10:1223–1241, 2002.

[185] Jean Baptiste Joseph Fourier. *The Analytical Theory of Heat*. The University Press, 1878.

[186] Joseph Fourier. *Theorie analytique de la chaleur, par M. Fourier*. Chez Firmin Didot, père et fils, 1822.

[187] J. E. Fowler. Compressive-projection principal component analysis. *IEEE Transactions on Image Processing*, 18(10):2230–2242, 2009.

[188] Yoav Freund and Robert E. Schapire. A decision-theoretic generalization of on-line learning and an application to boosting. *Journal of Computer and System Sciences*, 55(1):119–139, 1997.

[189] Jerome H. Friedman. Greedy function approximation: a gradient boosting machine. *Annals of Statistics*, pages 1189–1232, 2001.

[190] Alan Frieze, Ravi Kannan, and Santosh Vempala. Fast Monte-Carlo algorithms for finding low-rank approximations. *Journal of the ACM*, 51(6):1025–1041, 2004.

[191] Xing Fu, Steven L. Brunton, and J. Nathan Kutz. Classification of birefringence in mode-locked fiber lasers using machine learning and sparse representation. *Optics Express*, 22(7):8585–8597, 2014.

[192] Koji Fukagata, Stefan Kern, Philippe Chatelain, Petros Koumoutsakos, and Nobuhide Kasagi. Evolutionary optimization of an anisotropic compliant surface for turbulent friction drag reduction. *Journal of Turbulence*, 9(35):1–17, 2008.

[193] F. Fukushima. A self-organizing neural network model for a mechanism of pattern recognition unaffected by shift in position. *Biological Cybernetic*, 36:193–202, 1980.

[194] H. Gao, J. Lam, C. Wang, and Y. Wang. Delay-dependent output-feedback stabilisation of discrete-time systems with time-varying state delay. *IEE Proceedings-Control Theory and Applications*, 151(6):691–698, 2004.

[195] Carlos E. Garcia, David M. Prett, and Manfred Morari. Model predictive control: theory and practice: A survey. *Automatica*, 25(3):335–348, 1989.

[196] Jorge L. Garriga and Masoud Soroush. Model predictive control tuning methods: A review. *Industrial & Engineering Chemistry Research*, 49(8):3505–3515, 2010.

[197] Carl-Friedrich Gauss. *Theoria combinationis observationum erroribus minimis obnoxiae*, volume 1. Henricus Dieterich, 1823.

[198] C. F. Gauss. Nachlass: Theoria interpolationis methodo nova tractata, volume werke. *Königliche Gesellschaft der Wissenschaften, Göttingen*, 1866.

[199] Nicolas Gautier, J-L. Aider, Thomas Duriez, B. R. Noack, Marc Segond, and Markus Abel. Closed-loop separation control using machine learning. *Journal of Fluid Mechanics*, 770:442–457, 2015.

[200] M. Gavish and D. L. Donoho. The optimal hard threshold for singular values is $4/\sqrt{3}$. *IEEE Transactions on Information Theory*, 60(8):5040–5053, 2014.

[201] Mattia Gazzola, Oleg V. Vasilyev, and Petros Koumoutsakos. Shape optimization for drag reduction in linked bodies using evolution strategies. *Computers & Structures*, 89(11):1224–1231, 2011.

[202] Gregor Gelbert, Jonas P. Moeck, Christian O. Paschereit, and Rudibert King. Advanced algorithms for gradient estimation in one-and two-parameter extremum seeking controllers. *Journal of Process Control*, 22(4):700–709, 2012.

[203] A. S. Georghiades, P. N. Belhumeur, and D. J. Kriegman. From few to many: Illumination cone models for face recognition under variable lighting and pose. *IEEE Transactions on Pattern Analysis and Machine Intelligence (PAMI)*, 23(6):643–660, 2001.

[204] Jan J. Gerbrands. On the relationships between SVD, KLT and PCA. *Pattern Recognition*, 14(1):375–381, 1981.

[205] A. C. Gilbert and P. Indyk. Sparse recovery using sparse matrices. *Proceedings of the IEEE*, 98(6):937–947, 2010.

[206] A. C. Gilbert, J. Y. Park, and M. B. Wakin. Sketched SVD: Recovering spectral features from compressive measurements. *ArXiv e-prints*, 2012.

[207] A. C. Gilbert, M. J. Strauss, and J. A. Tropp. A tutorial on fast Fourier sampling. *IEEE Signal Processing Magazine*, pages 57–66, 2008.

[208] Bryan Glaz, Li Liu, and Peretz P Friedmann. Reduced-order nonlinear unsteady aerodynamic modeling using a surrogate-based recurrence framework. *AIAA Journal*, 48(10):2418–2429, 2010.

[209] Philip J Goddard and Keith Glover. Controller approximation: approaches for preserving H_∞ performance. *IEEE Transactions on Automatic Control*, 43(7):858–871, 1998.

[210] David E Goldberg. *Genetic Algorithms*. Pearson Education India, 2006.

[211] G. H. Golub and C. Reinsch. Singular value decomposition and least squares solutions. *Numerical Mathematics*, 14:403–420, 1970.

[212] Gene Golub and William Kahan. Calculating the singular values and pseudo-inverse of a matrix. *Journal of the Society for Industrial & Applied Mathematics, Series B: Numerical Analysis*, 2(2):205–224, 1965.

[213] Gene Golub, Stephen Nash, and Charles Van Loan. A Hessenberg-Schur method for the problem $ax + xb = c$. *IEEE Transactions on Automatic Control*, 24(6):909–913, 1979.

[214] Gene H. Golub and Charles F. Van Loan. *Matrix Computations*, volume 3. JHU Press, 2012.

[215] R. Gonzalez-Garcia, R. Rico-Martinez, and I. G. Kevrekidis. Identification of distributed parameter systems: A neural net based approach. *Comp. & Chem. Eng.*, 22:S965–S968, 1998.

[216] Ian Goodfellow, Yoshua Bengio, and Aaron Courville. *Deep Learning*. MIT Press, 2016. http://www.deeplearningbook.org.

[217] Ian Goodfellow, Jean Pouget-Abadie, Mehdi Mirza, Bing Xu, David Warde-Farley, Sherjil Ozair, Aaron Courville, and Yoshua Bengio. Generative adversarial nets. In *Advances in Neural Information Processing Systems*, pages 2672–2680, 2014.

[218] Michael Grant, Stephen Boyd, and Yinyu Ye. Cvx: Matlab software for disciplined convex programming, 2008.

[219] Alex Graves, Greg Wayne, and Ivo Danihelka. Neural turing machines. *arXiv preprint arXiv:1410.5401*, 2014.

[220] Anne Greenbaum. *Iterative Methods for Solving Linear Systems. SIAM*, 1997.

[221] Mohinder S. Grewal. Kalman filtering. In *International Encyclopedia of Statistical Science*, pages 705–708. Springer, 2011.

[222] M. Grilli, P. J. Schmid, S. Hickel, and N. A. Adams. Analysis of unsteady behaviour in shockwave turbulent boundary layer interaction. *Journal of Fluid Mechanics*, 700:16–28, 2012.

[223] Jacob Grosek and J. Nathan Kutz. Dynamic mode decomposition for real-time background/-foreground separation in video. *arXiv preprint arXiv:1404.7592*, 2014.

[224] Ming Gu. Subspace iteration randomization and singular value problems. *SIAM Journal on Scientific Computing*, 37(3):1139–1173, 2015.

[225] F. Gueniat, L. Mathelin, and L. Pastur. A dynamic mode decomposition approach for large and arbitrarily sampled systems. *Physics of Fluids*, 27(2):025113, 2015.

[226] Fredrik Gustafsson, Fredrik Gunnarsson, Niclas Bergman, Urban Forssell, Jonas Jansson, Rickard Karlsson, and P-J. Nordlund. Particle filters for positioning, navigation, and tracking. *IEEE Transactions on signal processing*, 50(2):425–437, 2002.

[227] Alfred Haar. Zur theorie der orthogonalen funktionensysteme. *Mathematische Annalen*, 69(3):331–371, 1910.

[228] N. Halko, P. G. Martinsson, and J. A. Tropp. Finding structure with randomness: Probabilistic algorithms for constructing approximate matrix decompositions. *SIAM Review*, 53(2):217–288, 2011.

[229] Nathan Halko, Per-Gunnar Martinsson, Yoel Shkolnisky, and Mark Tygert. An algorithm for the principal component analysis of large data sets. *SIAM Journal on Scientific Computing*, 33:2580–2594, 2011.

[230] Nathan Halko, Per-Gunnar Martinsson, and Joel A. Tropp. Finding structure with randomness: Probabilistic algorithms for constructing approximate matrix decompositions. *SIAM Review*, 53(2):217–288, 2011.

[231] Sven J. Hammarling. Numerical solution of the stable, non-negative definite Lyapunov equation. *IMA Journal of Numerical Analysis*, 2(3):303–323, 1982.

[232] Sangbo Han and Brian Feeny. Application of proper orthogonal decomposition to structural vibration analysis. *Mechanical Systems and Signal Processing*, 17(5):989–1001, 2003.

[233] Nikolaus Hansen, André S. P. Niederberger, Lino Guzzella, and Petros Koumoutsakos. A method for handling uncertainty in evolutionary optimization with an application to feedback control of combustion. *IEEE Transactions on Evolutionary Computation*, 13(1):180–197, 2009.

[234] David Harrison Jr. and Daniel L. Rubinfeld. Hedonic housing prices and the demand for clean air. *Journal of Environmental Economics and Management*, 5(1):81–102, 1978.

[235] Richard A. Harshman. Foundations of the PARAFAC procedure: Models and conditions for an "explanatory" multi-modal factor analysis. *UCLA working papers in phonetics*, 16:1–84, 1970. Available at www.psychology.uwo.ca/faculty/harshman/wpppfac0.pdf.

[236] Trevor Hastie, Robert Tibshirani, Jerome Friedman, T Hastie, J. Friedman, and R. Tibshirani. *The Elements of Statistical Learning*, volume 2. Springer, 2009.

[237] Kaiming He, Xiangyu Zhang, Shaoqing Ren, and Jian Sun. Deep residual learning for image recognition. In *Proceedings of the IEEE conference on computer vision and pattern recognition*, pages 770–778, 2016.

[238] M. T. Heath, A. J. Laub, C. C. Paige, and R. C. Ward. Computing the singular value decomposition of a product of two matrices. *SIAM Journal on Scientific and Statistical Computing*, 7(4):1147–1159, 1986.

[239] Michael Heideman, Don Johnson, and C Burrus. Gauss and the history of the fast Fourier transform. *IEEE ASSP Magazine*, 1(4):14–21, 1984.

[240] Werner Heisenberg. Über den anschaulichen inhalt der quantentheoretischen kinematik und mechanik. In *Original Scientific Papers Wissenschaftliche Originalarbeiten*, pages 478–504. Springer, 1985.

[241] Maziar S. Hemati, Clarence W. Rowley, Eric A. Deem, and Louis N. Cattafesta. De-biasing the dynamic mode decomposition for applied Koopman spectral analysis. *Theoretical and Computational Fluid Dynamics*, 31(4):349–368, 2017.

[242] Maziar S. Hemati, Matthew O. Williams, and Clarence W. Rowley. Dynamic mode decomposition for large and streaming datasets. *Physics of Fluids (1994-present)*, 26(11):111701, 2014.

[243] Kyle K. Herrity, Anna C. Gilbert, and Joel A. Tropp. Sparse approximation via iterative thresholding. In *Acoustics, Speech and Signal Processing, 2006. ICASSP 2006 Proceedings. 2006 IEEE International Conference on*, volume 3, pages III–III. IEEE, 2006.

[244] Jan S. Hesthaven, Gianluigi Rozza, and Benjamin Stamm. Certified reduced basis methods for parametrized partial differential equations. *SpringerBriefs in Mathematics*, 2015.

[245] Tony Hey, Stewart Tansley, Kristin M. Tolle, et al. *The Fourth Paradigm: Data-Intensive Scientific Discovery*, volume 1. Microsoft research Redmond, WA, 2009.

[246] Geoffrey E. Hinton and Terrence J. Sejnowski. Learning and releaming in boltzmann machines. *Parallel Distributed Processing: Explorations in the Microstructure of Cognition*, 1(282-317):2, 1986.

[247] B. L. Ho and R. E. Kalman. Effective construction of linear state-variable models from input/output data. In *Proceedings of the 3rd Annual Allerton Conference on Circuit and System Theory*, pages 449–459, 1965.

[248] Sepp Hochreiter and Jürgen Schmidhuber. Long short-term memory. *Neural Computation*, 9(8):1735–1780, 1997.

[249] Arthur E. Hoerl and Robert W. Kennard. Ridge regression: Biased estimation for nonorthogonal problems. *Technometrics*, 12(1):55–67, 1970.

[250] John H. Holland. *Adaptation in natural and artificial systems: An Introductory Analysis with Applications to Biology, Control, and Artificial Intelligence*. University of Michigan Press, 1975.

[251] P. Holmes, J. L. Lumley, G. Berkooz, and C. W. Rowley. *Turbulence, Coherent Structures, Dynamical Systems and Symmetry*. Cambridge University Press, Cambridge, 2nd paperback edition, 2012.

[252] Philip Holmes and John Guckenheimer. *Nonlinear oscillations, dynamical systems, and bifurcations of vector fields*, volume 42 of *Applied Mathematical Sciences*. Springer-Verlag, Berlin, Heidelberg, 1983.

[253] Eberhard Hopf. The partial differential equation $u_t + uu_x = \mu u_{xx}$. *Communications on Pure and Applied Mathematics*, 3(3):201–230, 1950.

[254] John J. Hopfield. Neural networks and physical systems with emergent collective computational abilities. *Proceedings of the National Academy of Sciences*, 79(8):2554–2558, 1982.

[255] Kurt Hornik, Maxwell Stinchcombe, and Halbert White. Multilayer feedforward networks are universal approximators. *Neural Networks*, 2(5):359–366, 1989.

[256] H. Hotelling. Analysis of a complex of statistical variables into principal components. *Journal of Educational Psychology*, 24:417–441, September 1933.

[257] H. Hotelling. Analysis of a complex of statistical variables into principal components. *Journal of Educational Psychology*, 24:498–520, October 1933.

[258] C. Huang, W. E. Anderson, M. E. Harvazinski, and V. Sankaran. Analysis of self-excited combustion instabilities using decomposition techniques. In *51st AIAA Aerospace Sciences Meeting*, pages 1–18, 2013.

[259] D. H. Hubel and T. N. Wiesel. Receptive fields, binocular interaction and functional architecture in the cat's visual cortex. *Journal of Physiology*, 160:106–154, 1962.

[260] Peter J. Huber. Robust statistics. In *International Encyclopedia of Statistical Science*, pages 1248–1251. Springer, 2011.

[261] S. J. Illingworth, A. S. Morgans, and C. W. Rowley. Feedback control of flow resonances using balanced reduced-order models. *Journal of Sound and Vibration*, 330(8):1567–1581, 2010.

[262] Eric Jacobsen and Richard Lyons. The sliding DFT. *IEEE Signal Processing Magazine*, 20(2):74–80, 2003.

[263] Herbert Jaeger and Harald Haas. Harnessing nonlinearity: Predicting chaotic systems and saving energy in wireless communication. *Science*, 304(5667):78–80, 2004.

[264] Gareth James, Daniela Witten, Trevor Hastie, and Robert Tibshirani. *An Introduction to Statistical Learning*. Springer, 2013.

[265] M. C. Johnson, S. L. Brunton, N. B. Kundtz, and J. N. Kutz. Extremum-seeking control of a beam pattern of a reconfigurable holographic metamaterial antenna. *Journal of the Optical Society of America A*, 33(1):59–68, 2016.

[266] Richard A. Johnson and Dean Wichern. *Multivariate Analysis*. Wiley Online Library, 2002.

[267] W. B Johnson and J. Lindenstrauss. Extensions of Lipschitz mappings into a Hilbert space. *Contemporary Mathematics*, 26(189-206):1, 1984.

[268] Ian Jolliffe. *Principal Component Analysis*. Wiley Online Library, 2005.

[269] Siddharth Joshi and Stephen Boyd. Sensor selection via convex optimization. *IEEE Transactions on Signal Processing*, 57(2):451–462, 2009.

[270] Mihailo R. Jovanović, Peter J. Schmid, and Joseph W. Nichols. Sparsity-promoting dynamic mode decomposition. *Physics of Fluids*, 26(2):024103, 2014.

[271] J. N. Juang. *Applied System Identification*. Prentice Hall PTR, Upper Saddle River, New Jersey, 1994.

[272] J. N. Juang and R. S. Pappa. An eigensystem realization algorithm for modal parameter identification and model reduction. *Journal of Guidance, Control, and Dynamics*, 8(5):620–627, 1985.

[273] J. N. Juang, M. Phan, L. G. Horta, and R. W. Longman. Identification of observer/Kalman filter Markov parameters: Theory and experiments. Technical Memorandum 104069, NASA, 1991.

[274] Simon J. Julier and Jeffrey K. Uhlmann. A new extension of the Kalman filter to nonlinear systems. In *Int. symp. aerospace/defense sensing, simul. and controls*, volume 3, pages 182–193. Orlando, FL, 1997.

[275] Simon J. Julier and Jeffrey K. Uhlmann. Unscented filtering and nonlinear estimation. *Proceedings of the IEEE*, 92(3):401–422, 2004.

[276] E. Kaiser, J. N. Kutz, and S. L. Brunton. Data-driven discovery of Koopman eigenfunctions for control. *arXiv preprint arXiv:1707.01146*, 2017.

[277] Eurika Kaiser, J. Nathan Kutz, and Steven L. Brunton. Sparse identification of nonlinear dynamics for model predictive control in the low-data limit. To appear in *Proceedings of the Royal Society A. arXiv preprint arXiv:1711.05501*, 2017.

[278] Eurika Kaiser, Bernd R. Noack, Laurent Cordier, Andreas Spohn, Marc Segond, Markus Abel, Guillaume Daviller, Jan Östh, Siniša Krajnović, and Robert K Niven. Cluster-based reduced-order modelling of a mixing layer. *Journal of Fluid Mechanics*, 754:365–414, 2014.

[279] Rudolph Emil Kalman. A new approach to linear filtering and prediction problems. *Journal of Fluids Engineering*, 82(1):35–45, 1960.

[280] K. Karhunen. Über lineare methoden in der wahrscheinlichkeitsrechnung, vol. 37. *Annales AcademiæScientiarum Fennicæ, Ser. A. I*, 1947.

[281] Kévin Kasper, Lionel Mathelin, and Hisham Abou-Kandil. A machine learning approach for constrained sensor placement. In *American Control Conference (ACC), 2015*, pages 4479–4484. IEEE, 2015.

[282] A. K. Kassam and L. N. Trefethen. Fourth-order time-stepping for stiff PDEs. *SIAM Journal on Scientific Computing*, 26(4):1214–1233, 2005.

[283] Michael Kearns and Leslie Valiant. Cryptographic limitations on learning boolean formulae and finite automata. *Journal of the ACM (JACM)*, 41(1):67–95, 1994.

[284] Anthony R. Kellems, Saifon Chaturantabut, Danny C. Sorensen, and Steven J. Cox. Morphologically accurate reduced order modeling of spiking neurons. *Journal of Computational Neuroscience*, 28(3):477–494, 2010.

[285] J. Kepler. *Tabulae Rudolphinae, quibus Astronomicae scientiae, temporum longinquitate collapsae Restauratio continetur*. Ulm: Jonas Saur, 1627.

[286] Gaëtan Kerschen and Jean-Claude Golinval. Physical interpretation of the proper orthogonal modes using the singular value decomposition. *Journal of Sound and Vibration*, 249(5):849–865, 2002.

[287] Gaetan Kerschen, Jean-claude Golinval, Alexander F. Vakakis, and Lawrence A. Bergman. The method of proper orthogonal decomposition for dynamical characterization and order reduction of mechanical systems: an overview. *Nonlinear Dynamics*, 41(1-3):147–169, 2005.

[288] I. G. Kevrekidis, C. W. Gear, J. M. Hyman, P. G. Kevrekidis, O. Runborg, and C. Theodoropoulos. Equation-free, coarse-grained multiscale computation: Enabling microscopic simulators to perform system-level analysis. *Communications in Mathematical Science*, 1(4):715–762, 2003.

[289] N. J. Killingsworth and M. Krstc. PID tuning using extremum seeking: online, model-free performance optimization. *IEEE Control Systems Magazine*, February:70–79, 2006.

[290] Diederik P. Kingma and Max Welling. Auto-encoding variational bayes. *arXiv preprint arXiv:1312.6114*, 2013.

[291] M. Kirby and L. Sirovich. Application of the Karhunen-Loève procedure for the characterization of human faces. *IEEE Transactions on Pattern Analysis and Machine Intelligence (PAMI)*, 12(1):103–108, 1990.

[292] V. C. Klema and A. J. Laub. The singular value decomposition: Its computation and some applications. *IEEE Transactions on Automatic Control*, 25(2):164–176, 1980.

[293] Stefan Klus, Feliks Nüske, Péter Koltai, Hao Wu, Ioannis Kevrekidis, Christof Schütte, and Frank Noé. Data-driven model reduction and transfer operator approximation. *Journal of Nonlinear Science*, pages 1–26, 2018.

[294] Richard Koch. *The 80/20 Principle*. Nicholas Brealey Publishing, 1997.

[295] Richard Koch. *Living the 80/20 Way*. Audio-Tech Business Book Summaries, Incorporated, 2006.

[296] Richard Koch. *The 80/20 Principle: The Secret to Achieving More with Less*. Crown Business, 2011.

[297] Richard Koch. *The 80/20 Principle and 92 other Powerful Laws of Nature: the Science of Success*. Nicholas Brealey Publishing, 2013.

[298] Teuvo Kohonen. The self-organizing map. *Neurocomputing*, 21(1-3):1–6, 1998.

[299] Tamara G. Kolda and Brett W. Bader. Tensor decompositions and applications. *SIAM Review*, 51(3):455–500, September 2009.

[300] B. O. Koopman. Hamiltonian systems and transformation in Hilbert space. *Proceedings of the National Academy of Sciences*, 17(5):315–318, 1931.

[301] B. O. Koopman and J.-v. Neumann. Dynamical systems of continuous spectra. *Proceedings of the National Academy of Sciences of the United States of America*, 18(3):255, 1932.

[302] Milan Korda and Igor Mezić. Linear predictors for nonlinear dynamical systems: Koopman operator meets model predictive control. *Automatica*, 93:149–160, 2018.

[303] Milan Korda and Igor Mezić. On convergence of extended dynamic mode decomposition to the Koopman operator. *Journal of Nonlinear Science,* 28(2): 687–710, 2018.

[304] Petros Koumoutsakos, Jonathan Freund, and David Parekh. Evolution strategies for automatic optimization of jet mixing. *AIAA Journal*, 39(5):967–969, 2001.

[305] Krzysztof Kowalski, Willi-Hans Steeb, and K. Kowalksi. *Nonlinear Dynamical Systems and Carleman Linearization*. World Scientific, 1991.

[306] John R. Koza. *Genetic Programming: On the Programming of Computers by Means of Natural Selection*, volume 1. MIT press, 1992.

[307] John R. Koza, Forrest H. Bennett III, and Oscar Stiffelman. Genetic programming as a darwinian invention machine. In *Genetic Programming*, pages 93–108. Springer, 1999.

[308] Boris Kramer, Piyush Grover, Petros Boufounos, Mouhacine Benosman, and Saleh Nabi. Sparse sensing and dmd based identification of flow regimes and bifurcations in complex flows. *SIAM Journal on Applied Dynamical Systems*, 16(2):1164–1196, 2017.

[309] J. P. Krieger and M. Krstic. Extremum seeking based on atmospheric turbulence for aircraft endurance. *Journal of Guidance, Control, and Dynamics*, 34(6):1876–1885, 2011.

[310] Alex Krizhevsky, Ilya Sutskever, and Geoffrey E. Hinton. Imagenet classification with deep convolutional neural networks. In *Advances in Neural Information Processing Systems*, pages 1097–1105, 2012.

[311] M. Krstic, A. Krupadanam, and C. Jacobson. Self-tuning control of a nonlinear model of combustion instabilities. *IEEE Tr. Contr. Syst. Technol.*, 7(4):424–436, 1999.

[312] M. Krstić and H. H. Wang. Stability of extremum seeking feedback for general nonlinear dynamic systems. *Automatica*, 36:595–601, 2000.

[313] Tejas D Kulkarni, William F Whitney, Pushmeet Kohli, and Josh Tenenbaum. Deep convolutional inverse graphics network. In *Advances in Neural Information Processing Systems*, pages 2539–2547, 2015.

[314] Solomon Kullback and Richard A Leibler. On information and sufficiency. *The Annals of Mathematical Statistics*, 22(1):79–86, 1951.

[315] Karl Kunisch and Stefan Volkwein. Optimal snapshot location for computing pod basis functions. *ESAIM: Mathematical Modelling and Numerical Analysis*, 44(3):509–529, 2010.

[316] J. N. Kutz. *Data-Driven Modeling & Scientific Computation: Methods for Complex Systems & Big Data*. Oxford University Press, 2013.

[317] J. N. Kutz, S. L. Brunton, B. W. Brunton, and J. L. Proctor. *Dynamic Mode Decomposition: Data-Driven Modeling of Complex Systems*. SIAM, 2016.

[318] J. N. Kutz, X. Fu, and S. L. Brunton. Multi-resolution dynamic mode decomposition. *SIAM Journal on Applied Dynamical Systems*, 15(2):713–735, 2016.

[319] J. Nathan Kutz, Syuzanna Sargsyan, and Steven L Brunton. Leveraging sparsity and compressive sensing for reduced order modeling. In *Model Reduction of Parametrized Systems*, pages 301–315. Springer, 2017.

[320] Sanjay Lall, Jerrold E. Marsden, and Sonja Glavaški. Empirical model reduction of controlled nonlinear systems. In *IFAC World Congress*, volume F, pages 473–478. International Federation of Automatic Control, 1999.

[321] Sanjay Lall, Jerrold E. Marsden, and Sonja Glavaški. A subspace approach to balanced truncation for model reduction of nonlinear control systems. *International Journal of Robust and Nonlinear Control*, 12(6):519–535, 2002.

[322] Yueheng Lan and Igor Mezić. Linearization in the large of nonlinear systems and Koopman operator spectrum. *Physica D: Nonlinear Phenomena*, 242(1):42–53, 2013.

[323] Alan Laub. A Schur method for solving algebraic Riccati equations. *IEEE Transactions on automatic control*, 24(6):913–921, 1979.

[324] Yann LeCun, Yoshua Bengio, and Geoffrey Hinton. Deep learning. *Nature*, 521(7553):436, 2015.

[325] Yann LeCun, Léon Bottou, Yoshua Bengio, and Patrick Haffner. Gradient-based learning applied to document recognition. *Proceedings of the IEEE*, 86(11):2278–2324, 1998.

[326] Jay H. Lee. Model predictive control: Review of the three decades of development. *International Journal of Control, Automation and Systems*, 9(3):415–424, 2011.

[327] K.C. Lee, J. Ho, and D. Kriegman. Acquiring linear subspaces for face recognition under variable lighting. *IEEE Transactions on Pattern Analysis and Machine Intelligence (PAMI)*, 27(5):684–698, 2005.

[328] Adrien Marie Legendre. *Nouvelles méthodes pour la détermination des orbites des comètes*. F. Didot, 1805.

[329] V. Lenaerts, Gaëtan Kerschen, and Jean-Claude Golinval. Proper orthogonal decomposition for model updating of non-linear mechanical systems. *Mechanical Systems and Signal Processing*, 15(1):31–43, 2001.

[330] Ian Lenz, Ross A. Knepper, and Ashutosh Saxena. Deepmpc: Learning deep latent features for model predictive control. In *Robotics: Science and Systems*, 2015.

[331] R. Leyva, C. Alonso, I. Queinnec, A. Cid-Pastor, D. Lagrange, and L. Martinez-Salamero. MPPT of photovoltaic systems using extremum-seeking control. *Ieee Transactions On Aerospace and Electronic Systems*, 42(1):249–258, January 2006.

[332] Qianxiao Li, Felix Dietrich, Erik M. Bollt, and Ioannis G. Kevrekidis. Extended dynamic mode decomposition with dictionary learning: A data-driven adaptive spectral decomposition of the Koopman operator. *Chaos: An Interdisciplinary Journal of Nonlinear Science*, 27(10):103111, 2017.

[333] Y. C. Liang, H. P. Lee, S. P. Lim, W. Z. Lin, K. H. Lee, and C. G. Wu. Proper orthogonal decomposition and its applications- part i: Theory. *Journal of Sound and vibration*, 252(3):527–544, 2002.

[334] Edo Liberty. Simple and deterministic matrix sketching. In *Proceedings of the 19th ACM SIGKDD International Conference on Knowledge Discovery and Data Mining*, pages 581–588. ACM, 2013.

[335] Edo Liberty, Franco Woolfe, Per-Gunnar Martinsson, Vladimir Rokhlin, and Mark Tygert. Randomized algorithms for the low-rank approximation of matrices. *Proceedings of the National Academy of Sciences*, 104:20167–20172, 2007.

[336] Timothy P. Lillicrap, Jonathan J. Hunt, Alexander Pritzel, Nicolas Heess, Tom Erez, Yuval Tassa, David Silver, and Daan Wierstra. Continuous control with deep reinforcement learning. *arXiv preprint arXiv:1509.02971*, 2015.

[337] Zhouchen Lin, Minming Chen, and Yi Ma. The augmented lagrange multiplier method for exact recovery of corrupted low-rank matrices. *arXiv preprint arXiv:1009.5055*, 2010.

[338] L. Ljung. *System Identification: Theory for the User*. Prentice Hall, 1999.

[339] Stuart Lloyd. Least squares quantization in PCM. *IEEE Transactions on Information Theory*, 28(2):129–137, 1982.

[340] M. Loeve. *Probability Theory*. Van Nostrand, Princeton, NJ, 1955.

[341] J.-C. Loiseau and S. L. Brunton. Constrained sparse Galerkin regression. *Journal of Fluid Mechanics*, 838:42–67, 2018.

[342] J.-C. Loiseau, B. R. Noack, and S. L. Brunton. Sparse reduced-order modeling: sensor-based dynamics to full-state estimation. *Journal of Fluid Mechanics*, 844:459–490, 2018.

[343] Richard W. Longman. Iterative learning control and repetitive control for engineering practice. *International Journal of Control*, 73(10):930–954, 2000.

[344] E. N. Lorenz. Empirical orthogonal functions and statistical weather prediction. Technical report, Massachusetts Institute of Technology, December 1956.

[345] Edward N. Lorenz. Deterministic nonperiodic flow. *Journal of the Atmospheric Sciences*, 20(2):130–141, 1963.

[346] D. M. Luchtenburg and C. W. Rowley. Model reduction using snapshot-based realizations. *Bulletin of the American Physical Society*, 56, 2011.

[347] J. L. Lumley. Toward a turbulent constitutive relation. *Journal of Fluid Mechanics*, 41(02):413–434, 1970.

[348] Bethany Lusch, Eric C. Chi, and J. Nathan Kutz. Shape constrained tensor decompositions using sparse representations in over-complete libraries. *arXiv preprint arXiv:1608.04674*, 2016.

[349] Bethany Lusch, J. Nathan Kutz, and Steven L. Brunton. Deep learning for universal linear embeddings of nonlinear dynamics. *Nature Communications. arXiv preprint arXiv:1712.09707*, 2018.

[350] F. Lusseyran, F. Gueniat, J. Basley, C. L. Douay, L. R. Pastur, T. M. Faure, and P. J. Schmid. Flow coherent structures and frequency signature: application of the dynamic modes decomposition to open cavity flow. In *Journal of Physics: Conference Series*, volume 318, page 042036. IOP Publishing, 2011.

[351] Z. Ma, S. Ahuja, and C. W. Rowley. Reduced order models for control of fluids using the eigensystem realization algorithm. *Theor. Comput. Fluid Dyn.*, 25(1):233–247, 2011.

[352] Wolfgang Maass, Thomas Natschläger, and Henry Markram. Real-time computing without stable states: A new framework for neural computation based on perturbations. *Neural Computation*, 14(11):2531–2560, 2002.

[353] Alan Mackey, Hayden Schaeffer, and Stanley Osher. On the compressive spectral method. *Multiscale Modeling & Simulation*, 12(4):1800–1827, 2014.

[354] Michael W. Mahoney. Randomized algorithms for matrices and data. *Foundations and Trends in Machine Learning*, 3:123–224, 2011.

[355] Andrew J. Majda and John Harlim. Physics constrained nonlinear regression models for time series. *Nonlinearity*, 26(1):201, 2012.

[356] Andrew J. Majda and Yoonsang Lee. Conceptual dynamical models for turbulence. *Proceedings of the National Academy of Sciences*, 111(18):6548–6553, 2014.

[357] Stéphane Mallat. *A Wavelet Tour of Signal Processing*. Academic Press, 1999.

[358] Stéphane Mallat. Understanding deep convolutional networks. *Phil. Trans. R. Soc. A*, 374(2065):20150203, 2016.

[359] Stephane G. Mallat. A theory for multiresolution signal decomposition: the wavelet representation. *IEEE Transactions on Pattern Analysis and Machine Intelligence*, 11(7):674–693, 1989.

[360] John Mandel. Use of the singular value decomposition in regression analysis. *The American Statistician*, 36(1):15–24, 1982.

[361] Niall M. Mangan, Steven L. Brunton, Joshua L. Proctor, and J. Nathan Kutz. Inferring biological networks by sparse identification of nonlinear dynamics. *IEEE Transactions on Molecular, Biological, and Multi-Scale Communications*, 2(1):52–63, 2016.

[362] Niall M. Mangan, J. Nathan Kutz, Steven L. Brunton, and Joshua L. Proctor. Model selection for dynamical systems via sparse regression and information criteria. *Proceedings of the Royal Society A*, 473(2204):1–16, 2017.

[363] Jordan Mann and J. Nathan Kutz. Dynamic mode decomposition for financial trading strategies. *Quantitative Finance*, pages 1–13, 2016.

[364] K. Manohar, S. L. Brunton, and J. N. Kutz. Environmental identification in flight using sparse approximation of wing strain. *Journal of Fluids and Structures*, 70:162–180, 2017.

[365] K. Manohar, J. N. Kutz, and S. L. Brunton. Greedy Sensor and Actuator Placement Using Balanced Model Reduction. *Bulletin of the American Physical Society*, 2018.

[366] Krithika Manohar, Bingni W. Brunton, J. Nathan Kutz, and Steven L. Brunton. Data-driven sparse sensor placement. *IEEE Control Systems Magazine*, 38:63–86, 2018

[367] Krithika Manohar, Eurika Kaiser, S. L. Brunton, and J. N. Kutz. Optimized sampling for multiscale dynamics. *SIAM Multiscale Modeling and Simulation. arXiv preprint arXiv:1712.05085*, 2017.

[368] Andreas Mardt, Luca Pasquali, Hao Wu, and Frank Noé. VAMPnets: Deep learning of molecular kinetics. *Nature Communications,* 9(1), 2018.

[369] J. E. Marsden and T. S. Ratiu. *Introduction to Mechanics and Symmetry*. Springer-Verlag, 2nd edition, 1999.

[370] Per-Gunnar Martinsson. Randomized methods for matrix computations and analysis of high dimensional data. *arXiv preprint arXiv:1607.01649*, 2016.

[371] Per-Gunnar Martinsson, Vladimir Rokhlin, and Mark Tygert. A randomized algorithm for the decomposition of matrices. *Applied and Computational Harmonic Analysis*, 30:47–68, 2011.

[372] John L. Maryak, James C. Spall, and Bryan D. Heydon. Use of the Kalman filter for inference in state-space models with unknown noise distributions. *IEEE Transactions on Automatic Control*, 49(1):87–90, 2004.

[373] L. Massa, R. Kumar, and P. Ravindran. Dynamic mode decomposition analysis of detonation waves. *Physics of Fluids (1994-present)*, 24(6):066101, 2012.

[374] Lionel Mathelin, Kévin Kasper, and Hisham Abou-Kandil. Observable dictionary learning for high-dimensional statistical inference. *Archives of Computational Methods in Engineering*, 25(1):103–120, 2018.

[375] R. Maury, M. Keonig, L. Cattafesta, P. Jordan, and J. Delville. Extremum-seeking control of jet noise. *Aeroacoustics*, 11(3&4):459–474, 2012.

[376] I. Mezić. Spectral properties of dynamical systems, model reduction and decompositions. *Nonlinear Dynamics*, 41(1-3):309–325, 2005.

[377] I. Mezić. Analysis of fluid flows via spectral properties of the Koopman operator. *Ann. Rev. Fluid Mech.*, 45:357–378, 2013.

[378] I. Mezić. *Spectral Operator Methods in Dynamical Systems: Theory and Applications*. Springer, 2017.

[379] Igor Mezić and Andrzej Banaszuk. Comparison of systems with complex behavior. *Physica D: Nonlinear Phenomena*, 197(1):101–133, 2004.

[380] Igor Mezić and Stephen Wiggins. A method for visualization of invariant sets of dynamical systems based on the ergodic partition. *Chaos: An Interdisciplinary Journal of Nonlinear Science*, 9(1):213–218, 1999.

[381] Michele Milano and Petros Koumoutsakos. Neural network modeling for near wall turbulent flow. *Journal of Computational Physics*, 182(1):1–26, 2002.

[382] T. M. Mitchell. *Machine Learning*. McGraw Hill, 1997.

[383] Y. Mizuno, D. Duke, C. Atkinson, and J. Soria. Investigation of wall-bounded turbulent flow using dynamic mode decomposition. In *Journal of Physics: Conference Series*, volume 318, page 042040. IOP Publishing, 2011.

[384] Volodymyr Mnih, Adria Puigdomenech Badia, Mehdi Mirza, Alex Graves, Timothy Lillicrap, Tim Harley, David Silver, and Koray Kavukcuoglu. Asynchronous methods for deep reinforcement learning. In *International Conference on Machine Learning*, pages 1928–1937, 2016.

[385] Volodymyr Mnih, Koray Kavukcuoglu, David Silver, Alex Graves, Ioannis Antonoglou, Daan Wierstra, and Martin Riedmiller. Playing atari with deep reinforcement learning. *arXiv preprint arXiv:1312.5602*, 2013.

[386] Volodymyr Mnih, Koray Kavukcuoglu, David Silver, Andrei A. Rusu, Joel Veness, Marc G. Bellemare, Alex Graves, Martin Riedmiller, Andreas K. Fidjeland, Georg Ostrovski et al. Human-level control through deep reinforcement learning. *Nature*, 518(7540):529, 2015.

[387] J. P. Moeck, J.-F. Bourgouin, D. Durox, T. Schuller, and S. Candel. Tomographic reconstruction of heat release rate perturbations induced by helical modes in turbulent swirl flames. *Experiments in Fluids*, 54(4):1–17, 2013.

[388] B. C. Moore. Principal component analysis in linear systems: Controllability, observability, and model reduction. *IEEE Transactions on Automatic Control*, AC-26(1):17–32, 1981.

[389] Calvin C. Moore. Ergodic theorem, ergodic theory, and statistical mechanics. *Proceedings of the National Academy of Sciences*, 112(7):1907–1911, 2015.

[390] Kevin L. Moore. *Iterative Learning Control for Deterministic Systems*. Springer Science & Business Media, 2012.

[391] Manfred Morari and Jay H. Lee. Model predictive control: past, present and future. *Computers & Chemical Engineering*, 23(4):667–682, 1999.

[392] T. W. Muld, G. Efraimsson, and D. S. Henningson. Flow structures around a high-speed train extracted using proper orthogonal decomposition and dynamic mode decomposition. *Computers & Fluids*, 57:87–97, 2012.

[393] T. W. Muld, G. Efraimsson, and D. S. Henningson. Mode decomposition on surface-mounted cube. *Flow, Turbulence and Combustion*, 88(3):279–310, 2012.

[394] S. D. Müller, M Milano, and P. Koumoutsakos. Application of machine learning algorithms to flow modeling and optimization. *Annual Research Briefs*, pages 169–178, 1999.

[395] Iulian Munteanu, Antoneta Iuliana Bratcu, and Emil Ceanga. Wind turbulence used as searching signal for MPPT in variable-speed wind energy conversion systems. *Renewable Energy*, 34(1):322–327, January 2009.

[396] Kevin P. Murphy. *Machine Learning: A Probabilistic Perspective*. MIT press, 2012.

[397] Vinod Nair and Geoffrey E. Hinton. Rectified linear units improve restricted boltzmann machines. In *Proceedings of the 27th international conference on machine learning (ICML-10)*, pages 807–814, 2010.

[398] D. Needell and J. A. Tropp. CoSaMP: iterative signal recovery from incomplete and inaccurate samples. *Communications of the ACM*, 53(12):93–100, 2010.

[399] J. v Neumann. Proof of the quasi-ergodic hypothesis. *Proceedings of the National Academy of Sciences*, 18(1):70–82, 1932.

[400] N. C. Nguyen, A. T. Patera, and J. Peraire. A best points interpolation method for efficient approximation of parametrized functions. *International Journal for Numerical Methods in Engineering*, 73(4):521–543, 2008.

[401] Yves Nievergelt and Y. Nievergelt. *Wavelets Made Easy*, volume 174. Springer, 1999.

[402] B. R. Noack, K. Afanasiev, M. Morzynski, G. Tadmor, and F. Thiele. A hierarchy of low-dimensional models for the transient and post-transient cylinder wake. *Journal of Fluid Mechanics*, 497:335–363, 2003.

[403] B. R. Noack, T. Duriez, L. Cordier, M. Segond, M. Abel, S. L. Brunton, M. Morzyński, J.-C. Laurentie, V. Parezanovic, and J.-P. Bonnet. Closed-loop turbulence control with machine learning methods. *Bulletin Am. Phys. Soc.*, 58(18):M25.0009, p. 418, 2013.

[404] Bernd R. Noack, Marek Morzynski, and Gilead Tadmor. *Reduced-Order Modelling for Flow Control*, volume 528. Springer Science & Business Media, 2011.

[405] Frank Noé and Feliks Nuske. A variational approach to modeling slow processes in stochastic dynamical systems. *Multiscale Modeling & Simulation*, 11(2):635–655, 2013.

[406] E. Noether. Invariante variationsprobleme nachr. d. könig. gesellsch. d. wiss. zu göttingen, math-phys. klasse 1918: 235-257. *English Reprint: physics/0503066, http://dx.doi.org/10.1080/00411457108231446*, page 57, 1918.

[407] Feliks Nüske, Bettina G. Keller, Guillermo Pérez-Hernández, Antonia S. J. S. Mey, and Frank Noé. Variational approach to molecular kinetics. *Journal of Chemical Theory and Computation*, 10(4):1739–1752, 2014.

[408] Feliks Nüske, Reinhold Schneider, Francesca Vitalini, and Frank Noé. Variational tensor approach for approximating the rare-event kinetics of macromolecular systems. *J. Chem. Phys.*, 144(5):054105, 2016.

[409] H. Nyquist. Certain topics in telegraph transmission theory. *Transactions of the A. I. E. E.*, pages 617–644, FEB 1928.

[410] Goro Obinata and Brian D. O. Anderson. *Model reduction for control system design*. Springer Science & Business Media, 2012.

[411] C. M. Ostoich, D. J. Bodony, and P. H. Geubelle. Interaction of a Mach 2.25 turbulent boundary layer with a fluttering panel using direct numerical simulation. *Physics of Fluids (1994-present)*, 25(11):110806, 2013.

[412] Samuel E. Otto and Clarence W. Rowley. Linearly-recurrent autoencoder networks for learning dynamics. *arXiv preprint arXiv:1712.01378*, 2017.

[413] Y. Ou, C. Xu, E. Schuster, T. C. Luce, J. R. Ferron, M. L. Walker, and D. A. Humphreys. Design and simulation of extremum-seeking open-loop optimal control of current profile in the DIII-D tokamak. *Plasma Physics and Controlled Fusion*, 50:115001–1–115001–24, 2008.

[414] Vidvuds Ozoliņš, Rongjie Lai, Russel Caflisch, and Stanley Osher. Compressed modes for variational problems in mathematics and physics. *Proceedings of the National Academy of Sciences*, 110(46):18368–18373, 2013.

[415] C. Pan, D. Yu, and J. Wang. Dynamical mode decomposition of Gurney flap wake flow. *Theoretical and Applied Mechanics Letters*, 1(1):012002, 2011.

[416] V. Parezanovic, J.-C. Laurentie, T. Duriez, C. Fourment, J. Delville, J.-P. Bonnet, L. Cordier, B. R. Noack, M. Segond, M. Abel, T. Shaqarin, and S. L. Brunton. Mixing layer manipulation experiment – from periodic forcing to machine learning closed-loop control. *Journal Flow Turbulence and Combustion*, 94(1):155–173, 2015.

[417] Vladimir Parezanović, Thomas Duriez, Laurent Cordier, Bernd R. Noack, Joël Delville, Jean-Paul Bonnet, Marc Segond, Markus Abel, and Steven L. Brunton. Closed-loop control of an experimental mixing layer using machine learning control. *arXiv preprint arXiv:1408.3259*, 2014.

[418] K. Pearson. On lines and planes of closest fit to systems of points in space. *Philosophical Magazine*, 2(7–12):559–572, 1901.

[419] B. Peherstorfer, D. Butnaru, K. Willcox, and H.-J. Bungartz. Localized discrete empirical interpolation method. *SIAM Journal on Scientific Computing*, 36(1):A168–A192, 2014.

[420] Benjamin Peherstorfer and Karen Willcox. Detecting and adapting to parameter changes for reduced models of dynamic data-driven application systems. *Procedia Computer Science*, 51:2553–2562, 2015.

[421] Benjamin Peherstorfer and Karen Willcox. Dynamic data-driven reduced-order models. *Computer Methods in Applied Mechanics and Engineering*, 291:21–41, 2015.

[422] Benjamin Peherstorfer and Karen Willcox. Online adaptive model reduction for nonlinear systems via low-rank updates. *SIAM Journal on Scientific Computing*, 37(4):A2123–A2150, 2015.

[423] Sebastian Peitz and Stefan Klus. Koopman operator-based model reduction for switched-system control of PDEs. *arXiv preprint arXiv:1710.06759*, 2017.

[424] S. D. Pendergrass, J. N. Kutz, and S. L. Brunton. Streaming GPU singular value and dynamic mode decompositions. *arXiv preprint arXiv:1612.07875*, 2016.

[425] Roger Penrose. A generalized inverse for matrices. In *Mathematical proceedings of the Cambridge philosophical society*, volume 51, pages 406–413. Cambridge University Press, 1955.

[426] Roger Penrose and John Arthur Todd. On best approximate solutions of linear matrix equations. In *Mathematical Proceedings of the Cambridge Philosophical Society*, volume 52, pages 17–19. Cambridge Univ Press, 1956.

[427] Lawrence Perko. *Differential Equations and Dynamical Systems*, volume 7. Springer Science & Business Media, 2013.

[428] M. Phan, L. G. Horta, J. N. Juang, and R. W. Longman. Linear system identification via an asymptotically stable observer. *Journal of Optimization Theory and Applications*, 79:59–86, 1993.

[429] Mark A. Pinsky. *Introduction to Fourier analysis and wavelets*, volume 102. American Mathematical Soc., 2002.

[430] T. Poggio. Deep learning: mathematics and neuroscience. *Views & Reviews, McGovern Center for Brains, Minds and Machines*, pages 1–7, 2016.

[431] Philippe Poncet, Georges-Henri Cottet, and Petros Koumoutsakos. Control of three-dimensional wakes using evolution strategies. *Comptes Rendus Mecanique*, 333(1):65–77, 2005.

[432] Christopher Poultney, Sumit Chopra, Yann L Cun, et al. Efficient learning of sparse representations with an energy-based model. In *Advances in Neural Information Processing systems*, pages 1137–1144, 2007.

[433] J. L. Proctor, S. L. Brunton, B. W. Brunton, and J. N. Kutz. Exploiting sparsity and equation-free architectures in complex systems (invited review). *The European Physical Journal Special Topics*, 223(13):2665–2684, 2014.

[434] Joshua L. Proctor, Steven L. Brunton, and J. Nathan Kutz. Dynamic mode decomposition with control. *SIAM Journal on Applied Dynamical Systems*, 15(1):142–161, 2016.

[435] Joshua L. Proctor and Philip A. Eckhoff. Discovering dynamic patterns from infectious disease data using dynamic mode decomposition. *International Health*, 7(2):139–145, 2015.

[436] H. Qi and S. M. Hughes. Invariance of principal components under low-dimensional random projection of the data. IEEE International Conference on Image Processing, October 2012.

[437] Shie Qian and Dapang Chen. Discrete Gabor transform. *IEEE Transactions on Signal Processing*, 41(7):2429–2438, 1993.

[438] S. J. Qin and T. A. Badgwell. An overview of industrial model predictive control technology. In *AIChE Symposium Series*, volume 93, pages 232–256, 1997.

[439] S. Joe Qin and Thomas A. Badgwell. A survey of industrial model predictive control technology. *Control Engineering Practice*, 11(7):733–764, 2003.

[440] Qing Qu, Ju Sun, and John Wright. Finding a sparse vector in a subspace: Linear sparsity using alternating directions. In *Advances in Neural Information Processing Systems 27*, pages 3401–3409, 2014.

[441] A. Quarteroni and G. Rozza. *Reduced Order Methods for Modeling and Computational Reduction*, volume 9 of *MS&A – Modeling, Simulation & Appplications*. Springer, 2013.

[442] Alfio Quarteroni, Andrea Manzoni, and Federico Negri. *Reduced Basis Methods for Partial Differential Equations: An Introduction*, volume 92. Springer, 2015.

[443] J. Ross Quinlan. Induction of decision trees. *Machine Learning*, 1(1):81–106, 1986.

[444] J Ross Quinlan. *C4. 5: Programs for Machine Learning*. Elsevier, 2014.

[445] Maziar Raissi and George Em Karniadakis. Hidden physics models: Machine learning of nonlinear partial differential equations. *Journal of Computational Physics*, 357:125–141, 2018.

[446] C. Radhakrishna Rao. The utilization of multiple measurements in problems of biological classification. *Journal of the Royal Statistical Society. Series B (Methodological)*, 10(2):159–203, 1948.

[447] James B. Rawlings. Tutorial overview of model predictive control. *IEEE Control Systems*, 20(3):38–52, 2000.

[448] Soumya Raychaudhuri, Joshua M. Stuart, and Russ B. Altman. Principal components analysis to summarize microarray experiments: application to sporulation time series. In *Pacific Symposium on Biocomputing. Pacific Symposium on Biocomputing*, page 455. NIH Public Access, 2000.

[449] Rolf H. Reichle, Dennis B. McLaughlin, and Dara Entekhabi. Hydrologic data assimilation with the ensemble Kalman filter. *Monthly Weather Review*, 130(1):103–114, 2002.

[450] B. Ren, P. Frihauf, R. J. Rafac, and M. Krstić. Laser pulse shaping via extremum seeking. *Control Engineering Practice*, 20:674–683, 2012.

[451] Branko Ristic, Sanjeev Arulampalam, and Neil James Gordon. *Beyond the Kalman Filter: Particle Filters for Tracking Applications*. Artech house, 2004.

[452] Anthony John Roberts. *Model Emergent Dynamics in Complex Systems*. SIAM, 2014.

[453] Charles A. Rohde. Generalized inverses of partitioned matrices. *Journal of the Society for Industrial & Applied Mathematics*, 13(4):1033–1035, 1965.

[454] Vladimir Rokhlin, Arthur Szlam, and Mark Tygert. A randomized algorithm for principal component analysis. *SIAM Journal on Matrix Analysis and Applications*, 31:1100–1124, 2009.

[455] C. W. Rowley, T. Colonius, and R. M. Murray. Model reduction for compressible flows using POD and Galerkin projection. *Physica D*, 189:115–129, 2004.

[456] C. W. Rowley, I. Mezić, S. Bagheri, P. Schlatter, and D. S. Henningson. Spectral analysis of nonlinear flows. *J. Fluid Mech.*, 645:115–127, 2009.

[457] Clarence W. Rowley and Jerrold E. Marsden. Reconstruction equations and the Karhunen–Loève expansion for systems with symmetry. *Physica D: Nonlinear Phenomena*, 142(1):1–19, 2000.

[458] C.W. Rowley. Model reduction for fluids using balanced proper orthogonal decomposition. *Int. J. Bifurcation and Chaos*, 15(3):997–1013, 2005.

[459] S. Roy, J.-C. Hua, W. Barnhill, G. H. Gunaratne, and J. R. Gord. Deconvolution of reacting-flow dynamics using proper orthogonal and dynamic mode decompositions. *Physical Review E*, 91(1):013001, 2015.

[460] S. H. Rudy, S. L. Brunton, J. L. Proctor, and J. N. Kutz. Data-driven discovery of partial differential equations. *Science Advances*, 3(e1602614), 2017.

[461] Themistoklis P. Sapsis and Andrew J. Majda. Statistically accurate low-order models for uncertainty quantification in turbulent dynamical systems. *Proceedings of the National Academy of Sciences*, 110(34):13705–13710, 2013.

[462] S. Sargsyan, S. L. Brunton, and J. N. Kutz. Nonlinear model reduction for dynamical systems using sparse sensor locations from learned libraries. *Physical Review E*, 92(033304), 2015.

[463] S. Sarkar, S. Ganguly, A. Dalal, P. Saha, and S. Chakraborty. Mixed convective flow stability of nanofluids past a square cylinder by dynamic mode decomposition. *International Journal of Heat and Fluid Flow*, 44:624–634, 2013.

[464] Tamas Sarlos. Improved approximation algorithms for large matrices via random projections. In *Foundations of Computer Science. 47th Annual IEEE Symposium on*, pages 143–152, 2006.

[465] T. Sayadi, P. J. Schmid, J. W. Nichols, and P. Moin. Reduced-order representation of near-wall structures in the late transitional boundary layer. *Journal of Fluid Mechanics*, 748:278–301, 2014.

[466] Taraneh Sayadi and Peter J. Schmid. Parallel data-driven decomposition algorithm for large-scale datasets: with application to transitional boundary layers. *Theoretical and Computational Fluid Dynamics*, pages 1–14, 2016.

[467] H. Schaeffer, R. Caflisch, C. D. Hauck, and S. Osher. Sparse dynamics for partial differential equations. *Proceedings of the National Academy of Sciences USA*, 110(17):6634–6639, 2013.

[468] Hayden Schaeffer. Learning partial differential equations via data discovery and sparse optimization. In *Proc. R. Soc. A*, volume 473, page 20160446. The Royal Society, 2017.

[469] Hayden Schaeffer and Scott G. McCalla. Sparse model selection via integral terms. *Physical Review E*, 96(2):023302, 2017.

[470] Robert E. Schapire. The strength of weak learnability. *Machine learning*, 5(2):197–227, 1990.

[471] M. Schlegel, B. R. Noack, and G. Tadmor. Low-dimensional Galerkin models and control of transitional channel flow. Technical Report 01/2004, Hermann-Föttinger-Institut für Strömungsmechanik, Technische Universität Berlin, Germany, 2004.

[472] P. J. Schmid. Dynamic mode decomposition for numerical and experimental data. *J. Fluid. Mech*, 656:5–28, 2010.

[473] P. J. Schmid, L. Li, M. P. Juniper, and O. Pust. Applications of the dynamic mode decomposition. *Theoretical and Computational Fluid Dynamics*, 25(1-4):249–259, 2011.

[474] P. J. Schmid and J. Sesterhenn. Dynamic mode decomposition of numerical and experimental data. In *61st Annual Meeting of the APS Division of Fluid Dynamics*. American Physical Society, November 2008.

[475] P. J. Schmid, D. Violato, and F. Scarano. Decomposition of time-resolved tomographic PIV. *Experiments in Fluids*, 52:1567–1579, 2012.

[476] E. Schmidt. Zur theorie der linearen und nichtlinearen integralgleichungen. i teil. entwicklung willkürlichen funktionen nach system vorgeschriebener. *Math. Ann.*, 3:433–476, 1907.

[477] Michael Schmidt and Hod Lipson. Distilling free-form natural laws from experimental data. *Science*, 324(5923):81–85, 2009.

[478] Michael D. Schmidt, Ravishankar R. Vallabhajosyula, Jerry W. Jenkins, Jonathan E. Hood, Abhishek S. Soni, John P. Wikswo, and Hod Lipson. Automated refinement and inference of analytical models for metabolic networks. *Physical Biology*, 8(5):055011, 2011.

[479] Bernhard Schölkopf and Alexander J. Smola. *Learning with Kernels: Support Vector Machines, Regularization, Optimization, and beyond*. MIT press, 2002.

[480] Gideon Schwarz et al. Estimating the dimension of a model. *The Annals of Statistics*, 6(2):461–464, 1978.

[481] A. Seena and H. J. Sung. Dynamic mode decomposition of turbulent cavity flows for self-sustained oscillations. *International Journal of Heat and Fluid Flow*, 32(6):1098–1110, 2011.

[482] Ervin Sejdić, Igor Djurović, and Jin Jiang. Time–frequency feature representation using energy concentration: An overview of recent advances. *Digital Signal Processing*, 19(1):153–183, 2009.

[483] O. Semeraro, G. Bellani, and F. Lundell. Analysis of time-resolved PIV measurements of a confined turbulent jet using POD and Koopman modes. *Experiments in Fluids*, 53(5):1203–1220, 2012.

[484] Onofrio Semeraro, Francois Lusseyran, Luc Pastur, and Peter Jordan. Qualitative dynamics of wavepackets in turbulent jets. *Physical Review Fluids*, 2(9):094605, 2017.

[485] Gil Shabat, Yaniv Shmueli, Yariv Aizenbud, and Amir Averbuch. Randomized LU decomposition. *Applied and Computational Harmonic Analysis*, 2016.

[486] C. E. Shannon. A mathematical theory of communication. *Bell System Technical Journal*, 27(3):379–423, 1948.

[487] Ati S. Sharma, Igor Mezić, and Beverley J. McKeon. Correspondence between Koopman mode decomposition, resolvent mode decomposition, and invariant solutions of the Navier-Stokes equations. *Physical Review Fluids*, 1(3):032402, 2016.

[488] Eli Shlizerman, Edwin Ding, Matthew O. Williams, and J. Nathan Kutz. The proper orthogonal decomposition for dimensionality reduction in mode-locked lasers and optical systems. *International Journal of Optics*, 2012, 2011.

[489] Valeria Simoncini. A new iterative method for solving large-scale Lyapunov matrix equations. *SIAM Journal on Scientific Computing*, 29(3):1268–1288, 2007.

[490] L. Sirovich. Turbulence and the dynamics of coherent structures, parts I-III. *Q. Appl. Math.*, XLV(3):561–590, 1987.

[491] L. Sirovich and M. Kirby. A low-dimensional procedure for the characterization of human faces. *Journal of the Optical Society of America A*, 4(3):519–524, 1987.

[492] S. Skogestad and I. Postlethwaite. *Multivariable Feedback Control*. Wiley, Chichester, 1996.

[493] Paul Smolensky. Information processing in dynamical systems: Foundations of harmony theory. Technical report, Colorado Univ at Boulder Dept of Computer Science, 1986.

[494] Giovanni Solari, Luigi Carassale, and Federica Tubino. Proper orthogonal decomposition in wind engineering. part 1: A state-of-the-art and some prospects. *Wind and Structures*, 10(2):153–176, 2007.

[495] G. Song, F. Alizard, J.-C. Robinet, and X. Gloerfelt. Global and Koopman modes analysis of sound generation in mixing layers. *Physics of Fluids (1994-present)*, 25(12):124101, 2013.

[496] Danny C. Sorensen and Yunkai Zhou. Direct methods for matrix Sylvester and Lyapunov equations. *Journal of Applied Mathematics*, 2003(6):277–303, 2003.

[497] Mariia Sorokina, Stylianos Sygletos, and Sergei Turitsyn. Sparse identification for nonlinear optical communication systems: SINO method. *Optics Express*, 24(26):30433–30443, 2016.

[498] James C. Spall. The Kantorovich inequality for error analysis of the Kalman filter with unknown noise distributions. *Automatica*, 31(10):1513–1517, 1995.

[499] Nitish Srivastava, Geoffrey Hinton, Alex Krizhevsky, Ilya Sutskever, and Ruslan Salakhutdinov. Dropout: A simple way to prevent neural networks from overfitting. *The Journal of Machine Learning Research*, 15(1):1929–1958, 2014.

[500] W-H. Steeb and F. Wilhelm. Non-linear autonomous systems of differential equations and Carleman linearization procedure. *Journal of Mathematical Analysis and Applications*, 77(2):601–611, 1980.

[501] Robert F. Stengel. *Optimal Control and Estimation*. Courier Corporation, 2012.

[502] Gilbert W. Stewart. On the early history of the singular value decomposition. *SIAM Review*, 35(4):551–566, 1993.

[503] George Sugihara, Robert May, Hao Ye, Chih-hao Hsieh, Ethan Deyle, Michael Fogarty, and Stephan Munch. Detecting causality in complex ecosystems. *Science*, 338(6106):496–500, 2012.

[504] A. Surana. Koopman operator based observer synthesis for control-affine nonlinear systems. In *55th IEEE Conference on Decision and Control (CDC*, pages 6492–6499, 2016.

[505] Amit Surana and Andrzej Banaszuk. Linear observer synthesis for nonlinear systems using Koopman operator framework. *IFAC-PapersOnLine*, 49(18):716–723, 2016.

[506] Yoshihiko Susuki and Igor Mezić. A prony approximation of Koopman mode decomposition. In *Decision and Control (CDC), 2015 IEEE 54th Annual Conference on*, pages 7022–7027. IEEE, 2015.

[507] Richard S. Sutton and Andrew G. Barto. *Reinforcement Learning: An Introduction*, volume 1. MIT press Cambridge, 1998.

[508] Adam Svenkeson, Bryan Glaz, Samuel Stanton, and Bruce J. West. Spectral decomposition of nonlinear systems with memory. *Phys. Rev. E*, 93:022211, Feb 2016.

[509] S. A. Svoronos, D. Papageorgiou, and C. Tsiligiannis. Discretization of nonlinear control systems via the Carleman linearization. *Chemical Engineering Science*, 49(19):3263–3267, 1994.

[510] D. L. Swets and J. Weng. Using discriminant eigenfeatures for image retrieval. *IEEE Transactions on Pattern Analysis and Machine Intelligence (PAMI)*, 18(8):831–836, 1996.

[511] K. Taira and T. Colonius. The immersed boundary method: a projection approach. *Journal of Computational Physics*, 225(2):2118–2137, 2007.

[512] Naoya Takeishi, Yoshinobu Kawahara, Yasuo Tabei, and Takehisa Yairi. Bayesian dynamic mode decomposition. *Twenty-Sixth International Joint Conference on Artificial Intelligence*, 2017.

[513] Naoya Takeishi, Yoshinobu Kawahara, and Takehisa Yairi. Learning Koopman invariant subspaces for dynamic mode decomposition. In *Advances in Neural Information Processing Systems*, pages 1130–1140, 2017.

[514] Naoya Takeishi, Yoshinobu Kawahara, and Takehisa Yairi. Subspace dynamic mode decomposition for stochastic Koopman analysis. *Physical Review*, E 96.3:033310, 2017.

[515] F. Takens. Detecting strange attractors in turbulence. *Lecture Notes in Mathematics*, 898:366–381, 1981.

[516] Z. Q. Tang and N. Jiang. Dynamic mode decomposition of hairpin vortices generated by a hemisphere protuberance. *Science China Physics, Mechanics and Astronomy*, 55(1):118–124, 2012.

[517] Roy Taylor, J. Nathan Kutz, Kyle Morgan, and Brian Nelson. Dynamic mode decomposition for plasma diagnostics and validation. *Review of Scientific Instruments,* 89 (5):053501, 2018.

[518] Robert Tibshirani. Regression shrinkage and selection via the lasso. *Journal of the Royal Statistical Society. Series B (Methodological)*, pages 267–288, 1996.

[519] Zhou Ting and Jiang Hui. Eeg signal processing based on proper orthogonal decomposition. In *Audio, Language and Image Processing (ICALIP), 2012 International Conference on*, pages 636–640. IEEE, 2012.

[520] Santosh Tirunagari, Norman Poh, Kevin Wells, Miroslaw Bober, Isky Gorden, and David Windridge. Movement correction in DCE-MRI through windowed and reconstruction dynamic mode decomposition. *Machine Vision and Applications*, 28(3-4):393–407, 2017.

[521] Christopher Torrence and Gilbert P. Compo. A practical guide to wavelet analysis. *Bulletin of the American Meteorological Society*, 79(1):61–78, 1998.

[522] Giang Tran and Rachel Ward. Exact recovery of chaotic systems from highly corrupted data. *Multiscale Modeling & Simulation,* 15 (3):1108–1129, 2017.

[523] Lloyd N. Trefethen. *Spectral methods in MATLAB. SIAM*, 2000.

[524] Lloyd N. Trefethen and David Bau III. *Numerical linear algebra*, volume 50. *SIAM*, 1997.

[525] J. A. Tropp. Greed is good: Algorithmic results for sparse approximation. *IEEE Transactions on Information Theory*, 50(10):2231–2242, 2004.

[526] J. A. Tropp. Recovery of short, complex linear combinations via l_1 minimization. *IEEE Transactions on Information Theory*, 51(4):1568–1570, 2005.

[527] J. A. Tropp. Algorithms for simultaneous sparse approximation. part ii: Convex relaxation. *Signal Processing*, 86(3):589–602, 2006.

[528] J. A. Tropp. Just relax: Convex programming methods for identifying sparse signals in noise. *IEEE Transactions on Information Theory*, 52(3):1030–1051, 2006.

[529] J. A. Tropp and A. C. Gilbert. Signal recovery from random measurements via orthogonal matching pursuit. *IEEE Transactions on Information Theory*, 53(12):4655–4666, 2007.

[530] J. A. Tropp, A. C. Gilbert, and M. J. Strauss. Algorithms for simultaneous sparse approximation. part i: Greedy pursuit. *Signal Processing*, 86(3):572–588, 2006.

[531] J. A. Tropp, J. N. Laska, M. F. Duarte, J. K. Romberg, and R. G. Baraniuk. Beyond Nyquist: Efficient sampling of sparse bandlimited signals. *IEEE Transactions on Information Theory*, 56(1):520–544, 2010.

[532] Joel A. Tropp, Alp Yurtsever, Madeleine Udell, and Volkan Cevher. Randomized single-view algorithms for low-rank matrix approximation. *arXiv preprint arXiv:1609.00048*, 2016.

[533] J. H. Tu and C. W. Rowley. An improved algorithm for balanced POD through an analytic treatment of impulse response tails. *J. Comp. Phys.*, 231(16):5317–5333, 2012.

[534] J. H. Tu, C. W. Rowley, E. Aram, and R. Mittal. Koopman spectral analysis of separated flow over a finite-thickness flat plate with elliptical leading edge. *AIAA Paper 2011*, 2864, 2011.

[535] J. H. Tu, C. W. Rowley, D. M. Luchtenburg, S. L. Brunton, and J. N. Kutz. On dynamic mode decomposition: theory and applications. *J. Comp. Dyn.*, 1(2):391–421, 2014.

[536] Jonathan H. Tu, Clarence W. Rowley, J. Nathan Kutz, and Jessica K. Shang. Spectral analysis of fluid flows using sub-Nyquist-rate PIV data. *Experiments in Fluids*, 55(9):1–13, 2014.

[537] M. Turk and A. Pentland. Eigenfaces for recognition. *Journal of Cognitive Neuroscience*, 3(1):71–86, 1991.

[538] Rudolph Van Der Merwe. *Sigma-point Kalman Filters for Probabilistic Inference in Dynamic State-Space Models*. 2004.

[539] Charles Van Loan. *Computational Frameworks for the Fast Fourier Transform*. SIAM, 1992.

[540] Daniele Venturi and George Em Karniadakis. Gappy data and reconstruction procedures for flow past a cylinder. *Journal of Fluid Mechanics*, 519:315–336, 2004.

[541] Pascal Vincent, Hugo Larochelle, Yoshua Bengio, and Pierre-Antoine Manzagol. Extracting and composing robust features with denoising autoencoders. In *Proceedings of the 25th international conference on Machine learning*, pages 1096–1103. ACM, 2008.

[542] Stefan Volkwein. Model reduction using proper orthogonal decomposition. *Lecture Notes, Institute of Mathematics and Scientific Computing, University of Graz. see http://www.uni-graz.at/imawww/volkwein/POD.pdf*, 1025, 2011.

[543] Stefan Volkwein. Proper orthogonal decomposition: Theory and reduced-order modelling. *Lecture Notes, University of Konstanz*, 4:4, 2013.

[544] Sergey Voronin and Per-Gunnar Martinsson. RSVDPACK: Subroutines for computing partial singular value decompositions via randomized sampling on single core, multi core, and GPU architectures. *arXiv preprint arXiv:1502.05366*, 2015.

[545] Avery Wang et al. An industrial strength audio search algorithm. In *Ismir*, volume 2003, pages 7–13. Washington, DC, 2003.

[546] H. H. Wang, M. Krstić, and G. Bastin. Optimizing bioreactors by extremum seeking. *Adaptive Control and Signal Processing*, 13(8):651–669, 1999.

[547] H. H. Wang, S. Yeung, and M. Krstić. Experimental application of extremum seeking on an axial-flow compressor. *IEEE Transactions on Control Systems Technology*, 8(2):300–309, 2000.

[548] W. X. Wang, R. Yang, Y. C. Lai, V. Kovanis, and C. Grebogi. Predicting catastrophes in nonlinear dynamical systems by compressive sensing. *Physical Review Letters*, 106:154101-1–154101-4, 2011.

[549] Zhu Wang, Imran Akhtar, Jeff Borggaard, and Traian Iliescu. Proper orthogonal decomposition closure models for turbulent flows: a numerical comparison. *Computer Methods in Applied Mechanics and Engineering*, 237:10–26, 2012.

[550] Christoph Wehmeyer and Frank Noé. Time-lagged autoencoders: Deep learning of slow collective variables for molecular kinetics. *The Journal of Chemical Physics*, 148(24):241703, 2018.

[551] Greg Welch and Gary Bishop. An introduction to the Kalman filter, 1995.

[552] Peter Whitle. *Hypothesis Testing in Time Series Analysis*, volume 4. Almqvist & Wiksells, 1951.

[553] O. Wiederhold, R. King, B. R. Noack, L. Neuhaus, L. Neise, W. an Enghard, and M. Swoboda. Extensions of extremum-seeking control to improve the aerodynamic performance of axial turbomachines. In *39th AIAA Fluid Dynamics Conference*, pages 1–19, San Antonio, TX, USA, 2009. AIAA-Paper 092407.

[554] K. Willcox and J. Peraire. Balanced model reduction via the proper orthogonal decomposition. *AIAA Journal*, 40(11):2323–2330, 2002.

[555] Karen Willcox. Unsteady flow sensing and estimation via the gappy proper orthogonal decomposition. *Computers & Fluids*, 35(2):208–226, 2006.

[556] Matthew O. Williams, Ioannis G. Kevrekidis, and Clarence W. Rowley. A data-driven approximation of the Koopman operator: extending dynamic mode decomposition. *Journal of Nonlinear Science*, 6:1307–1346, 2015.

[557] Matthew O. Williams, Clarence W. Rowley, and Ioannis G. Kevrekidis. A kernel approach to data-driven Koopman spectral analysis. *Journal of Computational Dynamics*, 2(2):247–265, 2015.

[558] Daniela M. Witten and Robert Tibshirani. Penalized classification using Fisher's linear discriminant. *Journal of the Royal Statistical Society: Series B (Statistical Methodology)*, 73(5):753–772, 2011.

[559] Franco Woolfe, Edo Liberty, Vladimir Rokhlin, and Mark Tygert. A fast randomized algorithm for the approximation of matrices. *Journal of Applied and Computational Harmonic Analysis*, 25:335–366, 2008.

[560] J. Wright, A. Yang, A. Ganesh, S. Sastry, and Y. Ma. Robust face recognition via sparse representation. *IEEE Transactions on Pattern Analysis and Machine Intelligence (PAMI)*, 31(2):210–227, 2009.

[561] C. F. Jeff Wu. On the convergence properties of the EM algorithm. *The Annals of Statistics*, pages 95–103, 1983.

[562] Xindong Wu, Vipin Kumar, J. Ross Quinlan, Joydeep Ghosh, Qiang Yang, Hiroshi Motoda, Geoffrey J. McLachlan, Angus Ng, Bing Liu, S. Yu Philip et al. Top 10 algorithms in data mining. *Knowledge and Information Systems*, 14(1):1–37, 2008.

[563] Hao Ye, Richard J. Beamish, Sarah M. Glaser, Sue C. H. Grant, Chih-hao Hsieh, Laura J. Richards, Jon T. Schnute, and George Sugihara. Equation-free mechanistic ecosystem forecasting using empirical dynamic modeling. *Proceedings of the National Academy of Sciences*, 112(13):E1569–E1576, 2015.

[564] Enoch Yeung, Soumya Kundu, and Nathan Hodas. Learning deep neural network representations for Koopman operators of nonlinear dynamical systems. *arXiv preprint arXiv:1708.06850*, 2017.

[565] B. Yildirim, C. Chryssostomidis, and G. E. Karniadakis. Efficient sensor placement for ocean measurements using low-dimensional concepts. *Ocean Modelling*, 27(3):160–173, 2009.

[566] Xiaoming Yuan and Junfeng Yang. Sparse and low-rank matrix decomposition via alternating direction methods. *preprint*, 12, 2009.

[567] M. D. Zeiler, D. Krishnan, G. W. Taylor, and R. Fergus. Deconvolutional networks. In *IEEE Computer Vision and Pattern Recognition (CVPR)*, pages 2528–2535, 2010.

[568] C. Zhang and R. Ordó nez. Numerical optimization-based extremum seeking control with application to ABS design. *IEEE Transactions on Automatic Control*, 52(3):454–467, 2007.

[569] Hao Zhang, Clarence W. Rowley, Eric A. Deem, and Louis N. Cattafesta. Online dynamic mode decomposition for time-varying systems. *arXiv preprint arXiv:1707.02876*, 2017.

[570] T. Zhang, G. Kahn, S. Levine, and P. Abbeel. Learning deep control policies for autonomous aerial vehicles with MPC-guided policy search. In *IEEE Robotics and Automation (ICRA)*, pages 528–535, 2016.

[571] Weiwei Zhang, Bobin Wang, Zhengyin Ye, and Jingge Quan. Efficient method for limit cycle flutter analysis based on nonlinear aerodynamic reduced-order models. *AIAA Journal*, 50(5):1019–1028, 2012.

[572] Sanjo Zlobec. An explicit form of the moore-penrose inverse of an arbitrary complex matrix. *SIAM Review*, 12(1):132–134, 1970.

[573] Hui Zou and Trevor Hastie. Regularization and variable selection via the elastic net. *Journal of the Royal Statistical Society: Series B (Statistical Methodology)*, 67(2):301–320, 2005.

Index

Printed in the United States
By Bookmasters